Oracle 7.0

Administration & Management

ORACLE 7.0
Administration
& Management

Michael R. Ault

JOHN WILEY & SONS, INC.
NEW YORK • CHICHESTER • BRISBANE • TORONTO • SINGAPORE

Library of Congress Cataloging-in-Publication Data

Ault, Michael R.
 Oracle 7.0 administration and management / Michael Ross Ault.
  p.   cm.
 "A Wiley-QED publication."
 Includes index.
 ISBN 0-471-60857-2 (alk. paper)
 1. Relational data bases. 2. Oracle (Computer file) I. Title.
QA76.9.D3A937 1994
005.75'65—dc20   94-2010
                                                                  CIP

Printed in the United States of America

10 9 8 7 6 5 4 3 2 1

Trademarks

Many of the designations used by manufacturers and sellers to distinguish their products are claimed as trademarks. Where those designations appear in this book, and John Wiley & Sons was aware of a trademark claim, the designations have been printed in caps or initial caps.

Postscript is a registered trademark of Adobe Systems, Inc.

INGRES is a registered trademark of ASK Corporation.

UNIX and Shell are registered trademarks of AT&T.

DCL, DEC, DECNET, DIGITAL, Ultrix, VAX, VAX/VMS, and VMS are registered trademarks of Digital Equipment Corporation.

Hewlett-Packard, HP, and HP/ux are registered trademarks of Hewlett-Packard Comapny.

INFORMIX is a registered trademark of INFORMIX, Inc.

AIX, IBM, and OS/2 are registered trademarks of International Business Machines Corporation.

X-Windows and X Window System are registered trademarks of Massachusetts Institute of Technology.

MS-DOS is a registered trademark of Microsoft Corporation.

ORACLE, Pro*COBOL, Pro*FORTRAN, Pro*Pascal, Pro*PL/I, SQL*DBA, SQL*Forms, SQL*Graph, SQL*Menu, SQL*Net, SQL*Plus, and SQL*ReportWriter are registered trademarks, and Oracle Book, Oracle7, Oracle Graphics, Oracle*Terminal, Oracle Toolkit, PL/SQL, and Pro*C are trademarks of Oracle Corporation.

Important Note

Permissions

All appropriate permission for the use of SQL listings have been granted by the authors of the scripts. Wherever known the authors of scripts are credited.

Limits of Liability and Disclaimer or Warranty

The author makes no warranty, express or implied, with regard to the programs or the documentation contained in this book. The author shall not be liable in any event for incidental or consequential damages in conjunction with, or arising out of, the furnishing, performance, or use of these programs.

Contents

2 Administration of Oracle, or, After the Bloom Is Off the Rose . . .

3 Administration of Database Objects 73

8 Backup and Recovery Procedures for Oracle   283

9 Managing the Oracle Tools   315

Preface

Why am I writing this book? This is a question I have asked myself often over the last several months. I want to provide to the novice database administrator/manager a single reference for ideas, answers, and methods on maintaining a database.

I remember how frustrating it was for me to go from reference to reference seeking the answer to a problem that appeared simple. It is ridiculous to have to wade through five different manuals for the answer to a simple question. It is even more frustrating to search through both the manuals and then the system for the latest README file. Hopefully this book will spare you some of that difficulty.

I have attempted to combine several DBAs' experiences and material from several sources to provide not just the "whats" but also the "hows." I have also attempted to provide guidelines for user, space, and product administration and control. I hope I have succeeded in the above goals.

In the final analysis it is you, the buyer of this book, who will make the determination if I have succeeded in meeting the above goals. As with any reference, if you don't use the information provided, be it actual scripts, techniques, or just philosophy, you have wasted your money. I assure you that if you use the scripts and follow the guidelines presented, you will benefit from this book.

Well, I hate long prefaces, so I'll cut this short. Let me just say that the companion disk contains all of the scripts, plus many others, the SQL*Menu load scripts for the SQL*Menu menus, copies of the DCL com, and UNIX shell procedures for a menu system. It's a bargain. End of commercial. I hope you get good use from this book. I enjoyed writing it.

Dedication

I would like to dedicate this book to my loving and patient wife and daughters, Susan, Cynthia and Michelle, who have put up with my ill-humor, raging at the computer and in-general unrefined behavior during its writing. I would also like to thank Oracle Corporation for their excellent classes and references. Lastly I would like to thank Mike Brouilette, Tim Olesen, Cary Millsap, and Gary Dodge for their contributions.

Acknowledgments

This book would not exist without the generous support and assistance of the people at John Wiley and QED, and especially Edwin Kerr and Maureen Drexel.

Introduction

So You've Chosen Oracle . . . Now What?

Good question. Oracle is one of the leading Relational Database Management systems available today. So what can it do for you?

Oracle's power comes from its ability to allow users quick and accurate data retrieval. This is the main strength of a relational system. Relational databases provide a logical, generally straightforward presentation of data. This allows users to query information and easily get the data they need and only the data they need. This is accomplished through the tabular format of a relational database. The logical collection of *related* data and the data tables' *relationships* to each other form the database. Through its SQL, SQL*Plus, SQL*Forms and other tools, Oracle allows developers, users, and administrators to get a look at their data as never before.

The purpose of this book is to provide the administrator responsible for maintaining and administrating the Oracle database a set of tools to make their job easier. It is hoped that through example and real-world scenarios the database administrator, or manager, will gain valuable insight into the workings of the Oracle database management system. Numerous examples of reports and the SQL, SQL*Plus, and PL/SQL code used to generate them will be given. The interpretation of these reports will also be covered.

Oracle provides a great database administration toolset. Unfortunately few beginning DBAs have the prerequisite knowledge to put these tools to good use. This book is intended to remedy that. In the chapters that follow, all phases of Oracle database administration and management will be covered: initial installation, day-to-day maintenance, the all-important backup, recovery, and disaster recovery procedures that could mean the difference between being a successful DBA and one given the boot.

A Brief Overview of Oracle

Oracle is a *relational database management system*, or RDBMS for short. As was discussed before, an RDBMS stores data in tables called *relations*. These relations are two dimensional representations of data where the rows—called *tuples* in relational jargon—represent records, and the columns—called *attributes*—are the pieces of information contained in the record.

Oracle provides a rich set of tools to allow design, and maintenance, of the database. The major Oracle tools are listed below.

RDBMS Kernel	This is the database engine, the workhorse of Oracle.
SQL	This is the relational language—structured query language.
SQL*Plus	This is Oracle's addition to SQL.
PL/SQL	Stands for procedural language SQL, allows procedural processing of SQL statements.
SQL*DBA	Database administrator's toolset, includes a monitor utility.
SQL*Loader	This allows data entry from ASCII flat files into Oracle tables.
EXPORT/IMPORT	These tools allow data and structure information to be removed and inserted from Oracle databases into or out of archives.
SQL*Report	This is Oracle's first report writer language.
SQL*Forms	If the RDBMS is the workhorse, this is the jockey. Forms allows ease of access to data, reports, and procedures.
SQL*ReportWriter	This is Oracle's standard report writer. It is pseudo-forms based.
SQL*Menu	This is Oracle's menu system. It allows access to forms, reports, procedures, and operating system level procedures.
SQL*Textretrieval	This allows access to text-based data stored in Oracle.
DataQuery	This is a forms-based query tool for endusers.
Oracle DataBrowser	This is a GUI-based query tool for endusers.
Oracle*Card	This provides HyperCard stack programming for Oracle data.
Oracle*Graphics	This product allows graphic representation of query results.
CASE*Dictionary	This stands for: *c*omputer *a*ided *s*oftware *e*ngineering data dictionary for Oracle. It is forms based.
CASE*Designer	This allows generation of *ERD*, *FHD*, *Matrix,* and *Dataflow* diagrams from CASE*Dictionary.
CASE*Generator	From data in the Dictionary, this generates applications for use with Oracle.

In order to fully understand the structures that make up an Oracle database, the ability to use the above tools is critical. As a database administrator or manager you will become intimately familiar with at least the first eleven of the above tools, with the possible exception of SQL*Report.

Oracle is more than just a collection of programs that allow ease of data access. Oracle can be compared to an operating system that overlays the operating system of the computer on which it resides. Oracle has its own file structures, buffer structures, global areas, and tunability above and beyond those provided within the operating system. Oracle controls its own processes, monitors its own records and consistencies, and cleans up after itself.

Oracle as it exists on your system (with the exception of DOS or OS/2) consists of executables, five to nine detached processes, a global memory area, data files, and maintenance files. It can be as small as a couple of megabytes or as large as a massive globe spanning construction of gigabytes.

Typical version 6 and ORACLE7 environments are shown in Figures 1 and 2. You may want to refer to these diagrams as you read the next sections.

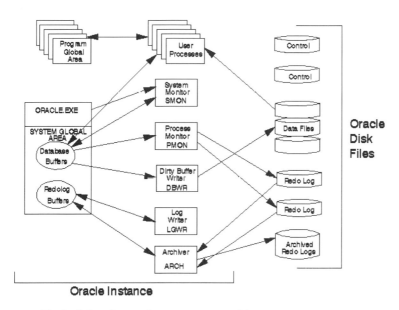

Figure 1. Typical Oracle version 6 system architecture.

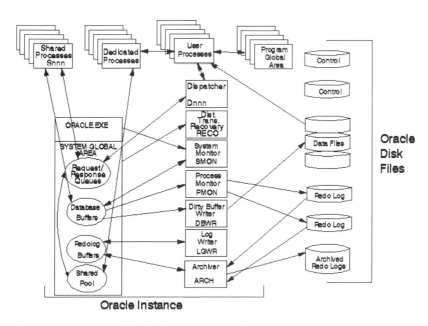

Figure 2. Typical ORACLE7 system architecture.

Let's look at a typical Oracle system that operates in either VMS or UNIX environments. On VMS or UNIX there may be up to six detached processes for Oracle version 6; for ORACLE7, this jumps to eight. Four of these are the base Oracle processes, and these processes are started every time Oracle is started up on a system; the additional processes may be started if the database is using archiving, uses TCPIP, or is being run in parallel and/or distributed mode. These processes are listed below.

DBWR—Database Writer	This process handles data transfer from the buffers in the SGA to the database files.
LGWR—Log Writer	This process transfers data from the redo log buffers to the redo log database files.
SMON—System Monitor	This process performs instance recovery on instance startup and is responsible for cleaning up temporary segments. In a parallel environment, this process recovers failed nodes.
PMON—Process Monitor	This process recovers user processes that have failed and cleans up the cache. This process recovers the resources from a failed process.
ARCH—Archiver Process	This process is only active if archive logging is in effect. This process writes the redo log data files that are filled into the archive log data files.
RECO—Distributed Transaction Recoverer	This is an ORACLE7 process that resolves failures involving distributed transactions.
LCK*n*—Lock Process	This process is used for inter-instance locking in an ORACLE7 parallel server environment.
D*nnn*—Dispatcher	This process allows multiple processes to share a finite number of ORACLE7 servers. It queues and routes process requests to the next available server.
S*nnn*—Servers	This ORACLE7 process makes all the required calls to the database to resolve a user's requests. It returns results to the D*nnn* process that calls it.
ORASRV—TCPIP server	If you are running TCPIP, this process, known as the listener process, will be running as well (only one per node).

On a UNIX system, this additional process may be present:

ARCHMON—Archive Monitor	This is a process on UNIX that monitors the archive process and writes the redo logs to the archives. It will require a dedicated window or terminal on BSD systems.

On both VMS and UNIX, each user process may spawn several subprocesses, depending on the type of activities being done by that process. Each time a tool such as SQL*Menu calls another tool such as SQL*Forms, another process is created.

The global memory area—called the system global area, or SGA—is an area of CPU memory that is reserved for Oracle use only. It contains buffers that are used to speed transaction throughput and help maintain the system integrity and consistency. No data is altered directly on the disk; it all passes through the SGA. The size and configuration of the SGA is defined by a file called the INIT.ORA file, which can contain information on each type of buffer or cache area in the SGA.

There are also shared programs that make up a typical instance. These can be as few as one (e.g., the ORACLE kernel) or as complex as the entire toolset. Placing the toolset into shared memory (on VMS) reduces the memory requirements for each user.

As said before, Oracle can be viewed as an operating system that overlays your existing operating system. It has structures and constructs that are unique to it alone. The major area of an Oracle installation is of course the database. In order to access an Oracle database you must first have at least one *instance* of Oracle that is assigned to that Database. An instance consists of the subprocesses, global area, and related structures that are assigned to it. Multiple instances can attach to a single database. Many of both the instance's and database's characteristics are determined when it is created. A single VMS or UNIX platform can have several instances in operation simultaneously. On VMS they can be attached to their own database, or they may share one. The document set for Oracle weighs in at over 60 pounds. Not light reading by any means.

A Brief Overview of Relational Jargon

Some of you are no doubt wondering what the heck this book is talking about. Relations, tuples, attributes—what are they? Ninety percent of any field is learning the jargon—the language specific to that field. With Oracle, the terminology is that of relational databases. Much of this jargon can be attributed to Dr. E. F. Codd, who formulated the rules, called "normal forms," for data and the relational algebra upon which relational databases are designed.

You may have already been exposed to such topics as "normal form," "tuples," and "primary and foreign keys." Others have not. It is not the intention of this book to give a full course in relational theory. It will, however, attempt to clarify the meanings of this "relational speak" so those without any formal ground in relational terminology can find the book as valuable as those who know it all.

We've already mentioned tables, tuples, attributes, and we've touched on relationships. Let's look at relationships a bit more as they apply to relational databases. Stop for a moment and consider the company where you work, or perhaps are consulting for. The company has employees, or let's say the company employs workers. The reverse is also true; a worker is employed by a company. This is a relationship. A relationship is a logical tie between information that is contained in entities. In this case, the information is from the entities—A, the company, and B, the workers.

Can a worker have more than one job? Of course. Can a company have more than one worker? Yes. So let's restate the relationship: A company might employ one or more workers. A worker may be employed by one or more Companies. This is called a "many-to-many" relationship. Of course other types of relationships exist. Within a company, a worker usually only works for one department at a time, while a department may have many workers. This is called a "one-to-many" relationship. Generally speaking, most many-to-many relationships can be broken down into one-to-many relationships; one-to-many relationships form a majority of the relationships in a relational database. A relationship is between two *entities*. In the above example, "worker" and "company" are entities. An entity is always singular in nature. In most cases, an entity will map into a table. A diagram showing the logical structure of a relational database is called an entity relation diagram, or ERD for short. Figure 3 shows a simple entity relationship diagram.

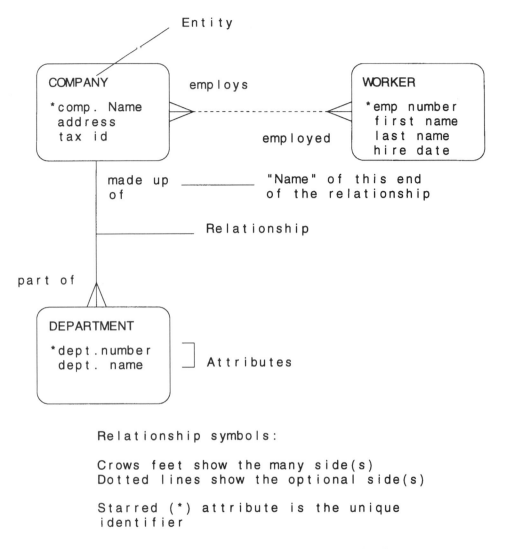

Figure 3. Example of an ERD diagram showing M:M and 1:M relationships.

Another aspect of a relational database is its functions. Without functions a database would have no purpose for being. Functions start at a high level, for example, "Provide a means of tracking and reporting the work history of employees." Functions can be broken down, or, if you wish, decomposed, until they are atomic in nature. A fanatic would break down a function until it consisted of operations involving individual attributes such as add, delete, update, retrieve.

For example, say we wished to retrieve a record (or *tuple)* from a table, update one of its columns (or *attributes),* and then return the row to the table. In one case, it could be considered one function, *update of attribute x.* In a different light, it could be decomposed into the individual

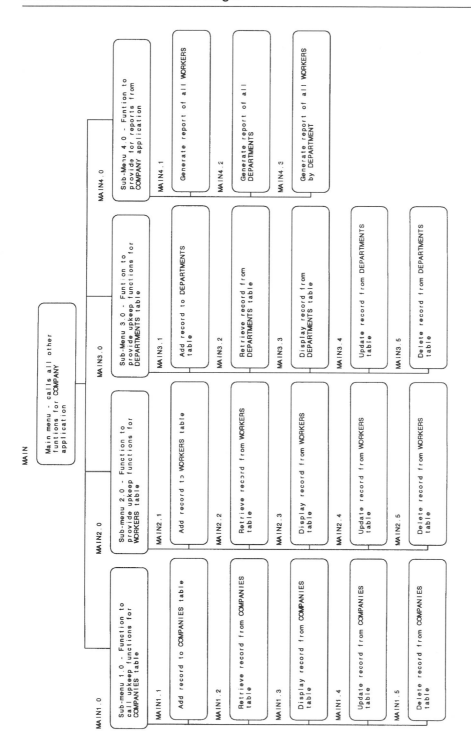

Figure 4. Example of a simple function hierarchy diagram.

retrieves, modifies, and updates of the columns. In most cases it isn't required to go into great and gory detail. The functions a database performs are shown in a function hierarchy diagram. Entities (and hence, tables) and relations map into functions. Figure 4 shows a simple function hierarchy diagram (FHD).

The final aspect of a relational database is its modules. A module may perform one or more *functions*. A module may map into a form, a report, a menu, or a procedure. For example, a single module representing a form can handle numerous atomic functions such as add, update, retrieve, and delete a table's or even a group of table's, data records.

Let's summarize. A relational database is made up of entities consisting of attributes. These entities and attributes can be mapped into a table. Each occurrence of an entity adds a row to the table it maps to. These rows are called tuples. Each entity relates to one or more other entities by means of relationships. Relationships must be valid in both directions and must have degree such as *one to many* or *many to many*. Relationships must also show optionality, such as *may be* or *must be*.

Functions are used to tell what is done with the entities and relations. Entities and relations map into functions. Modules implement functions and map into forms, reports, menus, or procedures. All of this depends on Dr. Codd's rules. The entire set of rules are complex and to most of us, rather obtuse at times. Luckily, they have been used to produce the rules of normalization.

Precursor:	*Each occurrence of an entity is uniquely identifiable by a combination of attributes and/or relationships.*
First Normal Form:	*Remove repeated attributes or groups of attributes to their own entity.*
Second Normal Form:	*Remove attributes dependent on only part of the unique identifier.*
Third Normal Form:	*Remove attributes dependent on attributes that are not a part of the unique identifier.*

In short, to be in third normal form all attributes in an entity must relate directly to the identifier and only to the identifier.

This unique identifier is called the *primary key*. It can be a unique number, such as a social security number, or a combination of attributes, called a concatenated or combination key, such as last name and date of birth. Generally speaking these primary keys are used to enforce relations by mapping the keys into related entities where they become *foreign keys*.

For those who want a more detailed discussion of entity relation diagrams, Normalization and other related (no pun intended) topics, these books are recommended:

Introduction to Database Systems, Volume 1, 4th Edition, C. J. Date, Addison-Wesley Publishing Co., Inc., Reading, Massachusetts.

CASE*METHOD Tasks and Deliverables, Richard Barker, Addison-Wesley Publishing Co., Inc., Reading, Massachusetts.

CASE*METHOD Entity Relationship Modeling, Richard Barker, Addison-Wesley Publishing Co., Inc., Reading, Massachusetts.

CASE*METHOD Function and Process Modeling, Richard Barker, Addison-Wesley Publishing Co., Inc., Reading, Massachusetts.

Data Base: Structured Techniques for Design, Performance and Management, S. Atre, J. Wiley, New York, New York.

RELATIONAL DATABASES Concepts, Design and Administration, K. S. Brathwaite, McGraw-Hill, Inc., New York, New York.

What Exactly Is a Database Administrator?

A database administrator (DBA) should not be confused with a data administrator (DA). While a data administrator is responsible for administering data via naming conventions and data dictionaries, a database administrator is responsible for administering the physical implementation of a database. This can include or overlap the database management function. In fact, this book will blur the two together since one's functions are closely related to the other. The DBA provides support and technical expertise to the DA and users.

The DBA position is constantly changing and expanding. It may encompass physical design and implementation, performance monitoring and tuning, even testing and configuration of interface programs such as X-Window emulators for use with the database.

The database administrator must have the freedom required to move data files in coordination with the system manager to optimize database access. The DBA should work hand in hand with the system administrator to ensure proper use is made of available resources. There is no more certain formula for failure than a company where the database administrator and the system administrator are at war.

Let's list the major jobs of a database administrator according to the *ORACLE7 Server Administrator's Guide*, DEC. 1992:

1. Installing and upgrading the ORACLE server and application tools.
2. Allocating system storage and planning future storage requirements for the database.
3. Creating primary database storage structures (tablespaces) once developers have designed an application.
4. Creating primary database objects (tables, views, indexes) once application developers have designed an application.
5. Modifying the database structure, as necessary, from information given by application developers.
6. Enrolling users and maintaining system security.
7. Ensuring compliance with Oracle license agreements.
8. Controlling and monitoring user access to the database.
9. Monitoring and optimizing the performance of the database.
10. Planning for backup and recovery of database information.
11. Maintaining archived data on appropriate storage devices.
12. Backing and restoring the database.
13. Contacting Oracle Corporation for technical support.

In an ideal structure, there is a data administrator who is a direct report to a director or other senior manager. This DA is "off to the side," rather like the executive officer on a Navy ship. Also reporting to this level of management should be the database administrator. The DA and DBA need to work closely together to be sure that the physical and logical structure of the database, through the data dictionary, are closely tied. The database administrator may also hold the database management function, or this may be a separate position. Beneath this level are the application administrators who control individual applications. Beneath the application administrators may be the development and maintenance staffs, or these may be in a separate directorate. This structure is shown in Figure 5. If the database is sufficiently large, especially under ORACLE7, due to its more complex security requirements, a security administrator may also be required.

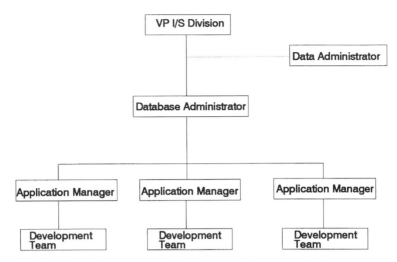

Figure 5. Sample information systems data administration organization.

All of the above positions must work closely together. The DA must talk to the DBA, and the DBM and DBA must work closely together to optimize the database system. The application managers need to ensure their applications meet naming rules and conventions and coordinate their resource utilization with the DBM and DBA. As can be seen, the DBA is central to the proper running of a database system. They coordinate activities related to the database; assist with design, development, and testing; and provide monitoring and tuning.

Hopefully, this book will provide database administrators, database managers, and application managers with a set of tools that will make their jobs easier and more enjoyable.

1

Installation of Oracle

Oracle installation is a complex topic. The method used to install the database system and toolset is very platform dependent. There are universal topics, however, that involve structure and layout issues. This chapter will present those areas and give a general idea of the way to proceed with your installation.

This chapter is not intended to replace the *Installation and User's Guide* provided with the software. You should install Oracle by following the manufacturer's specifications. The procedures provided at the end of this chapter are only examples.

1.1 Things to Consider Before Installation

Regardless of what system you are installing Oracle on, there are several major considerations that you must address before you install. When thinking about these items, allow for your data space needs for at least a year in advance:

- How many data files will the database require?
- What size global area will the database require?
- What are the database's archive requirements?
- How many disk drives are available for Oracle files?
- How many instances and/or databases does your installation require?
- Is there a need for shared instances?
- Will the database be distributed?
- Do you want single-task or independent tools?

The answers to the above questions will determine the entire course of the installation.

Serious thought should go into the structure of your database environment. You may have to administer this environment for a long time to come. Oracle has a method for laying out Oracle environments that provides the maximum stability and manageability. This is known as *OFA compliant* (OFA - optimal flexible architecture). Essentially, this involves spreading the Oracle database and its files across several platters and using environmental variables, such as VMS logicals, to enforce naming conventions for disks, directories, and locations.

1.1.1 Optimal Flexible Architecture (OFA)

In accordance with Cary V. Millsap of the Oracle National Technical Response Team, the OFA process involves three rules:

1. Establish an orderly operating system directory structure in which any database file can be stored on any disk resource.
    a. Name all devices that might contain Oracle data in such a manner that a wild card or similar mechanism can be used to refer to the collection of devices as a unit.
    b. Make a directory explicitly for storage of Oracle data at the same level on each of these devices.
    c. Beneath the Oracle data directory on each device, make a directory for each different Oracle database on the system.
    d. Put a file X in the directory /u??/ORACLE/D (or on VMS DISK2:[ORACLE.D]) if and only if X is a control file, redo log file, or data file of the Oracle database whose DB_NAME is D. X is any database file.
        Note: You may wish to add an additional directory layer if you will have multiple Oracle versions running at the same time. This additional layer includes the version level.
2. Separate groups of segments (data objects) with different behaviors into different tablespaces.
    a. Separate groups of objects with different fragmentation characteristics in different tablespaces (e.g., don't put data and rollback segments together).
    b. Separate groups of segments that will contend for disk resources in different tablespaces (e.g., don't put data and indexes together).
    c. Separate groups of segments representing objects with differing behavioral characteristics in different tablespaces (e.g., don't put tables that require daily backup in the same tablespace with those that require yearly backup).
3. Maximize database reliability and performance by separating database components across different disk resources.
    a. Keep at least three active copies of a database control file on at least three different physical drives.
    b. Use at least three database redo log files in version 6, and three groups in ORACLE7. Isolate them to the greatest extent possible on hardware serving few or no files that will be active while the RDBMS is in use.
    c. Separate tablespaces whose data will participate in disk resource contention across different physical disk resources. (You should also consider disk controller usage.)

1.1.2 Minimum OFA Configuration

The minimum suggested configuration would consist of five data areas, either disks, striped sets, RAID sets, or whatever else comes down the pike in the next few years. These areas should be as separate as possible, ideally operating off of different device controllers to maximize throughput. The more heads you have moving at one time, the faster your database will be. The disk layout should minimize disk contention, for example:

DISK1:   Oracle executables and user areas, a control file, the SYSTEM tablespace, redo logs.
DISK2:   Data—Data files, a control file Tool—Data files.
DISK3:   Index—Data files, a control file.
DISK4:   Rollback segment—Data files, export files.
DISK5:   Archive log files.

Of course, the more disks you can use, the better off you will be. For large databases, entire disks may be dedicated to a single data file. One rule of thumb: The more spread out the database files, the happier Oracle will be. Some small installations have gotten by with as few as two disks, but eventually, if more than just a few users are accessing Oracle, performance will degrade.

Oracle stores all information in data files. These data files can be likened to disks. They have a predetermined structure and may contain hundreds of tables of data. On VMS you are limited to 255 total data files in version 6, 1022 for ORACLE7. On UNIX the limit is 62. Other systems have limits as well. Consult your operating documentation to determine your limits. When you create your database, you will specify the number of data files it can ultimately have, some initial file placement, and whether you want archive logging or not.

1.2 Oracle Structures and How They Affect Installation

So, we can see an Oracle database is not a simple construct. Much thought must go into file placement, size of global areas, number of control files, and numerous other structural issues before installation. It is a testament to the resiliency of the Oracle RDBMS that even if most of the decisions are made incorrectly, the database that results will still function, albeit inefficiently.

For installation, the structures that should concern the DBA are:

- Oracle executables
- Data files—data, index, temporary, rollback
- Redo logs
- Control files
- Export files
- Archive logs

Let's examine each of these.

1.2.1 Executables

The Oracle executables are the heart of the system. Without them the system is, of course, worthless since the data files are only readable by Oracle processes. The Oracle executables should be on a disk reserved for executables and maybe some user files. Disk speed is not a big issue, but availability is of major concern. The executables will require 60 to 150 megabytes or more of disk space. The installation process will create a directory structure starting at a user-specified root directory. There will usually be a subdirectory for each major product installed.

1.2.2 Data Files

Data files are the physical implementations of Oracle tablespaces. Tablespaces are the logical units of storage that would roughly compare to disks in an operating system. Hundreds of tables, indexes, rollback segments, constraints, and other internal structures can be mapped into a single tablespace. In return, these are then mapped into the data files that correspond to the tablespaces. Only a limited number of data files can be associated with a tablespace. The total number of data files for the entire database is set by the MAXDATAFILES parameter at creation (VMS defaults to 32, UNIX, 16).

The ideal situation would be to have each data file on a separate disk. But, most of us don't have that many disks, let alone that many exclusively available to Oracle. Placing the different types of data files on different drives is a reasonable compromise. As a minimum, separate data files that contain *data* from data files that contain *indexes*. Trying to read the same disk for both data and its related indexes immediately results in disk contention. Rollback segments are used to store data about transactions so if the transaction aborts for any reason, it can be rolled back to a consistent state. Rollback segments are high-activity areas and should be separated from data and index files.

Each Oracle database will have a SYSTEM tablespace for storage of data dictionary information. The SYSTEM tablespace will grow as development proceeds and then will stabilize at a maximum size (this can be avoided by placing non-data dictionary tables in a separate tablespace instead of in the SYSTEM area, but we will discuss this later). It may be advisable to place it by itself on the same platter as the executables.

You will want several additional tablespaces. As a minimum you will need one for rollback segments, one for users, one as a temporary area, and one for the Oracle tool tables. Each application should be placed in its own tablespace, as should each application's indexes. So for an Oracle database supporting one application you will have seven tablespaces, each with one or more data files.

1.2.3 Redo Logs

As their name implies, redo logs are used to restore transactions after a system crash or other system failure. The redo logs store data about transactions that alter database information. Each database should have at least two if no archive logging is taking place, three or more with archive logging in effect. These are relatively active files, and if made unavailable, the database cannot function. They can be placed anywhere except in the same location as the archive logs. Archive logs are archive copies of filled redo logs and are used for point-in-time recovery from a major disk or system failure. Since they are backups of the redo logs it would not be logical to place the redo logs and archives in the same physical location. The size of the redo logs will determine how much data is lost due to a disaster affecting the database. The smaller the redo log, the less data lost. On the other hand, the larger the redo log, the smaller the impact on system performance. The size is set at creation.

1.2.4 Control Files

An Oracle database cannot be started without at least one control file. The control file contains data on system structures, log status, and other important information about the database. The control file is generally less than one megabyte in size. It is wise to have at least two copies of your control file on different disks, three for OFA compliance. Oracle will maintain them as mirror images of each other. This ensures that loss of a single control file will not knock your database out of the water. You cannot bring a control file back from a backup; it is a living file that corresponds to current database status. In later versions of Oracle version 6, and in ORACLE7, there is a CREATE CONTROL FILE command that allows recovery from loss of a control file. However, you must have detailed knowledge of your database to use it properly. It is easier to maintain extra control file copies.

1.2.5 Exports and Archives

Export and archive files affect the recoverability of your database should some disaster befall it. Export files, created by the export utility supplied by Oracle, are copies of a database's data and structure at a given point in time. There are several types of exports that will be covered in the section on backup and recovery. Export files should be stored in a separate location from archive files.

Archive files, as stated before, are archived copies of the redo logs. They provide the capability to recover to a specific point-in-time for any tablespace in the database. For any application considered to be production or mission critical, archive logging must be turned on. These files can be stored to disk, tape, or even optical storage such as WORM. Using operating system backups such as BACKUP on VMS or TAR on UNIX, and with the application of archive logs, a database can be quickly recovered after disaster.

After each successful backup of a shutdown Oracle database, the associated archive and export files may be removed and either placed in storage or deleted. In an active database these files may average tens of megabytes per day; storage for this amount of data must to be planned for. As an example, at one installation doing Oracle development with no active production databases, 244 megabytes of archives and over 170 megabytes of exports were generated in a one-week period. If archive logging is turned on, and you run out of archive disk space, the database stops after the last redo log is filled. Plan ahead and monitor disk usage for instances using archive logging.

1.3 System Considerations

Within each Oracle installation there are several operating system considerations that must be taken into account. These affect how Oracle uses global memory and process memory areas. The DBAs will be responsible for tuning and maintaining these areas.

1.3.1 What Is a PAD?

The PAD is used only on VMS systems. The SGA PAD file size is specified when you create the database for the first time. This parameter determines how much process memory is reserved for the system global area (SGA). If your settings in the INIT.ORA file (to be covered later) cause the SGA to be larger than the SGA PAD, the instance will not start up. Make the PAD as large as you ever expect to need. The SGA will use only as much as it needs. Increasing the PAD requires a recreation of the database on version 6 and a complete relink of all products on ORACLE7; either should be avoided if possible.

On UNIX systems, the shared memory parameters determine your maximum SGA. The critical parameters are SHMMAX and SHMSEG under HP-UX, for example. Please refer to your system documentation and the current version of your installation guide for information on setting these parameters. On both systems, increasing SGA size will increase performance, but, too large of an SGA will result in swapping and severe performance degradation.

1.3.2 What Is an SGA and How Does It Apply to Me?

SGA is a shared global area. As the term *global* implies, this area is accessible to all Oracle processes and users. Each instance will have its own SGA. Oracle processes and users must share large amounts of data. If all of the processes had to get the data from the disk, the IO load would soon render response times that would be totally unacceptable. To prevent this, Oracle uses global memory areas—that is, CPU memory. This memory is dedicated to use for Oracle alone. In Oracle version 6, the global area is divided into two general areas: the data dictionary caches/database buffers and the redo log buffers. For ORACLE7 an area is added to keep track of queues associated with requests and responses and a shared SQL area. Each area is important to the database overall performance.

The data dictionary caches and database buffers provide immediate access to data that has been preread from either the data dictionary tables or the data tables. The Oracle kernel process uses an LRU (least recently used) algorithm to write data back to the disks. Data is never altered on the disks directly but is altered in memory first.

The redo buffers contain row change information, transaction commit history, and checkpoint history. This data is written into the redo logs and eventually to the archive logs. A commit will force a disk write as will the filling of a redo log buffer or the reaching of a predefined checkpoint.

For ORACLE7 the queue and request areas store data that is being transferred between processes such as servers and other ORACLE7 processes. The shared SQL area stores all SQL statements in a parsed form. When a user or process issues an SQL command, the shared SQL area is checked to see if the command already exists in parsed form; if it does, this shared version is used.

1.3.3 What Is a PGA and How Does It Apply to Me?

The PGA is the process global area. This is memory reserved for each process that uses Oracle. It contains the context area. On VMS this is controlled via the INIT.ORA files context control parameters, CONTEXT_AREA and CONTEXT_INCR, and the VMS UAF working set and page file quota parameters.

If you are using UNIX, there is no OS level control in most flavors. That is, if a poorly written application opens too many context areas due to improper cursor usage, you can crash the system due to total depletion of system memory.

1.4 Some System-Specific Notes

Under each operating system there are items a DBA needs to be aware of and take into account when installing Oracle. This section is an attempt to consolidate these system-specific notes in one location.

1.4.1 VMS Specific Notes

As was stated before, UNIX defaults to a MAXDATAFILES of 16. If you don't correct this, the system must be exported, dropped, and recreated to increase it. You are limited to an SGA of 32 Mb in version 6 and ORACLE7, but since most run around 8 Mb to 32 Mb, this probably won't be a problem for you.

Memory Requirements. To run Oracle on VMS you must have at least 16 Mb of system memory. Loading the complete product set requires 112,000 blocks of disk space (512 K blocks) for Version 6 or 325,000 blocks of disk space for ORACLE7. If you comply to OFA rules you will need additional disk space to accommodate the tablespaces required.

VMS SYSGEN Parameters. SYSGEN parameters of interest are listed below.

PARAMETER	V6 VALUE	V7 VALUE
GBLPAGES	2200	8000 + 2 for every 1K of PAD for either V6 or V7
VIRTUALPAGECNT	10240	> than Max. User PGFLQUO
GBLSECTIONS	17	17

There are other requirements that may change with time and versions of the software. Please be sure to check your installation and administration guide for all values before altering them.

Data files. The limit for maximum open files for VMS on Oracle version 6 is 255; the limit for ORACLE7 is 1022. The minimum data file size for ORACLE7 is 5 Mb for the *first* file, but there is no limit after that. The maximum number of redo logs allowed is 255. For VMS, the maximum number of extents—that is, the number of times a table, rollback segment, or index can be extended—is based on database block size. For the VMS system, the minimum block size is 2K bytes; this yields a maximum number of extents of 121. For a 4K-byte block size the maximum is 249, and for an 8K-byte block size it will be 505.

1.4.2 UNIX Specific Notes

Data Files. As was stated before, UNIX defaults to a MAXDATAFILES of 16 and cannot exceed 60 due to the file number limit of 0 to 59 on UNIX systems. This can be overcome by altering the OPEN_MAX value in the limits.h file. Under some versions of UNIX this may be different; look under configurable kernel parameters. Another UNIX-specific limit is on the total number of file extents. It has been reported, but not documented, that a maximum of 121 extents per database object is allowed under version 6. The initial release of the ORACLE7 documentation gives the following information on maximum extents for various block sizes: .5K block size—25 extents, 1K block—57, 2K block—121, 4K block—249, 8K—505. This implies that a close watch on database table extents must be maintained for UNIX and that proper design and table sizing is critical.

System Global Area (SGA). In some cases, the SGA may exceed the available shared memory. The UNIX administrator must relink the kernel to allow larger programs if this occurs. There are system-specific shared memory parameters that control the maximum size of the SGA. These should be reviewed under configurable kernel parameters for your version of UNIX. The installation guide for your Oracle system will delineate which parameters to look at for your UNIX system. Under the HP-UX implementation, the size of the SGA is limited to the size of swap space on the available disk drives. The parameters that control how the SGA grows on a HP-UX system are SHMMAX, the size of a shared memory area, and SHMSEG, the number of shared memory areas a process can access.

Rollback Segments. There are three major concerns when dealing with rollback segments. These are: the number of rollback segments, the size of the rollback segments and extents, and whether to use private or public rollback segments. The number and size issues are determined by the number of users and the size of the expected transactions. The issue of whether to use private or public rollback segments is not so clear.

The major difference between public and private rollback segments is determined by how an instance uses them. With private rollback segments, the instance acquired the segments it requires at startup via the ROLLBACK_SEGMENTS parameter in the INIT.ORA file. These acquired rollback segments are the only segments that the instance will use unless there are public rollback segments available. Generally speaking, most DBAs will have a good idea as to the usage levels of the database and can create sufficient private segments so that all users are serviced properly. Public rollback segments are acquired as needed by an instance. The number of segments initially acquired is determined by the rollback ratio of the INIT.ORA parameters TRANSACTIONS and TRANSACTIONS_PER_ROLLBACK_SEGMENT. TRANSACTIONS is a derived parameter based on the value of the PROCESSES parameter. Once the instance acquires its initial segments, it will attempt to acquire an additional segment each time the number of transactions exceeds the value of TRANSACTIONS. This leads to not knowing which public rollback segments are active and which are available. In fact, it may be almost impossible to take a public segment offline for maintenance without use of the special INIT.ORA parameter _OFFLINE_ROLLBACK_SEGMENTS.

Public rollback segments are most useful when the database is being operated in parallel mode. In parallel mode, several instances of Oracle access the same central database file system. Parallel instances can share a common pool of public rollback segments reducing the required number of segments verses what would be required if all of the segments were private. Under UNIX, some platforms can support parallel instances; some cannot. For your implementation of UNIX, check your installation guide to see if parallel instances are supported.

In most cases public rollback segments on UNIX can cause more problems than they solve. Unless there is some overriding reason to use public segments under a UNIX environment, they should be avoided. If you will have large transactions, such as batch jobs with numerous updates and adds between commits, a second INIT.ORA file should be created, which brings online a single large rollback segment to be used during batch operations.

Raw Devices. If you use normal UNIX file devices, there is no guarantee that all updates will be written to disk in a timely manner. This is due to the UNIX file buffers. If a system crash should occur between the time data leaves the Oracle buffers and transits through the UNIX buffers, data could be lost. To correct this, use UNIX raw devices or disable the UNIX file buffers. Oracle is capable of reading and writing directly to raw devices. This can increase Oracle performance for disk IO by over 50 percent and ensures data integrity is maintained. One limitation is that Oracle data file names are restricted to a specified syntax when raw devices are used. This will require the DBA to keep an accurate map of what devices belong to which tablespaces, log files, and so on.

Another method is to turn off UNIX buffering. Whether the option of removing UNIX buffering is open to you depends on the version of UNIX you are using.

Archives. To implement archive logging on BSD type systems, the archmon process must be started as a separate process that communicates via SQL*NET over TCP/IP to the arch process. This will require that the SQL*NET TCP/IP process *orasrv* be running. The archmon process must be run from a dedicated window or terminal.

1.5 Oracle and Disk Usage

One of the major arguments against relational database systems has been speed. It is said that relational systems are slow. It has been found, however, that with proper tuning of Oracle, applications and operating system, as well as proper file placement, Oracle performance is excellent. Conversely, if you try to place Oracle on an insufficient number of disks, performance will suffer.

1.5.1 How Many Is Enough?

Some applications will do fine with two disks. Not great mind you, but the system will function. Other applications, such as large complex systems involving numerous indexes, data tables, and tablespaces, may require dozens. To reduce disk contention and maximize database reliability, it is suggested that the DBA utilize OFA procedures to place database files. The next sections cover file placement for some basic disk layouts.

1 Disk (Surely you jest). For other than DOS, OS/2, WINDOWS-NT, or MAC-based, single-user databases it is foolish and very dangerous to even consider using a single disk to hold all Oracle files. A single-disk failure or crash could completely destroy your system. Since there are no file placement options with one disk, let's go on to the next configuration.

2 Disks (Just barely adequate). At least with two disks you can achieve separation of data and indexes and can separate redo logs from archive log files. This at least gives you some redundancies in recovery options. The file placement is shown below.

DISK1:   Oracle executables, index data files, redo logs, export files, a copy of the control file.

DISK2:   Data data files, rollback segment data file, temporary user data files, archive log files, a copy of the control file.

As you can see, an attempt is made to spread IO between the two disks. Indexes and data are on separate platters, as are redo logs and rollback segments. Additional recoverability in case of disk crash is given by having exports on one drive and archive log files on the other. While infinitely better than only one disk, having only two disks is still an extremely vulnerable condition and is not recommended.

3 Disks (Nearly there). With three drives available we improve the chances that the database can be recovered from disk crashes. We can also reduce the disk contention caused by sharing disks between highly active files in flagrant disregard for OFA rules. Let's look at the three disk layout:

DISK1:   Executables, redo logs, rollback segments, export files, copy of the control file
DISK2:   Data data files, temporary user data files, a copy of the control file
DISK3:   Archive log files, indexes, a copy of the control file

Again, an attempt is made to spread IO evenly across the platters. While this is better than one or two disks, there is still contention between redo logs and rollback segments, indexes, and archives.

4 Disks (Just about right). Four disks are much better. Now we can spread the disk-intensive rollbacks and redo logs. In addition, we can isolate the archives away from the indexes. Let's look at the structure:

DISK1:   Executables, redo log files, export files, a copy of the control file
DISK2:   Data data files, temporary user data files, a copy of the control file
DISK3:   Indexes, a copy of the control file
DISK4:   Archive logs, rollback segments

Now we have succeeded in spreading IO even further. Redo logs and rollback segments have been separated, and because archive logs will not be as active as redo logs, there will be less contention in this configuration. Since in most installations exports will be done during off hours, there should be little contention between the redos and exports.

5 Disks (Oracle nirvana). Well, this may not be nirvana, but it is an excellent minimum configuration. Five disks allow OFA compliance and permit maximum spread of IO load. Let's look at a five-disk spread:

DISK1:   Executables, a copy of the control file, redo logs, the SYSTEM tablespace data files
DISK2:   Data data files, temporary user data files, a copy of the control file
DISK3:   Index data files, a copy of the control file
DISK4:   Rollback segment data files, export files
DISK5:   Archive log files

Now we have minimum contention. By moving export files to tape, we can eliminate one additional source of database lockup. By monitoring DISK5 and periodically removing archive log files to tape, we can eliminate another. If we really wanted to push OFA, we could add a disk for redo logs.

As was previously stated, the more we can spread our tablespaces across multiple disks the better Oracle likes it. If you have the disk resources, spread Oracle as thin as you can. While a five-disk configuration performs well and is easy to maintain, the more the merrier.

1.5.2 Disk Striping, Shadowing, RAID, and Other Topics

Unless you've been living in seclusion from the computer mainstream, you will have already heard of the above topics. Let's take a brief look at them and how they will affect Oracle.

Disk Striping. Disk striping is the process by which multiple smaller disks are made to look like one large disk. This allows extremely large databases, or even extremely large single-table tablespaces, to occupy one logical device. This makes managing the resource easier since backups must address only one logical volume instead of several. This also provides the advantage of spreading IO across several disks. If you will need several gigabytes of disk storage for your application, striping may be the way to go. One disadvantage to striping: If one of the disks in the set crashes, you lose them all.

Disk Shadowing. If you will have mission-critical applications that you absolutely cannot allow to go down, consider disk shadowing. As its name implies, disk shadowing is the process whereby each disk has a shadow disk that data is written to simultaneously. This redundant storage allows the shadow disk or set of disks to pick up the load in case of a disk crash on the primary disk or disks, so the users never see a crashed disk. Once the disk is brought back on-line, the shadow process brings it back in sync. This also allows for backup, since the shadow set can be broken (e.g., the shadow separated from the primary), a backup taken, and then the set resynchronized.

The main disadvantage of disk shadowing is the cost: For a two-gigabyte disk farm, you must purchase four gigabytes of disk storage.

RAID—Redundant Arrays of Inexpensive Disks. The main strength of RAID technology is its dependability. In a RAID 5 array, the data is stored as are check sums and other information about the contents of each disk in the array. If one disk is lost, the others can use this stored information to recreate the lost data. This makes RAID very attractive. RAID has the same advantages as shadowing and striping at a lower cost. It has been suggested that if the manufacturers would use slightly more expensive disks (RASMED—redundant array of slightly more expensive disks) performance gains could be realized. A RAID system appears as one very large, reliable disk to the CPU. There are several levels of RAID:

RAID-0—Known as disk striping

RAID-1—Known as disk shadowing

RAID-0/1—Combination of RAID-0 and RAID-1

RAID-2—Data is distributed in extremely small increments across all disks and adds one or more disks that contain a hamming code for redundancy. RAID-2 is not considered commercially viable due to the added disk requirements (10 percent to 20 percent must be added to allow for their hamming disks).

RAID-3—This also distributes data in small increments but adds only one parity disk. This results in good performance for large transfers, but small transfers show poor performance.

RAID-4—In order to overcome the small transfer performance penalties in RAID-3, RAID-4 uses large data chunks distributed over several disks and a single parity disk. This results in a bottleneck at the parity disk. Due to this performance problem RAID-4 is not considered commercially viable.

RAID-5—This solves the bottleneck by distributing the parity data across the disk array. The major problem is that it requires several write operations to update parity data. The performance hit is only moderate, and the other benefits outweigh this minor problem.

RAID-6—This adds a second redundancy disk that contains error-correction codes. Read performance is good due to load balancing, but write performance suffers due to RAID-6 requiring more writes than RAID-5 for data update.

The main drawbacks to RAID are its relative newness, thus lack of performance data and lack of performance gain.

1.5.3 Other Related Topics

It is realized that this is a rather broad area—rather like defining the universe and giving three examples. However, it is a good place to talk about optical storage, RAM drives, and use of tape systems.

Optical Disk Systems. WORM (write once, read many) or MWMR (Multiple Write, Multiple Read) optical disks can be used to great advantage in an Oracle system. Their main use will be in storage of export and archive log files. Their relative immunity to crashes and long shelf life provide an ideal solution to the storage of the immense amount of data that proper use of archive logging and exports produce. As access speeds improve, these devices will be worth considering for these applications in respect to Oracle.

Tape Systems. Nine-track, 4 mm, 8 mm, and the infamous TK series from DEC can be used to provide a medium for archive logs and exports. One problem with this is the need at most installations for Operator monitoring of the tape devices to switch cartridges and reels. The newcomer in this field, laser tape, is still in the gates, but with the immense potential it promises, it may soon eclipse even the Optical disk. A WORM optical tape system recently released by Creo Products offers 1000 gigabytes of storage with an average access time of 37 seconds and data transfer rate of up to 3 MBps.

RAM Drives (Random Access Memory). While RAM drives have been around for several years, they have not seen the popularity their speed and reliability should be able to claim. One of the problems has been their small capacity in comparison to other storage mediums. Several manufacturers offer solid state drives of steadily increasing capacities. For index storage these devices are excellent. Their major strength is their innate speed. They also have onboard battery backup sufficient to back up their contents to their built-in hard drives. This backup is an automatic procedure invisible to the user, as is the reload of data upon power restoration. The major drawback to RAM drives is their high cost. The rapid reductions in memory chip costs with the equally rapid increase in amount of storage per chip may soon render this drawback nonexistent.

1.6 Installation Guidelines

Installation of Oracle is a complex topic. On the one hand, Oracle has automated the process to a large extent, but on the other hand, if you don't have your ducks in a row before you start, your success is doubtful. This section will cover installation on VMS and UNIX and attempt to point out the pitfalls that may be obstacles to a proper installation. Since the product is growing and changing with each release, this section cannot, nor is it intended to, replace the installation guides provided by Oracle. Instead, this section should provide general guidelines for the DBA who is facing installation or upgrade of the Oracle products.

1.6.1 Generic Installation Issues

In any installation, whether it be on UNIX or VMS, there are certain items that must be addressed:

Disk space availability
DBA account setup
Training
File layout
Tablespace layout
Database-specific topics

We will cover these topics and hopefully provide the DBA the information to arrive at logical answers to installation questions that may arise.

Disk Space Availability. More than any other single item, disk space availability probably messes up more installations than any other. On VMS Oracle requires contiguous space for its tablespace data files. When you are talking about files that at a minimum are megabytes in size, this can become quite an issue. Disk fragmentation doesn't seem to be a problem under UNIX.

With most modern systems, disk space is allocated dynamically. This means that as a file needs space, it is granted space wherever it is available on a disk. On active systems, where files are created, updated, deleted, or moved to different disks, this results in fragmentation—and problems for the DBA.

Under VMS, the fragmentation of disk assets is a performance issue for the system administrator; for a DBA attempting to install Oracle, it can be a show stopper. A disk may show that it has several megabytes available, but if those megabytes are spread out in 512K chunks across the platter, they are useless to Oracle. It is very frustrating to get a message telling you the system cannot allocate enough contiguous space when multiple megabytes are available. How can this be prevented?

The best way to prevent disk fragmentation from stopping an Oracle install is to install to freshly formatted, or virgin, disks. Unfortunately, most DBAs' will be installing on existing systems, and this won't be an option. The next best way is to coordinate with the system administrator to have the disks defragmented before the installation. On VMS this means either using an online defragmentation utility (be sure it is Oracle compatible) or using VMS BACKUP to back up and restore the disks involved in the installation. Since this can take several hours if the disks are large and the only available backup media a TK70, you don't spring this on the system administrator an hour or two before the install; it will need to be coordinated days in advance.

The Oracle DBA Account. Other than the SYSTEM account on VMS and the ROOT or SUPERUSER account on UNIX, the Oracle DBA account—usually called ORACLE, or with ORACLE7, ORACLE7—will be one of the most powerful accounts on the system. This is required because the Oracle system is more like an operating system than just a set of executables. In order to start up and shut down, create the required files, and allow global sharing of the kernel and perhaps the tools, the Oracle DBA account needs much broader privileges than a normal user account. The account must have the privilege to create directories, files, and other system objects. It will also require the ability to place objects in shared memory.

The second-largest contributor to a bad install experience is an underprivileged Oracle DBA account. The account *must* be set up as stated in the installation documentation for the install to be successful. After the installation, some adjustment of account privileges can be made if the system administrator just can't tolerate an account out of his realm of control having such broad privileges—but not until *after* the install is complete.

In most cases, the privileges removed by an overzealous system administrator will have to be periodically reinstated for code relinks, special file work, and, of course, upgrades. This will soon convince most system administrators to set them and leave them. After all, if you can't be trusted with the required privileges to do your job, should you be trusted with the job? It is advised that the Oracle DBA be sent to at least an introductory course in system administration so as to know what not to do with the privileges. A course in system tuning is also advised.

Training. It has been said that success in a new venture usually depends on three things:

training, training, and training

This is especially true in the realm of the Oracle DBA. Oracle Corporation offers numerous classes at locations across the US and Europe. These classes are Oracle specific and address issues that DBAs , developers, and managers need to be aware of and take into account. With most Oracle purchases you can negotiate training units, or TUs. Use them—they are worth their weight in gold. While there have been a few successful seat-of-the-pants Oracle installations, most end up in trouble. The Oracle Masters programs are especially useful in that they take the guesswork out of what classes you should take. Consult with Oracle training about schedules and classes. For large Oracle installations with numerous developers and administrators, Oracle will provide onsite classes that may significantly reduce your training costs. If you have training onsite, don't allow outside interruptions to intrude upon the class. These can be disruptive and are rude to the instructor. Besides, it is a waste of your training money not to allow the instructor to have the proper environment.

Would you allow a first-time driver to just jump into the car and drive off? It is amazing how many sites turn new and complex systems over to personnel with perhaps a good background in databases but no experience whatsoever in Oracle. Yes, there are generic issues, but there are enough details specific to Oracle alone that training is highly recommended. If it costs $6,000 to train a DBA, isn't it worth it? How much money would it cost if the system were down for several days while an inexperienced DBA waded through the manuals and tried to communicate intelligently with the Oracle help line? What if a critical application was destroyed because of something the DBA did or didn't do? At one site, an experienced DBA, new to the Oracle database system, didn't follow the normal database data file naming convention recommended by Oracle. Even though backups were taken, they didn't get the one SYSTEM data file that was named incorrectly. As a result, when an application required recovery due to data corruption, the system couldn't be restored. This resulted in the users abandoning the application and investing hundreds of hours reinventing it on MAC systems.

1.6.2 Disk Layout

If you've read up to this point you should realize that disk layout is critical to efficient operation of Oracle systems. There are several topics you need to consider when designing your disk layout.

1. What are the sizes and available space on the disks to be used with Oracle?
2. Is this disk used for other non-Oracle applications?
3. Has the disk been defragmented (if VMS)?
4. Is this a RAW device (If UNIX)?
5. What is the speed of the disk?
6. Is this a RAM or Optical disk?

Let's look at each of these questions and how the answers affect Oracle.

What are the sizes and available space on the disks to be used with Oracle? Obviously if there isn't enough space on the disk, you can't use it. If the size is too small to handle projected growth, then you might want to look at another disk. Oracle files can be moved, but not with that section of the database active. If you enjoy coming in after or before hours or on weekends, then by all means put your database files on an inappropriately sized disk.

Is this disk used for other non-Oracle applications? This is in actuality a many-sided question. From the Oracle point of view, if you have a very active non-Oracle application, it will be in contention for the disk with Oracle at every turn. If the non-Oracle application, such as word processing or a calculation program that uses intermediate result files, results in disk fragmentation (on VMS), this is bad if the data file co-located with it has to grow and can't allocate more contiguous space.

From the viewpoint of the other application, if we are talking about export files, archive log files, or growing data files, an asset we need to operate may be consumed, thus preventing our operation. Look carefully at the applications with which you will be sharing the disk assets, talk with their administrators, and make logical usage projections.

Has the disk been defragmented (for VMS)? This was covered before but bears repeating. A fragmented disk is of little use to Oracle on VMS. Oracle needs contiguous disk space for its data files. If the disk hasn't been defragmented, have it checked by the system administrator for fragmentation and defragmented if required.

Is the disk a RAW device (for UNIX)? If the disk is a RAW device, this restricts your capability for file naming. Be sure you maintain an accurate log of tablespace mapping to raw devices. Map tablespace and other asset's locations ahead of time.

What is the speed of the disk? By speed of disk we are referring to the access and seek times. The disk speed will drive disk throughput. Another item to consider when looking at disk speed is whether or not the disk is on a single or shared controller. Is the DSSI chained? All of these questions affect device throughput. Generally data files and indexes should go on the fastest drives; if you must choose one or the other, put indexes on the fastest. Rollback segments and redo logs can go on the slowest drives as can archive logs and exports.

Is the disk a RAM or optical disk? Ultimately the RAM and Optical usage ties back to disk speed. A RAM drive should be used for indexes due to its high speed. It is probably not a good candidate for data files because of its current size limitations; this may change in the future. An optical drive, due to its relative slowness, is excellent for archives and exports but probably shouldn't be used for other Oracle files. A possible exception might be large image files (BLOBS) or large document files.

With the storage capacities of most Optical drives, they make excellent resources for archive logs and exports. They can conceivably provide a single-point-of-access for all required recovery files, even backups. This solves the biggest recovery bottleneck: restoration of required files from tape.

1.6.3 Database Specific Topics

There are numerous items to consider before installation:

- Number and size of database tablespaces, file placement, number of potential applications.
- SGA and PAD issues (just SGA for UNIX).
- Number of users, both developer and application.
- Number and placement of control files.
- Number and placement of redo logs.
- Number and placement of rollback segments.
- Will this database be shared between multiple instances?
- Will this database be distributed?
- Should the tools be linked single task or independent (two task)?

Let's examine each of these as they relate to installation of Oracle.

Number and size of database tablespaces, file placement, number of potential applications.
This is a disk space and create-script-related issue. The number of potential applications will drive
the number and size of database tablespaces above and beyond the five base tablespaces. To remind
you of what these are:

> SYSTEM—Contains files owned by the SYS and SYSTEM user.
>
> TOOLS—Contains files usually owned by SYSTEM but that apply to the Oracle developer's
> toolset; these files contain base information and details of forms, reports, and menus.
>
> ROLLBACK—Contains the private rollback segments; its size will depend on number of
> rollback segments and expected transaction size.
>
> DEFAULT USER—Tablespace in which users can create and destroy temporary,
> nonapplication-related tables such as those used in SQL*REPORT for intermediate que-
> ries.
>
> TEMPORARY USER—Tablespace for sorts, joins, and other operations that require tempo-
> rary disk space for intermediate operations. If this tablespace is not available and default
> tablespace is not set for each user, these tables will be created and dropped in the SYSTEM
> tablespace, resulting in fragmentation. Additionally, a poorly designed join or overly am-
> bitious select statement could result in filling the SYSTEM area and halting the database.

Each application should have its own tablespace. If there are several small applications, you
might want to put them in a single large tablespace, but if you can avoid this, it makes application
management easier. Each application should also have its own index tablespace. This results in a
simple formula for determining the number of tablespaces:

5 + 2 × the number of applications expected.

Some applications may require multiple tablespaces such as in the case where, for performance, you want to separate large tables from the rest of the application. In one case, a single application generated 13 tablespaces. Most applications aren't as complicated as this and will only require 2 tablespaces. Of course, the purists will claim each table should be in its own tablespace, but
this is overkill in many cases.

Sizing of tablespaces is a difficult question. Each tablespace will have unique requirements.
The following are general guidelines:

> The SYSTEM tablespace, if you split out the tool tables, should only require 10 to 20 mega-
> bytes of disk space.
>
> The TOOLS tablespace will depend entirely on the amount of development you expect. At
> one site with 16 applications being developed, nearly 90 megabytes were required for the
> TOOLS tables.
>
> The ROLLBACK tablespace will again be driven by the number and size of rollback seg-
> ments you require. The number and size of rollback segments is driven by the number of
> transactions per rollback segment, the number of users, and the maximum size of nonbatch
> transactions. With Oracle 6.0.36 and later releases (including ORACLE7) you can create a
> large rollback segment and leave it offline until it is needed for a large transaction and then
> use the SET TRANSACTION USE ROLLBACK SEGMENT command to utilize it after

bringing it online. The number of rollback segments is driven by the number of expected transactions and can be estimated by the equation:

NUMBER OF TRANSACTIONS / TRANSACTIONS PER ROLLBACK SEGMENT

The number of transactions will be driven by the number of users and types of database operations they will be doing. In fact, if the Oracle kernel sees a violation of the above formula, it will bring online any available public rollback segments.

The DEFAULT USER tablespace size will depend on the number of users you want to assign to it and the estimated size of tables they will be using. In most cases 10 to 20 megabytes is sufficient. If you expect heavy usage, assign quotas to each user.

The TEMPORARY USER tablespace should be 10 to 20 megabytes and is also dependent on the number of users and the size of sorts or joins they perform. An improperly designed join between large tables can fill a temporary area fast. For example, an unrestricted outside join of two thousand-row tables will result in a one-million-row temporary table. If those rows are each several hundred bytes long, there goes your temporary space. Unfortunately, there isn't much that can be done other than training developers or ad-hoc query generators not to do unrestricted joins of large tables. If a temporary tablespace gets filled, the users who are assigned to it cannot perform operations requiring temporary space, or, worse, the temporary space may be taken from the SYSTEM area. There is a valid argument for having several temporary areas if you have a large number of users. In one instance, a 10-megabyte temporary tablespace was completely filled by a single, multi-table outside join using DECODE statements.

If you have the disk space, placing the TEMPORARY USER tablespaces on a disk of its own will improve query and report performance due to reduction of disk contention, especially for large reports or queries.

If you will be using the Oracle CASE products, you will require two additional tablespaces for the CASE tables and indexes. These tablespaces must be created before you attempt to install the CASE tables. The same rules as for the TOOLS tablespace apply for these tablespaces.

SGA and PAD Issues. As was discussed previously, in VMS, PAD size governs the maximum size to which the SGA can grow. In UNIX the parameters controlling shared memory usage are the limiting factor. In either case, before you create the database, serious thought has to be given to how much you expect the SGA to grow over the next year. Sizing the PAD larger than what you need right now will not harm the VMS system, nor will overspecifying the shared memory parameters on a UNIX platform.

The two major components of the SGA are the database buffers and the redo log buffers. The SGA also contains the data dictionary cache parameters. The ideal situation would be to size the SGA to hold the entire database in memory. For small systems, this may be a real situation, but for most, it is not feasible. Therefore, you must decide how much to allocate. Many times, especially for development databases, this will be a rough SWAG (scientific wild assed guess). For systems already designed with detailed data storage estimates, it may be better defined.

Oracle provides tools to analyze buffer performance. Unfortunately, they can only be used once a system is operating and running under a normal load; so for our discussion of installation, they are useless. The estimate, therefore, will depend on average query or report size expected times the number of expected concurrent users plus a 50 percent fudge factor for recursive gets (when an unindexed row is queried, and the database has to rifle through its records recursively). This yields the formula:

(# users × size of average query or report in bytes) × 1.5.

The average report size can be estimated by taking the average line length times the number of lines. If you have no idea whatsoever, make it 8 meg or so (you will usually outgrow the 2 meg default rather quickly).

We will discuss the actual parameters in the INIT.ORA file that control SGA size when we get to the section on tuning. The PAD size is specified during the installation and the shared memory parameters should be set before installation as well.

One thing to remember: If you overspecify the shared memory or PAD size, you may get into a situation known as swapping. This is where all or part of your application is swapped out to disk because physical memory just isn't large enough to hold it all. Needless to say, this has a very negative impact on performance.

Number of Users, Administrative, Developer, and Application. We've already looked at the responsibilities of the DBA or administrative user. What are the normal responsibilities of the other user types? According to the *ORACLE7 Server Administrator's Guide* they are the following:

Developmental Responsibilities:

1.   Design and develop database applications.
2.   Design the database structure for an application.
3.   Estimating storage requirements for an application.
4.   Specifying modifications of the database structures for an application.
5.   Keeping the database administrator informed of required changes.
6.   Tuning the *application* (not the database!) during development.
7.   Establishing an application's security requirements during development.

Application Users' Responsibilities:

1.   Entering, modifying, and deleting data, where permitted.
2.   Generating reports of data.

All Oracle databases have these three types of users: administrative, developmental, and application. As their names imply, administrative users administer and maintain the database itself; developmental users develop applications and systems; application users use the developed applications and systems.

These three types of users have different needs. The space and disk needs of a developer are usually greater than that of an application user. For example, a developer using Oracle CASE tools and SQL*ReportWriter on a VMS system may require 150,000 blocks of paged memory, while an application user may do fine with only 20,000. A developer system may get by with a smaller SGA because, generally speaking, developers will work with a subset of all the data expected, while a production database user will need a larger SGA because the data set is much larger. Administration users usually have the same quotas as a developmental user, but their privileges are greater.

On VMS the process global area, as governed by the working set variables in the user's UAF file, will determine the number of database cursors the user can have open. On UNIX the user environment control variables in the kernel will perform the same function. These variables may have to be tailored for each type of user.

Generally speaking, you will need at least five or more subprocesses available to each Oracle user. This will allow a menu to call a form to call a report, and so on. This may mean that parameters affecting total system process counts and individual user process counts may have to be modified. It is suggested that you and the system administrator sit down and hammer out the requirements for your Oracle system before you install it. This will prevent unpleasant surprises for both of you. It may also require upgrading your system's memory. It is best to be forewarned of the limits for your operating platform before you run into them.

The number of each of these types of users will tell you about required SGA sizing, disk resource requirements, and required system memory. Sixteen-megabytes is required just to run Oracle. How much will your users require on top of this?

Number and Placement of Control Files. Control files are probably the smallest and most important files in the Oracle system. They contain the following data:

Names of the database and redo log files
Timestamp of database creation
Begin/end of rollback segments
Checkpoint information
Current redo log file sequence number

This data is critical for database operation, and at least one control file is required for database startup. There are methods for rebuilding a control file, but they aren't always 100 percent reliable. It is much easier to maintain, or rather have Oracle maintain, multiple copies of the control file.

Oracle recommends two copies on separate disk resources. For OFA compliance, three are required. Obviously if they are on the same platter, the same disaster can waste all of them; therefore, they should be placed on different physical disks. More than three copies is a bit paranoid, but if it makes you feel safer, have as many as you wish; only one usable, current, file is required for startup.

Number and Placement of Redo Logs. Oracle recommends at least two redo logs. If you are archiving, three are suggested. In a number of installations up to six have been defined. If you do a lot of update activity with numerous users, more than six may be required. When a log fills, the next one in the queue is opened, and the previously active log is marked for archive (if you have archiving enabled). The logs are archived on a first-in, first-out basis, so, depending on the speed that the log can be written to disk or tape, more than one log may be waiting to be archived. One redo log is used at a time with multiple users writing into it at the same time. The size of the redo logs depends on one critical piece of information: How much data can you afford to lose on a system crash?

You see, the smaller the log, the more often it is written to disk and the less data (timewise) is lost. The larger the log, the less often it is written to disk and the more data (timewise) is lost. For instance, if your logs are filling every ten minutes, then you may lose ten minutes' worth of data if the disk that holds that redo log file should crash. It has been demonstrated on an active system that a one-megabyte redo log may last only a few minutes. In an inactive or read-only type situation, a one-megabyte log may last for hours. It all depends on how the database is being used and the size of the redo log.

You have to balance the needs for restoration and minimal data loss against time to recover data. Obviously if you have archiving happening every minute and your normal work day is eight hours, you will have 480 logs written to disk daily. Over a five-day work week, this turns into 2400 files. If you have to restore from a crash or other disaster, you may have to apply all of these to your last backup to bring the database current to the time of the crash. In one case, a DBA had to apply 9000+ files to recover his system because he hadn't looked at how often his redo logs were archiving: Needless to say, he pays more attention now.

The minimum size for redo logs is 50K. In the section on database tuning we will discuss how to determine if you have a sufficient number of redo logs and how to optimize your archive process.

Number and Placement of Rollback Segments. Another item controlled by the number of users and the transaction load on the system is the number of rollback segments. The formula, as stated before, is:

NUMBER OF TRANSACTIONS / # OF TRANSACTIONS PER ROLLBACK SEGMENT

This will yield the number of rollback segments needed. They should be sized to handle the maximum expected live transaction. The number of transactions is determined by $1.1 \times$ the value of the PROCESSES INIT.ORA parameter.

The placement of rollback segments is decided based on resource contention prevention. Put them where they won't cause contention with other Oracle files. Transactions are spread across all active rollback segments. Usually it is a good idea to locate the rollback segments in a tablespace or tablespaces dedicated to just rollback segments. This allows the DBA to easily manage these resources. Remember, a tablespace with an active rollback segment cannot be taken offline.

The size of rollback segments is based on three items:

- Average number of simultaneous active transactions
- Average number of bytes modified per transaction
- Average duration of each transaction

The longer a transaction, the larger a rollback segment it will require. One is automatically created when the database is created. This initial rollback segment is for SYSTEM tablespace use. If you have plans for more than one tablespace, you will need a second rollback segment. Of course, this second segment will have to be created in the SYSTEM tablespace. Once the ROLLBACK tablespace is defined, and additional rollback segments created, the second rollback segment in the SYSTEM tablespace should be dropped.

Each rollback segment should be created with a MINEXTENTS value of at least two and a MAXEXTENTS based on the number of rollback segments in the tablespace, the size specified for each extent, and the size of the ROLLBACK tablespace. Each of the extents should be the same size; that is, initial should equal next and pctincrease should be set to zero percent (look at the STORAGE statement specification in Appendix A for an explanation of these parameters). If you intend to do large batch transactions, it may be advisable to create a large rollback segment used only for batch operations. This single large segment can be left offline until needed and then activated and used for a specific transaction using the SET TRANSACTION USE ROLLBACK SEGMENT command. For Oracle7 MINEXTENTS parameter defaults to 2 and you are not allowed to use the PCTINCREASE parameter when creating rollback segments.

Will the tools be linked single-task or independent (two-task)? This question deals with the way the Oracle tools, such as SQL*Forms, SQL*ReportWriter or CASE, address the Oracle kernel. See Figure 1.1 for a graphical demonstration of this concept.

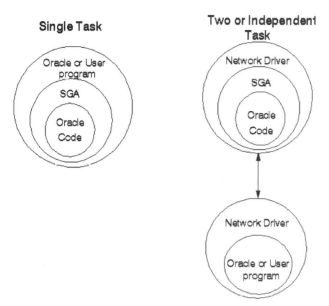

Figure 1.1 Single-task versus two-task structure.

If the tools are linked single-task, they address a specific node's Oracle kernel by default. To access another node or another system, a connect string must be used (connect strings will be covered in a later section). This mode is useful for a single-node database situation and saves on memory and task usage. This is generally used where a client-server architecture is not used.

If the tools are linked independent, or two-task, a connect string must always be used. It is called two-task because the tools must run as one task while the Oracle executable runs as another. Two-task is generally used in a client-server situation. This allows the following benefits:

1. This allows client machines to perform CPU-intensive tasks, offloading these tasks from the server.
2. This allows movement of tools from one environment to another (such as from a development area to a production one) without relinking.
3. It allows the ORACLE7 server to be relinked without relinking all the tools.

Depending on the machine they are installed on, two-task tools can reduce throughput. The DBA needs to consider the costs versus the benefits when deciding whether to use single- or two-task linked tools.

Will this database be shared between multiple instances? A shared database allows a number of instances to access the same database. This allows the DBA to spread the SGA usage for a large database system across the CPUs of several machines. The CPUs must be part of the same CLUSTER. This is also known as a *parallel* database.

A parallel database requires what is known as a *loosely coupled system*; a set of clustered VAX machines is an excellent example. This Parallel Server mode has the following characteristics according to the *ORACLE Parallel Server Administrator's Guide, Version 7:*

1. An Oracle instance can be started on each node in the loosely coupled system.
2. Each instance has its own SGA and set of detached processes.
3. All instances share the same database files and control files.
4. Each instance has its own set of redo log files or groups.
5. The database files, redo log files, and control files reside on one or more disks of the loosely coupled system.
6. All instances can execute transactions concurrently against the same database and each instance can have multiple users executing transactions concurrently.
7. Row locking is preserved.

Since the instances must share locks, a lock process is started, LCKn. In addition, the GC_ parameters must be configured in the INIT.ORA files.

This parallel database question is really only applicable to VMS users since under UNIX this doesn't seem to be possible according to Oracle documentation. If the answer to the above question is yes, the DBA needs to know how many instances will be sharing this database. This parameter will be used to determine INIT.ORA parameters. This answer is also important when determining the number and type of rollback segment. Rollback segments can either be private and only used by a single instance, or public and shared between all instances that access the database. The DBA will need to know the names for all instances sharing a database. They should also know the number of users per instance. Figure 1.2 illustrates this concept.

Another aspect of this concept of a parallel instance is the multithreaded database. Essentially this uses queue logic and shared processes (the Dnnn processes) to allow multiple users to share the same executable image. Under the other implementations a single process was allotted to each user. Each thread is associated with its own set of redo logs.

Will this database be distributed? A distributed database, as its name implies, has its data files spread across several databases in different locations. This requires that there be DBA's in these distributed locations. The major consideration will be network reliability. This is especially true if the two-phase commit available in ORACLE7 is used. Under two-phase commit, if one of your distributed database nodes goes down, you can't update tables that undergo two-phase commit with that node's data.

According to the *ORACLE7 Server Administrator's Guide*, the DBA needs to consider the following items in a distributed environment:

1. The number of transactions posted from each location.
2. The amount of data (portion of table) used by each node.
3. The performance characteristics and reliability of the network.
4. The speed of various nodes and the capacities of its disks.
5. The criticality of success if a node or link is down.
6. The need for referential integrity between tables.

A distributed database appears to be one database to the user but is in fact a collection of database tables in separate databases spread across several locations. These databases are of course on different computer systems that are connected by a network.

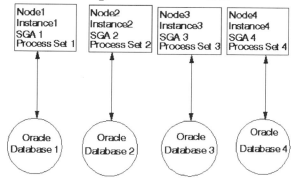

Figure 1.2 Parallel versus shared databases.

The computers, or *nodes* in a distributed database environment will act as both clients and servers depending on whether they are requesting data from another database on a different node or providing data to a different node as it is requested.

Each site is autonomous—that is, managed independently. The databases are distinct, separate entities that are sharing their data. According to the *ORACLE7 Server Concepts Manual*, Dec. 1992, the benefits of site autonomy are:

1. The various databases cooperating in the distributed environment can mirror the local organization's needs and desires. This is especially useful at sites where there may be two organizations that need to share some, but not all, data. An example would be two aerospace companies cooperating on the space platform. They may need to share data about design but not want to share financial information.

2. Local data is controlled by the local database administrator. This limits the responsibility to a manageable level.

3. Failure at one node is less likely to affect other nodes. The global system is at least partially available as long as a single node of the database is active. No single failure will halt all processing or be a performance bottleneck. For example, if the Pittsburgh node

goes down, it won't effect the Omaha node, as long as Omaha doesn't require any of Pittsburgh's data.

4. Failure recovery is on a per node basis.
5. A data dictionary exists for each local database.
6. Nodes can upgrade software independently, within reason.

As DBA you will need to understand the structures and limits of the distributed environment if you are required to maintain a distributed environment. The features of a two-phase commit as well as naming resolution and the other distributed topics will be covered later in the book. Figure 1.3 shows a distributed database structure.

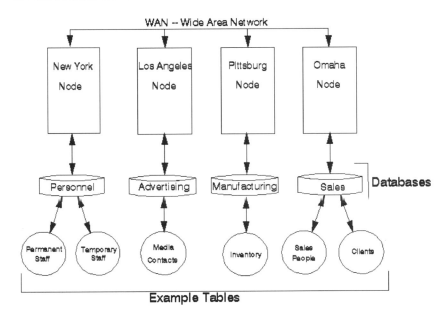

Figure 1.3 Example of a distributed database.

1.7 Installation Guidelines

Before beginning installation, the DBA needs to consider a very important topic. This topic deals with the question: Why am I installing Oracle? The answer drives the way Oracle is installed and how you configure your disk system for its installation. It depends on if you are installing Oracle to support a third-party-provided system, such as DLB's Monitor or Recorder products, PE-Nelson's LIMS, or even Oracle's Financials. Each of these has specific requirements and should be reviewed before you start installation. Another case in its entirety is when you are installing Oracle in support of in-house development. In this case, you have to consider the entire development environment and how to structure it to take full advantage of the Oracle product. Let's examine this.

1.7.1 The Development Environment

The location and access methods for the Oracle and Oracle CASE toolsets is fixed and not alterable by the developer. How the developer uses these tools and locates the modules thus created is, however, under their control. The developer has the choice of co-locating all modules in one directory, leading to confusion and difficulty in isolating one module or subtype of modules from the rest, or logically organizing a directory structure that facilitates access to each type of module. Obviously, the latter form of organization is more efficient and should be used.

The Development Directories. It is suggested that the development environment directory structure be set up as follows:

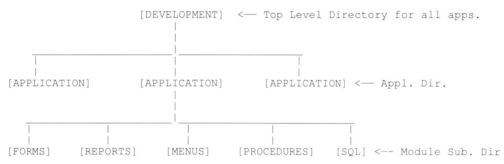

As can be seen, this provides a directory for each application and under each application all of its modules.

Environmental Logicals or Symbols. To prevent the developer from having to use excessively long path names, a logical symbol definition for each of the subdirectories is created. For an application called CDMS, for example, the logical definitions for VMS would be:

```
$! CDMS_LOGICALS.COM - Example DCL routine for VMS to set Logicals
$!
$ DEFINE CDMS$FORMS  DIA1:[M_ORACLE.DEVELOPMENT.CDMS]
$ DEFINE CDMS$REPORT DIA1:[M_ORACLE.DEVELOPMENT.CDMS]
$ DEFINE CDMS$MENU   DIA1:[M_ORACLE.DEVELOPMENT.CDMS]
$ DEFINE CDMS$PROC DIA1:[M_ORACLE.DEVELOPMENT.CDMS]
$ DEFINE CDMS$SQL    DIA1:[M_ORACLE.DEVELOPMENT.CDMS]
$ EXIT
```

Once these definitions are set for a particular developer, via a command file executed upon entry to the development environment, the developer can use them in place of the full path specification in reports, menus, and procedures.

This also facilitates transfer to a production environment. The entire directory structure is transferred to production from the application level down. The logical definitions are altered to reflect this move, and the rest of the code can remain as is.

VMS Symbol Definitions. To facilitate movement to and from the different subdirectories, symbols or keys can be defined to provide the SET DEFAULT commands as needed, for example:

```
$! CDMS_SYMBOLS.COM - Example command procedure for VMS symbols
$!
$ CDMSF :== "SET DEFAULT CDMS$FORMS"
$ CDMSR :== "SET DEFAULT CDMS$REPORTS"
```

```
$ CDMSM :== "SET DEFAULT CDMS$MENUS"
$ CDMSP :== "SET DEFAULT CDMS$PROC"
$ CDMSS :== "SET DEFAULT CDMS$SQL"
$!
$ EXIT
```

VMS Key Definitions. For developers desiring to use keystrokes to facilitate movement between the directories, the numeric PF1-PF4 and 0–9 keys can be defined as direct key strokes to execute these commands, for example:

```
$! CDMS_KEYS.COM - Example key definintion file for DCL
$!
$ DEFINE/KEY PF1 "SET DEFAULT CDMS$FORMS"/TERMINATE
$ DEFINE/KEY PF2 "SET DEFAULT CDMS$REPORTS"/TERMINATE
$ DEFINE/KEY PF3 "SET DEFAULT CDMS$MENUS"/TERMINATE
$ DEFINE/KEY PF4 "SET DEFAULT CDMS$PROC"/TERMINATE
$ DEFINE/KEY KP0 "SET DEFAULT CMDS$SQL"/TERMINATE
$!
$ EXIT
```

Use of the Development Environment. Once the development environment is established, the developer uses the symbols or key strokes to move between the subdirectories as needed. Each type of module is generated in its own subdirectory. The logicals are used in forms, menus, procedures, and SQL scripts to identify module locations.

When the developer switches between projects, they simply execute a single command procedure that alters all logical, symbol, and key definitions to reflect the new application's locations. For example, to enter the CDMS application development environment, a developer could run the following DCL script:

```
$! CDMS_SETUP.COM - DCL Command procedure for CDMS Environment
$!
$ @DIA1:[M_ORACLE.DEVELOPMENT.CDMS.PROCEDURES]CDMS_LOGICAL.COM
$ @CDMS$PROC:CDMS_SYMBOLS.COM
$ @CDMS$PROC:CDMS_KEYS.COM
$ SET DEFAULT DIA1:[M_ORACLE.DEVELOPMENT.CDMS]
$!
$ EXIT
```

A similar script would be developed for each application being developed.

A similar method uses a predefined list of applications and a DCL menu to automatically assign a developer to their environment. The DBA can even utilize SQL*Menu to provide ease of access to all tools, including CASE, and the developer only needs to enter his user name and password for Oracle once for the entire work session.

1.7.2 A Generic VMS Installation Procedure

The following guidelines assume you will be installing Oracle in compliance with OFA guidelines and with an eye toward the information provided in all of the previous sections. If you follow this general procedure, along with the installation guide provided by Oracle, you should have a successful Oracle installation.

1.   Review all installation documents sent with the software.

2. Using the guides provided in the documentation, establish the proper operating system environment. This will entail coordinating changes to the SYSGEN parameters with the system manager and possibly require alterations to the basic system user account quotas.

Example of VMS SYSGEN Parameters For Version 6 and ORACLE7

Oracle will run best under a properly tuned VMS environment. In order to ensure that a minimal tuning for Oracle is specified, the following SYSGEN parameters should be set as indicated.

Parameter	Oracle V6 Setting	Reason
GBLPAGES	CUR + 16,384 (For 8 Meg SGA)	2200 for base products + 4 × (8meg/2048). 4 global pages are required for each 2K Oracle block.
VIRTUALPAGECNT	>10240 free 500,000 sug. 80,000 MIN. 16,384 for 8 Meg SGA.	Oracle requires at least 10,240 virtual pages for a default 2 meg instance. For 8 meg instances (8 meg/512) = 16,384 minimum free pages or will get "insufficient virtual address space" error. ORACLE7 requires at least 16,500 free pages plus 2 pages for each 1K of additional SGA space over the SGA created by the supplied INIT.ORA.
GBLSECTIONS	CUR + 17	Must have at least 17 free global sections for Oracle to use. 1 for each SGA, 16 for products.
KFILSTCNT	CUR + 2 + Oracle Products	2 for RDBMS.

Product	Entries
Export/Import	2
Precompilers	1
CRT	1
SQL*Net	1
SQL*Plus	1
SQL*Forms	5
SQL*Menu	3

Parameter	Setting	Reason
SRPCOUNT	10,475 (7000 MIN)	From "Sizing, Positioning and Tuning of Oracle Applications on Digital Platforms" 21-Apr-1993, Joe Finocchiaro, DEC
IRPCOUNT	6000	
LRPCOUNT	1600 (250 MIN)	
TBSKIPWSL	64	From "VAX/VMS: How Many Memory Quotas Relate to the SGA," 1992 IOUG, Paper 420, S. Buxton, Oracle Corp.
MPW_HILIMIT	15% of Physical Memory.	

The AUTOGEN program should be used to ensure all related parameters are altered.

Oracle also requires several detached processes. These detached parameters should be set as follows:

Detached Process Parameters

Parameter	Setting	Reason
PQL_DASTLM	1000 (60 MIN)	From "Sizing, Positioning and Tuning of Oracle Applications on Digital Platforms" 21-Apr-1993, Joe Finocchiaro, DEC
PQL_DBIOLM	1000 (40 MIN)	
PQL_DBYTLM	1,000,000 (128,000 MIN)	
PQL_DIOLM	1000 (40 MIN)	
PQL_DENQLM	1000 (100 MIN)	
PQL_DFILLM	200	

PQL_DJTQUOTA   1024
PQL_DPRCLM   8
PQL_DTQELM   1000 (100 MIN)
PQL_DWSDEFAULT   1024 (478 MIN)
PQL_DWSQUOTA   4096 (2048 MIN)
PQL_DWSEXTENT   32,768 (4096 MIN)

Example of VMS UAF Parameters for Oracle

The Oracle system will not run if the user's UAF parameters are not set properly. Errors such as "Failure to extend context area," "Access violation," and "Exceed quota" indicate problems with the UAF parameters for a given user. The following user UAF profile is suggested for an 8 meg SGA environment.

Parameter	Interactive Setting	Batch Setting
ASTLM	1000	1000
BIOLM	1000	1000
BYTLM	1,000,000	1,000,000
DIOLM	1000	1000
ENQLM	1000	1000
FILLM	200	200
JTQUOTA	1024	1024
TQELM	1000	1000
WSDEFALUT	1024 (478 MIN)	1024
WSQUOTA	4096 (2048 MIN)	4096
WSEXTENT	32,768 (4096 MIN)	32,768
PGFLQUO	120,000 (75,000 MIN)	120,000
PROCLM	10 (5 MIN)	5
MAXJOBS	0	0 (UNLIMITED)
MAXACCTJOBS	0	0 (UNLIMITED)
MAXDETACH	0	0 (UNLIMITED)
QUEPRIO	0	0 (UNLIMITED)
SCHRFILLM	0	0 (UNLIMITED)
PBYTLM	0	0 (UNLIMITED)

Examples of SYSGEN Parameters for Oracle Version 7 (parallel):

MIN_GBLSECTIONS should be increased by (8 * #images) + #instances + #global sections
    for each product installed shared in memory.
MIN_GBLPAGES should be equal to or greater than: (15,100 * #instances) + #global pages
    for each product installed shared in memory.
Formulas for ORACLE7 increase to node-based parameters in parallel mode:
    SRPCOUNT — (ORACLE7 locks) × (# of instances in the cluster)
    SRPCOUNTV — (ORACLE7 locks) × (# of instances in the cluster)
    IRPCOUNT — ORACLE7 locks
    IRPCOUNTV — ORACLE7 locks
    LOCKIDTBL — (ORACLE7 locks) × (# of instances in the cluster)
    LOCKIDTBL_MAX — ORACLE7 locks) × (# of instances in the cluster)
    RESHASHTBL — (1/4) × (LOCKIDTBL) with a maximum of 8192
    LOCKDIRWT — Use the Digital Equipment Corporation documentation for the proper setting
        of this parameter for your system.

3. Provide a detailed description of the Oracle DBA account requirements with explanations of the reasons behind the quota and privilege requirements to the system manager, and have him/her create the required account.

   Set quotas in the high range of those listed above. In addition, the DBA account will require the following privileges:

   SYSNAM
   GRPNAM
   CHMKNL
   PRMMBX (If TCPIP is to be used)
   GROUP
   WORLD
   ORA_DB Rights Identifier.

   Note: ORA_DBA is the generic rights identifier that can access, start up and shut down all instances. If you wish finer control of who has access to what databases, use the SID in the identifier. For example, if the SID is PROD, then the rights identifier would be ORA_PROD_DBA. This would restrict the user to only being able to start up and shut down the PROD database. The ORACLE7 administrator may also require the OSOPER and OSDBA identifiers.

4. Have the system administrator review the available disks for space availability, speed of access, and fragmentation status. If needed, have the system administrator defragment the disks.

5. Obtain from the system manager the disks, their speeds, and their available capacities. Prepare an installation map showing file placement.

Disk space requirements for Oracle 6 code:	Disk space requirements for Oracle 7 code:
50,000 blocks for full product set	100,000 blocks for basic product set
50,000 blocks for link space	15,000 blocks for link space
18,500 blocks for SQL*ReportWriter	115,000 blocks for ORACLE7 code and executables
114,000 blocks for all CASE tools	25,000 blocks for a minimal instance

6. Define a list of required system logicals to point to disk locations. These should be descriptive and allow use of wild cards to address the entire setup. For example:

   ORA_MAIN, ORA_DATA, ORA_INDEXES, ORA_RBK, ORA_ARCHIVE.

7. Define the required directory structure on each disk. The structure should start with a generic top-level directory, such as ORACLE6 or ORACLE7, and then have subdirectories for each application. If desired, use the Oracle convention of DB_ followed by the SID name of the database to name these directories. Under these secondary directories it might be advisable to further subdivide the directory into file types if multiple file types will be stored there. Remember, if you have fewer than five disks available, you can still assign five logicals in preparation for the time when you may have more room to spread the files. This will allow you to redefine logicals instead of entire file names.

8. Write down how many users are you planning on.

9. Write down how many redo logs you will need.

10. Write down how many rollback segments you will need.

11. Write down which disks you want to place the CONTROL files on.

12. Write down what you want to call your instance (SID). This can be up to six characters long.

13. Write down what you want to call your database. This can be up to eight characters long.

14. Write down what the size for your PAD file (in K, default is 2048K or 2 meg).

15. Write down the number of data files will you need. (Remember, you will need at least five, with two additional for each application.) What size should they be, in megabytes? Write it all down. Map out locations if you have more than one data disk. Do you have any large tables that might require their own tablespace area?

16. Write down where you want your archive logs written to.

17. Write down where exports should go.

18. Make a list of your initial users, their default applications, any that require the ability to create files.

19. If you have space available, have the system manager copy the installation save sets from tape onto a disk. Your access time will be dramatically increased. Place each tape in its own subdirectory. This is required because each set of files will have its own BOOT.BCK file. If you put the save sets in one large directory, these files will become confused and cause installation problems. If you are installing from compact disk, this step is not required.

20. Set your default directory to the top-level directory on the executable drive. The VMS command is "SET DEFAULT disk:[directory]". It is suggested that the actual executables not be installed into a directory used as a login directory. Set up a subdirectory under the top-level directory such as [ORACLE7.DBA], and have the DBA account login at that directory.

21. Once you are in the top-level directory, unbundle the RDBMS save set using the following commands:
    Note: If you didn't have the disk space to unload the save sets from tape, do the following first (otherwise, proceed to step b):
    a. Mount the RDBMS tape into or onto the tape drive, issue the command:
        $ MOUNT/FOREIGN devicename
    b. Unbundle the BOOT.BCK save set using the following command:
        $ BACKUP/LOG devicename:BOOT.BCK/SAVE []*.*/NEW/OWN=PARENT

22. Use the Oracle install procedure, ORACLEINS.COM, to load the required products from the RDBMS save sets.
    a. This procedure is invoked by the following command:
        $ @ORACLEINS
    b. When ORACLEINS displays the "ORACLE Installation Startup Menu" choose the first selection, "Create a new ORACLE system."
    c. When prompted for the Oracle root directory, press enter to accept the default value and continue. If it is not, enter the proper directory and press enter.
    d. When prompted for the location of the save sets you want to load, enter the directory for the next save set if you used the preloaded save sets, or enter the tape drive from which you are loading the save sets.

e. When the "Main Menu" appears, choose the "Software Installation and Upgrade Menu."

f. When the "Software Installation and Upgrade Menu" appears, choose the "Select Products to Load" option.

g. When the list of applicable products from the save set is displayed, choose those you are licensed for from the menu by entering their number from the list. If you want to load all of the products, enter an "A." To exit the menu with your selections, enter an "E." If you make a mistake, exit the menu with a "Q" entry and start over.

h. When the "Software Installation and Upgrade Menu" is displayed, choose the "Load and Build Selected Products" menu item.
   Note: The products will be loaded first; then the procedure will prompt you "Do you want to reconfigure the products or exit before building? (N):" Enter a "Y" unless this is the last product save set you wish to unbundle.

i. If this is not the last save set, return to step 21 and load the next BOOT.BCK.

j. If this is the last save set, go on by selecting the "Select Build Configuration Options." Configure all products per your system requirements, and then exit the item with an "E" to return to the "Software Installation and Upgrade Menu." Be sure that in the RDBMS Configuration Options you specify the maximum PAD size you will require from step 14.

k. Select the "Build Selected Products" item. It is suggested that the OPTION item be built first if you are using the TPO option, and then build SQL*NET followed by any tools not built by the previous procedures. If you select all tools to be built from the first, it may result in products being linked multiple times.
   Note: The OPTION product must be loaded and built if you ever intend to use TPO. If it is not selected, it will not be built by the other build procedures.

23. Use steps 21 and 22 to unbundle the other product save sets. (You will have to load the BOOT.BCK save sets for each product from their own save set directory or tape.)
   Note: The first BOOT.BCK is unloaded into the top level or ROOT directory; all others are loaded into the INSTALL directory created when the first BOOT.BCK was unbundled.

24. Load all desired products before building any of them. Many of the products are dependent upon each other and will relink several times if you build the products as you load them. Use the load and build option from the ORACLEINS menu. Once the product is linked, answer "Y" when the procedure asks if you wish to reconfigure; then exit from the reconfigure menu.

25. Once all products are loaded, you can begin building them. Build the products in the following order:
   OPTION (TPO)
   SQL*NET (SQL*NET is used by virtually all of the products; it will link just about all of them for you)
   Any tools not linked by the SQL*NET build.

26. Once all of the products have been successfully built, use ORACLEINS to create an instance by selecting the "Instance Creation, Startup, and Shutdown Menu" item.

27. From the "Instance Creation, Startup, and Shutdown Menu," select the "Create a New Instance and Database" option.
28. Enter a unique SID (the one you wrote down in step 12).
29. Enter a unique database name (the one from step 13).
30. Check the defaults for the various system files displayed.
    a. Ensure redo logs are placed as you desire.
    b. Verify that the size of the redo logs is what you need.
    c. Insure the database (actually the SYSTEM tablespace) is sized for future expansion.
    d. Verify control files are placed properly.
    e. Enter your needed MAXDATAFILES from step 15. Enter your MAXLOGFILES from step 9.
    For ORACLE7 installs:
    f. Enter MAXINSTANCES, the maximum number of instances that may access a single database.
    g. Enter MAXLOGMEMBERS, the maximum number of copies against a single log file.
    h. Enter MAXLOGHISTORY, the maximum number of redo logs that can be recorded in the archive history of the control file.
    Once you are completely satisfied with the defaults, exit with an "E" to begin instance setup.
31. The procedure will build the instance directory structure, create database build and maintenance scripts, and create database startup and shutdown scripts. When asked if you want to continue, you have two options:
    a. If you don't want more than two control files and two redo logs created at this point, and don't want archive logging, answer "Y" or press return.
    b. If you need to add more control files, redo logs, or want archive logging, you must add this additional data to the creation script. Answer "N" and exit the ORACLEINS procedure.
    If you answered "Y," the procedure will build and start your initial instance.
32. If you chose "Y" in step 31, go on to step 34. If you choose "N" and exited the ORACLEINS procedure, return to the Oracle root directory (use a SET DEFAULT [-]) and execute a directory command (DIR).
33. If you have returned to the root directory, set your default directory to DB_<value of your SID> and then use the EDT or EVE editor to modify the CREATE_<SID>.SQL file so it includes the additional redo logs, control files, and archive log parameters. (Refer to Appendix A for the proper syntax to use.) Once you have finished the modifications, there is a .COM procedure named the same as the .SQL procedure to create your instance.
34. Once the instance is created and operational, add a second rollback segment using the procedure in the administration manual. Once this second rollback segment is created, shut down the instance and add the ROLLBACK_SEGMENTS statement to your INIT.ORA file with the name of the new rollback segment as its parameter. Restart the instance.
    Note: Every Oracle database is created with two default users. These users are SYS, who owns all the base tables, and SYSTEM, which is intended to be the DBA account for

high-level DBA work. These accounts are created with the default passwords "CHANGE_ON_INSTALL" and "MANAGER". These passwords should be changed immediately after all products have had their tables loaded. If you don't, you are left with a significant security hole in your database. Remember, everyone who has a copy of this book, or has ever looked at an Oracle database management book, knows these passwords.

35. Create any additional tablespaces you require using the CREATE TABLESPACE command shown in Appendix A. Be sure to create a tablespace for ROLLBACK SEGMENTS.

    Note: For documentation purposes, and to save you from having to enter the commands over and over again, it is suggested you create a .SQL script to create these initial tablespaces. Look at the example scripts in Appendix B for guidelines on format for this script.

36. Using the CREATE ROLLBACK SEGMENTS command from Appendix A, add the rollback segments you require from step 10. (It is suggested that simple names be used, such as RBK1, RBK2, RBK3, etc.) Use the TABLESPACE option of the command to be sure they are placed in the ROLLBACK tablespace.

    Note: For documentation and for future use, it is suggested you create a .SQL script to perform this function. An example script is in Appendix B.

37. Once step 36 is complete, shut down the database and edit the INIT.ORA file to remove the rollback segment name added in 34 from the ROLLBACK_SEGMENTS parameter, and add the names of the rollback segments just created. Restart the instance.

38. Drop the now offline rollback segment from step 34 using the DROP ROLLBACK SEGMENT command from Appendix A, or keep it for future maintenance of the other rollback segments.

39. Once the instance is created and operational, proceed with loading your toolset tables.

    Note: If you want the tools to be loaded in a tablespace different from the SYSTEM tablespace, use the SQLDBA program, connect internal, and issue an ALTER USER SYSTEM command to change the default tablespace for the SYSTEM user to the desired tools tablespace. You should also use the REVOKE command to remove the global RESOURCE privilege from the SYSTEM user. Use the GRANT command to grant resource on the new default tablespace to the SYSTEM user.

40. Type "ORACLEINS" at the command line. Once in the ORACLEINS procedure, select the "Reconfigure existing products, manage the database, or load demo tables" option from the menu.

41. From the "Oracle Product Installation and Upgrade" menu, select the "Build or Upgrade Database Tables Menu" option. When the list of products is displayed, select the ones to load the tables for and then exit the menu using the "E" option. The procedure will load all required tables, prompting you for any required data. Once this step is completed, the database is set up.

42. Shut down and cut a full backup of the Oracle installation. This is a base installation backup and should be saved.

    Note: Once a complete backup is taken, any archive logs accumulated during the install may be disposed of.

43. Consult the DBA guide for any SQL scripts, such as MONITOR.SQL, DBA SYNONYMS.SQL, and so forth, that should be run against the SYSTEM user. *Note:* Once this step is complete, the database is fully operational.
44. Using the editor of your choice, create a .SQL script to add the users listed in step 18. Use
    GRANT CONNECT TO user name IDENTIFIED BY password;
    ALTER USER username DEFAULT TABLESPACE default tablespace name
    TEMPORARY TABLESPACE temporary tablespace name;
    GRANT RESOURCE ON default ts name TO username;
    as a template for creating this file. A sample script with example names is shown in Appendix B.

Congratulations! If you have survived this far, your Oracle database is ready for business!

1.7.3 Installation of Oracle on UNIX

Unlike VMS, which is the same regardless of platform, the UNIX operating system varies considerably from platform to platform. This makes it difficult, if not impossible, to write a generic installation procedure for UNIX. It is strongly suggested that the DBA use the installation guide provided by Oracle for his/her own release of UNIX. The following procedure is just a general set of guidelines and is not intended to replace the installation procedures provided by Oracle.

1. Review all installation documents sent with the software.
2. Using the guides provided in the documentation, establish the proper operating system environment, coordinating changes to the shared memory parameters with the system manager.
   Sample Changes to UNIX System Shared Memory and Semaphore Parameters:

	HP-UX RELEASE 7.0	DYNIX / AT&T UNIX SYS V	SUN 4
SHMMAX	0x4000000		
SHMMNI	100		
SHMSEG	12		
SHMMNS	128	140	Depends
SEMMNI	10	20	Depends
NOFILEEXT		65	
MAXNOFILE		65	
SEMMSL		85	Depends

3. Provide a detailed description of the Oracle DBA account requirements with explanations of the reasons behind requirements to the system manager and have the required account created.
   Note: The oracle account on UNIX must belong to the DBA group, as must root.

4. Have the system administrator review the available disks for space availability and speed of access.
5. Obtain from the system manager the disks, their speeds, and their available capacities. Using the charts provided for your system in the installation guide, determine your disk and memory requirements. Prepare an installation map showing file placement.
6. Write down how many users are you planning on.
7. Write down many redo logs you will need.
8. Write down how many rollback segments you will need.
9. Write down which disks you want to place the CONTROL files on.
10. Write down what you want to call your instance (SID). This can be up to six characters long.
11. Write down what you want to call your database. This can be up to eight characters long.
12. Write down the number of data files will you need. (Remember, you will need at least five, with two additional for each application.) What size should they be, in megabytes? Write it all down. Map out locations if you have more than one data disk. Do you have any large tables that might require their own tablespace area? If you are using RAW devices, map out placement.
13. Write down where you want your archive logs written to.
14. Write down where exports should go.
15. Make a list of your initial users, their default applications, and make note of any that require the ability to create files.
16. Once you have the required information gathered in one place, use the installation checklists for your system. Due to the differences for each release of UNIX that Oracle supports, it would be difficult and confusing to try and cover every possible combination in this procedure.
17. The next step is to read the products into the directories using the cpio and tcio utilities. Some releases of UNIX may support the use of the oracle.boot program. This program automates the installation procedure. For example, on the SUN and DYNIX systems:
    a. Mount the distribution media, log in as oracle.
    b. For SUN, use tar xvf /dev/rst0; on DYNIX, att cpio -icBdmv < /dev/rts0.
       For HP-UX, tcio, and cpio must be used for each product.
    c. Use the cd command to move to the install directory: cd install.
    d. Run the oracle.install script by entering "oracle.install" at the command line.
    e. The script will prompt for data it needs and tell you when to reload the tape unit with a new tape. Once it is complete, it will instruct you to log in as root and rerun the oracle.install script.
    f. Log in as root and cd to the install directory, for example, cd /usr/oracle/install. Run the oracle.install script, for example, ./oracle.install. The script will prompt for oracle environment variables; these will be found in the data you wrote down for the first few steps of this procedure. Answer all questions and the script will prepare the system level environment for oracle.
    g. Log in as oracle and rerun the oracle.install script. As the script installs each product, you will be prompted for its setup variables. Once this process completes, the base install is complete.

18. Once the base install is complete, add control files, tablespaces, redo logs, and rollback segments. To start, a second rollback segment must be added
    a. Log on as oracle. Log in to the SQLDBA program, and use the CONNECT INTERNAL command to become the SYS user.
    b. Use the CREATE ROLLBACK SEGMENT command as specified in Appendix A to add a second rollback segment to the SYSTEM tablespace.
    c. Disconnect from the database by using the DISCONNECT command; then shut down the instance using the SHUTDOWN command.
    d. Exit the SQLDBA program, and edit the INIT.ORA file, which will be located in the /usr/oracle/dbs directory as the init*sid*.ora file. Add the ROLLBACK_SEGMENTS parameter, and list the second rollback segment.
    e. Login to the SQLDBA program, and start up the database using the STARTUP OPEN command, or use the dbstart script to restart the instance.
19. Add the additional tablespaces you require. This can be done from SQLDBA or from SQLPLUS.
    Note: It is suggested that a script be created similar to the example script in Appendix B. This will provide documentation and reduce the possibility of error. The CREATE TABLESPACE command from Appendix A is used to create new tablespaces.
20. Once the additional tablespaces are created, add the required number of rollback segments, calculated by taking the PROCESSES value from the INIT.ORA file and fitting it into this equation:
    PROCESSES * 1.1 / TRANSACTIONS_PER_ROLLBACK_SEGMENT
    (1.1 * PROCESSES = TRANSACTIONS).
    These rollback segments should be placed in their own tablespace.
21. Shut down the database, edit the INIT.ORA file to delete the second rollback in the SYSTEM tablespace, and place the names of the new rollback segments in its place.
22. Restart the instance.
23. If you want the tools tables in a separate tablespace from the SYSTEM tablespace, it may be required to export them from SYSTEM, alter the SYSTEM user so that they use the new tools tablespace as a default and only have resource on tools, then import the tables into the tools tablespace. The tables can then be dropped from the SYSTEM area. (*Note:* It may be required to drop the export/import tables and reload them; refer to the DBA manual provided by Oracle for the name of the script to use for this.)

If you have followed the installation guide provided by Oracle and paid attention to the heads up data provided so far, you should have a working Oracle installation. Congratulations!

Administration of Oracle, or, After the Bloom Is Off the Rose . . .

If you are at this point, one of three things has happened. You successfully installed your Oracle system using the guidelines in Chapter 1 and are anxiously awaiting further enlightenment, or you didn't successfully install your Oracle system using the guidelines in Chapter 1 but are bighearted enough to give this book another chance at proving that it's worth the purchase price, or you either don't have Oracle yet or have an existing system and just want to see what system administration tools this book can provide. In any case, the next few chapters are the heart of this book and are really what you paid for.

In this next chapter we will look at Oracle database level administration and management in detail. We will cover the tools available to the DBA and administration of the physical database and tablespaces. In the following chapters we will examine object, space, and user administration, techniques for using the tools, tuning issues and solutions, backup and recovery, and security.

Each of the subsections of Chapter 2 are designed to be standalone. They contain everything needed to manage that aspect of the Oracle database environment. It is suggested, however, that DBAs have the Oracle manuals that cover administration for their version of Oracle. While this book will try to be as comprehensive as it can be, there is still gold to be found in the Oracle manuals themselves. You just have to dig for it.

As the title of this chapter implies, Oracle administration isn't always a rose garden; sometimes it is the thorns. Hopefully, by using this book you can avoid some of the thorns that have gouged Oracle DBAs in the past. In writing this and subsequent chapters use was made of the Oracle documentation set, articles from *Oracle Magazine*, IOUG (International Oracle User's Group) presentations, and real-life experiences of several Oracle database experts.

In order to make full use of this chapter, it is suggested that the DBA either load the reports, menus, and forms from this book's companion disk, or load each by hand. The account used to run these scripts, menus, and forms should have DBA privilege under version 6, or the DBA role under ORACLE7, and have a default and temporary tablespace other than SYSTEM. The account should not be the SYSTEM account. It is suggested that a small (generally around 3 megabytes or less) tablespace be created to hold the temporary tables and permanent tables required to run the various utilities. The DBA_SYNONYMS.SQL or equivalent script should be run for this user, so the DBA_ views are created and available. The MONITOR.SQL script should also be run so the V$ views are created (if it is desired that the views not be made available to the general user population, this script should be copied to a new location and modified accordingly). On the companion disk, the file CT_DBAEN.SQL will create the DBA environment and a DBA user for you. If you are on UNIX you will have to alter the file specification in the CREATE TABLESPACE command to a UNIX full-path file specification.

This chapter assumes that the DBA is familiar with basic SQL and SQL*Plus commands. None of the scripts is overly complex, however, and even if you aren't a SQL virtuoso, some sense should be able to be made of them.

In any case, you should have the *SQL Language Reference Manual*, the *SQL*Plus Reference Manual*, the *Oracle Database Administrator's Guide*, the *PL/SQL Reference Guide*, the *Oracle RDBMS Performance Tuning Guide,* and the appropriate Installation and administration guide for your operating system, or the equivalent ORACLE7 server guides handy when using this chapter. The document set provided by Oracle is detailed and provides excellent information if you know where to find the data you need in all of the information provided. Wherever possible, this book will give references to the appropriate manual sections.

The scripts and procedures presented in this chapter are being used at several sites to manage and administrate Oracle databases. Each has been tested under version 6 and ORACLE7 and under both VMS and UNIX implementations of Oracle databases. It is suggested that the scripts be called from a centralized menu, either an operating system script or SQL*Menu application. An example script for both DCL and HP-UX KORNE Shell are shown in Appendix C. This provides for a single entry of your Oracle user name and password instead of having to invoke SQL*Plus each time you want to run a script. The scripts are kept simple to allow ease of understanding and to ensure that those who may not have the transaction processing option or other advanced Oracle features implemented may still find this book of use. Only a few of the scripts use PL/SQL. Every attempt has been made to follow the KISS principle (Keep It Simple, Stupid!).

2.1 Generic Tools Available to All DBAs

In almost every Oracle database, the DBA will have access to SQL, SQL*Plus, and SQLDBA. In some runtime versions of Oracle, such as those used with some CAD/CAM packages for drawing tracking, only SQLDBA may be provided. Unless the transaction processing option under version 6 or the procedural option under ORACLE7 was purchased, PL/SQL may not be available.

2.1.1 SQL—The Standard RDBMS Language

SQL, short for Standard Query Language, is the lingua franca of all RDBMS systems. The American National Standards Institute (ANSI) accepted SQL as the standard relational database language in October 1986 (ANSI X3.135-1986). SQL has also been accepted by the International Standards Organization (ISO standard 9075) as well as by the U.S. government in the Federal Information Processing Standard FIPS-127. A security enhancement has been added and is covered in ANSI SQL Addendum I and issued as X3.135-1989 and 9075-1989.

SQL is considered to be a nonprocedural language. This is because of the way it processes sets of records and provides automatic data access or navigation. SQL also uses query optimization—that is, the RDBMS kernel determines the optimum method to reach the desired data, so you don't have to. Under version 6 this optimization is rules based; under ORACLE7, a cost-based or a rules-based approach can be used. SQL is designed to be simple to learn and use. Despite this simplicity, SQL provides a rich command set under which virtually any combination of data in a database can be retrieved and reported.

The major statement in SQL is the SELECT statement. SELECT allows the retrieval of data from the database. Multiple selects can be nested into a single statements, and, using SQL*NET, selects can even span databases. SQL also allows insertion, update, and deletion of data as well as creation, modification, and deletion of database objects such as tables, sequences, indexes, tablespaces, and so forth. SQL provides for database security and consistency. Unlike other systems where entirely different command sets governed the different areas of database activities, SQL combines these functions into an integrated command set. Some of the SQL language is shown in Appendix A. Refer to the appropriate reference manual for more details on the command usages.

SQL is also portable. If two RDBMS are ANSI compliant, then a SQL statement that works in one will work in the other, assuming the data structures are the same. This only applies to standard SQL commands. Naturally, system-specific extensions won't transport to other systems. A good example of this is the Oracle storage clause.

If the DBA is not familiar with SQL, it is suggested that he or she look through the *SQL Language Reference Manual* and familiarize themselves with the basic commands. The SQL language is utilized by use of either SQL*Plus or SQLDBA. In fact, with ORACLE7 the SQLDBA statement acceptance has been extended to make it easier to use it alone for DBA tasks.

Appendix A shows the general formats for all SQL commands referenced in this book. For more detailed explanations the DBA should refer to the *SQL Language Reference Manual* for the release of the Oracle database they are operating under.

2.1.2 SQL*Plus—An Oracle Extension to Standard SQL

The SQL*Plus program allows users to access SQL and the Oracle SQL extensions. This combination of commands, SQL and the Oracle SQL extensions, allows users and the DBA to access the database via standard SQL and to format input and output using the SQL*Plus extensions to the language.

SQL*Plus has a command buffer that stores the current command and allows the user to edit the command using the native system editor or via command line input. SQL*Plus also allows the user to store, retrieve, and execute SQL/SQL*Plus command scripts as well as PL/SQL command scripts. It also allows use of abbreviated commands and calls to the host system command language. SQL*Plus allows local variables to be assigned as well as system variable control.

SQL*Plus can also be used to dynamically create command scripts that can then be used to perform en-mass changes to users, tables, or other Oracle objects. This is a very powerful feature that will be used in many of the example scripts. If DBAs are not familiar with SQL*Plus, it is suggested they review the SQL*Plus reference guide to aquaint themselves with the SQL*Plus commands.

SQL*Plus is accessed once the user has run the appropriate ORAUSER and instance-specific ORAUSER_instance files. The format for invoking SQL*Plus follows.

```
SQLPLUS username/password@connect string @command file
```

Where:

username/password—This is the user's Oracle username and password, which is usually different from the operating system username and password. If the user is assigned an autologin type of account, only the / is required.

@connect string—This is a connect string that connects the user to databases other than the default database. It can be used with SQL*NET over networks to access other systems.

@command file—This allows the user to specify a SQL command file that is run automatically.

If the DBA account is what is known as an OPS$ account (not recommended), the format would be as follows.

```
SQLPLUS /
```

Since an OPS$ account allows the user to get into the Oracle system without specifying a password if they are logging in from their normal account, the use of OPS$ accounts should be restricted to "captive"-type users—users who can only access the system via an appropriate secure menu system. Under ORACLE7 the OPS$ format is the default, but the system manager can assign whatever prefix they desire by use of the OS_AUTHENT_PREFIX parameter in the INIT.ORA file.

2.1.3 SQLDBA—A Database Administrator's Toolset

As its name implies, SQLDBA is designed for the DBA and only for the DBA. The SQLDBA program provides access to the database internals and allows access to all database objects. To use SQLDBA, the user must have the ORA_DBA identifier in VMS or must belong to the DBA group under UNIX.

There is no SQLDBA manual under version 6. Its use is covered in the *Database Administrator's Guide*. In ORACLE7, the use of SQLDBA is covered in the *ORACLE7 Server Utilities User's Guide*.

Monitor. SQLDBA also allows access to the monitor utility. Monitor provides views of the database virtual performance tables. Monitor also allows the DBA to observe user processes as they interact with the Oracle system. Monitor is a very powerful tool for viewing database status, but in Version 6 it suffers from giving to much information. Under version 6 several pages of data may be shown when the DBA only needs to examine perhaps six parameters, and, of course, those six will be spread between the different tables, making monitoring them difficult. While the format and access have improved considerably in ORACLE7, it appears the plethora of data in the monitor display screens has not. In some of the screens, file and name filters are added; in the statistics windows, they were not. This still leaves dozens of parameters to sort through when a DBA is only interested in a few.

Changes under ORACLE7. Under version 6, SQLDBA is command driven. Under ORACLE7, the use of pull-down menus and fill-in screens has automated many of the more tedious administration tasks such as addition of data files, tablespaces, users, dealing with startup/shutdown, and dealing with various logs. With ORACLE7, SQLDBA has come a long way toward being the tool to administer a database with, but, addition of customizable monitor screens would be a big help. Unfortunately, one of the major limitations in SQLDBA under Version 6, the lack of hard copy reports, has not been addressed even in ORACLE7. In fact, the SPOOL OUT option that allowed some reporting was removed. This is unfortunate. With some good, understandable reports, SQLDBA would be a powerful tool. It is hoped that in future releases, reports and graphic display of parameters over time will be added to SQLDBA to make it a true online administration tool in every sense of the word.

Operation of SQLDBA. To use SQLDBA, the DBA must have first run the appropriate ORAUSER procedure, usually located in the ORA_UTIL directory. In addition, if the DBA wants to run SQLDBA against a specific instance, the ORAUSER_instance file in the directory specified by the ORA_INSTANCE logical on VMS must be run. For some commands the user must either belong to the DBA group under UNIX or have the ORA_DBA or ORA_instance_DBA identifiers under VMS for version 6. Under ORACLE7 the OSOPER and OSDBA roles must be assigned the DBA. These roles control the privileges granted, thus allowing limited power to users who must use the CONNECT INTERNAL command under SQLDBA for shutdown and startup of the database and don't need other privileges. The SYS user must have run the ORA_RDBMS:MONITOR.SQL for version 6 or ORA_RDBMS:MONTR.SQL for ORACLE7 script for users to access the Monitor screens. The SQLDBA command format follows.

```
SQLDBA
```

Once the SQLDBA program is running, the DBA uses the CONNECT command to connect to the appropriate instance.

```
CONNECT username or CONNECT username/password
```

A special form of the CONNECT command can be used by DBAs from accounts with the proper privileges. This form allows the DBA to access all of the structures in the database, including those owned by SYS under version 6, but can be restricted under ORACLE7. This special format follows.

```
CONNECT INTERNAL
```

The DBA is allowed certain commands and privileges while in SQLDBA. These also depend on database status. The database status can be one of the following:

CLOSED, not MOUNTED—SHUTDOWN, used for some maintenance activities.
CLOSED, MOUNTED—Used for some maintenance activities.
OPEN, MOUNTED, NORMAL EXCLUSIVE—Normal mode for nonshared database.
OPEN, MOUNTED, DBA MODE—Used for maintenance.
OPEN, MOUNTED, SHARED—Used for shared instance Oracle.

The DBA tasks include user administration, space administration (physical such as data files and virtual such as tablespace usage), and tools administration (SQL*ReportWriter, SQL*Menu, CASE). We will cover these tasks in the following sections.

2.2 Administration of the Database

A database consists of executables, global areas, and database files. Within the database files exist tables, indexes, sequences, views, clusters, and synonyms. The DBA will be involved in the creation, maintenance, and deletion of these objects on a frequent basis. The commands, CREATE, ALTER, and DROP, are fairly easy to master. A subset of the CREATE and ALTER command, the STORAGE clause, is also very important for the DBA to understand and use properly.

2.2.1 The Create Command

As its name implies, the CREATE statement is used to create databases, tablespaces, tables, clusters, database links, indexes, sequences, views, and rollback segments. It has a general format of

```
CREATE object_type object_name
create options,
STORAGE ( storage parameters).
```

2.2.2 The Storage Clause

The STORAGE clause specifies how an object uses the space that is allocated to it. Let's look at the format of the STORAGE clause.

```
STORAGE ( INITIAL integer NEXT integer
    MINEXTENTS integer MAXEXTENTS integer
    PCTINCREASE integer (0-100))
```

Where:

INITIAL—This is the size in bytes of the initial extent of the object. The default is 10,240 bytes. The minimum is 4096. The maximum is 4095 megabytes. All values are rounded to the nearest Oracle block size.

NEXT—This is the size for the next extent after the INITIAL is used. The default is 10,240 bytes. The minimum is 2048. The maximum is 4095 megabytes. This is the value that will be used for each new extent if PCTINCREASE is set to 0.

MINEXTENTS—This is the number of initial extents for the object. Generally, except for rollback segments, it is set to 1. If a large amount of space is required, and there is not enough contiguous space for the table, setting a smaller extent size and specifying several extents may solve the problem.

MAXEXTENTS—This is the largest number of extents allowed the object. This defaults to 99. The limit for VMS is block size dependent; for UNIX, a maximum of 121 extents are allowed.

PCTINCREASE—This parameter tells Oracle how much to grow each extent after the INITIAL and NEXT extents are used. A specification of 50 will grow each extent after NEXT by 50 percent *for each subsequent extent*. This means that for a table created with one initial and a next extent any further extents will increase in size by 50 percent over their predecessor. If the table grows by 20 more extents, the final one will be 1.50 raised to the 18th power larger (1478 times) than the extent specified by the NEXT parameter. This is set to 50 percent as a default. Be sure you reset it. Under ORACLE7 this parameter is only applied against the size of the previous extent.

Proper use of the STORAGE clause means that you will have to perform accurate estimates of table and index size before creation. This will be covered in the section on tables. The create options specify such things as size, location, and other important details about the created object.

2.3 Database Creation, Alteration, and Deletion

Like other objects under Oracle, databases themselves can be created, altered, and deleted. Let's look at these different processes.

2.3.1 Database Creation

To create a database, the CREATE command is run under SQLDBA. The Instance is started in an unmounted condition. This is accomplished with the following command.

```
STARTUP NOMOUNT PFILE=filename
```

Where:

PFILE—filename refers to the INIT.ORA file you will be using, unless it is located in the directory you are currently in, a path must also be provided.

Then the DBA must connect to the SYS user via the command:

```
CONNECT INTERNAL
```

Next, the database is created. The format would be:

```
CREATE DATABASE database name
    CONTROLFILE REUSE
    LOGFILE file specifications
    MAXLOGFILES integer
    DATAFILE datafile specifications
    MAXDATAFILES integer
    MAXINSTANCES integer
    ARCHIVELOG or NOARCHIVELOG;
    Additional ORACLE7 parameters:
    MAXLOGMEMBERS n
    MAXLOGHISTORY n (only used for Oracle in shared multithread operation)
    CHARACTER SET charset
```

Where:

database name—is the name of the database, maximum of eight characters long.
file specifications for data files are of the format: 'filename' SIZE integer K or M REUSE. K is for kilobytes, M is for Megabytes. REUSE specifies that if the file already exists, reuse it.
file specifications for log files depend on the operating system.
The MAXLOGFILES, MAXDATAFILES, and MAXINSTANCES set hard limits for the database. These should be set to the maximum you ever expect.

For ORACLE7, MAXLOGMEMBERS and MAXLOGHISTORY are hard limits.

For ORACLE7, CHARACTER SET determines the character set that data will stored in. This value is operating and system dependent.

If you need archive logging, set ARCHIVELOG. If you will never need it, set NOARCHIVELOG.

Databases are created in EXCLUSIVE mode. There is an EXCLUSIVE clause that is entirely optional (not shown).

What the system does when given a CREATE DATABASE command is easy. First, the system creates control, database, and redo log files. Next, the system creates the SYSTEM rollback segment in the SYSTEM tablespace, creates and loads data dictionary tables, and mounts and opens the database.

2.3.2 Alteration of Databases

Even the best-designed database eventually has to be changed. New log files may need to be added, data files may need to be renamed or moved, archive logging status must be changed, and so on. These all are accomplished through the use of the ALTER DATABASE command. Lets look at its format and options.

```
ALTER DATABASE database name
    ADD LOGFILE filespec, filespec ....
    DROP LOGFILE 'filename', 'filename' ...
    RENAME FILE 'filename', 'filename' ....
        TO 'filename', 'filename' ...
    ARCHIVELOG or NOARCHIVELOG
    MOUNT EXCLUSIVE or SHARED (EXCLUSIVE is the default)
    MOUNT or DISMOUNT
    OPEN
    CLOSE NORMAL or IMMEDIATE (NORMAL is the default)
```

Where

database name—is the maximum of eight-character database name. If it is not specified, the value in the INIT.ORA file will be used.

filespec—is a file specification in the format of 'filename' SIZE integer K or M REUSE with:

- filename a OS specific full-path name K or M specifies integer as kilobytes or megabytes.
- REUSE specifies to reuse existing file if it exists.
- If SIZE isn't specified, 500K will be used. REUSE is optional.

filename—is a full-path file name.

MOUNT—Database is available for some DBA functions, but not normal functions.

DISMOUNT—Database is dismounted.

OPEN—Database is mounted and opened for general use.

CLOSE—Database is not available for use, but may still be mounted. Immediate does it now; normal does it politely.

These are some examples of the use of ALTER DATABASE:

To mount a database shared:

```
ALTER DATABASE dbname MOUNT SHARED
```

To close an open database:

```
ALTER DATABASE dbname CLOSE
```

To drop a logfile:

```
ALTER DATABASE
    DROP LOGFILE 'TEST_LOG.RDO'
```

Under ORACLE7 the database can only be shut down, not closed. This forces the write of information to various files on any system changes. Under version 6, even if you altered the database status to something other than OPEN, you had to shut it down and restart it after any changes.

2.3.3 Database Startup and Shutdown

When the instance and database are created using ORACLEINS, the operating system command files START_EXCLUSIVE_sid.COM, START_PARALLEL_sid.COM, START_DBA_sid.COM and STOP_sid.COM are created in the directory assigned to the ORA_INSTANCE logical on VMS and in the /users/oracle/bin/dbstart and /users/oracle/bin/dbstop files on UNIX .

Startup. The database is open and ready for use after being created. Once the operating system is shut down, or the database is shut down, it must be started before it can be accessed.

VMS Startup. On VMS platforms the startup of the Oracle instances and databases can be automated by placing a call to the appropriate startup scripts in the SYSTARUP_V5.COM procedure in the SYS$MANAGER directory. The script files are located in the ORA_INSTANCE directory for the instance. The full-path name will have to be used in the startup command file, since the ORA_INSTANCE logical is set by the procedures called by the startup script. As was stated above, these startup scripts are the following:

> START_EXCLUSIVE_sid.COM—This script starts up the database in the default mode, EXCLUSIVE.
>
> START_PARALLEL_sid.COM—This script starts up the database in shared instance mode. More than one instance using the same database.
>
> START_DBA_sid.COM—This script starts the database up in DBA only mode. Only users with the ORA_DBA or in the UNIX DBA group and with DBA privilege can access the database.

UNIX Startup. On UNIX systems, the DBA has to perform the following steps to ensure the instance and database startup each time the system starts up.

1. Log in as root.
2. Edit the /etc/oratab file. Change the last field for your $ORACLE_SID to Y.
3. Add a line similar to the following to your /etc/rc file. Be sure you use the full path to the dbstart procedure.

```
su oracle_owner -c /users/oracle/bin/dbstart
```

Manual Startup. On both systems manual startup is accomplished via either the supplied scripts or through the SQLDBA program. To start up a database using SQLDBA, use the following procedure. The command used is the STARTUP command; its format follows.

```
STARTUP [DBA] [FORCE] [PFILE=filename]
    [EXCLUSIVE or SHARED]
    [MOUNT or OPEN] dbname
    [NOMOUNT]
```

1. Log in to SQLDBA
2. Issue one of the following commands:

    a. STARTUP OPEN dbname PFILE=filename—This command starts the instance, and opens the database named dbname using the parameter file specified by the filename following the PFILE= clause. This starts up the database in the default, EXCLU-SIVE mode.
    b. STARTUP DBA OPEN dbname PFILE=filename—This command starts the in-stance, and opens the database named dbname using the parameter file specified by the filename following the PFILE= clause. This starts up the database in the DBA only mode.
    c. STARTUP NOMOUNT—This command starts the instance but leaves the database dismounted and closed. Cannot be used with EXCLUSIVE, MOUNT, or OPEN.
    d. STARTUP MOUNT—This command starts the instance and mounts the database but leaves it closed.
    e. STARTUP OPEN dbname SHARED—This command starts the instance, opens the database, and puts the database in SHARED mode for multi-instance use. Cannot be used with EXCLUSIVE or NOMOUNT or if the INIT.ORA parameter SINGLE_PROCESS is set to TRUE.
    f. STARTUP OPEN dbname EXCLUSIVE—This command is functionally identical to "a" above. Cannot be specified if SHARED or NOMOUNT is also specified.
    g. The FORCE parameter can be used with any of the above options to force a shut-down and restart of the database into that mode. This is not normally done and is only used for debugging and testing.

Errors that can occur during a startup include missing files, improperly specified PFILE path or name, or corrupted file errors. If these occur, the database will immediately shut down.

Shutdown. The databases should be shut down before system shutdowns, before full backups, and anytime system operations require it to be shut down.

VAX Shutdown. The VAX shutdown script is generally located in the SYS$MANAGER di-rectory in a file named SYSHUTDOWN.COM. Just have the system manager add a call to the Oracle shutdown script to this file for each instance on the VAX node being shut down. The Oracle shutdown script is located in the ORA_INSTANCE location for VMS and will be named similar to SHUTDOWN_instance.COM.

UNIX Shutdowns. For UNIX there are several things that need to be done to ensure shutdown occurs. The following procedure, for the HP-UX version of UNIX, demonstrates these steps.

1. Log in as root.
2. Edit the /etc/oratab file. Make the last field a Y for the $ORACLE_SID you want shut down.
3. Add the following entry to your /etc/shutdown file. Be sure to use full path to the dbshut utility.

```
su - oracle_owner -c /usr/oracle/bin/dbshut
```

You should alter the shutdown scripts to do a SHUTDOWN IMMEDIATE. This allows IO operations to complete and then shuts down the database. If a normal SHUTDOWN is performed, the system politely waits for all users to log off of Oracle—so, if Joe is on vacation and left his terminal up in a form, you could have a long wait. The other shutdown, SHUTDOWN ABORT, should only be used for emergencies as it stops the database just as it is, with operations pending or not.

The above provides for automatic shutdown when the Operating system shuts down. For a normal shutdown, execute the dbshut procedure for UNIX, the SHUTDOWN_sid.COM procedure for VMS, where the sid is the SID for the database you want to shut down.

To perform a manual shutdown on either system, perform the following procedure.

1. Start the SQLDBA procedure.
2. Issue the appropriate SHUTDOWN command.

    a. No option means SHUTDOWN NORMAL—The database waits for all users to disconnect, prohibits new connects, then closes and dismounts the database, and shuts down the instance.
    b. SHUTDOWN IMMEDIATE—Cancels current calls like a system interrupt, and closes and dismounts the database, then shuts down the instance. PMON gracefully shuts down the user processes. No instance recovery is required on startup.
    c. SHUTDOWN ABORT—This doesn't wait for anything. It shuts the database down now. Instance recovery will probably be required on startup. You should escalate to this by trying the other shutdowns first.

2.3.4 Database Deletion

Databases are deleted by shutting them down and then removing all of their associated files from the system. There is no command to perform this that is provided by Oracle.

There are several files that contain data concerning the database and the instance. If deletion is required of both, it is suggested that a VMS "SEARCH" command, or a UNIX "GREP" command be used to locate the files that contain the instance or database name. The name and related data must be removed from these files, or the files deleted, if the user wishes to reuse the instance name. If only the database needs to be deleted and then recreated, edit the CREATE script and rerun it under SQLDBA. This will reinitialize the database.

Under Oracle version 6 in the directory pointed at by the system logical ORA_RDBMS there is a DCL program titled ORA_FIND_SID.COM. This DCL procedure will update the ORA_RDBMS_SIDS.DAT file in the ORA_RDBMS directory to allow deletion of a SID from a VMS system. The format for using this procedure follows.

```
$@ORA_RDBMS:ORA_FIND_SID D <node> <database> <SID>
```

For example:

```
$@ORA_RDBMS:ORA_FIND_SID D MMRDI5 MAIN TEST
```

would remove the definition for the TEST instance for the MAIN database on MMRDI5 node from the ORA_RDBMS_SIDS.DAT file, thus removing it from use.

2.3.5 Other Database Administration Tasks

Let's look at some of the other operations that may need to be performed against a Database.

Addition of Log Files. The number of redo logs is directly related to the number, size, and length of transactions that are performed in the database. Each transaction that alters the database is recorded in the redo log files. The size of redo logs is governed by the amount of data a database can afford to lose. If a database supports noncritical data, where loss of a few hours' worth of data is not important, then very large redo logs can be used. In a database where each piece of data is critical and loss of even minuscule portions of data could be catastrophic, then a very small redo log is in order. If you have larger redo logs, fewer are needed; if you have small redo logs, many may be needed. Under version 6 two redo logs are required, and at least three are suggested. Under ORACLE7 two groups of at least one redo log each are required; again, three are suggested. Having multiple group members allows shadowing of log files on multiple drives, thus reducing redo log loss type failures almost impossible.

Under ORACLE7 redo logs are members of groups. Each group should be located on a separate drive, and each can be associated with a single thread of the multithread server. In addition, ORACLE7 allows redo log mirroring, where a redo log can be simultaneously copied to two disks at the same time by the LGWR process. This ensures that loss of a group of log files will not affect operation. Groups are archived together. The MAXLOGMEMBERS parameter in the create database statement determines the maximum number of redo logs in a group. The MAXLOGFILES parameter in the create database statement determines the maximum number of groups.

Another factor is whether or not you are using archive logging. While a redo log (or log group in ORACLE7) is being archived, it cannot be used. If a log switch goes to a redo log (or log group) that is being archived, the database stops. This is why three is the minimum number of logs or log groups recommended for an archive situation: one in use, one waiting to be used, and one archiving. Generally, it is suggested that several be available for use. In several installations where the logs were archived to disk, during heavy use periods the disk would fill, causing archiving to be suspended; once the available logs filled, the database stopped.

With multiple logs or log groups, you can have time to respond to this type of situation before the database has to be stopped. This also points out that you should keep a close eye on disk space usage for your archive destination. If the redo logs or groups are archived to tape, ensure the log sizes are such that an equal number will fit on a standard tape to avoid space, and time wastage. For example, if you have redo logs that are 1 megabyte in size on a version 6 database, and your tape is 90 megabytes capacity, then 90 will fit on the tape (approximately) with little waste. The combined size of the redo group needs to be considered for ORACLE7 since the entire group is archived as a unit. It is suggested that several smaller archive logs be used instead of fewer larger ones under ORACLE7 in a group. This allows you to size the group such that it is easily archived.

After operating for a while, DBAs get a feel for how often their databases generate logs. This will tell them how many they will require and what size they will need to be. Unfortunately there is no convenient formula for determining this. Each DBA must determine this for their own database(s). To add a redo log, the following command is used:

```
ALTER DATABASE database name
    ADD LOGFILE file specification, file specification;
```

or for ORACLE7:

```
ALTER DATABASE database name
ADD LOGFILE THREAD y GROUP n (file specification, file specification) SIZE x;
```

or:

```
ALTER DATABASE database name
ADD LOGFILE MEMBER 'file specification' REUSE TO GROUP n;
```

or:

```
ALTER DATABASE database name
    ADD LOGFILE MEMBER 'file specification' REUSE TO
        ('file specification', 'file specification');
```

Where:

For ORACLE7—n is the group number. If the GROUP n clause is left out, a new group will be added that consists of the specified log files.

For ORACLE7—x is the size for all members of the group.

For ORACLE7—y is the tread number to which the group is assigned. File specification is a system-specific, full-path file name.

UNIX:

```
'/etc/usr/ora_redo1.rdo' SIZE 1M REUSE
```

For ORACLE7 the size parameter is not with the file specification.

VMS:

```
'DUA1:[M_ORACLE_1.DB_EXAMPLE]ORA_REDO1.RDO' SIZE 1M REUSE
```

The SIZE clause specifies the size of the new log (it should be the same size as all of the other redo logs), M means megabytes, K kilobytes, and no specification—just a number—means bytes. REUSE tells oracle if the file exists, reuse it.

Dropping Log Files. The alter command is also used to drop redo logs.

```
ALTER DATABASE database name
   DROP LOGFILE 'filename';
```

For ORACLE7:

```
ALTER DATABASE database name
   DROP LOGFILE GROUP n --OR--('filename', 'filename');
```

or:

```
ALTER DATABASE database name
   DROP LOGFILE MEMBER 'filename';
```

Where 'filename' is just the file name, no SIZE or REUSE clause.

Addition of Rollback Segments. Another database structure is the ROLLBACK segment. ROLLBACK segments can be placed in any tablespace, but it is suggested that they be placed in a tablespace that only contains other rollback segments. This makes administration easier. Rollback segments can be either PUBLIC, which means that for a multi-instance database, any instance can use the rollback segment, or PRIVATE, which means only the instance that has the rollback segments name in its ROLLBACK_SEGMENTS clause of its INIT.ORA file can use the rollback segment. For UNIX it is suggested that PUBLIC rollback segments not be used since multiple instance databases are not allowed on all versions of UNIX.

Rollback segments are created using the CREATE command. The format for this command follows.

```
CREATE [PUBLIC] ROLLBACK SEGMENT rollback name
   TABLESPACE tablespace name
   STORAGE storage clause;
```

Where:

Rollback name is the name for the rollback segment; this name must be unique.

Tablespace name is the name of the tablespace where the segment is to be created.

Storage clause is a storage clause that specifies the required storage parameters for the rollback segment. It is strongly suggested the following guidelines be used:

```
INITIAL = NEXT
MINEXTENTS = 2 (see note below for ORACLE7)
MAXEXTENTS--calculated maximum based on size of the rollback segment
   tablespace, size of rollback segments extents and number of rollback
   segments.
PCTINCREASE--0 (see note below for ORACLE7)
```

For ORACLE7 a new parameter, OPTIMAL, is allowed. This parameter reflects the size that the system will restore the rollback segment to after it has been extended by a large transaction.

For ORACLE7 the MINEXTENTS will default to 2, and the PCTINCREASE will always be 0. In fact, if PCTINCREASE is specified in the create command, an error will result unless compatibility is set to version 6.

When a rollback segment is created, it is not online. To be used, it must be brought online using the ALTER ROLLBACK SEGMENT name ONLINE; command, or the database must be shutdown, the INIT.ORA parameter ROLLBACK_SEGMENTS modified, and the database restarted. In any case, the INIT.ORA file parameter should be altered if the rollback segment is to be used permanently or else it will not be acquired when the database is shut down and restarted.

Altering a Rollback Segment. The rollback segment can be altered using the alter command. However, this can result in mismatched extent sizes and is not recommended. You cannot alter a rollback segment from public to private or private to public. It must be dropped and recreated for this type of change. The format of the command follows.

```
ALTER [PUBLIC] ROLLBACK SEGMENT rollback name
    STORAGE storage clause
```

Where:

Storage clause cannot contain new values for INITIAL or MINEXTENTS.
For ORACLE7 a new OPTIMAL value can be set as well.

Dropping a Rollback Segment. Periodically it will be required that the DBA drop a rollback segment. This is required when the rollback segment has overextended due to a large transaction, has too many extents in general, or a larger size is desired for all rollback segments. This is accomplished through the DROP command. The format of this command follows.

```
DROP [PUBLIC] ROLLBACK SEGMENT rollback name;
```

A rollback segment must not be in use or it cannot be dropped. Once dropped it must be removed from the INIT.ORA-ROLLBACK_SEGMENTS clause, or the database cannot be restarted.

Moving Database Files. Periodically, DBAs will need to move database files, such as the SYSTEM tablespace data files or redo logs, from one location to another. This is accomplished through the following procedure:

1. Shut down the database.
2. Use the operating system to copy the file(s) to their new location.
3. Using SQLDBA MOUNT the database, but don't OPEN it.
4. Use the CONNECT INTERNAL command to connect to the database.
   Note: for ORACLE7 you will need to reverse steps 4 and 5.
5. Issue the ALTER DATABASE command to rename the file.

   ```
   ALTER DATABASE database name
       RENAME DATAFILE 'OLD FILE NAME' TO 'NEW FILE NAME';
   ```

6. Shut down and restart the database.
7. Use SQLDBA or SQLPLUS to look at the view DBA_DATA_FILES to be sure the file is renamed.

8. Delete the old file via the appropriate operating system command. (Be sure the database is started before you delete the file. If the database is running, it will prevent you from deleting files that are still active.)

2.4 Tablespace Administration

Tablespaces take the place of disks if we carry through with the analogy that Oracle is an operating system. Only with this disk, you, the DBA, can specify its size and how it will create and store data (via the DEFAULT STORAGE clause) in its files (tables).

2.4.1 Tablespace Creation

Let's look at the command for creating a tablespace.

```
CREATE TABLESPACE tablespace name
    DATAFILE filespec, filespec ....
    DEFAULT STORAGE storage
    ON-LINE or OFFLINE
```

Where:

tablespace name—This is the name you choose for the tablespace. It can be up to 30 characters long.

filespec—This is the file specification for the data file(s) that the tablespace needs. The format for this is:

```
'filename' SIZE integer K or M REUSE
```

Where:

filename—This is an OS specific file name.

integer—This is the size in either kilobytes (K) or megabytes (M) of the file.

REUSE—This is an optional parameter that instructs Oracle to reuse the file if it exists and is the proper size.

storage—This is the storage clause that will be used for any table in the tablespace that isn't created with its own STORAGE clause.

ONLINE/OFFLINE—This tells Oracle to either create the tablespace for immediate access, ON-LINE (default), or leave it idle, OFFLINE.

2.4.2 Alteration of Tablespaces

Periodically, a tablespace may need to have its default storage changed, require addition of data files to increase its storage volume, require a name change, require to be taken offline for maintenance, or to be placed in backup status for a hot backup. The command used for all of these functions is the ALTER command. Let's look at its format.

```
ALTER TABLESPACE tablespace name
    ADD DATAFILE filespec, filespec ...
```

```
RENAME DATAFILE 'filename', 'filename' ...
             TO 'filename', 'filename' ....
DEFAULT STORAGE storage
ON-LINE
OFFLINE NORMAL or IMMEDIATE
BEGIN or END BACKUP
```

At least one of the lines following the ALTER command must be supplied—or else why issue the command? The definitions for the arguments are the same as for the CREATE command. One thing to note is the RENAME DATAFILE option. This option is used when you need to (1) alter the name of a data file, or (2) relocate a data file. Option 1 is obvious, but 2 needs some explanation. This is the procedure for moving a data file:

1. Using the ALTER TABLESPACE command, take the tablespace that uses the data file offline.

   ```
   ALTER TABLESPACE tablespace OFFLINE;
   ```

2. Using the operating system command appropriate for your system, copy the data file to the new location (don't "move" it—it needs to exist in both locations until renamed).
3. Using the ALTER TABLESPACE command, rename the data file.

   ```
   ALTER TABLESPACE tablespace
       RENAME DATAFILE 'old name' TO 'new name';
   ```

   where old and new names are full-path names.
4. Using the ALTER TABLESPACE command, bring the tablespace back online.

   ```
   ALTER TABLESPACE tablespace ONLINE;
   ```

5. Remove the extra copy of the data file from its old location using the appropriate operating system command (rm on UNIX, DELETE on VMS).

The OFFLINE qualifiers apply to how user processes are treated as the tablespace is taken OFFLINE. NORMAL tells Oracle to wait for user processes to finish with the tablespace. IMMEDIATE tells the system to take the tablespace offline regardless of who is using it.

If using ALTER to place a tablespace in BEGIN BACKUP, be sure that the backup procedure backs up all the redo and archive logs as well. Immediately after the backup concludes, bring the tablespace back to normal with the END BACKUP command, or the redo logs will get out of sync and the file will not be recoverable should you be required to recover it due to a problem.

2.4.3 Deletion of Tablespaces

At one time or another, such as when consolidating a rollback segment tablespace, the DBA will have to remove, or drop, a tablespace from the Oracle database system. Removing tablespaces is done through the DROP command. Its format follows.

```
DROP TABLESPACE tablespace name INCLUDING CONTENTS;
```

The INCLUDING CONTENTS clause is optional, but if it isn't included, the tablespace must be empty of tables or other objects. If it is included, the tablespace will be dropped regardless of its contents. The SYSTEM tablespace cannot be dropped.

2.4.4 Recreating Tablespaces

There may be times when the DBA has to drop and recreate tablespaces. For instance, if the physical drive that the tablespaces are on has been damaged the DBA will have to recreate the tablespaces on another volume, or recover from a backup and apply redo logs. If the DBA has good documentation of what the database physical structure was before the incident, there is no problem. If the DBA has inherited a legacy system, or the system has grown substantially without good documentation, the DBA could have his or her hands full with rebuilding it. The script in Figure 2.1 can be used to document existing tablespaces and their data files.

```
rem
rem   NAME: TS_RCT.sql
rem
rem   HISTORY:
rem   Date            Who                 What
rem   --------        ------------------  ------------------------------------------
rem   12/22/92   Michael Brouillette    Creation
rem
rem   FUNCTION: Build a script to re-create tablespaces in a database.
rem
rem   NOTES:  Must be run by a DBA.
rem
rem   ***********************************************************************
SET LINESIZE 79
COLUMN X WORD_WRAPPED
SPOOL TS_RCT.LIS
SELECT 'CREATE TABLESPACE '||UPPER('&&1')||' DATAFILE '||
       ''''||FILE_NAME||''''||' SIZE '||BYTES/1024||'K REUSE'||
       ' DEFAULT STORAGE(INITIAL '||INITIAL_EXTENT||' NEXT '||NEXT_EXTENT||
       ' MINEXTENTS '||MIN_EXTENTS||' MAXEXTENTS '||MAX_EXTENTS||
       ' PCTINCREASE '||PCT_INCREASE||');' X
  FROM DBA_TABLESPACES, DBA_DATA_FILES
 WHERE DBA_TABLESPACES.TABLESPACE_NAME=
   DBA_DATA_FILES.TABLESPACE_NAME
   AND DBA_TABLESPACES.TABLESPACE_NAME = UPPER('&&1')
   AND DBA_DATA_FILES.FILE_ID =
         (SELECT MIN(FILE_ID)
            FROM DBA_DATA_FILES
           WHERE DBA_DATA_FILES.TABLESPACE_NAME=UPPER('&&1'));
SELECT 'ALTER TABLESPACE '||UPPER('&&1')||' ADD DATAFILE '||
       ''''||FILE_NAME||''''||' SIZE '||BYTES/1024||'K REUSE;' X
  FROM DBA_TABLESPACES, DBA_DATA_FILES
 WHERE DBA_TABLESPACES.TABLESPACE_NAME =
   DBA_DATA_FILES.TABLESPACE_NAME
   AND DBA_TABLESPACES.TABLESPACE_NAME = UPPER('&&1')
   AND DBA_DATA_FILES.FILE_ID !=
         (SELECT MIN(FILE_ID)
            FROM DBA_DATA_FILES
           WHERE DBA_DAT_FILES.TABLESPACE_NAME=UPPER('&&1'));
SPOOL OFF
```

Figure 2.1 Script to create rebuild script for tablespaces.

2.4.5 Periodic Tablespace Maintenance

Periodic tablespace maintenance includes consolidation of extents, reorganization to push all the free space in the file to the front, and exports to ensure recoverability. Let's look at these topics.

Consolidation of Extents. As tables, indexes, and clusters are created and dropped in a tablespace, extents are dynamically assigned and deassigned to the objects. Like a disk system, which dynamically assigns space to files, this causes fragmentation. Fragmentation results in objects being stored all over the tablespace requiring more head moves to recover the information to fill user's queries. This reduces response time and makes the system slow. Unless you can exactly specify the required storage and sizing information for each and every table in each tablespace, some of this internal fragmentation will occur. Under ORACLE7 the SMON process automatically consolidates contiguous free extents into single large extents. This reduces but doesn't eliminate the problem. So, how do you correct it? There are two methods. Let's look at each of them.

Method 1: Use of export and import.

This method will consolidate all free space and will consolidate all tables into single extents. This method will work on both version 6 and ORACLE7. However, the database won't be available, and for large systems, the time required could be extensive.

1. Perform an export on all objects in the tablespace. Remember that you must export each owner's objects for all users who own objects in the tablespace.
2. Drop the tablespace using the INCLUDING CONTENTS clause.
3. Recreate the tablespace. (If you created a script to create the tablespace, you can just rerun the script. Be sure to include all active data files. It might be desirable to delete all of a tablespace's data files and consolidate them into one large data file at this time.)
4. Import all of the exports generated in step 1.

Another major problem with this method is it won't work on the SYSTEM tablespace.

Method 2: Create temporary tables in the tablespace that exactly occupy the available extents, and then drop them.

This option works for contiguous extent consolidation, but not on Swiss-cheese-type fragmentation. If ORACLE7 performs as promised, it won't be needed for ORACLE7 databases.

1. From a DBA level account in either SQL*Plus or SQLDBA, run the script shown in Figure 2.2. (The full listing for Figure 2.2 appears in Appendix B.) The script will create a DBA level account, a default tablespace for the account, synonyms, and tables for use with administration scripts.
2. Log in to SQL*Plus as the account created in step 1.
3. Execute the script in Figure 2.3. (The full listing for Figure 2.3 appears in Appendix B.)
4. From the displayed tablespaces, enter the names of the tablespaces to be defragmented using the specified format.
5. Exit SQL*Plus.

```
rem    *****************************************************************
rem    NAME: CT_DBAEN
rem    HISTORY:
rem    Date        Who                 What
rem    --------    ------------------  ----------------------------------------
rem    12/09/92  Michael Brouillette   Creation
rem    04/09/93  Michael Ault          Appended script to build DBA tables.
rem    FUNCTION: This script builds the initial environment for the DBA to work
rem              in. Specifically it:
rem                          Creates a separate tablespace for the DBA's objects.
rem                          Creates the DBA user id and sets its default
rem                          tablespace to the one just created and sets the
rem                          temporary tablespace to the one specified by &1.
rem                          Builds & runs script to grant access to SYS objects
rem                          and create synonyms for those objects.
rem                          Builds & runs script to grant access to SYSTEM objects
rem                          and create synonyms for those objects.
rem    INPUTS:
rem                          tsn     = Name of temporary tablespace for the DBA user
rem                          dbau    = User ID for the new DBA user
rem                          dbap    = Password for the new DBA user
rem                          sysp    = Password for the 'SYS' account
rem                          systemp = Password for the 'SYSTEM' account
rem
rem    NOTES: Runtime changes will probably have to be made to the command to
rem           create the tablespace. Format is for VMS, for UNIX must be
rem           changed to proper format.
rem    *****************************************************************
```

Figure 2.2 Script to create a DBA user, tablespace and objects for version 6 monitoring activities. (See Appendix B for the full script.)

```
rem    *****************************************************************
rem    NAME:   CONS_FS.sql
rem    HISTORY:
rem    Date        Who                 What
rem    --------    ------------------  ----------------------------------------
rem    12/04/92  Michael Brouillette   Creation
rem    12/15/92  Michael Brouillette   Changed to use FET$ and TS$ instead of
rem                                     DBA_FREE_SPACE
rem    12/18/92  Michael Brouillette   Incorporated option to keep temp file CONS$
rem    01/05/93  Michael Brouillette   Split CONS$ file into CREATE$ and DROP$.
rem                                    When the code was combined consolidation
rem                                    would not always occur due to timing. This
rem                                    may still happen but can be worked around
```

Figure 2.3 Script to consolidate free space in a version 6 database. (See Appendix B for complete caption.)

```
rem                                  by executing the CREATE$ and DROP$ scripts
rem                                  directly.
rem   01/06/93  Michael Brouillette  Modified creation of CREATE$ to include
rem                                  ALTER SYSTEM command to avoid timing
rem                                  problem. Not guaranteed but seems to work.
rem   04/09/93  Michael Ault         Added in script BLOKSIZ.SQL
rem   FUNCTION: This routine shows the true contiguous extents and will allow
rem             the user the option of consolidating one or more tablespaces.
rem
rem             If the user DOES consolidate it is IMPORTANT that the tablespace
rem             names be provided in the exact format shown.  That format is:
rem
rem                       'tsname1','tsname2',... ('keep')
rem
rem             The specification of the fake tablespace KEEP causes the temp
rem             files CREATE$ and DROP$ to be kept.
rem
rem   NOTES: There is an assumption that the following table, index, and view
rem          exist.  The DBA routine CT_DBAEN.SQL will create the objects.
rem          The table and view are required.  The index is needed only for
rem          performance reasons.
rem
rem                       TABLE:  TRUE_SPACE_T
rem                       INDEX:  TRUE_SPACE_T_I1
rem                       VIEW:   TRUE_SPACE_V
rem
rem   **********************************************************************
```

Figure 2.3 (continued)

The biggest problem with the script in Figure 2.3 is that this script will only consolidate extents in a tablespace that are adjacent to each other. If your tablespace is suffering from Swiss-cheese-type fragmentation—that is, where the table's extents wrap around blocks of empty space—then this procedure doesn't fix it. This can be detected by running the script in Figure 2.4 after running the CT_DBAEN.SQL script from Figure 2.2. (The CT_DBAEN.SQL script only needs to be run once but must be run for many of the scripts in the rest of the book to work properly.)

```
rem   NAME:   BOUND_OB.sql
rem   HISTORY:
rem   Date      Who                  What
rem   --------  ------------------   ----------------------------------------
rem   12/04/92  Michael Brouillette  Creation
rem   01/07/93  Michael Brouillette  Switched to title80
rem   04/09/93  Michael Ault         Included code for Bloksiz.sql
rem   FUNCTION: Shows the object name, type and owner for all objects with one
rem             or more extents bounded by free space.
```

Figure 2.4 Script to determine if there are objects with bound extents.   (continued)

```
start title80 'Objects With Extents Bounded by Free Space'
spool b_ob||&&db||.lis
column e     format a23        heading "TABLE SPACE"
column a     format a6         heading "OBJECT|TYPE"
column b     format a20        heading "OBJECT NAME"
column c     format a15        heading "OWNER ID"
column d     format 99,999,999 heading "SIZE|IN BYTES"
column bls new_value BLOCK_SIZE
break on e skip 1 on c
set feedback off verify off  termout off
select blocksize bls from sys.ts$
where name='SYSTEM';
select h.name e, g.name c, f.object_type a, e.name b, b.length*&&blocksize d
 from uet$ b, fet$ c, fet$ d, obj$ e, sys_objects f, user$ g, ts$ h
where b.block# = c.block# + c.length
 and b.block# + b.length = d.block# and f.header_file = b.segfile#
 and f.header_block = b.segblock# and f.object_id = e.obj#
 and g.user# = e.owner# and b.ts# = h.ts#
order by 1,2,3,4;                    /* group by g.name, f.object_type, e.name */
column a clear
column b clear
column c clear
column d clear
set feedback 10
ttitle ''
ttitle off
spool off
```

Figure 2.4 (continued)

After the script in Figure 2.4 is run, the DBA can create an export job to export these tables. Then they can be dropped, the consolidation script run, and then imported. This will consolidate the tables into contiguous areas.

2.5 Use of the ALTER SYSTEM Command

The ALTER SYSTEM command is used to dynamically alter the Oracle instance under an ORACLE7 database. This command is not available under version 6. The ALTER SYSTEM command allows the following system level items to be modified.

- Resource limits
- Create or terminate shared server or dispatcher processes.
- Switch redo log groups.
- Perform a checkpoint.
- Verify data file access.
- Restrict login to users with RESTRICTED SESSION privilege (replaces DBA mode).
- Perform distributed recovery in single-process environment.
- Disable distributed recovery.

- Manually archive redo logs or enable or disable automatic archiving.
- Clear the shared pool in the SGA.
- Terminate a session.

The ALTER SYSTEM command allows the DBA much greater control over the Oracle environment than was possible in previous releases.

2.5.1 ALTER SYSTEM Command Format

The ALTER SYSTEM command's format follows.

```
ALTER SYSTEM
[SET RESOURCE_LIMIT = TRUE --or-- FALSE]
[SET MTS_SERVER = n]
[SET MTS_DISPATCHERS = 'protocol, n']
[SWITCH LOGFILE]
[CHECKPOINT --or-- CHECK DATAFILES [GLOBAL --or-- LOCAL]]
[ENABLE --or-- DISABLE [DISTRIBUTED RECOVERY --or-- RESTRICTED SESSION]]
[ARCHIVE LOG archive_clause]
[FLUSH SHARED POOL]
[KILL SESSION 'sid, serial#'] (sid and serial# are in V$SESSION)
```

Where:

RESOURCE_LIMIT—This either enables (TRUE) or disables (FALSE) the use of resource limits.

MTS_SERVERS—The n specifies the number of shared server process to enable, up to the value of the MAX_SERVERS parameter.

MTS_DISPATCHERS—The protocol specifies the network protocol for the dispatcher(s). The n specifies the number of dispatchers for the specified protocols up to the value of MAX_DISPATCHERS (as a sum of all dispatchers under all protocols).

SWITCH LOGFILE—This switches the active log file groups.

CHECKPOINT—This performs either a GLOBAL (all open instances on the database) or LOCAL (current instance) checkpoint.

CHECK DATAFILES—This verifies access to data files. If GLOBAL is specified, all data files in all instances accessing the database are verified accessible. If LOCAL is specified only the current instance's data files are verified.

ENABLE RESTRICTED SESSION—This only allows users with RESTRICTED SESSION privilege to log in to the database.

DISABLE RESTRICTED SESSION—This allows any user to log on to the instance.

ENABLE RESTRICTED RECOVERY—This enables distributed recovery.

DISABLE RESTRICTED RECOVERY—This disables distributed recovery.

ARCHIVE LOG—Manually archives redo log files or enables or disables automatic archiving depending on the clause specified.

```
ARCHIVE LOG clauses:
  THREAD n
  [SEQ n] [TO 'location']
```

```
[CHANGE n] [TO 'location']
[CURRENT] [TO 'location']
[GROUP n] [TO 'location']
[LOGFILE 'filename'] [TO 'location']
[NEXT] [TO 'location']
[ALL] [TO 'location']
[START] [TO 'location']
[STOP]
```

2.5.2 A Detailed Look at ARCHIVE LOG Clauses

The ARCHIVE LOG clauses under ORACLE7 provide the functionality of the ARCHIVE LOG command in SQLDBA under version 6. The version 6 ARCHIVE LOG command has the following format.

```
ARCHIVE LOG [LIST] [STOP] [START --or-- n --or-- NEXT --or-- ALL]
['filespec']
```

Where:

LIST—This shows the current status of logs for the instance with a display of the format shown in Figure 2.5.

```
Database log mode                 ARCHIVELOG
Automatic archival                ENABLED
Archive destination               M_ORA_DISK4:[M_ORACLE6.DB_CASE.ARCHIVES]ARC
Oldest online log sequence        1023
Next log sequence to archive      1025
Current log sequence number       1025
```

Figure 2.5 Example of the ARCHIVE LOG LIST command output.

STOP—Disable automatic archival.

START—Enables automatic archiving.

n—Archives the log specified by the integer 'n'.

NEXT—Manually archives the next online redo log file that has been filled but not archived.

ALL—Manually archive all filed but not archived online log files.

filespec—This is the system specific file specification for the archive log destination.

For ORACLE7 the command is removed from SQLDBA (except for the pull-down display) and is placed under the ALTER SYSTEM command (shown above). The new command has additional clauses to handle the more complex archive log scheme under ORACLE7. The new syntax handles the threads and groups associated with the new archive logs. The new syntax follows.

```
ARCHIVE LOG clause
ARCHIVE LOG clauses:
    THREAD n
    [SEQ n] [TO 'location']
    [CHANGE n] [TO 'location']
    [CURRENT] [TO 'location']
    [GROUP n] [TO 'location']
    [LOGFILE 'filename'] [TO 'location']
    [NEXT] [TO 'location']
    [ALL] [TO 'location']
    [START] [TO 'location']
    [STOP]
```

Where:

THREAD—This specifies the specific redo log thread to effect. If this isn't specified, then
  the current instance redo log thread is affected.

SEQ—This archives the redo log group that corresponds to the integer specified by the integer given as the argument.

CHANGE—This corresponds to the SCN (system *change* number) for the transaction you
  want to archive. It will force archival of the log containing the transaction with the SCN
  that matches the integer given as the argument to the CHANGE argument.

GROUP—This manually archives the redo logs in the specified group. If both THREAD and
  GROUP are specified, the group must belong to the specified thread.

CURRENT—This causes all nonarchived redo log members of the current group to be
  archived.

LOGFILE—This manually archives the group that contains the file specified by 'filespec'. If
  thread is specified the file must be in a group contained in the thread specified.

NEXT—This forces manual archival of the next online redo log that requires it. If no thread
  is specified, Oracle archives the earliest available unarchived redo log.

ALL—This archives all online archive logs that are part of the current thread haven't been
  archived. If no thread is specified, then all unarchived logs from all threads are archived.

START—Starts automatic archiving of redo log file groups. This only applies to thread assigned to the current instance.

TO—This specifies the location to archive the logs to. This must be a full-path specification.

STOP—This disables automatic archiving of redo file log groups. This applies to your current instance.

2.6 The INIT.ORA (Initialization File) Parameters

It should be obvious the the most important file as far as database setup and operation is probably
the INIT.ORA or initialization file. This file contains the assignments for the database initialization
parameters.

Under version 6 there were over 120 of these parameters; for ORACLE7 there are 104. The
major cause of the reduction was the implementation of the shared pool concept. This removed the
21 DC_ parameters from use (much to the consternation of DBAs whose sole job was the tweeking

of these parameters). A list of the version 6 and ORACLE7 INIT.ORA parameters, their default values, and dependencies is shown in Appendix D.

The DBA should review the applicable administrator's and tuning guides before modifying any INIT.ORA parameters.

For further reading, the DBA should refer to the following.

ORACLE7 Server Administrator's Guide, PART# 6694-70-1292, Dec. 1992, Oracle Corp.

ORACLE7 Server SQL Language Reference Manual, PART# 778-70-1292, Dec. 1992, Oracle Corp.

ORACLE RDBMS Database Administrator's Guide, Version 6.0, PART# 3601-V6.0, Oct. 1990, Oracle Corp.

SQL Language Reference Manual, Version 6.0, PART# 778-V6.0, Feb. 1990, Oracle Corp.

Administration of Database Objects

In Chapter 2 we discussed the administration and management of the physical database and tablespaces. In Chapter 3 we will look at the administration of objects stored in the database.

Tables, indexes, sequences, and views are all objects that are contained in tablespaces. Hence, it makes sense to discuss them at this point. Since indexes, sequences, and views are all either used by or on tables, let's discuss the administration of tables first.

3.1 Table Administration

Tables are the primary storage division in Oracle. All data is stored in tables. Sequences and indexes support tables. Synonyms point to tables. Tables make Oracle work. The next sections describe the administration and maintenance of database tables in detail.

3.1.1 Creation of Tables

Tables are owned by users (renamed to schemas in ORACLE7). For a given application it is suggested that its tables reside in a single dedicated tablespace or group of tablespaces. This leads to the premise that all of an application's tables should be owned by a single user or reside in a single schema. This makes further maintenance such as exports, imports, synonym creation, table creates, and drops easier to deal with. As with the other database objects, tables are built using the CREATE command. Let's look at this command's format when used to create tables.

```
CREATE TABLE table name
( table column column format column constraint,
  table column column format column constraint...)
    [PCTFREE integer(0-100)] [PCTUSED integer(0-100)]
    [INITRANS integer] [MAXTRANS integer]
    [TABLESPACE tablespace name]
    [STORAGE storage clause]
```

```
[CLUSTER cluster name (column, column ....)]
[ENABLE --or-- DISABLE clause]
[AS query]
```

Where:

Table name—This is formatted either user.name or just the name, defaulting to the current user. This must be a unique name by user. This unique name applies to tables, views, synonyms, clusters, and indexes. For uniqueness, the user portion counts.

Column name—This is a unique name by table. The column name can be up to 30 characters long and cannot contain a quotation, slash or character other than A–Z, 0–9, _, $, and #. A column name must not duplicate an Oracle reserved word (see the *SQL Language Manual* for a list of these words). To use mixed case, include the mixed-case portion in quotation marks. For example:

```
EMPNAME
DOG
AULT.EXPENSE
"SELECT" (Even though select is a reserved word, if it is enclosed in
    quotes it is okay to use.)
"NIP AND TUCK" (Even spaces are allowed with quotes)
```

Names should be meaningful, not a bunch of symbols like A, B, C, and so on. The Oracle CASE products always pluralize the names of tables. If you will be using CASE, you might want to follow this convention.

Column format—This is one of the allowed SQL data types. They are listed in the SQL language manual. A brief list is:

```
CHAR(size) Character type data, max size 255 Under ORACLE7 this is
    replaced by VARCHAR2. Under ORACLE7 CHAR will be right-side padded to
    specified length.
VARCHAR2 Variable-length character up to 2000.
DATE Date format, from 1/1/4712 BC to 12/31/4712 AD. Standard Oracle
    fomat is dd-mmm-yy (10-APR-93)
LONG Character, up to 65,535 long. Only one LONG per table. 2 gig under
    ORACLE7.
RAW(size) Raw binary data, max of 255 size in version 6, 2000 under
    ORACLE7.
LONG RAW Raw binary data in hexadecimal format, 65,535 long. 2 gig under
    ORACLE7.
ROWID Internal data type, not user definable, used to uniquely identify
    table rows.
NUMBER(p,s) Numeric data with p being precision and s being scale.
    Defaults to 38 p, null s.
DECIMAL(p,s) Same as numeric.
INTEGER Defaults to NUMBER(38), no scale.
SMALLINT Same as INTEGER
FLOAT Same as NUMBER(38)
```

```
FLOAT(b) NUMBER with precision of 1 to 126.
REAL NUMBER(63)
DOUBLE PRECISION Same as NUMBER(38)
```

No scale specification means floating point.

Column constraint—This is used to specify constraints. Constraints are limits placed either on a table or column. Oracle version 6 supports the format of constraints and stores constraint definitions but does not enforce them. It is a statement of the format:

```
CONSTRAINT name constraint type
```

Constraints also may be of the form:

```
NULL CONSTRAINT constraint type
NOT NULL CONSTRAINT constraint type
PRIMARY KEY CONSTRAINT constraint type
UNIQUE CONSTRAINT constraint type
UNIQUE PRIMARY KEY CONSTRAINT constraint type
CHECK condition CONSTRAINT constraint type
REFERENCES table name (column name) CONSTRAINT constraint type
```

In the above formats the "CONSTRAINT constraint type" is optional.

Tables may also have the additional constraints:

```
FOREIGN KEY (column, column)
   REFERENCES table name (column, column)
   CONSTRAINT constraint type
```

The foreign key constraint IS enforced. However, no index is automatically generated. It is suggested that indexes be maintained on foreign keys or else excessive full table scans may result.

PCTFREE—This parameter tells Oracle how much space to leave in each Oracle block for future updates. This defaults to 10. If a table will have a large number of updates, a larger value is needed. If the table will be static, a small value can be used. This is very table and table usage specific. Improper specification can result in chaining or improper space usage and performance degradation.

PCTUSED—This parameter tells Oracle the minimum level of space in a block to maintain. PCTUSED defaults to 40. A block becomes a candidate for updates if its storage falls below PCTUSED. The sum of PCTFREE and PCTUSED may not exceed 100. A high PCTUSED value results in more efficient space utilization but higher overhead, as Oracle must work harder to maintain the free block list.

INITRANS—This option specifies the initial number of transactions that are allocated within each block.

MAXTRANS—This option species the maximum number of transactions that can update a block concurrently.

TABLESPACE—This specifies the tablespace if it is other than the user's default.

STORAGE—This specifies the storage options for the table.

CLUSTER—This specifies the table is to be part of the specified cluster through the specified columns. PCTFREE, PCTUSED, and TABLESPACE options will produce errors when used with the CLUSTER clause.

ENABLE—This enables constraints for an ORACLE7 database.
DISABLE—This disables constraints for an ORACLE7 database.

Let's look at a full example of a CREATE TABLE command with both column and table constraints.

```
CREATE TABLE puchase_order
   (po_number        INTEGER NOT NULL,
   line_no           INTEGER NOT NULL,
   line_description  CHAR(60),
   part_no           CHAR(30),
   no_items          NUMBER,
   unit_cost         FLOAT,
   line_comment      LONG,
   UNIQUE PRIMARY KEY (po_number, line_no) CONSTRAINT
   po_lno_pk,
   FOREIGN KEY (part_no)
      REFERENCES (po_dba.part_list) CONSTRAINT po_pn_fk,
   CHECK (line_no > 0) CONSTRAINT po_ck1,
   CHECK (no_items >0) CONSTRAINT po_ck2 )
```

This command creates the table purchase_orders with the columns po_number, line_no, line_description, part_no, no_items, unit_cost and line_comment. The primary key, or unique identifier is a concatination of po_number and line_no. Part_no references another table called part_list, that is owned by the user PO_DBA, no values can be entered into part_no unless they also exist in part_list. No values less than zero can be entered in either line_no or no_items. Po_number cannot be null; neither can line_no.

Notice that all of the constraints are named. If you allow the system to provide default names, it will punish you by making them very cryptic. Since they may need to be enabled, disabled, dropped, or rebuilt, it will make your life easier if you name them explicitly.

The DBA should read the *SQL Language Reference Manual* sections concerning constraints, table creation, and use of storage parameters, before creating tables.

To estimate a version 6 table's size for the storage clause, use the following procedures.

Case 1: You have a test database available.

If you have a test database available, perform the following to determine the required size for your production table:

1. Calculate the block header size using:

Block header = $57+(23 \times \text{INITRANS}) + (4 \times T) + (2 \times \text{RPB})$

Where:

T = Number of tables in cluster (1 for single table)

(*Note:* You can't figure RPB yet, so you get some integer plus $2 \times \text{RPB}$.)

2. Issue the following query against your test database:

```
SELECT AVG(NVL(VSIZE(col1), 1)) +
   AVG(NVL(VSIZE(col2), 1)) +
   ... +
   AVG(NVL(VSIZE(coln), 1)) "Average Data Length (ADL)"
   FROM Table name
```

Where:

```
        col1, col2, ... coln are the names of the columns in the table.
           Table name is the name of the table to be sized.
```

3. Calculate the average row length (ARL).

ARL = row header + TLB1b + TLB3b + ADL

Where:

Row header = 3 for each row in a nonclustered table

TLB1b = total length bytes of all columns with 1-byte column lengths

```
        (CHAR, NUMBER, DATE, ROWID)
```

TLB1b = (1 × # of 1 byte-records)

TLB3b = total length bytes of all columns with 3-byte column lengths

```
        (LONG, RAW, LONG RAW)
```

TLB3b = (3 × # of 3-byte records)

4. Now calculate RPB (substitute and solve for RPB).

RPB = (Data space in block / average row length (or 9 whichever is larger))

5. Now calculate the total amount of blocks needed for the table.

Total table space = estimated # rows/RPB

6. Finally, calculate bytes.

Space required in bytes = (Bytes/block) × (# of blocks)

If an example table exists that contains enough test data to be an accurate representation of the final table, the script in Figure 3.1 can be used to estimate the size of the final table's average row length.

For an ORACLE7 table's size, if it exists in a test database, use the ANALYZE command to calculate the table's statistics. Then simply look at the DBA_TABLES view to find average row length.

```
rem    ********************************************************************
rem    NAME: TB_RW_SZ.sql
rem    HISTORY:
rem    Date           Who                  What
rem    --------       ------------------   -----------------------------------------
rem    01/20/93       Michael Brouillette  Creation
rem    FUNCTION:  Compute the average row size for a table.
rem    NOTES:  Currently requires DBA.
rem    INPUTS:
rem        tname  = Name of table.
rem        towner = Name of owner of table.
rem                 cfile  = Name of output SQL Script file
rem    ********************************************************************
column dum1        noprint
```

Figure 3.1 Script used to determine the average row length for a table.   (continued)

```
column rsize        format 99,999.99
column rcount       format 999,999,999 newline
accept tname   prompt 'Enter table name: '
accept towner prompt 'Enter owner name: '
accept cfile   prompt 'Enter name for output SQL script file: '
set pagesize 999  heading off   verify off   termout off
set feedback off   sqlcase upper   newpage 3
spool &cfile..sql
select 0 dum1,
    'select ''Table '||'&towner..&tname'||
    ' has '',count(*) rcount,'' rows of '', ('   from dual
union
select column_id,
    'sum(nvl(vsize('||column_name||'),0)) + 1 +'  from dba_tab_columns
 where table_name = '&tname' and owner = '&towner'
   and column_id <> (select max(column_id)
            from dba_tab_columns
                                        where table_name = '&tname'
                                          and owner = '&towner')
union
select column_id,
    'sum(nvl(vsize('||column_name||'),0)) + 1)'
  from dba_tab_columns
 where table_name = '&tname' and owner = '&towner'
   and column_id = (select max(column_id)
            from dba_tab_columns
                                        where table_name  '&tname'
                                          and owner = '&towner')
union
select 997,  '/ count(*) + 5 rsize, '' bytes each.'''   from dual
union
select 999,  'from &towner..&tname.;'  from dual;
spool off
set termout on   feedback 15    pagesize 20   sqlcase mixed    newpage 1
start &cfile
clear columns
undef cfile
undef tname
undef towner
```

Figure 3.1 (continued)

Case 2: You don't have a test database.

If you don't have a test database, or the test database has an insignificant amount of data in it (you need at least enough data to provide good averages), then you will need to manually calculate the average data length (ADL).

1. Calculate the block header size using:
    Block header= $57+(23 \times \text{INITRANS}) + (4 \times T) + (2 \times \text{RPB})$
    Where:
    T = Number of tables in cluster (1 for single table)

(*Note:* You can't figure RPB yet, so you get some integer plus 2 X RPB.)

2. Calculate the data space available in the block (BLOCK SIZE is set on database creation, usually 2048).

    Data space in block = (block size - total block header) (1-PCTFREE)

3. Calculate the average data length per row (ADL).

    ADL = (total char. in fixed records + avg. char in var. length records)
    Where:
    Total char. in fixed records = (total of CHAR types + (7 × # of date fields))
    Total char in var. length records = ((ave_prec/2+1) + (ave_prec/2+1) +...)

4. Calculate the average row length (ARL).

    ARL = row header + TLB1b + TLB3b + ADL
    Where:
    Row header = 3 for each row in a nonclustered table
    TLB1b = total length bytes of all columns with 1-byte column lengths

    ```
    (CHAR, NUMBER, DATE, ROWID)
    ```

    TLB1b = (1 × # of 1 byte records)
    TLB3b = total length bytes of all columns with 3-byte column lengths

    ```
    (LONG, RAW, LONG RAW)
    ```

    TLB3b = (3 × # of 3 byte records)

4. Now calculate RPB (substitute and solve for RPB).

    RPB = (Data space in block / average row length (or 9 whichever is larger))

5. Now calculate the total amount of blocks needed for the table.

    Total table space = Estimated # rows/RPB

6. Finally, calculate bytes.

    Space required in bytes = (bytes/block) × (# of blocks)

For ORACLE7 the ANALYZE command can be used on an example table to give the data to get accurate size estimates. The format of this command follows.

```
ANALYZE TABLE [schema.]table COMPUTE--or--ESTIMATE
(for estimate) SAMPLE n ROWS --or-- PERCENT
STATISTICS ;
The results appear in the DBA_TABLES view.
```

3.1.2 Table Alteration

Face it, none of us are perfect. We don't design perfect applications. This means we sometimes have to change things. For tables this means adding, changing, or dropping columns, adding constraints, or even deleting all of the rows from the table. Let's look at how to accomplish these table changes.

Altering table structure: The command used to alter a table is the ALTER TABLE command. The ALTER TABLE command's format follows.

```
ALTER TABLE tablename
ADD (column name table constraint, column name table constraint)
MODIFY (column name)
```

```
DROP CONSTRAINT constraint
PCTFREE integer PCTUSED integer
INITRANS integer MAXTRANS integer
STORAGE storage
BACKUP
```

Here are some notes on the ALTER TABLE command. Things you can do are the following:

1. Add columns that can have NULL values to any table.
2. Modify columns to a larger size.
3. Modify columns that have all null values to be shorter, or to a different data type.
4. Alter the PCTFREE, PCTUSED, INITRANS, or MAXTRANS for any table.
5. Alter the storage clause for any table.
6. Tell the data dictionary that the table has been backed up as of the date of the ALTER command by use of BACKUP clause.

Here are some things you cannot do:

1. Modify a column that has values to be shorter or to a different data type.
2. Add a NOT NULL column to a table that has rows.
3. Alter a column to NOT NULL if it has rows with NULL values in that column.

To help a DBA determine if a tables data and indexes have integrity, ORACLE7 provides the ANALYZE command that can be used to analyze the structure of a table and its indexes. The format of this command follows.

```
ANALYZE TABLE [schema.]table
VALIDATE STRUCTURE [CASCADE]
```

The results are supplied to the DBA on screen.

Use of the CASCADE option causes the command to validate all indexes against the base table.

3.1.3 Deletion of a Table's Data

You can selectively delete data or delete all of a table's data using the DELETE command. The format for this command follows.

```
DELETE FROM table name WHERE condition
```

The table name can include an alias. If the WHERE clause is left out, all of the rows in the table are deleted. The first example follows.

```
DELETE FROM PER_DBA.JOBS A WHERE A.JOB_STATUS = 'COMPLETE';
```

This command would delete all rows with the data value COMPLETE in the column JOB_STATUS from the JOBS table owned by the PER_DBA user.

```
DELETE PER_DBA.OLD_JOBS;
```

This command would remove all rows from the table OLD_JOBS that belongs to the user PER_DBA.

In ORACLE7, a new command is supplied to perform removal of a table or cluster's data. This new command is the TRUNCATE command. One good feature of this command is that it can be used to reclaim the space used by the data that was in the table. In version 6 the table had to be dropped before the space was reusable. The format for this command follows.

```
TRUNCATE TABLE--or--CLUSTER [schema.]table--or--cluster name
DROP --or-- REUSE STORAGE;
```

Where:

DROP STORAGE deallocates the space previously used by the tables data. This is the default.

REUSE STORAGE leaves the space from the deleted rows in the table.

Both DROP and REUSE qualifiers also apply to whatever index space is regained.

The truncate command is faster than the delete command because it is a DDL command and generates no rollback data. If you are using truncate on a clustered table, the data must be removed from the entire cluster, not just the one table. Any referential integrity constraints on a table must be disabled before it can be truncated. A truncation is not recoverable. If a table is truncated, you cannot rollback if you made a mistake. Use TRUNCATE carefully.

3.1.4 Dropping a Table

To completely remove a table from the tablespace, use the DROP TABLE command. This command's format follows.

```
DROP TABLE table name;
```

Oracle will drop the table regardless of its contents. The only time a drop will fail is when a table's primary key is referenced by another table's foreign key via a restraint clause. The DBA can check for this situation by looking at the DBA_CONSTRAINTS and the DBA_CONS_COLUMNS views. A view called USER_CROSS_REFS provides this information on a user by user basis.

3.1.5 Rebuilding Tables

The DBA may have to rebuild a table or tables after maintenance, after a physical disk crash, or, the leading cause, operational stupidity. If the application designers were thoughtful enough to provide a build script, there is no problem. However, for legacy systems, systems that have been modified and not redocumented, or systems created on-the-fly, there may be no current build scripts, if there were even any to begin with. In this case, the DBA is in trouble. How can this situation be prevented? Require build scripts for each application and keep them up to date. For existing, undocumented systems, the script in Figure 3.2 will create a build script for existing tables. It must be run before any loss has occurred.

A similar script is provided for indexes in section 3.2 (Figure 3.3).

3.2 Administration of Indexes

Indexes allow queries to rapidly retrieve data with proper implementation. Single columns or groups of columns are indexed. A DBA can specify whether or not an index is unique. Remember: For proper table design, each table must have a unique identifier. In Oracle version 6 the unique identifier is enforced with a unique index. Indexes can be created and dropped. The unique index is not needed with ORACLE7.

```
rem   ********************************************************************
rem   NAME:  TB_RCT.sql
rem   HISTORY:
rem   Date            Who               What
rem   _____        _____    _____
rem   02/25/91  R. Gaydos              Created
rem   03/18/92  Gary Dodge             Improved format, changed SPOOL file name
rem   FUNCTION:  Build a script to re-create tables
rem   ********************************************************************
COLUMN CPR NOPRINT
COLUMN NPR NOPRINT
SET PAGESIZE 0
SPOOL creatab2
Select table_name cpr, 10 npr, 1 npr,
      'Create table  '||table_name||' ( '  from user_tables
UNION
select table_name cpr, 20 npr, column_id npr,
      '           '||
      decode( column_id, 1, ' ',',')||
      rpad(column_name,31)||decode(data_type,
                'CHAR', 'CHAR ('||data_length||')',
                'RAW', 'RAW ('||data_length||')',
                'NUMBER','NUMBER '||
                        decode( nvl(data_precision 0 , ' ',
                                '('||data_precision||','||data_scale||')')' ),
                'DATE', 'DATE','LONG', 'LONG',
                'Error in script '||data_type||' not handled '
                ||' length '||to_char(data_length)
                ||' precision '||to_char(data_precision)
                ||' scale '||to_char(data_scale) )
              ||decode( nullable, 'Y', '          ', ' NOT NULL' ) from
user_tab_columns
 where table_name in ( select table_name from user_tables ) UNION
select table_name cpr, 30 npr, 1 npr, ' )    ' from user_tables UNION
select table_name cpr, 40 npr, 1 npr, '        pctfree '||pct_free  from
user_tables
UNION
select table_name cpr, 45 npr, 1 npr, '        pctused '||pct_used  from
user_tables
UNION
select table_name cpr, 50 npr, 1 npr, '        initrans '||ini_trans  from
user_tables
UNION
select table_name cpr, 55 npr, 1 npr, '        maxtrans '||max_trans  from
user_tables
```

Figure 3.2 Script to create a table rebuild script for undocumented systems.

```
UNION
select table_name cpr, 60 npr, 1 npr, '          tablespace '||tablespace_name
from user_tables  UNION
select table_name cpr, 70 npr, 1 npr, ' Storage ('  from user_tables  UNION
select table_name cpr, 80 npr, 1 npr, '          initial   '||initial_extent
from user_tables
UNION
select table_name cpr, 90 npr, 1 npr, '          next      '||next_extent
from user_tables
UNION
select table_name cpr, 100 npr, 1 npr, '          minextents '||min_extents
from user_tables UNION
select table_name cpr, 110 npr, 1 npr, '          maxextents '||max_extents
from user_tables UNION
select table_name cpr, 120 npr, 1 npr, '          pctincrease '|| pct_increase
from user_tables UNION
select table_name cpr, 130 npr, 1 npr, '          ) ' from user_tables UNION
select table_name cpr, 140 npr, 1 npr, ' ; ' from user_tables UNION
select table_name cpr, 150 npr, 1 npr, '   '  from user_tables
 order by 1,2,3;
SPOOL OFF
```

Figure 3.2 (continued)

Indexes speed the search for queries when approximately 10 percent to 15 percent of the table is being retrieved. For large retrievals, insert and updates to index columns and deletes, indexes slow response.

The way columns are indexed will effect their efficiency. The order columns are specified should reflect the way a select will retrieve them. Put the column expected to be accessed most often first. Remember the leading portion of the index is used to speed queries. A composite index can be created on up to 16 columns.

3.2.1 Creation of an Index

Create indexes with the CREATE INDEX command.

```
CREATE [UNIQUE] INDEX Index name ON
   table name (column ASC|DESC, column ASC|DESC ...)
   [CLUSTER cluster name]
   [INITRANS n MAXTRANS n]
   [TABLESPACE tablespace name]
   [STORAGE storage clause]
   [PCTFREE]
   [NOSORT]
```

Where:

Index name—is a user unique index name
Table name—is the name of the table to be indexed; the table must exist.
Column—is the name of the column to include in the index, maximum of 16.

The order of a concatenated key is important. Only queries that access columns in this order will use the index. For example, table EXAMPLE has 16 columns. The first three are used as the concatenated index. Only queries that contain columns 1, 2, 3—or—1, 2—or—1 will use the index.

Tablespace name—is the name of the tablespace in which to store the index.

Storage clause—is a standard storage clause

NOSORT—tells oracle to not sort the index, since the table is already loaded into Oracle in ascending order.

The UNIQUE clause causes Oracle to enforce uniqueness of the entire key. If UNIQUE is left out, the index is nonunique. In ORACLE7 the primary key and unique key constraints automatically generate the required indexes. This renders the UNIQUE clause obsolete in ORACLE7.

To estimate the size of an index for the storage clause, use the following procedure.

1. Calculate the required database block header size (BHS).
   BHS = fixed header + variable transaction header
   Where:
   Fixed header = 113
   variable transaction header = 23 × INITRANS
2. Calculate available data space (ADS).
   ADS = ((Block size - BHS) X (PCTFREE/100))
3. Calculate the average data length per row (ADL)
   ADL = (total char. in fixed records + avg. char in var. length records)
   Where:
   total char. in fixed records = (total of CHAR types + (7 × # of date fields))
   total char in var. length records = ((ave_prec/2+1) + (ave_prec/2+1) +...)
4. Calculate the average row length (ARL).
   ARL = entry header + ROWID length + TLB1b + TLB3b + ADL
   Where:
   entry header = 1 for each entry
   ROWID length = 6
   TLB1b = total length bytes of all columns with 1-byte column lengths
   (CHAR, NUMBER, DATE, ROWID)
   TLB1b = (1 × # of 1-byte records)
   TLB3b = total length bytes of all columns with 3-byte column lengths
   (LONG, RAW, LONG RAW)
   TLB3b = (3 × # of 3-byte records)
   For UNIQUE indexes the entry header is 0.
5. Calculate number of blocks for index.
   # of Blocks = 1.1 × (((# of NOT NULL rows × ADL) / (ADS)) × ARL)
6. Calculate the number of bytes required.
   Size in bytes = BLOCK SIZE × number of blocks

If the table that the index is based on exists, the script in Figure 3.3 is used to estimate the size of the index that is generated from a given list of columns. The DBA enters the table name, the table owner name, and a list of columns and the procedure does the rest.

For ORACLE7 the ANALYZE command can be used to get the average index size from an example index. The format of this command follows.

```
ANALYZE INDEX [schema.]index COMPUTE--or--ESTIMATE
(for estimate) SAMPLE n ROWS --or-- PERCENT
STATISTICS ;
```

The results appear in the DBA_INDEXES view.

```
rem     *********************************************************************
rem  NAME:  IN_ES_SZ.sql
rem  HISTORY:
rem  Date            Who                 What
rem  --------        -----------------   -------------------------------------------
rem  01/20/93    Michael Brouillette    Creation
rem  FUNCTION:  Compute the space used by an entry for an existing index.
rem  NOTES:  Currently requires DBA.
rem  INPUTS:
rem          tname  = Name of table.
rem          towner = Name of owner of table.
rem          clist  = List of column names enclosed in quotes.
rem                   i.e 'ename', 'empno'
rem     cfile  = Name of output SQL Script file
rem     *********************************************************************
column dum1       noprint
column isize      format 99,999.99
column rcount     format 999,999,999 newline
accept tname  prompt 'Enter table name: '
accept towner prompt 'Enter table owner name: '
accept clist  prompt 'Enter column list: '
accept cfile  prompt 'Enter name for output SQL script file: '
set pagesize 999 heading off verify off termout off feedback off sqlcase upper
set newpage 3
spool &cfile..sql
select -1 dum1,
       'select ''Proposed Index on table ''||' from dual
union
select 0,
       '''&towner..&tname'||' has '',count(*) rcount,'' entries of '', ('  from
dual union
select column_id,
      'sum(nil(vsize('||column_name||'),0)) + 1 +'
  from dba_tab_columns
 where table_name = '&tname'  and owner = '&towner'
   and column_name in (&clist)
      and column_id <> (select max(column_id)
                   from dba_tab_columns
      where table_name = '&tname' and owner = '&towner'
                     and column_name in (&clist)) union
```

Figure 3.3 Script to calculate index space requirements for a proposed index.   (continued)

```
select column_id,
       'sum(nil(vsize('||column_name||'),0)) + 1)'
  from dba_tab_columns
 where table_name = '&tname'
   and owner = '&towner' and column_name in (&clist)
   and column_id = (select max(column_id)
                      from dba_tab_columns
       where table_name = '&tname'
       and owner = '&towner'
                         and column_name in (&clist)) union
select 997, '/ count(*) + 11 isize, '' bytes each.''' from dual union
select 999,
       'from &towner..&tname.;'  from dual;
spool off
set termout on feedback 15 pagesize 20 sqlcase mixed newpage 1
start &cfile
clear columns
exit
```

Figure 3.3 (continued)

3.2.2 Alteration of Indexes

If the DBA suspects that an index's storage clause is improper, the script in Figure 3.4 is run to show the space used for the average entry in the index. This data can then be input into the space calculation formula to get a more accurate sizing estimate. The DBA can then use the ALTER IN-DEX command to alter the indexes storage clause for future extents, or drop and recreate the index with better parameters.

Indexes may only be altered to change their storage clauses. The alteration will only affect the storage allocations of future extents. To alter rows used in the index, unique versus nonunique, or all of the storage extents for an existing index, it must be dropped and recreated. To alter the storage within an existing index, use the ALTER INDEX command.

```
rem    ********************************************************************
rem
rem    NAME:  IN_CM_SZ.sql
rom
rem    HISTORY:
rem    Date            Who               What
rem    --------        ------------------    -----------------------------------------
rem    01/20/93     Michael Brouillette  Creation
rem
rem    FUNCTION:  Compute the space used by an entry for an existing index.
```

Figure 3.4 Script to calculate average length of an index entry.

```
rem
rem  NOTES:  Currently requires DBA.
rem
rem  INPUTS:
rem         tname  = Name of table.
rem         towner = Name of owner of table.
rem         iname  = Name of index.
rem         iowner = Name of owner of index.
rem         cfile  = Name of output file SQL Script.
rem  ********************************************************************
column dum1        noprint
column isize       format 99,999.99
column rcount      format 999,999,999 newline
accept tname  prompt 'Enter table name: '
accept towner prompt 'Enter table owner name: '
accept iname  prompt 'Enter index name: '
accept iowner prompt 'Enter index owner name: '
accept cfile  prompt 'Enter name for output SQL script file: '
set pagesize 999 heading off verify off termout off feedback off
set sqlcase upper newpage 3
spool &cfile..sql
select -1 dum1,
       'select ''Index '||'&iowner..&iname'||' on table '
  from dual
union
select 0,
       '&towner..&tname'||' has '',count(*) rcount,'' entries of '', ('
  from dual
union
select column_id,
      'sum(nil(vsize('||column_name||'),0)) + 1 +'
  from dba_tab_columns
 where table_name = '&tname'
   and owner = '&towner' and column_name in
                    (select column_name from dba_ind_columns
                       where table_name = '&tname'
                         and table_owner = '&towner'
                         and index_name = '&iname'
                         and index_owner = '&iowner')
   and column_id <> (select max(column_id)
                       from dba_tab_columns
    where table_name = '&tname'
      and owner = '&towner'
                          and column_name in
                              (select column_name from dba_ind_columns
                                 where table_name = '&tname'
                                   and table_owner = '&towner'
                                   and index_name = '&iname'
                                   and index_owner = '&iowner'))
union
select column_id,
```

Figure 3.4 (continued)   (continued)

```
       'sum(nil(vsize('||column_name||'),0)) + 1)'
  from dba_tab_columns
 where table_name = '&tname' and owner = '&towner'
   and column_name in
                     (select column_name from dba_ind_columns
                       where table_name = '&tname'
                         and table_owner = '&towner'
                         and index_name = '&iname'
                         and index_owner = '&iowner')
   and column_id = (select max(column_id)
                      from dba_tab_columns
     where table_name = '&tname' and owner = '&towner'
                      and column_name in
                            (select column_name from dba_ind_columns
                              where table_name = '&tname'
                                and table_owner = '&towner' and index_name = '&iname'
                                and index_owner = '&iowner'))
union
select 997,
       '/ count(*) + 11 isize, '' bytes each.'''  from dual
union
select 999,  'from &towner..&tname.;'  from dual;
spool off
set termout on feedback 15 pagesize 20 sqlcase mixed newpage 1
start &cfile
clear columns
undef tname
undef towner
undef iname
undef iowner
undef cfile
exit
```

Figure 3.4 (continued)

The ALTER INDEX command's format follows.

```
ALTER INDEX index
   INITRANS integer MAXTRANS integer
   STORAGE storage clause;
```

Where the parameters are as described in the CREATE TABLE command.

3.2.3 Dropping an Index

An index is dropped using the DROP INDEX command.

```
DROP INDEX index;
```

3.2.4 Rebuilding Indexes

Occasionally, the DBA may be required to drop and recreate indexes. If the scripts used to initially create the system are available, this is a relatively simple matter. If the scripts used to build the indexes are not available, or were never created in the first case, the script in Figure 3.5 can be run to create a script that will recreate existing indexes when run.

Under version 6 the structure of an index can be checked for consistency using the VALIDATE INDEX command. The format of this command follows.

```
VALIDATE INDEX [user.]index
```

Under ORACLE7 the DBA can use the ANALYZE command to validate an index's structures. The format of this command follows. This data can help the DBA determine if a specific index has become corrupted and must be rebuilt.

```
ANALYZE INDEX [schema.]index
VALIDATE STRUCTURE;
```

The results are supplied to the DBA on screen and are placed in a view called index_stats, which is dropped upon session exit.

```
rem    **********************************************************************
rem    NAME:  IN_RCT.sql
rem    HISTORY:
rem    Date         Who                What
rem    _____     _____       _____
rem    01/27/93     Michael Brouillette   Created
rem    FUNCTION:  Build a script to re-create indexes.
rem    **********************************************************************
column dum1 noprint
column dum2 noprint
column dum3 noprint
set termout off feedback off verify off echo off heading off pagesize 0
spool in_rct.lis
select index_name dum1, 10 dum2, 0 dum3,
       'create '||decode(uniqueness,'UNIQUE', 'UNIQUE','')||
       ' index '||index_name||' on ' from user_indexes   union
select index_name, 20, 0, table_owner||'.'||table_name||' ('  from user_indexes union
select index_name, 30, column_position,
       decode(column_position,1,' ',',')||column_name from user_ind_columns UNION
select index_name, 40, 99,' )    '  from user_indexes UNION
select index_name, 50, 99,'           pctfree  '||pct_free  from user_indexes UNION
select index_name, 70, 99,'           initrans '||ini_trans from user_indexes UNION
select index_name, 80, 99,'           maxtrans '||max_trans from user_indexes UNION
select index_name, 90, 99,'         tablespace '||tablespace_name  from user_indexes
UNION
select index_name, 100, 99, ' Storage ('  from user_indexes UNION
select index_name, 110, 99,'         initial    '||initial_extent from user_indexes
 UNION
```

Figure 3.5 Script to create rebuild script for indexes.   (continued)

```
select index_name, 120, 99,'          next        '||next_extent from user_indexes
UNION
select index_name, 130, 99,'          minextents '||min_extents from user_indexes
 UNION
select index_name, 140, 99,'          maxextents '||max_extents from user_indexes
 UNION
select index_name, 150, 99,'          pctincrease '|| pct_increase from user_indexes
 UNION
select index_name, 160, 99, '            ) from user_indexes UNION
select index_name, 170, 99, '; ' from user_indexes UNION
select index_name, 180, 99, '   '  from user_indexes
 order by 1,2,3;
SPOOL OFF
set termout on feedback 15 verify on pagesize 20 linesize 80 space 1 heading on
exit
```

Figure 3.5 (continued)

3.3 Administration of Synonyms

Synonyms are a database shorthand. They allow the specifications of long or complex object names to be shortened. This is especially useful for shared tables or views. In addition, use of DATABASE LINK3 in synonyms allows transparent access to other databases on other nodes or even other entire systems halfway around the globe. Synonyms are a very power feature of Oracle and other SQL-compliant relational database systems.

3.3.1 Creation of Synonyms

Synonyms are created using the CREATE SYNONYM command. Synonyms can be either PRIVATE (the default) or PUBLIC. Private synonyms can only be used by the user creating them. In Oracle 6 anyone can create synonyms. In ORACLE7 you must have a specific grant or one of the special ROLES assigned to you before you can create synonyms. Only DBAs can create PUBLIC synonyms. PRIVATE synonyms are more secure.

The format of the CREATE SYNONYM command follows.

```
CREATE [PUBLIC] SYNONYM synonym FOR owner.table [@database link]
```

Where:

Synonym—is an allowed name. (It cannot be the name of an existing object for this user. For
     purposes of uniqueness, the owner name is considered as a part of the name for an object.)
Owner.table—is an existing table, view, or sequence name.
Database link—is an existing database link (covered later)

Synonyms provide both data independence and location transparency. With proper use and assignment, they allow an application to function regardless of table ownership, location, or even database.

3.3.2 Alteration of Synonyms

Synonyms cannot be altered. To change a synonym's definition it must be dropped and recreated.

3.3.3 Dropping Synonyms

Synonyms are dropped via the DROP command.

```
DROP [PUBLIC] SYNONYM synonym;
```

3.4 Administration of Sequences

Sequences are special database objects that provide numbers in sequence for input to a table. They are useful for providing generated unique key values, input of number type columns such as purchase order, employee number, sample number, sales order number, where the input must be unique and in numerical sequence.

3.4.1 Creation of Sequences

Sequences are created by use of the CREATE SEQUENCE command. The command's format follows.

```
CREATE SEQUENCE sequence name
   INCREMENT BY n
   START WITH n
   MAXVALUE n or NOMAXVALUE
   MINVALUE n or NOMINVALUE
   CYCLE or NOCYCLE (default)
   CACHE n or NOCACHE
   ORDER or NOORDER
```

Where:

Sequence name—is the name you want the sequence to have. This may include the user name if created from an account with DBA privilege.

n—is an integer, positive or negative.

INCREMENT BY—tells the system how to increment the sequence. If it is positive the values are ascending, negative, descending.

START WITH—tells the system what integer to start with.

MINVALUE—tells the system how low the sequence can go. For ascending sequences it defaults to 1; for descending, the default value is 10e27-1.

MAXVALUE—tells the system the highest value that will be allowed. for descending sequences the default is 1; for ascending, sequences the default is 10e27-1.

CYCLE—This option causes the sequence to automatically recycle to minvalue when maxvalue is reached for ascending sequences. For descending sequences it will cause recycle from minvalue back to maxvalue.

CACHE—This option will cache the specified number of sequence values into the buffers in the SGA. This speeds access, but all cached numbers are lost when the database is shut down. Default value is 20; maximum value is maxvalue-minvalue.

ORDER—This option forces sequence numbers to be output in order of request. In cases where they are used for time stamping, this may be required. In most cases, the sequence numbers will be in order anyway, and ORDER is not required.

Sequences avoid the performance problems associated with sequencing numbers generated by application triggers of the form:

```
DECLARE
    TEMP_NO NUMBER;
BEGIN
    LOCK TABLE PO_NUM IN EXCLUSIVE MODE NOWAIT;
    SELECT MAX(PO_NUM)+1 INTO TEMP_NO FROM SALES ;
END;
```

If the application requires numbers that are exactly in sequence (e.g., 1, 2, 3 . . .), then the trigger shown above may be your only recourse because if a statement that references a sequence is rolled back (cancelled), that sequence number is lost.

3.4.2 Alteration of Sequences

There may be times when a sequence must be altered, such as when a maximum or minimum value is reached. The ALTER SEQUENCE command is used to accomplish this. The format of the command follows.

```
ALTER SEQUENCE sequence name
    INCREMENT BY n
    MAXVALUE n or NOMAXVALUE
    MINVALUE n or NOMINVALUE
    CYCLE or NOCYCLE
    ORDER or NOORDER
```

Only future sequence numbers are affected by this statement. To alter the START WITH clause, the sequence must be dropped and recreated. For ascending sequences, the MAXVALUE cannot be less than the current sequence value. For descending sequences, the MINVALUE cannot be greater than the current sequence value.

3.4.3 Dropping a Sequence

Sequences are dropped using the DROP SEQUENCE command. The format of this command follows.

```
DROP SEQUENCE sequence name
```

If triggers and procedures reference the sequence, these triggers and procedures will fail if the sequence is dropped. It may be advisable to add an exception that will perform the trigger in section 3.4.1 in this situation.

3.4.4 Use of Sequences

Sequences are used by selecting using the sequence name and the parameters CURRVAL AND NEXTVAL. For example:

```
INSERT INTO purchase_orders (po_num, po_date, originator)
VALUES (po_seq.NEXTVAL, SYSDATE, USER) FROM dual;
```

In the above example po_seq is the name of a sequence. The above INSERT would update the po_num, po_date and originator fields of the purchase_orders table with the next sequence value from po_seq, the current system date and the current user name.

CURRVAL will retrieve the same value into multiple fields in the same session. CURRVAL cannot be used unless the NEXTVAL for the sequence has already been referenced in the current session.

The following lists contain restrictions and uses of NEXTVAL and CURRVAL.

Uses:
*   With the VALUES clause on an INSERT command.
*   With the SELECT subclause of a SELECT command.
*   In the SET clause of an UPDATE command.

Restrictions:
*   Neither one can be used in a subquery.
*   Neither can be used in a view or snapshot query.
*   Neither can be used with a DISTINCT clause.
*   Neither can be used with GROUP BY or ORDER BY.
*   Neither can be used in a SELECT command in combination with another SELECT using UNION, MINUS, or INTERSECT.
*   Neither can be used in the WHERE clause.
*   Neither can be used in the DEFAULT column value in a CREATE TABLE or ALTER TABLE command.
*   Neither can be used in a CHECK in a constraint.

3.5 Administration of Table Clusters

A cluster can be used when several tables store a row that is of the same data type and size in the same location. This reduces storage requirements and in some cases can speed access to data. The major drawback is that in operations involving updates, inserts, and deletes there can be performance degradation. The DBA should look at the expected mix of transaction types on the tables to be clustered and only cluster those that are frequently joined and don't have numerous updates, inserts, and deletes.

Under ORACLE7 there is an additional cluster feature, the ability to specify a HASH cluster. A HASH cluster uses a HASH form of storage and no index rather than the normal B-Tree-type index. Hash structures should only be used for static tables. Hashing is the process where a value, either of a unique or nonunique row, is used to generate a hash value. This hash value is used to place the row into the hashed table. To retrieve the row, the value is simply recalculated. Hashes can only be used for equality operations.

3.5.1 Creation of Clusters

Cluster creation is actually a two-step process. The first step is to specify the cluster using the CRE-ATE CLUSTER command. Before any tables in the cluster can be accessed, the cluster index must also be created. Let's look at this process.

1. First create the cluster:

```
CREATE CLUSTER cluster name
    (cluster key)
    PCTUSED n PCTFREE n
    SIZE n
    INITRANS n MAXTRANS n
    TABLESPACE tablespace
    STORAGE storage
    INDEX --or-- HASH IS column [HASHKEYS n]
```
   or:
```
    HASH IS--column [HASHKEYS n]
```

Where:

cluster name—is the name for the cluster; if the user has DBA privilege, a user name may be specified (user.cluster).

cluster key—is a list of columns and their data types. The names for the columns do not have to match the table column names, but the data types, lengths, and precisions do have to match.

n—is an integer (not all of the n's are the same value; n is just used for convenience).

SIZE—This is the expected size of the average cluster. This is calculated by:

     $19 + $ (sum of column lengths) $ + (1 \times $ num of columns)

SIZE should be rounded up to the nearest equal divisor of your block size. For example, if your block size is 2048 and the cluster length is 223, round up to 256.

storage—This storage clause will be used as the default for the tables in the cluster.

INDEX—This specifies to create an indexed cluster (default).

HASH IS—This specifies to create a HASH cluster. The specified column must be a zero precision number.

HASHKEYS—This creates a hash cluster and specifies the number (n) of keys. The value is rounded up to the nearest prime number.

The other parameters are the same as for the CREATE TABLE command.

2. Create the cluster index:

```
CREATE INDEX index name ON CLUSTER cluster name
```

Note that you don't specify the columns. This is taken from the CREATE CLUSTER command that was used to create the named cluster.

3. Create the tables that will be in the cluster (16 maximum for Oracle version 6):

```
CREATE TABLE cluster table
    (column list)
    CLUSTER cluster name (cluster column(s))
```

Where:

> cluster table—is a table name for a table that will be a part of the cluster.
>
> column list—is a list of columns for the table, specified identically to the CREATE TABLE command's normal format.

Remember: The cluster columns need not have the same name, but they must be the same data type, size, and precision and must be specified in the same order as the columns in the CREATE CLUSTER command.

3.5.2 Alteration of Clusters

Clusters are altered via the ALTER CLUSTER command. Only the sizing and storage parameters may be altered. No additional columns may be added to the cluster, or removed, using the ALTER CLUSTER command. The format of the command follows.

```
ALTER CLUSTER cluster name
    PCTUSED n PCTFREE n
    SIZE n
    INITRANS n MAXTRANS n
    STORAGE storage
```

The definitions for the above parameters are the same as for the CREATE TABLE, CREATE CLUSTER, and storage clause definitions.

In ORACLE7 the structure of a cluster and its associated index and tables can be analyzed for consistency and for sizing data using the ANALYZE CLUSTER command. The format of this command follows.

```
ANALYZE CLUSTER [schema.]cluster COMPUTE--or--ESTIMATE
(for estimate) SAMPLE n ROWS --or-- PERCENT
STATISTICS ;
```

The results appear in the DBA_CLUSTERS view.

To verify a clusters integrity, the following version of the ANALYZE command is used.

```
ANALYZE CLUSTER [schema.]cluster
VALIDATE STRUCTURE [CASCADE]
```

The CASCADE option forces analysis of all indexes and tables in the cluster.

3.5.3 Dropping a Cluster

As with the creation of clusters, dropping a cluster is a multipart function. The first step is to drop the tables in the cluster using the DROP TABLE command. Next, the cluster is dropped with the DROP CLUSTER command. There is an INCLUDING TABLES clause that will allow the DBA to drop both the cluster and tables at the same time. The format of the command follows.

```
DROP CLUSTER cluster name
    [INCLUDING TABLES]
```

3.5.4 Declustering Tables

Rather than dropping a cluster's tables completely, it may be desirable to decluster them and then just drop the cluster and cluster index with the DROP CLUSTER command. The procedure to decluster a table follows.

1. Create a new table that is a mirror of the existing clustered table—only of course it isn't clustered.

   ```
   CREATE TABLE new table
       AS SELECT * FROM cluster table
   ```

   (*Note:* "New table" is a different name from "cluster table.")

2. Drop the clustered table.

   ```
   DROP TABLE cluster table
   ```

3. Rename the replacement table.

   ```
   RENAME new table TO cluster table
   ```

4. Regrant all grants, create required indexes.
   Note: In the example SQL scripts there is a dynamic SQL script that will create a grant script for a specified database object. The script must of course be run before the object is dropped.

3.6 Administration of Database Links

Database links allow users to access tables in other databases, even other databases on other computers running different operating systems. To use database links, the systems involved must have the SQL*NET product installed. All systems need to have network links as well.

3.6.1 Creation of Database Links

Database links are created with the CREATE DATABASE LINK command. The format of this command follows.

```
CREATE [PUBLIC] DATABASE LINK link name
    [CONNECT TO user IDENTIFIED BY password]
    USING 'connect string'
```

Where:

database link—Under version 6 SQLXNETV1 this was a user specified name. Under ORACLE7 SQLXNETV2 this is the GLOBAL db name and the DB_DOMAIN.

PUBLIC—This is specified for database links that are to be used by all users. The user must have DBA privilege to specify a PUBLIC link.

CONNECT TO—This clause is used to force connection to a specific database user at the database being connected to. This allows the DBA to restrict access to confidential or sensitive information for one user instead of all users. If this clause isn't specified, the user's user name and password will be used in its place.

'connect string'—This is the protocol specific connection command. For VMS the format is:

```
D:NODE"""USER PASSWORD""":::"""TASK=ORDNsid"""
```

(*Note:* The TASK specifies a file that is located in the user's login directory. This can lead to management problems if multiple people need access. One way around this is to specify a network object that all users log in through, or by specifying a special user that all users log in to, such as SQLNET.)

The ORDNsid.COM file on a VMS machine contains:

```
$ DEFINE ORA_SID sid
$ DEFINE ORA_RDBMS oracle location
$ SRV=="$ORA_RDBMS:SRV.EXE"
$ SRV DECNET_NSP
```

The use of proxies and net objects needs to be coordinated with the system administrator. T*he SQL*Net FOR DEC VAX/VMS Installation and User's Guide* should be consulted for a more detailed explanation.

For a TCPIP (UNIX) installation, the connect string would be of the format:

```
T:HOST:SYSTEM ID,BUFFER
```

Where:

T—Tells Oracle this is TCPIP.

HOST—Name of a node that is in your system HOSTS file.

SYSTEM ID—This is one or more characters that correspond to the sid for the database on the remote system. It must exist in the database listing file.

BUFFER—This is the size in bytes of the context area used between TCPIP and ORACLE. The value can be set between 4 and 4096. The default is 4096.

Some or all of these parameters can be aliased on UNIX.

Connect strings are very system specific and DBAs should read all documentation provided by Oracle on their system's SQL*Net version before attempting to use them.

The database link would be used in the following manner:

```
SELECT * FROM emp@link;
```

The combination of table name and link can be placed into a single synonym for ease of use.

```
CREATE PUBLIC SYNONYM BOS_EMP FOR EMP@BOSTON;
```

(*Note:* Assuming BOSTON is a defined database link)

Until version 2.0 of SQL*Net is released, the selection of LONG table types via a database link is not allowed. Some get around this by constructing a view on tables with LONG data types that chop the long fields into multiple CHAR fields.

3.6.2 Alteration of Database Links

Database links cannot be altered. To modify a database link, it must be dropped and recreated.

3.6.3 Dropping Database Links

Database links are dropped via the DROP DATABASE LINK command. For public database links the word public must be inserted after DROP. Only DBAs can drop public database links. The format of the DROP command follows.

```
DROP [PUBLIC] DATABASE LINK link
```

3.7 Administration of Views

Views are virtual looks at tables. They don't exist until queried except as a specification statement stored in the database. A single view can be very efficient, but the "stacking" of views, that is, views that reference views that reference views, can show a performance problem. Views allow the DBA to restrict access to certain columns within a table or tables. Views can also act as preprocessing for reports. Views can also be used to perform calculations and display the results alongside of the data as if the results where stored in a table. Views can also be used to "filter" data. A view can be constructed from virtually any SELECT statement. Depending on how a view is constructed, updates and inserts can be done through them.

3.7.1 Creation of Views

Creation of views is accomplished with the CREATE VIEW command. Let's look at this command.

```
CREATE VIEW view name (alias, alias,...)
AS query
[WITH CHECK OPTION [CONSTRAINT constraint]]
```

Where:

view name—is the name for the view.

alias—is a valid column name. It isn't required to be the same as the column it is based on. If aliases aren't used, the names of the columns are used. If a column is modified by an expression, it must be aliased. If four columns are in the query, there must be four aliases.

query—This is any valid SELECT statement that doesn't include an ORDER BY or FOR UPDATE clause.

WITH CHECK—This clause specifies that inserts and updates through the view must be selectable from the view. This can be used in a view based on a view (ORACLE7).

CONSTRAINT—This specifies the name associated with the WITH CHECK constraint (ORACLE7).

A view is just a window to data, it can't store data itself. Views can be used in a SQL statement just like a table, with the following exceptions:

You can't update a view if:

* it contains a join.
* it contains a GROUP BY, CONNECT BY, or START WITH clause.

- it contains a DISTINCT clause, pseudo-columns like ROWNUM, or expressions like "AMOUNT+10" in the column list.
- it doesn't reference all NOT NULL columns in the table (all "not nulls" must be in the view and assigned a value by the update).

You can update a view that contains pseudo-columns or columns modified by expressions if the update doesn't effect these columns. An example of a view that uses aliases and expressions to modify columns is shown in Figure 3.6.

```
create view free_space
    (tablespace, file_id, pieces, free_bytes, free_blocks, largest_bytes,
    largest_blks) as
select tablespace_name, file_id, count(*),
    sum(bytes), sum(blocks),
    max(bytes), max(blocks) from sys.dba_free_space
group by tablespace_name, file_id;
```

Figure 3.6 Example of a view with expressions.

In Figure 3.6 the SUM, MAX, and COUNT expressions (functions) are used to provide summary data on space usage. This view could not be updated. Further reading will show it is also based on a view DBA_FREE_SPACE that is based on several data dictionary tables owned by the SYS user. An example of a view that performs calculations and filters the data provided is shown in Figure 3.7.

```
REM Title           : DD_VIEW.SQL
REM Purpose         : View of the Data Dictionary caches
REM                   showing only parameters that have usage
REM                   and the percent of GETMISSES/GETS
REM USE             : Use as a selectable table only
REM Limitations     : User must have access to V$ views.
REM Revisions:
REM                   Date      Modified By    Reason For change
REM                   4/28/93   Mike Ault      Initial Creation
REM
CREATE VIEW dd_cache
AS SELECT PARAMETER,GETS,GETMISSES,GETMISSES/GETS*100 PERCENT        ,COUNT,USAGE
FROM V$ROWCACHE
WHERE GETS > 100 AND GETMISSES > 0;
```

Figure 3.7. View using expressions and filtering.

3.7.2 Alteration of Views

Views cannot be altered under version 6, to be changed they must be dropped and recreated. Grants can be made on views, as can synonyms.

Under ORACLE7 there is a single option for the ALTER VIEW command—the COMPILE option. If a view's underlying views or tables are marked as invalid or changed, the view is marked as invalid and must be recompiled. This can be done automatically when the view is next called, or it can be done explicitly with the ALTER VIEW command. It is best to do this explicitly so that any problems are found before the users attempt to use the view. The format for the ALTER VIEW command follows.

```
ALTER VIEW [schema.]view name COMPILE;
```

3.7.3 Dropping Views

Views are dropped with the DROP VIEW command. Its format follows.

```
DROP VIEW [owner --or-- schema.]view name
```

3.8 Administration of Triggers In ORACLE7

In ORACLE7, several new database objects have been added. The first we shall discuss is the database level trigger. Database triggers are triggers stored in the database and associated with specific actions on a database level. Previously, in version 6 and other earlier versions of Oracle, the triggers had to be associated with a form. With ORACLE7 this is no longer needed. Form triggers are still used within the context of SQL*Forms, but database triggers are a completely seperate entitiy.

3.8.1 Creation of Database Triggers

Database triggers are created using the CREATE TRIGGER command. There are three basic types of triggers, BEFORE, AFTER, and FOR EACH ROW. Since the FOR EACH ROW clause can be combined with the other two, this gives four types of triggers: before and after statement triggers and before and after row triggers. In addition, each of the four types can be tied to the three basic actions, DELETE, INSERT, and UPDATE, giving 12 possible triggers per table. Only one of each type of trigger is allowed. A trigger is ENABLED when it is created. This command's format follows.

```
CREATE [OR REPLACE] TRIGGER [schema.]trigger
BEFORE--or--AFTER DELETE--or--INSERT--or--UPDATE
OF column --or-- ON [schema.]table
(The above is mandatory section, what follows is optional)
[[REFERENCING OLD--or--NEW AS old--or--new] --or- [FOR EACH ROW]
WHEN (condition)]
pl/sql block
```

Where:

OR REPLACE—replaces trigger if it exists, this can be used to change the definition of a
 trigger without dropping it first.
schema—This takes the place of the owner argument from version 6.
trigger—This is the trigger's name.
BEFORE—This specifies the trigger is fired before the specified action.
AFTER—This indicates the trigger is fired after the specified action.
DELETE / INSERT / UPDATE—These are the specified actions, only one per trigger.
OF—This limits the action response to the listed columns.
ON—This specifies the table name of the table the trigger is for.
REFERENCING—This deals with correlation names. This allows specification of old and
 new values for a column.
FOR EACH ROW—This forces the trigger to fire on each affected row, making it a row
 trigger. The trigger is fired for each row that is affected by the trigger and that meets the
 WHEN clause constraints.
WHEN—This specifies any constraints on the trigger. This is a trigger restriction clause. This
 contains a standard SQL clause.
pl/sql Block—This is the trigger body and is in the standard pl/sql format.

One thing to note concerns AFTER ROW triggers and table snapshot logs. Table snapshot
logs create an after row trigger. If there is already an after row trigger in existence, the CREATE
SNAPSHOT LOG command will fail. It is suggested that the text of whatever after row trigger you
have be saved out into a text file, the after row trigger dropped, the snapshot log created, and the
text of your trigger added to that of the snapshot log trigger. It is anticipated that at some point after
7.0.12 of ORACLE7 the snapshot log trigger will be specified as a seperate type of trigger avoiding
this problem.

3.8.2 Alteration of Triggers

As was stated in section 3.8.1, the CREATE command has the OR REPLACE option to allow a
trigger to be recreated without being dropped. To alter the contents of a trigger, this create or replace option is used. A trigger has one of two possible states, either ENABLED or DISABLED.
This state is changed with either the ALTER TRIGGER or ALTER TABLE command.

```
ALTER TRIGGER [schema.]trigger ENABLE--or--DISABLE;
```

or:

```
ALTER TABLE [schema.]table ENABLE [UNIQUE] (column, column...)
PRIMARY KEY --or-- CONSTRAINT constraint [EXCEPTIONS INTO [schema.]table]
USING INDEX (index clause)
ALL TRIGGERS;
```

Where the index clause consists of:

```
INITRANS n MAXTRANS n TABLESPACE ts_name
STORAGE (storage clause) PCTFREE n
Where n are integers.
```

There can be multiple enables in a single alter.

The ALTER TABLE command can also use a DISABLE clause.

```
DISABLE UNIQUE
or
CONSTRAINT constraint
or
PRIMARY KEY
or
ALL TRIGGERS
(column, column)
[CASCADE];
```

Where CASCADE disables any integrity constraints that depend on a specified constraint. If a unique or primary key is referenced in this clause the CASCADE option must be specified.

One limit on the usefulness of the ALTER TABLE in either disabling or enabling triggers is that it is an all-or-nothing proposition. It is better to use the ALTER TRIGGER command unless you want all triggers enabled or disabled at one time.

3.8.3 Dropping a Trigger

Triggers are dropped using the DROP TRIGGER command.

```
DROP TRIGGER [schema.]trigger;
```

3.9 Administration of Functions and Procedures Under ORACLE7

Functions and procedures under ORACLE7 are virtually identical. The major exceptions are that functions always return a value, while procedures don't. This leads to the second difference, the procedure can use the OUT and IN OUT arguments in the create command, while the function can't. In fact, the function doesn't have to specify the IN argument since input to a function is required.

Why use functions and procedures? The benefits are numerous. Functions and procedures provide a consistent means of accessing, altering, and deleting database information. They allow enhanced security by giving the DBA the ability to grant access to the procedures and functions instead of the actual tables or views. The procedure or functions can have elevated privileges that are in effect while the procedure or function is active but go away when it completes. This is synonymous with using installed images under the VMS operating system.

Functions and procedures enhance productivity by allowing a given process to be coded once and then referenced by all developers. Instead of each form requiring coded triggers for data access, the stored procedures and functions can be referenced instead. This drives consistency down to the database level instead of requiring it from each developer.

Performance is enhanced by allowing multiple users to access the same shared image. Since the procedures and functions are loaded into the cached memory area, only one I/O is required for each procedure or function to be available to all users. In a distributed environment, network traffic is reduced since the procedures and functions are stored at the database level rather than at the distributed location. Let's look at administration of functions and procedures.

3.9.1 Creation of Functions and Procedures

Before a function or procedure can be created, the DBA must have run the DBMSSTDX.SQL script. The user creating the function or procedure must have CREATE PROCEDURE to create a procedure or function in their own schema or CREATE ANY PROCEDURE system privilege. Functions and procedures are created using the CREATE command. The format for each differs slightly.

For functions the format is:

```
CREATE [OR REPLACE] FUNCTION [schema.]function
[( argument IN datatype, argument IN datatype,...)]
RETURN datatype
IS
```

or

```
AS pl/sql body
```

For procedures the format is:

```
CREATE [OR REPLACE] PROCEDURE [schema.]procedure
[( argument IN--or--OUT--or--IN OUT datatype,
argument IN--or--OUT--or--IN OUT datatype,...)]
IS--or--AS pl/sql body
```

For both procedures and functions the command arguments are listed below.

OR REPLACE—This optional statement specifies that if the procedure or function exists, replace it; if it doesn't exist, create it.

schema—This is the schema to place the procedure or function into. If other than the user's default schema, the user must have CREATE ANY PROCEDURE system privilege.

procedure or function—This is the name of the procedure or function being created.

argument(s)—This is the argument to the procedure or function. There may be more than one of these.

IN—This specifies that the argument must be specified when calling the procedure or function. For functions, an argument must always be provided.

OUT—This specifies the procedure passes a value for this argument back to the calling object. Not used with functions.

IN OUT—This specifies both the IN and OUT features are in effect for the procedure. This is not used with functions.

datatype—This is the data type of the argument. Precision, length, and scale cannot be specified; they are derived from the calling object.

pl/sql body—This is a SQL, PL/SQL body of statements.

It is suggested that each function and procedure be created under a single owner for a given application. This makes administration easier and allows ease of use of dynamic SQL to create packages. It is also suggested that the procedure or function be created as a text file for documentation and later ease of update. The source files for related procedures and functions should be stored under a common directory area.

3.9.2 Alteration of Procedures and Functions

To alter the logic or variables of a procedure or function, the CREATE OR REPLACE form of the command in section 3.9.1 should be used. The only option for the ALTER command for functions and procedures is the COMPILE option. This option recompiles the procedure or function after a modification to their references objects has occurred. The format of this command follows.

```
ALTER FUNCTION--or--PROCEDURE [schema.]function --or-- procedure
COMPILE;
```

If a function or procedure is called that has been invalidated by a change to a table, view, or other referenced procedure or function, it is automatically recompiled. Whenever possible, explicit recompilation via the ALTER command should be used. This will pinpoint any problems before the users find them for you.

3.9.3 Dropping Procedures or Functions

Periodically it may be required for a DBA to remove a function or procedure from the database. This is accomplished with the DROP command. The format of this command follows.

```
DROP FUNCTION--or--PROCEDURE [schema.]function or procedure.
```

This will invalidate any related functions or procedures, and they will have to be recompiled before use.

3.10 Administration of Packages

Under ORACLE7 packages are collections of related functions, variables, and procedures. All of the functions and procedures for a specific application can be grouped under one or more packages and handled as units. A package is loaded into shared memory whenever one of its parts is referenced. The package stays in memory until the least recently used algorithm (LRU) determines it hasn't been recently used. This determination of use is for all database users, not just the originating user.

Packages allow public and private functions, procedures, and variables. Public functions, procedures, and variables are named in the package definition and are available to all users with the privilege to access the package. Private procedures, functions, and variables are not referenced in the package definition but are contained in the package body. They are only referenced by the package internal objects.

As is hinted at above, the package consists of two possible parts, a definition and a body. Each of the parts of a package are created separately. In the case of a package that has no private functions, procedures, or variables, no package body is required. However, each of the referenced public objects must exist.

Not using private objects allows the DBA and developers to maintain the individual objects separately instead of as a single entity. If a package has private objects, it must have a body. The package definition contains the names of all public functions, procedures, and variables. The package body contains the pl/sql and SQL code for all of the public and private package objects.

If the DBA has enforced use of script files to create database functions and procedures, creating the package body involves simply concatenating the various scripts together and making minor changes to the syntax of the statements. By use of the DBA_SOURCE view, the DBA can use dynamic SQL to create script listings. An example of this is shown in Figure 3.8. This will create one large file with all of the type of objects that the DBA specifies for a specific owner. This script can also be used to document existing package definitions and package bodies.

Let's look at the processes and commands used to administrate packages.

```
rem     ************************************************************************
rem     NAME:  FPRC_RCT.sql
rem     HISTORY:
rem     Date        Who             What
rem     _____     _____     _____
rem     05/22/93    Michael Ault    Created
rem     FUNCTION:   Build a script to re-create functions, procedures,
rem                 packages or package bodies.
rem     ************************************************************************
set verify off  feedback off lines 80 pages 0 heading off
spool cre_fprc.sql
select 'create '||s1.type||' '||s1.owner||'.'||s1.name,
                 substr(s2.text,1,80)||';'
from
                DBA_SOURCE s1,
                DBA_SOURCE s2
WHERE
                s1.type = UPPER('&object_type') AND
                s1.owner = UPPER('&object_owner') AND
                s1.type = s2.type AND
                s1.owner = s2.owner AND
                s1.name = s2.name
GROUP BY
                s1.owner,
                s1.name
ORDER BY
                s2.line;
rem
spool off
exit
```

Figure 3.8 Example of script to rebuild function and procedure objects.

3.10.1 Creation of Packages

Package creation involves one or two steps. The first step, creation of the package definition, is required for all packages. The second step, creation of the package body, is required only for those packages that have private components. The command for creating package definitions follows.

```
CREATE [OR REPLACE] PACKAGE [schema.]package
IS--or--AS pl/sql package specification;
```

Where:

OR REPLACE—This is used when the user wishes to create or replace a package. If the package definition exists, it is replaced; if it doesn't exist, it is created.

schema—This is the schema the package is to be created in. If this is not specified, the package is created in the user's default schema.

package—This is the name of the package to be created.

pl/sql package specification—This is the list of procedures, functions, or variables that make up the package. All components listed are considered to be public in nature.

Example:

```
CREATE PACKAGE admin.employee_package
AS
   FUNCTION new_emp(ename CHAR, position CHAR, supervisor NUM,
      catagory NUM, hiredate DATE)
      RETURN NUMBER;
   FUNCTION fire_them(ename CHAR, reason VARCHAR2, term_date DATE)
      RETURN DATE;
   PROCEDURE new_dept(ename CHAR, dept CHAR, new_dept CHAR,
      date_of_change DATE);
   bad_catagory EXCEPTION;
   bad_date EXCEPTION;
   END employee_package
```

This example creates the package employee_package. The package contains the functions new_emp and fire_them, the procedure new_dept, and the exceptions bad_catagory and bad_date. All of the objects are available to whoever has privileges on employee_package.

Creation of the Package Body. The package body contains all of the SQL and PL/SQL scripts that make up the procedures, functions, exceptions, and variables used by the package. If the package only contains public items, a package body may not be required. The format for the CREATE PACKAGE BODY command follows.

```
CREATE [OR REPLACE] PACKAGE BODY [schema.]package
IS--or--AS pl/sql package body;
```

Where:

OR REPLACE—When this is used, if the package body exists, it is replaced; if it doesn't exist, it is created.

schema—This specifies the schema to create the package in. If this is not specified, the package body is created in the user's default schema.

pl/sql package body—This is the collection of all of the SQL and pl/sql text required to create all of the objects in the package.

Figure 3.9 is an example of the CREATE PROCEDURE BODY command. The exceptions listed in the package definition are contained within the procedures.

```
CREATE OR REPLACE PROCEDURE BODY admin.employee_package AS
FUNCTION new_emp(ename CHAR, position CHAR, supervisor NUM, catagory NUM,
hiredate DATE)
                RETURN NUMBER IS
                emp_number number(5);
                BEGIN
                .
                .
                .
                END;
FUNCTION fire_them(ename CHAR, reason VARCHAR2, term_date DATE)
                RETURN NUMBER AS
                years_of_service NUMBER (4,2);
                BEGIN
                .
                .
                .
                END;
PROCEDURE new_dept(ename CHAR, dept CHAR, new_dept CHAR, date_of_change DATE)
                IS
                BEGIN
                .
                .
                .
                END;
                END employee_package
```

Figure 3.9. Example of format for package body.

3.10.2 Alteration of the Package

It will be required for the DBA to alter a package when the tables, views, sequences, and so forth. that the package procedures and functions reference change. This is accomplished through use of the CREATE OR REPLACE PACKAGE [BODY] form of the CREATE PACKAGE command. The format for the command is identical to the CREATE PACKAGE [BODY] command. Remember that all procedures, variables, and functions referenced in the CREATE PACKAGE command must be present in the CREATE OR REPLACE PACKAGE BODY command. If you just use the command with a single procedure or function you want altered, that will be the only object left in the body when you are finished. Perhaps with a future release we will see the ability to use the package definition as a link list, and this won't be required. There is also an ALTER PACKAGE BODY command that is used only to recompile the package body. The format of the ALTER command follows.

```
ALTER PACKAGE [schema.]package COMPILE PACKAGE--or--BODY;
```

3.10.3 Dropping a Package

Even such wonderful things as packages have limited lifetimes. Applications are replaced or are no longer needed; entire database practices are rethought and changed. This leads to the requirement to be able to drop packages that are no longer needed. This is accomplished through the DROP PACKAGE command. The format of this command follows.

```
DROP PACKAGE [BODY] [schema.]package;
```

Exclusion of the keyword BODY results in the drop of both the definition and the body. Inclusion of BODY drops just the package body leaving the definition intact.

When a package is dropped, all dependent objects are invalidated. If the package is not recreated before one of the dependent objects is accessed, ORACLE7 tries to recompile the package. This will return an error and cause failure of the command.

3.11 Administration of Snapshots

Another feature of ORACLE7 that needs administration is the snapshot. Snapshots are read-only copies of either an entire single table or set of its rows (simple snapshot) or a collection of tables, views, or their rows using joins, grouping, and selection criteria (complex snapshots). Snapshots are very useful in a distributed environment where remote locations need a queriable copy of a table from the master database. Instead of paying the penalty for using the network to send out the query and get back the data, the query is against a local table image and is thus much faster.

Snapshots are asynchronous in nature. They reflect a table's or a collection's state at the time the snapshot was taken. A simple snapshot can be periodically refreshed by either use of a snapshot log containing only the changed rows for the snapshot (fast refresh) or a totally new copy (complete refresh). In most cases, the fast refresh is quicker and just as accurate. A fast refresh can only be used if the snapshot has a log and that log was created prior to the creation or last refresh of the snapshot. For a complex snapshot, a complete refresh is required. It is also possible to allow the system to decide which to use, either a fast or complete refresh.

One problem with a snapshot log is that it keeps a copy of each and every change to a row. Therefore, if a row undergoes 200 changes between one refresh and the next, there will be 200 entries in the snapshot log that will be applied to the snapshot at refresh. This could lead to the refresh of the snapshot taking longer than a complete refresh. Each snapshot should be examined for the amount of activity it is seeing, and if this is occurring with any of them, the snapshot log should be eliminated or the refresh mode changed to COMPLETE. Since the snapshot log must be created prior to the snapshot itself for a simple snapshot, let's examine the administration of snapshot logs first.

3.11.1 Creation of Snapshot Logs

A snapshot log is created for the master table of a snapshot. In the case of a simple snapshot, there is only one table. Creation of a snapshot log for a complex snapshot does no good since a complex snapshot requires a complete refresh that doesn't use a snapshot log. Before a snapshot log can be created, the DBMDDNAP.SQL procedure must have been run by the DBA, and the ORACLE7 system must have the procedural option. The user creating the snapshot must have the CREATE TRIGGER privilege on the table the log is being created for.

The CREATE SNAPSHOT LOG command is used to create a snapshot log. The format of the command follows.

```
CREATE SNAPSHOT LOG ON [schema.]table
[PCTFREE n]
[PCTUSED n]
[INITRANS n]
[MAXTRANS n]
[TABLESPACE tablespace]
[STORAGE ( storage clause)];
```

Where:

schema—This is the schema in which to store the log. If not specified, this will default to the user's own schema.

table—This is the table name to create the snapshot log for.

PCTFREE—These are the values for these creation parameters to use for

PCTUSED—the created log file.

INITRANS

MAXTRANS

TABLESPACE—This specifies the tablespace in which to create the snapshot log. This will default to the user's default tablespace if not specified.

STORAGE—This is a standard storage clause.

Example use of the CREATE SNAPSHOT LOG command:

```
CREATE SNAPSHOT LOG ON admin.personnel
   PCTFREE 10
   PCTUSED 70
   TABLESPACE remote_admin_data
   STORAGE (  INITIAL 50K NEXT 50K
             MINEXTENTS 1 MAXEXTENTS 50
             PCTINCREASE 0);
```

As was noted before, the CREATE SNAPSHOT LOG command creates an after-row trigger on the affected table. If the table already has an after-row trigger, the CREATE command will fail. In this case, save the text of the existing after-row trigger into a text file, drop the existing trigger, create the snapshot log, and then add the text of the old after-row trigger to the after-row trigger created by the snapshot log CREATE process.

3.11.2 Alteration of Snapshot Logs

Periodically, snapshot logs may need to be altered. Storage needs may change, or the storage dynamics may need to be altered on a snapshot log. These are accomplished by use of the ALTER SNAPSHOT LOG command. The format for this command follows.

```
ALTER SNAPSHOT LOG ON [schema.]table
[PCTFREE n]
```

```
[PCTUSED n]
[INITRANS n]
[MAXTRANS n]
[STORAGE ( storage clause)];
```

Where:

schema—This is the schema in which to store the log. If not specified, this will default to the user's own schema.

table—This is the table name to create the snapshot log for.

PCTFREE—These are the values for these creation parameters to use for

PCTUSED—the created log file.

INITRANS

MAXTRANS

STORAGE—This is a standard storage clause.

To change a snapshot log's location either an export/import or a drop/create of the snapshot log is required.

3.11.3 Dropping a Snapshot Log

A snapshot log is dropped using the DROP SNAPSHOT LOG command. The format for the command follows.

```
DROP SNAPSHOT LOG ON [schema.]table;
```

3.11.4 Creation of Snapshots

Once any required snapshot logs are created, the snapshots themselves can be created. This is accomplished through the CREATE SNAPSHOT command. Snapshots can be either simple or complex. A simple snapshot consists of either an entire single table or a simple selection of rows from a single table. A complex snapshot consists of joined tables, views, or grouped or complex select statement queries. Snapshots are built using the CREATE SNAPSHOT command.

```
CREATE SNAPSHOT [schema.]snapshot
[[PCTFREE n]
[PCTUSED n]
[INITRANS n]
[MAXTRANS n]
[TABLESPACE tablespace]
[STORAGE ( storage clause)]]--or-- [ CLUSTER (column, column,....)]
[REFRESH FAST--or--COMPLETE--or--FORCE
[START WITH date]
[NEXT date]]
AS subquery;
```

Where:

schema—This is the schema in which to store the log. If not specified, this will default to the user's own schema.

table—This is the table name to create the snapshot for.

PCTFREE—These are the values for these creation parameters to use for

PCTUSED—the created snapshot file.

INITRANS

MAXTRANS

TABLESPACE—This specifies the tablespace in which to create the snapshot. This will default to the user's default tablespace if not specified.

STORAGE—This is a standard storage clause.

CLUSTER—This is used to designate the snapshot as part of the specified cluster. The values before the —or— will default to the clusters values so they are not used. In addition, the STORAGE clause for the cluster is used, so it is not needed.

REFRESH—This specifies the refresh mode, either FAST, COMPLETE, or FORCE. FAST uses a SNAPSHOT LOG; COMPLETE reperforms the subquery and is the only valid mode for a complex snapshot; FORCE causes the system to first try a FAST, and if this is not possible, then a COMPLETE. FAST is the default mode.

START WITH—This specifies the date for the first refresh.

NEXT—This specifies either a date or a time interval for the next refresh of the snapshot.

START WITH and NEXT values are used to determine the REFRESH cycle for the snapshot. If just START WITH is specified, only the initial REFRESH is done. If both are specified, the first is done on the START WITH date and the next is evaluated against the START WITH to determine future refreshes. If just the NEXT value is specified, it computes based on the date the snapshot is created. If neither is specified, the snapshot is not automatically refreshed.

AS subquery—The subquery is a valid select statement on one or more tables.

Snapshots cannot be created on tables owned by the SYS user. Data can only be selected from a snapshot; no updates, inserts, or deletions are allowed. For verification and lookup purposes snapshots are ideal.

Figure 3.10 shows the use of the CREATE SNAPSHOT command for a simple snapshot. Figure 3.11 shows use of the CREATE SNAPSHOT command with a complex snapshot. The sizing considerations should mirror those for the source table. If the source table is stable, a large initial extent with smaller subsequent extents should be used. Since snapshots will most likely be on slow growth tables, set pctincrease to zero in most cases.

```
CREATE SNAPSHOT new_drugs
PCTFREE 10 PCTUSED 70
TABLESPACE clinical_tests
STORAGE (INITIAL 50K NEXT 50K PCTINCREASE 0)
REFRESH
                START WITH ROUND(SYSDATE + 7) + 2/24
                NEXT NEXT_DAY(TRUNC(SYSDATE, 'TUESDAY') + 2/24
AS select * from test_drugs@kcgc;
```

Figure 3.10 Example of the CREATE SNAPSHOT command for a simple snapshot.

In the snapshot in Figure 3.10 the entire test_drugs table is used to create a snapshot from its location at a remote database identified in the kcgc connect string into the tablespace clinical_trials in the current database. It will be first refreshed in seven days at 2 A.M. and subsequently at seven-day intervals on every Tuesday at 2 A.M thereafter. Since no refresh mode is specified, if the table has a snapshot log, the fast mode will be used since it is a simple snapshot. If no snapshot log is available, then the complete mode will be used. If you specify the FORCE option, it will always try to do a FAST first.

The script in the Figure 3.11 produces a complex snapshot called trail_summary with data from the test_drugs, trial_doctors, and trial_summaries tables in the database specified in the connect string kcgc. The snapshot is refreshed using the complete mode since it is a complex query and is created in the clinical_tests tablespace of the local database.

```
CREATE SNAPSHOT trial_summary
PCTFREE 5 PCTUSED 60
TABLESPACE clinical_tests
STORAGE (INITIAL 100K NEXT 50K PCTINCREASE 0)
REFRESH COMPLETE
                 START WITH ROUND(SYSDATE + 14) + 6/24
                 NEXT NEXT_DAY(TRUNC(SYSDATE, 'FRIDAY') + 19/24
AS
select td.drug_name, s.trial_number, dr.doctor_id, s.comment_line,s.comment
from
                 test_drugs@kcgc td,
                 trial_doctors@kcgc dr,
                 trial_summaries@kcgc s
where
                 td.drug_id = s.drug_id and
                 s.trial_id = dr.trial_id and
                 s.doctor_id=dr.doctor_id;
```

Figure 3.11 Script to produce a complex snapshot.

3.11.5 Altering a Snapshot

A snapshot is altered using the ALTER SNAPSHOT command. The user may alter such items as storage and space usage parameters and type and frequency of refresh. The format for this command follows.

```
ALTER SNAPSHOT [schema.]snapshot
[[PCTFREE n]
[PCTUSED n]
[INITRANS n]
[MAXTRANS n]
[STORAGE ( storage clause)]]--or-- [ CLUSTER (column, column,....)]
```

```
[REFRESH FAST--or--COMPLETE--or--FORCE
[START WITH date]
[NEXT date]];
```

Where:

schema—This is the schema in which to store the snapshot. If not specified, this will default
    to the user's own schema.

table—This is the table name to create the snapshot for.

PCTFREE—These are the values for these creation parameters to use for

PCTUSED—the created snapshot file.

INITRANS

MAXTRANS

STORAGE—This is a standard storage clause.

REFRESH—This specifies the refresh mode, either FAST, COMPLETE, or FORCE. FAST
    uses a SNAPSHOT LOG; COMPLETE reperforms the subquery and is the only valid mode
    for a complex snapshot; FORCE causes the system to first try a FAST, and if this is not
    possible, then a COMPLETE. FAST is the default mode.

START WITH—This specifies the date for the first refresh.

NEXT—This specifies either a date or a time interval for the next refresh of the snapshot.

START WITH and NEXT values are used to determine the refresh cycle for the snapshot. If
just START WITH is specified, only the initial REFRESH is done. If both are specified, the first is
done on the start with date, and the next is evaluated against the start with to determine future
REFRESHES. If just the next value is specified, it computes based on the date the snapshot is created. If neither is specified, the snapshot is not automatically refreshed.

3.11.6 Dropping a Snapshot

A snapshot is dropped using the DROP SNAPSHOT command. The command's format follows.

```
DROP SNAPSHOT [schema.]snapshot;
```

When a snapshot is dropped, if it has a snapshot log associated with it, only the rows required
for maintaining that snapshot are dropped. Dropping a master table on which a snapshot is based
doesn't drop the snapshot. However, any subsequent refreshes will fail.

3.12 Administration of Schemas Under ORACLE7

Another new feature that has been mentioned but not explained in the previous sections is the feature known as SCHEMAS. Those DBAs familiar with other database systems may already be familiar with this concept as it has been used in other systems such as INFORMIX for several years.
However, schemas are new to Oracle as of ORACLE7.

A schema is a logical grouping of related database objects. It roughly compares to the owner
of the objects in a version 6 database. Just as in version 6 and object owners, objects in a given
schema do not have to be in the same tablespace. In fact, each user has a default schema that corresponds to his user name in Oracle. A user may only create objects in their own schema (that schema

named the same as the user they are logged in under) unless they have proper privileges. Schemas are populated via the CREATE SCHEMA command.

3.12.1 Creation of Schemas

The CREATE SCHEMA statement can include the creation commands for tables, views, and grants. The user issuing the command must have the appropriate privileges to create each of the objects mentioned in the CREATE SCHEMA command. The format of this command follows.

```
CREATE SCHEMA AUTHORIZATION schema
[CREATE TABLE command]
[CREATE VIEW command]
[GRANT command];
```

Where:

schema—This is the user's schema; it must be the user name.
command—This corresponds to the appropriate CREATE object command.

The individual create commands are not separated with a command terminator. The terminator is placed at the end of the entire create sequence of commands for the schema. You cannot specify storage parameters in the create commands. They will only support the extensions of standard rather than Oracle extended SQL.

Schemas cannot be altered or dropped; only individual schema objects can. It is anticipated that under future releases there will be stand-alone schemas allowed that don't require an owning user. For now, you can only issue a CREATE SCHEMA command on the name of the SCHEMA that you own (i.e., your own name). Until that time arrives, you can create a user that doesn't have CREATE SESSION privilege to own the schema to get the same effect if desired. The DBA should consult the following references for more detailed information.

ORACLE7 Server Administrator's Guide, PART# 6694-70-1292, Dec. 1992, Oracle Corp.

ORACLE7 Server SQL Language Reference Manual, PART# 778-70-1292, Dec. 1992, Oracle Corp.

ORACLE RDBMS Database Administrator's Guide, Version 6.0, PART# 3601-V6.0, Oct. 1990, Oracle Corp.

SQL Language Reference Manual, Version 6.0, PART# 778-V6.0, Feb. 1990, Oracle Corp.

An Internal Look at Rollback Segments, Nguyen, L., Lindsay, W., Oracle World Wide Support RDBMS Group. 1991 IOUG Proceedings Paper #537, Miami, Fla.

Space, The Final Frontier, Jou, K., Wetzler, V., Oracle World Wide Technical Support. 1991 IOUG Proceedings, Miami, Fla.

ORACLE7: PL/SQL Stored Procedures and Triggers, Kooi, R., Oracle Corp. 1992 IOUG Proceedings, San Francisco, Calif., Paper # 534.

Administration of Oracle Users

Without users databases would be of no value. Administration of users is a critical function of the DBA and cannot be approached in a haphazard manner. The proper assignment of system privileges, object privileges, default, and temporary tablespaces under version 6 is critical if your database is to be managed. Under ORACLE7 the creation, maintenance, and assignment of roles and profiles is just as critical.

4.1 Oracle User Administration Under Version 6

Of all the things a DBA is responsible for, user administration is probably the most important. Database file placement, tuning, and all other DBA functions will not amount to much if a single misconfigured user wipes out your SYSTEM tablespace or fills a critical area with temporary tables just in time to cause an important report to fail. User administration is also the most visible of the DBA activities. The DBA is advised that creation of SQL scripts that provide standard methodologies for configuring users is recommended. This will ensure things such as default and temporary tablespace assignment aren't forgotten. They also speed the process of assigning users to the database.

The users should have a default and a temporary tablespace other than the SYSTEM tablespace that they are assigned to. This prevents formation of nonsystem-related tables in the SYSTEM tablespace and prevents formation of temporary segments that will fragment the SYSTEM area. Generally, generic tablespaces are created to hold the user's accounts, such as ORA_USER_tablespace_1 and ORA_TEMP_TABLESPACE_1. The default tablespace should be sized according to the number of users and their data needs. For instance, if you have 20 users, and each is granted a one megabyte quota, then the default should be 20 megabytes in size. It has been found that unless users are doing extremely large transactions that do a number of decodes, group-bys, or nonindexed joins, ten megabytes per temporary area is enough. Creation of database objects should be reserved to nonsystem user-related accounts. This makes management of database objects easier. For example, GCDM_DBA create tables and objects for the GCDM application, not user SMITH.

4.1.1 User Database Privileges in Version 6

Under Oracle version 6, user setup is fairly easy. You have three basic database privileges to watch. These privileges are listed below.

PRIVILEGE	WHO SHOULD HAVE IT	WHY
DBA	Nobody but the DBA	This gives the user all of the other privileges and allows them to wreak havoc on your database.
RESOURCE	Only personnel requiring the ability to put a table anywhere they want—in other words, the DBA	This allows the user the ability to create objects in any tablespace. This is not a good idea.
CONNECT	Everybody	If they can't connect, they aren't a user.

4.1.2 User Connection to Oracle

You are probably saying: "Wait a minute. Don't give anything but connect to users? How will they create tables?" The answer is through the tablespace level grant. In Oracle version 6 there is a single tablespace grant. This is the RESOURCE grant. Get the picture? Just grant resource on the tablespaces that the individual users need to create tables in. Don't give away one of the keys to the kingdom by giving global resource. Look back at section 1 under step 43 of the VMS installation procedure. The "GRANT RESOURCE ON tablespace TO username" command allows the users who receive this type of grant to create tables, but only in the tablespace named in the command. A single user may have multiple tablespaces in which they have resource granted. However, for each create statement they issue, they *must* specify the tablespace or else the table will be created in their default tablespace.

To reiterate what was said in section 1, no user should be allowed to have the SYSTEM tablespace as either a DEFAULT or a TEMPORARY tablespace with the exception of SYS, SYS-TEM, and PUBLIC. For SYS and SYSTEM, the temporary tablespace should be set away from SYSTEM. If you have installed the TOOLS tables in another tablespace, set the SYSTEM user's default to that tablespace. This will help prevent excessive fragmentation in the SYSTEM tablespace. If the temporary tablespace for any user except PUBLIC is set to SYSTEM, there is a distinct possibility that a runaway query or large outside join could freeze the entire database.

The automation of the user addition process will prevent the overlooking of default and temporary tablespace assignment. An sample script is shown in Figure 4.1.

Some things are important to note about this script. First, note the set command in line 9. This prevents the lines with the &'ed variables from being displayed as the variables are substituted for (a single ampersand says, "Get a value for this"; two ampersands say, "Substitute the value you have for this into this spot, too"). Another thing to notice is that in accordance with the guidelines stated above, only "connect" is granted at the database level. Without the "verify off," each time a

```
1:    REM NAME        : add_user.sql
2:    REM PURPOSE     : adds a user to the database
3:    REM USE         : called from SQL*Plus, SQL*Menu or OS script
4:    REM Limitations : None
5:    REM Revisions   :
6:    REM               Date       Modified By    Reason For change
7:    REM               5 DEC 90   Mike Riggs     Initial Checkin
8:    REM               3 AUG 91   MIKE AULT      DONT USE SYSTEM
9:    set verify off
10:   grant connect to &user_name identified by &password;
11:   alter user &&user_name default tablespace &default_ts;
12:   alter user &&user_name temporary tablespace &temporary_ts;
13:   grant resource on &&default_ts to &&user_name;
14:   exit
```

Figure 4.1. Example of version 6 user addition script.

variable is substituted, the line is redisplayed. This procedure will prompt for user_name, default_ts, and temporary_ts, and then will perform the commands as shown. This will work on both VMS and UNIX.

Note: You don't have to grant resource on the temporary tablespace. This is done automatically.

4.1.3 Altering a User

A user's database level privileges are altered using the GRANT and REVOKE commands. For instance, to grant global resource to a user, use the following format for the GRANT command:

```
GRANT RESOURCE TO user name;
```

To remove a privilege, the revoke command is used. The format to remove RESOURCE from a user would be:

```
REVOKE RESOURCE FROM user name;
```

Other than DBA accounts, there should be no need to grant global RESOURCE to a user. Global RESOURCE allows users to create tables, indexes, sequences, clusters, and views anywhere they wish in the database structure. Like RESOURCE, the DBA privilege should only be granted to those that really need it. With the DBA privilege a user can create, alter, or delete any item in the database. With the DBA privilege a user can also grant access and privilege to others. Careful consideration should be given to granting more than CONNECT to any account. In several years of experience with numerous user scenarios there have been few, if any, valid reasons to give global RESOURCE to a development user.

Periodically you may have to alter a user's default and temporary tablespace assignments. This can be done manually using the ALTER USER command as follows:

```
ALTER USER user
DEFAULT TABLESPACE new default
TEMPORARY TABLESPACE new temporary;
```

If there are several users to alter, the DBA can use dynamic SQL to create an entire set of these commands:

```
SET HEADING OFF TERMOUT OFF ECHO OFF PAGES 0 VERIFY OFF
SET FEEDBACK OFF
SPOOL ALTER_USERS.SQL
SELECT 'ALTER USER '||USERNAME||-
' DEFAULT TABLESPACE new_default
TEMPORARY TABLESPACE new_temporary;'
FROM DBA_USERS
WHERE DEFAULT_TABLESPACE = 'old_default' AND
    TEMPORARY_TABLESPACE = 'old_temporary' AND
    USERNAME NOT IN ('SYSTEM','SYS','PUBLIC','_NEXT_USER');
SPOOL OFF
```

Once the above script completes, the DBA should edit the ALTER_USERS.SQL file to be sure all users that are in it are supposed to be altered. Once the DBA is sure, the script is run from either SQLDBA or SQLPLUS with the following command from a DBA account:

```
START ALTER_USERS.SQL
```

4.1.4 Removing a User in Oracle Version 6

The other side of the user coin is dropping a user. In Oracle version 6, you can't drop a user. The only way to remove access from a user is to revoke connect from them. The command is:

```
REVOKE CONNECT FROM username;
```

This only removes the connect privilege from the user. The user's tables, synonyms, indexes, and so on still exist. For older version 6 databases, there may be more inactivated users than there are active ones. If a user's tables are no longer required, a script can be built using the SQL routine in Figure 4.2 that will drop all of a user's objects.

```
rem ***************************************************************************
rem NAME: RM_US.sql
rem HISTORY:
rem Date        Who                 What
rem --------    ------------------  ----------------------------------------
rem 10/25/92    Cary Millsap        Creation
rem FUNCTION: To build a script to remove all the object owned by a specified
rem           user.
rem INPUTS:
rem         1 = User name
rem         2 = File name of the resulting script.
rem ***************************************************************************
set verify off  feedback off  heading off     pagesize 0
def uname       = &&1
```

Figure 4.2 Script to create a SQL procedure to drop a user's objects.

```
def fname      = &&2
spool &fname
select 'set echo on' from system.dual;
select
  'DROP '||object_type||' '||owner||'.'||object_name||';'
from  dba_objects
where
  (object_type not in ('INDEX'))
    and
  (owner = upper('&uname'));
select 'set echo off' from system.dual;
spool off
set newpage 1
select 'To drop &uname''s objects:' from dual;
select '  1. Examine the file &fname' from dual;
select '  2. SQL> start &fname' from dual;
select '  3. Remove the file &fname' from dual;
start login
```

Figure 4.2 (continued)

4.1.5 Creating User Quotas

If you wish to use tablespace quotas—that is, limit the amount of space a user can take up in a tablespace—add the quota variable followed by "K" for kilobytes or "M" for megabytes after the GRANT RESOURCE on line 17. Thus, if you use "M," line 17 would become:

```
GRANT RESOURCE &quota||'M' on &&default_ts to &&user_name;
```

and the script would prompt you for "quota" along with the other items.

If you wish to find out what quotas have been assigned to users for a tablespace, the script in Figure 4.3 can be run from SQLPLUS from a DBA account.

```
rem   ********************************************************************
rem   NAME: TS_QO_US.sql
rem   HISTORY:
rem   Date      Who                 What
rem   --------  ------------------  ----------------------------------------
rem   06/17/91  G. Godart-Brown     Creation
rem   07/14/91  G. Godart-Brown     Clears & clean up
rem   12/14/92  Michael Brouillette Add ability to specify only one user
rem   05/11/93  Mike Ault           Remove use of ALL and use wild card
rem   FUNCTION: Print the tablespace quotas of users.
rem   ********************************************************************
prompt Percent signs are wild cards
accept username prompt 'Enter user name or wild card '
```

Figure 4.3 Script to generate quota report.   (continued)

```
prompt Print the details of the Users Tablespace Quotas
start title80 "Database Users Space Quotas by Tablespace"
col un               format a25 heading 'User Name'
col ta               format a25 heading 'Tablespace'
col usd              format 9,999,999 heading 'K Used'
col maxb             format 9,999,999 heading 'Max K '
set verify off feedback off newpage 0 heading on
spool tsquotas&db..lst
set break on ta skip 2
select
 TABLESPACE_NAME                ta,
 USERNAME                       un,
 BYTES/1024      usd,
 MAX_BYTES/1024                 maxb
from dba_ts_quotas
   where username = upper('&&username')
order by tablespace_name,username;
prompt End of Report
spool off
set verify on
undef username
clear breaks
clear columns
clear computes
```

Figure 4.3 (continued)

There is no need to grant quotas on the temporary tablespace. The system ignores any quotas set on temporary areas.

4.2 Administration of Object Level Privileges in Oracle Version 6

Hand in hand with user administration is object-level-privilege administration. Once users are granted access to the database and have been assigned to a default and temporary tablespace, they must be granted privileges on an application's tables in order to use the application.

4.2.1 Object Level Privileges in Oracle Version 6

Some applications require very little security. There is a grant "ALL" that can be given to everyone; "PUBLIC" to grant all privileges on the object to everyone. It is not recommended. Instead, thought should be given to each table in an application, and privileges established for each type of user. These user profiles of privileges can then be loaded into a grant script that can be run for a user, depending on their level of access, when they are created. The object permissions for version 6 follow.

PRIVILEGE	PURPOSE	TABLE	VIEW	COLUMN	SEQUENCE
ALTER	Allows a user to alter the object (not data).	Yes	No	No	Yes
AUDIT	Allows a user to audit actions taken against the object.	Yes	No	No	No
COMMENT	Allows a user to enter comments about tables and rows.	Yes	No	No	No
DELETE	Allows a user to delete rows from the object.	Yes	Yes*	No	No
GRANT	Allows the user to grant privilege to other users.	Yes	No	No	No
INDEX	Allows a user to create an index on the object.	Yes	No	No	No
INSERT	Allows a user to insert rows into an object.	Yes	Yes*	No	No
LOCK	Allows a user to lock access to an object.	Yes	No	No	No
REFERENCES	Allows a user to refer to an object in another table or constraint.	Yes	No	No	No
RENAME	Allows a user to rename the object.	Yes	No	No	No
SELECT	Allows a user to select rows from the object.	Yes	Yes	No	Yes
UPDATE	Allows a user to update rows in the object.	Yes	Yes*	Yes*	No

4.2.2 Granting Object Level Privileges

The above privileges are bestowed using the GRANT statement. To use the GRANT statement, the user must either have DBA privilege or have been granted their privileges on the table or tables on which they are issuing the grants with the grant option. The format of this command is:

```
GRANT priv, priv, priv...ON object TO username;
```

To grant all privileges on an object the format is:

```
GRANT ALL PRIVILEGES ON object TO username;
```

To grant the ability for the user to grant the privileges to other users:

```
GRANT priv, priv, priv...ON object TO username WITH GRANT OPTION;
```

4.2.3 Tablespace Level Grants

As was stated before, for tablespaces there is only one grant, and that is resource. The format of this command is:

```
GRANT RESOURCE ON tablespace TO username;
```

To establish a resource quota, specify the limit with either K for kilobytes or M for megabytes after the RESOURCE specified, for example:

```
GRANT RESOURCE 1M ON tablespace TO username;
```

would grant 1 megabyte of space to the user in the specified tablespace.

If a user has been granted a quota on a tablespace, he or she will be assigned that quota value in the view DBA_TS_QUOTAS. If a user has unlimited resource, that is, no quota, the assigned quota in DBA_TS_QUOTAS will be negative.

4.3 User Administration Under ORACLE7

Compared to ORACLE7, Oracle version 6 user administration is a piece of cake. Remember what was said about Oracle version 6 and the three database—or, if you prefer, system—level privileges? ORACLE7 has 80. Okay, close your mouth. It would be a real administration nightmare if you had to wade through these 80 different privileges for each user, but ORACLE7 simplifies it just a bit through the use of roles. Roles are named collections of system and application privileges. Thus, by assigning users to prespecified roles, you can assign them a full set of privileges for a specific type of database use.

4.4 Administration of System Privileges Under ORACLE7

Under ORACLE7 database or system level privileges are controlled either by direct grant (not recommended) or by use of roles (the preferred method). The major job for a DBA in user administration under ORACLE7 will be managing the roles used to assign privileges to users. Once the roles are created, user assignment is simply a matter of starting up SQLDBA, connecting as a DBA user and using the appropriate pull-down menus. Alternatively, the DBA can create a standard set of scripts similar to the version 6 scripts that create the users and set up default roles as needed. DDL-type commands such as CREATE require that the appropriate privilege be a direct grant, not a grant through a role.

4.4.1 Creation of Roles Under ORACLE7

Roles are defined the same way as users, through SQLDBA. Roles can also be created through the use of the CREATE ROLE command. The format of the CREATE ROLE command follows.

```
CREATE ROLE role NOT IDENTIFIED --or-- IDENTIFIED
[BY password] --or-- [EXTERNALLY];
```

Where:

role—This names the role to be created.

NOT IDENTIFIED—This indicates the user using the role doesn't need to be verified (doesn't have to supply a password) to use the role.

This is the default option.

IDENTIFIED—This indicates all users are verified with a specified password or by the operating system.

BY password—This gives the password that the users must use to access the role.

EXTERNAL—This indicates verification will be performed by the operating system.

The roles have unique names and have one or more system and object privileges assigned to them. Roles can also be assigned to other roles. For example, an application may have an administrator role that is simply a role with all other roles for the application assigned to it.

Assigning Privileges to a Role. When a role is created, it has no assigned privileges or roles. To assign the privileges or roles to a new role, use the following command:

```
GRANT priv1, priv2,...,role1, role2,... TO role name or user name;
```

The ALTER USER command can also be used to assign roles to a user; its format follows.

```
ALTER USER user DEFAULT ROLE role, role...
```

Only roles that have been granted to the user with the GRANT command can be assigned via the default role option of the alter command.

Only operating system privileges and roles can be granted together. Database object privileges must be granted separately. For convenience, there are five preset roles available in the database. These are listed below.

ROLE	PRIVILEGES
CONNECT	ALTER SESSION, CREATE CLUSTER, CREATE DATABASE LINK, CREATE SEQUENCE, CREATE SESSION, CREATE SYNONYM, CREATE TABLE, CREATE VIEW
RESOURCE	CREATE CLUSTER, CREATE PROCEDURE, CREATE SEQUENCE, CREATE TABLE, CREATE TRIGGER
DBA	ALL PRIVILEGES with admin option (allows grants to other users or roles)

(continued)

ROLE	PRIVILEGES
EXP_FULL_DATABASE	SELECT ANY TABLE, BACKUP ANY TABLE, IN-SERT, DELETE, and UPDATE on the tables SYS.INCVID, SYS.INCFIL, and SYS.INCEXP
IMP_FULL_DATABASE	BECOME USER, WRITEDOWN (trusted Oracle only)

NOTES FOR PRIVILEGE LIST:

CONNECT, RESOURCE, and DBA are created by the SQL.BSQ procedure on database creation. RESOURCE and DBA are also granted the UNLIMITED TABLESPACE privilege. DBA includes the EXP_FULL_DATABASE and IMP_FULL_DATABASE roles if the CATEXP.SQL script has been run.

EXP_FULL_DATABASE and IMP_FULL_DATABASE roles are created by the CATEXP.SQL script. These roles are required to be granted to users who perform exports and imports.

Assigning Object Level Privileges to a User or Role. In addition to the system level grants, there are also object level grants. The object level grants deal with the insert, update, delete, select, and so forth of data within database objects. The object level privileges can be granted at the object, or in some cases, column level. The format for granting these privileges follows.

```
GRANT object_priv, object_priv,...--or-- ALL PRIVILEGES [(column, column,...)]
ON [schema.]object TO user--or--role--or--PUBLIC
[WITH GRANT OPTION];
```

Where:

object_priv—This corresponds to:

ALTER for tables, sequences
DELETE for tables, views, columns in tables
EXECUTE for procedures, packages, functions
INDEX for tables
INSERT for tables, views, columns in tables
REFERENCES for tables (not to a role)
SELECT for tables, views, sequences, columns in tables, and snapshots
UPDATE for tables, views, columns in tables

ALL PRIVILEGES—Grants all privileges applicable to the item to the user or role.

column—This is a column in the table referenced in the command.

ON—This identifies the object on which the privileges are granted. If schema is not specified, the user's default schema is used. In addition to tables, views, sequences, functions, procedures, packages, and snapshots, synonyms that refer to these objects can be used here.

TO—This identifies the user or role to which the privilege is granted. If PUBLIC is used, all users receive the grant.

WITH GRANT OPTION—This allows the user to grant the privilege. This cannot be given to a role.

Grants are immediately available if given to a specific user or to PUBLIC. If a grant is given to a role, it must be enabled using the ALTER USER command. A privilege cannot appear more than once in a privilege list. A user or role cannot appear more than once in the TO clause.

4.4.2 System Grants Under ORACLE7

The system privileges for ORACLE7 follow.

PRIVILEGE TYPE	PRIVILEGE NAME	DESCRIPTION
ANALYZE	ANALYZE ANY	This allows the user to analyze any table, cluster, or index in the database.
AUDIT	AUDIT ANY	This allows the user to audit any schema object in the database.
	AUDIT SYSTEM	This allows the user to enable and disable statement and privilege audit options.
CLUSTER	CREATE CLUSTER	This allows the user to create a cluster in their own schema.
	CREATE ANY CLUSTER	This allows the user to create a cluster in any schema. Behaves like the CREATE ANY TABLE privilege.
	ALTER ANY CLUSTER	This allows the user to alter any cluster in the database.
	DROP ANY CLUSTER	This allows the user to drop any cluster in the database.
DATABASE	ALTER DATABASE	This allows the user to alter the database; add files to the operating system via Oracle, regardless of OS privileges.
DATABASE LINK	CREATE DATABASE LINK	This allows the user to create private database links in their own schema.
INDEX	CREATE ANY INDEX	This allows the user to create an index anywhere on any table.
	ALTER ANY INDEX	This allows the user to alter any index in the database.
	DROP ANY INDEX	This allows the user to drop any index in the database.

(continued)

PRIVILEGE TYPE	PRIVILEGE NAME	DESCRIPTION
PRIVILEGE	GRANT ANY PRIVILEGE	This allows the user to grant any system privilege (not object privilege).
PROCEDURE	CREATE PROCEDURE	This allows the user to create stored procedures, functions, and packages in their own schema.
	CREATE ANY PROCEDURE	This allows the user to create stored procedures, functions, and packages in any schema. (Requires that user also have ALTER ANY TABLE, BACKUP ANY TABLE, DROP ANY TABLE, LOCK ANY TABLE, COMMENT ANY TABLE, SELECT ANY TABLE, INSERT ANY TABLE, UPDATE ANY TABLE, DELETE ANY TABLE, or GRANT ANY TABLE.)
	ALTER ANY PROCEDURE	This allows the user to compile any stored procedures, functions, and packages in any schema.
	DROP ANY PROCEDURE	This allows the user to drop any stored procedures, functions, and packages in any schema.
	EXECUTE ANY PROCEDURE	This allows the user to execute any stored procedures, functions, and packages in any schema.
PROFILE	CREATE PROFILE	This allows the user to create profiles.
	ALTER PROFILE	This allows the user to alter any profile in the database.
	DROP PROFILE	This allows the user to drop any profile in the database.
	ALTER RESOURCE COST	This allows the user to set costs for resources used in all user sessions.
PUBLIC DATABASE LINK	CREATE PUBLIC DATABASE LINK	This allows the user to create public database links.

PRIVILEGE TYPE	PRIVILEGE NAME	DESCRIPTION
	DROP PUBLIC DATABASE LINK	This allows the user to drop public database links.
PUBLIC SYNONYM	CREATE PUBLIC SYNONYM	This allows the user to create public synonyms.
	DROP PUBLIC SYNONYM	This allows the user to drop public synonyms.
ROLE	CREATE ROLE	This allows the user to create roles.
	ALTER ANY ROLE	This allows the user to alter any role in the database.
	DROP ANY ROLE	This allows the user to drop any role in the database.
	GRANT ANY ROLL	This allows the user to grant any role in the database.
ROLLBACK SEGMENT	CREATE ROLLBACK SEGMENT	This allows the user to create rollback segments.
	ALTER ROLLBACK SEGMENT	This allows the user to alter rollback segments.
	DROP ROLLBACK SEGMENT	This allows the user to drop rollback segments.
SESSION	CREATE SESSION	This allows the user to connect to the database.
	ALTER SESSION	This allows the user to issue the ALTER SESSION command.
	RESTRICTED SESSION	This allows the user to connect when the database has been started up using the STARTUP RESTRICT command. (The OSOPER and OSDBA roles contain this privilege.)
SEQUENCE	CREATE SEQUENCE	This allows the user to create a sequence in their own schema.
	CREATE ANY SEQUENCE	This allows the user to create any sequence in any schema.
	ALTER ANY SEQUENCE	This allows the user to alter any sequence in any schema.

(continued)

PRIVILEGE TYPE	PRIVILEGE NAME	DESCRIPTION
	DROP ANY SEQUENCE	This allows the user to drop any sequence in any schema.
	SELECT ANY SEQUENCE	This allows the user to reference any sequence in any schema.
SNAPSHOT	CREATE SNAPSHOT	This allows the user to create snapshots in their own schema. (Must also have CREATE TABLE.)
	CREATE ANY SNAPSHOT	This allows the user to create snapshots in any schema. (Must have CREATE ANY TABLE.)
	DROP ANY SNAPSHOT	This allows the user to drop snapshots in any schema. (Must also have DROP ANY TABLE.)
SYNONYM	CREATE SYNONYM	This allows the user to create synonym in their own schema.
	CREATE ANY SYNONYM	This allows the user to create any synonym in any schema.
	DROP ANY SYNONYM	This allows the user to drop any synonym in any schema.
SYSTEM	ALTER SYSTEM	This allows the user to issue the ALTER SYSTEM command.
TABLE	CREATE TABLE	This allows the user to create table in own schema. This also allows user to create indexes (including those for integrity constraints) on tables in their own schema. (The grantee must have a quota for the tablespace or the UNLIMITED TABLESPACE privilege.)
	CREATE ANY TABLE	This allows the user to create table in any schema.
	ALTER ANY TABLE	This allows the user to alter any table in any schema and to compile any view in any schema.
	BACKUP ANY TABLE	This allows the user to back up, via incremental export, any table in any schema.

PRIVILEGE TYPE	PRIVILEGE NAME	DESCRIPTION
	DROP ANY TABLE	This allows the user to drop any table in any schema.
	LOCK ANY TABLE	This allows the user to lock any table or view in the database.
	COMMENT ANY TABLE	This allows the user to enter a comment for any table, view, or column in any schema.
	SELECT ANY TABLE	This allows the user to query any table, view, or snapshot in the database.
	INSERT ANY TABLE	This allows the user to insert rows into any table or view in the database.
	UPDATE ANY TABLE	Update rows in any table or view in the database.
	DELETE ANY TABLE	This allows the user to delete rows from any table or view in any schema.
TABLESPACE	CREATE TABLESPACE	This allows the user to create tablespaces; this also allows addition of files to the operating system regardless of the user's OS privileges.
	ALTER TABLESPACE	This allows the user to alter tablespaces; this also allows addition of files to the operating system regardless of the user's OS privileges.
	MANAGE TABLESPACE	This allows the user to take any tablespace offline, bring any tablespace online, and perform hot backups.
	DROP TABLESPACE	This allows the user to drop any tablespace.
	UNLIMITED TABLESPACE	This allows the user to use an unlimited amount of space in any tablespace, overriding any quotas set. This can only be granted to users, not roles. This should not normally be granted.

(continued)

PRIVILEGE TYPE	PRIVILEGE NAME	DESCRIPTION
TRANSACTION	FORCE TRANSACTION	This allows the user's process to force the commit or rollback of its own in-doubt distributed transactions in the local database.
	FORCE ANY TRANSACTION	This allows the user's process to force the commit or rollback of any in-doubt distributed transactions in the local database.
TRIGGER	CREATE TRIGGER	This allows the user to create a trigger in their own schema.
	CREATE ANY TRIGGER	This allows the user to create a trigger in any schema.
	ALTER ANY TRIGGER	This allows the user to alter a trigger in any schema.
	DROP ANY TRIGGER	This allows the user to drop a trigger in any schema.
USER	CREATE USER	This allows a user to create other users.
	BECOME USER	This allows a user to become another user. This privilege must be granted to users that perform full database imports.
	ALTER USER	This privilege allows a user to alter other users in the following ways: passwords, quotas, default and temporary tablespaces, profiles and default rolls. This privilege is not required to alter user's own password.
	DROP USER	This allows the user to drop any other user.
VIEW	CREATE VIEW	This allows the user to create views in their own schema.
	CREATE ANY VIEW	This allows the user to create views in any schema. (Requires that user also have ALTER ANY TABLE, BACK UP ANY TABLE, DROP ANY TABLE, LOCK ANY TABLE, COMMENT ANY TABLE,

PRIVILEGE TYPE	PRIVILEGE NAME	DESCRIPTION
		SELECT ANY TABLE, INSERT ANY TABLE, UPDATE ANY TABLE, DELETE ANY TABLE, or GRANT ANY TABLE.)
	DROP ANY VIEW	This allows the user to drop any view in any schema.

4.4.3 Alteration of a Role

The method of authorization or the authorization password may be changed for a role using the following command:

```
ALTER ROLE roll name IDENTIFIED authorization password;
```

or

```
ALTER ROLE roll name IDENTIFIED EXTERNALLY.
```

To use this command you must have the ALTER ANY ROLE privilege or have been granted the role with the ADMIN OPTION.

4.4.4 Dropping a Role

To remove a role from a database, use the DROP ROLE role name; command. To use this command you must have the DROP ANY ROLE privilege or have been granted the role with the ADMIN OPTION. The format of this command follows.

```
DROP ROLE role;
```

Where:

role—This is the role name to be dropped.

To drop a role you must have been given the role with the ADMIN OPTION or have the DROP ANY ROLE privilege at the system level.

The ADMIN OPTION for a privilege or role allows the grantee to do the following:

- Grant or revoke the privilege or role to another user.
- Grant or revoke the privilege or role to another user with the ADMIN OPTION.
- Alter or drop the role.

Giving this much authority to anyone is a heavy responsibility. Be sure the user will treat these abilities with proper respect.

4.4.5 Use of SQLDBA and Roles

All of those activities—creation of users, roles, grants, dropping of roles, altering of users, roles—can be done via the SQLDBA screens in ORACLE7. This makes the operations easier, but you have no hard copy of exactly what was done as you would if you had created a script to do the above operations. It is not suggested you create a script for each individual user added or modified, but for initial startup or addition of an application when a large number of users are added or altered, or if you create a new role or set of roles, having a script for documentation is a good idea.

4.5 Administration of Profiles Under ORACLE7

Another item that concerns user administration in ORACLE7 are profiles. Profiles assign resource limits to a specified set of users. The idea of resource quotas is a new one implemented under ORACLE7. The resource quotas themselves can be modified by the ALTER RESOURCE COST command.

4.5.1 Creation of Profiles

Profiles are created using the CREATE PROFILE command. The format of the CREATE PROFILE format follows.

```
CREATE PROFILE profile LIMIT
SESSIONS_PER_USER n --or--
CPU_PER_SESSION n (in hundredths of seconds)--or--
CPU_PER_CALL n (in hundredths of seconds)--or--
CONNECT_TIME n (in minutes)--or--
IDLE_TIME n (in minutes)--or--
LOGICAL_READS_PER_SESSION n (in blocks)--or--
LOGICAL_READS_PER_CALL n (in blocks)--or--
COMPOSIT_LIMIT n (in service units)--or--
PRIVATE_SGA [n K--or--M]--or--UNLIMITED--or--DEFAULT
```

Each of the n's above can be replaced with the keyword UNLIMITED or DEFAULT. Unlimited means there is no limit on this resource; default causes the resource to use the value from the default profile. The default profile as provided has all resource quotas set at unlimited.

Here is an example of CREATE PROFILE command:

```
CREATE PROFILE mega_user
   LIMIT    SESSIONS_PER_USER        UNLIMITED
       CPU_PER_SESSION              UNLIMITED
       CPU_PER_CALL                 30000
       CONNECT_TIME                 240
       IDLE_TIME                    30
       LOGICAL_READS_PER_SESSION    UNLIMITED
       LOGICAL_READS_PER_CALL       UNLIMITED
       PRIVATE_SGA                  UNLIMITED
       COMPOSITE_LIMIT              5000000;
```

In this example a profile called mega_user is created with the following characteristics:

- The user can have any number of concurrent sessions.
- The user can consume an unlimited amount of CPU time.
- The maximum CPU time per call is limited to 30 seconds.
- The connect time per session is limited to 4 hours.
- The time a session can remain idle is 30 minutes before it is terminated.
- Logical reads per session and per call are unlimited.
- The users SGA use is unlimited.
- The composite cost of a single session cannot exceed 5 million service units.

If a given parameter is not specified, it defaults to the default profile value. If the INIT.ORA parameter RESOURCE_LIMIT is set to false, resource quotas will not be used.

4.5.2 Alteration of a Profile

A profile can be altered using the ALTER PROFILE command. It has the same format as the CREATE PROFILE command.

4.5.3 Dropping a Profile

A profile is dropped using the DROP PROFILE command. The command's format follows.

```
DROP PROFILE profile [CASCADE];
```

Users assigned to the dropped profile are automatically assigned to the DEFAULT profile.

4.6 Security Administration Under ORACLE7

Needless to say, with large databases, each with numerous applications and development efforts running concurrently, the administration of ORACLE7 may require a separate security administrator. Even if the database is small, procedures and policies should be established in accordance with Chapter 10 of the *ORACLE7 Server Administrator's Guide*. This policy should cover at a minimum, the following items.

General user security—This includes password security and privilege management.
End-user security— This includes the use of roles.
Administrator security—This includes protecting SYS and SYSTEM, connection from SQLDBA as INTERNAL (SYS), and use of roles.
Application developer security—This includes required privileges, the environment, the amount of control over development activities, roles required, and control of developer space usage.
Application administrator security—This applies to large databases with numerous applications. It should address who controls space usage—the DBA or AA, who controls roles and security, and other administration issues.
Audit control—This policy should determine the what, when, and how much of the auditing of the database. Too much and performance can suffer; not enough and you leave holes through which problems can enter.

4.7 Adding, Altering, and Dropping Database Users

Once profiles and roles are ready and a viable security plan is in effect, the DBA under ORACLE7 should be ready to actually manage the users. Let's look at what commands the DBA will use.

4.7.1 Creating Database Users

Database users are created using the CREATE USER command. This command replaces the GRANT CONNECT TO user IDENTIFIED BY password; command in version 6. The format of this command follows.

```
CREATE USER user IDENTIFIED BY password--or-- IDENTIFIED EXTERNALLY
[DEFAULT TABLESPACE tablespace]
[TEMPORARY TABLESPACE tablespace]
[QUOTA n K--or--M --or-- UNLIMITED ON tablespace]
[PROFILE profile]
```

Where:

user—This is the user name of the user to be created. Use of the prefix specified in the OS_AUTHENT_PREFIX parameter of the INIT.ORA file will create a user accessible only to the user whose operating system login matches the specified user name plus the prefix. The prefix defaults to OPS$ but can be changed if desired.

password—This is the password the user must enter to use oracle.

IDENTIFIED EXTERNALLY—This says that if the user can log on the system, he can use the account.

Tablespace—This is the name for the specific tablespace the command option applies to. If DEFAULT or TEMPORARY tablespaces aren't assigned, they are defaulted to the SYS-TEM tablespace.

QUOTA—This is used to assign quota on a tablespace. Multiple quota assignments can be made in the same command.

n—This is the amount of quota assigned in the specified tablespace; if not specified, it defaults to 0.

PROFILE—This assigns a specific profile to a user. If this is not specified, the user is assigned to the default profile.

Example use of the CREATE USER command:

```
CREATE USER admin_dba
   IDENTIFIED BY super_user
   DEFAULT TABLESPACE dba_ts
   TEMPORARY TABLESPACE temp_user_1
   QUOTA UNLIMITED ON dba_ts
   QUOTA 500K ON SYSTEM
   PROFILE mega_user;
```

The user admin_dba will be created an assigned a password of super_user. The user is created with a default tablespace of dba_ts and a temporary tablespace of temp_user_1. The user has unlimited quota in the dba_ts and 500k of quota on the SYSTEM tablespace. The user is assigned to the mega_user profile.

The assignment of this user isn't complete. At create the user is assigned ALL for roles, which gives them the default roles. To complete user assignment the GRANT and the ALTER USER commands as described in section 4.4.2 are used to assign roles to the user.

4.7.2 Alteration of a User

As with version 6, users periodically must be altered to reflect status changes within the database. Different default or temporary tablespaces, new quotas, and so on. all require user alteration. The command to alter a user is ALTER USER. The ALTER USER command's format follows.

```
ALTER USER user
[IDENTIFIED BY password] --or-- [IDENTIFIED EXTERNALLY]
[DEFAULT TABLESPACE tablespace]
[TEMPORARY TABLESPACE tablespace]
[QUOTA n K--or--M--or--UNLIMITED ON tablespace] (this can be repeated)
[PROFILE profile]
[DEFAULT ROLE [role, role.]--or--[ALL [EXCEPT role, role.]--or--[NONE]];
```

Where:

user—This is the user to be altered.

password—Allows alteration of specified user's password. Must be single byte. This is not case sensitive and is not delimited by quotes.

tablespace—This is a specific tablespace.

n—Integer specification for quota in bytes, Kbytes or Mbytes

UNLIMITED—This means the user has unlimited quota on the specified tablespace.

profile—This changes the user's profile.

role—One of the predefined roles available to be assigned.

ALL—This assigns all of the roles GRANTED to be DEFAULT roles

NONE—This assigns none of the roles GRANTED to be DEFAULT roles.

EXCEPT—This grants all the roles except those listed.

4.7.3 Dropping Database Users

Unlike version 6, under ORACLE7 the DBA can drop users from the database. The user's objects should be transferred to another user via an export and import, or be dropped prior to the DROP USER command, or the DROP USER specified with the CASECADE option. If the user's objects are still in use, you must transfer their ownership to maintain them in the database.

This supports the good practice of assigning nonuser-affiliated database accounts to hold all database objects. For example, an application called ADMIN would be owned by the database account ADMIN_DBA. This allows the various users and developers to access the account, create objects with the account, and when they are no longer users, the dropping of their account has no effect on database objects.

The command to drop a user follows.

```
DROP USER user [CASCADE];
```

Where:

user   This is the user name to be dropped.
CASCADE—This tells ORACLE7 to also drop all of the user's objects.

If the cascade option is used, ORACLE7 also drops all referential integrity constraints associated with the objects. The system will also invalidate views, synonyms, procedures, functions, and packages that are associated with the dropped objects.

5

Monitoring Database Objects

Once the database, tablespaces, tables, users, and other database objects are created, the DBA is also tasked with monitoring these numerous constructs. Luckily Oracle has numerous tables and views available for this purpose. The data dictionary tables are owned by the SYS user and normally shouldn't be accessed. Oracle has provided DBA_ and V$ views into these tables that should be used whenever possible.

5.1 All Those DBA Views

Oracle has provided many windows into the data dictionary that is central to the Oracle database. These windows are the DBA_ series of views. A view is a look at a table or tables that may be displayed and may be updated. The following is a list of the DBA_ views and their function.

5.1.1 Version 6 and ORACLE7 Views

VIEW NAME	FUNCTION
DBA_AUDIT_CONNECT	Synonym for USER_AUDIT_CONNECT, a view that provides audit trail for user logons/logoffs.
DBA_AUDIT_DBA	Provides look at audit trail for audit trail entries created by the AUDIT DBA command (audits use of commands requiring DBA type access).
DBA_AUDIT_EXISTS	Provides a look at entries created by the AUDIT EXISTS command.

(continued)

VIEW NAME	FUNCTION
DBA_AUDIT_RESOURCE	Provides a look at entries created by the AUDIT RESOURCE command (any actions that require the resource privilege).
DBA_AUDIT_TRAIL	Provides comprehensive look at all user actions that auditing is enabled for.
DBA_CATALOG	A look at all database tables, views, synonyms, and sequences (internal database objects).
DBA_CLUSTERS	A look at the descriptions of all CLUSTERS in the database. (A cluster is a collection of tables that share some common rows.)
DBA_CLU_COLUMNS	A look at how table columns map into cluster columns.
DBA_COL_COMMENTS	A look at all of the comments on all of the tables and views in the database.
DBA_COL_GRANTS	A look at all of the grants on all columns in the database.
DBA_CONSTRAINTS	A look at all of the constraint definitions for accessible tables in the database.
DBA_CONS_COLUMNS	Information about the accessible columns in the constraint definitions.
DBA_CROSS_REFS	A look at all of the cross-references between all views and synonyms in the database.
DBA_DATA_FILES	A look at key information concerning all database data files (external objects).
DBA_DB_LINKS	A look at all database links in the data base. (Database links link the database to other databases or to itself.)
DBA_EXP_FILES	This view gives a description of the export files currently in use.
DBA_EXP_OBJECTS	This view lists internal database objects that have been incrementally exported.
DBA_EXP_VERSION	Version number of the last export session.
DBA_EXTENTS	This is a view of the file extent map.
DBA_FREE_SPACE	This view lists the free extents for all files in the database.

VIEW NAME	FUNCTION
DBA_INDEXES	This view shows the description for all indexes in the database.
DBA_IND_COLUMNS	This view shows all of the columns used in indexes on all tables and clusters.
DBA_OBJECTS	This view lists all objects in the database.
DBA_ROLLBACK_SEGS	This view lists data concerning rollback segments.
DBA_SEGMENTS	This is a view of all storage allocations for all database segments (table, cluster, index, rollback, deferred rollback).
DBA_SEQUENCES	This view shows descriptions of all the sequences used in the database.
DBA_SYNONYMS	This view shows all of the SYNONYMS in the database.
DBA_SYS_AUDIT_OPTS	This view shows what types of auditing are active in the database.
DBA_TAB_AUDIT_OPTS	This view shows all of the table-level auditing enabled for the database.
DBA_TAB_COLUMNS	This view shows all of the columns for all tables, views and clusters.
DBA_TAB_COMMENTS	This view shows all of the comments on tables and views in the database.
DBA_TAB_GRANTS	This view shows all of the grants on all of the internal objects in the database.
DBA_TABLES	This view shows the descriptions of all tables in the database.
DBA_TABLESPACES	Description of all of the tablespace in the database.
DBA_TS_QUOTAS	This view lists all of the tablespace quotas assigned for the database. (If a user has resource privilege on a tablespace, their name will be in here.)
DBA_USERS	This view shows data on all users in the database (if CONNECT_PRIV is 1, the user is active; 0, inactive).
DBA_VIEWS	This view shows data on all of the views in the database, including the DBA_ views.

5.1.2 Additional ORACLE7 Views

VIEW	PURPOSE
DBA_2PC_NEIGHBORS	This view keeps information about incoming and outgoing connections for pending transactions.
DBA_2PC_PENDING	This view shows information about failed distributed transactions that are in the PREPARED state.
DBA_AUDIT_OBJECTS	This view shows all audit trail records for all objects in the system.
DBA_AUDIT_SESSION	Replaces DBA_AUDIT_CONNECTS.
DBA_AUDIT_STATEMENT	Replaces DBA_AUDIT_DBA.
DBA_BLOCKERS	This view shows all users who have someone waiting on a lock they hold, who are not themselves waiting on a lock.
DBA_COL_PRIVS	Replaces DBA_COL_GRANTS.
DBA_DDL_LOCKS	This view shows all DDL locks held and all outstanding DDL lock requests.
DBA_DEPENDENCIES	This view shows dependencies to and from all objects.
DBA_DML_LOCKS	This view shows all DML locks held and all outstanding DML lock requests.
DBA_ERRORS	This view shows current errors on all stored objects in the database.
DBA_LOCKS	This view shows information on all locks or latches held and all outstanding requests for a lock or latch. This includes DML and DDL locks.
DBA_OBJECT_SIZE	This view shows all PL/SQL objects in the database and their sizing data.
DBA_OBJ_AUDIT_OPTS	This replaces DBA_TAB_AUDIT_OPTS.
DBA_PRIV_AUDIT_OPTS	This view shows results from privilege auditing.
DBA_PROFILES	This view shows limits assigned to each database profile.
DBA_ROLES	This is a view of all the rolls that exist in the database.
DBA_ROLE_PRIVS	This view gives the description of roles granted to users and to rolls.
DBA_SNAPSHOTS	This view shows all the snapshots in the database.

VIEW	PURPOSE
DBA_SNAPSHOT_LOGS	This view shows all snapshot logs in the database.
DBA_SOURCE	This view shows all of the sources for all stored objects in the database.
DBA_STMT_AUDIT_OPTS	This view describes the current system auditing options across the system and by user.
DBA_SYS_PRIVS	This view gives descriptions of system privileges granted to users and roles.
DBA_TRIGGERS	This view describes all of the triggers stored in the database.
DBA_TRIGGER_COLS	This view shows the usages of columns in triggers defined by any user or on any user's table.
DBA_WAITERS	This view shows all sessions waiting for locks and the session that holds the lock (look at DBA_BLOCKERS).

5.1.3 The Dynamic Performance Tables (DPTs)

These views are based on the dynamic performance tables (DPT). The DPTs are views whose names begin with V_$ and have public synonyms beginning with V$. The views are created by running the CATALOG.SQL script. Access is granted to all users by running the MONITOR.SQL script while connected to the SYS user under version 6, the UTLMONTR.SQL script under ORACLE7. The DBA may want to alter this script to restrict access. If you need version 5 views under version 6, the CATALOG5.SQL script should be run. The views and their purposes are listed below.

5.1.4 Version 6 DPTs

VIEW	PURPOSE
* V$ACCESS	This view describes the owners of tables.
* V$BGPROCESS	This view describes the background processes.
* V$DBFILE	This view gives information about each database file in the database.
* V$FILESTAT	This view gives information about file read/write statistics.
* V$LATCH	This view gives information about each type of latch. There is a one-to-one correspondence between this view and V$LATCHNAME.

(continued)

VIEW	PURPOSE
* **V$LATCHHOLDER**	This view gives information the current latch holders.
* **V$LATCHNAME**	This view contains the decoded latch names shown in the view V$LATCH.
V$_LOCK	This view shows the addresses of locks, re-sources, and processes holding locks.
* **V$LOCK**	This view gives information about locks and resources.
* **V$LOGFILE**	This view gives information about redo log files.
* **V$PARAMETER**	This view gives the values of current oracle parameters (init.ora).
* **V$PROCESS**	This view gives information about the current processes.
* **V$RESOURCE**	This view gives information about resources.
* **V$ROLLNAME**	This view gives the names of rollback segments. The rows in this table correspond one-to-one with the rows in V$ROLLSTAT.
* **V$ROLLSTAT**	This view contains rollback segment statistics.
* **V$ROWCACHE**	This view contains the statistics for data dictionary activity; each row contains data for one type of data dictionary cache.
* **V$SESSION**	This view contains session information for each active session.
* **V$SESSTAT**	This view contains statistics on current sessions.
* **V$SGA**	This view contains information about the system global area.
* **V$STATNAME**	This view contains the decoded statistic names for the statistics shown in tables V$SESSTAT and V$SYSSTAT.
* **V$SYSSTAT**	This view contains the current system-wide value for each statistic in table V$SESSTAT.
* **V$TRANSACTION**	This view contains information about transactions.
* **V$WAITSTAT**	This view gives block-contention statistics.

* - Also an ORACLE7 view, although structure may be changed.

5.1.5 Additional ORACLE7 DPTs

For ORACLE7, the script CATALOG.SQL to create the V$ views; UTLMONTR.SQL grants public access to the V$ tables. To create version 6 V$ tables, run the CATALOG6.SQL script.

VIEW	PURPOSE
V$ARCHIVE	This view shows information on system archive logs for each thread in the system. There is one row for each thread.
V$BACKUP	This view shows the backup status of all online data files.
V$CIRCUIT	This view shows information about virtual circuits. Virtual circuits are user connections through dispatchers and servers.
V$DATABASE	This view gives the database information from the control file.
V$DATAFILE	This view shows data file information from the control file.
V$DB_OBJECT_CACHE	This view shows database objects that are cached in the library cache. These objects include tables, indexes, synonym definitions, PL/SQL procedures and packages, clusters and triggers.
V$DISPATCHER	This view shows information concerning the dispatcher processes.
V$ENABLEDPRIVS	This view shows which privileges are enabled.
V$FIXED_TABLE	This view shows all fixed tables, views, and derived tables in the database.
V$INSTANCE	This view shows the state of the current instance.
V$LIBRARYCACHE	This view shows statistics concerning library cache management.
V$LICENSE	This view gives information about license limits.
V$LOADCSTAT	This view gives information on SQL*Loader statistics compiled during a direct load.
V$LOADSTAT	This view gives information on SQL*Loader statistics compiled during a direct load.
V$LOG	This view gives the log file information from the control file.
V$LOGHIST	This file shows log history information from the control file. (Use LOG_HISTORY instead.)

(continued)

VIEW	PURPOSE
V$LOG HISTORY	This view replaces V$LOGHIST; it contains archived log names for all logs in the log history by thread.
V$NLS_PARAMETERS	This view shows the current values of the National Language Support parameters.
V$OPEN_CURSOR	This view shows cursors that each user session currently has open and parsed.
V$QUEUE	This view contains information on the multithread process message queues.
V$RECOVERY_LOG	This view is derived from V$LOG_HISTORY and is limited by the initialization value of MAX_LOG_HISTORY. The view contains information on archived logs that will be needed to complete media recovery.
V$RECOVER_FILE	This view shows the status of files that require media recovery.
V$REQDIST	This view is a histogram of request times, divided into 12 ranges of time.
V$SECONDARY	A TRUSTED ORACLE view that lists secondary mounted databases.
V$SESSION_WAIT	This view lists the resources or events that active sessions are waiting for.
V$SESS_IO	This view shows I/O statistics for each user session.
V$SGASTAT	This view gives detailed size information for each SGA component.
V$SHARED_SERVER	This view gives information on the shared server processes.
V$SQLAREA	This view has information on the shared cursor cache. One row per each cursor.
V$SQLTEXT	This view shows the text of each SQL cursor in the shared cache of the SGA.
V$SYSLABEL	A TRUSTED ORACLE view that lists the system labels.
V$THREAD	This view shows thread information from the control file.
V$TIMER	This view shows the current time in hundredths of a second.

VIEW	PURPOSE
V$TYPE_SIZE	This view shows the sizes of various database components used for estimation data block capacity.
V$VERSION	This view contains information on the versions of core library components of the ORACLE server. It has one row per component.

As you can see there is no dearth of information available about the database.

5.1.6 What Do You Use Them For?

These views provide detailed information about the system, the data dictionary, and the processes for the Oracle database. Reports can access these views to give the DBA just about any cut on the data he or she desires. Many, if not all, of the reports in the following sections utilize these views either directly or indirectly via the DBA_ views.

Most, if not all, of the additional ORACLE7 views deal with the dispatcher and server processes. The scripts in the following sections use version 6 views. Wherever required, the changes to allow them to be functional on ORACLE7 are shown.

The views can also be queried interactively during a DBA user session to find the current status of virtually any system parameter. Use of dynamic SQL against these views can shorten a DBA task—such as switching users from one temporary tablespace to another or dropping a set of tables—by a factor of 10 or more.

5.1.7 The View's Relationship to SQLDBA Monitor

As was stated above, the views are also used by the monitor utility in SQLDBA. A breakdown of how the views are used by monitor follows.

MONITOR SCREEN OR DISPLAY	VIEW(S) USED
* FILE (FILE IO in 7)	V$DBFILE, V$FILESTAT
IO	V$STATNAME, V$PROCESS, V$SESSION, V$SESSTAT, V$SYSSTAT
* LATCH	V$LATCHNAME, V$LATCHHOLDER, V$LATCH
* LOCK	V$LOCK, V$PROCESS, V$RESOURCE FOR 7: V$LOCK, V$SESSION
* PROCESS	V$PROCESS
ROLLBACK	V$ROLLNAME, V$ROLLSTAT

(continued)

MONITOR SCREEN OR DISPLAY	VIEW(S) USED
STATISTICS	V$STATNAME, V$PROCESS, V$SESSION V$SYSSTAT, V$SESSTAT
* TABLE (TABLE ACCESS in 7)	V$ACCESS
USER	V$PROCESS, V$SESSION, V$BGPROCESS, V$LATCH, V$LATCHNAME, V$LOCK, V$RESOURCE, V$TRANSACTION

* Also in ORACLE7

ORACLE7 ADDITIONAL SCREENS:

SHARED SERVER	V$SHARED_SERVERS
DISPATCHER	V$DISPATCHER
CIRCUIT	V$CIRCUIT, V$DISPATCHER, V$SESSION V$SHARED_SERVER
QUEUE	V$QUEUE
LIBRARY	V$LIBRARYCACHE
SESSION	V$PROCESS, V$SYSSTAT
SESSION STATISTIC	V$SESSTAT, V$SYSSTAT
SYSTEM STATISTIC	V$SYSSTAT
SQL AREA	V$SQLAREA

The SQLDBA program under version 6 is difficult to use since you must at times cycle through numerous displays to get to the one you require. ORACLE7 has improved by filtering some screens. Filtering is the process by which a user entered value is used to produce selection criteria for the display, such as only processes 1 to 10 or only user X.

However, both versions lack adequate report capabilities. To remedy this shortfall, DBAs must be prepared to create SQL*Plus, PL/SQL, and SQL*ReportWriter reports that provide just the cut of information they require. The next sections discuss these reports and show example scripts used to generate them. It is suggested that the DBA review the contents of the V$ and DBA_ views as listed in either the *ORACLE RDBMS Database Administrator's Guide Version 6.0*, or for ORACLE7; *ORACLE7 Server Administrator's Guide*. Additional information is contained in the *ORACLE7 Server Utilities User's Guide* for ORACLE7.

5.2 Using the Views and DPTs to Monitor Objects

Now that we know all about the views and DPTs, let's look at how they are used to monitor various database constructs.

5.2.1 Using the V$ and DBA_ Views for Monitoring Users

What do DBAs need to know about the users of their databases? There are many important facts about each user the DBA needs to keep track of—for instance, privileges, quotas, tables owned, file space used, database default locations.

How can the DBA keep track of this information for hundreds or thousands of possible users? Scribble it down as it flashes across the SQLDBA screen? Hardly. To keep track of this information the DBA needs reports. Whether they store the reports online or use a three-ring binder, good reports tell the DBA exactly what they need to know. Let's address the above listed topics.

The first report we will look at uses the DBA_USERS view to provide information on users, user default and temporary tablespace assignments, and user database level privileges. The script for this report is listed in Figure 5.1.

```
1:   REM
2:   REM NAME    : USER_REPORT.SQL
3:   REM PURPOSE: GENERATE USER_REPORT
4:   REM USE    : CALLED BY USER_REPORT.COM
5:   REM Limitations : None
6:   REM Revisions:
7:   REM  Date            Modified By      Reason For change
8:   REM 21-AUG-1991      MIKE AULT        INITIAL CREATE
9:   REM
10:  set flush off  term off  set pagesize 58  set linesize 131
11:  column username heading User
12:  column default_tablespace heading Default
13:  column temporary_tablespace heading Temporary
14:  column dba_priv heading DBA
15:  column resource_priv RESOURCE
16:  column connect_priv CONNECT
17:  start oracle$sql:title132 'ORACLE USER REPORT'
18:  define output = ORA_STATUS_REPORTS:user_report&db.lis'
19:  spool &output
20:  select username, default_tablespace, temporary_tablespace,
21:  dba_priv, resource_priv, connect_priv from sys.dba_users
22:  where connect_priv != 0
23:  order by username;
24:  spool off
25:  exit
```

Figure 5.1 Example of user report listing.

Several items bear mentioning about this report script. First, notice the header format in lines 1 through 9. It is suggested that each report contain a header section similar to this one. It tells what the report script does, who wrote it, and most important, what changes have been done on it. Next, notice the *start* command in line 17. This command is calling a script that generates a standard 132 column header for use in reports. This script is included on the companion disk. The report header programs also return the database name so that it may be included in the file name. This report was written for use on the VMS platform. To use in on the UNIX platform, the file specification format will have to be modified; other than that, it will work as is. The output from this report is shown in Figure 5.2.

```
Date: 04/05/93              "Your Companies Name"              Page: 1
Time: 06:55 AM                ORACLE USER REPORT              "User's Name"
                          "Database Name" Database


User            Default      Temporary     DBA   RESOURCE    CONNECT
------------    -----------  ------------  ----  ---------   --------
ADHOC_DBA       DEF_USER     TEMP_USER     0     0           1
CASE            CASE_WORK    TEMP_USER     0     0           1
CASE$TEST       DEF_USER     TEMP_USER     0     0           1
.               .            .             .     .           .
.               .            .             .     .           .
.               .            .             .     .           .
OPS$NM90950     DEF_USER     TEMP_USER     0     0           1
OPS$NM90964     DEF_USER     TEMP_USER     0     0           1
OPS$NM90995     DEF_USER     TEMP_USER     0     0           1
OPS$NM91469     DEF_USER     TEMP_USER     0     0           1
OPS$NM91498     DEF_USER     TEMP_USER     0     0           1
PC_DBA          DEF_USER     TEMP_USER     0     0           1

52 rows selected
```

Figure 5.2 Example of user report format.

As you can see, this report takes care of several of our requirements: user names, Default tablespace assignments, temporary tablespace assignments, and database level privileges. The report could be enhanced by using the decode statement to convert the 1's and 0's to "GRANTED" or "NOT GRANTED". This report can be quickly scanned and problems swiftly located. The report is currently sorted, via the "order by" in line 23, by username. If you want, it could be sorted by default or temporary tablespace, or by individual privilege. You should also note that this report only lists users with connect privilege (the where clause in line 22). This is required in version 6 because no user is ever removed from the database. Therefore, if a database gets to be several years old, the number of inactive users (those without connect privilege) may exceed the number of active (those with connect privilege), and the report will become hard to read. A report showing those users that are inactive could be generated by simply changing the "!=" in line 22 to an "=".

The above report is good for tracking user's set up and base level of privilege for version 6, but it is not sufficient for tracking users, profiles, roles, privileges, and licensing issues for ORACLE7. Oracle version 6 has three database level privileges: connect, resource, and DBA. In ORACLE7 there are 80 distinct database-level privileges. A sample script for ORACLE7 is shown in Figure 5.3, with the resulting output in Figure 5.4.

```
 1:   REM
 2:   REM NAME        : USER_REPORT.SQL
 3:   REM PURPOSE     : GENERATE USER_REPORT
 4:   REM USE         : CALLED BY USER_REPORT.COM
 5:   REM Limitations : None
 6:   REM Revisions:
 7:   REM Date          Modified By      Reason For change
 8:   REM 08-Apr-1993   MIKE AULT        INITIAL CREATE
 9:   REM
10: set flush off term off pagesize 58 linesize 131
11: column username   heading User
12: column default_tablespace     heading Default
13: column temporary_tablespace   heading Temporary
14: column granted_role           heading Roles
15: column default_role           heading Default?
16: column admin_option           heading Admin?
17: column profile   heading 'Users Profile'
18: start title132 'ORACLE USER REPORT'
19: spool user7_report
20: select username, default_tablespace, temporary_tablespace, profile,
21: granted_role, admin_option, default_role
22: from sys.dba_users a, sys.dba_dba_role_privs b
23: where a.username = b.grantee and  b.granted_role='CONNECT'
24: group by username, default_tablespace, temporary_tablespace, profile;
25: spool off
26: exit
```

Figure 5.3 Example of user report listing for ORACLE7.

```
Date: 06/12/93                      "Your Company"                      Page:   1
Time: 07:56 AM                    ORACLE USER REPORT                    DEV7_DBA
                                   "Your Database"
```

User	Default Tablespace	Temporary Tablespace	Users Profile	Roles	Admin?	Default?
DEV7_DBA	DBA_TS	ORA_TEMP	DEFAULT	DBA	NO	YES
SYS	SYSTEM	ORA_TEMP	DEFAULT	CONNECT	YES	YES
			DBA	YES	YES	
				EXP_FULL_DATABASE	YES	YES
				IMP_FULL_DATABASE	YES	YES
				RESOURCE	YES	YES
SYSTEM	ORA_TOOLS	ORA_TEMP	DEFAULT	DBA	YES	YES

```
7 rows selected.
```

Figure 5.4 Example of output from script in Figure 5.3.

Note that in the version 6 script in Figure 5.1, only one report row per user is generated. In the Figure 5.3 script there will be one row for each role granted to the user. A companion script to show roles and administration options is also required. This is shown in Figure 5.5, with output in Figure 5.6. As you can see, it will be very important under ORACLE7 to assign users to roles. If you assign each privilege as it is required to each user, it will soon be impossible to manage your user base. Start by only assigning the default roles and then expanding those roles as required. For example, for a user who needs to create tables and indexes a role called CREATOR could be constructed that has the role CONNECT plus the CREATE_TABLE and CREATE_INDEX privileges. It should also be obvious that the DBA will need to track the roles and have them available at a moment's notice in hard copy to refer to as users are assigned to the system.

```
1:  REM
2:  REM NAME        : ROLE_REPORT.SQL
3:  REM PURPOSE     : GENERATE ROLES REPORT
4:  REM USE         : CALLED BY ROLE_REPORT.COM
5:  REM Limitations : None
6:  REM Revisions:
7:  REM Date          Modified By     Reason For change
8:  REM 08-Apr-1993   MIKE AULT       INITIAL CREATE
9:  REM
10: set flush off term off pagesize 58  linesize 78
11: column grantee heading 'User or Role'
12: column admin_option heading Admin?
13: start oracle$sql:title80 'ORACLE ROLES REPORT'
14: define output = ORA_STATUS_REPORTS:role_report&db.lis'
15: spool &output
16: select grantee, privilege, admin_option
17: from sys.dba_sys_privs
18: group by grantee;
19: spool off
20: exit
```

Figure 5.5 Example of role report listing for ORACLE7.

```
Date: 06/09/93              "Your Company Name"              Page:    1
Time: 03:12 PM              ORACLE ROLES REPORT             SYSTEM
                              "Your Database"

User or Role       PRIVILEGE                                Adm
-----------------  ------------------------------------     ---
CONNECT            ALTER SESSION                            NO
                   CREATE CLUSTER                           NO
```

Figure 5.6 Example of output from script in Figure 5.5.

	CREATE DATABASE LINK	NO
	CREATE SEQUENCE	NO
	CREATE SESSION	NO
	CREATE SYNONYM	NO
	CREATE TABLE	NO
	CREATE VIEW	NO
DBA	ALTER ANY CLUSTER	YES
	ALTER ANY INDEX	YES
	ALTER ANY PROCEDURE	YES
	ALTER ANY ROLE	YES
	CREATE SEQUENCE	YES
	CREATE SESSION	YES
	CREATE SNAPSHOT	YES
	.	
	.	
	.	
DEV7_DBA	UNLIMITED TABLESPACE	NO

Figure 5.6 (continued)

Now a complete picture of the user is known. A third script, to show the different user profiles, is shown in Figure 5.7. Output is in Figure 5.8.

```
1:   REM NAME      : PROFILE_REPORT.SQL
2:   REM PURPOSE   : GENERATE USER PROFILES REPORT
3:   REM USE       : CALLED BY PROFILE_REPORT.COM
4:   REM Revisions:
5:   REM Date           Modified By     Reason For change
6:   REM 08-Apr-1993   MIKE AULT        INITIAL CREATE
7:   set flush off term off pagesize 58 linesize 78
8:   column profile    heading Profile
9:   column resource_name      heading 'Resource:'
10: column limit                heading Limit
11: start oracle$sql:title80 'ORACLE PROFILES REPORT'
12: define output = ORA_STATUS_REPORTS:profile_report&db.lis'
13: spool &output
14: select profile, resource_name, limit  from sys.dba_profiles
15: group by profile;
16: spool off
17: exit
```

Figure 5.7 Script to generate a report on ORACLE7 user resource profiles.

```
Date: 06/09/93                    "Your Company Name"              Page:   1
Time: 03:10 PM                  ORACLE PROFILES REPORT             SYSTEM
                                    "Your Database"

Profile             Resource:                     Limit
---------------     ---------------------------   ------------------------------
DEFAULT             COMPOSITE_LIMIT               UNLIMITED
                    CONNECT_TIME                  UNLIMITED
                    CPU_PER_CALL                  UNLIMITED
                    CPU_PER_SESSION               UNLIMITED
                    IDLE_TIME                     UNLIMITED
                    LOGICAL_READS_PER_CALL        UNLIMITED
                    LOGICAL_READS_PER_SESSION     UNLIMITED
                    PRIVATE_SGA                   UNLIMITED
                    SESSIONS_PER_USER             UNLIMITED
9 rows selected.
```

Figure 5.8 Example of output from the report in Figure 5.7.

One thing to notice about the report in Figure 5.8 is that it displays the values for the DE-FAULT profile. As you can see, the default profile has unlimited resources. This is fine if you are a DBA-type account, but for the rank and file of general users, you will probably want to restrict some of the quotas and define a new profile for general users. Remember to set the RESOURCE_LIMIT parameter in the INIT.ORA file to TRUE in order to enable resource quota usage.

In most environments, weekly monitoring of users is sufficient. In some high use, rapidly changing environments where several DBAs or other types of administrative personnel are adding users, the reports may have to be run more frequently.

The user profiles are used in ORACLE7 to ensure a user doesn't consume more resources than are allowed. By default each user is assigned to the DEFAULT profile, which you should tailor for your specific environment.

5.2.2 Using the V$ and DB_ Views to Monitor Tablespaces

The DBA needs to monitor more than just users. Tablespaces also require watching. Tablespaces are not unchanging objects. They are subject to becoming filled and becoming fragmented. Luckily it is a fairly easy thing to monitor tablespaces using the V$ and DB_ views. Let's examine a report that covers these two critical parameters, available space and fragmentation.

The report in Figure 5.9 uses the view FREE_SPACE, which is based on the DBA view DBA_FREE_SPACE. This view is shown in Figure 5.10. The resulting report is in Figure 5.11.

In an ideal situation the tablespace data file(s) (there will be one line in the above report for each tablespace data file) will show one extent, and the biggest area will match the free area. In most cases if the tablespace has been used for any length of time, there will be several extents, and the free area (which corresponds to total free space in the tablespace) and the biggest area (which corresponds to the biggest area of contiguous free space) will not be equal. If the number of extents isn't large—say, less than 20—and the mismatch between the two sizes is small—say, less than 10 percent difference between biggest and free—then there is probably nothing to worry about. If either of these values are exceeded, the DBA should consider using the defragmentation methods described earlier. Under ORACLE7 the tablespaces are automatically defragmented by the SMON process.

```
REM   TITLE       : FREE_SPACE.SQL
REM   PURPOSE     : Generate a report showing Tablespace free space and
REM                 fragmentation
REM   USE         : Called from SQLPLUS, a user menu or other front end
REM   LIMITS      : None
REM   REVISIONS:
REM                 DATE      NAME       CHANGE
REM                 12/15/91  Mike Ault  Initial Creation
clear columns
set pages 56 linesize 80 feedback off verify off
column tablespace      heading Name format a10
column file_id         heading File# format 99999
column pieces          heading Frag format 9999
column free_bytes      heading 'Free Byte'
column free_blocks     heading 'Free Blk'
column largest_bytes   heading 'Biggest Bytes'
column largest_blks    heading 'Biggest Blks'
start ORACLE$SQL:TITLE80 "FREE SPACE REPORT"
spool ORACLE1:[ORACLE6.COM]free_space&DB.report
select tablespace,file_id,pieces,free_bytes,
                  free_blocks,largest_bytes,largest_blks
                  from free_space;
                  spool off
clear columns
SET FLUSH ON TERM ON
exit
```

Figure 5.9 A report on tablespace space usage and fragmentation.

```
create view free_space
    (tablespace, file_id, pieces, free_bytes, free_blocks, largest_bytes,
    largest_blks) as
select tablespace_name, file_id, count(*),
    sum(bytes), sum(blocks),
    max(bytes), max(blocks) from sys.dba_free_space
group by tablespace_name, file_id;
```

Figure 5.10 Free space view listing.

```
Date: 04/26/93                "Your Company Name"                  Page:    1
Time: 11:07 AM              ORACLE FREE SPACE REPORT               RECRUN_DBA
                               "Your" Database

Name          File#   Frag   Free Byte    Free Blk    Biggest Bytes   Biggest Blks
----------    ------  ----   ----------   ----------  ------------    ------------
DBA_TS        6       1      2527232      1234        2527232         1234
ORA_TEMP      3       1      10483712     5119        10483712        5119
ORA_USERS     2       1      10483712     5119        10483712        5119
RCRUN         4       1      15235072     7439        15235072        7439
RCRUN_ROLL    5       1      6387712      3119        6387712         3119
BACKS
SYSTEM        1       1      38270976     18687       38270976        18687

6 rows selected.
```

Figure 5.11 Example of report from free space report script.

If you find yourself adding several data files to a single tablespace in a relatively short period of time, it may be wise to extrapolate the growth and then export, drop, and recreate the tablespace to the size required to prevent excessive addition of data files. Of course, spreading data files for large databases across several drives may be desirable for equalizing disk IO. This is a database-specific question and needs to be answered on a database-by-database consideration. If you have several large tables that would benefit from being spread across several disks, you might consider placing them in their own tablespaces, then sizing the data files for the tablespaces such that the data contained in the tables is spread. For instance, if you have a single table that contains a gigabyte of data, it may be advisable to spread this file across several platters. To do this, create a table-specific tablespace on each of the platters to hold the file, each a fraction of the total size of the table. That is, if you want to spread the file across four drives, each data file would be 250 megabytes in size. Then, when you import the table, it will be spread across the four drives. The database will see the table as one contiguous entity, but you will gain IO speed by having spread the table across the drives available.

You should create each tablespace with default storage parameters that takes into account the performance-critical tables in the application that resides in it. You should also do the best job you can estimating the size requirements for the tables as they are created and only default to the default storage for minor tables. Ideally, this size estimation should be pushed down to the developers of the applications.

5.2.3 Monitoring Tables with the V$ and DBA_ Views

For tables, the DBA has four major concerns: Who owns them? Where are they created? Are they clustered? What is their space utilization?

Monitoring Ownership, Placement, and Clustering. The first three items on this list can be determined with a single report. This report for tables is shown in Figure 5.12, with the output in Figure 5.13. It is also important to monitor tables right after they have been created for proper sizing and storage parameters. This can be accomplished through use of the script in Figure 3.2 that documents how a table was created. If the table was created under ORACLE7 using the CREATE SCHEMA command, then the parameters will have to be altered since they will default to the tablespace default parameters.

```
REM
REM NAME          : TABLE_RP.SQL
REM PURPOSE       : GENERATE TABLE REPORT
REM USE           : FROM BOW_WEEKLY_STATUS.COM
REM Limitations   : None
REM Revisions:
REM Date            Modified By       Reason For change
REM 21-AUG-1991     MIKE AULT         INITIAL CREATE
REM 28-OCT-1992     MIKE AULT         ADD CALL TO TITLE132
clear columns
column table_name     heading Table
column tablespace_name     heading Tablespace
column cluster_name                  heading Cluster
START TITLE132 "ORACLE TABLE REPORT"
DEFINE OUTPUT = 'table_report&DB..lis'
spool &OUTPUT
select owner,table_name,tablespace_name,cluster_name from sys.dba_tables
where OWNER NOT IN ('SYSTEM', 'SYS')
order by tablespace_name, owner;
spool off
clear columns
EXIT
```

Figure 5.12 Tables Report Script.

```
Date: 05/10/93               "Your Company Name"              Page:   5
Time: 08:00 AM               ORACLE TABLE REPORT              OPS$NM91263
                              "Your" Database

OWNER          Table                    Tablespace           Cluster
----------     --------------------     -------------------  ----------------
CASE           CDI_DELTAB               CASE_WORKING_AREA
CASE           CDI_DICTIONARY_VERSION   CASE_WORKING_AREA
CASE           SDD_ERRORS               CASE_WORKING_AREA
KCGC_DBA       TEMP_SIZE_TABLE          DBA_TS               TEMP_CLUST
KCGC_DBA       LOCK_HOLDERS             DBA_TS
KCGC_DBA       DBA_TEMP                 DBA_TS               TEMP_CLUST
  .              .                        .                    .
  .              .                        .                    .
  .              .                        .                    .
RND_DBA        SDD_CC_ATTRIBUTES        DEFAULT_USER
RND_DBA        CG_FORM_HELP             DEFAULT_USER
405 rows selected.
```

Figure 5.13 Example of the table report script output.

One thing to notice about the script in Figure 5.12 is that it excludes the tables owned by SYSTEM and SYS. Since a good DBA never uses these users unless absolutely required, no extraneous tables should be created after product loads; therefore the data won't change. We are more concerned with new tables for the purposes of this report. The items the DBA should watch for in the output of this report script follow.

1. Tables that should belong to the specific application owner showing ownership of a regular user.
2. Excessive use of clusters.
3. Tables showing up in the SYSTEM tablespace, or in tablespaces other than where they belong.

You will also note this report gives no sizing information. This is covered next. Determining if table size is correct is one of the important tasks of the DBA.

Monitoring Size of Tables. One method to determine if your default storage sizing is correct for a tablespace is to monitor the extents for each of the tables that reside in the tablespace. Another method is to monitor the used space against the available space for each table. Scripts to perform these functions are shown in Figures 5.14 (output in Figure 5.15) and 5.16 (output in Figure 5.17).

```
REM
REM NAME        : EXTENTS.SQL
REM PURPOSE     : Generate extents report
REM USE         : From SQLPlus or other front end
REM Limitations : None
REM Revisions:
REM Date         Modified By    Reason For change
REM 15-jan-91    Mike Ault      Initial Creation
REM
CLEAR COLUMNS
column segment_name heading 'Segment' format a30
column tablespace_name heading 'Tablespace' format a20
set pagesize 58 NEWPAGE 0
SET LINESIZE 79
set feedback off  echo off   termout off   newpage 0
BREAK ON TABLESPACE_NAME SKIP PAGE
START ORACLE$SQL:TITLE80 "EXTENTS REPORT"
DEFINE OUTPUT = 'ora_status_reports:EXTENT&DB..LIS'
spool &OUTPUT
select TABLESPACE_NAME,segment_name,EXTENTS "Extents"
FROM SYS.DBA_SEGMENTS
order by tablespace_name,segment_name;
SPOOL OFF
EXIT
```

Figure 5.14 SQL*Plus report to show extents for each table in each tablespace.

```
Date: 05/10/93                    "Your Company"              Page:   1
Time: 08:19 AM                    EXTENTS REPORT              RECDEV_DBA
                                  "Your" Database

Tablespace              Segment                             Extents
-------------------     -----------------------------       ----------

DBA_TS                  APS_CFET$                           1
                        DBA_OBJ_TEMP                        1
                        DBA_TEMP                            1
                        HIT_RATIOS                          3
                        HR_INDEX                            2
                        LOCK_HOLDERS                        1
                        PLAN_TABLE                          1
                        TEMP_SIZE_TABLE                     1
                        TRUE_SPACE_T                        1
                          .                                   .
                          .                                   .
                          .                                   .
                        TRUE_SPACE_T_I1                     1
```

Figure 5.15 Example of output of the extents script.

```
rem   NAME: ACT_SIZE.sql
rem   HISTORY:
rem   Date       Who                What
rem   --------    ------------------ ----------------------------------------
rem   09/??/90    Maurice C. Manton   Creation for IOUG
rem   12/23/92    Michael Brouillette Changed to assume TEMP_SIZE_TABLE
rem                                   exists
rem                                   Changed to use DBA info and prompt for  the
rem                                   user name
rem                                   Changed spool file name to = owner
rem   FUNCTION:  Will show actual block used vs allocated for all tables for a user.
rem   INPUTS:
rem             owner = Table owner name.
accept owner prompt 'Enter table owner name: '
def aps_prog = act_size.sql
def aps_title = 'Table Space Utilization Effectiveness | for | &&owner'
start title80
set term off  pagesize 0  verify off  heading off  recsep off  feedback off ttitle off
delete temp_size_table;
SPOOL fill_size_table.sql
SELECT 'INSERT INTO temp_size_table',
       ' SELECT ','&'||'temp_var.' || segment_name ||'&'||'temp_var',
',COUNT( DISTINCT( SUBSTR( ROWID,1,8))) blocks',
```

Figure 5.16 Actual size report from IOUG.   (continued)

```
' FROM &&owner..'||segment_name, ';'
FROM dba_segments
WHERE segment_type = 'TABLE' AND owner = upper('&&owner');
SPOOL OFF
DEFINE temp_var = ''''
START fill_size_table;
HOST            DEL fill_size_table.sql;*
SET TERM ON TTITLE ON
SET VERIFY ON  HEADING ON  LINESIZE 79  PAGESIZE 58  NEWPAGE 0
COLUMN t_date    NOPRINT new_value t_date
COLUMN user_id   NOPRINT new_value user_id
COLUMN segment_name       FORMAT A20 HEADING "SEGMENT|NAME"
COLUMN segment_type       FORMAT A7 HEADING "SEGMENT|TYPE"
COLUMN extents            FORMAT 999 HEADING "EXTENTS"
COLUMN bytes    FORMAT A6 HEADING "BYTES"
COLUMN blocks FORMAT 9,999,999 HEADING "ORACLE|BLOCKS"
COLUMN act_blocks FORMAT 9,999,999 HEADING "ACTUAL|USED|BLOCKS"
COLUMN pct_block FORMAT 999.99 HEADING "PCT|BLOCKS|USED"
SPOOL &&owner
SELECT segment_name, segment_type, extents, to_char( bytes/1024)||'K' bytes,
 a.blocks, b.blocks act_blocks, b.blocks/a.blocks*100 pct_block
  FROM sys.user_segments a, temp_size_table b
 WHERE segment_name = UPPER( b.table_name );
SPOOL OFF;
   delete temp_size_table;
```

Figure 5.16 (continued)

```
Date: 03/16/93                "Your Company Name"                Page:  1
Time: 04:41 PM          SYS ACTUAL VS ALLOCATED STORAGE REPORT       SYS
                             "Your" Database

                                                  ACTUAL     PCT
SEGMENT    SEGMENT                                 ORACLE     BLOCKS
NAME       TYPE     EXTENTS   BYTES     BLOCKS     BLOCKS     USED
--------   -------  -------   -----     ------     ------     ------
AUD$       TABLE    1         10K       5          4          80.00
COLAUTH$   TABLE    1         10K       5          .00
COM$       TABLE    5         96K       48         44         91.67
CON$       TABLE    4         60K       30         23         76.67
DUAL       TABLE    1         10K       5          1          20.00
FILE$      TABLE    1         10K       5          1          20.00
INCEXP     TABLE    8         356K      178        138        77.53
INCFIL     TABLE    2         20K       10         5          50.00
INCVID     TABLE    1         10K       5          1          20.00

9 rows selected.
```

Figure 5.17 Example of output of actual size report.

Each of the above reports gives specific information. In the report from Figure 5.15, if a table shows greater than three extents, the DBA should review its size usage via the report in Figure 5.17 and rebuild the table with better storage parameters. In the report in Figure 5.17, if a table shows that it is using far less space than it has been allocated, it should be recreated accordingly.

Under ORACLE7 the DBA_TABLES view has several additional columns that document table specific data such as number of rows, number of allocated blocks, number of empty blocks, average percent of free space in a table, number of chained rows, and average row length. This provides the DBA with a more detailed view of the tables in the database than ever before. This shows the need for a new report to document this data in hard copy format so a DBA can easily track a table's growth, space usage, and chaining. The example script in Figure 5.18 shows such a report. An example of its output is in Figure 5.19.

```
rem
rem   NAME: tab_stat.sql
rem   HISTORY:
rem   Date       Who                 What
rem   --------   ------------------  ----------------------------------------
rem   5/27/93    Mike Ault           Initial creation
rem
rem   FUNCTION:  Will show table statistics for a user's tables or all tables.
rem
 set pages 56 lines 132 newpage 0 verify off echo off feedback off
rem
column owner format a12 heading "Table Owner"
column table_name format a20 heading "Table"
column tablespace_name format a20 heading "Tablespace"
column num_rows format 999999999 heading "Rows"
column blocks format 999999 heading "Blocks"
column empty_blocks format 999999 heading "Empties"
column space_full format 9999999999999 "Percent Full"
column chain_cnt format 999999 "Chains"
column avg_row_len format 999999999999999999 "Avg Length (Bytes)"
rem
start title132 "Table Statistics Report"
spool tab_stat&db
rem
select owner, table_name, tablespace_name, num_rows, blocks,
                empty_blocks,
                1-((blocks * avg_space)/(blocks * 2048)) space_full,
                chain_cnt, avg_row_len
from dba_tables
where owner = upper('&owner') and tablespace_name = upper('&tablespace')
order by owner, tablespace_name;
spool off
exit
```

Figure 5.18 Script to report additional statistics provided in ORACLE7.

```
Date: 06/10/93                          "Your Company Name"                          Page:    1
Time: 01:14 PM                         Table Statistics Report                       SYSTEM
                                          "Your Database"


Table Owner   Table               Tablespace   Rows   Blocks   Empties Percent Full   Chains   Avg Length (Bytes)
-----------   ----------------    ----------   ----   ------   ------- -----------    ------   ----------------
SYSTEM        MENU_B_APPL         ORA_TOOL        6                 1      22.56                              77
              MENU_B_CIRCLE                                         1        .00
              MENU_B_GROUP                        1                 1        .98                              20
              MENU_B_GRP_PRIV                   164                 3      61.39                              23
              MENU_B_OBJ_TEXT                   142                 5      72.11                              52
              MENU_B_OPTION                     141                 8      80.90                              94
              MENU_B_PARAM                                         1        .00
              MENU_B_PARM_XREF                                     1        .00
              MENU_B_PRIV                       141                 3      75.73                              33
              MENU_B_PROCEDURE                                     1        .00
              MENU_B_REF                                           1        .00
              MENU_B_USER                         2                 1       1.95                              20
              PRODUCT_ACCESS                                       1        .00
              PRODUCT_PROFILE                     1                 1       2.00                              41
              SRW_CMD_NAMES                      77                 1      67.68                              18

17 rows selected.
```

Figure 5.19 Example of output of report in Figure 5.18.

If indicated by the actual space report in version 6, or if the report shown in Figure 5.19 for ORACLE7 shows improper space utilization or excessive chaining, the table(s) involved should be rebuilt.

One method of rebuilding a table is:

1. Using a SQL script, unload the table into a flat file.
2. Drop the table and recreate it with a more representative storage clause.
3. Use SQLLOADER to reload the table data.

A second method would be:

1. Using the CREATE TABLE ... AS SELECT ..... FROM command, build a second table that is an image of the first table (SELECT * FROM first table) with a storage clause that specifies a larger initial extent.
2. Delete the first table.
3. Use the RENAME command to rename the second table with the first table's name.

Management of Keys. As per the requirements of third normal form, each table is required to have a unique identifier that consists of one or more of the table's columns. This is called the *primary key* (see Figures 5.20 and 5.21) of the table. This primary key should be identified using a constraint clause when the table is created. A second type of key, called a *foreign key* (see Figures 5.22 and 5.23), is also present in most tables. The foreign key is used to enforce relationships between two or more tables. Usually the foreign key consists of the primary key from the related table. Again, this foreign key should be identified by a constraint clause when the table is created. If the two types of keys have been identified via the constraint clause during table creation, they can be readily monitored via a SQL script report.

```
rem    ************************************************************************
rem    NAME: PKEYLIST.sql
rem
rem    HISTORY:
rem    Date       Who                  What
rem    --------    ------------------    -------------------------------------------
rem    06/18/91   Gary Dodge           Creation
rem    12/14/92   Michael Brouillette  Modified to accept an owner name.
rem
rem    FUNCTION:  This routine prints a report of all primary keys defined
rem               in the data dictionary (for owners other than SYS and SYSTEM).
rem               As written, it must be run by a DBA.  By changing the query to
rem               run against ALL_CONSTRAINTS, etc. it could be used by any user
rem               to see the primary keys which are "available" to them.
rem
rem    NOTES:
rem
rem    INPUTS: Owner for tables
rem
rem    ************************************************************************
ACCEPT OWNER PROMPT 'ENTER OWNER NAME OR "ALL" '
rem
COLUMN OWNER  FORMAT A15  NOPRINT NEW_VALUE OWNER_VAR
COLUMN TABLE_NAME         FORMAT A25 HEADING 'Table Name'
COLUMN CONSTRAINT_NAME    FORMAT A20  HEADING 'Constraint Name'
COLUMN COLUMN_NAME        FORMAT A25 HEADING' Column Name'
rem
BREAK ON OWNER SKIP PAGE ON TABLE_NAME SKIP 1 ON CONSTRAINT_NAME
rem
start title80 "Primary Keys For Database Tables"
SPOOL pkeylist
rem
SELECT C.OWNER, C.TABLE_NAME, C.CONSTRAINT_NAME,
               CC.COLUMN_NAME
   FROM DBA_CONSTRAINTS C, DBA_CONS_COLUMNS CC
 WHERE C.CONSTRAINT_NAME = CC.CONSTRAINT_NAME
   AND C.OWNER = CC.OWNER
   AND C.CONSTRAINT_TYPE = 'P'
   AND C.OWNER <> 'SYS'
   AND C.OWNER <> 'SYSTEM'
   AND C.OWNER = UPPER('&&OWNER') OR UPPER('&&OWNER') = 'ALL'
 ORDER BY C.OWNER, C.TABLE_NAME, CC.POSITION;
SPOOL OFF
UNDEF OWNER
exit
```

Figure 5.20 SQL script to list primary keys in tables from a specified owner.

```
Date: 05/11/93                    "Your Company Name"                    Page: 1
Time: 02:03 PM              PRIMARY KEY REPORT FOR ADHOC DBA              SYSTEM
                                  "Your" Database


Table Name                    Constraint Name            Column Name
----------------------        --------------------       -----------------------

ACCOUNT_CATEGORIES            CAT_PK                     ACT_CAT

ACCOUNT_CODES                 ACT_PK                     ACT_COD

ACTIVITIES                    ACY_PK                     ATY_COD

COST_CENTERS                  CCTR_PK                    COST_CTR

CURRENCY_RATES                CURR_PK                    PST_DT
                              SCENARIO
                              SIT_COD

FUNCTIONS                     FUNC_PK                    FCT_COD

HEAD_COUNTS                   HDCNT_PK                   COST_CTR
                              SCENARIO
                              PST_DT

MTD_EXPENSES                  MTDEXP_PK                  SEQ

PRODUCTS                      PROD_PK                    PRD_ID_COD

REGIONS                       REGION_PK                  REGION

REPORTING_ENTITIES            REPORTING_PK               RLT_ENT

SCENARIOS                     SCEN_PK                    SCENARIO

SITES                         SITE_PK                    SIT_COD

STRATEGIC_OBJECTIVES          SR_PK                      SR_COD

SUB_ACTIVITIES                SAC_PK                     SAC_COD

SYSTEM_TYPES                  SYS_PK                     SYS

UNIT_OF_CURRENCIES            UOC_PK                     CURR_DSC

WORK_EFFORTS                  WKEFF_PK                   SEQ
```

Figure 5.21 Example of output from primary key report.

```
rem     *************************************************************************
rem     NAME: FKEYLIST.sql
rem
rem     HISTORY:
rem     Date        Who                 What
rem     --------    ------------------  ------------------------------------------
rem     06/18/91    Gary Dodge          Creation
rem     06/28/91    Gary Dodge          Alter sort order
rem     05/10/93    Mike Ault           Alter select order to speed query,
rem                                     alter line and page size
rem     FUNCTION: This routine prints a report of all foreign keys defined in the
rem               data dictionary (for owners other than SYS and SYSTEM).  As
rem               written, it must be run by a DBA.  By changing the query to run
rem               against ALL_CONSTRAINTS, etc. it could be used by any user to
rem               see the foreign keys which are "available" to them.
rem     *************************************************************************
SET LINES 130 PAGES 56
rem
COLUMN OWNER   FORMAT A10   NOPRINT NEW_VALUE OWNER_VAR
COLUMN TABLE_NAME           FORMAT A24    HEADING'TABLE NAME'
COLUMN REF_TABLE            FORMAT A24    HEADING'REF TABLE'
COLUMN R_OWNER              FORMAT A10    NOPRINT
COLUMN CONSTRAINT_NAME      FORMAT A30    HEADING 'CONST NAME'
COLUMN R_CONSTRAINT_NAME    FORMAT A30    NOPRINT
COLUMN COLUMN_NAME          FORMAT A20    HEADING'COLUMN'
COLUMN REF_COLUMN           FORMAT A20    HEADING'REF COLUMN'
rem
start ORACLE$SQL:title132 "FOREIGN KEY REPORT"
rem
BREAK ON OWNER SKIP PAGE ON TABLE_NAME SKIP 1 -
      ON CONSTRAINT_NAME ON REF_TABLE
SPOOL fkeylist&DB
rem
SELECT C.OWNER, C.TABLE_NAME, C.CONSTRAINT_NAME,
       CC.COLUMN_NAME,
       R.TABLE_NAME REF_TABLE, RC.COLUMN_NAME REF_COLUMN
  FROM DBA_CONSTRAINTS C,
       DBA_CONSTRAINTS R,
       DBA_CONS_COLUMNS CC,
       DBA_CONS_COLUMNS RC
 WHERE C.CONSTRAINT_TYPE = 'R' AND C.OWNER NOT IN ('SYS','SYSTEM')
   AND C.R_OWNER = R.OWNER and
   C.R_CONSTRAINT_NAME = R.CONSTRAINT_NAME
   AND C.CONSTRAINT_NAME = CC.CONSTRAINT_NAME
   AND C.OWNER = CC.OWNER AND
   R.CONSTRAINT_NAME = RC.CONSTRAINT_NAME
   AND R.OWNER = RC.OWNER AND CC.POSITION = RC.POSITION
ORDER BY C.OWNER, C.TABLE_NAME, C.CONSTRAINT_NAME, CC.POSITION;
SPOOL OFF
EXIT
```

Figure 5.22 SQL script to show foreign keys.

```
Date: 05/11/93                  "Your Company Name"              Page:   1
Time: 03:10                     PMFOREIGN KEY REPORT             SYSTEM
                                 "Your" Database

TABLE NAME        CONST NAME              COLUMN        REF TABLE         REF COLUMN
-------------     ---------------------   ----------    ---------------   -----------
-
ACCOUNT_CODES     ACT_CATEGORIED_BY       ACT_CAT       ACCOUNT_CATS      ACT_CAT
ACTIVITIES        ACY_CHARGED_AGNST       SR_COD        STRATEGIC_OBJ     SR_COD
COST_CENTERS      CCTR_A_SUBSET_OF        SIT_COD       SITES             SIT_COD
                  CCTR_RESPNSBLE_TO       FCT_COD       FUNCTIONS         FCT_COD
CURRENCY_RATS     CURR_CLASSIFIED_BY      SCENARIO      SCENARIOS         SCENARIO
                  CURR_TIED_TO            SIT_COD       SITES             SIT_COD
HEAD_COUNTS       HDCNT_CLSSIFD_BY        SCENARIO      SCENARIOS         SCENARIO
                  HDCNT_RPRTED_BY         COST_CTR      COST_CENTERS      COST_CTR
MTD_EXPENSES      MTDEXP_ALLCTD_TO        COST_CTR      COST_CENTERS      COST_CTR
                  MTDEXP_CTGRZD_BY        SCENARIO      SCENARIOS         SCENARIO
                  MTDEXP_CHRGED_TO        ACT_COD       ACCNT_CODES       ACT_COD
                  MTDEXP_CHRGED_TO2       ATY_COD       ACTIVITIES        ATY_COD
                  MTDEXP_CHRGED_TO3       SR_COD        STRAT_OBJ         SR_COD
                  MTDEXP_CHRGED_TO4       SAC_COD       SUB_ACTIVITIES    SAC_COD
```

Figure 5.23 Example of output of foreign key report.

Monitoring for Chained Rows. Chaining occurs as data is added to an existing record. When there is insufficient room for the addition, the row is chained to another block and added there. This can lead to significant performance degradation if chaining is occurring regularly. This degradation is caused by the requirements to read multiple blocks to retrieve a single record. An example of a script to monitor a single table under version 6 for chained rows is shown in Figure 5.24.

The Analyze Command. In ORACLE7 a new command is provided that can be used to find if a table has chained rows. This is the ANALYZE command. The general format of this command follows:

```
ANALYZE TABLE--or--CLUSTER [schema.]table--or--cluster
LIST CHAINED ROWS INTO [schema.]table;
```

```
rem   NAME: CHAINING.sql
rem   HISTORY:
rem   Date         Who                  What
rem   01/11/93     Michael Brouillette    Creation
rem   FUNCTION:    Produce a report showing the number of chained rows in a table.
rem        REQUIREMENTS:
rem1.The user running this routine must have DBA privileges.
rem2.The table must have at least one column that is both the leading portion of an
rem      index and defined as not null.
```

Figure 5.24 Interactive SQL script to determine chained rows in a table.

```
rem    WARNINGS:
rem 1. This routine will use the V$SESSTAT table where the USERNAME
rem    is the current user.  This will cause a problem if there is
rem    more than one session active with that USERID.
rem 2. This routine uses the V$SESSTAT statistics.  These statistics
rem    may change between releases and platforms.  If the routine
rem    fails, check to make sure that the name of the statistic has
rem    not changed.  The current name is: 'table fetch continued row'
rem INPUTS:  obj_own = Name of table owner,  obj_nam = Name of the table
rem ********************************************************************
accept obj_own prompt 'Enter the table owners name: '
accept obj_nam prompt 'Enter the table name: '
set echo off  feedback off  verify off  heading off  termout off
rem find out what statistic we want
column statistic# new_value stat_no
select statistic# from v$statname n
 where n.name = 'table fetch continued row';
rem  find out who we are it terms of sid
col sid new_value user_sid
select sid from sys.v_$session
 where audsid = userenv('SESSIONID');
col  column_name new_value last_col
select column_name  from sys.dba_tab_columns
 where table_name = upper('&&obj_nam')
 order by column_id;
col name new_value indexed_column
select c.name  from sys.col$ c, sys.obj$ idx, sys.obj$ base, sys.icol$ ic
 where base.obj# = c.obj#
   and ic.bo# = base.obj# and ic.col# = c.col#
   and base.owner# =(select user# from sys.user$  where name = upper('&&obj_own'))
   and ic.obj# = idx.obj#
   and base.name = upper('&&obj_nam') and ic.pos# = 1 and c.null$ > 0;
col value new_value before_count
select value from v$sesstat
 where v$sesstat.sid = &user_sid and v$sesstat.statistic# = &stat_no;
select &last_col from &obj_own..&obj_nam
 where &indexed_column <=(select max(&indexed_column)
                  from &obj_own..&obj_nam);
col value new_value after_count
select value  from v$sesstat
 where v$sesstat.sid = &user_sid and v$sesstat.statistic# = &stat_no;
set termout on
select upper('&obj_own')||'.'||upper('&obj_nam')||' contains '||
    (to_number(&after_count) - to_number(&before_count))||' chained rows.'
  from sys.dual;
select 'No indexed not null columns in table '||
    upper('&obj_own')||'.'||upper('&obj_nam') from sys.dual
where rtrim('&indexed_column') is null;
set heading on feedback on
```

Figure 5.24 (continued)

Also provided in ORACLE7 is a column showing chained rows for a specific table in the DBA_TABLES view (see Figure 5.18). If you don't care what rows are chained, a simple query against this view will tell you if changing is occuring.

Monitoring Grants on a Table. The DBA also needs to monitor grants on tables. It is good to know who is granting what privileges to whom. The script to determine this is shown in Figure 5.25, with an example of its output in Figure 5.26.

Using the above report it is easy to monitor the grants on specific version 6 objects. A close look at the generation script shows that this report is very selective, down to the individual object level or as general as the entire database base. Using this script the DBA can find out the level of protection for any and all version 6 database objects.

```
rem  ***********************************************************************
rem  NAME: GRANTS.sql
rem  HISTORY:
rem  Date       Who                 What
rem  --------   ------------------  -------------------------------------------
rem  05/24/91   Gary Dodge          Creation
rem  12/12/92   Michael Brouillette  Allow specification of a owner.
rem
rem  FUNCTION: Produce report of table grants showing GRANTOR, GRANTEE and
rem            specific GRANTS.
rem  INPUTS: Owner name
rem  ***********************************************************************
ACCEPT OWNER PROMPT 'ENTER OWNER NAME OR "ALL" '
rem
COLUMN GRANTEE           FORMAT A15
COLUMN OWNER             FORMAT A15
COLUMN TABLE_NAME        FORMAT A25
COLUMN GRANTOR           FORMAT A15
COLUMN SELECT_PRIV       FORMAT A1        HEADING'S|E|L'
COLUMN INSERT_PRIV       FORMAT A1        HEADING'I|N|S'
COLUMN DELETE_PRIV       FORMAT A1        HEADING'D|E|L'
COLUMN UPDATE_PRIV       FORMAT A1        HEADING'U|P|D'
COLUMN REFERENCES_PRIV   FORMAT A1        HEADING'R|E|F'
COLUMN ALTER_PRIV        FORMAT A1        HEADING'A|L|T'
COLUMN INDEX_PRIV        FORMAT A1        HEADING'I|N|D'
COLUMN CREATED           FORMAT A11       HEADING'GRANTED ON:'
rem
BREAK ON OWNER SKIP 4 ON TABLE_NAME SKIP 1 ON REPORT
SET LINESIZE 130
start title132 "TABLE GRANTS BY OWNER AND TABLE'"
rem
BTITLE SKIP 2 CENTER -
   'Y = Granted, N = Not Granted, G = Granted WITH GRANT OPTION, ' -
   'S = Granted on Specific Columns, A = Granted on All Columns' -
   left 'produced by ' &aps_prog
```

Figure 5.25 SQL script to show object level grants.

```
SPOOL grants
rem
SELECT OWNER, TABLE_NAME, GRANTEE, GRANTOR, CREATED,
       SELECT_PRIV, INSERT_PRIV, DELETE_PRIV, UPDATE_PRIV,
       REFERENCES_PRIV, ALTER_PRIV, INDEX_PRIV
  FROM DBA_TAB_GRANTS
 WHERE OWNER NOT IN ('SYS','SYSTEM')
   AND OWNER = UPPER('&&OWNER') OR UPPER('&&OWNER') = 'ALL'
   ORDER BY OWNER, TABLE_NAME, GRANTOR, GRANTEE;
rem
SPOOL OFF
exit
```

Figure 5.25 (continued)

```
Date: 05/10/93                "Your Company Name"               Page:   1
Time: 09:43 AMTable authorizations by Grantor, Grantee, Owner Object name
RECRUN_DBA
                           "Your" Database

                                                 S I U D A I R
                                                 E N P E L N E
GRANTOR    GRANTEE    Object Owner    Object Name L S D L T D F  Created
--------   --------   -------------   ----------- - - - - - - -  --------

SYSTEM     REC_DBA    SYSTEM          MENU_B_A    G G G G N N N  26-APR-93
                                      MENU_B_CIRC G G G G N N N  26-APR-93
                                      MENU_B_GRP  G G G G N N N  26-APR-93
                                      MENU_B_INFO G G G G N N N  26-APR-93
                                      MENU_B_OPT  G G G G N N N  26-APR-93
                                      MENU_B_PRM  G G G G N N N  26-APR-93
                                      MENU_B_PRIV G G G G N N N  26-APR-93
                                      MENU_B_PRC  G G G G N N N  26-APR-93
                                      MENU_B_REF  G G G G N N N  26-APR-93
                                      MENU_B_USR  G G G G N N N  26-APR-93
                                      MENU_V_APL  G G G G N N N  26-APR-93
                                      MENU_V_CiRC G G G G N N N  26-APR-93
                                      MENU_V_GRP  G G G G N N N  26-APR-93
                                      MENU_V_INFO G G G G N N N  26-APR-93
                                      MENU_V_OPT  G G G G N N N  26-APR-93
                                      MENU_V_PRM  G G G G N N N  26-APR-93
                                      MENU_V_PRIV G G G G N N N  26-APR-93

17 rows selected.
```

Figure 5.26 Example of report from grant script.

Under ORACLE7 the DBA_TAB_GRANTS view is replaced by the DBA_TAB_PRIVS table and several of the columns in the view have been modified. The example script in Figure 5.27 (output in Figure 5.28) shows an updated version of this report script. Rather than have 1 or 0 for a specified list of privileges, the actual privilege name is stored in the database field. This allows future enhancements without changing view definitions. Notice that the column GRANTABLE has also been added. This column documents that the privilege was granted with the ADMIN OPTION if it is set to YES.

```
rem    ********************************************************************
rem    NAME: GRANTS.sql
rem
rem    HISTORY:
rem    Date      Who                What
rem    --------  -----------------  -------------------------------------------
rem    05/24/91  Gary Dodge         Creation
rem    12/12/92  Michael Brouillette  Allow specification of a owner.
rem    05/27/93  Mike Ault          Updated to ORACLE7
rem
rem    FUNCTION: Produce report of table grants showing GRANTOR, GRANTEE and
rem             specific GRANTS.
rem
rem    INPUTS: Owner name
rem    ********************************************************************
ACCEPT OWNER PROMPT 'ENTER OWNER NAME OR "ALL" '
rem
COLUMN GRANTEE                FORMAT A15
COLUMN OWNER                  FORMAT A15
COLUMN TABLE_NAME             FORMAT A25
COLUMN GRANTOR                FORMAT A15
COLUMN PRIVILEGE              FORMAT A10 "Privilege"
COLUMN GRANTABLE    FORMAT A19   HEADING "With Grant Option?"
rem
BREAK ON OWNER SKIP 4 ON TABLE_NAME SKIP 1 ON REPORT
REM
SET LINESIZE 130 PAGES 56 VERIFY OFF FEEDBACK OFF
start title132 "TABLE GRANTS BY OWNER AND TABLE"
SPOOL grants&db
REM
SELECT OWNER, TABLE_NAME, GRANTEE, GRANTOR,
            PRIVILEGE, GRANTABLE
  FROM DBA_TAB_PRIVS
 WHERE OWNER NOT IN ('SYS','SYSTEM')
   AND OWNER = UPPER('&&OWNER') OR UPPER('&&OWNER') = 'ALL'
   ORDER BY OWNER, TABLE_NAME, GRANTOR, GRANTEE;
REM
SPOOL OFF
exit
```

Figure 5.27 Grants script updated for ORACLE7.

```
Date: 06/09/93              "Your Company Name"              Page:  1
Time: 03:09 PM        TABLE GRANTS BY OWNER AND TABLE        SYSTEM
                            "Your Database"

OWNER      TABLE_NAME           GRANTEE    GRANTOR   Privilege   With Grant Option?
---------  -------------------- ---------  --------- ----------  ------------------
DEV7_DBA   APS_ROLLBACK_SEGS    PUBLIC     DEV7_DBA  SELECT      NO
           INSTANCE             PUBLIC     DEV7_DBA  SELECT      NO
```

Figure 5.28 Example of output from report in Figure 5.27.

5.2.4 Using the V$ and DB_ Views for Monitoring Sequences

Sequences are used to generate integer numbers for use in keys or any other column that requires either repeating or nonrepeating numbers. Essentially the only monitoring that the DBA can do is to identify the sequences, their owners, and so on. The DBA can query the sequence's values, but then those values are lost. The view used in the SQL script in Figure 5.29 (example in Figure 5.30) holds the last value written to disk. This is all the data on the actual sequence value the DBA can get nondestructively.

The DBA should monitor the last value written against the maximum value for ascending and the minimum value for descending sequences. If the sequence is near its limit and is not a cycled sequence, the DBA will have to alter the minimum or maximum values using the ALTER SEQUENCE command if the sequence value is approaching the minimum or maximum value. If this isn't done, the tables depending on the sequence will fail any selects to retrieve sequence values.

As with other objects, if sequences are used in applications, they should be owned by a central DBA account for the application. This report if used with the wild card (%) option, will report on all sequences, thus showing privately owned sequences. To alter the ownership of a sequence, it must either be dropped and recreated, with possible loss of continuity in sequence numbers, or it can be exported and then imported into the new owner with no loss of values.

In addition, the DBA should monitor the number of values being cached. If this value is excessive, large numbers of cached sequence values are lost during shutdown. If the value is too small, performance can suffer if the sequence is accessed frequently. The default value for cache is 20 under version 6 and 10 under ORACLE7.

5.2.5 Using the V$ and DB_ Views for Monitoring Indexes

The DBA will have to monitor table indexes to verify uniqueness, determine if the appropriate columns are indexed, and to determine if ownership of indexes for a given application is proper. In addition, the DBA needs a convenient reference to show what tables have indexes and what is indexed in case of loss of a table, or for use during table maintenance. The report in Figure 5.31 provides a convenient format for the DBA to review indexed tables and columns. It is selective down to the single-table, single-owner level. The report should be run after database maintenance involving table rebuilds, exports and imports, or database rebuilds. An example is in Figure 5.32.

```
rem   NAME: Sequence.sql
rem
rem   HISTORY:
rem   Date        Who                   What
rem   --------    ------------------    ------------------
rem   5/10/93     Mike Ault             Creation
rem   FUNCTION:
rem               Generate report on Sequences
rem   INPUTS:
rem
rem               1 - Sequence Owner or Wild Card
rem               2 - Sequence Name or Wild Card
rem
rem   ***************************************************************************
SET HEADING OFF VERIFY OFF PAUSE OFF
PROMPT ** Sequence Report **
PROMPT
PROMPT Percent signs are wild
ACCEPT sequence_owner char  'Enter Oracle account to report on (or wild):';
ACCEPT sequence_name char  'Enter object name to report on (or wild): ';
PROMPT
PROMPT Report file name is SEQUENCE_DBNAME.LIS
SET HEADING ON
SET LINESIZE 130 PAGESIZE 56 NEWPAGE 0 TAB OFF SPACE 1
SET TERMOUT OFF
BREAK ON SEQUENCE_OWNER SKIP 2
COLUMN SEQUENCE_OWNER    FORMAT A30    HEADING 'Sequence Owner'
COLUMN SEQUENCE_NAME     FORMAT A30    HEADING 'Sequence Name'
COLUMN MIN_VALUE                       HEADING 'Minimum'
COLUMN MAX_VALUE                       HEADING 'Maximum'
COLUMN INCREMENT_BY      FORMAT 9999   HEADING 'Incr.'
COLUMN CYCLE_FLAG                      HEADING 'Cycle'
COLUMN ORDER_FLAG                      HEADING 'Order'
COLUMN CACHE_SIZE        FORMAT 99999  HEADING 'Cache'
COLUMN LAST_NUMBER                     HEADING 'Last Value'
START TITLE132 "SEQUENCE REPORT"
SPOOL SEQUENCES&DB.LIS
SELECT  SEQUENCE_OWNER, SEQUENCE_NAME, MIN_VALUE, MAX_VALUE,
            INCREMENT_BY,
            DECODE(CYCLE_FLAG,'Y','YES','N','NO') CYCLE_FLAG,
            DECODE(ORDER_FLAG,'Y','YES','N','NO') ORDER_FLAG,
            CACHE_SIZE, LAST_NUMBER
FROM   DBA_SEQUENCES
WHERE  SEQUENCE_OWNER LIKE UPPER('&SEQUENCE_OWNER') AND
           SEQUENCE_NAME LIKE UPPER('&SEQUENCE_NAME')
ORDER BY  1,2;
SPOOL OFF
EXIT
```

Figure 5.29 SQL script to generate a sequence report.

```
Date: 05/11/93                "Your Company Name"              Page:   1
Time: 11:03 AM                 SEQUENCE REPORT                 SYSTEM
                               "Your" Database

Sequence Own Sequence Name Minimum  Maximum     Incr. Cyc  Ord  Cache  Last Value
------------ ------------- --------  ----------  ----  ---  ---  -----  ----------
ADHOC_DBA    MTD_EXPENSE   1         1.0000E+27  1     NO   NO   20     1
             WORK_EFFRT    1         1.0000E+27  1     NO   NO   20     1
CT_DBA       AUDITOR       1         1.0000E+27  1     NO   NO   20     21
GRTS_DBA     COUNTRY       1         999         1     NO   NO   20     10
             DEGREE        1         99999       1     NO   NO   20     28
             DEGREE_T      1         99999       1     NO   NO   20     3
             DEPT          1         999         1     YES  NO   20     4
             MMD_PER       1         99999999    1     NO   NO   20     5
             POSITION      1         99999999    1     NO   NO   20     44
             REGION        1         999         1     NO   NO   20     6

10 Rows Selected
```

Figure 5.30 Example of report format from sequence script.

```
rem    ********************************************************************
rem    NAME: Index_rp.sql (Originally ODD005.sql)
rem    HISTORY:
rem    Date        Who                 What
rem    --------    ------------------  ------------------------------------------
rem    7/25/91     Tim Olesen          Creation
rem    01/07/93    Mike Ault           Switched to title132 altered line size
rem    05/10/93    Mike Ault           Added Header
rem    FUNCTION: Generate report on Indexes.
rem    INPUTS:
rem          1 = Oracle Account
rem          2 = Table name
rem    ********************************************************************
SET HEADING OFF VERIFY OFF PAUSE OFF
PROMPT **  Index Column Report  **
PROMPT
PROMPT Percent signs are wild
ACCEPT OWNER CHAR PROMPT 'Enter Oracle account to report on (or wild): ';
ACCEPT TABLE_NAME CHAR PROMPT 'Enter table name to report on (or wild): ';
PROMPT
PROMPT Report file name is  INDEXES.LIS
SET HEADING ON
SET LINESIZE 130 PAGESIZE 56 NEWPAGE 0 SPACE 1 TAB OFF
```

Figure 5.31 SQL script to generate index report.   (continued)

```
SET TERMOUT OFF
BREAK ON TABLE_OWNER SKIP PAGE ON TABLE_TYPE ON TABLE_NAME
ON UNIQUENESS ON INDEX_NAME SKIP 1
COLUMN TABLE_OWNER    FORMAT A30   HEADING 'Object Owner'
COLUMN TABLE_TYPE     FORMAT A6    HEADING 'Type'
COLUMN TABLE_NAME     FORMAT A30   HEADING 'Object Name'
COLUMN INDEX_NAME     FORMAT A30   HEADING 'Index Name'
COLUMN UNIQUENESS     FORMAT A1    HEADING 'U|N|I|Q|U|E'
COLUMN COLUMN_NAME    FORMAT A30   HEADING 'Column Name'
START ORACLE$SQL:TITLE132 "Index Columns by Owner and Table Name"
SPOOL   indexes&db.LIS
SELECT   I.TABLE_OWNER
        , DECODE(TABLE_TYPE,'CLUSTER','CLUSTR','TABLE') TABLE_TYPE
        , I.TABLE_NAME, I.INDEX_NAME
        , SUBSTR(UNIQUENESS,1,1) UNIQUENESS, IC.COLUMN_NAME
    FROM DBA_INDEXES I, DBA_IND_COLUMNS IC
   WHERE I.INDEX_NAME = IC.INDEX_NAME
     AND OWNER      = INDEX_OWNER  AND I.OWNER      LIKE upper('&OWNER')
     AND I.TABLE_NAME LIKE upper('&TABLE_NAME')
ORDER BY 1,2,3,5 DESC,4,COLUMN_POSITION;
SPOOL OFF
EXIT
```

Figure 5.31 (continued)

Date: 05/11/93		"Your Company Name"			Page: 1
Time: 11:06 AM		Index Columns by Owner and Table Name			KCGC_DBA
		"Your" Database			
				U	
				N	
				I	
				Q	
				U	
Object Owner	Type	Object Name	Index Name	E	Column
------------	------	--------------------	---------------	--	-----------
ADHOC_DBA	TABLE	ACCOUNT_CATEGORIES	CAT_PK_PRIM	U	ACT_CAT
		ACCOUNT_CODES	ACT_PK_PRIM	U	ACT_COD
			ACT_CAT_BY_FR	N	ACT_CAT
		ACTIVITIES	ACY_PK_PRIM	U	ATY_COD
			ACY_AGST_FRN	N	SR_COD
		ADHOC_RPT_FRM_HLP	X_AH_RP_FM_HP	N	HLP_IDX
					HLP_TYPE
					HLP_APPLN
					HLP_SEQ
		AD_FUNTREE	AD_FUNTREE1	N	EL_ID
		AD_FUNTREE2	PARENT		
		AD_MODNOTES	ADM_PRIME	N	MOD_ID

12 rows selected.

Figure 5.32 Example of output from index report.

Another useful report is one that shows the index statistics such as most used keys, head space used, rows per key, and so forth. The script for this report is shown in Figure 5.33, with output in Figure 5.34.

```
rem   NAME: IN_STAT.sql
rem   HISTORY:
rem   Date        Who                     What
rem   10/25/92    Cary Millsap            Creation
rem   01/07/93    Michael Brouillette     Switched to title80
rem   05/11/93    Mike Ault               Reformatted
rem   FUNCTION: Report on index statistics
rem   INPUTS:     1 = Index owner    2 = Index name
def iowner= &&1
def iname            = &&2
set heading off
col name                newline
col headsep             newline
col height              newline
col blocks              newline
col lf_rows             newline
col lf_blks             newline
col lf_rows_len         newline
col lf_blk_len          newline
col br_rows             newline
col br_blks             newline
col br_rows_len         newline
col br_blk_len          newline
col del_lf_rows         newline
col del_lf_rows_len     newline
col distinct_keys       newline
col most_repeated_key   newline
col btree_space         newline
col used_space          newline
col pct_used            newline
col rows_per_key        newline
col blks_gets_per_access newline
validate index &iowner..&iname;
start title80 "Index Statistics for &iowner..&iname"
spool in_stat
select name,  '----------------------------------------------------'  headsep,
   'height              '||to_char(height,     '999,999,990') height,
   'blocks              '||to_char(blocks,     '999,999,990') blocks,
   'del_lf_rows         '||to_char(del_lf_rows,'999,999,990') del_lf_rows,
   'del_lf_rows_len     '||to_char(del_lf_rows_len,'999,999,990') del_lf_rows_len,
   'distinct_keys       '||to_char(distinct_keys,'999,999,990') distinct_keys,
   'most_repeated_key   '||to_char(most_repeated_key,'999,999,990')
    most_repeated_key,
   'btree_space         '||to_char(btree_space,'999,999,990') btree_space,
   'used_space          '||to_char(used_space,'999,999,990') used_space,
```

Figure 5.33 Script to produce index statistics reports.   (continued)

```
'pct_used                        '||to_char(pct_used,'990') pct_used,
'rows_per_key            '||to_char(rows_per_key,'999,999,990') rows_per_key,
'blks_gets_per_access '||to_char(blks_gets_per_access,'999,999,990')
 blks_gets_per_access,
'lf_rows        '||to_char(lf_rows,    '999,999,990')||'        '||+
'br_rows        '||to_char(br_rows,    '999,999,990') br_rows,
'lf_blks        '||to_char(lf_blks,    '999,999,990')||'        '||+
'br_blks        '||to_char(br_blks,    '999,999,990') br_blks,
'lf_rows_len    '||to_char(lf_rows_len,'999,999,990')||'        '||+
'br_rows_len    '||to_char(br_rows_len,'999,999,990') br_rows_len,
'lf_blk_len     '||to_char(lf_blk_len, '999,999,990')||'        '||+
'br_blk_len     '||to_char(br_blk_len, '999,999,990') br_blk_len from
index_stats;
spool off
exit
```

Figure 5.33 (continued)

```
Date: 05/12/93                  "Your Company Name"              Page:   1
Time: 02:06 PM           Index Statistics for case.elem_10       SYSTEM
                                "Your" Database


ELEM_10
-----------------------------------------------
height                                    ?
blocks                                   86
del_lf_rows                               2
del_lf_rows_len                          32
distinct_keys                             6
most_repeated_key                     4,843
btree_space                         149,262
used_space                           78,820
pct_used                                 53
rows_per_key                            808
blks_gets_per_access                    407
lf_rows              4,848      br_rows                 77
lf_blks                 78      br_blks                  1
lf_rows_len         77,588      br_rows_len          1,232
lf_blk_len           1,889      br_blk_len           1,920
```

Figure 5.34 Example of output from index statistics report.

This report (Figure 5.34) shows how efficiently the index is being used. By examining distinct keys and rows per key, the DBA can determine how well data is being indexed—that is, the selectivity of the index. In this example report with 808 rows per key, the selectivity appears low. It might be advisable to examine the structure of the index columns and determine if selectivity can be increased—that is, if the key can be made more selective. Of course, this index may be designed to provide rapid access to only a select group of data items, and selectivity isn't really an issue—for example, all of the CASE elements that belong to a single application.

Under ORACLE7 the DBA_INDEXES view has been extended to include b-tree level, number of leaf blocks, number of distinct keys, average number of leaf blocks per key, average number of data blocks per key, and the index clustering factor. In addition, a column to show the index status, either DIRECT LOAD or VALID, has been added.

The new column clustering factor shows how well the table being indexed is ordered. If the value for clustering factor is near the number of table blocks, the table is well ordered. If instead it is near the number of rows in the table, the table is not well ordered (unless the row size is close to block size).

A script for reporting these statistics for an ORACLE7 database is shown in Figure 5.35 (output in Figure 5.36).

```
rem   NAME: IN_STAT.sql
rem   HISTORY:
rem   Date        Who           What
rem   05/27/93    Mike Ault     Initial creation
rem
rem   FUNCTION: Report on index statistics
rem   INPUTS:    1 = Index owner    2 = Index name
rem
def iowner= &&1
def iname  = &&2
set pages 56 lines 130 verify off feedback off
column owner format a20 heading "Owner"
column index_name format a20 heading "Index"
column status format a11 heading heading "Status"
column blevel format 9,999,999,999 heading "Tree Level"
column leaf_blocks format 999,999,999 heading "Leaf Blk"
column distinct_keys format 999,999 heading "# Keys"
column avg_leaf_blocks_per_key format 999,999,999 heading "Avg. LB/Key"
column avg_data_blocks_per_key format 999,999,999 heading "Avg. DB/Key"
column clustering_factor format 999,999,999 heading "Clstr Factor"
rem
start title132 "Index Statistics Report"
spool ind_stat&db
rem
select owner, index_name, status, blevel, leaf_blocks.
            distinct_keys, avg_leaf_blocks_per_key,
            avg_data_blocks_per_key, clustering_factor
from dba_indexes
where
owner like upper('&&iowner') and index_name like upper('&&iname')
order by 1,2;
rem
spool off
exit
```

Figure 5.35 Example statistics report for ORACLE7 indexes.

```
Date: 06/12/93                           "Your Company Name"                          Page:   1
Time: 11:21 AM                          Index Statistics Report                       DEV7_DBA
                                           "Your Database"

Owner      Index            STATUS    Tree Level    Leaf Blk    # Keys    Avg. LB/Key    Avg. DB/Key   Clstr Factor
--------   --------------   -----     ----------    --------    ------    -----------    -----------   ------------
DEV7_DBA   DBA_OB_DESC      VALID          1            33        254           1              3            835
           INDEX_LIST_1_PK  VALID
           SYS_C00440       VALID          2            88       1,013          1              1            353
           SYS_C00441       VALID
           TABLE_LIST_1_PK  VALID
           TRUE_SPACE_T_1   VALID
```

Figure 5.36 Example of report output from script in Figure 5.35.

The various values in the report in Figure 5.36 are interpreted as follows:

BLEVEL—This is the depth, or number of levels, from the root block of the index to its leaf blocks. A depth of 1 will indicate that they are all on the same level.

LEAF_BLOCKS—This is the number of leaf blocks in the index.

AVG_LEAF_—This indicates a nonunique index if its value is greater than 1.

BLOCKS_PER_KEY—If greater than 1, it indicates the key has duplicate values.

AVG_DATA_—This indicates the average number of data blocks in the

BLOCKS_PER_KEY—indexed table that are pointed to by a distinct value in the index

CLUSTERING_FACTOR—This value indicates the orderliness of the table being indexed. If it is near the number of blocks in the table, it indicates a well-ordered table. If it is near the number of rows, it indicates a disordered table.

5.2.6 Monitoring Synonyms Using the V$ and DBA_ Views

In all of the reports reviewed for this book, not one seemed to cover synonyms. Yet synonyms are the key to providing cross-database access for queries and a means of implementing distributed data across nodes, systems, and databases. If you will remember, a synonym allows a shorthand version of an object name to be specified. The parts of a synonym are the object name (which usually includes an owner), sometimes a connect string that uses a protocol specification (D: or T:), and some connection string that usually consists of a node, username password combination, and a task specification such as D:MMRD01"SQLNET SQLNET"::"TASK=ORDNKCGC." This connect string can be loaded into a database link that will also provide an Oracle username and password. A complete report will show all of these items. See Figure 5.37.

Why is it important to monitor synonyms? Synonyms can be used to access data, sometimes data that shouldn't be accessed if object grants have been too widely distributed. In addition, they are the means for reaching other nodes and databases. If a connect string becomes invalid, a

```
REM
REM NAME            : SYNONYM.SQL
REM PURPOSE         : GENERATE REPORT OF A USERS SYNONYMS
REM USE             : FROM SQLPLUS
REM Limitations     : None
REM Revisions:
REMDate          Modified By    Reason For change
REM12/MAY/93     Mike Ault      Initial Creation
REM
prompt Percent signs are Wild Cards
prompt
accept own prompt 'Enter the user who owns synonym: '
set pages 56 lines 130 verify off feedback off term off
start oracle$sql:title132 "Synonym Report"
spool synonym&db
column host         format a24 heading "Connect String"
column owner        format a15
column table        format a35
column db_link      format a6 heading Link
column username     format a15
select a.owner, synonym_name , table_owner ||'.'|| table_name "Table" , b.db_link,
username, host from dba_synonyms a, dba_db_links b
where            a.db_link = b.db_link(+) and
                 a.owner like upper('&own');
spool off
exit
```

Figure 5.37 Script for synonym report.

username is disconnected or its password changes, a node name changes it. It is good to be able to see what object synonyms will be affected.

Something to note about the report in Figure 5.38: The connect string specification for those synonyms using database links is not in the format we specified above. This report was taken from a VAX-VMS-based system. VAX-VMS allows specification of SYSTEM, GROUP, and PRIVATE logical symbols. In this case, the logicals DEVCON and CASECON take the place of the connect string and do in fact point to connect strings identical in format to that specified above.

5.2.7 Monitoring Database Links Using V$ and DBA_ Views

Database links provide connection paths to external databases. They specify protocol, user name, password, and connection string data. Database links can be either private, used by a single user, or public and accessible to all users. Database links can be used on the fly in queries or can be made invisible to the common user by use of synonyms. The DBA_DB_LINKS view is used to monitor them.

```
Date: 05/12/93              "Your Company Name"              Page:    1
Time: 05:35 PM                Synonym Report              OPS$NM91263
                              "Your" Database


OWNER         SYNONYM_NAME     Table                Link    USER        Conn
String
-----------   ---------------  ---------------      ------- ----------------------
-----------   -----------
OPS$NM91263   DEV_INSTANCE     DEV_DBA.INSTANCE     DEV     OPS$NM91263 d:devcon
OPS$NM91263   DEV_HIT_RATIOS   DEV_DBA.HIT_RATIO    DEV     OPS$NM91263 d:devcon
OPS$NM91263   KCGC_INSTANCE    KCGC_DBA.INSTANCE    KCGC    OPS$NM91263 d:casecon
OPS$NM91263   KCGC_HIT_RATIO   KCGC_DBA.HIT_RATIO   KCGC    OPS$NM91263 d:casecon
  .               .               .                   .       .           .
  .               .               .                   .       .           .
  .               .               .                   .       .           .
OPS$NM91263   CDI_MCUI         CASE.CDI_MCUI
OPS$NM91263   ENTITIES         CASE.ENTITIES
OPS$NM91263   CDI_MTUI         CASE.CDI_MTUI
OPS$NM91263   CDI_NET_CHDRN    CASE.CDI_NET_CHILDREN
OPS$NM91263   CDI_NET_PRNTS    CASE.CDI_NET_PARENTS
OPS$NM91263   CDI_SEQUENCES    CASE.CDI_SEQUENCES
OPS$NM91263   SDD_DATASTRS     CASE.SDD_DATASTORES
OPS$NM91263   SDD_DATAFLWS     CASE.SDD_DATAFLOWS
OPS$NM91263   SDD_COLUMNS      CASE.SDD_COLUMNS
```

Figure 5.38 Example of output from synonym script.

```
REM NAME          : DB_LINKS.SQL
REM PURPOSE       : GENERATE REPORT OF DATABASE LINKS
REM USE           : FROM SQLPLUS
REM Limitations   : None
REM Revisions:
REM Date          Modified By    Reason For change
REM 12/MAY/93     Mike Ault      Initial Creation
set pages 56 lines 130 verify off feedback off term off
start oracle$sql:title132 "Database Links Report"
spool db_links&db
column host format a60 heading "Connect String"
column owner format a15 heading "Creator"
```

Figure 5.39 Script to produce DB links report.

```
column db_link format a10 heading "Link Name"
column username format a15 heading "User"
column password format a15 heading "Password"
column create heading "Date Created"
select host, owner, db_link, username, password, created
   from dba_db_links;
exit
```

Figure 5.39 (continued)

```
Date: 05/12/93                "Your Company Name"              Page:   1
Time: 05:35 PM              Database Links Report              OPS$NM91263
                             "Your" Database


Connect String                          DB Link   Creator  Passwd    Date Created
-----------------------------------     --------- -------  --------  ------------
-
D:MMRD01"SQLNET SNET"::"TASK=ORDNKCGC"   CASECON   KC_DBA   CASE_DB   15-MAY-1993
D:MMRD15"SQLNET SNET"::"TASK=ORDNDEV"    DEVCON    KC_DBA   CASE_DB   10-APR-1993
D:MMR203"SQLNET SNET"::"TASK=ORDNDREC"   DLBDCON   KC_DBA   CASE_DB   10-MAY-1993
D:MMR203"SQLNET SNET"::"TASK=ORDNRREC"   DLBRCON   KC_DBA   CASE_DB   10-MAY-1993
D:MMR102"SQLNET SNET"::"TASK=ORDNLIMSA"  LIMSACON  KC_DBA   CASE_DB   12-MAY-1993
D:MMR102"SQLNET SNET"::"TASK=ORDNLIMSB"  LIMSBCON  KC_DBA   CASE_DB   12-MAY-1993
T:ELWOOD                                 ELCON     KC_DBA   CASE_DB   10-APR-1993
D:WINLIMS"WINNET WNET"::TASK=ORDNWINS"   WINCON    KC_DBA   CASE_DB   05-FEB-1993
```

Figure 5.40 Example of listing from DB link report script.

5.2.8 Monitoring Database Rollback Segments Using V$ and DBA_ Views

Rollback segments must be monitored. Their tablespace area is monitored through the free space and extents reports shown in previous sections. It would be good to have a report just for rollback segments to present rollback-related data in one convenient location. The script in Figure 5.41 (output in Figure 5.42) does this. The V$ROLLSTAT and V$WAITSTAT views are most important for monitoring rollback activity. The DBA_ view, DBA_ROLLBACK_SEGS is based on these two tables.

The parameters of concern to the DBA in the report shown in Figure 5.42 consist of location, status, and sizing data. The DBA needs to verify that no rollback segments have been created outside of the prescribed locations for rollback segments. In addition, the DBA should verify that all rollback segments that are supposed to be online are in fact online, and that those that are supposed to be offline, such as the second SYSTEM rollback segment used for maintenance, are offline. The overall size of the segments should be monitored in Oracle version 6 because there is no dynamic reallocation of the rollback space in version 6. So depending on the size of your transactions, the rollback segments should be periodically dropped and redefined. The type column in the report tells whether the rollback is a private (SYS) or public (PUBLIC) rollback segment.

```
rem   ************************************************************************
rem   NAME: DB_RBS.sql
rem   HISTORY:
rem   Date        Who                 What
rem   --------    ------------------  -------------------------------------------
rem   10/25/92    Cary Millsap        Creation
rem   01/07/93    Michael Brouillette Switched to title80
rem   05/15/93    Mike Ault           Added spool to file
rem                                   added sets
rem   FUNCTION: To report on database rollback segments.
rem   NOTES:
rem           The outer join (+) is needed on RBSNAMESTAT because there are only
rem           rows in RBSNAMESTAT for segments in DBA_ROLLBACK_SEGS with
rem           status='IN USE'. We want this report to list all rollback
rem           segments, regardless of status.
rem   ************************************************************************
set pages 56  lines 130  verify off  feedback off
start title132 "Database Rollback Segments"
col segment       format  a20        heading 'Segment Name'  justify c trunc
col status        format  a14        heading 'Status'        justify c
col tablespace    format  a20        heading 'Tablespace'    justify c trunc
col extents       format  9,990      heading 'Extents'       justify c
col rssize        format  9,999,999,990 heading 'Size|in Bytes' justify c
col owner         format  a6         heading 'Type'
spool rbs_rpt&db
select
  r.segment_name      segment,
  r.status            status,
  r.tablespace_name       tablespace,
  n.extents           extents,
  n.rssize            rssize,
  r.owner             owner
from
  sys.dba_rollback_segs  r,  aps_rollback_segs       n
where
  (r.segment_name = n.name(+))
order by  r.status, r.segment_name;
spool off
exit
```

Figure 5.41 SQL script to generate a rollback segment report.

```
Date: 05/20/93                  "Your Company Name"              Page:    1
Time: 11:10 AM              Database Rollback Segments           KCGC_DBA
                                 "Your" Database

                                                      Size
Segment Name    Status      Tablespace       Extents  in Bytes    Type
------------    ----------  ---------------  -------  ----------   ------
RBS2            AVAILABLE   SYSTEM                                 SYS
ROLLBACK_1      IN USE      CASE_ROLLBACK_SEGMENT  3   1,508,486   SYS
ROLLBACK_2      IN USE      CASE_ROLLBACK_SEGMENT  3   1,508,486   SYS
ROLLBACK_3      IN USE      CASE_ROLLBACK_SEGMENT  3   1,508,486   SYS
ROLLBACK_4      IN USE      CASE_ROLLBACK_SEGMENT  11  5,536,486   SYS
ROLLBACK_5      IN USE      CASE_ROLLBACK_SEGMENT  11  5,536,486   SYS
SYSTEM          IN USE      SYSTEM                 3   175,218     SYS
```

Figure 5.42 Example of rollback report output.

To identify what users are using which rollback segments, the script in Figure 5.43 should be run. The report generated (Figure 5.44) shows the Oracle process ID, the System process ID, and the rollback segment in use.

```
rem   Name      : TX_RBS.SQL
rem   Purpose   : Generate a report of active rollbacks
rem   Use       : From SQL*Plus
rem   History:
rem   Date       Who              What
rem   Sept 91    Lan Nguyen       Presented in paper at IOUG
rem              Walter Lindsey
rem   5/15/93    Mike Ault        Added Title80, sets and output
rem*********************************************************************************
column  name    format a20         heading "Rollback Segment Name"
column  pid     format 9999999999  heading "Oracle PID"
column  spid    format 9999999999  heading "Sys PID"
set pages 56   lines 130 verify off feedback off
start title132 "Rollback Segments in Use"
spool tx_rbs&db
select   r.name, l.pid, p.spid,
NVL(p.username, 'no transaction) "Transaction",
p.terminal "Terminal"
from  v$lock l, v$process p, v$rollname r
where l.pid = p.pid (+)
and    TRUNC(l.id1(+) / 65536) = r.usn and l.type(+) = 'TX' and l.lmode(+) = 6
order by r.name
spool off
exit
```

Figure 5.43 Example of SQL script to generate active rollback report.

```
Date: 05/20/93                   "Your Company Name"             Page:   1
Time: 10:44 AM                  Rollback Segments in Use         KCGC_DBA
                                   "Your" Database

Rollback Segment Name   Oracle PID    Sys PID    Transaction      Terminal
---------------------   ----------    ---------  -------------    ------------
ROLLBACK_1                                       no transaction
ROLLBACK_2                  23        2C401AE9    NM91498-T        FTA125-T
ROLLBACK_3                                       no transaction
ROLLBACK_4                                       no transaction
ROLLBACK_5                                       no transaction
SYSTEM                                           no transaction

6 rows selected.
```

Figure 5.44 Example of output from active rollback report.

```
rem*************************************************************
rem  Name          : UNDO.SQL
rem  Purpose        : Document rollback usage for a single transaction
rem  Use            : Note: You must alter the UNDO script and add a
rem                   call to the transaction at the indicated line
rem  Restrictions:  : The database should be placed in DBA mode and
rem                   these be the only transaction running.
rem  History:
rem   Date      Who              What
rem   Sept 91   Lan Nguyen       Presented in paper at IOUG
rem             Walter Lindsey
rem   5/15/93   Mike Ault        Changed to use one table
rem
set feedback off  termout off
column name format a40
define undo_overhead=54
drop table undo_data;
create table undo_data (tran_no number, start_writes number, end_writes number);
insert into undo_data
select 1, SUM(writes) from v$rollstat;
set feedback on  termout on
rem
rem    INSERT TRANSACTION HERE
rem
set feedback off  termout off
```

Figure 5.45 Script to generate total rollback bytes used in a transaction.

```
update undo_data end_writes = SUM(writes) from v$rollstat;
 where tran_no=1;
set feedback on termout on
select ((end-writes - start_writes) - &undo_overhead)
"Number of Rollback Bytes Generated"
from undo_data;
set termout off feedback off
drop table undo_data;
exit
```

Figure 5.45 (continued)

If the DBA has one transaction that he or she is concerned about as far as rollback usage is concerned. The script in Figure 5.45 can be run with the transaction in question executed in the indicated spot in the script. The data generated will tell the DBA the exact amount of rollback usage for the transaction. This data can then be used to create a custom rollback segment that can be brought online and used during that transaction. The script and test run of the transaction must be the only active transactions in the database when the test is run.

Under Oracle version 6 rollback segments were either online, available, offline, or inactive. The system automatically creates deferred rollbacks in the system tablespace when statements cannot be rolled back because the tablespace they refer to is offline or otherwise unavailable. If a DBA thinks this may have occurred, or wishes to find out if for some reason deferred rollbacks have been created and not dropped, the following script will report on any deferred rollbacks in the database.

```
SELECT segment_name, segment_type, tablespace_name
FROM    sys.dba_segments
WHERE segment_type = 'DEFERRED ROLLBACK';
```

Under Oracle version 6 if a rollback segment had active transactions, it could not be taken offline. Under ORACLE7, its status is changed to PENDING OFFLINE, and it is taken offline as soon as its pending transactions complete. The select statement shown above could be used to determine if any of these active transactions are in a deferred state. To determine if a rollback segment under ORACLE7 has outstanding transactions, the following select statement is used.

```
SELECT name, xacts 'ACTIVE TRANSACTIONS'
FROM    v$rollname, v$rollstat
WHERE  status = 'PENDING OFFLINE'
AND     v$rollname.usn = v$rollstat.usn;
```

Remember to be sure your database has a sufficient number of online rollback segments. If the ratio TRANSACTIONS/TRANSACTIONS_PER_ROLLBACK is exceeded, the system automatically brings online any available public rollback segments. If the only available rollback happens to be the maintenance segment in the system space, it is brought online and could cause havoc in the system tablespace as it extends to accommodate transactions.

5.2.9 Monitoring Redo Activity With V$ and DBA_ Views

The redo logs provide the information to redo entries into the database. These logs are kept in redo logs that are created as needed (see section 1.1.3) by the DBA. There should be at least three for a version 6 database. For an ORACLE7 database, redo logs are placed in log groups that have members that consist of individual log files. For ORACLE7 there should be mirrored groups of log files on separate drives. We will first look at monitoring version 6 logs, then at ORACLE7 and its new requirements.

In version 6 there are no groups or members, just logs. The number of logs is selected by the DBA and limited to the value of MAXLOGFILES specified in the database creation script. In version 6 there are no views that will allow the user to look at a log files data directly. Instead of direct views, we must look at statistics based on redo log and log writer process statistics. These views are the V$STATNAME, V$SESSION, V$PROCESS, V$SESSTAT, V$LATCH, and V$LATCHNAME. An example report that uses these views is shown in Figure 5.46. An example of the script's output is shown in Figure 5.47.

```
REM
REM NAME        : rdo_stat.sql
REM PURPOSE     : Show REDO latch statisitics
REM USE         : from SQLPlus
REM Limitations : Must have access to v_$ views
REM Revisions:
REM Date          Modified By    Reason For change
REM 20 May 93   Mike Ault      Initial creation
REM (From "Using SQL to ID DB Performance Bottlenecks"
REM  by Deepak Gupta and Sameer Patkar of Oracle Corp)
REM************************************************************************
set pages 56 lines 78 verify off feedback off termout off
start oracle$sql:title80 "Redo Latch Statistics"
spool rdo_stat&db
column name format a30
column percent format 999.999
select
                name,
                waits Total,
                immediates Successes,
                timeouts,
                100.*(timeouts/waits) Percent
from
sys.v_$latch l1, sys.v_$latchname l2
where
l1.latch#=l2.latch# and
l1.latch# in (11,12);
rem
start oracle$sql:title80 "Redo Log Statistics"
```

Figure 5.46 Script to generate report on redo statistics.

```
select
                n.name name,
                sum(st.value) value
from
sys.v_$sesstat st, sys.v_$statname n, sys.v_$session s, sys.v_$process p
where
                st.statistic# = n.statistic# and
                s.paddr = p.addr and
                p.pid = '5' and
                n.statistic# between 64 and 78
                group by n.name;
spool off
exit
```

Figure 5.46 (continued)

```
Date: 05/20/93                "Your Company Name"              Page: 1
Time: 12:51 PM               Redo Latch Statistics           KCGC_DBA
                               "Your" Database

NAME                   TOTAL          SUCCESSES      TIMEOUTS      PERCENT
-------------------    ----------     --------------  ------------  ----------
redo allocation        481621          481058         778            .162
redo copy                   3               0           3         100.000

Date: 05/20/93                "Your Company Name"              Page: 1
Time: 12:51 PM               Redo Log Statistics             KCGC_DBA
                               "Your" Database

NAME                           VALUE
----------------------------   --------
redo blocks written             174537
redo buffer allocation retries       5
redo chunk allocations             855
redo entries                      1044
redo entries linearized              0
redo log space requests              3
redo log space wait time             0
redo log switch interrupts           0
redo log switch wait failure         0
redo size                       211082
redo small copies                 1027
redo wastage                   1050943
redo write time                      0
redo writer latching time            0
redo writes                       7338
```

Figure 5.47 Example of output from redo report script.

The script in Figure 5.46 checks for a PID value of 5; if archiving is not being used, change this check to one for a value of 4. You might also notice that the report actually will generate two pages of output, one with redo latch data and one with redo statistics data. If desired, these two report sections could be split into separate SQL scripts and run individually.

Of course, right about now you are probably asking what good all these numbers do you. Let's look at what they mean and how you can use them. Actually, the first section of the report in Figure 5.47 is self-explanatory. There are two latches that the redo logs use, the REDO ALLOCATION latch and the REDO COPY latch.

In general, if the PERCENT statistic (actually the ratio of timeouts to waits) is greater than 10 percent contention is occurring, and the DBA needs to examine the way they are doing redo logs to figure out why. More about this in a second. You should notice that the REDO_COPY latch percent is 100. This is caused when there is contention for the REDO_COPY latch. This latch is granted to a user when the size of their entry is greater than the LOG_SMALL_ENTRY_MAX_SIZE parameter in the INIT.ORA file. If there is more than one user that requires this latch, you get contention. The number of REDO_COPY latches is limited to twice the number of CPUs on the system. If you have a single CPU, only one is allowed. It is normal to see high contention for this latch on single CPU systems, and there is nothing the DBA can do to increase the number of REDO_COPY latches. On multiple CPU systems, increase the number of REDO_COPY latches to twice the number of CPUs.

The DBA can also reduce contention for the REDO_COPY latch by forcing the redo entries to be prebuilt. This is accomplished by increasing the size of the INIT.ORA parameter LOG_ENTRY_PREBUILD_THRESHOLD (obsolete under ORACLE7). Unless your system has a fast CPU and good memory-to-memory copy algorithms, this value should remain at zero for single CPU systems. In order to use this parameter, the LOG_SIMULTANEOUS_COPIES needs to be set to a nonzero value.

In the second half of the report, statistics from the caches are shown that affect redo operations. Let's look at what these numbers are telling us. The most important of the listed statistics are "redo blocks written," "redo entries lineralized," "redo small copies," and "redo writes."

The "redo blocks written" statistic is useful when two entries are compared for a specified time period. This will indicate how much redo is generated for the period between the two checks.

"Redo entries lineralized" is useful only if LOG_ENTRY_PREBUILD_THRESHOLD and LOG_SIMULTANEOUS_COPIES parameters are set. This statistic tells the total number of entries that were prebuilt. Large values of this statistic in comparison to the "redo entries" statistic indicates effective prebuilding.

"Redo small copies" tells how many times the entry was effectively written on a "redo allocation" latch. This indicates a "redo copy" latch was not required for this entry. This statistic should be compared with the "redo entries" parameter. If there is close to a one-to-one relationship, then your system is making effective use of the "redo allocation" latch. If there is a large difference, then the LOG_SMALL_ENTRY_MAX_SIZE INIT.ORA parameter should be increased. If the LOG_SIMULTANEOUS_COPIES parameter is zero, this value is ignored.

The "redo writes" statistic is the total number of redo writes to the redo buffer. If this value is too large compared to the "redo entries" parameter value, then the DBA should tune the INIT.ORA parameters mentioned in the above sections to force prebuilding of the entries. If the entries are not prebuilt, the entry may require several writes to the buffer before it is fully entered; if it is prebuilt, it only requires one.

"Redo log space wait" is the statistic that tells you if users are having to wait for space in the redo buffer. If this value is nonzero, increase the size of the LOG_BUFFER in the INIT.ORA file.

"Redo buffer allocation retries" is the statistic that tells the DBA the number of repeated attempts to allocate space in the redo buffer. If this value is high in comparison to redo entries, it indicates that the redo logs may be too small and should be increased in size. Normally this value should be much less than the redo entries statistic. In the example it has a value of 5 compared to the entries value of 1044; this is satisfactory.

"Rcdo size" tells the total number of redo bytes generated for the time since the database was started. Comparison of two readings will give the amount generated over time. This value can then be used to determine if the log switch interval is proper. Too many log switches over a small amount of time can impair performance. Use the following formula to look at log switches over time:

```
(X / (dN / dt)) / interval of concern
```

Where:

X—the value of LOG_CHECKPOINT_INTERVAL or size of the redo log in system blocks.
dN—the change in the "redo size" over the time interval
dt—the time differential for the period (usually minutes)

Once the number of log switches is known, the DBA can use this value to determine size of redo logs based on system IO requirements. If you need to reduce the number of log switches, increase the redo log size. Of course, this may impact system availability since it takes longer to write out a large redo log buffer to disk than a small one. A balance must be struck between undersizing the redo logs and taking a database performance hit or making the logs too large and taking an IO hit.

5.2.10 Monitoring Clusters Using DBA_ and V_$ Views

Clusters can be indexed, as in Oracle version 6, or indexed or hashed in ORACLE7. Using the various views and tables available to the DBA they can be readily monitored. The DBA_CLUSTERS, DBA_CLU_COLUMNS, and DBA_TABLES views are utilized to monitor clusters in version 6. A script for generating a cluster report is shown in Figure 5.48 (output in Figure 5.49).

```
rem
rem File:       CLU_REP.SQL
rem Purpose:    Document Cluster Data
rem Use:        From user with access to DBA_ views
rem
rem When        Who          What
rem ------      ----         ------
rem 5/27/93     Mike Ault    Initial Creation
```

Figure 5.48 Example script to produce a cluster report. (continued)

```
rem
column owner format a10
column cluster_name format a15 heading "Cluster"
column tablespace_name format a20 heading "Tablespace"
column table_name format a20 heading "Table"
column tab_column_name format a20 heading "Table Column"
column clu_column_name format a20 heading "Cluster Column"
set pages 56 lines 130 feedback off
start title132 "Cluster Report"
break on owner skip 1on cluster on tablespace
spool cluster&db
select a.owner,a.cluster_name,tablespace_name,
            table_name,tab_column_name,clu_column_name
            from dba_clusters a,dba_clu_columns b
where
            a.owner = b.owner and
            a.cluster_name=b.cluster_name
order by 1,2,3,4
/
spool off
exit
```

Figure 5.48 (continued)

```
Date: 05/26/93               "Your Company Name"              Page:   1
Time: 09:17 PM                 Cluster Report                 KCGC_DBA
                              "Your" Database


OWNER      Cluster          Tablespace      Table      Table Column    Cluster Column
--------- --------------- --------------- ------- ------------- --------------
SYS        C_COBJ#          SYSTEM          CCOL$      OBJ#            OBJ#
                                            CDEF$      OBJ#            OBJ#
           C_FILE#_BLOCK#                   SEG$       BLOCK#          SEGBLOCK#
                                            SEG$       FILE#           SEGFILE#
                                            UET$       SEGFILE#        SEGFILE#
                                            UET$       SEGBLOCK#       SEGBLOCK#
           C_OBJ#                           CLU$       OBJ#            OBJ#
                                            COL$       OBJ#            OBJ#
                                            ICOL$      BO#             OBJ#
                                            IND$       BO#             OBJ#
                                            TAB$       OBJ#            OBJ#
           C_TS#                            FET$       TS#             TS#
                                            TS$        TS#             TS#
           C_USER#                          TSQ$       USER#           USER#
                                            USER$      USER#           USER#
```

Figure 5.49 Example of output from cluster report.

As a DBA you may be interested in the storage statistics used to create each cluster. This data is found in the DBA_CLUSTERS view. The script in Figure 5.50 is an example of this type of report. An example of the script's output is shown in Figure 5.51.

The reports in Figures 5.49 and 5.51 give the DBA information on cluster keys, cluster columns, cluster tables and columns, and cluster sizing. Combined with the actual size and extent reports previously shown, the DBA can have a complete picture of clusters in his or her database.

Under ORACLE7 the view DBA_CLUSTERS view has several additional columns. These additional columns provide a more detailed glimpse of cluster status. The additional columns in the DBA_CLUSTERS view are AVG_BLOCKS_PER_KEY, CLUSTER_TYPE, FUNCTION, and HASHKEYS. The above report script can either be modified to include these columns (since 132 is about the widest you can go, not a good choice) or a new report can be created. An example of this report is shown in Figure 5.52 (output in Figure 5.53).

```
rem
rem File:      CLU_SIZ.SQL
rem Purpose:   Document Cluster Space
rem Use:       From user with access to DBA_ views
rem
rem When       Who          What
rem ------     ----         ------
rem 5/27/93    Mike Ault    \Initial Creation
rem
column owner format a10
column cluster_name format a15 heading "Cluster"
column tablespace_name format a10 heading "Tablespace"
column pct_free format 999999 heading "% Free"
column pct_used format 999999 heading "% Used"
column key_size format 999999 heading "Key Size"
column ini_trans format 999 heading "IT"
column max_trans format 999999 heading "MT"
column initial_extent format 999999999 heading "Initial Ext"
column next_extent format 999999999 heading "Next Ext"
column max_extents format 9999 heading "Max Ext"
column pct_increase format 9999 heading "% Inc"
set pages 56 lines 130 feedback off
start oracle$sql:title132 "Cluster Sizing Report"
break on owner skip 1 on tablespace_name
spool cluster_size&db
select owner,cluster_name,tablespace_name,
          pct_free,pct_used,key_size,ini_trans,max_trans,
          initial_extent, next_extent, min_extents, max_extents,
   pct_increase
from dba_clusters
order by 1,3
/
spool off
exit
```

Figure 5.50 Example script to produce a cluster sizing report.

```
Date: 05/26/93                    "Your Company Name"              Page:    1
Time: 09:57 PM                    Cluster Sizing Report            KCGC_DBA
                                    "Your" Database
```

OWNER	Cluster	Tablespace %	Free %	Used	Key Size	IT	MT	Initial Ext	Next Ext	Min Ex	Max Ext	% Inc
SYS	C_COBJ#	SYSTEM	50		300	2	255	51200	10240	1	99	50
	C_FILE#_BLOCK#		10	40	225	2	255	20480	10240	1	99	50
	C_OBJ#		5	40	800	2	255	122880	10240	1	99	50
	C_TS#		10	40		2	255	10240	10240	1	99	50
	C_USER#		10	40	315	2	255	10240	10240	1	99	50

Figure 5.51 Example of output of the cluster sizing report.

```
rem Name:        clu_typ.sql
rem Purpose:     Report on new DBA_CLUSTER columns
rem Use:         From an account that accesses DBA_ views
rem
rem   When        Who             What
rem   --------    --------        ------------------
rem   5/26/93     Mike Ault       Initial Creation
rem
column owner format a10 heading "Owner"
column cluster_name format a15 heading "Cluster"
column tablespace_name format a10 heading "Tablespace"
column avg_blocks_per_key format 999999 heading "Blocks per Key"
column cluster_type format a8 Heading "Type"
column function format 999999 heading "Function"
column hashkeys format 99999 heading "# of Keys"
set pages 56 lines 79 feedback off
start title80 "Cluster Type Report"
spool cluster_type&db
select owner,cluster_name,tablespace_name,
            avg_blocks_per_key, cluster_type, function,
            hashkeys
from dba_clusters
order by 2
/
spool off
exit
```

Figure 5.52 Report script for new ORACLE7 DBA_CLUSTERS columns.

```
Date: 06/12/93                "Your Company Name"              Page:   1
Time: 12:15 PM              Cluster Statistics Report          DEV7_DBA
                              "Your" Database

Owner  Cluster Name        Tablespace     Blk/Key   Type     Function   # of Keys
------  ----------------    -------------  --------  -------  ---------  -----------
-
SYS    C_COBJ#             SYSTEM         INDEX
       C_FILE#_BLOCK#
       C_MLOG#
       C_OBJ#
       C_TS#
       C_USER#
       HIST$
```

Figure 5.53 Example of output from cluster statistics report script.

5.2.11 Monitoring of Snapshots and Snapshot Logs Using DBA_ and V_$ Type Views

Snapshots and snapshot logs are strictly ORACLE7 features. These allow read-only copies of a table or columns from multiple tables to be maintained in several locations. The refresh rate of the snapshots can be varied and accomplished automatically. The DBA needs tools to monitor snapshots and snapshot logs. It is more convenient at times to have a hard copy listing documenting snapshots and snapshot logs. The scripts in Figures 5.54 (output in Figure 5.55) and 5.56 document a database's snapshots and snapshot logs.

```
rem
rem Name:      snap_rep.sql
rem Purpose:   Report on database Snapshots
rem Use:       From an account that accesses DBA_ views
rem
rem   When        Who          What
rem   --------    --------     ------------------
rem   5/27/93     Mike Ault     Initial Creation
rem
set pages 56 lines 130 feedback off
rem
column owner format a10 heading "Owner"
column snapshot format a30 heading "Snapshot"
```

Figure 5.54 Example script to document snapshots.   (continued)

```
column source format a30 heading "Source Table"
column link format a20 heading "Link"
column log heading "Use Log?"
column refreshed heading "Refreshed?"
column error format a20 heading "Error?"
column type format a10 heading "Refresh Type"
column refreshed heading "Last Refresh"
column start format a13 heading "Start Refresh"
column error heading "Error"
column type heading "Type Refresh"
column next format a13 heading "Next Refresh"
rem
start oracle$sql:title132 "Snapshot Report"
spool snap_rep&db
rem
select owner, name||'.'||table_name Snapshot, master_view,
              master_owner||'.'||master Source, master_link Link,
              can_use_log Log, last_refresh Refreshed, start_with start,
              error, type , next,
              start_with Started, query
from dba_snapshots
order by 1,3,5;
rem
spool off
exit
```

Figure 5.54 (continued)

```
Date: 06/10/93                        "Your  Company Name "                   Page:   1
Time: 04:28 PM                         Snapshot Report                       DEV7_DBA
                                       "Your Database"


Owner     Snapshot        VIEW     Source Table  Link Log  Last Ref   Start Ref  R Type  Next Ref    STARTED    QUERY
DEV7_DBA  TEST.SNAP$_TEST  MVIEW$_  DEV7_DBA.     YES       10-JUN-93  10-JUN-93  FAST    SYSDATE+7   10-JUN-93  SELECT CHECK_DATE
                           TEST     HIT_RATIOS                                                                  FROM   HIT_RATIOS
```

Figure 5.55 Example of output of the script in Figure 5.54.

The reports from Figures 5.54 and 5.56 will provide the DBA with hard copy documentation of all snapshots and snapshot logs in the database. With use of "where" clauses each can be made more restrictive by selecting on a specific set of values such as owner or log_owner, type, or date since last refresh (last_refresh > &date —or— current_snapshots > &date).

```
rem
rem Name:      snap_log_rep.sql
rem Purpose:   Report on database Snapshot Logs
rem Use:       From an account that accesses DBA_ views
rem
rem   When       Who          What
rem   --------    --------      ------------------
rem   5/27/93    Mike Ault     Initial Creation
rem
set pages 56 lines 130 feedback off
start title132 "Snapshot Log Report"
spool snap_log_rep&db
rem
column log_owner format a10 heading "Owner"
column master format a20 heading "Master"
column log_table format a20 heading "Snapshot"
column trigger format a20 heading "Trigger Text"
column current heading "Last Refresh"
rem
select log_owner, master, log_table table,
          log_trigger trigger, current_snapshots current
from dba_snapshot_logs
order by 1;
rem
spool off
exit
```

Figure 5.56 Example script to generate snapshot log report.

The DBA may find these references of interest when planning to do monitoring activities:

ORACLE RDBMS Performance Tuning Guide, Version 6.0, PART# 5317-V6.0 Feb. 1990, Oracle Corp.

ORACLE RDBMS Database Administrator's Guide, Version 6.0, PART# 3601-V6.0 Oct. 1990, Oracle Corp.

ORACLE7 Server Administrator's Guide, PART# 6694-70-1292, Dec. 1992, Oracle Corp.

Using Oracle Tools to Administer Oracle Databases (ODMS v2.0), Olesen, T., UC Davis, 1991 IOUG Proceedings, Paper #270.

*SQL*DBA Monitor, A Powerful Tool for the Database Administrator*, Fardoost, M., Oracle Corp. 1991 IOUG Proceedings, Paper #520.

Dynamic Performance Tables in Version 6, Walsh, K.R., Oracle Corp., 1991 IOUG Proceedings. Paper #523.

An Internal Look at Rollback Segments, Nguyen, L., Lindsay, W., Oracle Corp., 1991 IOUG Proceedings, Paper #537.

Surviving With ORACLE V6.0 in a UNIX Environment, Jambu, A.A., Colonial Mutual Investment Management, 1992 IOUG Proccedings, Paper #30.

Tuning Oracle Databases

In a previously used analogy, the Oracle relational database management system (RDBMS) has been compared to an operating system that overlays the existing VMS or UNIX operating system. The Oracle RDBMS handles its own buffering, caching, and file management within pseudo-disks known as tablespaces. All of these internal Oracle functions can add or detract from performance. Oracle provides numerous tuning options to optimize these functions under both version 6 and ORACLE7.

Under version 6 the *ORACLE RDBMS Performance Tuning Guide, Version 6* provides guidelines to tuning the various functions within Oracle. Under ORACLE7 Chapters 20 to 24 in Part VII of the *ORACLE7 Server Administrator's Guide* provides insight into the various aspects of tuning ORACLE7 databases. In most cases the tuning that applies to version 6 will also apply to ORACLE7. Where differences exist, this book will try to point them out.

Tuning of Oracle is a two-part process, in which the old 80/20 rule applies. This rule states that 80 percent of the gains will be accomplished through 20 percent of the work. With Oracle, this 20 percent corresponds to the first part of the process. The first part of the process is application tuning.

Eighty percent of your performance gains will be accomplished through proper application tuning. In one situation, involving the script in Figure 5.22, altering the select order and the where clause improved the query response time severalfold. Imagine what performance gains can be made over an entire application?

The remaining 20 percent of the performance gains can be realized through tuning the processes that make up the Oracle system. Reducing disk, memory, and IO contention and improving sort and checkpoint speed will all improve performance. Of course, if all of these functions are really out of tune, database performance may show more than a 20 percent gain. In general, the 20 percent gain is a good rule of thumb.

6.1 Application Tuning

Application tuning is a severalfold concept. It involves both the design (logical as well as physical) and execution of an application. Depending on how your company's organization is laid out, you may or may not have any control over application development. In the case where you have no control, try to show management the value you can add by providing application tuning skills to the developers. It is strongly suggested that each developer attend the application tuning class provided by Oracle Corporation for the release of Oracle you are using. If they cannot be sent to training, see if you can sponsor a workshop where the application tuning concepts can be presented to the developers.

Application tuning involves several steps:

1. Proper logical design

    a. Normalization of data
    b. Denormalization of selected tables for performance

2. Proper physical layout of application areas

    a. Placement of tables in multiple tablespaces
    b. Placement of indexes away from tables
    c. Placement of other database objects

3. Tuning of application statements

    a. Determination of index requirements
    b. Proper use, and nonuse, of indexes
    c. Query tuning — the use of TKPROF and EXPLAIN PLAN

4. Application processing scheduling

    a. Concurrent processes
    b. Batch jobs

Let's examine each of these areas.

6.1.1 Proper Logical Design

Normalization. Take a minute and review the introduction section: A Brief Discussion of Relational Jargon. Specifically pay attention to the normalization rules. Following these rules will lead to a proper *logical* design. Simply stated, a fully normalized design is one in which all attributes for a specific entity's relate to and only to the entity's unique identifier. To say this in laymen's terms, they relate to the whole key and nothing but the key.

Denormalization. Sometimes, for performance of special reports or frequently run important queries, it may be desirous to denormalize a table or tables in your design. Denormalization is the process by which columns from multiple tables are combined into a single table to speed queries on the data contained in those columns. In cases where the data from two or more tables is accessed repeatedly for reports or special queries, denormalization will speed access. It may be better to cluster the tables rather than denormalize. This will depend on how often the tables are to have update or insert activity.

Denormalization will involve redundant storage of database information. If denormalization is used, be sure that your application performs updates to all of the data storage locations. The major problems with denormalized data are update, delete, and insert anomalies. In version 6, this will have to be performed on a procedure-by-procedure, form-by-form process.

In ORACLE7, the use of database-stored triggers is suggested to handle the possible storage problems. Build stored triggers for each redundant field so that an update, delete, or insert activity must affect all values in the database.

One very powerful tool that can assist developers and DBAs in checking logical design is a good CASE (computer-aided software engineering) tool. Since we are dealing with Oracle, it is suggested that the Oracle CASE tool set be used. The Oracle CASE system has both design— CASE*DICTIONARY and CASE*DESIGNER—and implementation—CASE*GENERATOR for FORMS, MENUS, and REPORTS—of database applications. The dictionary and design tools provide numerous reports to allow the cross-checking of designs for possible problems.

6.1.2 Proper Physical Design

Physical design involves the physical design of the tables themselves. In this area you as the DBA are concerned with the table, index, and cluster, and sizing and storage parameters. Let's look at these issues and attempt to give you some guidelines in their proper use.

Sizing. Use of the sizing formulas provided in the various subsections of Chapter 2 should provide you with detailed sizing data for the database objects. Be sure that you have sized the tables for at least a year's worth of activity (unless, of course, the application's expected lifetime is less than a year). If the amount of storage used is not of prime consideration, oversizing is better than undersizing. Whenever possible you don't want dynamic space extension in database objects.

Dynamic space extension is the process by which a database object grows past its initial settings. If the database objects have been created too small, this can result in the Swiss-cheese-type of tablespace fragmentation that is very detrimental to performance. You want as few a number of extensions per table as possible. The report in Figure 4.13 for version 6 or the report in Figure 4.15 for ORACLE7 will give you information on extents for existing objects and help pinpoint those with excessive extents. This is where a test database can be helpful.

Use of a Test Database. A small test database should be created and loaded with test data that is representative of what you expect the data in the real database to look like. In order to get good sizing estimates, you should load at least 10 percent of the data you expect in the final database into the test database. Run the various sizing reports, and check the database objects for dynamic extension. Once you are satisfied that the best sizing parameters have been used, ratio up the sizing parameters for your production installation. This involves deriving the ratio of how much data is expected in the actual table against how much was loaded into the test database table. This number is then applied to the sizing numbers from the test database.

Key Sizing Parameters. The INITIAL, NEXT, and PCTINCREASE values are the key sizing parameters. If you are dealing with legacy systems where a great deal of existing data is to be loaded, make the INITIAL extent large enough to handle this existing data *plus a year's worth* of additional data. Make the NEXT parameter big enough to deal with an additional year's worth of expected entries for the table. If you aren't sure how much the data entry requirements will be that far in the future, perform a SWAG (scientific wild-assed guess) and use the PCTINCREASE parameter to take up the slop. Remember, the PCTINCREASE is an incrementally applied value. The first extent added after the extent that uses the NEXT parameter will be (1 + pctincrease/100) times larger than the NEXT parameter; the next extent after that one will be another (1 + pctincrease/100) times larger and so on. If you alter the PCTINCREASE on an existing table with n multiple extents, this factor will be carried through ((1 + pctincrease/100) raised to the nth power times). (So, if you have 10 extents and alter the pctincrease up from 10 to 20, the 11th extent will be 1.2 [11] or 7.43 times larger than the value specified in the NEXT parameter.) For tables or objects with numerous extents, this factor can be substantial. Since the multiplier is calculated based on number of extents and not just applied to the next extent to be created, the DBA must consider this when setting or resetting the PCTINCREASE parameter. In one case a table had 90 extents; the factor was raised from 0 percent to 50 percent, and the next extent the database tried to create was over a *gigabyte*. Obviously, it didn't work.

The actual value for the INITIAL and NEXT extent values should be carefully calculated to allow as close as possible to an even number of entries per extent for the table. For some fixed-length entries this is easy; for entries that vary in length, it will require a careful determination of the average row length. Again, the scripts in Figures 5.16 and 5.18 can be helpful if there is an existing database. If not, the calculations in Chapter 3 will be useful. To facilitate the DBWR and other processes—and make extent reuse easier—some experts say to make table extents a standard size. Most feel this wastes more space than it saves.

Table Placement. Read the section in Chapter 1 concerning the optimal flexible architecture (OFA). If these principles are applied, file placement can be easily accomplished. Generally speaking, you want to distribute an Oracle database across as many drives as possible. Ideally one table per tablespace and one tablespace per drive would give the ultimate in performance. Of course few if any of us can afford such an extensive disk array as would be required in this scenario, nor would any of us wish to manage this complex of an environment. The next best thing is to spread the disk IO across available platters as evenly as possible.

High-volume, high-activity files should be placed in their own tablespaces on their own platters if possible. Low-volume, low-activity tables, such as static lookup tables, can be placed together in a single tablespace, preferably away from the high-volume tables. Other database tables such as redo logs, rollback segments, and system tablespaces should be placed to reduce disk contention and maximize dependability and recoverability. A few rules of thumb are

1. Place redo logs and archive files on separate platters.

   - Since one is a backup to the other, this only makes sense.

2. Place redo logs and rollback segments on different platters.

   - Both of these tend to be high activity; separation reduces disk contention.

3. Separate the system tablespace from other application tablespaces if possible.

   - The system tablespace is called by all others; separation reduces contention.

4. Run exports to a separate drive from archive logs.

   - These provide two of the three legs of recovery: archives, exports, and system backups. Separation of each from the others improves recoverability.

5. Place archive logs away from active disks, preferably on their own platter.

    •   These files can be large and numerous. If there isn't adequate space to store these
        archive files, the database will stop.

Table Striping. As DBA you will also make decisions regarding striping of tables. Large tables
may exceed the storage capacity of a single disk. In other cases, it may be desirous to place a table
across several disks to optimize performance. This can be accomplished in the following manner:

1. Determine the size of each table fragment. It is suggested that each be the same size.
2. Create a tablespace that has data files spread across the platters. The data files should
    each be sized to hold one table fragment.

```
CREATE TABLESPACE ACCOUNT_SPREAD
DATAFILE 'm_ora_disk1:[m_oracle.db_example]account_file1.dbs' SIZE 500M REUSE,
DATAFILE 'm_ora_disk2:[m_oracle.db_example]account_file2.dbs' SIZE 500M REUSE,
DATAFILE 'm_ora_disk3:[m_oracle.db_example]account_file3.dbs' SIZE 500M REUSE
ONLINE;
```

3. Create the table in the tablespace from step 2 with X initial extents, each close to the
    same size as the data files from step 2 (you need to allow for overhead).

```
CREATE TABLE accounts(acct_no number CONSTRAINT pk_acct PRIMARY KEY,
    acct_name varchar2 CONSTRAINT nn_act_name NOT NULL,
    acct_size number,
    acct_desc varchar)
PCTFREE 5 PCTUSED 90
TABLESPACE ACCOUNT_SPREAD
STORAGE (INITIAL 495M NEXT 495M
    MINEXTENTS 3 MAXEXTENTS 3
    PCTINCREASE 0)
```

4. Load the data into the table, either using SQL loader or IMPORT.

If you choose to spread a table in this manner, attempt to sort the data before is loaded. If the
data is already loaded into existing tables, use a query to load the data that presorts the records. If
the data is in flat files or in another database, attempt to use operating system utilities or existing
database reporting capabilities to sort the data. This will improve the accessibility of the data to
your users once it is loaded into the spread data table.

6.1.3 Tuning of Application Query Statements

Tuning of application queries is a complex topic. Such factors as index use, index nonuse, order of
query where clauses, and Oracle optimizer settings can all effect query performance. In addition,
the number of data dictionary caches and database buffers also affect query performance as does the
sort area size. As an example, look at the two queries in Figure 6.1.

```
Query 1:
SELECT C.OWNER, C.TABLE_NAME, C.CONSTRAINT_NAME,
CC.COLUMN_NAME, R.TABLE_NAME REF_TABLE,
RC.COLUMN_NAME REF_COLUMN
FROM DBA_CONSTRAINTS C, DBA_CONSTRAINTS R, DBA_CONS_COLUMNS CC, DBA_CONS_COLUMNS RC
WHERE C.R_CONSTRAINT_NAME = R.CONSTRAINT_NAME
AND C.R_OWNER = R.OWNER AND C.CONSTRAINT_NAME = CC.CONSTRAINT_NAME
AND C.OWNER = CC.OWNER AND R.CONSTRAINT_NAME = RC.CONSTRAINT_NAME
AND R.OWNER = RC.OWNER AND CC.POSITION = RC.POSITION
AND C.CONSTRAINT_TYPE = 'R' AND C.OWNER <> 'SYS'
AND C.OWNER <> 'SYSTEM'
ORDER BY C.OWNER, C.TABLE_NAME, C.CONSTRAINT_NAME, CC.POSITION

query 2:
SELECT C.OWNER, C.TABLE_NAME, C.CONSTRAINT_NAME,
CC.COLUMN_NAME, R.TABLE_NAME REF_TABLE,
RC.COLUMN_NAME REF_COLUMN
FROM DBA_CONSTRAINTS C, DBA_CONSTRAINTS R, DBA_CONS_COLUMNS CC, DBA_CONS_COLUMNS RC
WHERE C.CONSTRAINT_TYPE = 'R'
AND C.OWNER NOT IN ('SYS','SYSTEM')
AND C.R_OWNER = R.OWNER
and C.R_CONSTRAINT_NAME = R.CONSTRAINT_NAME
AND C.CONSTRAINT_NAME = CC.CONSTRAINT_NAME
AND C.OWNER = CC.OWNER
AND R.CONSTRAINT_NAME = RC.CONSTRAINT_NAME
AND R.OWNER = RC.OWNER
AND CC.POSITION = RC.POSITION
ORDER BY C.OWNER, C.TABLE_NAME, C.CONSTRAINT_NAME, CC.POSITION
```

Figure 6.1 Example queries.

Both of the queries are complex queries against views. Both of the queries retrieve the same information from the database. Close examination reveals that the only difference between them is the order of the where clause columns. Figure 6.2 shows the results of analyzing the above queries with the TKPROF tool. As you can see, the second query performs better. This is due to placing the most restrictive columns first, thus reducing the volume of subsequent merges and sorts. Unfortunately a query against views that are not owned by the user running TKPROF cannot be run through EXPLAIN PLAN, so since the queries involve views from multiple owners, an explain plan output was not available.

As you can see, the rearrangement of the where clause has reduced the cpu, elap, phys, and cr statistics for both the parse and execute phases of the query processing. The improvements in these areas far outweigh the slight increase in fetch statistics.

```
TKPROF from Query 1:
         count  cpu    elap  phys  cr     cur   rows    count = number of times OPI
                                                                procedure was
Parse:   1      33     50    8     54     0     executed
Execute: 1      2715   3274  710   86720  2     0       cpu = cpu time executing in
                                                              hundreths of seconds
Fetch:   18     2      4     0     0      0     260     elap = elapsed time executing
                                                               in hundreths of seconds
TKPROF from Query 2:                                    phys = number of physical
                                                               reads from disk
         count  cpu    elap  phys  cr     cur   rows    cr = number of buffers
                                                             gotten for consistent
Parse:   1      11     18    1     16     0     read
Execute: 1      2652   2782  293   86716  2     0       cur = number of buffers
                                                              gotten in current mode
Fetch:   18     5      6     0     0      0     260     rows = number of rows
                                                               processed by OPI call
```

Figure 6.2 TKPROF results from queries in Figure 6.1.

To use the TKPROF tool the TIMED_STATISTICS parameter in the INIT.ORA file must be set to TRUE. To limit the size of the generated trace file, set the INIT.ORA parameter MAX_DUMP_FILE_SIZE to the desired file size limit. If you want the files to be created in other than the ORA_INSTANCE, ORA_TRACE, or the ORACLE$HOME directory, set the USER_DUMP_DEST to the desired file location. In order for these parameters to take effect, the instance has to be shut down and restarted. Once testing is finished, reset the TIMED_STATISTIC parameter to FALSE or there will be a performance hit due to continuous statistics collection.

Setting TIMED_STATISTICS to TRUE will allow individual users to set the SQL_TRACE value for their process to TRUE, which will then generate a trace file in the ORA_TRACE or selected directory. The users should then execute the statements from within SQLPLUS. To enable the trace facility while using SQL*FORMS, issue the RUNFORM command using the -S option. To use the trace facility in SQL*Plus, the ALTER SESSION command is used, for example:

```
ALTER SESSION SET SQL_TRACE TRUE;
```

Use of TKPROF. Once the SQL statements or forms have been run, exit SQLPLUS or the forms-based application, and look for the proper trace file that corresponds to the PID of the process that generated it. For example, if the database is testb, the PID in Oracle is 5, and the program being run is SQLPLUS, the trace file will be SQLPLUS_F30_TESTB_005.TRC. If you try to look at this file without processing through TKPROF, you will receive little benefit. TKPROF formats the trace files into a user-readable form. The format of the TKPROF command follows.

```
TKPROF tracefile outputfile
    [SORT = sort option --or-- (sort option, sort option,...)]
    [EXPLAIN = user/password]
```

The EXPLAIN Option of TKPROF. To use the EXPLAIN option, a user must have resource privilege on a tablespace so the needed tables can be created. The command is issued at the operating system level. To split the command on multiple lines in VMS, place a dash at the end of each line. For UNIX you simply place a "/" (backslash) character at the end of the line to be continued.

The above command will generate a file named whatever you specified the output file to be. If you include the SORT qualifier, the output will be sorted accordingly. If you include the EXPLAIN qualifier, a temporary table will be created in the user's default tablespace, and the various SQL statements will be "explained" in accordance with the formats of the explain plan command.

TKPROF Sort Option. The SORT option of TKPROF has the following possible arguments:

PRSCNT—Number of times parsed.
PRSCPU—The amount of time the CPU spent parsing.
PRSELA—The elapsed time spent parsing.
PRSPHR—The number of disk accesses during the parse.
PRSCR—The number of consistent mode block reads during the parse step.
PRSCU—The number of current mode block reads during the parse.
EXECNT—The number of executes performed.
EXECPU—The amount of time the CPU spent executing.
EXEELA—The amount of time spent executing.
EXEPHR—The number of disk accesses during execution.
EXECR—The number of consistent mode block reads during the execute step.
EXECU—The number of current mode block reads during the execute step.
EXEROW—The number of rows processed during execute.
FCHCNT—The number of fetches.
FCHCPU—The amount of time the CPU spent fetching.
FCHELA—The amount of time spent fetching.
FCHPHR—The number of disk accesses during the fetches.
FCHCR—The number of current mode block reads during the fetches.
FCHCU—The number of current mode block reads during the fetches.
FCHROW—The number of rows fetched.

TKPROF Statistics. Each line of statistics will correspond to either the parse, execute, or fetch part of the query operation. These parts of a query are defined as:

Parse—The query is translated into an execution plan. If the user doesn't have the proper security or table authorization, or the objects in the query don't exist, this step will catch it as well.
Execute—The execution plan is executed against the RDBMS.
Fetch—n this final step, all rows that satisfy the query are retrieved from the database.

For each step the following parameters are traced:

count—This is the number of times this step was repeated.
cpu—This is the total cpu time for the step in hundredths of a second.
elap—This is the total elapsed time for the step in hundredths of a second.
phys—This is the total number of database blocks read from disk for the step. In ORACLE7 this column is called *disk*.
cr—This is the number of buffers retrieved in a consistent read mode. In ORACLE7 this column is called *query*.

cur—This is the number of buffers retrieved in current mode. In ORACLE7 this column is called *current*.

rows—This is the number of rows processed during the SQL statement execution step.

TKPROF Examples. Let's look at some example outputs from the TKPROF using EXPLAIN. The descriptions for tables being used for these examples are shown in Figure 6.3.

```
DESC TKP_EXAMPLE
Name                            Null?       Type
------------------------------  --------    ----
USERNAME                        NOT NULL    CHAR(30)
USER_ID                         NOT NULL    NUMBER
PASSWORD                                    CHAR(30)
CONNECT_PRIV                    NOT NULL    NUMBER
RESOURCE_PRIV                   NOT NULL    NUMBER
DBA_PRIV                        NOT NULL    NUMBER
DEFAULT_TABLESPACE              NOT NULL    CHAR(30)
TEMPORARY_TABLESPACE            NOT NULL    CHAR(30)
CREATED                         NOT NULL    DATE
EXPIRES                                     DATE

DESC TKP_EXAMPLE2
Name                            Null?       Type
------------------------------  --------    ----
OWNER                           NOT NULL    CHAR(30)
TABLE_NAME                      NOT NULL    CHAR(30)
TABLESPACE_NAME                 NOT NULL    CHAR(30)
```

Figure 6.3 Structures of tables used in TKPROF examples.

In the first examples, let's look at the TKPROF output from some queries using these tables without having indexes. Of course, what we expect is that the RDBMS will do full table scans no matter how complex the query. Remember one thing: It isn't always a bad move to do a full table scan. It depends entirely on the selectivity of your query. If you are only returning a few rows, index use is advised. The old rule of thumb is if your query returns less than 10 percent to 15 percent of rows in the table, use an index. The select statement in Figure 6.4 is a two-table join, stripping out system tables, of the two tables in Figure 6.3. Experienced system managers will recognize these tables as a copy of portions of the DBA_USERS and the DBA_TABLES views. They were created using the CREATE TABLE command with the AS clause.

As you can see, the performance isn't as bad as we thought it might be. Even with stripping out the hundred or so system tables, there were still 300 rows returned. As we expected, the query performed two full table scans. But what are MERGE JOIN, SORT(JOIN), and so on? These are part of the execution plan that the parse step generated. In addition to the information presented in Figure 6.4, ORACLE7's TKPROF also provides the number of misses in the library cache during the parse step and adds a ROWS column to the query plan. Let's look at the possible outputs from the EXPLAIN portion of the TKPROF output.

```
select
            username,
            default_tablespace,
            tablespace_name,
            table_name
from
            tkp_example,
            tkp_example2
where
            USERNAME != 'SYS' AND
            USERNAME != 'SYSTEM' AND
            DEFAULT_tablespace = tablespace_NAME AND
            OWNER = USERNAME

          count   cpu    elap   phys    cr    cur    rows
Parse:      1      1      0      0      0      0
Execute:    1      4      8      5      8      2      0
Fetch:     21      8      8      0      3      2     300

Execution plan:
MERGE JOIN
  SORT (JOIN)
    TABLE ACCESS (FULL) OF 'TKP_EXAMPLE2'
  SORT (JOIN)
    TABLE ACCESS (FULL) OF 'TKP_EXAMPLE'
```

Figure 6.4 Query against example tables with no indexes.

ACTION	WHAT IT MEANS
AND-EQUAL	If the where clause contains references to unique indexed columns only, the system will choose to use the ROWIDs from the indexes to perform the table intersections. This is faster than a full-table-scan-type of intersection.
CONNECT-BY	This only shows up in queries that use a connect clause. When a CONNECT-BY is executed, it forces a tree-walk of the table structure to perform the operation.
CONCATENATION	This is a full union of two or more tables. With small tables, it won't hurt; with large tables, it can kill you.

(continued)

ACTION	WHAT IT MEANS
COUNTING	This action happens if the query uses the COUNT aggregate to return the number of rows.
FILTER	This is a process by which rows not meeting the selection criteria are removed from the returned set of values.
FIRST ROW	This shows that only the first row of a query was returned; this shows activity with a cursor.
FOR UPDATE	This shows the query operation involved a possible update situation (such as in a form or SELECT....FOR UPDATE). This indicates that the rows involved were write locked during the operation.
INDEX (UNIQUE—or—RANGE SCAN)	This action shows that a query used and index to resolve the needed values. The UNIQUE qualifier shows that the index was scanned for specific unique values. The RANGE qualifier shows that a specific range of values was searched such as that specified in a BETWEEN or less-than–greater-than construct.
INTERSECTION	This shows that the query retrieved the rows from the tables in the query that were common to each of the tables based on the conditions in the where clause. The rows are sorted.
MERGE JOIN (OUTER)	This shows that two sorted sets of operations were joined to resolve the query. The OUTER qualifier shows that an outer join was performed.
MINUS	This shows that an INTERSECTION-type operation was performed, but instead of similar rows being returned, only rows that didn't match the specified criteria where returned.
NESTED LOOPS (OUTER)	This shows that for each of the first child operation, one or more of the other child operations that follow it were performed. If the OUTER qualifier is present, it signifies that an outer join was performed between the results.
PROJECTION	This shows that a subset of a table's columns was returned.
REMOTE	This shows that a retrieval from other than the current database was performed to resolve the query.

ACTION	WHAT IT MEANS
SEQUENCE	This shows that a sequence was accessed during a query.
SORT (UNIQUE GROUP BY JOIN ORDER BY)	This shows a query used one of the ordering clauses; the type of clause will be listed as a qualifier.
TABLE ACCESS (BY ROWID FULL CLUSTER)	This shows that a table access was performed. Some queries can be resolved by an INDEX scan only. The type of access performed is showed by the included qualifier. ROWID is generally the fastest form of table access and shows an index scan was also used.
UNION	This shows that a retrieval of unique rows from each table was performed with the duplicates removed from the output.
VIEW	This shows the query accessed a view to resolve the query.

Additional ORACLE7 operations:

AGGREGATE—This shows the use of a grouping function such as MAX, MIN, and so on.
INDEX (RANGE SCAN DESCENDING)—This shows retrieval of one or more ROWIDs
    from an index scanned in descending order (normal scan is ascending).
TABLE ACCESS (HASH)—This shows the retrieval of a value based on the value of a hash
    cluster.

Let's look at this first query's EXPLAIN output in light of the above.
Execution plan:

MERGE JOIN—This shows that the results from the following operations are merged.
SORT (JOIN)—This shows that the results are sorted before being passed to the MERGE
    TABLE ACCESS (FULL) OF 'TKP_EXAMPLE2'—This indicates the full table was
    scanned.
SORT (JOIN)—This shows that the results are sorted before being passed to the MERGE.
TABLE ACCESS (FULL) OF 'TKP_EXAMPLE'—This indicates the full table was scanned.

So what does this tell us? First, both tables were fully scanned to retrieve the rows that met the where clause's criteria. Next, the results from each were sorted. Finally, the results were merged based on the selection criteria. Can these results be improved on for this type of query? Let's add some indexes (listed in Figure 6.5) and find out.

The attempt has been made to ensure the indexes have high selectivity and that columns most accessed in the tables are the leading portion of one or more indexes. Let's reissue the select in Figure 6.4 and see what happens.

```
SQL> CREATE UNIQUE INDEX TKP_EXP_INDEX
  2  ON TKP_EXAMPLE(
                   USERNAME,
                   DEFAULT_TABLESPACE,
                   TEMPORARY_TABLESPACE);
SQL> CREATE UNIQUE INDEX TKP_EXP_INDEX2
  2  ON TKP_EXAMPLE(
                   TEMPORARY_TABLESPACE,
                   USERNAME,
                   DEFAULT_TABLESPACE);
SQL> CREATE UNIQUE INDEX TKP_EXP_INDEX3
  2  ON TKP_EXAMPLE(
                   DEFAULT_TABLESPACE,
                   TEMPORARY_TABLESPACE,
                   USERNAME);
SQL> CREATE UNIQUE INDEX TKP_EXP2_INDEX ON
  2  TKP_EXAMPLE2(
                   OWNER,
                   TABLE_NAME);
SQL> CREATE UNIQUE INDEX TKP_EXP2_INDEX2 ON
  2  TKP_EXAMPLE2(
                   OWNER,
                   TABLESPACE_NAME,
                   TABLE_NAME);
SQL> CREATE UNIQUE INDEX TKP_EXP2_INDEX3 ON
  2  TKP_EXAMPLE2(
                   TABLESPACE_NAME,
                   OWNER,
                   TABLE_NAME);
```

Figure 6.5 Indexes added to tables from Figure 6.3.

As you can see, the indexes didn't improve performance. In fact, they made performance worse. A key indicator that something is wrong is that the cr parameter jumped by several orders of magnitude. This is an example of a query that returns more than 15 percent of a table. How can we restore performance? If we use the NOT or LIKE clause instead of the comparison operators ("!=", "="), are indexes used? Let's look at the same query with the NOT clause replacing the "!=" in the select statement. Figure 6.6 shows the TKPROF results from this query. Did performance improve? No, in fact, the results are almost identical even down to the execution plan. NOT and "!=" are treated identically. Figures 6.7 and 6.8 show the results of other substitutions.

```
select
                username,
                default_tablespace,
                tablespace_name,
                table_name
from
                tkp_example,
                tkp_example2
where
                USERNAME != 'SYS' AND
                USERNAME != 'SYSTEM' AND
                DEFAULT_tablespace = tablespace_NAME AND
                OWNER = USERNAME

          count   cpu    elap    phys    cr      cur    rows
Parse:      2      1      0       0       0       0
Execute:    2      4      8       5       8       4       0
Fetch:     42     44     42       5    1228       2     600

Execution plan:
NESTED LOOPS
   TABLE ACCESS (FULL) OF 'TKP_EXAMPLE2'
   INDEX (RANGE SCAN) OF 'TKP_EXP_INDEX' (UNIQUE)
```

Figure 6.6 The results on the query from Figure 6.3 of indexes.

```
select
                username, default_tablespace,
                tablespace_name, table_name
from
                tkp_example,
                tkp_example2
where
                USERNAME NOT IN ('SYS','SYSTEM') AND
                DEFAULT_tablespace = tablespace_NAME and
                OWNER = USERNAME

          count   cpu    elap    phys    cr      cur    rows
Parse:      2      2      0       0       0       0
Execute:    2      4      6       4       8       4       0
Fetch:     42     47     42       7    1228       2     600

Execution plan:
NESTED LOOPS
   TABLE ACCESS (FULL) OF 'TKP_EXAMPLE2'
   INDEX (RANGE SCAN) OF 'TKP_EXP_INDEX' (UNIQUE)
```

Figure 6.7 Results of replacing the != with a NOT IN.

```
SELECT
                 USERNAME,
                 DEFAULT_TABLESPACE,
                 TABLESPACE_NAME,
                 TABLE_NAME
FROM
                 TKP_EXAMPLE,
                 TKP_EXAMPLE2
WHERE
                 USERNAME NOT IN ('SYS','SYSTEM') AND
                 DEFAULT_TABLESPACE LIKE TABLESPACE_NAME AND
                 OWNER LIKE USERNAME

          count    cpu   elap   phys    cr    cur   rows
Parse:        1      1      2      0     0      0
Execute:      1      0      0      0     0      2      0
Fetch:       21     45     50      8  1236      0    300

Execution plan:
NESTED LOOPS
  TABLE ACCESS (FULL) OF 'TKP_EXAMPLE2'
  INDEX (RANGE SCAN) OF 'TKP_EXP_INDEX3' (UNIQUE)
```

Figure 6.8 Results of replacing the = with LIKE.

Why are the results the same? In this query the controlling table will be TKP_EXAMPLE2. The NOT doesn't affect the TKP_EXAMPLE2 table, which was already using a full table scan. Let's replace the "=" operator with a LIKE statement and see what happens (Figure 6.8).

Even by replacing the "=" with LIKE, we have not forced full table scans. Performance still isn't as good as with the original nonindexed tables. The index scanned was changed from TKP_EXP_INDEX to TKP_EXP_INDEX3. The performance is still poor because for each row of the TKP_EXAMPLE2 table, there is a scan of the TKP_EXP_INDEX3 index, with the scans rejecting tables owned by SYS and SYSTEM. Notice that the number of fetch steps were cut in half.

To achieve the results from the first query, supposedly we can defeat the use of indexes by adding a zero to a number column or concatenating a null to a character column. Let's look at this and see if we can get back to the performance we want to achieve.

As can be seen in Figure 6.9, the index was still used. Look at the last section of the where clause. The order compares OWNER to USERNAME. This causes the TKP_EXAMPLE2 table to drive the query. If we switch the order of this comparison, we can use the shorter table TKP_EXAMPLE instead of TKP_EXAMPLE2. The index is still used, but the shorter table significantly reduces the query execution time (see Figure 6.10).

As you can see, performance is back to the levels we had before we created the indexes. Did the use of null concatenation really affect performance for this query? Leaving the where clause the same, let's go back to the standard comparison and see if the results change (see Figure 6.11).

```
SELECT
                USERNAME,
                DEFAULT_TABLESPACE,
                TABLESPACE_NAME, TABLE_NAME
FROM
                TKP_EXAMPLE, TKP_EXAMPLE2
WHERE
                USERNAME NOT IN ('SYS','SYSTEM') AND
                DEFAULT_TABLESPACE||''= TABLESPACE_NAME AND
                OWNER||''= USERNAME

          count    cpu   elap   phys    cr    cur   rows
Parse:       1       1      2      0     0      0
Execute:     1       0      0      0     0      2        0
Fetch:      21      41     48      8  1225      0      300

Execution plan:
NESTED LOOPS
   TABLE ACCESS (FULL) OF 'TKP_EXAMPLE2'
   INDEX (RANGE SCAN) OF 'TKP_EXP_INDEX' (UNIQUE)
```

Figure 6.9 Use of null concatenation to defeat indexes.

```
SELECT
                USERNAME,
                DEFAULT_TABLESPACE,
                TABLESPACE_NAME,
                TABLE_NAME
FROM
                TKP_EXAMPLE,
                TKP_EXAMPLE2
WHERE
                USERNAME NOT IN ('SYS', 'SYSTEM') AND
                DEFAULT_TABLESPACE||''= TABLESPACE_NAME AND
                USERNAME||''= OWNER

          count    cpu   elap   phys    cr    cur   rows
Parse:       1       1      0      0     0      0
Execute:     1       0      0      0     0      2        0
Fetch:      21      11     12      0   201      0      300

Execution plan:
NESTED LOOPS
   TABLE ACCESS (FULL) OF 'TKP_EXAMPLE'
   INDEX (RANGE SCAN) OF 'TKP_EXP2_INDEX2' (UNIQUE)
```

Figure 6.10 Results of switching the where order.

```
SELECT
                USERNAME,
                DEFAULT_TABLESPACE,
                TABLESPACE_NAME,
                TABLE_NAME
FROM
                TKP_EXAMPLE,
                TKP_EXAMPLE2
WHERE
                USERNAME NOT IN ('SYS', 'SYSTEM') AND
                DEFAULT_TABLESPACE = TABLESPACE_NAME AND
                USERNAME = OWNER

          count    cpu    elap    phys    cr    cur    rows
Parse:        1      1       0       0     0      0
Execute:      1      0       0       0     0      2       0
Fetch:       21     46      68       8  1225      0     300

Execution plan:
NESTED LOOPS
   TABLE ACCESS (FULL) OF 'TKP_EXAMPLE2'
   INDEX (RANGE SCAN) OF 'TKP_EXP_INDEX3' (UNIQUE)
```

Figure 6.11 Effects of the switched where clause and no null concatenation.

```
select
                username,
                default_tablespace,
                tablespace_name,
                table_name
from
                tkp_example,
                tkp_example2
where
                USERNAME = 'DLBB_DBA' AND
                DEFAULT_TABLESPACE = TABLESPACE_NAME and
                OWNER = USERNAME

          count    cpu    elap    phys    cr    cur    rows
Parse:        1      1       0       0     0      0
Execute:      1      8      30       8     8      2       0
Fetch:        1      5       4       0     3      2      12

Execution plan:
MERGE JOIN
   SORT (JOIN)
     TABLE ACCESS (FULL) OF 'TKP_EXAMPLE2'
   SORT (JOIN)
     TABLE ACCESS (FULL) OF 'TKP_EXAMPLE'
```

Figure 6.12 Restricted query with full table scans (no indexes).

As can be seen, the results look virtually identical to those we had before we switched the where clause. So, for this type of statement it would be best to defeat as many indexes as possible and force execution driven by the shortest table. Again, this underscores the need to understand the application, the size and use of its tables, and how its indexes are constructed. If the DBA doesn't understand the application, the tuning of the application should be the developer's job with the DBA assisting.

When do indexes do us any good? If the query returns a small percent of the table values, an index will improve performance. An example of a restricted query with no index is shown in Figure 6.12. Figure 6.13 shows the same query using indexes.

```
select
                username,
                default_tablespace,
                tablespace_name,
                table_name
from
                tkp_example,
                tkp_example2
where
                USERNAME = 'DLBB_DBA' AND
                DEFAULT_TABLESPACE = TABLESPACE_NAME AND
                OWNER = USERNAME

            count   cpu   elap   phys    cr    cur   rows
Parse:          1     1      0      0      0      0
Execute:        1     0      0      0      0      0      0
Fetch:          1     0      0      0      5      0     12

Execution plan:
NESTED LOOPS
   INDEX (RANGE SCAN) OF 'TKP_EXP_INDEX' (UNIQUE)
   INDEX (RANGE SCAN) OF 'TKP_EXP2_INDEX2' (UNIQUE)
```

Figure 6.13 Same query as in 6.12, but using indexes.

As you can see, the performance gains, even for these small tables, is rather large, especially in the execute step. An additional indicator of problems with a query is a high cr to rows ratio. A rule of thumb is if this ratio exceeds 15, the query needs tuning.

So, what have we learned? First off, statement tuning is complex. The optimizer built in to the SQL processor makes choices based on built in optimization rules that are based on statement rank in version 6, or on cost under ORACLE7. At times this optimizer doesn't always use the right index or truly optimize the statement.

For unrestricted queries that return most if not all of the values in a table or group of tables, use methods to restrict the use of indexes as much as possible. With unrestricted queries start the where clause by restricting the values to be retrieved as much as possible, as rapidly as possible. Try to get full table scans on small tables first and use their results to search other tables.

There is some debate as to whether making the small table the controlling table really improves performance. If the small table can be completely cached in memory, it may make more sense to drive from the larger table since multiblock reads can then be used rather than random reads, which may reread the same block several times. This would have the effect of reducing time-consuming physical block reads for the query. Since this will be application and index controlled, in situations were this happens, use TKPROF to find out the facts before simply following a possibly outmoded rule.

Indexing Guidelines. For restricted queries that retrieve a small percent of the table's entries, create indexes that will assist the query. The guidelines for indexing columns follow.
Index columns that:

- are used frequently in where clauses.
- are used frequently in MIN or MAX selects.
- are used to join tables.
- have high selectivity.

Remember—You can concatenate two low-selectivity columns to form a higher-selectivity index than either column has singly.
Don't index:

- columns that don't have high selectivity.
- columns in small tables (less than five blocks).
- columns that are frequently modified.

Remember, you never get something **for nothing**. The more indexes you have, the longer inserts, updates, and deletes will take. Optimizing queries doesn't gain you much if you pay a stiff penalty for update activity.

Concatenated indexes are only used when the predicate value is equality (i.e., e.jobname = f.jobname). The full key is only used if all the concatenated values are referenced in the where clause. If the concatenated key is used, it makes little difference in what order the columns are referenced since the structure is a B-tree structure.

It would be wonderful if the rules for optimizing your tables, indexes, and queries could be simply stated and listed and you could be guaranteed that if they were followed your application would run as you hope. Unfortunately, this is not the case. Just when we think we have the proper cast on optimization, Oracle will release a new version that throws a monkey wrench into our logic and makes us start again. You as a DBA will have to keep abreast of changes to Oracle and filter the new ways of optimization down to the developers.

Query Paths and Ranks. The paths a query can take are ranked according to speed. The lower the rank, the higher the speed. The paths for version 6 follow.

RANK	PATH
1	ROWID = constant
2	unique column = constant
3	entire unique concatenated index = constant

RANK	PATH
4	entire cluster key = corresponding cluster key in another table in the same cluster
5	entire cluster key = constant
6	entire non-unique concatenated index = constant
7	nonunique index = constant
8	entire concatenated index = lower bound
9	most leading concatenated index specified
10	unique indexed column between low value and high value, or unique indexed column LIKE 'C%' (bounded query)
11	nonunique indexed column between low value and high value or nonunique indexed column LIKE 'C%' (bounded query)
12	unique indexed column or constant (unbounded range)
13	nonunique indexed column or constant (unbounded range)
14	sort/merge (joins only)
15	MAX or MIN of single indexed column
16	ORDER BY entire index
17	full-table scans
18	unindexed column = constant or column IS NULL, or column LIKE '%C%' (full table scan)

These ranks are used in rules-based optimization in version 6. The revised list used in ORACLE7 follows.

RANK	PATH
1	single row by ROWID
2	single row by cluster join
3	single row by hash cluster key with unique or primary key
4	single row by unique or primary key
5	cluster join
6	hash cluster key
7	indexed cluster key
8	composite Index
9	single-column index

(continued)

RANK	PATH
10	bounded range search on indexed columns
11	unbounded range search on indexed columns
12	sort-merge join
13	MAX or MIN on indexed column
14	ORDER BY indexed columns
15	full-table scan

ORACLE7 Optimization. Under ORACLE7 the optimizer uses cost-based optimization and can be forced to use rules-based optimization. Cost-based optimization assigns a cost to each possible execution path based on data distribution statistics for the objects used in the SQL statement being optimized. These statistics are loaded into the various object tables and views using the ANALYZE command.

Use of ANALYZE. This indicates that for various applications this ANALYZE command must be run on a periodic nature, perhaps based on table growth. In systems using similar schemes the analyzer had to be run for each 30 percent change in a table's contents. Note that this is for a change in contents—not just size. If a table has a fairly constant size, but its contained data is being altered frequently thus affecting the row size and index structure, then ANALYZE needs to be run on it as well. A simple script can be built using dynamic SQL that will analyze all the tables for a specific user. The script will resemble Figure 6.14.

```
rem
rem name          : ANLYZIT.SQL
rem purpose       : Build analyze script and run it for a user's tables
rem use           : Gather statistics for cost based optimization
rem limitations   : None
rem revisions:
rem Date:    Who:        What:
rem 6/10/93  Mike Ault   Initial Creation
rem
set lines 80 pages 0 heading off feedback off echo off
prompt Creating analyze script for tables
set termout off
spool analyze.sql
select 'analyze table '||table_name||' compute statistics;' from user_tables;
spool off
set termout on
prompt Analyzing all tables for user
start analyze
exit
```

Figure 6.14 Script to automatically analyze a user's tables.

The DBA needs to watch the growth of the main tables in an application. The reports shown in section 4 should provide the needed data. If the DBA isn't using an automated script like the one in Figure 6.14, once the required threshold for percent change is reached, the ANALYZE command should be run. The ANALYZE command format follows.

```
ANALYZE TABLE [schema.]table COMPUTE--or--ESTIMATE
   --or-- INDEX [schema.]index
   --or-- CLUSTER [schema.]schema
```

(for estimate) SAMPLE n ROWS —or— PERCENT

```
STATISTICS ;
```

Where:

COMPUTE—Calculates statistics on all rows. This may take a long period of time.

ESTIMATE—Calculates statistics based on the SAMPLE clause. If you don't specify the number of ROWS or a value for PERCENT, 1064 rows are sampled. If over 50 percent of the table is specified, the entire table is computed.

The results are loaded into the SYS tables and can be examined via the DBA_, USER_, or ALL_ views. For an excellent discussion of how ORACLE7 uses cost-based optimization, look at Chapter 13 of the *ORACLE7 Server Concepts Manual.*

Other Application Tuning Tips. There are other things an application tuner can use to boost performance. The best tips follow.

- Use PL/SQL to speed processing. A PL/SQL statement is parsed once and allows loop processing. This reduces reparsing. The statements in a PL/SQL block are passed at the same time, reducing the number of RDBMS calls.
- Use sequence generators. Sequence numbers are cached, speeding access to numbers used for keys or in applications for tracking entries. This eliminates the SQL calls used in a trigger that calls up the current MAX value and then increments it by 1.
- Use clusters for frequently joined tables. However, if the tables are frequently updated clustering can have a negative effect on performance. Use the TKPROF tool to check a test database that is clustered versus one that is not clustered.
- Use array processing in applications were multiple values are required. This will reduce RDBMS calls.

Use of Standalone EXPLAIN PLAN. The EXPLAIN PLAN program can be used in standalone fashion without the TKPROF application. In order to use EXPLAIN PLAN in this way, the user must create a "PLAN" table in their tablespace. This can either be done with the supplied SQL script XPLAINPL.SQL, which is located in the directory pointed at by the ORA_RDBMS logical in VMS, or in the oracle/rdbms/admin directory on most UNIX systems. Under ORACLE7 the script has been renamed to UTLXPLAIN.SQL.

The XPLAINPL.SQL procedure creates the PLAN_TABLE. As an alternative, the user can create a table with any name they choose, but the table must have the columns and data types shown in Figure 6.15.

```
Characteristics of file to hold EXPLAIN PLAN output:

Column                    Column Data Type
statement_id              char(30)
timestamp                 date
remarks                   char(80)
operation                 char(30)
options                   char(30)
object_node               char(30)
object_owner              char(30)
object_name               char(30)
object_instance           numeric
object_type               char(30)
search_columns            numeric
id                        numeric
parent_id                 numeric
position                  numeric
other                     long
```

Figure 6.15 Columns and data types for the EXPLAIN PLAN output table.

When TKPROF is run using the EXPLAIN option, the table is created and dropped automatically. If it is created for use in EXPLAIN PLAN, it is permanent. The table should have the DELETE command issued against it between runs of EXPLAIN PLAN, or duplicate rows will be inserted into the table and into any output generated based on the table.

The columns from Figure 6.15 are defined as follows:

COLUMN	DESCRIPTION
Statement_id	The value of the descriptor for the SQL statement (see command syntax that follows).
Timestamp	Date and time statement was analyzed.
Remarks	A comment that is associated with this row of the table. This comment is added via an UPDATE to the table to modify the row.
Operation	One of the operations listed previously. For ORACLE7 the first row will describe the overall type for the statement, this will be DELETE STATEMENT, INSERT STATEMENT, SELECT STATEMENT, or UPDATE STATEMENT.
Options	Any options (FULL, OUTER, JOIN, etc.) to the operation.
Object_node	The database link used to access external data sources.
Object_owner	The owner of the object accessed in the command.
Object_name	Name of the database object accessed by the command.

COLUMN	DESCRIPTION
Object_instance	The sequential order that the object appeared in the statement. For views this is unpredictable.
Object_type	Descriptive information about the object, such as UNIQUE for an index.
Search_columns	Not used in version 6.
ID	A number assigned for the step in the execution plan.
Parent_id	The ID of the step that uses the output of this step.
Position	Order for sub-steps within a parent ID. For ORACLE7 the value for the first row of a SQL statement's plan will contain the cost of the statement, if rules based processing was used, it will be null.
Other	Miscellaneous information such as the text of a SQL statement sent to a remote node in a subquery.

Once this table is generated, the user issues the EXPLAIN PLAN command from within SQLPLUS to generate output to the table. The EXPLAIN PLAN command format follows.

```
EXPLAIN PLAN [SET STATEMENT_ID = 'descriptor']
   [INTO table]
FOR SQL statement;
```

Where:

descriptor—This is a short name to identify the SQL statement by. If not specified, the entire statement will be used as the identifier.

table—If other than the PLAN_TABLE is used, this is where it is named.

SQL statement—This is the SQL statement to analyze.

An example of the use of the EXPLAIN PLAN command is shown in Figure 6.16.

```
SQL> EXPLAIN PLAN
  2  SET STATEMENT_ID = 'EXP PLAN EXAMPLE'
  3  FOR
  4  select t.owner,t.table_name,t.tablespace_name,
  5  i.index_name, i.tablespace_name
  6  from TKP_EXAMPLE t, TKP_EXAMPLE2 i
  7  where
  8  t.table_name = i.table_name and
  9* t.owner not in ('SYS','SYSTEM')
Explained.
```

Figure 6.16 Example of use of the EXPLAIN PLAN command.

To get the results of the EXPLAIN PLAN command, the table PLAN_TABLE, or whatever table was specified in the EXPLAIN PLAN command, must be queried. Let's look at a simple query of this table for the above SQL statement. The query and output from the query are shown in Figure 6.17. While this type of query will provide useful information, it leaves the logical arrangement of the information retrieved to the user. With use of the padding options and connect features available in SQL, the user can generate a pseudo-execution plan comparable to the one generated in the TKPROF command. The query used for this and the output generated in place of the tabular information in Figure 6.17, is shown in Figure 6.18.

This new format shown in Figure 6.18 is easier to understand. The TKPROF output for each statement also needs to be reviewed as was shown in the first part of this chapter. Just because index rather than table scans are used it doesn't mean the query executed faster.

```
SQL> COLUMN POSITION FORMAT 99999999
SQL> COLUMN OBJECT_NAME FORMAT A12
SQL> COLUMN OPTIONS FORMAT A7
SQL> COLUMN OPERATION FORMAT A15
SQL> SELECT OPERATION, OPTIONS, OBJECT_NAME, ID, PARENT_ID, POSITION
  2   FROM PLAN_TABLE
  3   WHERE STATEMENT_ID='EXP PLAN EXAMPLE'
  4*  ORDER BY ID
```

OPERATION	OPTIONS	OBJECT_NAME	ID	PARENT_ID	POSITION
MERGE	JOIN		1		
SORT	JOIN		2	1	1
TABLE ACCESS	FULL	TKP_EXAMPLE2	3	2	1
SORT	JOIN		4	1	2
TABLE ACCESS	FULL	TKP_EXAMPLE	5	4	1

```
5 rows selected.
```

Figure 6.17 Example of query of the PLAN_TABLE.

```
SQL> COLUMN QUERY_PLAN FORMAT A60
SQL> SELECT LPAD(' ',2*LEVEL)||OPERATION||' '||OBJECT_NAME QUERY_PLAN
  2   FROM PLAN_TABLE WHERE STATEMENT_ID IS NOT NULL
  3   CONNECT BY PRIOR ID = PARENT_ID
  4*  START WITH ID=1
QUERY_PLAN
------------------------------------------------------------
  MERGE JOIN
    SORT
      TABLE ACCESS TKP_EXAMPLE2
    SORT
      TABLE ACCESS TKP_EXAMPLE
```

Figure 6.18 SQL statement to generate an execution plan from the PLAN_TABLE.

One thing to remember is that these plans need to be read from the bottom up. For example, in the plan in Figure 6.18, the TKP_EXAMPLE table is accessed, and all rows that don't have the OWNER SYS or SYSTEM are retrieved. Then, the TKP_EXAMPLE2 table is accessed for each row in the TKP_EXAMPLE table and all rows that have matches in the TABLE_NAME column are selected. The results for both accesses are then sorted and merged to form the final output.

Use of the IDXSTAT Utility. Another tuning tool provided with Oracle is the IDXSTAT utility. This utility consists of three scripts, IDXSTAT.SQL, ONEIDXS.SQL, and DIPIDXS.SQL under version 6, and UTLSIDXS.SQL, UTLOIDXS,SQL, and UTLDIDXS.SQL under ORACLE7. These scripts are located in the directory specified in the ORA_RDBMS logical under VMS and in the oracle/rdbms/admin directory on most UNIX systems. These scripts provide detailed statistics on indexes used for a specific table.

The scripts provide the following functionality:

IDXSTAT.SQL—This script starts the ONEIDXS.SQL script on multiple tables and columns. It requires the input of the table name and the column name. Its main use is to provide the selectivity information on key candidates.

ONEIDXS.SQL—This script is called by IDXSTAT.SQL

DISPIDXS.SQL—This script is run after ONEIDXS.SQL (IDXSTAT.SQL) is run. It takes the same arguments as IDXSTAT.SQL and can take % as a wild card value. DIPIDXS.SQL generates a report based on the statistics. The report is only shown on screen; to have hard copy output you must modify the script to add SPOOL and SPOOL OFF statements.

To use the scripts, the tables and columns must exist. The scripts are used on single column indexes, generally speaking. To run the scripts on a concatenated index, create a test table that consists of a single column that simulates the concatenated index as a single column. For example, if your index is on po_num, po_date create a test table that concatenates these into a single column:

```
CREATE TABLE test_index AS SELECT po_num||po_date po_ind FROM
purchase_order;
```

Once the test table is created, the script is run the same as for if the user where analyzing a normal single column index candidate. This is essentially a three-step process:

1. Choose the candidate columns from the table.
2. Logon to SQLPLUS and run IDXSTAT.SQL for entire applications and ONEIDXS.SQL for single tables, giving it the table and column name.
3. Use DISPIDXS.SQL to generate a report on the index candidate(s).

An example run of IDXSTAT, including a sample DISPIDXS report is shown in Figure 6.19

As you can see from examining the DISPIDXS reports in Figure 6.19, OWNER would not make a very good index. It has a low selectivity and its db_gets_per_key_hits is 50 percent lower than its db_gets_per_key_misses, which means it misses a row twice as much as it finds it. This is further witnessed by its high badness of 143 and low keys_count where the badness is low (badness ratings are summarized by the number of keys that exhibit that amount of badness). On the other hand, TABLE_NAME makes a good index because of its high selectivity, its nearly unity hit/miss ratio, and its low badness ratings, but how often will we look for a table strictly by its name? What would the performance be if we made a concatenated index of both OWNER and TABLE_NAME? Let's find out (see Figure 6.20).

```
SQL> @IDXSTAT TKP_EXAMPLE OWNER
TKP_EXAMPLE OWNER
SQL> @DISPIDXS TKP_EXAMPLE OWNER

TAB_NAME                              COL_NAME
----------------------------         ----------------------------
TKP_EXAMPLE                           OWNER
TABLE_NAME        COLUMN_NAME        STAT_NAME                   STAT_VALUE
-------------     -------------      ----------------------      -----------
TKP_EXAMPLE       OWNER              Rows - Null                       0.00
TKP_EXAMPLE       OWNER              Rows - Total                    398.00
TKP_EXAMPLE       OWNER              Rows per key - avg               36.18
TKP_EXAMPLE       OWNER              Rows per key - dev               43.95
TKP_EXAMPLE       OWNER              Rows per key - max              143.00
TKP_EXAMPLE       OWNER              Rows per key - min                1.00
TKP_EXAMPLE       OWNER              Total Distinct Keys              11.00
TKP_EXAMPLE       OWNER              db_gets_per_key_hit              42.65
TKP_EXAMPLE       OWNER              db_gets_per_key_miss             84.72

TABLE_NAME       COLUMN_NAME    BADNESS    KEYS_COUNT    ROW_PERCENT    KEY_PERCENT
-------------    ------------   ---------  -----------   ------------   ------------
TKP_EXAMPLE      OWNER          143        1             35.93          9.09
TKP_EXAMPLE      OWNER          70         1             17.59          9.09
TKP_EXAMPLE      OWNER          65         1             16.33          9.09
TKP_EXAMPLE      OWNER          4          2             2.01           18.18
TKP_EXAMPLE      OWNER          1          1             0.25           9.09
SQL> @ONEIDXS TKP_EXAMPLE TABLE_NAME
TKP_EXAMPLE          TABLE_NAME
SQL> @DISPIDXS TKP_EXAMPLE TABLE_NAME
TAB_NAME          COL_NAME
----------------------------      ----------------------------

TKP_EXAMPLE                       OWNER
TABLE_NAME        COLUMN_NAME     STAT_NAME                   STAT_VALUE
-------------     -------------   ----------------------      -----------
TKP_EXAMPLE       TABLE_NAME      Rows - Null                       0.00
TKP_EXAMPLE       TABLE_NAME      Rows - Total                    398.00
TKP_EXAMPLE       TABLE_NAME      Rows per key - avg                1.01
TKP_EXAMPLE       TABLE_NAME      Rows per key - dev                0.10
TKP_EXAMPLE       TABLE_NAME      Rows per key - max                2.00
TKP_EXAMPLE       TABLE_NAME      Rows per key - min                1.00
TKP_EXAMPLE       TABLE_NAME      Total Distinct Keys             394.00
TKP_EXAMPLE       TABLE_NAME      db_gets_per_key_hit               1.00
TKP_EXAMPLE       TABLE_NAME      db_gets_per_key_miss              1.02

TABLE_NAME       COLUMN_NAME    BADNESS    KEYS_COUNT    ROW_PERCENT    KEY_PERCENT
-------------    ------------   ---------  -----------   ------------   ------------
TKP_EXAMPLE      TABLE_NAME     2          4             2.01           1.02
TKP_EXAMPLE      TABLE_NAME     1          390           97.99          98.99
```

Figure 6.19 Example of use of INDXSTAT, ONEIDXS, DISPIDXS.

```
SQL> REM     TEST_INDEX is a table made by selecting "owner||table_name"  into
SQL> REM     the column TEST_COL. The column values are selected from
SQL> REM     TKP_EXAMPLE. It demonstrates the performance of a concatenated index
SQL> REM     on these two columns.
SQL>
SQL> @ONEIDXS TEST_INDEX TEST_COL

TEST_INDEX   TEST_COL
SQL> @DISPIDXS TEST_INDEX TEST_COL

TAB_NAME                         COL_NAME
----------------------------     -----------------------------
TEST_INDEX      TEST_COL
TABLE_NAME      COLUMN_NAME      STAT_NAME               STAT_VALUE
-------------   -------------    ---------------------   -----------
TEST_INDEX      TEST_COL         Rows - Null                   0.00
TEST_INDEX      TEST_COL         Rows - Total                398.00
TEST_INDEX      TEST_COL         Rows per key - avg            1.00
TEST_INDEX      TEST_COL         Rows per key - dev            0.00
TEST_INDEX      TEST_COL         Rows per key - max            1.00
TEST_INDEX      TEST_COL         Rows per key - min            1.00
TEST_INDEX      TEST_COL         Total Distinct Keys         398.00
TEST_INDEX      TEST_COL         db_gets_per_key_hit           1.00
TEST_INDEX      TEST_COL         db_gets_per_key_miss          1.00

TABLE_NAME      COLUMN_NAME   BADNESS    KEYS_COUNT   ROW_PERCENT    KEY_PERCENT
-------------   -----------   --------   ----------   ------------   ------------
TEST_INDEX      TEST_COL          1         398        100.00         100.00
SQL> EXIT
```

Figure 6.20 Example of test of a pseudoconcatenated index.

As can be seen by making the same comparisons as with either OWNER or TABLE_NAME, this new concatenated index would perform better than either of the previous single-column indexes. It has the added benefit of allowing us to search on OWNER with no performance penalties. In fact for a simple query looking for OWNERs and TABLE_NAMEs performance should be much better since it can be resolved completely in the index. Under ORACLE7 these scripts are called UTLDIDXS.SQL, UTLSIDXS.SQL, and UTLOIDXS.SQL.

Using Hints in ORACLE7 to Force Behavior. One important new feature of ORACLE7 is the ability to issue hints to the optimizer. Under version 6 you could only force the optimizer by the hit-and-miss methods shown above. IN ORACLE7 you can tell the optimizer directly to use a specific type of action for your queries. This gives the DBA or application developer more control than was ever possible in version 6. Let's look at how this feature is used.

Hints are enclosed within comments to the SQL commands DELETE, SELECT, or UPDATE, or are designated by two dashes and a plus sign. To show the format, the SELECT statement only will be used, but the format is identical for all three commands.

```
SELECT          /*+ hint --or-- text */
statement body
   -- or --
SELECT          --+ hint --or-- text
statement body
```

Where:

/*—This is the comment delimiter.
+—This tells Oracle a hint follows; it must come immediately after the /*.
hint—This is one of the allowed hints.
text—This is the comment text.

HINT	MEANING
ALL_ROWS	Use the cost-based approach for best throughput.
FIRST_ROWS	Use the cost-based approach for best response time.
RULE	Use rules-based approach; this cancels any other hints specified for this statement. This will not be available after ORACLE7.
FULL(table)	This tells the optimizer to do a full scan of the specified table
ROWID (table)	Forces a rowid scan of the specified table.
CLUSTER(table)	Forces a cluster scan of the specified table.
INDEX(table [index])	Forces an index scan of the specified table using the specified index(s). If a list of indexes is specified, the optimizer chooses the one with the lowest cost. If no index is specified, then the optimizer chooses the available index for the table with the lowest cost.
INDEX_ASC (table [index])	Same as INDEX, only performs an ascending search of the index chosen; this is functionally identical to the INDEX statement.
INDEX_DESC(table [index])	Same as INDEX, except performs a descending search. If more than one table is accessed, this is ignored.
AND_EQUAL(table index index [index index index])	This hint causes a merge on several single-column indexes. Two must be specified, five can be.
ORDERED	This hint forces tables to be joined in the order specified. If you know table X has fewer rows, then ordering it first may speed execution in a join.

HINT	MEANING
USE_NL(table)	This operation forces a nested loop using the specified table as the controlling table.
USE_MERGE(table,[table,...])	This operation forces a sort-merge-join operation of the specified tables.

As you can see, our dilemma in the first part of this chapter with the stubborn index usage could have been easily solved using ORACLE7 and hints. You must know the application to be tuned. The DBA can provide guidance to developers, but in all but the smallest development projects, it will be nearly impossible for a DBA to know everything about each application. It is clear that responsibility for application tuning rests solely on the developer's shoulders with help and guidance from the DBA.

Suggested Additional Reading. If you want more detailed information on use of TKPROF, EXPLAIN PLAN, rules, and cost-based optimization, the following references are suggested:

ORACLE RDBMS Performance Tuning Guide Version 6.0, Chapter 7, Oracle Corp. part number 5317-V6.0.

ORACLE RDBMS Database Administrator's Guide Version 6, Chapter 19, Oracle Corp. part number 3601-V6.0 Oct. 1990.

ORACLE7 Server Concepts Manual, Chapter 13, Oracle Corp. part number 6693-70-1292 Dec. 1992.

ORACLE7 Server Application Developer's Guide, Appendix B, Oracle Corp., part number 6695-70-1292 Dec. 1992.

Put the Smallest Table Last and Other Tuning Myths, Gardner, M., Oracle Corp., IOUG Proceedings, 1991 IOUG Symposium, Miami, Florida.

Performance Optimization Through SQL Query Decomposition Testing, Rausch, R.J., Pacific Bell Directory, IOUG Proceedings, 1991 IOUG Symposium, Miami, Florida.

How to Translate TKPROFS and IDXSTAT into Meaningful Applications Changes, Manton, M.C. III, TESTMARK, IOUG Proceedings, 1991 IOUG Symposium, Miami, Florida.

Query and Application Tuning Using EXPLAIN and TKPROF Utility, Presley, D.L., Oracle Corp., IOUG Proceedings, 1991 IOUG Symposium, Miami, Florida.

Performance Optimization: The Next Step, Rausch, R.J., Pacific Bell Directory, IOUG Proceedings, 1992 IOUG Symposium, Los Angeles, California.

Optimizing Distributed Queries, Bakker, A., Oracle Netherlands, IOUG Proceedings, 1992 IOUG Symposium, Los Angeles, California.

Explain Plan: An Aid to Query Optimization, Sankar, H., Fardoost, M., Oracle Corp., IOUG Proceedings, 1992 IOUG Symposium, Los Angeles, California.

Optimizing Query Performance in ORACLE7, Peeler, E., Oracle Corp., IOUG Proceedings, 1992 IOUG Symposium, Los Angeles, California.

Oracle for UNIX Performance Tuning Tips, Boeheim, C., Oracle Corp. Part number 53134-0293, February 1993.

DBAs and developers can use TKPROF and EXPLAIN PLAN to tune their SQL statements so an application performs in the most efficient manner. Once the applications are as efficient as is possible, the DBA's job as far as tuning really begins.

6.2 Database Internals Tuning

As was said at the end of the last section, once the application is tuned, the DBA's job really begins. Now you can begin tuning the Oracle system itself to take advantage of the tuned application from section 6.1. This second step of the tuning process is typically a four-part process:

1. Tuning memory allocation
2. Elimination of IO bottlenecks
3. Tuning resource contention
4. Tuning sorts, free lists, and checkpoints

6.2.1 The BSTAT and ESTAT Scripts and Their Use

Oracle provides the ESTAT.SQL and BSTAT.SQL scripts in version 6 to assist the DBA in tuning the various performance areas. Under ORACLE7 these scripts become CATBSTAT.SQL and CATESTAT.SQL. These scripts take a beginning snapshot (BSTAT) and an ending snapshot (ESTAT) of database statistics and generate a set of differences reports.

Use of ESTAT/BSTAT. After shutting down the database, setting the TIMED_STATISTICS parameter of the INIT.ORA file to TRUE, and then restarting the database, the script BSTAT is run from the SQLDBA program after the database has reached equilibrium (i.e., after the database has been started and the buffers and caches have stabilized). If you don't wait until the database has reached a steady state condition, the statistics will reflect "startup noise" from the various process startups and will not give a true baseline. Once BSTAT has been run, the application you wish to test is then run through its paces. Once you are satisfied that the application has been fully rung out under as close to as possible actual running conditions (a 1-user test of a 20-user application isn't going to tell you much), the ESTAT script is run, again from SQLDBA. The ESTAT script calculates various statistics for the database and generates several reports that can then be used for tuning. Let's look at these reports and see how they can help with the various aspects of tuning.

The BSTAT/ESTAT Script Reports. Figure 6.21 shows the first of the BSTAT/ESTAT reports. These reports cover virtually every aspect of internals and general database tuning.

Statistic Report. The first report is the statistics report. All database statistics are shown regardless of their tuning value to the DBA. An attempt has been made to list the important parameters after the figure.

```
Statistic                        Total           Per Trans
-----------------------------    ----------      ----------
DBWR exchange waits              0               0
background timeouts              683             136.6
buffer busy waits                0               0
busy wait time                   0               0
calls to kcmgcs                  1887            377.4
calls to kcmgns                  13              2.6
calls to kcmgrs                  107             21.4
```

Figure 6.21 First BSTAT/ESTAT report.

change write time	6	1.2
cluster key scan block gets	6987	1397.4
cluster key scans	3902	780.4
consistent changes	27	5.4
consistent forceouts	0	0
consistent gets	1952856	390571.2
consistent lock get time	0	0
consistant lock gets	0	0
cumulative opened cursors	194	38.8
current lock get fails	0	0
current lock get time	0	0
current lock gets	0	0
current logons	0	0
current open cursors	0	0
db block changes	532	106.4
db block gets	820	164
dbwr buffers scanned	3970	794
dbwr checkpoints	0	0
dbwr free low	1	0.2
dbwr free needed	0	0
dbwr interrupts	0	0
dbwr interrupts deferred	0	0
dbwr timeouts	341	68.2
enqueue conversions	0	0
enqueue deadlocks	0	0
enqueue releases	800	160
enqueue requests	800	160
enqueue timeouts	0	0
enqueue waits	0	0
exchange deadlocks	0	0
free buffer inspected	2	0.4
free buffer requested	6453	1290.6
free buffer scans	6453	1290.6
free buffer waits	0	0
free wait time	0	0
instance lock convert time	0	0
instance lock converts (async)	0	0
instance lock converts (non as	0	0
instance lock get time	0	0
instance lock gets (async)	0	0
instance lock gets (non async)	0	0
instance lock release time	0	0
instance lock releases (async)	0	0
instance lock releases (non as	0	0
logons	12	2.4
messages received	20	4
messages sent	20	4
parse count	231	46.2
parse time cpu	329	65.8
parse time elapsed	774	154.8
physical reads	6420	1284

Figure 6.21 (continued)   (continued)

physical writes	109	21.8
recursive calls	2321	464.2
redo blocks written	00	17,6
redo buffer allocation retries	0	0
redo chunk allocations	0	0
redo delayed write sync	0	0
redo entries	226	45.2
redo entries linearized	0	0
redo log space requests	0	0
redo log space wait time	0	0
redo log switch interrupts	0	0
redo log switch wait failure	0	0
redo size	38348	7669.6
redo small copies	225	45
redo synch time	50	10
redo synch writes	13	2.6
redo wastage	5122	1024.4
redo write time	68	13.6
redo writer latching time	0	0
redo writes	20	4
sorts (disk)	0	0
sorts (memory)	77	15.4
sorts (rows)	1656	331.2
table fetch by rowid	771241	154248.2
table fetch continued row	1	.2
table scan blocks gotten	19105	3821
table scan rows gotten	119200	23840
table scans (long tables)	32	6.1
table scans (short tables)	92	18.4
transaction lock background ge	0	0
transaction lock background ge	0	0
transaction lock foreground re	0	0
transaction lock foreground wa	0	0
user calls	21194	4238.8
user commits	5	1
user rollbacks	0	0
write complete waits	0	0
write wait time	0	0
96 rows selected.		

Figure 6.21 (continued)

Don't let the size of the report in Figure 6.21 scare you off. Actually there are only a few of its numbers that we are concerned with. Let's examine the performance critical parameters.

Buffer busy waits—This statistic shows contention for data blocks containing undo blocks, undo segment headers, data blocks, and segment headers. To find if this value is high, divide it by the sum of "consistent gets" and "db_buffer_gets." If this number is in excess of 10 percent, issue the following version 6 query to find the offending area:

```
SELECT class, SUM(count) "total waits"
FROM sys.v$waitstat
WHERE operation = 'buffer busy waits' AND
class IN  ('undo block', 'undo segment header', 'data block', 'segment
          header')
GROUP BY class;
```

For ORACLE7 the query becomes:

```
SELECT class, count
FROM v$waitstat
WHERE class IN ('free list', 'system undo header', 'system undo block',
                'undo header', 'undo block')
GROUP BY class;
```

If the value is high for one or more of the parameters, then take the following action(s):

- If "data block" and or "segment header" values are high, then increase the available free lists by increasing the INIT.ORA parameter FREE_LIST_PROC in version 6 and then dropping and recreating the affected tables. If "data block" and or "segment header" values in ORACLE7 are high, recreate the tables in the application that were accessed during the test with a higher value for FREELIST.

- If the values are high for "undo block" and or "undo segment headers," then additional rollback segments are needed.

- If the ratio of "logical reads" minus the value of "physical reads" to "logical reads" ((logical reads—physical reads)/logical reads), otherwise known as "hit ratio," is less than 70 percent increase the INIT.ORA parameter DB_BLOCK_BUFFERS for version 6 and ORACLE7.

dbwr checkpoints—If the number of database checkpoints for the test period is high, increase the INIT.ORA parameter LOG_CHECKPOINT_INTERVAL. If this value is greater than the size of the redo log, then checkpoints will only occur on log switches. To increase the number of checkpoints, reduce the value of LOG_CHECKPOINT_INTERVAL. The more checkpoints you have, the faster database recovery, but performance may degrade, the fewer, the longer database recovery will take.

dbwr free low—If this is nonzero, it indicates the number of times the dirty-buffer-writer process, DBWR, was activated because a user process found DB_BLOCK_WRITE_BATCH / 2 number of buffers on the dirty buffer list. This parameter is used in conjunction with "dbwr free low" to determine if DB_BLOCK_WRITE_BATCH should be modified. This parameter is replaced by "free buffer requested" in ORACLE7. This parameter is obsolete in ORACLE7 and DB_BLOCK_WRITE_BATCH is no longer an INIT.ORA parameter.

dbwr free needed—This parameter increments whenever a user process scans DB_BLOCK_MAX_SCAN_CNT number of buffers without finding a clean one. If this parameter is nonzero, increase the value of DB_BLOCK_WRITE_BATCH until "write complete waits" and "write wait time" show an increase. If the problem persists, try increasing the value of DB_BLOCK_BUFFERS. This parameter is obsolete in ORACLE7 and DB_BLOCK_MAX_SCAN_CNT and DB_BLOCK_WRITE_BATCH are no longer INIT.ORA parameters.

enqueue timeouts—This parameter should always be zero. It indicates the number of times an enqueue lock was requested and wasn't immediately granted. If this value is nonzero, increase the value of the INIT.ORA parameter ENQUEUE_RESOURCES.

recursive calls—This parameter shows that segment extension is occurring and indicate cache misses. If this parameter in relation to the number of processes is high (some sources say greater than 4/process), then one or both of the following should be done:

- Tune the data dictionary cache.
- Drop and recreate tables showing dynamic extension with better sizing parameters (INITIAL, NEXT, PCTINCREASE, MINEXTENTS, MAXEXTENTS).

redo logs space wait—If this parameter is nonzero, it shows that user processes are waiting for space in the redo buffer. If this is nonzero, increase the INIT.ORA parameter LOG_BUFFER to increase the redo log buffer size.

redo chunk allocations—Nonzero values for this parameter indicates that the users are requiring more space than is available in the online redo logs. The INIT.ORA parameter LOG_ALLOCATION is used to set the number of blocks allocated for each extension. It should be set to a value larger than the size of the redo logs. If "redo chunk allocations" is high in proportion to the number of processes, increase the LOG_BUFFER parameter, the LOG_ALLOCATION parameter, and possibly the size of your redo logs. Under ORACLE7 the LOG_ALLOCATION parameter is no longer available in INIT.ORA.

sorts(disk)—If this value is nonzero, it indicates that the SORT_AREA_SIZE parameter may need to be increased. This parameter indicates the number of times the user processes had to write temporary files to disk during a sort rather than being able to cache them in the memory area reserved for sorts. Sorts are performed for the following operations:

- Index creation
- Use of GROUP BY
- Use of ORDER BY
- Use of DISTINCT
- Sort merge joins
- UNION/INTERSECT/MINUS statements

You want sorts in the sort area in memory, not on disk. The parameter "sorts (memory)" shows how many sorts were accomplished in memory. "Sort (rows)" shows the total number of rows sorted.

table scans (long tables)—This parameter shows the number of times the system had to scan tables that were in excess of five oracle blocks in length. If this value is excessive, it indicates that your applications need better indexes. Ideally, all scans should be accomplished via short table scans. The parameter "table scans (short tables)" shows the number of short table scans performed. This number should be greater than "table scans (long tables)" by a large margin. In the example report the parameters indicate the application needs better indexing.

table fetch by rowid—This parameter shows that rowid fetches, the most efficient retrieval, are being used.

table fetch by continued row—This parameter indicates that chaining is occurring in the application. If the application uses a number of LONG type fields, this can't be helped. If the application doesn't use LONG, or if the number seems inconsistent with the amount LONG data types that are used, it indicates improper PCTUSED and PCTFREE and possible problems with the application's table's storage parameters.

File IO Statistics. The next BSTAT/ESTAT report deals with disk file input and output statistics. This information is useful in helping the DBA to pinpoint disks where excessive IO could be a problem. The format of this report is shown in Figure 6.22.

TABLE_SPACE	FILE_NAME	PHS_RDS	PHS_BKS_RD	PHS_RD_TIM	PHS_WRTS	PHS_BLKS_WR	PHS_WRT_TIM
CASE_GHOST	DIA1:[ORA.DB_B]GHOST_TS.DBS	0	0	0	0	0	0
MONITOR	DIA1:[ORA.DB_B]MONTOR_1.DBS	0	0	0	0	0	0
RCDEV	DIA1:[ORA.DB_B]RCDEV_1.DBS	0	0	0	0	0	0
RCRUN	DIA1:[ORA.DB_B]RCRUN_1.DBS	0	0	0	0	0	0
ORA_USERS	DIA1:[ORA.DB_B]USERS_1.DBS	761	4361	2044	1	1	4
SYSTEM	DIA1:[ORA.DB_B]SYSTEM.DBS	831	927	1308	27	27	74
DLBB_DBA	DIA2:[ORA.DB_B]DLBB_DBA_1.DBS	3	9	4	1	1	2
ORA_MONTR_INDEX	DIA3:[ORA.DB_B]MONTR_ID_1.DBS	0	0	0	0	0	0
ORA_ROLLBACKS	DIA4:[ORA.DB_B]ROLLBACK_1.DBS	6	6	14	26	26	66
SYSTEM	DIA2:[ORA.DB_B]SYSTEM_2.DBS	983	1166	1076	38	38	164
SYSTEM	DIA2:[ORA.DB_B]SYSTEM_3.DBS	0	0	0	16	16	100
ORA_TEMP	DIA5:[ORA.DB_B]TEMP_1.DBS	0	0	0	0	0	0

12 rows selected.

Figure 6.22 Example of file IO report from BSTAT/ESTAT.

As was said before, we want to spread disk IO out across multiple platters and attempt to even out the IO between these platters. The above report was taken during activity that accessed the system tablespace almost exclusively so it is not really a valid indication of system IO. In addition, the application (running system tuning reports) did a majority of read-type operations. You can see that few rollback transactions were monitored and no disk sorts as shown by the zero values for the ORA_TEMP tablespace and low values for the Redo log and archive activities aren't shown.

The meanings for the headers in this report follow.

Table Space—This is the tablespace that the data file in this line belongs to.

File Name—This is the name of the physical data file on disk.

Phys Read—This is the number of physical reads from the file.

Phys Blks Rd—This is the number of physical blocks read from the file.

Phys Rd Time—This is the time required to perform the physical reads (if timed statistics are turned on).

Phys Writes—This is the number of physical writes to the file.

Phys Blks Wr—This is the number of blocks written to the file.

Phys Wrt Time—This is the time required to perform the physical writes (if timed statistics are turned on).

By summing the physical reads and writes the total IO activity for a specific disk can be determined. The system manager can be consulted as to the limitations and other IO requirements for the disk and a good picture of disk usage will result. This disk usage picture can then be used to decide Oracle file placement and as to whether or not high-activity tables should be split out to another tablespace on a different disk.

Latches Statistics Successes/Timeouts The next BSTAT/ESTAT report deals with database latches and their statistics. This report will show which latches may need tuning and which can be left alone. The report is shown in Figure 6.23. Latches in this report fall into two general categories: those that are willing to wait and those that aren't. Those that were willing to wait have statistics in the waits, immediates, and timeouts columns. Those that couldn't wait are shown in the nowaits and successes columns. In general, Immediates plus timeouts should equal waits, but this is not always true since a latch may try several times before being successful. The ratio of timeouts to waits should not exceed 10 percent in version 6 or 1 percent in ORACLE7. If it does, check the INIT.ORA parameter that corresponds to that latch (shown later). If the ratio of successes to nowaits is less than 90 percent in version 6, or 99 percent in ORACLE7, then the INIT.ORA parameters should be altered.

NAME	WAITS	IMMEDIATE	TIMEOUTS	NOWAITS	SUCCESSES
archive control	0	0	0	0	0
cache buffer handles	862	862	0	0	0
cache buffers chains	3922950	3922949	1	14030	14026
cache buffers lru chain	7228	7224	4	1940306	1940306
dml/ddl allocation	1038	1038	0	0	0
enqueues	3292	3292	0	0	0
inter-instance buffer lock	0	0	0	0	0
messages	1854	1854	0	0	0
multiblock read objects	1506	1506	0	0	0
process allocation	28	28	0	0	0
redo allocation	1415	1415	0	0	0
redo copy	0	0	0	90	90
row cache objects	9576	9576	0	0	0
sequence cache	55	55	0	0	0
session allocation	8676	8676	0	0	0
system commit number	2814	2814	0	0	0
transaction allocation	170	170	0	0	0
undo global data	138	138	0	0	0
18 rows selected.					

Figure 6. 23 Example of the latches statistics ESTAT/BSTAT report.

Let's look at the latches mentioned in this report and the associated INIT.ORA parameter associated with the latch. In general, you as DBA will only be concerned with the values or the enqueues, cache buffers, and redo latches. The others are of more concern to Oracle technical support personnel.

Cache Buffers Chain—This latch indicates user processes are waiting to scan the SGA for block access. The latch is related to the INIT.ORA parameter DB_BLOCK_HASH_BUCKETS, which is related to DB_BLOCK_BUFFERS. To tune this latch, adjust DB_BLOCK_BUFFERS.

Cache Buffers LRU Chains—This latch indicates waits when user attempts to scan the LRU (least recently used) chain that contains all the used blocks in the database buffers. To reduce waits on this latch, increase the INIT.ORA parameter DB_BLOCK_BUFFERS or the INIT.ORA parameter DB_BLOCK_WRITE_BATCH.

Enqueues—This latch is controlled by the INIT.ORA parameter, ENQUEUE_RESOURCES. If the ratio of timeouts to total exceeds 10 percent in version 6 or 1 percent in ORACLE7, increase ENQUEUE_RESOURCES.

Redo Allocation—This latch controls the allocation of space in the redo buffer. There is only one allocation latch per instance in version 6 and ORACLE7. To reduce contention for this latch, reduce the value of the INIT.ORA parameter LOG_SMALL_ENTRY_MAX_SIZE on multi-CPU systems to force use of a redo copy latch. On single-CPU systems the value of CPU_COUNT in the INIT.ORA file is set to zero. This indicates no redo copy latches are allowed. Setting the CPU_COUNT to 1 and LOG_SIMULTANEOUS_COPIES to 2 is not recommended by Oracle for single-CPU machines, even though two redo copy latches are allowed per CPU. In the example report 90 uses of the redo copy latch are shown even though the CPU count for the computer was set to zero. This indicates there are redo copy latches even on single-CPU machines.

Redo copy—This latch is used when an entry's size exceeds LOG_SMALL_ENTRY_SIZE and use of a redo copy latch is forced. This happens on both single- and multi-CPU computers as is witnessed by the above example report for a single-CPU computer.

On multi-CPU computers you can reduce redo copy latch contention by increasing LOG_SIMULTANEOUS_COPIES to twice the value of CPU_COUNT, and — or, increasing the value of LOG_ENTRY_PREBUILD_THRESHOLD. On single-CPU systems, changing LOG_ENTRY_PREBUILD_THRESHOLD has no effect since the CPU_COUNT is set to zero and LOG_SIMULTANEOUS_COPIES and LOG_ENTRY_PREBUILD_THRESHOLD have no effect.

LOG_ENTRY_PREBUILD_THRESHOLD determines the size of redo entry that will be prebuilt before being passed to the log buffer. By prebuilding the entry the time the redo copy latch is held is reduced, thus reducing the contention for the latch.

row cache objects—This latch shows waits for the user processes attempting to access the cached data dictionary values. To reduce contention for this latch the data dictionary cache is tuncd. This will be covered in a later section.

Other than those listed above, the rest of the latches shouldn't require tuning. If excessive contention is shown for them, contact the Oracle support group.

Rollback Segment Statistics. The next report in the BSTAT/ESTAT series deals with the database rollback segment performance. This report is shown in Figure 6.24. The report shows statistics for rollback segment accesses (trans_tbl_gets), the number of times a user process had to wait on a rollback segment (trans_tbl_waits), the number of bytes written to a rollback segment (undo_bytes_wr), and the size of the particular rollback segment in bytes (segment_size_byt). This report shows if contention for rollback segments is occurring if the ratio of trans_tbl_waits to trans_tbl_gets is greater than 5 percent. As you can, for the example database, there is no rollback contention indicated as all values for TRANS_TBL_WAITS are zero.

You should also verify that the rollback segments are of nearly equal size. If they aren't, drop and recreate them. The only segment showing a big difference in size is the first one listed in the report. This corresponds to the system rollback and is not of concern. The order of rows in this report corresponds to the rollback segment creation order and file number. The first row will correspond to the SYSTEM rollback segment.

TRANS_TBL_GETS	TRANS_TBL_WAITS	UNDO_BYTES_WRITTEN	SEGMENT_SIZE_BYTES
4	0	0	175218
89	0	6223	1004986
144	0	10691	1004986
260	0	19765	1508486
4 rows selected			

Figure 6.24 Example of rollback segment report from BSTAT/ESTAT.

Data Dictionary Cache Statistics. The next report is the Data Dictionary Cache Statistics report. The output of this report is shown in Figure 6.25.

In version 6, each of the data dictionary caches was independently tunable. This led to some being too large and consuming valuable memory resources and others being set too small, thus being starved for resources. Under ORACLE7 the data dictionary caches are tuned as a single entity, the data dictionary cache, and each of the individual caches share this resource. This makes the DBA's job much easier as far as the data dictionary cache is concerned. Only 1 INIT.ORA parameter under ORACLE7 is tuned, instead of the 22 individual parameters under version 6.

If the ratio of get_miss to get_req for any individual data dictionary cache exceeds 10 percent under version 6, increase that cache's INIT.ORA parameter. The version 6 INIT.ORA parameter that corresponds to the cache will be "DC_cache name." Under ORACLE7, increase the SHARED_POOL_SIZE parameter in the INIT.ORA file (this parameter an ORACLE7 parameter only).

Under ORACLE7, the get_reqs and get_miss columns should be summed and then ratioed. If the overall ratio of get_misses to get_reqs is greater than 10 percent, then increase the SHARED_POOL_SIZE parameter. For a quick look at this, use the following query of the V$ROWCACHE table:

```
SELECT (SUM(getmisses) / SUM(gets)) 'DD CACHE MISS RATIO'
FROM V$ROWCACHE;
```

One important thing to remember is that the ratio of get_miss to get_req doesn't apply if the value of the cur_usag column is less than the objects "DC_" INIT.ORA parameter. If this is the case it indicates that either the cache is being accessed so infrequently for this type of entry that the LRU algorithm is cleaning it out before it can be reused, or the requests for this type of cache entry are so varied that it is difficult to cache accurately.

INIT.ORA Parameters. The next BSTAT/ESTAT report is a listing of the INIT.ORA parameters in effect while the BSTAT/ESTAT was run. This report is used to show existing conditions and provide a reference for parameter adjustment. The output from this report is shown in Figure 6.26.

If the INIT.ORA parameter isn't explicitly listed in the INIT.ORA file, the system assigns a default value to the parameter. These default values are listed in the database administrator's manual for the version of Oracle you are using or in the *Installation and User's Guide* for the CPU type you are using in the case of system specific parameters.

NAME	GET_REQS	GET_MISS	SCAN_REQ	SCAN_MIS	MOD_REQS	CUR_USAG
dc_free_extents	16	4	12	0	20	34
dc_used_extents	12	4	0	0	12	28
dc_segments	36	4	0	0	32	25
dc_tablespaces	16	0	0	0	0	10
dc_tablespaces	8	0	0	0	8	2
dc_tablespace_quotas	0	0	0	0	0	1
dc_files	0	0	0	0	0	0
dc_users	111	1	0	0	0	4
dc_rollback_segments	20	0	0	0	0	6
dc_objects	735	25	0	0	20	187
dc_constraints	2	1	0	0	2	27
dc_object_ids	209	4	0	0	0	5
dc_tables	770	18	0	0	12	119
dc_synonyms	41	8	0	0	0	24
dc_sequences	11	0	0	0	0	1
dc_usernames	105	2	0	0	0	5
dc_columns	3249	64	139	8	43	698
dc_table_grants	0	0	0	0	0	0
dc_column_grants	0	0	0	0	0	0
dc_indexes	554	2	612	10	0	38
dc_constraint_defs	0	0	0	0	1	12
dc_sequence_grants	0	0	0	0	0	0

22 rows selected.

Figure 6.25 Example of data dictionary cache statistic report from BSTAT/ESTAT.

NAME	TYPE	VALUE
audit_trail	boolean	FALSE
background_dump_dest	string	ORA_DUMP
calls	integer	130
cleanup_rollback_entries	integer	20
context_area	integer	4096
context_incr	integer	4096
control_files	string	DIA1:[ORACLE.DB_B]ORA_TESTB_CO
cpu_count	integer	0
db_block_buffers	integer	500
db_block_cache_protect	boolean	FALSE
db_block_compute_checksums	boolean	FALSE
db_block_hash_buckets	integer	125
db_block_lru_extended_statistics	integer	0

Figure 6.26 Example of INIT.ORA report from BSTAT/ESTAT.   (continued)

```
db_block_lru_statistics                 boolean     FALSE
db_block_max_scan_cnt                    integer     30
db_block_multiple hashchain_latches      boolean     TRUE
db_block_size                            integer     2048
db_block_write_batch                     integer     8
db_file_multiblock_read_count            integer     8
db_file_simultaneous_writes              integer     4
db_files                                 integer     32
db_handles                               integer     292
db_handles_cached                        integer     2
db_name                                  string      TESTB
db_writer_max_scan_cnt                   integer     50
dc_column_grants                         integer     150
dc_columns                               integer     1000
dc_constraint_defs                       integer     600
dc_constraints                           integer     450
dc_files                                 integer     32
dc_free_extents                          integer     200
dc_indexes                               integer     150
dc_object_ids                            integer     150
dc_objects                               integer     500
dc_rollback_segments                     integer     25
dc_segments                              integer     150
dc_sequence_grants                       integer     60
dc_sequences                             integer     60
dc_synonyms                              integer     300
dc_table_grants                          integer     150
dc_tables                                integer     250
dc_tablespace_quotas                     integer     160
dc_tablespaces                           integer     32
dc_used_extents                          integer     200
dc_usernames                             integer     150
dc_users                                 integer     150
ddl_locks                                integer     400
dml_locks                                integer     400
enqueue_debug_multi_instance             boolean     FALSE
enqueue_hash                             integer     181
enqueue_locks                            integer     730
enqueue_resources                        integer     500
event                                    string
fixed_date                               string
free_list_inst                           integer     1
free_list_proc                           integer     1
gc_db_locks                              integer     500
gc_rollback_locks                        integer     20
gc_rollback_segments                     integer     20
gc_save_rollback_locks                   integer     20
gc_segments                              integer     10
gc_sort_locks                            integer     500
gc_tablespaces                           integer     5
ifile                                    file
```

Figure 6.26 (continued)

init_sql_files	string	ORA_INITSQL
instances	integer	16
language	string	AMERICAN_AMERICA.US7ASCII
log_allocation	integer	200
log_archive_dest	string	ORA_ARCHIVE:ARCH
log_archive_start	boolean	FALSE
log_blocks_during_backup	boolean	TRUE
log_buffer	integer	32768
log_buffers_debug	boolean	FALSE
log_checkpoint_interval	integer	10000
log_debug_multi_instance	boolean	FALSE
log_entry_prebuild_threshold	integer	0
log_files	integer	255
log_io_size	integer	0
log_simultaneous_copies	integer	1
log_small_entry_max_size	integer	800
max_dump_file_size	integer	1000000
messages	integer	146
nls_sort	boolean	FALSE
open_cursors	integer	383
open_links	integer	4
pre_page_sga	boolean	FALSE
processes	integer	73
rollback_segments	string	ROLLBACK1, ROLLBACK2, ROLLBACK3
row_cache_buffer_size	integer	200
row_cache_cursors	integer	10
row_cache_enqueues	integer	400
row_cache_instance_locks	integer	100
row_cache_multi_instance	boolean	TRUE
row_cache_pct_free	integer	10
row_locking	string	default
savepoints	integer	5
scn_increment	integer	2048
scn_threshold	integer	512
sequence_cache_entries	integer	10
sequence_cache_hash_buckets	integer	7
serializable	boolean	FALSE
sessions	integer	80
single_process	boolean	FALSE
sort_area_size	integer	81920
sort_read_fac	integer	5
sort_spacemap_size	integer	512
sql_trace	boolean	FALSE
timed_statistics	boolean	TRUE
transactions	integer	80
transactions_per_rollback_segment	integer	30
use_row_enqueues	boolean	TRUE
user_dump_dest	string	ORA_DUMP
user_sessions	integer	1
wait_for_sync	boolean	TRUE

Figure 6.26 (continued)

Date and Time. The final report is simply a listing of the dates and times for the start and stop of the BSTAT/ESTAT run. This report is shown in Figure 6.27.

```
STATS_GATHER_TIMES
-------------------
02-jun-93 07:45:35
02-jun-93 08:02:56

2 rows selected.
```

Figure 6.27 Example of date and time report from BSTAT/ESTAT.

Be sure that the dates and times in this report correspond to the expected dates and times. It would be terribly embarrassing to retune your database to outmoded data!

For more information on tuning using BSTAT/ESTAT and on tuning in general, the following extra reading is suggested:

ORACLE RDBMS Performance Tuning Guide Version 6.0, Chapters 3, 7 Oracle Corp. part number 5317-V6.0.

ORACLE RDBMS Database Version 6, Chapter 12, Appendix B, Oracle Corp. Part number 3601-V6.0 Oct. 1990.

ORACLE7 Server Administrator's Guide, Chapter 21, Oracle Corp. Part number 6694-70-1292, Dec. 1992.

ORACLE7 Server Application Developer's Guide, Appendix B, Oracle Corp. Part number 6695-70-1292 Dec. 1992.

Performance Tuning with BSTAT/ESTAT, Powell, K., Oracle Corp., 1991 IOUG Proceedings, Miami, Florida.

SQL*DBA Monitor, A Powerful Tool for the Database Administrator, Fardoost, M., Oracle Corp., 1991 IOUG Proceedings, Miami, Florida.

6.2.2 Other Tools for Internals Tuning

The BSTAT/ESTAT scripts are a powerful tool for the DBA to use. However, to use them on a day-to-day basis would be a bit much for most DBAs to handle. This section will give the DBA several additional tuning and reporting tools to add to their tuning toolbox. The tuning guides for Oracle list several areas where tuning is required. These are:

Tuning memory allocation

- SQL and PL/SQL areas
- Data dictionary caches (shared pool in ORACLE7)
- Database buffer cache

Tuning input and output

- Disk IO
- Space allocation

- Dynamic extension

Tuning contention

- Rollback segments
- Redo logs
- For ORACLE7—multithread server

Other tuning topics

- Sorts
- Free lists
- Checkpoints

Tuning Memory Contention. Memory contention will make the best-tuned application perform poorly. If the application is constantly having to go to disk to get data dictionary and actual data, then performance will suffer. If you will remember, the SGA is divided into three major areas in version 6: the data dictionary cache (shared pool under ORACLE7), the redo log buffer, and the database buffers. Under ORACLE7 there is an additional area in the SGA for databases using the multithreaded database option and SQL*NET version 2.0.

Under version 6 and ORACLE7 the major effort at tuning will be with the data dictionary cache (shared pool in ORACLE7), the database buffers, and the redo log buffers, in that order.

Tuning the Data Dictionary Caches (Shared Pool). Missing a get on the data dictionary or shared pool area of the SGA is more costly than missing a get on a data buffer or waiting for a redo buffer. Therefore we will look at a SQL script that allows the DBA to look at the current status of the data dictionary or shared pool area. This SQL script is shown in Figure 6.28. Under ORACLE7 this report is still useful but the summary SQL statement shown below is more meaningful.

Some things to notice about the script in Figure 6.28 is that the script only selects statistics that have been used greater than 100 times and have had getmisses occur. Obviously if the parameter has had no getmisses, it should be satisfactory. The factor of 100 gets was selected to ensure that the parameter has had enough activity to generate valid statistics. You might also notice that the percentage of misses is automatically calculated and reported for each parameter. If the DBA desires, the percent value could be used to generate a decoded value of "RAISE" if the percent is greater than 10, or "LOWER" if the value is less than a predetermined value. An example of this script's output is shown in Figure 6.29.

```
REM
REM NAME          : DD_CACHE.SQL
REM PURPOSE       : GENERATE REPORT TO SHOW DATA DICTIONARY CACHE CONDITION
REM USE           : FROM EOW_WEEKLY_STATUS.COM
REM Limitations   : None
REM Revisions:
REM Date            Modified By    Reason For change
REM 21-AUG-1991     MIKE AULT      INITIAL CREATE
REM 27-NOV-1991     MIKE AULT      ADD % CALCULATION TO REPORT
```

Figure 6.28 Script to generate data dictionary cache statistics report.   (continued)

```
REM 28-OCT-1992   MIKE AULT     ADD CALL TO TITLE PROCEDURE
REM SET FLUSH OFF
REM SET TERM OFF
SET PAGESIZE 59
SET LINESIZE 79
COLUMN PARAMETER FORMAT A20;
COLUMN T_DATE NOPRINT NEW_VALUE T_DATE;
COLUMN PERCENT FORMAT 999.99 HEADING "%";
SELECT SYSDATE T_DATE FROM DUAL;
START ORACLE$SQL:TITLE80 "DATA DICTIONARY CACHE STATISTICS REPORT"
DEFINE OUTPUT = 'CACHE_STAT&DB..LIS'
SPOOL &OUTPUT
SELECT
                 PARAMETER,
                 GETS,
                 GETMISSES,
                 ( GETMISSES / GETS * 100) PERCENT,
                 COUNT,
                 USAGE
FROM V$ROWCACHE
WHERE
                 GETS > 100 AND
                 GETMISSES > 0
ORDER BY PARAMETER;
SPOOL OFF
EXIT
```

Figure 6.28 (continued)

```
Date: 06/04/93               "Your Company Name"              Page:   1
Time: 04:17 PM         DATA DICTIONARY CACHE STATISTICS       DEV_DBA
                            "Your" Database

PARAMETER                GETS        GETMISSES     %      COUNT        USAGE
--------------------  ----------   ----------   ------  ----------   ----------
dc_columns              141779       15072       10.63    1000         1000
dc_indexes               27280         188         .69     150          149
dc_object_ids             4293           7         .16      75            6
dc_objects               27178         757        2.79     500          500
dc_rollback_segments      8456           6         .07      25            7
dc_sequences               375           4        1.07      30            4
dc_synonyms               3721         209        5.62     350          209
dc_table_grants           4704         257        5.46     150          110
dc_tables                26963         296        1.10     250          249
dc_tablespaces             171          12        7.02      30           12
dc_usernames              5636          40         .71     100           40
dc_users                  5735          30         .52     100           30

12 rows selected.
```

Figure 6.29 Example of data dictionary cache report.

In reviewing this report the following things should be checked:

1. Review count and usage columns. If usage is equal to count, the cache area is being fully utilized. If usage is consistently low compared to count, consider reducing the INIT.ORA parameter that controls the cache.
2. If count and usage are equal and percent is greater than 10 percent, consider increasing the INIT.ORA parameter that controls the cache.

For ORACLE7, the above report will still function, and the above items still hold true, except only one INIT.ORA parameter is effected. Since under ORACLE7 we are talking about a shared cache area called the shared pool, the INIT.ORA parameter SHARED_POOL_SIZE controls this shared cache area. The query:

```
SELECT (SUM(getmisses) / SUM(gets)) 'DD CACHE MISS RATIO'
FROM V$ROWCACHE;
```

can be issued to give an instant indication of shared pool status.

An additional area of the shared pool deals with the tuning of the library cache. The library cache is used to store information concerning the shared objects that are new to ORACLE7. These consist of the SQL AREA, TABLE/PROCEDURE, BODY, and TRIGGER type objects. These areas are monitored via the V$LIBRARYCACHE table which is new with ORACLE7. This table has the columns: NAMESPACE, PINS, and RELOADS.

NAMESPACE refers to the type of object (listed above). PINS refers to the number of times the object was executed. RELOADS shows the number of library cache misses on execution steps. If the ratio of reloads to pins exceeds 1 percent, the SHARED_POOL_SIZE parameter should be increased. This can be determined by a simple query:

```
SELECT (SUM(reloads)/SUM(pins)) * 100 'Miss %'
FROM v$librarycache;
```

To fully utilize the higher value for SHARED_POOL_SIZE, you may also want to increase the number of cursors available to each user. This is accomplished via the OPEN_CURSORS INIT.ORA parameter.

Additional gains can be realized by making your SQL statements identical, not just in content but in form as well, right down to the spaces, capitalization, and punctuation. This will allow the SQL statements to share the shared SQL area.

Tuning the BUFFER CACHE. The buffer cache is the area in memory where data is stored from data tables, indexes, rollback segments, clusters, and sequences. By ensuring that enough buffers are available for storage of these data items, you can speed execution by reducing required disk reads.

The statistics "logical reads" and "physical reads" from the V$SYSSTAT table show the relationship between "logical," or cache, hits verses "physical," or disk hits, while retrieving the above type of data. The statistic called "hit ratio" is determined by the simple formula: hit ratio(%) = ((logical reads - physical reads) / logical reads) * 100 . If hit ratio is less than 80 percent to 90 percent in a loaded and running database, this indicates that there may be insufficient buffers allocated. If the hit ratio is less than 80 percent to 90 percent, increase the INIT.ORA parameter DB_BLOCK_BUFFERS.

Monitoring Hit Ratio. A PL/SQL script that can be used to periodically load hit ratio, usage, and number of users into a table for later review is shown in Figure 6.30. The script in Figure 6.30 can be run hourly, every half hour, every four hours—in short, at what ever periodicity the DBA decides to monitor for with minor changes. This can provide valuable information about peak usage times and hit ratio at those peak times. The table to store this information must be created, its structure is:

```
create table hit_ratios (
    CHECK_DATE          DATE,
    CHECK_HOUR          NUMBER,
    DB_BLOCK_GETS       NUMBER,
    CONSISTENT          NUMBER,
    PHY_READS           NUMBER,
    HITRATIO            NUMBER,
    PERIOD_HIT_RATIO    NUMBER,
    PERIOD_USAGE        NUMBER
    USERS               NUMBER)
storage (initial 10k next 10k pctincrease 0);
```

In addition, a unique index on CHECK_DATE, CHECK_HOUR should be created to prevent duplicate entries.

```
REM
REM NAME             :RUN_B_HRATIO.SQL
REM PURPOSE          :RUN PL/SQL PROCEDURE TO LOAD HIT RATIO AND USAGE DATA
REM USE              :FROM RUN_B_HRATIO.COM
REM Limitations      : None
REM Revisions:
REM    Date          Modified By    Reason For change
REM    10-JUL-1992   M. AULT        INITIAL CREATE
REM
get batch_hratio.sql
run
exit
```

Figure 6.30 SQL script used to run hit ratio PL/SQL procedure.

The script in Figure 6.30 can the be scheduled on SYS$BATCH under VMS or via the CHRON program on UNIX to run hourly. If you want it to run with greater or lessor periodicity, the PL/SQL script will have to be modified. The commands to run this script are executed in the SQLPLUS environment, so a small file consisting of a GET and a RUN command needs to be built and this file is what is actually run by the batch scheduling program. The file should look something like the script in Figure 6.30.

```
DECLARE
    C_DATE DATE;
    C_HOUR NUMBER := 0;
    H_RATIO NUMBER := 0;
    CON_GETS NUMBER := 0;
    DB_GETS NUMBER := 0;
    P_READS NUMBER := 0;
    STAT_NAME CHAR(64);
    temp_NAME CHAR(64);
    STAT_VAL NUMBER := 0;
    USERS  NUMBER := 0;
BEGIN
  select to_char(sysdate,'DD-MON-YY') into c_date from dual;
  select to_char(sysdate,'HH24') into c_hour from dual;
  STAT_NAME := 'db block gets';
      select a.name, b.value  into temp_name, db_gets from v$statname a, v$sysstat b
   where a.statistic# = b.statistic# AND A.NAME = STAT_NAME;
  STAT_NAME := 'consistent gets';
      select a.name,b.value into temp_name, con_gets from v$statname a, v$sysstat b
   where a.statistic# = b.statistic# AND A.NAME = STAT_NAME;
  STAT_NAME := 'physical reads';
      select a.name,b.value into temp_name, p_reads from v$statname a, v$sysstat b
   where a.statistic# = b.statistic# AND A.NAME = STAT_NAME;
   select count(*)-4 into users from v$session;
   H_RATIO := (((DB_GETS+CON_GETS-p_reads)/(DB_GETS+CON_GETS))*100);
   INSERT INTO  hit_ratios
      VALUES (c_date,c_hour,db_gets,con_gets,p_reads,h_ratio,0,0,users);
commit;
update hit_ratios set period_hit_ratio =
    (select round((((h2.consistent-h1.consistent)+(h2.db_block_gets-h1.db_block_gets)-
    (h2.phy_reads-h1.phy_reads))/((h2.consistent-h1.consistent)+
        (h2.db_block_gets-h1.db_block_gets)))*100,2) from hit_ratios h1, hit_ratios h2
    where h2.check_date = hit_ratios.check_date and h2.check_hour = hit_ratios.check_hour
    and ((h1.check_date = h2.check_date and h1.check_hour+1 = h2.check_hour) or
    (h1.check_date+1 = h2.check_date and h1.check_hour = '23' and h2.check_hour='0')))
where period_hit_ratio = 0;
  COMMIT;
update hit_ratios set period_USAGE =
    (select ((h2.consistent-h1.consistent)+(h2.db_block_gets-h1.db_block_gets))
    from hit_ratios h1, hit_ratios h2 where h2.check_date = hit_ratios.check_date
    and h2.check_hour = hit_ratios.check_hour  and ((h1.check_date = h2.check_date
    and h1.check_hour+1 = h2.check_hour) or (h1.check_date+1 = h2.check_date and
    h1.check_hour = '23' and h2.check_hour='0'))) where period_USAGE = 0;
  COMMIT;
EXCEPTION
    WHEN ZERO_DIVIDE THEN
    INSERT INTO  hit_ratios  VALUES (c_date,c_hour,db_gets,con_gets,p_reads,0,0,0,users);
    COMMIT;
END;
```

Figure 6.31 PL/SQL script to monitor hit ratio.

The script in Figure 6.31 is designed for hourly monitoring of hit ratio. The script is called from a standard SQL script similar to Figure 6.30. Once the script completes, it is rescheduled to run the next hour. The hit ratio for the previous hour is calculated as is the cumulative hit ratio and usage as a function of read/write activity. Some example results from this script, generated by the script in Figure 6.32, are shown in Figure 6.33. Using the decode and pad statements the hit ratio data can be plotted on any printer as a graph. This program is shown in Figure 6.36.

```
REM
REM NAME           :HITRATIO_SUMMARY.SQL
REM PURPOSE        :GENERATE SUMMARY REPORT OF PERIOD HIT RATIOS AND USAGE
REM PURPOSE        :BETWEEN TWO DATES
REM USE            :FROM STATUS_REPORTS.COM
REM Limitations    : None
REM Revisions:
REM    Date            Modified By     Reason For change
REM    10-JUL-1992     M.AULT          INITIAL CREATE
REM
set verify off pages 58 newpage 0
start title80 "HIT RATIO AND USAGE FOR &&CHECK_DATE1 TO &&CHECK_DATE2"
define output = 'hitratio_summary&db..lis'
spool &output
select
                CHECK_DATE,
                CHECK_HOUR,
                PERIOD_HIT_RATIO,
                PERIOD_USAGE,
                USERS
                from
                hit_ratios
where
                CHECK_DATE BETWEEN '&&CHECK_DATE1' AND '&&CHECK_DATE2'
order by
                CHECK_DATE,CHECK_HOUR;
SPOOL OFF
PAUSE PRESS RETURN TO CONTINUE
EXIT
```

Figure 6.32 Script to generate hit ratio and usage report.

The problem with sporadic monitoring of hit ratios is that the DBA may catch the system at a low point, or just when the database usage has switched from one user to another on a different application. All of this can contribute to incorrect hit ratio results. The use of a periodic script to monitor hit ratio tends to even out these fluctuations and provide a better look at the statistic.

Another problem with looking at hit ratio as it is described in the Oracle manuals is that you are looking at a running average, a cumulative value. This will result in low readings when the database is started and high readings after it has been running. Graphs showing actual periodic hit ratio and cumulative hit ratio are shown in Figures 6.34 and 6.35.

The above graphs were generated by a script similar to the script in Figure 6.36. For the cumulative graph, hit_ratio instead of period_hit_ratio is fed into the decode statements. As you can see, the cumulative hit ratio graph stayed fairly constant for the period, while the actual or period hit ratio varied between 18.78 and 92.95 percent. In fact, the cumulative hit ratio will reach a steady, slowly increasing value, shortly after startup.

If your hit ratio for periods of high usage is below 70 percent, increase the DB_BLOCK_BUFFERS INIT.ORA parameter. As you can see from the listing in Figure 6.33, when database usage was minimal, the hit ratio hovered at 18 percent to 20 percent. Once usage increased above 10,000 to 20,000, hit ratio jumped to greater than 90 percent, as would be expected.

If DB_BLOCK_BUFFERS is set too high, you may run out of PAD area under VMS or exceed shared memory size on UNIX for your instance. Another possible result is that the entire Oracle process could be swapped out due to memory contention with other processes. In either case, it is not a desirable condition. To avoid exceeding your PAD or shared memory areas, be sure you set these values high when the instance is created. To avoid swapping, know how much memory you are able to access. Discuss this with your system administrator.

```
Date: 06/05/93              "Your Company Name"            Page:   1
Time: 03:39 PM    HIT RATIO AND USAGE FOR 18-may-93 TO 18-may-93   DEV_DBA
                          "Your" Database


CHECK_DAT     CHECK_HOUR     PERIOD_HIT_RATIO    PERIOD_USAGE    USERS
---------     ----------     ----------------    ------------    ----------
18-MAY-93     0              18.78               2172            1
18-MAY-93     1              19.01               2178            1
18-MAY-93     2              19.01               2178            1
18-MAY-93     3              18.78               2172            1
18-MAY-93     4              18.78               2172            1
18-MAY-93     5              18.78               2172            1
18-MAY-93     6              18.78               2172            1
18-MAY-93     7              18.78               2172            1
18-MAY-93     8              21.7                2253            4
18-MAY-93     9              24.41               2360            5
18-MAY-93     10             55.27               3946            6
18-MAY-93     11             92.95               28578           6
18-MAY-93     12             50.21               3547            5
18-MAY-93     13             18.78               2172            5
18-MAY-93     14             20.89               2259            5
18-MAY-93     15             19.08               2180            5
18-MAY-93     16             20.07               2207            5
18-MAY-93     17             19.08               2180            5
18-MAY-93     18             19.08               2180            1
18-MAY-93     19             19.21               2186            1
18-MAY-93     20             19.08               2180            1
18-MAY-93     21             19.08               2180            1
18-MAY-93     22             19.08               2180            1
18-MAY-93     23             19.08               2180            1
24 rows selected
```

Figure 6.33 Example of output of periodic hit ratio report.

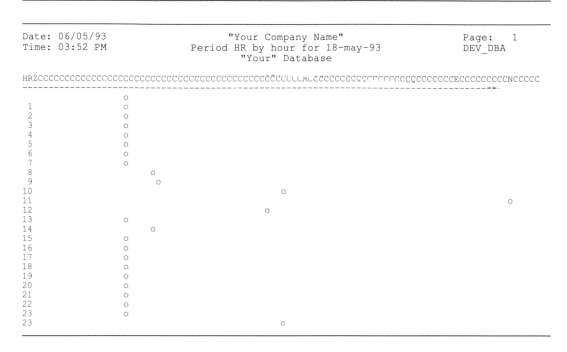

Figure 6.34 Periodic hit ratio for May 1993.

Figure 6.35 Graph of cumulative hit ratio for 18 May 1993.

```
REM
REM NAME          :HRATIO_REPORT.SQL
REM PURPOSE       :CREATE PLOT OF PERIOD HIT RATIO FOR 1 DAY
REM USE           :FROM STATUS_REPORTS.COM
REM Limitations   : None
REM Revisions:
REM   Date          Modified By      Reason For change
REM   10-JUL-1992   M. AULT          INITIAL CREATE
REM
host SET TERM/WID=132 REM: For VMS only, won't work under UNIX
set lines 131 newpage 0 VERIFY OFF pages 180 space 0 feedback off column hr
format 99
start title132 "Period HR for &&check_date1 TO &&check_date2"
define output = 'hratio_graph_BT_DATES&db.lis'
spool &output
select
    check_hour hr,
    decode(round(period_hit_ratio),0,'o',null) zchk0,
    decode(round(period_hit_ratio),1,'o',null) chk1,
    decode(round(period_hit_ratio),2,'o',null) chk2,
    decode(round(period_hit_ratio),3,'o',null) chk3,
    decode(round(period_hit_ratio),4,'o',null) chk4,
    decode(round(period_hit_ratio),5,'o',null) chk5,
    .
    .
    .
    decode(round(period_hit_ratio),94,'o',null) chk94,
    decode(round(period_hit_ratio),95,'o',null) chk95,
    decode(round(period_hit_ratio),96,'o',null) chk96,
    decode(round(period_hit_ratio),97,'o',null) chk97,
    decode(round(period_hit_ratio),98,'o',null) chk98,
    decode(round(period_hit_ratio),99,'o',null) chk99,
    decode(round(period_hit_ratio),100,'o',null) chk100
from hit_ratios
WHERE CHECK_DATE BETWEEN '&&CHECK_DATE1' AND '&&CHECK_DATE2'
order by CHECK_DATE,check_hour;
spool off
PAUSE 'PRESS RETURN TO CONTINUE'
host SET TERM/WID=80  rem: Only for VMS, will not work on UNIX
exit
```

Figure 6.36 SQL script to generate a 132-column hit ratio graph.

Use of X$CBRBH and X$CBCBH Tables. Oracle provides a virtual table owned by the SYS user to provide information on the effects of adding buffers to the buffer cache. This is the X$CBRBH table. This table has two columns, INDX and COUNT. The table is activated by setting the value of the INIT.ORA parameter DB_BLOCK_LRU_EXTENDED_STATISTICS to a non-zero value indicating the number of buffers you wish to add. The value you set this parameter to will determine the number of rows in the X$CBRBH table. There is one row for each additional buffer.

Once DB_BLOCK_LRU_EXTENDED_STATISTICS is set, the database will have to be shut down and restarted. This parameter should not be left enabled as it will cause a performance hit. The magnitude of the performance hit is directly proportional to the number of additional buffers data is collected about.

There are two methods for reviewing the statistics collected in V$CBRBH: The first is to select the sum of the values of COUNT over a specific interval:

```
SELECT SUM(count) "interval total"
   FROM v$kcbrbh
   WHERE indx BETWEEN ( interval start, Interval end);
```

The second gives more detailed information and is the suggested method. It provides summation over several intervals and gives the DBA more detail on which to base their choice of number of buffers to add:

```
SELECT
   50 * TRUNC(indx/50)+1||' to '||50 * (TRUNC(indx/50)+1) "Interval",
   SUM(count) "Buffer Cache Hits"
FROM  sys.x$kcbrbh
GROUP BY TRUNC(indx/50);
```

The output from the above select looks like the following:

Interval	Buffer Cache Hits
1 to 50	17350
51 to 100	9345
101 to 150	404
151 to 200	19568

The value 50 can be changed to any appropriate value. The output of this report shows the interval and the expected increase in buffer cache hits that could be expected from adding that many buffers to the cache. The above examples shows that adding 50, 100, or 200 buffers would add to the number of hits significantly. Adding 150 buffers would add very few hits. Therefore, add 50, 100, or 200 additional buffers, but not 150.

```
rem    *******************************************************************
rem
rem    NAME: SGA_INC.sql
rem
rem    HISTORY:
rem    Date          Who                   What
rem    --------      -----------------     ----------------------------------
rem    10/25/92      Cary Millsap          Creation
```

Figure 6.37 More detailed report of DD cache increment results.

```
rem  01/07/93      Michael Brouillette    Switched to title80
rem  06/05/93      Mike Ault              Added capability to input buffer interval
rem
rem  FUNCTION: Examine the statistice in the X$KCBRBH table with the intent to
rem            increase the size of the SGA.
rem
rem  *************************************************************************
col bufval new_value nbuf noprint
col thits new_value tot_hits noprint
select  value  bufval
from  v$parameter
where
  lower(name) = 'db_block_lru_extended_statistics';
select sum(count)  thits from v$kcbrbh;
start title80 "Prospective Hits if &nbuf Cache Buffers were Added"
col interval   format          a20 justify c heading 'Buffers'
col cache_hits format 999,999,990 justify c heading -
  'Cache Hits that would have been|gained by adding Buffers'
col cum format 99.99 heading 'Percent of Gain'
set termout off feedback off verify off echo off
spool sga_inc&db
select
  lpad(to_char((&nbuf/&incr)*trunc(indx/(&nbuf/&&incr))+1,'999,990'),8)||' to '||
  lpad(to_char((&nbuf/&&incr)*(trunc(indx/(&nbuf/&&incr))+1),'999,990'),8) interval,
  sum(count) cache_hits, sum(count)/&tot_hits * 100 cum
from
  v$kcbrbh
group by
  trunc(indx/(&nbuf/&&incr));
spool off
set termout on feedback 15 verify on
undef nbuf
exit
```

Figure 6.37 (continued)

A more detailed report is demonstrated in Figure 6.37. This report prompts for the value to increment the summation by and then generates a report that also lists the percent gain for each increment.

Of course, the analysis of the buffer cache may indicate that the buffers have been overallocated. The X$KCBCBH table will provide data on the results of removing buffers from the buffer cache. There is a row for each buffer in the current buffer cache in the table. The collection of statistics is enabled by setting the DB_BLOCK_LRU_STATISTICS to TRUE, shutting down, and restarting the database. This data collection will cause a performance hit, the severity is proportional to the number of current buffers in the buffer cache. Once data collection is complete, the DB_BLOCK_LRU_STATISTICS parameter should be set to FALSE.

To review data in the X$KCBCBH table, the methods are similar to those used for the X$KCBCBH table. You can select for a specific interval, or gather summation for ranges of buffers.

To determine the results from having, say, only 100 buffers in the cache, perform the following select:

```
SELECT SUM(count) "Hit Misses"
    FROM x$kcbcbh
    WHERE indx >= 100;
```

To summarize data over intervals of buffers, a select similar to the following could be used:

```
SELECT 10*TRUNC(indx/10)+1||' to '||10*(TRUNC(indx/10)+1) "Interval,"
SUM(copunt) 'Buffer Hits'
FROM x$kcbcbh
WHERE indx > 0
GROUP BY TRUNC(indx/10);
```

The results will look like the following:

Interval	Buffer Hits
1 to 10	2500
11 to 20	1345
21 to 30	1097
31 to 40	896
41 to 50	110

In this case if the number of buffers were reduced by 10 there would be few hits lost. If anything greater than 10 are dropped, significant losses in hits would occur. Therefore, drop only 10 buffers in this situation. A more detailed report can be generated with the script in Figure 6.37. See Figure 6.38. Once the buffer cache is tuned, you have completed the tuning of memory. The next step is to tune IO contention.

Tuning IO Contention. Once the data dictionary caches and buffer caches have been tuned, the DBA must turn his or her eyes to the IO performance of the disks and files associated with the Oracle system to realize further performance gains.

Tuning IO to Avoid Bottlenecks. Once the application and memory areas have been tuned, the next performance bottleneck can be the disk subsystem. This system is tuned by tuning the input and output processes that Oracle uses, reducing contention for disk resources, and reducing or eliminating dynamic space allocation within database data files.

```
rem    ************************************************************************
rem    NAME: SGA_DEC.sql
rem
rem    HISTORY:
rem    Date        Who                    What
rem    --------    ------------------     ----------------------------------------
rem    10/25/92    Cary Millsap           Creation
```

Figure 6.38 Example of buffer cache decrement detailed report script.

```
rem   01/07/93   Michael Brouillette   Switched to title80
rem   06/05/93   Mike Ault             Added selectable ranges
rem   FUNCTION: Examine statistice in the X$KCBCBH table with intent to shrink
rem             the SGA.
rem   ****************************************************************************
col bufval new_value nbuf noprint
col thits new_value tot_hits noprint
select value  bufval
from v$parameter
where
  lower(name) = 'db_block_buffers';

select sum(count) thits
from x$kcbhcbh;
start title80 "Lost Hits if &nbuf Cache Buffers were Removed"
col interval   format          a20 justify c heading 'Buffers'
col cache_hits format 999,999,990 justify c heading -
 'Hits that would have been lost|had Cache Buffers been removed'
col cum fromat 99.99 'Percent of loss'
set termout off feedback off verify off echo off
spool sga_dec&db

select
            lpad(to_char(&&incr*trunc(indx/&&incr)+1,'999,990'),8)||' to '||
            lpad(to_char(&&incr*(trunc(indx/&&incr)+1),'999,990'),8) interval,
            sum(count)  cache_hits,
            sum(count)/&tot_hits * 100 cum
from
            x$kcbcbh
where
            indx > 0
group by
  trunc(indx/&&incr) ;
spool off
set termout on feedback 15 verify on
exit
```

Figure 6.38 (continued)

The DBWR Process. The DBWR process manages the buffer cache. In this capacity it writes filled buffers from the buffer cache in the SGA to the disks. Obviously, a properly tuned DBWR process will be the first step in tuning IO for the Oracle system. The DBWR process, as was described in the section on BSTAT and ESTAT, uses the INIT.ORA parameters DB_BLOCK_WRITE_BATCH and DB_BLOCK_MAX_SCAN_CNT to determine when it should write used, or dirty, buffers to the disk, thus freeing them for further use. DBWR triggers on the following conditions:

1. A user process writes a used buffer to the dirty buffer list and finds it is DB_BLOCK_WRITE_BATCH / 2 long.
2. A user process searches DB_BLOCK_MAX_SCAN_CNT buffers without finding a clean one.
3. If DBWR has been inactive for three seconds.
4. When a checkpoint occurs LGWR signals DBWR triggering it to write.

The DBWR writes out DB_BLOCK_WRITE_BATCH buffers each time it is triggered. If there aren't that many buffers in the dirty buffer list, the buffers on the LRU list are written until DB_BLOCK_WRITE_BATCH buffers are written.

DBWR is monitored using the statistics dbwr_free_low and dbwr_free_needed. Dbwr_free_needed should always be zero. If dbwr_free_needed is nonzero, verify that DB_BLOCK_MAX_SCAN_CNT is set at 30 or greater. Normally, the default value of 30 is fine for this parameter. If you are dissatisfied with the performance of DBWR, try increasing the INIT.ORA parameter DB_BLOCK_WRITE_BATCH first. Increasing this parameter improves DBWR's ability to use operating system facilities to write to multiple disks and write adjacent blocks in a single IO operation. Unfortunately, dbwr_free_low and dbwr_free_needed are not available under ORACLE7, and what replaces them isn't clear.

Disk Contention. Once DBWR is tuned, the DBA needs to look at disk contention. Disk contention happens when one or more users attempt to read the same disk at the same time, or in some cases, access a different disk through the same controller path at the same time. This is prevented by spreading Oracle-related files across several platters—the more the better.

The DBA can monitor disk activity by looking at the statistics for disk IO stored in the database virtual tables. Using the hit ratio scripts from the previous section as a model, the DBA should be able to devise a periodic monitoring script that calculates periodic disk usage as well as the cumulative figures already stored in the virtual tables. The script in Figure 6.39 shows how to access the SYS tables for this cumulative information.

To perform periodic measurements simply perform the select shown in Figure 6.39 as part of an update to a DBA created table. In addition to the disk information, append a date and time stamp and then the table can be used to perform periodic disk IO calculations just like the HIT_RATIOS table in the previous pages. Instead of indexing by only date and hour, index by date, hour, and file name.

This report is a cumulative report that gives information based on IO since the Oracle instance was started. The report generated will list physical block reads and efficiency (the efficiency number measures the percent of time Oracle asked for and got the right block the first time. This is a function of type of table scan and indexing.

Some things to notice about the example report in Figure 6.40 are:

• The number of system data files. This indicates that the tools weren't split out into their own tablespace area.
• The relatively low efficiency of the SYSTEM areas in general. This is due to indexes and tables being mixed together in the SYSTEM area.

- If your temporary tablespace (ORA_TEMP1 in the example) shows an efficiency number, someone is using it for real instead of temporary tables.
- Rollback efficiency should always be 100 percent; if not, someone is using the rollback area for tables.

```
REM
REM NAME        :FILE_EFF.SQL
REM PURPOSE     :GENERATE FILE IO EFFICIENCIES REPORT
REM USE         :FROM STATUS_REPORTS.COM
REM Limitations :MUST BE RUN FROM ORACLE DBA ACCOUNT
REM Revisions:
REM Date           Modified By    Reason For change
REM 10-JUL-1992    M. AULT        INITIAL CREATE
REM 07-JUN-1993    M.AULT         Added reads to writes, reformatted
REM
$SET TERM/WIDT=132
$set term/noecho
connect  sys/&sys_password
$set term/echo
SET PAGES 58 NEWPAGE 0
SET LINES 131
COLUMN EFFICIENCY FORMAT 999.99 HEADING '% Eff'
COLUMN RW FORMAT 9,999,999,999 HEADING 'Phys Block read/writes'
COLUMN TS FORMAT A22 HEADING 'TABLESPACE NAME'
start title132 "FILE IO EFFICIENCY"
BREAK ON TS
DEFINE OUTPUT = 'file_io_eff&DB..rep'
spool &OUTPUT
SELECT
    SUBSTR(TS.NAME,1,30) TS,
    SUBSTR(i.kcffinam,1,40) name,
    x.kcfiopbr+x.kcfiopbw RW,
    decode(x.kcfiopbr,0,null,
                round(100*x.kcfiopyr/x.kcfiopbr,2))  efficiency
from x$kcfio x,ts$ ts, x$kcffi i, file$ f
where i.kcffiidn=f.file#
and ts.ts#=f.ts#
and x.kcfiofno=f.file# AND i.kcffinam IS NOT NULL ORDER BY I.KCFFINAM;
spool off
PAUSE 'PRESS RETURN TO CONTINUE'
$ SET TERM/WID=80
exit
```

Figure 6.39 SQL script for report on disk activity.

```
Date: 06/07/93                    "Your Company Name"                        Page:   1
Time: 10:46 AM                    FILE IO EFFICIENCY                         SYS
                                  "Your" Database

TABLESPACE NAME    NAME                                      Phys Block read/writes    % Eff
---------------    ------------------------------------      ----------------------    --------
CASE_RLBK_SEG      M_DISK6:[M_ORACLE6.DB_CASE]ORA_CASE_ROLL  14,411                    100
APPL_INDEXES       M_DISK8:[M_ORACLE6.DB_CASE]ORA_APPL_IDX_  791                       95.92
CASE_INDEX         M_DISK8:[M_ORACLE6.DB_CASE]ORA_CASE_INDE  3,279                     100
APPLICATIONS       M_DISK9:[M_ORACLE6.DB_CASE]ORA_APPL_1.DB  45,765                    23.07
CASE_TRAINING      M_DISK9:[M_ORACLE6.DB_CASE]ORA_CASE_TRAI  2,942                     21.47
                   M_DISK9:[M_ORACLE6.DB_CASE]ORA_CASE_TRAI  878                       18.36
CASE_W_AREA        M_DISK9:[M_ORACLE6.DB_CASE]ORA_CASE_WORK  259,531                   9.28
                   M_DISK9:[M_ORACLE6.DB_CASE]ORA_CASE_WORK  24,513                    13.75
DBA_TS             M_DISK9:[M_ORACLE6.DB_CASE]ORA_DBA_TS.DB  254                       61.72
DEFAULT_USER       M_DISK9:[M_ORACLE6.DB_CASE]ORA_DEFAULT_U  1,880                     36.09
SYSTEM             M_DISK9:[M_ORACLE6.DB_CASE]ORA_SYSTEM.DB  205,815                   22.85
                   M_DISK9:[M_ORACLE6.DB_CASE]ORA_SYSTEM_2.  198,757                   9.64
                   M_DISK9:[M_ORACLE6.DB_CASE]ORA_SYSTEM_3.  28,509                    21.12
                   M_DISK9:[M_ORACLE6.DB_CASE]ORA_SYSTEM_4.  20,507                    40.82
                   M_DISK9:[M_ORACLE6.DB_CASE]ORA_SYSTEM_5.  181,513                   10.11
                   M_DISK9:[M_ORACLE6.DB_CASE]ORA_SYSTEM_6.  193,892                   19.62
TEMP_USER1         M_DISK9:[M_ORACLE6.DB_CASE]ORA_TEMP_USER  3,703

17 rows selected.
```

Figure 6.40 Example of the output of File IO Efficiency report.

Index tablespace should always show high efficiencies; if they don't, then either the indexes are bad or someone is using the index areas for normal tables.

- An attempt should be made to even out IO. In the above example to much IO is being done on M_DISK9. Some of these data files should be spread to other disks.
- This report shows total IO for the time frame beginning with the Oracle system startup. The results could be stored for two or more dates and times and then subtracted to show the disk IO for a selected period of time. BSTAT/ESTAT should be used for this type of measurement.

With a copy of this report run before an application test run, and a copy run after the test run, an idea of the disk IO profile for the application can be developed. This profile combined with information concerning the maximum IO supported by each disk or each controller. The DBA can determine how best to split out the application's files between disks.

Further Reading. For more detailed information and further reading, take a look at the following:

HI/O HI/O Our System's WAY Too Slow a Collective Approach to Reducing Disk I/O, Brady, W.A., 1991 IOUG Proceedings, Miami, Florida.

SQL*DBA Monitor, A Powerful Tool for the Database Administrator, Fardoost, M., Oracle Corp., 1991 IOUG Proceedings, Miami, Florida.

Pushing Oracle to the Limit, Butler, B., Strehlo, K., DBMS Magazine, Dec. 1991.

Lies, Damned Lies, and Hit Ratios, Loney, K.M., Centocor, Inc., ORACLE Magazine, Summer 1992.

Using SQL to Identify Database Performance Bottlenecks, Gupta, G., Patkar, S., Oracle Corp., 1992 IOUG Proceedings, Los Angeles, California.

ORACLE RDBMS Performance Tuning Guide Version 6.0, Chapter 4, Oracle Corp. Part number 5317-V6.0.

ORACLE7 Server Administrator's Guide, Chapter 22, Oracle Corp. Part number 6694-70-1292, Dec. 1992.

Tuning to Prevent Contention. Contention occurs when a number of users attempt to access the same resource at the same time. This can occur for any database object but is most noticeable when the contention is for rollback segments, redo logs, latches, or locks. Under ORACLE7 you can also experience contention with the processes involved with the multithreaded server.

To correct contention you must first realize that it is occurring. The script shown in Figure 6.41 can be used to monitor for contention. The report generated by this script is shown in Figure 6.42.

```
REM
REM NAME          :CAL_STAT_REPORT.SQL
REM PURPOSE       :GENERATE CALCULATED STATISITICS REPORT USING CAL_STAT.SQL
REM USE           :FROM STATUS_REPORTS.COM
REM Limitations   :
REM Revisions:
REM Date          Modified By    Reason For change
REM 05-MAY-1992   Mike Ault      Initial Creation
REM
SET PAGES 58 NEWPAGE 0
COLUMN TODAY NEW_VALUE _DATE
GET ORACLE$SQL:CAL_STAT.SQL
R
START TITLE80 "CALCULATED STATISTICS REPORT"
DEFINE OUTPUT = 'CAL_STAT_REPORT&DB..LIS'
SPOOL &OUTPUT
SELECT * FROM DBA_TEMP;
SPOOL OFF

Listing of CAL_STAT.SQL - The called PL/SQL routine

DECLARE
    STAT_VAL NUMBER := 0;
    P_COUNT NUMBER := 0;
    PC_U NUMBER := 0;
    R_CALLS NUMBER := 0;
    H_RATIO NUMBER := 0;
    W_CONT  NUMBER := 0;
    DB_GETS NUMBER := 0;
    CON_GETS NUMBER := 0;
    P_READS NUMBER := 0;
    BB_WAITS NUMBER := 0;
    U_CALLS NUMBER := 0;
    CALLS_U NUMBER := 0;
    RLOG_WAIT NUMBER := 0;
    STAT_NAME CHAR(64);              /*Change to VARCHAR2 in ORACLE7*/
    TEMP_NAME CHAR(64);              /*Change to VARCHAR2 in ORACLE7*/
```

Figure 6.41 SQL and PL/SQL scripts to generate contention statistics.   (continued)

```
BEGIN
  DELETE DBA_TEMP;
  STAT_NAME := 'parse count';
     select a.name,b.value into TEMP_NAME, p_count
         from v$statname a, v$sysstat b   /* Selects can be made entirely */
         where a.statistic# = b.statistic#  AND A.NAME = STAT_NAME; /* from v$sysstat under
                              ORACLE7*/
  STAT_NAME := 'recursive calls';
     select a.name,b.value into TEMP_name, r_calls
         from v$statname a, v$sysstat b
         where a.statistic# = b.statistic#  AND A.NAME = STAT_NAME;
  STAT_NAME := 'user calls';
     select a.name,b.value into TEMP_NAME, u_calls
         from v$statname a, v$sysstat b
         where a.statistic# = b.statistic# AND A.NAME = STAT_NAME;
  STAT_NAME := 'db block gets';
     select a.name,b.value into TEMP_NAME, db_gets
         from v$statname a, v$sysstat b
         where a.statistic# = b.statistic# AND A.NAME = STAT_NAME;
  STAT_NAME := 'consistent gets';
     select a.name,b.value into TEMP_NAME, con_gets
         from v$statname a, v$sysstat b
         where a.statistic# = b.statistic#  AND A.NAME = STAT_NAME;
  STAT_NAME := 'physical reads';
     select a.name,b.value into TEMP_NAME, p_reads
         from v$statname a, v$sysstat b
         where a.statistic# = b.statistic#  AND A.NAME = STAT_NAME;
  STAT_NAME := 'buffer busy waits';
      select a.name,b.value into TEMP_NAME, bb_waits
          from v$statname a, v$sysstat b
          where a.statistic# = b.statistic#  AND A.NAME = STAT_NAME;
   PC_U    := (P_COUNT/U_CALLS);
   CALLS_U := (R_CALLS/U_CALLS);
   H_RATIO := (100*(DB_GETS+CON_GETS)/(DB_GETS+CON_GETS+P_READS));
   W_CONT  := (BB_WAITS/(DB_GETS+CON_GETS));
  STAT_NAME := 'RECURSIVE CALLS PER USER';
   INSERT INTO DBA_TEMP VALUES (STAT_NAME, CALLS_U);
  STAT_NAME := 'CUMMULATIVE HIT RATIO';
   INSERT INTO DBA_TEMP VALUES (STAT_NAME, H_RATIO);
  STAT_NAME := 'BUFFER ACCESS WAIT CONTENTION';
   INSERT INTO DBA_TEMP VALUES (STAT_NAME, W_CONT);
  STAT_NAME := 'CALLS PER PARSE';
   INSERT INTO DBA_TEMP VALUES (STAT_NAME, PC_U);
  STAT_NAME := 'dbwr free needed';   /* Obsolete in ORACLE7*/
     select a.name,b.value into TEMP_NAME, stat_val
         from v$statname a, v$sysstat b
         where a.statistic# = b.statistic# AND A.NAME = STAT_NAME;
   INSERT INTO DBA_TEMP VALUES (STAT_NAME, STAT_VAL);
  STAT_NAME := 'dbwr free low';   /*Obsolete in ORACLE7*/
     select a.name,b.value into TEMP_NAME, stat_val
         from v$statname a, v$sysstat b
         where a.statistic# = b.statistic# AND A.NAME = STAT_NAME;
   INSERT INTO DBA_TEMP VALUES (STAT_NAME, STAT_VAL);
  STAT_NAME := 'enqueue timeouts';
     select a.name,b.value into TEMP_NAME, stat_val
         from v$statname a, v$sysstat b
         where a.statistic# = b.statistic# AND A.NAME = STAT_NAME;
   INSERT INTO DBA_TEMP VALUES (STAT_NAME, STAT_VAL);
```

Figure 6.41 (continued)

```
STAT_NAME := 'table scans (short tables)';
   select a.name,b.value into TEMP_NAME, stat_val
      from v$statname a, v$sysstat b
      where a.statistic# = b.statistic#  AND A.NAME = STAT_NAME;
  INSERT INTO DBA_TEMP VALUES (STAT_NAME, STAT_VAL);
STAT_NAME := 'table scans (long tables)';
   select a.name,b.value into TEMP_NAME, stat_val
      from v$statname a, v$sysstat b
      where a.statistic# = b.statistic#  AND A.NAME = STAT_NAME;
  INSERT INTO DBA_TEMP VALUES (STAT_NAME, STAT_VAL);
STAT_NAME := 'table fetch continued row';
   select a.name,b.value into TEMP_NAME, stat_val
      from v$statname a, v$sysstat b
      where a.statistic# = b.statistic#  AND A.NAME = STAT_NAME;
  INSERT INTO DBA_TEMP VALUES (STAT_NAME, STAT_VAL);
STAT_NAME := 'sorts (memory)';
   select a.name,b.value into TEMP_NAME, stat_val
      from v$statname a, v$sysstat b
      where a.statistic# = b.statistic#  AND A.NAME = STAT_NAME;
  INSERT INTO DBA_TEMP VALUES (STAT_NAME, STAT_VAL);
STAT_NAME := 'sorts (disk)';
   select a.name,b.value into TEMP_NAME, stat_val
      from v$statname a, v$sysstat b
      where a.statistic# = b.statistic#  AND A.NAME = STAT_NAME;
INSERT INTO DBA_TEMP VALUES (STAT_NAME, STAT_VAL);
STAT_NAME := 'redo log space wait time';
   select a.name,b.value into TEMP_NAME, stat_val
      from v$statname a, v$sysstat b
      where a.statistic# = b.statistic#  AND A.NAME = STAT_NAME;
INSERT INTO DBA_TEMP VALUES (STAT_NAME, STAT_VAL);
 COMMIT;
EXCEPTION
   WHEN ZERO_DIVIDE THEN
      INSERT INTO DBA_TEMP VALUES (STAT_NAME,0);
   COMMIT;
END;
```

Figure 6.41 (continued)

Under ORACLE7 the statistic name is stored in the V$SYSSTAT table, so the select from the V$STATNAME is redundant. This simplifies the query. The reason multiple selects are used in the script is because the select is slightly different each time. Therefore a cursor and fetch cannot be used. In addition, a variable cannot be passed into a parsed cursor, so it is not possible to use a cursor. The query will become:

```
select name, value into TEMP_NAME, stat_val
from v$sysstat where NAME = STAT_NAME;
```

The first section of Figure 6.41 shows the SQL script used to call and run the PL/SQL script located in the second section of Figure 6.41. This script retrieves contention and database health related statistics and calculates other statistics based upon those it retrieves. An example of the report generated by these two scripts is shown in Figure 6.42.

```
Date: 06/04/93                "Your Company Name"              Page:   1
Time: 04:09 PM             CALCULATED STATISTICS REPORT        KCGC_DBA
                               "Your" Database


STAT_NAME                           STAT_VALUE
----------------------------------- ----------
RECURSIVE CALLS PER USER            1.28859702
CUMULATIVE HIT RATIO                88.2306292
BUFFER ACCESS WAIT CONTENTION       .000085936
CALLS PER PARSE                     .08003804
dbwr free needed                    0              Obsolete in ORACLE7
dbwr free low                       295            Obsolete in ORACLE7
enqueue timeouts                    17
table scans (short tables)          4255
table scans (long tables)           7497
table fetch continued row           61
sorts (memory)                      12745
sorts (disk)                        6
redo log space wait time            0

13 rows selected.
```

Figure 6.42 Example of calculated statistics report.

The statistics that are calculated in 6.40 are shown in upper case. The "raw" values are reported in lower case. What is this report telling us? Let's look at each of the statistics and see.

Recursive calls per user—This calculated statistic is the ratio between user calls and recursive calls. If this number is over four, you need to revisit how your applications are using indexes and how your data dictionary and buffers are tuned.

Cumulative hit ratio—This calculated statistic shows the cumulative hit ratio. In general, use period hit ratio from the hit ratio report. For a normal database this should be above 70 percent shortly after startup and shouldn't drop below this value. If your cumulative hit ratio is less than 70 percent to 90 percent you should look at buffer and data dictionary caches for possible tuning problems.

Buffer access wait contention—This is the total wait contention mentioned on page 5-3 of the *Oracle RDBMS Performance Tuning Guide Version 6*. If this parameter is greater than 5 percent to 10 percent, run the report shown in Figure 6.43 and determine the area where contention is occurring.

Calls per parse—This calculated statistic tells you if parses are being reused. The lower the number, the fewer cursors (parses) are being reused, and performance will suffer. If you database uses numerous ad hoc queries instead of PL/SQL and FORMS, then this number will always be low.

The other statistics listed were covered in detail in the section on BSTAT and ESTAT.

Buffer Contention. If you think there may be contention for buffers, as shown by the buffer busy waits statistic mentioned in previous sections, the report in Figure 6.43 can be run to show possible areas of contention.

```
REM
REM   NAME      : CONTEND.SQL
REM   PURPOSE   : SHOWS WHERE POSSIBLE CONTENTION FOR RESOURCES IN
REM               BUFFER BUSY WAITS
REM   USE       : TO PINPOINT ADDITIONAL TUNING AREAS.
REM REV 0. DOCUMENTED ON PAGE 5-6 OF TUNING MANUAL. M. AULT 14-AUG-1992
REM
SET VERIFY OFF FEEDBACK OFF
SET PAGES 58 LINES 79
START TITLE80 "AREA OF CONTENTION REPORT"
DEFINE OUTPUT = 'CONTEND_AREA&DB..LIS'
SPOOL &OUTPUT
SELECT CLASS,SUM(COUNT) TOTAL_WAITS, sum(time) TOTAL_TIME
FROM V$WAITSTAT
group by class;
SPOOL OFF
PAUSE PRESS RETURN TO CONTINUE
EXIT
```

Figure 6.43 SQL script for report to show possible contention areas.

```
Date: 06/03/93              "Your Company Name"          Page:    1
Time: 08:25 AM           AREA OF CONTENTION REPORT       ELWOOD_DBA
                            "Your" Database

CLASS                TOTAL_WAITS      TOTAL_TIME
------------------   ----------       ----------
data block           68               0
free list            0                0
save undo block      0                0
save undo header     0                0
segment header       1                0
sort block           0                0
system undo block    0                0
system undo header   0                0
undo block           0                0
undo header          1                0


10 rows selected
```

Figure 6.44 Example of output from CONTEND.SQL script.

The report in Figure 6.44 covers the following types of blocks in the buffer cache:

data block—This statistic shows waits for blocks in the data buffer cache.

free list—This statistic shows waits for free lists (free list contention).

system undo header—This statistic shows waits for header blocks of the system rollback segment.

system undo block—This statistic shows waits for buffers containing other than header blocks for the system rollback segment.

undo header—This statistic shows waits for buffers containing nonsystem rollback segment header blocks

undo blocks—This statistic shows waits for buffers containing other than header blocks for the nonsystem rollback segments.

Segment header, save undo header, save undo block and sort block are not used by DBAs for tuning.

The statistic with the highest value shows the area where the DBA should concentrate their tuning efforts. From the example report (no statistic is actually high enough to warrant action) the INIT.ORA parameter DB_BLOCK_BUFFERS could be increased to reduce data block buffer contention. If rollback contention is indicated ("undo" statistics), increase the number of rollback segments. Contention is indicated when any one area shows greater than a 1 percent value for the calculation:

parameter / (db block gets + consistent gets)

```
REM
REM NAME          : LATCH_CO.SQL
REM PURPOSE       : Genereate latch contention report
REM USE           : From SQLPlus or other front end
REM Limitations   : None
REM Revisions:
REM Date          Modified By    Reason For change
REM 5 DEC 92      Mike Ault      Initial Creation
REM
COLUMN NAME FORMAT A30
COLUMN RATIO FORMAT 999.999
SET PAGES 58 NEWPAGE 0
start title80 "LATCH CONTENTION REPORT"
define output = 'CONTENTION&db..LIS'
SPOOL &output
SELECT A.NAME,100.*B.TIMEOUTS/B.WAITS RATIO FROM
V$LATCHNAME A, V$LATCH B WHERE
A.LATCH# = B.LATCH# AND B.TIMEOUTS > 0;
SPOOL OFF
PAUSE PRESS RETURN TO CONTINUE
EXIT
```

Figure 6.45 SQL script to generate latch contention report.

Latch Contention. The next type of contention deals with latches. Look at the script in Figure 6.45. This script generates a report of latch contention. The script restricts output to only those latches that exhibit a greater than zero timeout value. Obviously if a latch shows zero timeouts, there is no contention for that latch. This restriction greatly reduces the amount of information the DBA has to review. The multipage monitor screen in SQLDBA is usually reduced to a few lines of output that gives the DBA exactly what is needed to get a good picture of latch activity in the database.

Note: Under ORACLE7 the column timeouts becomes sleeps and the column waits becomes misses. The immediate_misses and immediate_gets parameters, new to ORACLE7, should also be monitored. The query becomes:

```
SELECT
A.NAME,
100.*B.MISSES/B.GETS RATIO1
100.*B.IMMEDIATE_MISSES/(B.IMMEDIATE_GETS+b.IMMEDIATE_MISSES) RATIO2
FROM
V$LATCHNAME A, V$LATCH B WHERE
A.LATCH# = B.LATCH# AND B.MISSES > 0;
```

The report runs fine with the above query substitution under ORACLE7. See Figure 6.46. As you can see, this report is much easier to look at than the SQLDBA monitor screen. The suggested calculations are done behind the scenes, and the DBA can tell at a glance if any latches are suffering contention. One interesting thing to notice is that all of these values are fractional percentages with the exception of "redo copy," which is 200 percent due to having only one CPU on the example system. If these values get up into whole percentages, reduce contention in version 6 by increasing the latches DC_ parameter in the INIT.ORA file or by increasing the SHARED_POOL_SIZE parameter under ORACLE7.

```
Date: 06/04/93                  "Your Company Name"              Page:    1
Time: 04:04 PM               LATCH CONTENTION REPORT             KCGC_DBA
                                "Your" Database

NAME                          RATIO
----------------------------- --------
process allocation            .101
session allocation            .003
messages                      .002
enqueues                      .014
cache buffers chains          .000
cache buffers lru chain       .030
cache buffer handles          .001
multiblock read objects       .005
redo allocation               .032
redo copy                     200.000
dml/ddl allocation            .005
row cache objects             .008

12 rows selected.
```

Figure 6.46 Example report generated by LATCH_CO.SQL.

Some latches may not have exact correspondences (i.e., redo_copy, redo_allocation, etc.); these have been discussed in the section on BSTAT and ESTAT. The material from that section is recapped next, so if you've already read that section, you can skip over this to the next section.

The following latches are the major ones the DBA needs to be concerned about; the others shouldn't require tuning.

Cache Buffers Chain—This latch indicates user processes are waiting to scan the SGA for block access. The latch is related to the INIT.ORA parameter DB_BLOCK_HASH_BUCKETS, which is related to DB_BLOCK_BUFFERS. To tune this latch, adjust DB_BLOCK_BUFFERS.

Cache Buffers LRU Chains—This latch indicates waits when user attempts to scan the LRU (least recently used) chain that contains all the used blocks in the database buffers. To reduce waits on this latch, increase the INIT.ORA parameter DB_BLOCK_BUFFERS or the INIT.ORA parameter DB_BLOCK_WRITE_BATCH.

Enqueues—This latch is controlled by the INIT.ORA parameter ENQUEUE_RESOURCES. If the ratio of timeouts to total exceeds 10 percent in version 6 or 1 percent in ORACLE7 increase ENQUEUE_RESOURCES.

Redo Allocation—This latch controls the allocation of space in the redo buffer. There is only one allocation latch per instance in version 6 and ORACLE7. To reduce contention for this latch, reduce the value of the INIT.ORA parameter LOG_SMALL_ENTRY_MAX_SIZE on multi-CPU systems to force use of a redo copy latch. On single-CPU systems the value of CPU_COUNT in the INIT.ORA file is set to zero, this indicates no redo copy latches are allowed. Setting the CPU_COUNT to 1 and LOG_SIMULTANEOUS_COPIES to 2 is not recommended by Oracle for single CPU machines even though two redo copy latches are allowed per CPU. In the example report 90 uses of the redo copy latch are shown even though the CPU count for the computer was set to zero. This indicates there are redo copy latches even on single-CPU machines.

Redo Copy—This latch is used when an entry's size exceeds LOG_SMALL_ENTRY_SIZE and use of a redo copy latch is forced. This happens on both single- and multi-CPU computers as is witnessed by the above example report for a single-CPU computer. On multi-CPU computers you can reduce redo copy latch contention by increasing LOG_SIMULTANEOUS_COPIES to twice the value of CPU_COUNT, and — or, increasing the value of LOG_ENTRY_PREBUILD_THRESHOLD. The LOG_SMALL_ENTRY_SIZE parameter is changed to LOG_SMALL_ENTRY_MAX_SIZE under ORACLE7 and the parameter is used to specify the maximum size of a redo entry that can be copied on the redo allocation latch.

On single-CPU systems, changing LOG_ENTRY_PREBUILD_THRESHOLD has no effect since the CPU_COUNT is set to zero and LOG_SIMULTANEOUS_COPIES and LOG_ENTRY_PREBUILD_THRESHOLD have no effect.

LOG_ENTRY_PREBUILD_THRESHOLD determines the size of redo entry that will be prebuilt before being passed to the log buffer. By prebuilding the entry the time the redo copy latch is held is reduced thus reducing the contention for the latch.

Row Cache Objects—This latch shows waits for the user processes attempting to access the cached data dictionary values. To reduce contention for this latch the data dictionary cache is tuned. This will be covered in a later section.

Other than those listed above, the rest of the latches shouldn't require tuning. If excessive contention is shown for them, contact the Oracle Support group.

Additional Tuning Concerns. Once the DBA has tuned memory, tuned IO, and tuned contention, there are still a couple of minor items that he or she must consider. These items will improve performance, but any improvement would be masked by the other tuning areas if they are not taken care of first. This is why these are addressed last. The final tuning areas concern sorts, free lists, and checkpoints.

Sorts, Free Lists, and Checkpoints. Improvement of sort speed provides obvious benefits. Free lists provide information on the free blocks inside database tables. If there aren't enough free lists, this can have an impact on performance. Checkpoints are writes from buffers to disk. Checkpoints, if excessive, can adversely effect performance as well. If there aren't enough checkpoints, recovery from disasters can be impeded. The DBA needs to monitor these items on a regular basis and tune them as needed to get peak performance from the database.

Tuning Oracle Sorts. Sorts are done when Oracle performs operations that retrieve information and require the information retrieved to be an ordered set—in other words, sorted. Sorts are done when the following operations are performed:

- Index creation
- Group by or order by statements
- Use of the distinct operator
- Join operations
- Union, intersect, and minus set operators

Each of these operations requires a sort. There are two main indicators that your sorts are going to disk and therefore your sort area in memory is too small. This area is defined by the INIT.ORA parameter SORT_AREA_SIZE in both version 6 and ORACLE7.

One method involves running the sort while watching the SQLDBA monitor screen for file IO and monitoring the file IO to the temporary tablespace that the user performing the sort is assigned to. If there are numerous users assigned to the temporary tablespace, it may be difficult to determine who is actually performing IO to the temporary area. In this situation, create a small secondary temporary tablespace and assign the user performing the sort to the secondary space so all activity to that tablespace is due to the sort.

The second method involves the sorts (disk) statistic shown in Figure 6.40. If this parameter exceeds 10 percent of the sum of sorts(memory) and sorts(disk), increase the SORT_AREA_SIZE parameter. Large values for this parameter can induce paging and swapping, so be careful you don't over allocate.

Under ORACLE7 the SORT_AREA_SIZE parameter controls the maximum sort area. The sort area will be dynamically reallocated down to the size specified by the new INIT.ORA parameter SORT_AREA_RETAINED_SIZE.

Reducing Free List Contention. As was stated above, a free list is a list of data blocks that contain free lists. Every table has one or more free lists. This is determined by the INIT.ORA parameter FREE_LIST_PROC, its default value is 4. The setting of this parameter at the time the table is created determines the number of free lists for the table.

If you decide this parameter must be increased, the effected tables will have to be dropped and recreated for it to take effect under version 6. Ideally, the number of free lists should be equal to the number of individual processes that will be accessing the tables simultaneously.

Under ORACLE7 each table specifies its own number of free lists by use of the FREELISTS parameter of the CREATE TABLE command, this parameter will default to 1 if not specified explicitly.

Free list contention is shown by contention for data blocks in the buffer cache. If you get contention as shown in the report in Figure 6.44 under the data block area. This type of contention can also indicate there aren't enough data buffers.

Tuning Checkpoints. Checkpoints provide for rolling forward after a system crash. Data is applied from the time of the last checkpoint forward from the redo entries. Checkpoints also provide for reuse of redo logs. When a redo log is filled, the LGWR process automatically switches to the next available log. All data in the now inactive log is written to disk by an automatic checkpoint. This frees the log for reuse or for archiving.

Checkpoints occur when a redo log is filled, when the INIT.ORA parameter LOG_CHECKPOINT_INTERVAL under version 6 or ORACLE7 is reached (total bytes written to a redo log), under ORACLE7 the elapsed time has reached the INIT.ORA parameter LOG_CHECKPOINT_TIMEOUT expressed in seconds or every three seconds under version 6, or when an ALTER SYSTEM command is issued with the CHECKPOINT option specified under ORACLE7.

While frequent checkpoints will reduce recovery time, they will also decrease performance. Infrequent checkpoints will increase performance but increase required recovery times. To reduce checkpoints to only happen on log switches, set LOG_CHECKPOINT_INTERVAL to larger than your redo log size, and for ORACLE7 set LOG_CHECKPOINT_TIMEOUT to zero.

If checkpoints still cause performance problems, set the INIT.ORA parameter CHECKPOINT_PROCESS to TRUE to start the CKPT process running. This will free the LGWR from checkpoint and increase performance. The INIT.ORA parameter PROCESSES may also have to be increased.

Managing in a Distributed Environment

The Oracle database can be operated in one of several types of relational environments. These types are:

- Exclusive, non-shared database
- Parallel server database
- Distributed database
- Client/Server database
- Multi-threaded server database

For the most part, we have been discussing the database as if it were an exclusive type of database. The characteristics of this type of database are:

- Standalone operation. The database doesn't require other databases to be available to function.
- Single location and CPU. The database resides in one physical location and uses one CPU.
- Database administration is independent from other sites and little, if any, inter-site cooperation is required.

If you feel your applications will never operate outside of these parameters, then you can skip this chapter. If your applications will require a more complex environment involving multiple CPUs, sites, and databases, then read on.

7.1 Management in a Parallel or "Shared" Environment

In a shared or parallel database the CPUs involved are loosely coupled, such as in a VAX cluster, and share disk resources. This is usually only applicable to a VAX/VMS system since most UNIX systems can't be clustered. The database is called parallel or shared because the database files themselves are shared between several instances on several CPUs or nodes.

The benefits of this type of installation are severalfold.

- The data is maintained on one disk farm allowing ease of backup and management.
- The user processing load is spread across several CPUs, thus allowing more users and faster access to data.
- Different types of users can be placed on different machines to allow the distribution of types of processing. For example, users who require large sorts and intense CPU activity can be placed on a cluster node with a faster CPU and larger internal RAM (for a larger sort area), while users who only query limited sets of data can be placed on a smaller CPU.
- This type of configuration is good for databases without a lot of update activity or where the types of update activity can be distributed between the nodes in the cluster. For example, the group that uses node A only deals with tables A, B, and C on drive A, while the group that uses node B only deals with tables D, E, and F on drive B.

Figure 7.1 shows a comparison of a shared or parallel system and an exclusive system. The major disadvantage to a parallel configuration is that a single point of failure can result in loss of all database file access. For example, if the disk farm is hung off of a single disk controller on one VAX in the cluster and either the disk controller or VAX itself fails, access to the database is lost.

The following are disadvantages to this type of configuration:

- Since the instances are all part of the same cluster, they must have the same SGA size.
- Each instance must have its own SGA, which will have to be maintained in parallel with the main SGA.
- Additional overhead is required due to the parallel lock manager.

7.1.1 INIT.ORA Parameters for a Shared Database

Most of the INIT.ORA parameters that control a parallel instance are prefixed with "GC_." These parameters are listed in Figure 7.2. These parameters are subject to change, and this list is only a general guideline. You should use the most current version of the *ORACLE7 Parallel Server Administrator's Guide* for your database for the most current list. Another good reference will be the README files that come with the most current release tape.

The administrator's guide provides detailed guidelines for setting these parameters. There are also several normal server parameters that take on added significance. These are:

```
CONTROL_FILES, which must be set identically for all instances.
CPU_COUNT, which can be different for each instance.
DB_BLOCK_SIZE, which must be identical for all instances.
DB_FILES, which must be the same for all instances.
DB_NAME, which if specified must be the same for all instances.
LOG_FILES, which must be identical for all instances.
ROLLBACK_SEGMENTS, which must be different for each instance.
ROW_LOCKING, which must be identical for all instances
SERIALIZABLE, which must be identical for all instances.
SINGLE_PROCESS must be FALSE for all instances in the server
```

All other parameters can differ for each instance. The guidelines for the parallel server should be followed when a guideline for a specific parameter is given.

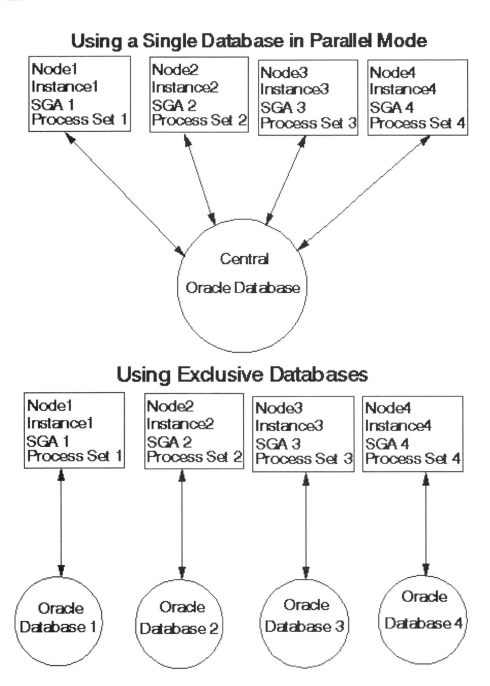

Figure 7.1 Parallel versus shared databases.

Use of SQLDBA. There are two types of instance in a parallel environment: the DEFAULT and the CURRENT instance. The DEFAULT instance is the instance that is resident on the node where the SQLDBA program is invoked. The CURRENT instance is the instance where you may have used the CONNECT command to attach to. The CURRENT and DEFAULT instances will be the same if you don't specify a connect string in the connect command.

The following commands apply under SQLDBA when you are connected to an instance:

```
ARCHIVE LOG
CONNECT
CONNECT INTERNAL
MONITOR
SHOW INSTANCE
SHOW PARAMETERS
SHOW SGA
SHUTDOWN
STARTUP
```

You change the DEFAULT instance by disconnecting from the CURRENT installation and issuing the "SET INSTANCE con string" command. Note there is no username or password.

V6 Parameter Name	Function	Used in ORACLE7
GC_DB_LOCKS	The total number of instance locks for an ORACLE parallel server. Identical for all instances in the server	Yes
GC_FILES_TO_LOCKS	Controls the hashing of locks from the database files to sets of instance locks. Identical for all instances in the server.	Yes
GC_LCK_PROCS	The total number of ORACLE7 PCM locks (Distributed locks) covering database blocks cached in the multiple SGAs of a parallel server. Must be identical for all instances in server.	only applicable for ORACLE7
GC_ROLLBACK_LOCKS	10 per instance for more than 2 instances, otherwise the default is adequate. Identical for all instances.	Yes
GC_ROLLBACK_SEGMENTS	Total number of rollbacks in all instances of the parallel database. Identical for all instances in the server.	Yes
GC_SAVE_ROLLBACK_LOCKS	10 per instance for more than 2 instances, otherwise the default is adequate. Must be identical for all instances in the parallel server.	Yes

Figure 7.2 INIT.ORA parameters that control parallel instance operation.

GC_SEGMENTS	10 per instance for more than 2 instances,otherwise the default is adequate. Identical for all instances.	**Yes**
GC_SORT_LOCKS	Total number of sort locks.	**OBSOLETE**
GC_TABLESPACES	The total number of tablespace for all instances that can be brought on or off line simultaneously. Must be the same for all instances in the database.	
INSTANCES	Current maximum number of instances that can be open on the database. Cannot exceed the CREATE DATABASE parameter MAXINSTANCES.	**OBSOLETE**
LOG_ALLOCATION	Number of redo log file blocks allocated to an instance each time it requires more space in a current online log file.	
MI_BG_PROCS	The number of lock background processes (LCK0 to LCK9) must be greater than 0 to use Parallel server.	**Replaced by GC_LCK_PROCS**
INSTANCE_NUMBER	This is an ORACLE7 parameter that uniquely identifies a particular instance to the parallel instance. It is used to map the instance to a set of free lists for each table.	
THREAD	This is an ORACLE7 parameter that tells the instance which redo log thread to use.	

Figure 7.2 (continued)

7.1.2 Basic Procedure for Creating a Shared Oracle Database

Everything must start somewhere. A parallel database starts with a single instance. This instance is created exactly like an exclusive instance. Once the instance is up and operating, the additional instances that will share the database are defined. The final step is to bring the INIT.ORA files into sync and start all the instances in shared mode.

There are several parts of the database that need to be considered when designing and starting up a parallel instance:

- File structures
- Data dictionary
- Sequence number generators
- Rollback segments
- Redo log files
- Database creation

By properly designing the above items, resource contention can be avoided, thus optimizing performance.

All instances in a parallel database use the same control files and data files. Each instance has its own SGA and redo logs and can have differing numbers of redo logs, and different degrees of mirroring. Each must have its own dedicated rollback segment(s).

What does all this mean? First, before we can start up a parallel instance, there must be sufficient redo logs and rollback segments available to split up among the instances. Next, there must be sufficient memory available on each node to handle the SGA requirements for each instance.

The rollback segments can be either public or private. It is suggested that they be made as private rollback segments so that they can be positioned on the disk farm for each instance and made exclusive to that instance. Additional rollback segments can be specified from any active instance. Each instance acquires its private rollback segments by specifying their name in the INIT.ORA parameter ROLLBACK_SEGMENTS. At least one rollback segment must be available for each instance. This can be guaranteed via use of the private rollback segments.

Let's look at a more detailed procedure.

1. Using ORACLEINS create the initial instance. Verify that the parameters MAXINSTANCES, MAXLOGFILES, ARCHIVELOG, and for ORACLE7, MAXLOGHISTORY are set in accordance with the values you require. You should alter the INIT.ORA parameter DB_BLOCK_SIZE to ensure the database can provide the number of freelists and extents you require. You should also set the DB_NAME parameter.

2. Add a second rollback segment to this new instance and then shut down, add the second name to the INIT.ORA file via the ROLLBACK_SEGMENTS parameter, and start up the instance. Under ORACLE7, there is no need to shut down; once the rollback segment is created, it can be brought online with the ALTER ROLLBACK SEGMENT command.

3. Add required tablespaces to the instance. As a minimum, add the following additional tablespaces:

   • TOOLS—For form, report, and menu files owned by SYSTEM
   • ORA_USERS—To use for the DEFAULT tablespace for users
   • ORA_TEMP—To use as the TEMPORARY tablespace for users
   • ORA_ROLLBACKSn—To use for rollbacks for this instance. If there are different disk strings attached to other nodes, you may want to add additional rollback segment tablespaces for each set of disks that will be used by the parallel instance. The "n" is an integer that specifies an arbitrary number assigned to each instance in the database.

4. Create additional rollback segments. There should be one rollback segment for every 4 users you expect for each instance. If you expect 50 users on instance 1, 24 users on instance 2, and 50 users on instance 3, assign 32 rollback segments total spread over the 3 ORA_ROLLBACK tablespaces (1 tablespace for each instance).

5. For version 6, create enough additional redo logs for the expected number of instances. There should be two redo logs per instance as a minimum; three are suggested. For ORACLE7 create enough redo log threads for all of the expected instances. Each thread must have at least two groups of one redo log each; three groups are suggested.

6. Shut down the instance, and deassign the rollback segment assigned in step 2 by removing it from the ROLLBACK_SEGMENTS parameter. Assign the rollback segments for this instance only by placing their names in the ROLLBACK_SEGMENTS parameter. Alter the GC_ROLLBACK_SEGMENTS parameter (or add it) to the total number of rollback segments expected to ever be created by all instances in the parallel database. For ORACLE7 you can take the additional system rollback segment offline with the ALTER ROLLBACK SEGMENT command, and bring on this instance's rollback segments with the same command without shutting down the instance.

7. For ORACLE7, add the THREAD parameter to the INIT.ORA file and set the THREAD value for this instance.

8. Set the ARCHIVE_LOG_DEST and for ORACLE7 the ARCHIVE_LOG_FORMAT parameters.

9. Set all INIT.ORA GC_ parameters.

10. Set the INIT.ORA parameter INSTANCE_NUMBER for the initial instance to 1. For additional instances, increment this number so each instance has a unique value. This value determines the free list used by the instance. If one instance uses this parameter, they all should. If it is not used, each instance acquires the lowest available instance number and the DBA has no control over it.

11. Be sure the SINGLE_PROCESS value is set to FALSE in the INIT.ORA file, for this and all other instances in the parallel instance.

12. If not already shut down, shut down and then restart the instance in parallel mode.

13. Create the additional instances, edit their INIT.ORA files in accordance with figure 7.2, and specify, for each instance, the appropriate rollback segments and for ORACLE7, the redo thread.

14. Create a common INITSHARE.ORA file in which the common initialization parameters are placed. For a parallel database all instances must have the same value for the following parameters:

```
CONTROL_FILES            GC_SEGMENTS
DB_BLOCK_SIZE            GC_TABLESPACES
DB_FILES                 LOG_FILES
DB_NAME                  LICENSE_MAX_SESSIONS
GC_DB_LOCKS              LICENSE_MAX_USERS
GC_FILES_TO_LOCKS        LICENSE_SESSIONS_WARNING
GC_LCK_PROCS             ROW_LOCKING
GC_ROLLBACK_LOCKS        SERAILIZABLE
GC_ROLLBACK_SEGMENTS     SINGLE_PROCESS
GC_SAVE_ROLLBACK_LOCKS
IFILE
```

The IFILE parameter should be specified in each of the instance's INIT.ORA file to point to the location of the INITSHARE.ORA file that contains the rest of the parameters.

15. Start the additional instances in parallel.

Archive Logging. Archive logging is controlled independently for each instance, however, if one archives it is suggested that all archive.

Backup. Backup can be either online or offline. Any instance can issue the ALTER TABLESPACE name BEGIN | END command. For ease of management it is suggested that the first instance created be used as the management instance and all backup and export actions be initiated there if possible.

Recovery. Recovery of a single failed node is accomplished by the SMON process of one of the other nodes when the failed node comes back on line. Recovery of data, redo, or rollback files can be accomplished from any instance in the database, but it is suggested that recovery be done with the other instances shut down and the instance used for recovery be in EXCLUSIVE mode. See Chapter 8 for database recovery instructions.

7.2 Distributed Database Management

The next form of database we will look at is the distributed database. The distributed database exists at numerous locations, perhaps even on different types of computers. The distributed database is linked via a network, be it LAN (local area network), WAN (wide area network), or a combination of both.

As its name implies, the database itself, the files that make up the database, are spread across the various nodes of the system. This could lead to duplication of data, bad updates due to network problems, indeed, a whole plethora of problems. Oracle, in ORACLE7, has solved many of these possible problems through several methods. These methods are the two-phase commit, table replication through database level triggers, and table snapshots.

Essentially you as DBA are responsible for seeing that the data someone needs is available when they need it, whether the data is on the VAX in the next room, or on the HP9000 UNIX platform in Ankara, Turkey. This can be a bit of a challenge. Let's examine the tools and techniques used to implement a distributed database.

First, the communication between the platforms will most likely be DECNET, NOVELL, TCPIP, or one of the other major protocols. For the purposes of this book we will limit ourselves to DECNET, the major DEC/VAX protocol, and TCP/IP, the major UNIX protocol.

No matter what protocol you use, you will have to have the Oracle SQL*NET package that is compatible. With version 6 of Oracle, these were separate packages, SQL*NET/DECNET or SQL*NET/TCPIP. Under ORACLE7 you will have a core module known as the TNS (transparent network substrate) and the drivers for the protocol you need. You can have as many drivers as you have supported protocols. Normally you will need both DECNET for your LAN and TCPIP for communication with a WAN.

7.2.1 Use of SQL*NET/DECNET

In its most basic form, a distributed database would consist of a link that allows update and query between two databases. Under version 6, you are able to query, except for LONG fields, across database links. You cannot update unless you are logged in to the node at which the data resides. This rather puts a crimp on the usefulness of distributed databases under version 6. However, let's look at what we can do.

Under version 6, the DBA should supply a DATABASE LINK to the database users. It is suggested that a logical definition be made to specify the "connect string" portion of the link. For example, if we have a database in Devonshire, England and one in Dallas, Texas, and we want to be able to query the database in Devonshire for the local price of fish and chips (which is, of course, stored in the LUNCH table of the PRICE database), we must specify a logical connect string and an internal database link specification.

Defining a VMS logical connection string:

```
$DEFINE  DEVONCON  DEVO1"""SQLNET SQLNET"""::"""TASK=ORDNPRICE"""
```

DEVONCON is a VMS logical that now contains the string:

```
DEVO1"""SQLNET SQLNET"""::"""TASK=ORDNPRICE"""
```

This string breaks down into:

DEV01—The node name of the system we are going to contact.
""""SQLNET SQLNET""""—The username and password for the user we wish to use (use of DECNET objects is better for security, but this isn't a DECNET book).
""""TASK=ORDNPRICE""""—The task, or procedure, to execute once connected.

The TASK defines a DCL (digital command language) command file that sets up the connection to the database on the server end of the connection. The DCL file should reside either in the login directory of the called user or in the SQLNETDNT directory. The contents of this file are as follows:

```
$ DEFINE ORA_SID PRICE
$ DEFINE ORA_RDBMS DEVON_ORA_DISK0:[M_ORACLE.ORACLE6.RDBMS]
$ SRV=="$ORA_RDBMS:SRV.EXE"
$ SRV DECNET_NSP:
```

The first line defines the SID (system identifier) for the database we want to talk to. The next line provides a path to the server executable. The third line defines a symbol that we can use to start the server, and the final line starts the server. The server uses the previously defined ORA_SID logical to connect us to the proper database if it is available.

Now we have our logical connection string defined. Next, we define an internal database link that tells Oracle how to use the logical connection string. For example:

```
SQLPLUS  JOHN/HUNGRY
SQL> CREATE DATABASE LINK DEVON
   2: CONNECT TO DEVON_USER IDENTIFED BY LOW_PRIVS
   3: USING 'D:DEVONCON'
   4:/
```

The first line names the database link. If we wanted to share and were using a DBA privileged account, we could have specified CREATE PUBLIC DATABASE LINK DEVCON instead. The next line of the command tells Oracle what user and password to connect to at the remote database. If this isn't specified, it will try to use your current database username and password. The next to last line tells Oracle to use the previously established logical connection string over the "D:" or SQL*NET/DECNET protocol. Once defined, the link is resident in the database until it is dropped.

Finally, we should tie a synonym to the table name—link name combination to make it easier to use.

```
CREATE SYNONYM LUNCH FOR LUNCH@DEVON;
```

Now, if DEVON_USER owns LUNCH, or has a synonym LUNCH pointing to the LUNCH table, all we need to do is query LUNCH to determine the data we wanted.

```
SQL>SELECT COST , FOOD_TYPE
  2: FROM LUNCH
  3: WHERE FOOD_TYPE='FISH AND CHIPS' AND
  4: DATE_OF_PRICE = (SELECT SYSDATE FROM DUAL);

COST      FOOD_TYPE
1.50      "FISH AND CHIPS"
```

Of course, we'll have to convert it from pounds sterling to dollars...

If you need to query more than a few remote databases, the OPEN_LINKS parameter of the INIT.ORA file needs to be bumped up. This parameter specifies the maximum number of open links any one user can have in one transaction. The OPEN_LINKS parameter defaults to four under version 6 and ORACLE7.

Once we establish the synonyms for all the tables of interest, we can then query at will as long as the other database is up and running. At one installation, a DBA used this technique to monitor 10 different instances from a central database. As long as you don't have to update, this works fine. The only method to update a table from one database to another is to select into the desired table from the remote table. This is limited to non-long-data fields. Long data fields can be copied using the COPY command.

7.2.2 Use of the COPY Command

The format of the COPY command follows.

```
COPY {FROM username [/password]@db_spec |
    TO username[/password]@db_spec |
    FROM username [/password]@db_spec TO
    username[/password]@db_spec}
    {APPEND|CREATE|INSERT|REPLACE| dest_table [(column list)]
    USING query
```

The COPY command can be used to copy entire tables, subsections based on the query used, or to append data into an existing table. For the append and replace options, if the destination table doesn't exist, the command creates it. The db_spec variable is the logical connect string. If you don't specify a password, the command prompts for it, without echoing it so security is maintained.

The copy command can be used to distribute data across a version 6 database that has been distributed across several nodes. A procedure would be created using a select into an intermediate table of new or changed rows and that then would cause this information to be copied into the other databases. The procedure would be run automatically at predefined intervals.

7.2.3 Use of SQL*NET/TCPIP

In the previous section we discussed the use of DECNET. It is always used the same way regardless of the platform. Unfortunately this is not so for UNIX and TCPIP. Each node that uses TCPIP must have its own listener process that listens for a IP connection request. Each flavor of TCPIP seems to require a slightly different logical connect string, and you will need to review the SQL*NET/TCPIP manual for your flavor. The simplest connect string is the UCX string on the VAX system.

$DEFINE DEVCON "DEVO1:price"

In this connect string the DEVO1 is the node or IP name and price is the SID for the database. On some UNIX systems this may be a single letter. The internet address or IP address can be substituted if desired. The system must be in the HOSTS file.

There is no need to start up a process as with DECNET since the SQL*NET/TCPIP listener process must be running at all times. The database link string is specified in the same manner as with DECNET with the exception that the D: is replace with T: to specify TCPIP as the network protocol.

Some TCPIP servers may require port identification, buffer specification, and numerous other parameters. It is best to review your system documentation thoroughly before attempting to define your connect strings. Under UNIX the connect string can be loaded into an environmental variable in the .login file and then exported for use outside of the script.

7.2.4 Connect Strings Under ORACLE7

Under ORACLE7 and its new network interface architecture, the structure of connect strings and database links is very different. The database specification now consists of a domain name and a database base name. These names look very similar to the internet address format. For example, if you had a database that was in the USA branch of the company, located in Nebraska, on the UOB campus, the domain name might be "UOB.NEBR.USA.EDU". If the database name is STUDENTS, the full specification for a database name in a connect string would be STUDENTS.UOB.NEBR.USA.EDU. Of course, this can be synonymed. Then, to specify a table you would add the table specification to the database identifier:

```
STUD_DBA.GRADES@STUDENTS.UOB.NEBR.USA.EDU
```

For this example, the database is STUDENTS, the domain is UOB.NEBR.USA.EDU, and the table is GRADES in the schema STUD_DBA (short for STUDENTS DBA of course).

In general, the link will follow the internet protocol. This protocol uses a general identifier, for educational institutions EDU, for commercial companies, COM, and for military, MIL. There are other identifiers, but these are the main ones. This is followed by an identifier for your activity, for example, Oracle uses ORACLE (ORACLE.COM). Then you can add further identifiers to give greater restriction, such as country, state, and branch of company, or user identification. The strings are read from right to left.

If the INIT.ORA parameter GLOBAL_NAME is set to TRUE, the link name is checked against the remote database name and the domain. The database domain is specified by use of the DB_DOMAIN INIT.ORA parameter, and the database name must be specified by the DB_NAME parameter. If the GLOBAL_NAME parameter is set to FALSE (the default value), no checking is performed. For SQL*NET 2.0 this format is still evolving and may be changed before the product gets out of BETA testing in fall, 1992.

The logical connection string now specifies a port number and a protocol. This allows the TNS to connect the user with the appropriate dispatcher process (Dnnn). Generally speaking there will be at least one dispatcher per protocol used in your network. For a database needing both DECNET and TCPIP, there would be two dispatchers.

There are two additional files that you will maintain under SQL*NET Version 2. These are the DNS_LISTENER.ORA and LISTENER.ORA files. These files define the number and type of listeners and the database logical connections.

INIT.ORA Parameters. There are several new INIT.ORA parameters for use with a distributed environment. These parameters are used to tell ORACLE7 how to set up the listener and dispatcher processes.

PARAMETER	PURPOSE
MTS_SERVICE	Specifies the database name; should usually be set to the SID for the database.
MTS_SERVERS	Specifies the number of servers (S00n) processes to be brought online at startup.
MTS_MAX_SERVERS	Specifies the maximum number of server processes.
MTS_DISPATCHERS	Specifies the type and number of dispatcher processes for the type of protocol specified. ("tcp, 1," "decnet, 3") Only one protocol specification for each MTS_DISPATCHERS parameter, parameter can be specified multiple times.
MTS_LISTENER_ADDRESS	The address that the listener process should use to listen for the specified protocol. There should be one MTS_LISTENER_ADDRESS for each protocol, the address must also be listed in the LISTENER.ORA file. Not every address in the LISTENER.ORA needs to be in the INIT.ORA.
COMMIT_POINT_STRENGTH	Used to determine if node is the commit point for a given distributed transaction. The node with the highest value for a session tree will be the commit point.

An example of a section of an INIT.ORA file using these parameters is shown in Figure 7.3.

Example of the LISTENER.ORA File. The LISTENER.ORA file specifies all addresses that the listener process can use to listen for connection requests. The file must contain all references from the INIT.ORA file and can contain alternatives should the addresses specified in the INIT.ORA file become inoperable. This file takes the place of the ORASRV.ORA file. An example of this file is shown in Figure 7.4.

```
#
#  Example MTS parameters
#
MTS_SERVICE = STUDENTS
MTS_SERVERS = 6
MTS_MAX_SERVERS = 10
MTS_DISPATCHERS = "DECNET,4"
MTS_DISPATCHERS = "TCP,3"
MTS_MAX_DISPATCHERS = 10      # This is the total for all protocols combined
MTS_LISTENER_ADDRESS = "(ADDRESS = (PROTOTCOL = DECNET) (NODE = MMRD01)
                                    (OBJECT = ORACLE_USER))"
MTS_LISTENER_ADDRESS = "(ADDRESS = (PROTOCOL = TCP) (HOST = ELWOOD)
                                    (PORT = 6576))"
COMMIT_POINT_STRENGTH = 125   # Maximum of 255
#
#
```

Figure 7.3 Example of distributed database/multithreaded server INIT.ORA parameters.

```
#
# ORACLE7 listener configuration file
#
# Example VMS connection
SQLNET SIDMAP STUDENTS = m_ora_disk1:[m_oracle.oracle7.db_students.rdbms]orasrv.com
#
# Example UNIX connection
SQLNET SIDMAP STUDENTS = /home/oraclev7
#
# Only one of the above formats would be specified dependent upon your system.
#
# You use the above formats to specify each of the databases you would need access to
#
SQLNET LISTEN = (address =    (protocol = decnet)
                              (object = oracle_user)
                              (node = mmrd01))
SQLNET LISTEN = (address =    (protocol = tcp)
                              (port = 6521)
                              (host = elwood))
#
# If there are any other objects or ports the DBA wants the listener to listen on,
# these should also be specified.
#
```

Figure 7.4 Example of the LISTENER.ORA file configuration.

The user under SQL*NET version 2 will use a new format for the logical connect string as well. This format for DECNET is:

```
(DESCRIPTION = (ADDRESS = (PROTOCOL = decnet) (OBJECT = oracle_user)
               (NODE = mmrd01) (CONNECT_DATA = (SID = students))
```

This format for TCP is:

```
(DESCRIPTION = (ADDRESS = (PROTOCOL = tcp) (PORT = 6521) (HOST = elwood)
               (CONNECT_DATA = (SID = students))
```

As with earlier versions of SQL*NET, these logical connection strings can be placed into logicals on VMS or environmental variables on UNIX.

The TNS_NAMES.ORA File. The TNS_NAMES.ORA file is used to establish a list of aliases for the long connect strings. If the TNS_NAMES file is used, there should be no need for a logical or environmental variable to be set for each connection string. The file consists of a list of aliases and connect string definitions of the following format:

```
CONNECT_ALIAS = CONNECT_STRING
```

7.2.5 ORACLE7 Data Duplication Features

Under ORACLE7 the DBA has a much wider selection of options. For tables in a distributed environment that have dependent values, such as sales, inventory, and required purchases tables, the two-phase commit should be employed. The two-phase commit should not be used to replicate data. Database replication triggers or snapshots were designed for this function. To avoid use of the two-phase-commit, update data on one node at a time followed by a commit.

For maintenance of duplicate copies of tables, or copying subsets of tables, database table replication triggers are available under ORACLE7. These triggers fire whenever rows are updated, inserted, or deleted and replicate the changes throughout the distributed environment. Unlike a simple update using the two-phase-commit process, if a database level trigger fails, you can build automated recovery procedures that wait for the condition to clear and resend the data from a journal. For high-use tables this can seriously degrade database performance. However, if it is important that all sites maintain up-to-the-minute data at all times, this may be the option of choice.

The other mechanism that can be used for table duplication under ORACLE7 is the snapshot method. This method is periodic in nature and only happens as specified by the snapshot parameters. This allows a frequently updated table to be replicated at low-use times. If it isn't critical that all sites have up-to-the-minute data, this method works well. The snapshot method can also be used to provide read-only copies of subsets of data for either a single table or several tables. Values can also be calculated for a snapshot.

The full use of these objects, other than two-phase-commit, was covered in Chapter 2. The two-phase-commit will be covered in the next section.

The DBA will have to coordinate the best method of data replication between the sites in a distributed database. The two-phase-commit, table replication triggers, and snapshotting provide a true distributed database environment.

It should be noted that anytime more than one node is involved in a transaction involving updates, inserts, or deletes the two-phase-commit is used. If the DBA wishes to avoid the use of the two-phase-commit, he or she should use single-point transaction logic—that is, only update the data on a single node at a time followed by a commit.

7.3 The Use of Two-Phase-Commit

What exactly is a "two-phase-commit," and how is it used? As more and more databases are distributed across multiple systems as companies grow, this question will have to be addressed by most DBAs. Let's examine these questions and hopefully give some concrete answers.

7.3.1 What Is a Two-Phase-Commit?

Under ORACLE7 the programmer or application developer doesn't have to do anything special for the two-phase-commit to be used. The DBA has several INI.ORA parameters to specify, but other than that, little or no action is required on their part either. Anytime a transaction updates data (insert, update, or delete functions) across multiple nodes with a single set of commands with no intervening commits, a two-phase-commit will be used.

The actual mechanism of a two-phase-commit is easily stated: Each transaction shall be committed, or rolled back, as a unit. How this is actually accomplished is another thing altogether.

As was stated before, the two-phase-commit (TPC) should only be used when there are data dependancies between two or more tables in a distributed environment. In most cases it shouldn't be used for simple data replication. The two-phase-commit, as its name implies, depends on two phases of activity to work. These are:

> The prepare phase—In this phase the initiating node (called the "global coordinator") asks the nodes participating in the TPC to prepare. This consists of being ready to commit or roll back the transaction even in the event of a network or node failure.
> The commit phase—In this phase all participants in the TPC commit. If they can't all commit, the coordinator tells all the nodes to roll back.

Under a TPC each transaction has a session tree. This is a structure that shows each site involved and its role in the TPC. These roles can be any one of the following:

1. Client
2. Database server
3. Global coordinator
4. Local coordinator
5. Commit point site

The role for each node is determined by where the transaction originates, the commit point strength as set in the INIT.ORA file, whether or not the data is available at the node or other nodes need to be referenced, and whether or not the node is read only. (If the data to be updated on the node is in a read-only snapshot, the node will not participate.) What do the various roles do in a TPC? Lets look and see.

> Clients—Clients are nodes that request data from other nodes in a distributed transaction.
> Database servers—Database servers are nodes that are directly referenced or are requested to participate by a referenced node in a distributed transaction.

The global coordinator—This is the node that has requested the distributed transaction. This is the parent or root of the session tree. The global coordinator performs the following:

- Sends all SQL statements used by the distributed transaction.
- Communicates with all directly referenced nodes other than the commit point sites.
- Once all nodes are prepared, asks the commit point site to initiate the commit of the transaction across all nodes.

Local coordinator—This is a node that references other nodes to complete a request. The local coordinator is responsible for coordination of the request activities among the nodes it references through the following activities:

- Relay of information to the referenced nodes
- Collection of information from the referenced nodes
- Return of collected data to the node that called it

Commit point site—The commit point site is the node or nodes that have the highest value of the COMMIT_POINT_STRENGTH parameter in their INIT.ORA file. There can be more than one commit point site for a given transaction. Generally speaking, if a session tree has several branches, there will be several commit point sites. The commit point site fulfills the following functions:

- This should be the site that is most reliable and thus holds the most critical data. Critical data is data that is never in doubt, even in a failure situation.
- The commit point site, as its name implies, determines if the data is committed or if it is rolled back. If the update fails at the commit point site, it is rolled back for all sites. If the data is successfully updated at the commit point site, it is updated at all sites. The global coordinator ensures all sites treat the data the same as the commit point site.

Commit Point Strength—As was stated above, the COMMIT_POINT_STRENGTH INIT.ORA parameter, set by the DBA, determines if a site is a commit point site. The global coordinator site determines the commit point site from within its branch of the session tree. If the commit point site sees another site within its own branch of the session tree with a greater value of commit point strength, it will not commit or roll back unless that site commits or rolls back, and so on down the branches of the session tree.

7.3.2 Examples of a Distributed Transaction

As was stated above, a distributed transaction is one with multiple updates to tables spread across multiple nodes with no intervening commits. For example, the transaction:

```
insert into grades@uob (student, class, grade) values ('9999','1072','3.8');
commit;
insert into grades@sui (student, class, grade) values ('9999','1072','3.8');
commit;
```

wouldn't be a distributed transaction since there are intervening commits between the actions on different nodes (uob and sui). However, the following transaction:

```
insert into grades@uob (student, class, grade) values ('9999','1072','3.8');
insert into grades@sui (student, class, grade) values ('9999','1072','3.8');
commit;
```

would be a distributed transaction since the commit follows both insert statements. In the first transaction a TPC wouldn't be used, while for the second transaction a TPC would occur. Let's look at the second transaction in more detail.

For the purpose of this discussion the transaction was started at node "central." The following are the commit point strengths for the nodes:

central—80
uob—255
sui—150

From this data you can see that the node "uob" would be the commit point, the node "central" would be the global coordinator, and the node "sui" is a client. Both "uob" and "sui" are database servers. The nodes are in a simple triangle connection with central at the apex and uob and sui at the legs.

What would the process look like for the TPC for the above transaction? Let's look. The SQL statements are sent out to each site, and the needed locks are established. The global coordinator issues a commit, initiating the TPC. First, the global coordinator, "central", determines who is the commit point site by looking at the directly connected node's commit point strengths. The global coordinator would compare its value of commit point strength to the other nodes and determine the commit point for the transaction. In this case, "uob" would be the commit point. The global coordinator would then send out a call for the clients involved to prepare.

Next, the client's report is prepared; for this transaction only "sui" is a client. Once "sui" reports that it is prepared, the global coordinator sends out a commit order to the commit point site "uob." If the commit point site can commit, all other sites commit; if the commit point site cannot commit, the transaction is rolled back.

If the transaction is not completed—say, the commit point site committed and then the database link failed due to a network error—there are two database views that will show the problem. These are the DBA_2PC_PENDING and DBA_2PC_NEIGHBORS views. If this situation occurs, the DBA has three possible actions:

1. Manually complete the transaction by having the remote site DBAs either roll back or commit the transaction number specified by the global transaction number.
2. Wait for the database link to be reestablished, and allow RECO to recover the transaction.
3. Respecify a different link by use of a synonym pointing to a link that is still active, and allow RECO to recover the transaction.

If the same recovery option isn't performed on all nodes, the databases will be left in an inconsistent state. It is always the best option to allow RECO to recover the transaction. To this end, it is suggested that all database links be specified via synonyms so that if an alternate connection is required a simple drop and redefine of the synonym is all that is needed to recover the transaction (assuming multiple paths are available).

For a detailed discussion of the two-phase-commit mechanism and other two-phase-commit topics, read Chapter 21 of the *ORACLE7 Server Concepts Manual*.

7.4 Client/Server Relational Databases

Client server databases are databases where a central node acts as database server, and connecting nodes do all or a part of the execution of tools and programs. An example of this configuration would be a CPU with a large disk farm that holds the database connected to by several other CPUs, each running their own version of the tools such as SQL*FORMS, SQL*REPORTWRITER, or SQL*MENU with the two-task link option.

The basic method for setting up a client server database is as follows:

1. Set up the main database server, and link all tools two-task (usually the "T" option). This consists of loading all the Oracle software and creating the required databases and instances on the server. The main server will have the RDBMS and all SQL*NET protocols running on it. The database files will be created on the server and will be owned by the server.
2. Set up the client machines with the tools and whatever SQL*NET protocol they require. Again, be sure the tools are linked two-task.
3. Configure SQL*NET protocols on each of the clients so that they reference the server.

Note that there are no database data files on any of the clients. All data files, control files, redo logs, rollbacks, and so on are located on the server. As the clients need data, they connect via a SQL*NET link over their own protocols (DECNET, TCPIP, ASYNC, etc.) and use the data on the server.

7.4.1 Benefits of Client/Server

The benefits of a client/server configuration are severalfold.

- The database can be placed on a machine optimized for speed of access.
- The tool processing overhead is offloaded to other CPUs. For example, the DECWINDOWS or X-Windows processing required by CASE*Designer or SQL*Forms4.0 could be offloaded to workstations.
- Processing can be compartmentalized to optimize the type of CPU required. CASE could be placed on high-speed workstations, forms applications on slower CPUs, and so on.

Client/server requires SQL*NET and the protocol drivers you will be using.

7.5 Use of the Multithreaded Server

The multithreaded server under ORACLE7 allows multiple-user processes to share the same Oracle-server process. This reduces the number of Oracle-related processes required to support multiple users under operating systems that require dedicated servers (UNIX). In other environments that may use two-task-linked Oracle, such as in the client/server configuration, the multithreaded server is also useful. The INIT.ORA parameters shown in Figure 7.3 control the multithreaded server. This should be obvious since their names begin with MTS.

The multithreaded server uses the listener process to assign users to specific types of servers. The listener is configured via the MTS parameters and controlled with the LSNRCTL program. The options on this program are similar to the TCPCTL process controller under version 6. The options are listed below.

start—Will start the listener on the node

stop—Will stop the listener on the node

status—Will report the status for the node

reload—Will reload parameters from the LISTENER.ORA file.

trace—Will request the listener process to start or stop tracing.

version - Will provide the version number of the TNS listener process being used.

The command format is LSNRCTL "command" "node". If no node is specified, the command operates on the current node. A general procedure to start the multithreaded server process follows.

1. Edit the INIT.ORA file in accordance with your systems requires. Figure 7.3 can be used as a template.
2. Create the LISTENER.ORA and TNS_NAMES.ORA (if required) files to configure the listener process. The format for the LISTENER.ORA file is shown in Figure 7.4.
3. Shut down and restart the instance(s) to reconfigure the INIT.ORA parameters.
4. Start the listener process using the appropriate LSNRCTL command.

Connecting to the Multithreaded Server. The users can connect to the multithreaded server by the same commands as were used in version 1.1 of SQL*NET. The multithreaded server requires a two-task-type of connection, so the users will generally specify a connect string. The listener will automatically assign them to a server process based on the type of protocol specified in the connect string.

The DBA needs to monitor the dispatcher, processes and if they exceed 80 percent busy as indicated by the BUSY column of the V$DISPATCHER table, he or she should start another dispatcher process by use of the ALTER SYSTEM SET MTS_DISPATCHERS (protocol, integer) command. The DBA can also increase the number of database servers by use of the ALTER SYSTEM SET MTS_SERVERS integer command.

The user can force a connect to a specific server by adding a connect string to their user login. This connect string can connect back to the node they are currently on. It is suggested that the DBA place several connect strings and aliases in the TNS_NAMES.ORA file that allow this type of connection.

For additional reading on distributed databases, multithreaded servers, client/server type topics, the DBA should consult the following references:

ORACLE RDBMS Database Administrator's Guide Addendum, Version 6.2 Apr. 1991, Part# 5990-V6.2, Oracle Corp.

ORACLE7 Parallel Server Administrator's Guide, Dec. 1992, Part# 5990-70-1292, Oracle Corp.

*SQL*Plus User's Guide and Reference Version 3.0*, 1991, Part# 5142-V3.0 0991, Oracle Corp.

ORACLE7 Server Concepts Manual, Chapters 1, 9, 21, and 22, Dec. 1992, Part# 6693-70-1292, Oracle Corp.

ORACLE7 Server Application Developer's Guide, Chapters 11 and 12. Dec. 1992, Part# 6695-70-1292, Oracle Corp.

ORACLE7 Server Administrator's Guide, Chapters 14, 15, and 16. Dec. 1992, Part# 6694-70-1292, Oracle Corp.

SQL*NET V2 Trilogy: SQL*Net V2 Administrator's Guide MultiProtocol Interchange Administrator's Guide Oracle Network Products Error Messages Manual, Beta Draft V2.0.9 3/27/92, Part# 6759-20-0392.

Backup and Recovery Procedures for Oracle

As should be obvious from the previous chapters, Oracle is a complex, interrelated set of files and executables. The database files include data segments, redo logs, rollback segments, control files, and system areas. Each of these files is not a separate entity but is tightly linked to the others. For instance: The data files are repositories for all table data, the data file structure is controlled by the control file, implemented by the system areas, and maintained by a combination of the executables, redo, and rollback segments. This complexity leads to the requirement for a threefold backup recovery methodology to ensure data recovery can be made.

The threefold recovery methodology consists of:

1. Normal VMS or UNIX backups
2. Exports and Imports
3. Archive logging of redo logs

Let's look at each of these and how they are used.

8.1 VMS and UNIX Backups

Normal system backups, referred to as either hot or cold backups, are used to protect from media failure. Each can and should be used when required.

8.1.1 Cold VMS Backups

A cold backup—that is, one done with the database in a shutdown state—provides a complete copy of the database that can be restored exactly. The procedure for using a cold backup is as follows:

1. Using the shutdown script(s) provided, shut down the Oracle instance(s) to be backed up.
2. Ensure there is enough backup media to back up the entire database.

3. Mount the first volume of the backup media (9 track, WORM, TK50, TK70, etc.) using the VMS mount command:

    ```
    $ mount/foreign dev: volume_name
    ```

4. Issue the VMS backup command to initiate the backup.

    ```
    $ backup/log=ora_<date>.log -
    $ ora_diskx:[oracle...]*.*,-
    $ ora_diskx+1:[oracle...]*.*-
    $ ora_diskx+2:[oracle...]*.*-
    .
    .
    .
    $ ora_diskx+n:oracle...] dev:ora_<date>.sav/save
    ```

    Where:

    ora_diskx....ora_diskn represent the system logicals in accordance with OFA rules with n being the highest numbered disk and x being the lowest.

    <date> represents the date for the backup.

    dev: represents the backup media device name such as mua0:

    /log=log_<date>.log names a file to log the results from the backup.

    /save tells BACKUP to archive the files in save set format. This requires less room than an image backup.

5. Once the backup is complete, be sure all backup volumes are properly labeled and stored *away from the computer.* The final volume is dismounted from the tape drive using the VMS DISMOUNT command.

    $ DISMOUNT dev:

6. Restart the Oracle instances using the appropriate startup script(s).

Note the italicized phrase in step 5. In visits to computer facilities it has been noted that a number of facilities keep backups close at hand, sometimes in the same room as the computer. What would happen if a site disaster destroyed the computer room? Not only the hardware, but all of the system backups and your data could be lost. It is suggested that backups be stored in another building—or even completely offsite somewhere. This assures that come fire, flood, or typhoon, you should be able to get back up one way or another.

8.1.2 VMS Hot Backups

A hot backup, or one taken while the database is active, can only give a read-consistent copy, but it doesn't handle active transactions. The hot backup differs from the cold backup in that only sections of the database are backed up at one time. This is accomplished by using the ALTER command to modify a tablespace's status to backup. Be sure that you restore the status to normal once the database is backed up, or else redo log mismatch and improper archiving/rollbacks can occur.

While it is quite simple (generally speaking) to do a cold backup by hand, a hot backup can be quite complex and should be automated. The automated procedure should then be thoroughly tested on a dummy database, for both proper operation and ability to restore, prior to use on the production database(s).

Limitations on hot or online backups:

1. The database must be operating in ARCHIVELOG mode for hot backups to work.
2. Hot backups should only be done during off-hour or low-use periods.
3. During the hot backups the entire block containing a changed record, and not just the changed record, is written to the archive log, requiring more archive space for this period.

Parts of a hot or online backup:

1. The tablespace data files are backed up.
2. The archived redo logs are backed up.
3. The control file is backed up.

These three parts have to be repeated for each tablespace in the database. For small databases this is relatively easy. For large complex databases with files spread across several drives, this can become a nightmare if not properly automated in VMS DCL command scripts. An example of this type of a backup DCL script is shown in Figure 8.1.

```
$!*********************************************************************************
$! Name        : Hot_backup.com
$! Purpose     : Perform a hot backup of an Oracle Database
$! Use         : @Hot_backup.com
$! Limitations : Creates a read consistent image, but doesn't backup in process
$!                 transactions
$!
$! Revision History:
$! Date          Who               What
$! -----------   ---------------   --------------------------------
$! June 1993     K. Loney          Featured in Oracle Mag. Article
$! 29-Jun-93     M. Ault           Modified, commented
$!*********************************************************************************
$!
$! Define symbol for backup command so don't have to fully specify it each time
$ dup_it = "backup/ignore=(noback,interlock,label) /log"
$ !
$ sqldba
    connect internal
    alter tablespace system begin backup;
    exit
$ dup_it m_ora_disk2:[m_oracle.oracle6.db_example]ora_system_1.dbs
  mua0:ora_system.bck/save
$!
```

Figure 8.1 Example of script to perform online "hot" backup.   (continued)

```
  sqldba
    connect internal
    alter tablespace system end backup;
    alter tablespace tools begin backup;
    exit
$ dup_it m_ora_disk3:[m_oracle.oracle6.db_example]ora_tools_1.dbs-
  mua0:ts_tools.bck/save
$!
sqldba
    connect internal
    alter tablespace tools end backup;
    alter tablespace user_tables begin backup;
    exit
$ dup_it m_ora_disk3:[m_oracle.oracle6.db_example]ora_user_tables_1.dbs-
  mua0:ts_tools.bck/save
$!
    sqldba
    alter tablespace user_tables end backup;
    exit
$! force write of all archive logs
$!
$ sqldba
    connect internal
    alter system switch logfile;
    archive log all;
    exit
$!
$ rename m_ora_disk5:[m_oracle.oracle6.db_example.archives]*.arc *.oldarc
$! Now backup a control file
$!
$ sqldba
    connect internal
    alter database example
    backup controlfile to
    'm_ora_disk1:[m_oracle.oracle6.db_example]ora_control.bac'
    reuse;
    exit
$ dup_it m_ora_disk1:[m_oracle.oracle6.db_example]ora_control1.con
mua0:ora_control.bac/save
$! now backup all archive logs
$!
$! you don't want to delete logs if an error causes them not to be backed up
$ on error goto end_it
$!
$ dup_it m_ora_disk5:[m_oracle.oracle6.db_example.archives]*.oldarc-
$! mua0:ora_archives.bck/save
$! Now delete logs
$!
$ delete/log m_ora_disk5:[m_oracle.oracle6.db_examples.archives]*.oldarc;*
$ end_it:
$ exit
```

Figure 8.1 (continued)

As you can see, this is a bit more complex than a full cold backup and requires more monitoring than a cold backup. Recovery from this type of backup consists of restoring all tablespaces and logs and then recovering.

8.1.3 UNIX Backups

The type of backup you perform in UNIX is dependent on whether you use RAW devices or not. RAW devices will require backup of the entire device, while use of the mounted file systems will allow partial backups.

8.1.4 Cold UNIX Backup

1. Using the shutdown script(s) provided, shut down the Oracle instance(s) to be backed up.
2. Ensure there is enough backup media to back up the entire database.
3. Mount the tape using the appropriate UNIX command.
4. Using the dump, tar, or cpio commands, make a backup of the Oracle subdirectories.
5. Once the backup is complete, dismount the final media volume using the appropriate UNIX command for your system. Be sure the backups are stored in a safe place, *preferably away from the system.*
6. Restart the Oracle instance(s) using the appropriate startup script(s).

Note the italicized phrase in step 5. In visits to computer facilities it has been noted that a number of facilities keep backups close at hand, sometimes in the same room as the computer. What would happen if a site disaster destroyed the computer room? Not only the hardware, but all of the system backups and your data could be lost. It is suggested that backups be stored in another building—or even completely offsite somewhere. This assures that come fire, flood, or typhoon, you should be able to get back up one way or another.

8.1.5 UNIX Hot Backups

A hot backup, or one taken while the database is active, can only give a read-consistent copy, but it doesn't handle active transactions. The hot backup differs from the cold backup in that only sections of the database are backed up at one time. Under UNIX this will require the use of normal mounted file systems and not RAW devices.

A hot backup is accomplished by using the ALTER command to modify tablespace status to begin backup. Be sure that you restore their status to normal once the tablespace is backed up, or else redo log mismatch and improper archiving/rollbacks can occur. This will cause the database to assume a full recovery of the affected tablespace is required upon the next startup of the database.

While it is quite simple (generally speaking) to do a cold backup by hand, a hot backup can be quite complex and should be automated. The automated procedure should then be thoroughly tested on a dummy database, for both proper operation and ability to restore, prior to use on the production database(s).

Limitations on hot or online backups:

1.   The database must be operating in ARCHIVELOG mode for hot backups to work.
2.   Hot backups should only be done during off-hour or low-use periods.
3.   During the hot backups the entire block containing a changed record, and not just the changed record, is written to the archive log, requiring more archive space for this period.

Parts of a hot or online backup:
The UNIX hot backup consists of three parts identical to the VMS hot backup:

1.   The tablespace data files are backed up.
2.   The archived redo logs are backed up.
3.   The control file is backed up.

These three parts have to be repeated for each tablespace in the database. For small databases, this is relatively easy. For large complex databases with files spread across several drives, this can become a nightmare if not properly automated in UNIX shell scripts. An example of this type of a backup KORNE shell script is shown in Figure 8.2.

```
#*******************************************************************************
# Name        : hot_backup
# Purpose     : Perform a hot backup of an Oracle Database
# Use         : sh hot_backup
# Limitations : Creates a read consistent image, but doesn't backup in process
                transactions
#
# Revision History:
# Date             Who                    What
# --------------   --------------------   --------------------------------
# June 1993        K. Loney               Featured in Oracle Mag. Article
# 29-Jun-93        M. Ault                Modified, commented
# 02-Aug-93        M.Ault                 Converted to UNIX script
# 03-Aug-93        M. Phillips            Added error detection
#*******************************************************************************
#
ERROR="FALSE"
LOGFILE="$ORACLE_HOME/ADHOC/scripts/hot_back_log"
while [ "$error"=FALSE ]
do
sqldba << ending1
                connect internal
                alter tablespace system begin backup;
                exit
ending1
                if ( tar cfv /oracle/backup /data/ORA_SYSTEM_1.DBF )
                then
                :
                else
```

Figure 8.2 Example of hot backup script for UNIX KORNE shell.

```
                              ERROR="TRUE";
                echo "Tar backup failed for ora_system1.dbf" >$LOGFILE
                    fi
sqldba << ending2
                    connect internal
                    alter tablespace system end backup;
                    exit
ending2

dup_it="tar rv /oracle/backup"
sqldba << ending3
                    connect internal
                    alter tablespace user_tables begin backup;
                    exit
ending3
if ( $dup_it /data/ora_user_tables_1.dbf )
then
                         :
else
    ERROR="TRUE";echo "Tar backup failed for ora_user tables_1.dbf">>$LOGFILE
fi #we must still end backup for tablespaces
sqldba << ending4
                    connect internal
                    alter tablespace user_tables end backup;
                    exit
ending4
# force write of all archive logs
sqldba << ending5
                    connect internal
                    alter system switch logfile;
                    archive log all;
                    exit
ending5
if ( cp /usr/oracle/oracle6/db_example.archives/*.arc *.oldarc )
then
    :
else
    ERROR="TRUE";echo "Copy of archive logs failed">>$LOGFILE
fi
# Now backup a control file
sqldba << ending6
                    connect internal
                    alter database example
                    backup controlfile to
                    '/usr/oracle/oracle6/db_example/ora_control.bac'
                    reuse;
                    exit
ending6
if ( $dup_it /usr/oracle/oracle6/db_example/ora_control.bac )
then
    :
```

Figure 8.2 (continued)   (continued)

```
else
    ERROR="TRUE";echo "Tar backup failed for control file">>$LOGFILE
fi
# now backup all archive logs
if ( $dup_it /usr/oracle/oracle6/db_example.archives/*.oldarc )
then
    :
else
    ERROR="TRUE";echo "Tar backup failed for archive files">>$LOGFILE
fi
# Now delete logs
if ( rm /usr/m_oracle/oracle6/db_examples.archives/*.oldarc;* )
then
    ERROR="TRUE"
else
    ERROR="TRUE";echo "Delete of archive files failed">>$LOGFILE
fi
done
exit
done
```

Figure 8.2 (continued)

8.2 Imports/Exports

Imports and exports extract or insert an ORACLE readable copy of the actual data and structures in the database. The exports can be used to recover single data structures to the date and time the export was taken. Exports come in three types: full, cumulative, and incremental. Full, as its name implies, provides a full logical copy of the database and its structures. A cumulative provides a complete copy of altered structures since the last full or the last cumulative export. Incrementals provide a complete copy of altered structures since the last incremental, cumulative, or full export.

Limitations on export/import:

1. A database must be running to perform either an export or import.
2. Export files shouldn't be edited and can only be used by import.
3. Import only imports full tables. It can't be used to do a conditional load.
4. Exported data is only a logical copy of the data. An export can only allow recovery to the date and time the export was taken.

Imports and exports are accomplished using the Oracle IMPORT and EXPORT utilities. For exports the EXPORT utility is used. The format for use of this command follows.

```
Format:  EXP KEYWORD=value --or-- KEYWORD=(list of values)
Example: EXP AULT/AUTHOR GRANTS=N TABLES=(CHAPTERS, EDITORS,ADVANCES)
```

KEYWORD	DESCRIPTION	KEYWORD	DESCRIPTION (DEFAULT)
USERID	username/password	FULL	export entire file (N)
BUFFER	size of data buffer	OWNER	list of owner usernames
FILE	output file (EXPDAT.DMP)	TABLES	list of table names
COMPRESS	import into one extent (Y)	RECORDLENGTH	length of IO record
GRANTS	export grants (N - V6, Y - V7)	INCTYPE	incremental export type
INDEXES	export indexes (Y)	RECORD	track incr. export (Y)
ROWS	export data rows (Y)	PARFILE	parameter filename
CONSTRAINTS	export table constraints (N - V6, Y - V7)		
CONSISTENT	cross-table consistency (New for ORACLE7)		
LOG	log file of screen output (New for ORACLE7)		
ANALYZE	analyze objects (ESTIMATE) (New for ORACLE7)		

Exports should be automated and scheduled to run automatically. An export methodology should be worked out such that the DBA is reasonably certain a deleted file can be recovered.

The format of the IMPORT command follows.

```
Format: IMP KEYWORD=value --or-- KEYWORD=(list of values)
Example: IMP AULT/AUTHOR IGNORE=Y TABLES=(EXPENSES, ADVANCES) FULL=N
```

KEYWORD	DESCRIPTION	KEYWORD	DESCRIPTION (DEFAULT)
USERID	username/password	FULL	import entire file (N)
BUFFER	size of data buffer	FROMUSER	list of owner usernames
FILE	output file (EXPDAT.DMP)	TOUSER	list of usernames
SHOW	just list file contents (N)	TABLES	list of table names
IGNORE	ignore create errors (Y - V6, N - V7)		
RECORDLENGTH	length of IO record		
GRANTS	import grants (Y)	INCTYPE	incremental import type
INDEXES	import indexes (Y)	COMMIT	commit array insert (N)
ROWS	import data rows (Y)	PARFILE	parameter filename

New for ORACLE7

Keyword	Description (Default)	Keyword	Description (Default)
LOG	log file of screen output	DESTROY	overwrite tablespace data (N)
INDEXFILE	write table/index info to specified file	CHARSET	char. set of export file (NLS_LANG)

As you can see, there are several new options for ORACLE7. These provide expanded functionality for the import and export processes. A quick overview of these new features follows:

EXPORT New Features

CONSISTENT—This command option provides cross-table consistency. Under version 6 each table was read consistently, but not absolutely consistently with other tables in the same database. For example, if table x and table y shared a foreign key relationship, and a user added to table y while table x was being exported, table x would not reflect the changes. This was handled via archive log restoration under Oracle version 6. Under 7 this won't be a problem if CONSISTENT is specified equal to Y (for yes). This cannot be specified for a cumulative or incremental export.

LOG—This command option causes Oracle to write a log file of screen output. This allows a record to be easily made of export operations.

ANALYZE—This command option forces Oracle to analyze objects (ESTIMATE is default) when they are imported from this export. The options are ESTIMATE, COMPUTE, and NONE.

IMPORT New Features

LOG—As with export, this command option will write a log file of the screen output to the specified file.

DESTROY—This command option causes the import to overwrite existing tablespace data.

INDEXFILE—This command option causes index creation commands to be written to the specified file

CHARSET—This command option allows the user to specify the export files character set from one of the NLS (national language system) character sets.

Under ORACLE7 the user must be granted the EXP_FULL_DATABASE role in order to do full exports. In order to perform a full import, the user must have the IMP_FULL_DATABASE role. The users with the DBA role are granted these implicitly.

An example of when the DBA would want to grant these roles to a user would be a user whose password is specified in the command script used for doing the automatic exports. If the only role granted to the user is CREATE_SESSION and EXP_FULL_DATABASE, even if the user's password is compromised, they won't be able to do much damage.

8.3 Archive Logs

The redo logs store all transactions that alter the database, all committed updates, adds, deletes of tables, structures, or data. If archiving is disabled, only data in the current offline and online redo logs can be recovered. If the system recycles through all redo logs, the old ones are reused, destroying their contents. If archive logging is enabled, the redo logs are written out to storage before reuse. Archive logging allows recovery to a specific point in time since the last full cold backup or complete offline backup.

Under ORACLE7 redo logs are specified in groups; each group is archived together. Under ORACLE7 archive logs can also be shadowed and assigned to threads. Redo logs cannot be used to recover a database brought back from a full export. A proper use of these backup/recovery tools allows the DBA to recover from any possible failure.

8.4 Backup Methodologies

8.4.1 VMS or UNIX System Backup

1. VMS (BACKUP) or UNIX system backups (such as TAR or DUMP) should be taken on at least a weekly basis. The Oracle database(s) should be shut down and a full cold backup taken. If this isn't possible, consider developing a hot back up procedure.
2. Once the full cold backup or full hot backup is taken, archive logs and exports from the time period prior to the backup can be copied to tape and removed from the system.
3. Hot backups, where Oracle is not shut down, can be taken periodically, but the DBA is cautioned that full recovery may not be possible if this is the sole backup method used. Great care must be taken to ensure all redo logs and a good copy of the control file are taken along with the hot backups of the data files.
4. It should be remembered that recovery is only to the time the backup was taken. All control, data, and redo logs must be backed up at the same time. The data from the backup forward is recovered from the archive and redo logs.

8.4.2 Import/Export

1. As a minimum the following export schedule should be used:

   Daily: Incremental export during offpeak time
   Weekly: Full export during offpeak time

2. Once the full export is taken, the DBA can remove previous full and incremental backups. This schedule should be implemented using batch queues and DCL or CRON and shell scripts.
3. A more aggressive export schedule could be:

   Daily: Incremental export
   Weekly: Cumulative export
   Monthly: Full export

4. The expired exports would be deleted as before. This would also be implemented using automated procedures.
5. All export procedures should be logged so that they can be reviewed. Some data corruption problems, such as unreadable characters in a record, will only be caught by the export process.

8.4.3 Archive Logging

1. Archive logging is strongly suggested for all Oracle databases. In version 6 of Oracle, you MUST specify ARCHIVE_LOG_MODE to TRUE when the database is created or you WILL NOT be able to start archive logging.
2. Archive logging is automatic. It may consume disk resources in a highly active environment. If recovery is required, the system will ask for the archive logs it needs and perform recovery from them. Archive logs allow point in time recovery.
3. Using Oracle INIT.ORA parameters, the destination, frequency, and size of archive logs can be controlled.

8.4.4 Recovery Types

Recovery depends entirely on how the backup methodology was employed. It also depends on what the DBA has to recover.

Recoveries can consist of:

REDO log recovery—offline or online log
ROLLBACK segment recovery
Tablespace recovery
Table recovery
Recovery of the entire database
Recovery of executables
Recovery of control files

Each recovery may consist of one or a combination of the above depending on file placement.

Recovery generally is required only after a physical insult to the database file system. Most internal errors are corrected automatically by Oracle using the REDO and rollback logs and data buffers.

Since each site will have differing file placement, and each recovery will most likely be unique, it is suggested that the DBA manual be consulted for the appropriate recovery methodology that applies to the situation(s) the DBA finds themselves in.

8.5 An Example Set of Recovery Procedures

Understanding how various system failures will affect the ORACLE database system requires an understanding of how the system is physically located on the disk farm. The purpose of this set of procedures is to provide a single source for database recovery options. The procedures below will have to be run, depending on the type of failure that occurs. Where important, the file names for the instance are referred to.

8.5.1 Disk Setup Information

We assume in these procedures that the DBA has spread the ORACLE files across several platters to reduce disk contention and speed access. The current configuration is as follows:

DISK	LOGICAL	CONTENTS
1	X_ORACLE	EXECUTABLES, FORMS, REPORTS, MENUS, COM FILES, ONE CONTROL FILE, TRACE FILES, LOGS, REDO LOGS
2	X_ORA_DB	THE DATA FILES INCLUDING SYSTEM, COPY OF THE CONTROL FILE, TEMPORARY TABLESPACE
3	X_ORA_RBK	COPY OF THE CONTROL FILE, INDEXES
4	X_ORA_IDX	ROLLBACK SEGMENTS, EXPORTS
5	X_ORA_ARC	ALL ARCHIVE LOGS

Recovery from loss of one of the above disks would depend on what files were contained on the disk. Detailed ORACLE recovery procedures are contained in Chapter 15 of the *ORACLE RDBMS Database Administrator's Guide,* Version 6.0, Apr. 1989, Part VI, Chapters 17, 18, and 19 of *ORACLE7 Server Administrator's Guide*, Dec. 1992, and in the RECOVERY ADDENDUM contained on disk in the X_ORACLE:[ORACLE.RDBMS]RECOVERY.DOC file. Although the above shows an ideal for a medium-sized database, the Oracle system is flexible enough to be installed on as few as two disks or may be installed across a massive disk farm. The DBA should ensure that proper separation of high-use files, redo logs, archives, and exports is accomplished should fewer than five disks be used.

8.5.2 General Discussion

1. Loss of X_ORACLE: X_ORACLE loss would require a backup restore operation (performed by the SYSTEM MANAGER from VMS backup tapes) to recover the system's executables, com (command), forms, reports, menus, log, trace, and most recent control file. The control file would have to be copied from a unaffected disk before starting the instance if changes to database structure had occurred since the last VMS backup. This is required due to the control file containing the latest data on archive log usage and data file locations. The CONTROL file on the backup contains out-of-date information. The REDO log loss would require a recovery to the most current archive log file.

2. Loss of X_ORA_DB: X_ORA_DB loss would be the most serious loss since it contains the majority of data files. Recovery would consist of restoration of the most current backup, then application of all archive logs from the last backup to the current date. A second method of recovery would be to recreate the database and then import the most recent full export and apply all cumulative and incremental exports. Once the exports were applied, a full recovery would be finished by applying the most recent redo logs.

3. Loss of X_ORA_IDX: X_ORA_IDX loss would slow data access but not necessarily require immediate recovery. If the index tablespaces are taken offline using the SQLDBA utility, users could still access the data for query-only operations in the database since indexes are not required. Updates involving keyed or indexed files would not be possible. The index tablespaces would then be recovered using the archive logs and the tablespace recovery procedure in the addendum.

4. Loss of X_ORA_RBK: X_ORA_RBK loss would require a complete restore of the database similar to loss of X_ORA_DB but only proceeding to the most current readable redo log. This could result in loss of several hours' worth of data depending on system usage levels.

5. Loss of X_ORA_ARC: X_ORA_ARC loss would require an immediate ORACLE shutdown and full backup or a full export followed by shutdown. This is to ensure data recoverability should recovery of the lost archives and exports be impossible. The DBA would then reset the archive log destination and restart ORACLE. If immediate shutdown is not possible, the DBA can reset the archive log destination and continue operation. This is not a safe condition for full recovery but will allow continued use until a full backup can be taken.
   Note: Since the backup of the archive disk would be one week old, it would be useless. Only those archive logs since the last backup are needed for a recovery.

6. Loss of a Single File: In the event that a user lost data due to inadvertent table deletion, the table would be recovered from the last full export and all incremental exports up to the day prior to the loss. If exports are not taken, recovery of a single table would require restoring the entire tablespace and applying archive logs up to the time just prior to the table loss (this requires the tablespace to be offline).

7. Partial Disk Loss: In the event that only a small section of a disk is lost, recovery would depend on the type of Oracle file that occupied that area of the disk.

8. Nonphysical Data Problems: Other than physical data loss, such as disk crash, all other recovery scenarios are handled automatically by the ORACLE kernel. These include program failure, CPU failure, instance failure due to bug, system failure due to power loss, or forced crash.

8.6 Detailed Procedures

8.6.1 Recovery of the Full Database Using Export Files

1. Create a new version of the affected database using a script similar to CREATE_DATABASE_SRM.SQL shown in Figure 8.3. The script for your database is

located in the appropriate ORA_INSTANCE or ORACLE$HOME for the instance of concern. This logical or environmental variable is set automatically.

```
rem     File:  M_ORA_Disk0:[M_Oracle.Oracle6.DB_prod]create_all_ts.SQL
rem  Created:  11jun93  M.Ault
rem
rem !!! Short !!! abstract about application
rem
rem ----------------- Disk Capacity Plan (MB) -------------------------
rem
rem
rem   M_ORA_DISK#->    1     2     3     4     5     6     7
rem                   ----  ----  ----  ----  ----  ----  ----
rem Data  -LOTS             5
rem Index -LOTS                   5
rem Roll Back                           20
rem Redo              4
rem Archive                                   1-10 vary w/ activity
rem DBA space               3
rem Ora_temp               10
rem Ora_user               10
rem system           10
rem tools            20
rem Control Files    .19   .19   .19
rem                  ----  ----  ----  ----  ----  ----  ----
rem  Disk Totals (MB) 34.2  28.2  5.2   20   10(max)
rem
rem
rem GRAND TOTAL DISK CONSUMPTION ==> 97.6 MB <==
rem -----------------------------------------------------------------

remark - Created by ORA_RDBMS_CDB.COM on 25-MAY-1993 13:16:29.62
remark - added monitor script call, database tablespace creates 27-may-1993  M. Ault

spool ora_instance:create_PROD.log
set echo on

remark - This will take some time, please wait.

startup nomount
connect internal
create database PROD controlfile reuse
      datafile 'm_ORA_DISK1:[M_ORACLE6.DB_PROD]ORA_SYSTEM_1.DBS' size 30M reuse
      logfile  'M_ORA_DISK1:[M_ORACLE6.DB_PROD]ORA_LOG1.RDO' size 1M reuse,
               'M_ORA_DISK1:[M_ORACLE6.DB_PROD]ORA_LOG2.RDO' size 1M reuse,
               'M_ORA_DISK1:[M_ORACLE6.DB_PROD]ORA_LOG3.RDO' size 1M reuse,
               'M_ORA_DISK1:[M_ORACLE6.DB_PROD]ORA_LOG4.RDO' size 1M reuse
      maxdatafiles 190
      maxlogfiles  32
      maxinstances 16
               archivelog;
```

Figure 8.3 Example of database creation script with tablespaces. (continued)

```
set termout off
@ora_system:catalog.sql    rem: This remains CATALOG.SQL in ORACLE7
@ora_system:expvew.sql     rem: This is called CATEXP.SQL in ORACLE7
@ora_system:monitor.sql    rem: This is called UTLMONTR.SQL in ORACLE7

create tablespace tools
datafile 'm_ora_disk1:[m_oracle6.db_prod]ora_tools_1.dbs' size 20m reuse
default storage (minextents 1 maxextents 110 initial 50k next 50k
pctincrease 50);

create tablespace ora_users
datafile 'm_ora_disk2:[m_oracle6.db_prod]ora_users_1.dbs' size 10m reuse
default storage (minextents 1 maxextents 110 initial 50k next 50k
pctincrease 0);

create tablespace ora_temp
datafile 'm_ora_disk2:[m_oracle6.db_prod]ora_temp_1.dbs' size 10m reuse
default storage (minextents 1 maxextents 110 initial 50k next 50k
pctincrease 0);

create tablespace ora_lots_data
datafile 'm_ora_disk2:[m_oracle6.db_prod]ora_lots_data_1.dbs' size 5m reuse
default storage (minextents 1 maxextents 110 initial 4k next 10k
pctincrease 0);

create tablespace ora_lots_index
datafile 'm_ora_disk3:[m_oracle6.db_prod]ora_lots_index_1.dbs' size 5m reuse
default storage (minextents 1 maxextents 110 initial 4k next 10k
pctincrease 0);

create tablespace ora_rollbacks
datafile 'm_ora_disk4:[m_oracle6.db_prod]ora_rollbacks_1.dbs' size 20m reuse
default storage (minextents 2 maxextents 40 initial 100k next 100k
pctincrease 0);    rem: No need to specify PCTINCREASE for ORACLE7
                   rem: it defaults to 0 and cannot be specified.

exit
```

Figure 8.3 (continued)

      Note: For UNIX the path names will have to be altered to reflect UNIX syntax.

2.   Add new rollback segments. Use steps 2 through 12 of procedure III.B.4.a of this document.

3.   If not done in step 1, create the required tablespaces in the new database using script similar to Figure 8.4. This script is created and maintained by the DBA.

4.   Recreate all users. The users should be documented using scripts from section 4. A script similar to Figure 8.5 or Figure 8.6 should be run periodically to keep an up-to-date user recreation script handy.

5. Get a list of the full (or complete) cumulative and incremental exports online. Use the most current full or complete and subsequent cumulative and/or incremental exports. The commands are executed after setting the default directory to

X_ORA_RBK:[ORACLE.DB_<DB_NAME>.EXPORTS] using the command:
>SET DEF X_ORA_RBK:[ORACLE.DB_<DB_NAME>.EXPORTS]

```
rem
rem  Name          : CREATE_TS_ALL_PROD.SQL
rem  Purpose       : Create all tablespaces for the PROD database
rem  Use           : From SQLDBA or SQLPLUS and a DBA account
rem  Limitations   : VMS or UNIX user must have create permission on disks used
rem  History
rem  When      Who           What
rem  --------  ------------  ----------------------
rem 27-May-93  M. Ault       Initial Creation
rem
create tablespace tools
datafile 'm_ora_disk1:[m_oracle6.db_prod]ora_users_1.dbs' size 10m reuse
default storage (minextents 1 maxextents 110 initial 50k next 50k
pctincrease 0);

create tablespace ora_users
datafile 'm_ora_disk2:[m_oracle6.db_prod]ora_users_1.dbs' size 10m reuse
default storage (minextents 1 maxextents 110 initial 50k next 50k
pctincrease 0);

create tablespace ora_temp
datafile 'm_ora_disk2:[m_oracle6.db_prod]ora_temp_1.dbs' size 10m reuse
default storage (minextents 1 maxextents 110 initial 50k next 50k
pctincrease 0);

create tablespace ora_lots_data
datafile 'm_ora_disk2:[m_oracle6.db_prod]ora_lots_data_1.dbs' size 5m reuse
default storage (minextents 1 maxextents 110 initial 4k next 10k
pctincrease 0);

create tablespace ora_lots_index
datafile 'm_ora_disk3:[m_oracle6.db_prod]ora_lots_index_1.dbs' size 5m reuse
default storage (minextents 1 maxextents 110 initial 4k next 10k
pctincrease 0);

create tablespace ora_rollbacks
datafile 'm_ora_disk4:[m_oracle6.db_prod]ora_rollbacks_1.dbs' size 20m reuse
default storage (minextents 2 maxextents 40 initial 100k next 100k
pctincrease 0);   rem : PCTINCREASE  not used for ORACLE7 rollbacks.

exit
```

Figure 8.4 Example of tablespace build script.

```
set heading off verify off termout off feedback off echo off
set pages 0 lines 132
spool recreate_users.sql

select
                'grant connect to '||username||' identified by new_user;'
from
                dba_users
where
                username not in ('SYSTEM','SYS','_NEXT_USER','PUBLIC')
/
select
                'alter user '||username||
                ' default tablespace '||default_tablespace||
                ' temporary tablespace '||temporary_tablespace||';'
from
                dba_users
where
                username not in ('SYSTEM','SYS','_NEXT_USER','PUBLIC')
/
spool off
exit
```

Figure 8.5 Script to build a recreate user's SQL script under version 6.

```
set heading off verify off termout off feedback off echo off
set pages 0 lines 132
spool recreate_users.sql

select 'create user '||username||
'default tablespace '||default_tablespace||
'temporary tablespace '||temporary_tablespace||
'profile '||profile||';'
/

spool off
exit
```

Figure 8.6 Script to build a recreate user's script for ORACLE7.

6. Import the most recent incremental export file (or cumulative export file if no incrementals have been taken) using the INCTYPE=SYSTEM option.

   ```
   >IMP SYSTEM/[PASSWORD] INCTYPE=SYSTEM FULL=Y FILE=last_incr
   ```

7. Import the most recent complete (FULL) export file using the INCTYPE = RESTORE option

   ```
   >IMP SYSTEM/[PASSWORD] INCTYPE=RESTORE FULL=Y FILE=last_full
   ```

8. Import all CUMULATIVE and INCREMENTAL exports using the INCTYPE = RE-STORE option.

```
>IMP SYSTEM/[PASSWORD] INCTYPE=RESTORE FULL=Y FILE=first_cum
>IMP SYSTEM/[PASSWORD] INCTYPE=RESTORE FULL=Y FILE=next_cum
>IMP SYSTEM/[PASSWORD] INCTYPE=RESTORE FULL=Y FILE=last_cum
>IMP SYSTEM/[PASSWORD] INCTYPE=RESTORE FULL=Y FILE=first_incr
>IMP SYSTEM/[PASSWORD] INCTYPE=RESTORE FULL=Y FILE=next_incr
>IMP SYSTEM/[PASSWORD] INCTYPE=RESTORE FULL=Y FILE=last_incr
```

Note that the last incremental export is applied twice, once in step 5 and once here. This will recover to the time of the last incremental export.

8.6.2 Procedures for Recovery From Individual Disk Lost

1. Recovery from loss of X_ORACLE:
Note: Since X_ORACLE contains all the executable files and system tablespace data files, database activity will cease upon loss of X_ORACLE

a. Have the system manager restore the X_ORACLE:[M_ORACLE...]* directory structures from the latest backup.
b. Overwrite the X_ORACLE:[ORACLE.DB_<DB_NAME>]ORA_CONTROL1.CON file using the VMS copy command from either the X_ORA_DB: or X_ORA_RBK: control file copies.
c. Use the procedure for individual tablespace recovery to restore the SYSTEM tablespace.
d. Login to the ORACLE user and using SQLDBA shutdown and restart the database.

2. Recovery from loss of X_ORA_DB or X_ORA_IDX: Loss of X_ORA_DB would mean loss of all data files for the database system. Loss of X_ORA_IDX would mean loss of all indexes. The loss of X_ORA_DB would result in the halting of all database activity. Loss of X_ORA_IDX would result in the slowing of all index based queries and loss of update capability to indexed fields unless the indexes are explicitly dropped.

a. Have the system manager recover either the

```
X_ORA_DB:[ORACLE.DB_<DB_NAME>...]* or the
X_ORA_IDX:[ORACLE.DB_<DB_NAME>...]* directory structures from
the latest ORACLE backup.
```

b. If the instance is still operating:

1. Log in to the ORACLE user.
2. Start the SQLDBA program.
3. Issue the SHUTDOWN ABORT <DATABASE> command.

c. Issue the following SQLDBA command to restart the instance:

    ```
    STARTUP DBA EXCLUSIVE MOUNT <DATABASE>
    ```

d. Connect to the database by issuing the following SQLDBA command:

    ```
    CONNECT INTERNAL
    ```

e. If the failure resulted in relocation of the affected files, you must rename the files using the following SQLDBA command:

    ```
    ALTER DATABASE RENAME FILE 'OLD' TO 'NEW'
    ```

    where old and new are full-path file names for each of the affected files.

f. To ensure all database files are online, issue the following SQLDBA command for each of the affected database files. If the database is recovered with the data file offline, all of its data will be lost.

    ```
    ALTER DATABASE DATAFILE [name] ONLINE
    ```

    where name is the full-path file name enclosed by single quotes.

g. Once all of the data files are online, issue the SQLDBA RECOVER command with no parameters:

    ```
    RECOVER DATABASE
    ```

h. ORACLE will prompt for the names of the ARCHIVE files required, beginning with the oldest file. The archive files are stored in X_ORA_ARC: [ORACLE.DB_<DB_NAME>]. All required logs should be online. Each file begins with a DBA-specified string followed by filler zeros, then the log number followed by '.ARC'. The total length is 19 characters under version 6; therefore the number of filler zeros for version 6 is:

    19 - length of string - length of log number

    For example, log number 506 could be 'SRM_ARC00000506.ARC'. For ORACLE7 this value depends on how parameters were specified in the LOG_ARCHIVE_FORMAT parameter in the INIT.ORA file.

i. After each log is applied, the system will prompt for the next one it requires. After the last one has been applied, the system will respond:

    Media recovery complete.

j. This concludes the recovery. The database can now be brought online by issuing the SQLDBA command:

    ```
    ALTER DATABASE [name] OPEN
    ```

    Note: In some cases, specification of the database name is not required.

3. Recovery from the loss of a single tablespace's data file(s) from X_ORA_DB or X_ORA_IDX.

a. Login to the ORACLE user.

b. If the tablespace that uses the data file is online, take it offline with the SQLDBA commands:

```
CONNECT INTERNAL
ALTER TABLESPACE [name] OFFLINE
```

where [name] is the tablespace name, such as DEV or PROD.

c. Correct the problem, or find a new location for the file(s).

d. Have the system manager recover the latest copy of the data file from the latest ORACLE backup tape into the selected location.

e. If the file had to be relocated, alter the name in the database with the following SQLDBA command to reflect the change:

```
ALTER DATABASE RENAME FILE 'old' TO 'new'
```

where 'old' and 'new' are full-path file names enclosed in single quotes.

f. Execute the SQLDBA RECOVER command using the TABLESPACE option as follows:

```
RECOVER TABLESPACE [name]
```

where [name] is the tablespace name such as DMS or AEONIC.

g. ORACLE will prompt for the names of the ARCHIVE files required, beginning with the oldest file. The archive files are stored in X_ORA_ARC:[ORACLE.DB_<DB_NAME>]. All required logs should be online. Each file begins with a DBA specified string followed by filler zeros, then the log number followed by '.ARC'. The total length is 19 characters under version 6; therefore the number of filler zeros is:

19 - length of string - 4 - length of log number

For example, log number 506 could be 'SRM_ARC00000506.ARC'. Under ORACLE7 the format is specified via the LOG_ARCHIVE_FORMAT parameter in the INIT.ORA file.

h. Once all logs have been applied to the affected tablespace, the system will respond:

Media recovery complete.

i. Bring the tablespace back online with the SQLDBA command:

```
ALTER TABLESPACE [name] ONLINE
```

where [name] is the tablespace name such as DEV or PROD. This completes the recovery of the data file.

4. Recovery from loss of X_ORA_RBK.
Note: Loss of X_ORA_RBK would result in loss of all rollback segments and exports.

a. Recovery from loss of all of the rollback segments

1. Login as the ORACLE user.
2. Use the editor of your choice to alter the INIT.ORA file in the ORA_INSTANCE directory to comment out the ROLLBACK_SEGMENTS entry. This prevents the system from trying to acquire anything but the rollback segment contained in the SYSTEM tablespace.
3. Shut down and restart the instance using SQLDBA.
4. Create a second rollback segment using the SQLDBA command:

```
CREATE ROLLBACK SEGMENT [segment name]
TABLESPACE [tablespace name]
```

where: [segment name] is the name of the rollback segment such as ROLLBACK_1.
[tablespace name] is the tablespace for the rollback segments or SYSTEM.
Since this segment will be dropped later, use the default storage parameters.

5. Edit the INIT.ORA file found in the ORA_INSTANCE directory to alter the ROLLBACK SEGMENTS entry to list only the name of the segment created in step 5.
6. Shut down and start up the instance using SQLDBA.
7. Drop the old rollback segment tablespace:
    DROP TABLESPACE ROLLBACK_SEGS INCLUDING CONTENTS
8. Use the SQLDBA command to create a new rollback segment tablespace:

```
CREATE TABLESPACE ROLLBACK_SEGS
DATAFILE 'FILE SPEC'
DEFAULT STORAGE (
INITIAL 500K NEXT 500K
MINEXTENTS 2 MAXEXTENTS 99
PCTINCREASE 0)      Note: Not required under ORACLE7
ONLINE
```

If the location is the same, use the REUSE option on the file spec. The size should be the same as before.
Note: Under ORACLE7, if you include the PCTINCREASE in the create command for a rollback segment, the statement will fail. Under ORACLE7 the PCTINCREASE for rollback segments is always zero. To use Figure 8.7 under ORACLE7, either add SET COMPATIBILITY V6 to the top of the file or remove the PCTINCREASE clauses from the storage statements.

9. Use the DBA created procedure similar to Figure 8.7 from SQLDBA to create the new rollback segments.
10. Shut down the database, then edit the INIT.ORA file to return it to the condition it was before the loss of the rollback segments (The ROLLBACK_SEGMENTS statement listing all the rollback segments and not listing the second segment in the SYSTEM tablespace). Restart the database.

```
rem
rem Name           : Create_prod_rollbacks.sql
rem Purpose        : Create production instance rollback segments
rem Use            : From SQLPLUS or SQLDBA using a DBA level account
rem Limitations    : None
rem History
rem When           Who              What
rem -----------    -------------    -----------------------
rem 5/28/93        M. Ault          Initial Creation
rem
create rollback segment rollback1
tablespace ora_rollbacks
storage (
                initial 100k next 100k
                minextents 2 maxextents 40
                pctincrease 0);

create rollback segment rollback2
tablespace ora_rollbacks
storage (
                initial 100k next 100k
                minextents 2 maxextents 40
                pctincrease 0);

create rollback segment rollback3
tablespace ora_rollbacks
storage (
                initial 100k next 100k
                minextents 2 maxextents 40
                pctincrease 0);

create rollback segment rollback4
tablespace ora_rollbacks
storage (
                initial 100k next 100k
                minextents 2 maxextents 40
                pctincrease 0);
exit
```

Figure 8.7 Example of script to recreate rollback segments.

11. Using SQLDBA, drop the rollback segment you created in the SYSTEM tablespace. This completes the recovery from the loss of the ROLLBACK SEGMENTS.
12. Since the export files have been lost, perform a full export.

b. Recovery from loss of the active rollback segment
If you notice ORA-600 series errors in the ALERT.LOG in reference to the rollback segment, this indicates that the rollback segment in use has become corrupted. To recover from this, perform the following steps:

1. Log in as ORACLE.
2. Edit the INIT.ORA file; add the following line:

```
_OFFLINE_ROLLBACK SEGMENTS = ([name])
```

3. While still in the editor, remove reference to the problem rollback segment from the ROLLBACK SEGMENTS entry. Exit the editor.
4. Shut down and restart the database using SQLDBA.
5. Using SQLDBA, drop the corrupted rollback segment using the SQLDBA commands:

```
CONNECT INTERNAL
DROP ROLLBACK SEGMENT [name]
```

6. Recreate the rollback segment using the SQLDBA command:

```
CREATE ROLLBACK SEGMENT [name]
TABLESPACE ROLLBACK_SEGS
STORAGE (INITIAL 500K NEXT 500K
MINEXENTS 2 MAXEXTENTS 99
PCTINCREASE 0) Note: PCTINCREASE cannot be specified under
ORACLE7.
```

7. Edit the file ORA_INSTANCE:INIT.ORA to remove the _OFFLINE_ROLL-BACK_SEGMENTS line and add back the name of the rollback segment to the ROLLBACK_SEGMENTS line. Exit the editor.
8. Shut down and restart the database using SQLDBA.
9. The integrity of the database should be checked after this procedure using the following steps:
   a. Set the default to the export directory:

   ```
   $ SET DEF X_ORA_RBK:[ORACLE.DB_<DB_NAME>.EXPORTS]
   ```

   —or—
   ```
   $cd /oracle/db_<db_name>/exports
   ```

   b. Issue the following command:

   ```
   EXP SYSTEM/[password] FULL=YES INDEXES=YES ROWS=NO
   ```

   If no errors are returned, the database is consistent; if the database is not consistent, use the SQLDBA command RECOVER DATABASE to recover the database.

c. Recovery from loss of an Inactive REDO log.

   1. Log in as ORACLE. Start SQLDBA, and issue the following command:

   SHUTDOWN ABORT

   2. Spawn out to the operating system and copy an archived or backup copy of the damaged file to

```
X_ORA_RBK:[ORACLE.DB_<DB_NAME>]
```
--or--
```
x_ora_rbk/oracle/db_<db_name>
```

3. Use SQLDBA to issue the following commands:

```
STARTUP MOUNT
CONNECT INTERNAL
```

4. If the failure was a result of media damage, which required moving the REDO log to a different disk, rename the log using the following SQLDBA command:

```
ALTER DATABASE RENAME FILE 'old' TO 'new'
```

where old and new are the full-path file names enclosed in single quotes.

5. Issue the SQLDBA command:

```
ALTER DATABASE OPEN
```

If no error occurs, recovery is complete.

6. If step 5 resulted in an error, the wrong archival copy may have been used. Check the file and if needed repeat steps 1 to 5. If you are certain that the file is correct and you still receive an error, go on to step 7.

7. Using SQLDBA, shut down the Oracle database and then have the system manager perform a full backup of the Oracle system.

8. Using SQLDBA, restart the database following the backup and using SQLDBA. Stop archiving with these commands:

```
CONNECT INTERNAL
ALTER DATABASE NOARCHIVELOG
```

9. Using SQLDBA, replace the lost redo file with a new one using the following commands:

```
CONNECT INTERNAL
ALTER DATABASE ADD LOGFILE 'new file'
```

where 'new file' is the full-path file name.

10. Still using SQLDBA, drop the damaged file using the command:

```
ALTER DATABASE DROP LOGFILE 'old name'
```

where 'old name' is the full-path file name.
If this results in an error, go to the procedure for recovering from loss of an active redo log.

11. Exit from SQLDBA and have the system manager back up all the redo logs including the one created in step 9.

12. Back up the current control file using the SQLDBA commands:

```
CONNECT INTERNAL
ALTER DATABASE BACKUP CONTROL FILE TO 'backup file'
```

where 'backup file' is the full-path file name.

13. Using SQLDBA, shut down the database and have the system manager back up the database files.

14. Restart the database using the menu option. Using SQLDBA, issue the following commands:

```
CONNECT INTERNAL
ALTER DATABASE ARCHIVELOG
```

15. Issue the following SQLDBA commands to shut down and restart the database:

```
DISCONNECT
SHUTDOWN
STARTUP OPEN
```

If this results in an error, go to the procedure for recovering an active redo log.

d. Recovery from loss of an active REDO log file.

1. Log in as ORACLE. Using SQLDBA, shut down the database using the following command:

```
SHUTDOWN ABORT
```

2. Exit SQLDBA and have the system manager backup all database files. This provides you with a restart point should the rest of the recovery fail.

3. Correct the problem that caused the failure, or find a new location for the redo logs.

4. Have the system manager restore all database files using the latest backup, not the backup from step 2.

5. Start the database and mount it using the SQLDBA command:

```
STARTUP MOUNT
```

6. Connect to the database using the SQLDBA command:

```
CONNECT INTERNAL
```

7. Make sure all database files are online by executing the following command for each file:

```
ALTER DATABASE DATAFILE 'filename' ONLINE;
```

where 'filename' is the full-path file name.
If a database is recovered with a data file off-line, that data file's data is lost.

8. If the original location of the redo logs has become invalid, rename the files with the SQLDBA command:

```
ALTER DATABASE RENAME FILE 'old' TO 'new';
```

where old and new are full-path file names enclosed in single quotes.

Each file must be renamed if its location has changed.

9. Recover the database in manual mode using the command:

```
RECOVER DATABASE MANUAL;
```

10. ORACLE will prompt for the names of the ARCHIVE files required, beginning with the oldest file. The archive files are stored in

```
X_ORA_ARC:[ORACLE.DB_<DB_NAME>].
--or--
x_ora_arc/oracle/db_<db_name>
```

All required logs should be online. Each file begins with a DBA-specified string followed by filler zeros, then the log number followed by '.ARC'. The total length is 19 characters for version 6; therefore the number of filler zeros is:

19 - length of string - 3 - length of log number

For example, log number 506 could be 'SRM_ARC00000506.ARC'.
The format for ORACLE7 is determined by the LOG_ARCHIVE_FORMAT parameter in the INIT.ORA file.

11. After each log is applied, the system will request the next one in sequence. When the log just prior to the damaged log is applied, issue the command:

```
CANCEL
```

to abort the restore operation. Recovery is complete at this point. All data in the damaged redo log is lost and must be reentered.

12. Restart the database with the SQLDBA command:

```
ALTER DATABASE OPEN RESETLOGS;
```

13. Once the database is open, immediately shutdown with the SQLDBA command:

```
SHUTDOWN NORMAL
```

14. Exit SQLDBA and have the system manager make a complete backup of the Oracle system. All previous archive logs are now invalid and may be disposed of.

15. Using SQLDBA, restart the Oracle system.

5. Recovery from loss of X_ORA_ARC

   a. If the system manager can fix the problem, shut down the system. Have the system manager perform a full backup and then restart the Oracle system using the menu.

   b. If the system operator cannot fix the problem and a new archive log location is set up, perform the following:

      1. Using the SQLDBA option from the ORACLE user menu, issue the commands:

```
CONNECT INTERNAL
ARCHIVE LOG 'DEST';
```

Where DEST is the new location, for example, if the new location is disk DATA_4:[ORACLE.DB_<DB_NAME>. ARCHIVES], DEST would be:

— or —
rdo4/oracle/db_<db_name>/archives
'DATA_4:[ORACLE.DB_<DB_NAME>]SRM_ARC'
— or —
'rdo4/oracle/db_<db_name>/archives'

2. Exit SQLDBA and edit the ORA_INSTANCE:INIT.ORA file to reflect the new archive log location.
3. Using SQLDBA shutdown the Oracle system.
4. Have the system manager perform a full backup of the Oracle system; then use SQLDBA to restart the system.

6. Recovery of a deleted table from a tablespace

a. Determine from the user when the table was deleted and when the last entry, modification, or deletions were made to the table.
b. Log in as ORACLE and get a list of the full export files and the incremental export files on the system. If a full export has been done since the last update, but before the file was deleted, use this file in step 4.
c. From the list of incremental exports, determine the export that is just after the date the file was last modified but before the date the file was deleted. If the date of modification and deletion are the same, select the last incremental after a file modification. If there is no file on the system, have the system manager restore the X_ORA_RBK:[ORACLE.DB_<DB_NAME>.EXPORTS] directory contents from the last backup and recheck. If the file still is not available, repeat the restore request with the backup previous to that. If the file needed is not on the available backups, the table is not recoverable. If the file was not modified, it will not be in the incremental export and must be recovered from a full export.
d. Once the export is located, spawn out to the operating system and set the default directory to the export file location using the command:

```
>SET DEF X_ORA_RBK:[ORACLE.DB_<DB_NAME>.EXPORTS]
--or--
cd x_ora_rbk/oracle/db_<db_name>/exports
```

e. Use the following import command from the system prompt to restore the table:

```
>IMP SYSTEM/[password] FROMUSER=[user] TOUSER=[user] -
TABLES=([table_name]) FILE=[export file name]
```

where: [password] is the DBA user - SYSTEM's password
[user] is the owner's user name
[table_name] is the name of the table to be recovered
[export file name] is the name of the export file

This recovers the table to the date of the export. If data was added or removed from the table since this export, the data must be reentered. This may result in loss of referential integrity, so any referential integrity constraints under ORACLE7 may have to be disabled until data is fully restored.

7. Recovery from loss of all control files.

If for some unimaginable reason you lose all copies of your control file (about the only way would be deliberate sabotage if you follow OFA guidelines) there is a command available to rebuild them. You must know the following information in order to rebuild the control files:

a. All redo log file names and locations
b. All database file data files and locations
c. The values for MAXLOGFILES, MAXDATAFILES, and MAXINSTANCES
d. The status of archive logging

Items a, c, and d should be available via the original CREATE_<db_name> script. Item b should be documented before it is needed with a script similar to the one shown in Figure 8.8, with an example of output in Figure 8.9.

```
REM Name        : SPACE.SQL
REM Purpose     : Document file sizes and locations
REM Use         : From SQLPLUS
REM History:
REM When    Who      What
REM 7/5/93  M. Ault   Initial creation
REM
COLUMN FILE_NAME FORMAT A55
COLUMN TABLESPACE_NAME FORMAT A20
START ORACLE$SQL:TITLE80 'DATABASE DATAFILES'
SPOOL FILE_LIST&DB..LIS
BREAK ON TABLESPACE_NAME SKIP 1 ON REPORT
COMPUTE SUM OF MEG ON TABLESPACE_NAME ON REPORT
SELECT
              TABLESPACE_NAME, FILE_NAME BYTES/1048576 MEG
FROM
              DBA_DATA_FILES
ORDER BY
              TABLESPACE_NAME
/
SPOOL OFF
EXIT
```

Figure 8.8 Example of script to document file sizes and locations.

```
Date: 06/24/93                "Your Company Name"               Page:  1
Time: 05:15 PM               TABLESPACE SPACE USAGE            ADHOC_DBA
                               "Your" Database

TABLESPACE_NAME        FILE_NAME                                      MEG
--------------------   -----------------------------------------------------
-
MTD_EXPENSES_INDEXES   M_DISK19:[M_ORACLE6.DB_ADHOC]ORA_MTD_INDEXES_1.DBS  400.00
                       M_DISK20:[M_ORACLE6.DB_ADHOC]ORA_MTD_INDEXES_2.DBS  400.00
                       M_DISK11:[M_ORACLE6.DB_ADHOC]ORA_MTD_INDEXES_3.DBS  400.00
******************************                                    --------
sum                                                              1,200.00

MTD_EXPENSES_SPREAD    M_DISK11:[M_ORACLE6.DB_ADHOC]ORA_MTD_SPREAD_1.DBS   250.00
                       M_DISK21:[M_ORACLE6.DB_ADHOC]ORA_MTD_SPREAD_3.DBS   250.00
                       M_DISK18:[M_ORACLE6.DB_ADHOC]ORA_MTD_SPREAD_2.DBS   250.00
******************************                                    --------
sum                                                                750.00

ORA_ROLLBACKS          M_DISK6:[M_ORACLE6.DB_ADHOC]ORA_ROLLBACKS_1.DBS      90.00
******************************                                    --------
sum                                                                 90.00

ORA_TEMP               M_DISK11:[M_ORACLE6.DB_ADHOC]ORA_TEMP_1.DBS         400.00
******************************
--------
sum                                                                400.00

TOOLS                  M_DISK8:[M_ORACLE6.DB_ADHOC]ORA_TOOLS_1.DBS          10.00
******************************                                    --------
sum                                                                 10.00

ORA_USERS              M_DISK9:[M_ORACLE6.DB_ADHOC]ORA_USERS_1.DBS          10.00
******************************                                    --------
sum                                                                 10.00

SYSTEM                 M_DISK9:[M_ORACLE6.DB_ADHOC]ORA_SYSTEM_1.DBS         10.00
******************************                                    --------
sum                                                                 10.00

YTD_EXPENSES           M_DISK21:[M_ORACLE6.DB_ADHOC]ORA_YTD_EXPENSES_1.DBS  60.00
                       M_DISK9:[M_ORACLE6.DB_ADHOC]ORA_YTD_EXPENSES_2.DBS   60.00
                       M_DISK11:[M_ORACLE6.DB_ADHOC]ORA_YTD_EXPENSES_3.DBS  60.00
******************************
--------
sum                                                                180.00

YTD_INDEXES            M_DISK20:[M_ORACLE6.DB_ADHOC]ORA_YTD_INDEXES_1.DBS  270.00
******************************                                    --------
sum                                                                270.00
                                                                 --------
sum                                                              2,920.00
```

Figure 8.9 Example of output from script in Figure 8.8.

The data files can either be the current files or files needing recovery. Any data file containing a rollback segment must be available, or recovery will fail. The CREATE CONTROLFILE command is used to rebuild a destroyed control file. The syntax of the CREATE CONTROLFILE command follows.

```
CREATE CONTROLFILE [REUSE]
   DATABASE name
   [LOGFILE  filespec, filespec,...filespec]
   RESETLOGS | NORESETLOGS
   [MAXLOGFILES n]
   [DATAFILE  filespec, filespec,...filespec]
   [MAXDATAFILES n]
   [MAXINSTANCES n]
   [MAXLOGFILES n]
   [MAXLOGHISTORY n]
   [ARCHIVELOG | NOARCHIVELOG]
   [SHARED | EXCLUSIVE]
```

Where:

REUSE—If this is specified, the control files may already exist. For example, if an improperly specified backup didn't allow recovery of the most current control files, you could use the REUSE option to overwrite the old version. If this option is not specified, the control files must not currently exist. If specified, the file locations from the INIT.ORA file will be used.

[SET] DATABASE—The name specified here must match the database names in the data and log files. The SET option allows changing the database name under ORACLE7.

LOGFILE [GROUP n]—This clause lists all online logs used for the database. If not specified, the platform specific defaults for either VMS or UNIX will be used.

RESETLOGS—This is the option of choice for this command. It will force the use of ALTER DATABASE OPEN RESETLOGS when starting the database. Media recovery is allowed before issuing the above command. This should always be used unless the logs online are the current logs. If the logs were restored from backup and all logs are listed, NORESETLOGS may be used, but it is not recommended.

MAXLOGFILES—May be larger than the value used in the original CREATE DATABASE command, but cannot be smaller than the number that the database ever contained, including dropped log files.

DATAFILES—All data files must be listed. All data files must be accessible since they are assumed to be online. The files may be backup copies needing recovery.

MAXDATAFILES—May be different from the original CREATE DATABASE, but cannot be smaller than the maximum number of data files ever used by the database.

MAXINSTANCES—May be different from the original control file.

[NO] ARCHIVELOG: NOARCHIVELOG is the default if not specified. If you intend to use archived logs, use ARCHIVELOG even though ALTER DATABASE can be used to reset the option at a later time.

SHARED —or— EXCLUSIVE : Same use as in a CREATE DATABASE command.

For ORACLE7 there are two additional options:

MAXLOGMEMBERS—This specifies the maximum number of members for a redo log group under ORACLE7. Defaults to 1.

MAXLOGHISTORY—This specifies the maximum number of archived redo logs that can be applied for recovery of an ORACLE parallel server. This is only used for parallel server-based databases.

To use the CREATE CONTROLFILE command, use the following procedure:

1. Back up all existing files.
2. Log in to SQLDBA
3. Issue the STARTUP NOMOUNT command.
4. Issue the CREATE CONTROLFILE command.
5. Issue the ALTER DATABASE MOUNT command.
6. Apply required recovery to the database files.
7. Shut down cleanly (SHUTDOWN with no options) and back up the recovered database.
8. Restart the database.

The DBA is encouraged to do the following additional reading on backup and recovery:

Integrating ORACLE Backup Strategies, Loney, K., Oracle Magazine, Summer 1993.

ORACLE RDBMS Database Administrator's Guide, Version 6, Oct. 1990, Oracle Corp. Part number 3601-V6.0, Chapter 15.

ORACLE7 Server Administrator's Guide, Dec. 1992, Oracle Corp. Part number 6694-70-1292, Part VI, Chapters 17 to 19.

CREATE CONTROLFILE readme file, Version 6.0.33 release tape, and subsequent V6 release tapes.

SQL Language Reference Manual, Oracle 7, Dec. 1992, Oracle Corp.

RECOVERY ADDENDUM readme file, Oracle release tapes.

A Case Study Determining a 10 Gbyte Backup/Recovery Scheme, Dunlap, S., Northern Telecom, 1991 IOUG Proceedings, Miami, Florida.

Managing the Oracle Tools

This last chapter concerns the management of the Oracle toolset. The tools such as SQL*FORMS, SQL*REPORTWRITER, SQL*MENUS, and CASE will be covered. A majority of the provided tools require little if any DBA intervention for their use. Others will require thought and planning to be used to their fullest extent. Hopefully this chapter will provide the food for that thought process.

9.1 User Management for Oracle Tools

User management for tools will consist of finding the right default quota settings under VMS and ensuring the proper group assignment and system quotas under UNIX. It would be great if a list existed for each machine that would tell you exactly what quotas to assign, but unfortunately only the guidelines presented in Chapter 4 exist.

9.1.1 Managing Tool Users Under VMS

If the DBA, under VMS, installs a majority of the tools in shared memory, the user quotas will decrease; if the SGA has to be large, they will increase. The quota for your users will have to be determined in a hit-and-miss method between you and the system manager. The guidelines as given are a good place to start, but you will find they will not fit all situations.

A general user will require less page file quota than a developer, for instance. However, if that user is running large reports, they may require more working set. It is best to start at the low end for the quotas and then test run your applications against them.

Two of the major indicators of lack of page file quota on VMS is a system-level fatal access error or a system-level exceeded quota error. If your users under VMS get these types of errors, generally during report generation, increase their page file quotas. The other major error will have to do with process count, and for once the error message will tell you exactly what is wrong.

9.2.1 Managing Tool Users Under UNIX

Generally speaking, UNIX users will require less management than VMS users. The user processes under UNIX are more privileged due to the lack of user process tunability in most flavors.

9.2 Managing SQL*FORMS

Once the form's product is installed, all users have access to it. The best way to prevent unauthorized use of the SQL*FORMS tool is to reset the operating system protections to restrict access to the SQLFORMS command to a specified group of individuals. Under UNIX this would be done via a group assignment. Under VMS the users could be assigned to a specific UIC code, or could be granted a special rights identifier and an ACL maintained on the SQLFORMS executables.

One thing to remember is that on VMS there is no SQLFORMS executable. The SQLFORMS, SQLFORMS30, and other forms related commands are actually symbols that point to an executable in the forms directory. These symbols and the programs they call are listed in Figure 9.1.

SYMBOL	PROGRAM	PURPOSE
SQLFORMS, SQLFORMS30	IAD	Forms Design
GENFORM	IAG	Generate Forms
RUNFORM	IAP	Execute forms
CONVERT	IAC	Convert forms

Figure 9.1 SQL*Forms symbol and program definitions.

The actual programs will have their protections altered. For a user to run forms the IAP, or RUNFORM, program will have to remain as a general access program; the general user will not require access to any of the other forms executables.

9.2.1 The ORACLE*TERMINAL Tool and SQLFORMS

The ORACLE*TERMINAL tool replaces the CRT tool from Oracle releases prior to version 6. This tool allows the definition of terminal characteristics for any terminal that Oracle will need to run on. ORACLE*TERMINAL, or ORATERM, allows the DBA to specify key mapping, screen characteristics, and help screens that will then be used by all of the other tools, such as SQLFORMS that access the modified terminal definition.

Under SQLFORMS the two biggest areas for the DBA to worry over will most likely be screen width and mapping of the KEY_Fn triggers. The screen width will generally be set to either 80 (the default) or 132 columns. The KEY_Fn, or "Hot Keys," can be mapped to any keys or combination of keys. Generally the KEY_Fn are mapped to a shifted Function key.

It is suggested that the DBA use the copy option from the main menu to make a copy of the terminal definition he or she is modifying before any modifications are made. The changes are then made on the copy, leaving the original as a fallback.

To change the screen width the DBA uses the DEVICE DISPLAY DEFINITION screen under the ORATERM program. The DBA simply enters the new screen width in the Screen Width field of the form and recompiles the definition.

To add the KEY_Fn (where n = 0 to 9) "Hot Key" definitions, the DBA will use the PRODUCT menu and select the KEYS section. The new keys added to the product section are listed in Figure 9.2.

KEY	KEY CODE
Key 0	10022
Key 1	10023
Key 2	10024
Key 3	10025
Key 4	10026
Key 5	10027
Key 6	10028
Key 7	10029
Key 8	10030
Key 9	10031

Figure 9.2 Key and key code definitions.

The second phase required to map the KEY_Fn keys requires the DBA to access the KEY MAPPING menu under ORATERM and enter the key mappings specified in Figure 9.3. The actual key strokes are the choice of the DBA; the ones listed are for example only.

KEY	KEY STROKES
Key 0	PF1 PF1 0
Key 1	PF1 PF1 1
Key 2	PF1 PF1 2
Key 3	PF1 PF1 3
Key 4	PF1 PF1 4
Key 5	PF1 PF1 5
Key 6	PF1 PF1 6
Key 7	PF1 PF1 7
Key 8	PF1 PF1 8
Key 9	PF1 PF1 9

Figure 9.3 Key and key stroke definitions.

Once the definitions are in place and the terminal definition compiled, the developers use the KEY_Fn triggers to map functionality into the keys.

9.2.2 User Exits and SQL*FORMS

Users may require 3GL user exits to perform calculations or special operations under forms. In order to do this, the user exits must be linked in with the forms code. This is accomplished by creating the GENXTB program and the table IAPXTB. This is a platform specific operation.

GENXTB and IAPXTB on VMS. To generate the GENXTB program and the IAPXTB table on a VMS system, perform the following procedure:

1. Link GENXTB.OBJ supplied with SQLFORMS30.

   ```
   $ ORA_RDBMS:LOUTL ORA_SQLFORMS:GENXTB -
   _$ ORA_SQLFORMS:GENXTB,ORA_UTIL:SQLLIB/LIB -
   _$ ORA_SQLFORMS:GENXTB S
   ```

2. Generate the required form:

   ```
   $ GENFORM ORA_SQLFORMS:GENXTB -TO
   ```

3. Run the GENXTB program to create the IAPXTB table.

   ```
   $ GENXTB username/password
   ```

   Note: This table is generated only once.

To add a line for a given user exit, use the form generated in step 2,

```
$RUNFORM ORA_SQLFORMS:GENXTB username/password
```

The form will require the following fields to be input:

NAME—This is the user exit name as called by the form or report, not the source file name.
   Note: This name is limited to 6–10 characters. In some compilers uniqueness is only guaranteed to 5 characters.
TYPE—This is the language of the exit (C, COB, FOR, PAS, ADA, PLI).
REMARKS—This is a brief description of the user exit.

Once the user exits are added, there are several more steps to be accomplished before they can be used. These are:

1. Generate a macro that will link the exits into forms:

   ```
   $ GENXTB username/password EXITTABLE.MAR
   ```

2. Assemble the macro:

   ```
   $MACRO/OBJ=EXITTABLE EXITTABLE
   ```

3. Use either LIAP.COM or GLIAP.COM to relink the forms IAP executable. LIAP places a copy of the new IAP executable in the ORA_SQLFORMS directory. GLIAP places a file called XAIP.EXE into your default directory. It is suggested you use GLIAP while testing your exits; then use LIAP when you are sure they function correctly.

The procedure for using GLIAP is as follows:

1. Copy ORA_SQLFORMS:GLIAP.COM into your working directory.
2. Run GLIAP with the objects created in 2 above.

   ```
   $@GLIAP objectlist MD
   ```

   Where objectlist is the EXITTABLE.OBJ and the exit object files.
3. Test the user exit by using the XIAP executable in place of RUNFORM (IAP).
4. Once you are satisfied that the exits perform as expected, enter the objects into the forms library and relink the forms executable.

   ```
   $ LIBRARY/REPLACE ORA_SQLFORMS:IAPLIB objectlist
   $ @ORA_SQLFORMS:LIAP S
   $ @ORA_SQLFORMS:LIAD S
   ```

Remember that the GENXTB and IAPXTB creation needs only to be done one time.

GENXTB and IAPXTB on UNIX. To generate the GENXTB program and the IAPXTB table on a UNIX system, perform the following:

To use user exits in UNIX for SQLFORMS refer to the installation and user guide for your system. The process varies for each type of source language and flavor of UNIX. You must have a C compiler.

9.2.3 Managing SQL*FORMS 4.0

Under SQL*FORMS 4.0 the functions of SQL*FORMS and SQL*MENUS have been combined. The added functionality of a GUI (Graphic User Interface) is also provided. As far as can be determined from examining the developer's release of the documentation and looking at the DOS Beta release, management of SQL*FORMS 4.0 will not be significantly different from management of SQL*FORMS 3.0 and the management of SQL*Menu 5.0. The major differences in the product(s) will be from the developer's viewpoint.

From the menu side of the new SQL*FORMS release, the management is actually easier because if a developer has access to SQL*FORMS 4.0, he or she will have access to the menus. No additional access grants such as those used in SQL*Menu 5.0 are required with the integrated product.

In order to create roles and grant other users access to those roles, developers must be granted administration privileges. This is done through the file menu, grant option for role access. Once a developer has administration privilege, he or she can create roles and grant users access to those roles by use of the file menu, grant option, and select role, then choose new to create a role.

The developers will need to become thoroughly familiar with the use of memory roles and how to enable and disable security within their menus. Chapter 18 of the *SQL*FORMS User's Guide Version 4 (Developer's Release)* details this information.

User exits are enabled in the same manner as for SQL*FORMS 3.0. The full procedure is documented in the *SQL*FORMS Reference Manual, Volume 2 Version 4 (Developer's Release)* Appendix F.

9.3 Managing the SQL*MENU Tool

SQL*MENU 5.0 management consists of the managing of roles and access privileges. The DBA will control types of access by use of the SQL*MENU Action Menu ADMIN option. Under the admin option there are three choices: grant access, security, and host.

The grant access option allows the DBA to grant three types of user access. These are "execute," "design," and "administrate." General users will require execute privilege. Designers will require design privilege, and users who will be able to assign roles and privileges to other users will require administrate privilege.

The security option allows the specification of roles and assignment of users to those roles. The roles are then used in the SQL*MENU Menus to restrict or grant access to various menus and commands within an application. These roles are different from ORACLE7 system roles and should not be confused with them. By default the SYSTEM user has administrate privileges and access to all roles.

The SQL*MENU system consists of four commands. These are listed below with their function. General users will only require access to RUNMENU. Designers will require SQLMENU, GENMENU, and DOCMENU. Generally speaking, access to SQLMENU will give users access to GENMENU and DOCMENU. Each designer can specify the security of their menus by specification of the required roles. See Figure 9.4.

```
COMMAND    FUNCTION
SQLMENU    Allows generation, modification and documentation of menus.
GENMENU    Allows generation of menus, and menu users.
RUNMENU    Allows users to run menus that have been created.
DOCMENU    Allows documentation of existing menus.
```

Figure 9.4 Menu commands and functions.

The DBA will generally assign users and roles under the direction of the application designers and security plan for a given application. The access to SQLMENU should be restricted to designers. General users only require access to RUNMENU.

9.4 Managing SQL*REPORTWRITER1.1

Oracle's report generation tools consist of SQL*REPORT, SQL*PLUS, and SQL*REPORTWRITER. Arguments could also be made for the SQL*Query and DATA*QUERY products, but these are PC based and thus out of the scope of this book. Of the three report-generation tools that are based on UNIX and VMS platforms, most would rate them from SQL*PLUS, to SQL*REPORTWRITER to SQL*REPORT as far as ease of use. The new release of SQL*REPORTWRITER, version 2.0 is supposed to be far superior to version 1.1, and promises ease of use that exceeds even that of SQLPLUS, but the jury is still out as of this date. Future releases of Oracle (probably release 8) will cease to support SQL*REPORT, so the major contenders for your report-writing needs will be SQL*PLUS and SQL*REPORTWRITER.

SQL*REPORTWRITER is a "forms"-based reporting tool. Unfortunately query generation for SQL*REPORTWRITER is sometimes obtuse and formatting output cumbersome. In spite of these shortfalls it is a usable tool and can give good results if a little care is given to the report development process.

9.4.1 System or Individual Report Writer Tables

The SQL*REPORTWRITER product has two installation options. You can have shared report tables owned by SYSTEM, or you can have each developer own their own set of report tables. Depending on your development environment, either is acceptable.

If your environment consists of groups of developers all working on a single large project, a shared set of tables makes sense. In this environment Joe may start a report only to have Becky finish it. If they each had individual tables, Joe would have to use the DUMPREP command to create a REX file that Becky would then use LOADREP to reload into her tables, and so on down the line until the report is finished. All of this is avoided if a central shared set of tables is used.

There is less overhead for the system with shared tables. Instead of 5 copies of 12 tables for 5 developers with an additional 3 SYSTEM owned tables for a total of 63 tables, only 16 tables are required. A single DBA can easily manage a shared set of tables, generating status reports and re-port listings in a much easier fashion than if the tables are spread across the entire database.

If on the other hand you have several developers all working on different projects, then indi-vidually owned tables might be better. This would allow an application to be handled as a unit for exports and imports, neglecting the forms tables of course. Another advantage with individually owned tables is in the security area. It is easier to maintain application security with distributed report tables. Shared or individual, you, the DBA, have to make that choice when installing the SQL*REPORTWRITER product.

9.4.2 User Administration for SQL*REPORTWRITER

The DBA is responsible for granting access to SQL*REPORTWRITER for developers. Users who only use the RUNREP command don't require SQL*REPORTWRITER access, just access to the tables referenced and suitable system quotas to successfully run reports. The SQL*ReportWriter process opens temporary files, which can be many times larger than the report generated. The users should have sufficient free disk space accessible to them or some reports may fail.

The Oracle manuals state to create SRW developers with CONNECT and RESOURCE privi-lege. This is not a good idea and can be dangerous. The developers only require CONNECT and tablespace level RESOURCE on tablespaces where they need to create objects. Only DBA users may require global RESOURCE.

On VMS it has been found that developers may require PGFLQUOs in excess of 120,000 to run SQL*ReportWriter to generate reports on reports. Since there is virtually no limit on UNIX users, until the system crashes, this doesn't apply to UNIX.

The DBA is also responsible for establishing the developer environment. This involves the selection of the default terminal type and the choice of shared or individual tables. An additional requirement is that of linking the executables when user exits are used. It has been found that the VT2200 report-writer terminal definition seems to work the best on most VMS platforms. UNIX terminals vary considerably and each platform will have a different specification.

9.4.3 The SRW_ADMIN Procedure

On VMS the major tool for maintaining the SQL*REPORTWRITER product is the SRW_ADMIN.COM procedure located in the directory pointed to by the logical ORA_SQLREPORTWRITER. This procedure provides the options shown in Figure 9.5.

```
 1 -  Add a new user
 2 -  Drop a user
 3 -  Add a page limit for a user
 4 -  Relink the executables with user exits
 5 -  Load the demo database and simple example reports
 6 -  Load the advanced sample reports
 7 -  Load reports which document your report definitions
 8 -  Set the default terminal definition
 9 -  Upgrade user exits names
10 -  Exit administration script
```

Figure 9.5 Example of SRW_ADMIN script options.

SCRIPT	FUNCTION
SRW_GRNT.SQL	Grants access to a user.
SRW_RVKE.SQL	Revokes access from user.
SRW_ILOC.SQL	Installs tables for a user.
SRW_DROP.SQL	Drops a specified report.
SRW_ICEN.SQL	Creates SYSTEM owned SRW tables.
SRW_LMT.SQL	Restricts a user to a specified page limit for reports.
SRW_DCEN.SQL	Drops all central tables. Reports should be UNLOADED or tables EXPORTED first.
SRW_UCEN.SQL	Upgrades version 1.1 reports in central tables to be able to use new 1.1.10 user exit names.
SRW_DLOC.SQL	Drops a users local report writer tables. If the user's reports are still required, they should be UNLOADED first.
SRW_ULOC.SQL	Same as SRW_UCEN only for local tables.
SRW_DR10.SQL	Drops version 1.0 tables after upgrade.
SRW_MAIL.COM --or--	
SRW_MAIL.SH	Allows report output to go to Oracle*Mail.
SRW_1104.SQL	Upgrades reports to 1.1.4 from earlier 1.1 version.
SRW_1110.SQL	Upgrades reports to 1.1.10 from earlier versions.
SRW_PRAC.SQL	Used by DBA to create PRODUCT_ACCESS table.
SRW_CMDN.SQL	Should only be run by the SYSTEM account. This script creates a table of SQL*ReportWriter command names that are used by the TERMDEF (VMS) --or-- TERMINAL (UNIX) routine.

The scripts for UNIX will be lowercase (srw_cmdn.sql vice SRW_CMDN.SQL).

Figure 9.6 ReportWriter administration scripts and their functions.

As can be seen from Figure 9.5, the SRW_ADMIN script allows the DBA to control all aspects of the SQL*REPORTWRITER program. On UNIX the script will be:

```
/oracle/sqlreport/admin/srw.admin
```

and the output from the UNIX shell script is virtually identical to the DCL command file output shown in Figure 9.5. In addition to the main script there are several other scripts available on both systems. These additional scripts are listed in Figure 9.6 with their functions.

9.4.4 SQL*REPORTWRITER Reports on Reports

Oracle provides several reports that can be used to document reports stored in the user's or in the central database report tables. These reports vary in width and are named accordingly. The reports will have to be loaded by the DBA and PUBLIC access granted for their security before they can be used by the general development community. Additional page file quota may be required for each user under VMS in order to run the reports.

The reports are:

- SRW80
- SRW132
- SRW175

9.4.5 User Exits and SQL*ReportWriter

Users may require 3GL user exits to perform calculations or special operations under SRW. In order to do this, the user exits must be linked in with the SRW code. This is accomplished by creating the GENXTB program and the table IAPXTB. This is a platform-specific operation.

GENXTB and IAPXTB on VMS. To generate the GENXTB program and the IAPXTB table on a VMS system, perform the following procedure:

1. Link GENXTB.OBJ supplied with SQLFORMS30.

   ```
   $ ORA_RDBMS:LOUTL ORA_SQLFORMS:GENXTB -
   _$ ORA_SQLFORMS:GENXTB,ORA_UTIL:SQLLIB/LIB -
   _$ ORA_SQLFORMS:GENXTB S
   ```

2. Generate the required form:

   ```
   $ GENFORM ORA_SQLFORMS:GENXTB -TO
   ```

3. Run the GENXTB program to create the IAPXTB table.

   ```
   $ GENXTB username/password
   ```

   Note: This table is generated only once.

   To add a line for a given user exit, use the form generated in step 2.

   ```
   $ RUNFORM ORA_SQLFORMS:GENXTB username/password
   ```

The form will require the following fields to be input:

NAME—This is the user exit name as called by the form or report, not the source file name. *Note:* This name is limited to 6 to 10 characters. Some precompilers only look at the first 5 characters for uniqueness.

TYPE—This is the language of the exit (C, COB, FOR, PAS, ADA, PLI).

REMARKS—This is a brief description of the user exit.

Once the user exits are added, there are several more steps to be accomplished before they can be used. These are:

1. Generate a macro that will link the exits into SRW:

   ```
   $ GENXTB username/password IAPXTB.MAR
   ```

2. Assemble the macro:

   ```
   $MACRO IAPXTB
   ```

3. Using the file IAPXTB.C as an example, add the demo exits to IAPXTB if you want to use them in addition to your own exits. This only needs to be done once.

4. Create an option file (.OPT) that tells the linker what .OBJ files contain your user exits. An example is contained in REPORT$HOME:[SRW_DEMO]DEMO.OPT file.

5. Using the SRW_ADMIN script, choose the relink option and relink the executables.

It is suggested that you refer to the installation and user's guide for your system to actually perform this operation. In different releases the process may vary.

GENXTB and IAPXTB on UNIX. To generate the GENXTB program and the IAPXTB table on a UNIX system, perform the following:

To use user exits in UNIX the same procedure is used as for VMS except no .OPT file is used and you must provide the full-path names of the .o files you wish to be linked with the SRW executables.

9.4.6 Management of SQL*ReportWriter 2.0

There are only centralized report writer tables for SQL*ReportWriter 2.0. It is no longer an option to have either local or centralized tables. The management scripts have been renamed and several have been dropped under version 2.0 of SQL*ReportWriter. The new scripts are listed with their functions in Figure 9.7.

To install the SQL*ReportWriter tables for version 2.0, a two-step process must be followed:

1. Run the TOOLICEN.SQL script to install the integrated tools tables.

2. Run the SRW2ICEN.SQL script to install the SQL*ReportWriter 2.0 tables. *Note:* These must be run in this order.

The executables have also changed slightly. The new executables are listed in Figure 9.8.

Under version 2.0 the DUMPREP, GENREP, LOADREP, PRINTDEF, and TERMDEF executables have been replaced by the CONVREP executable. PRINTDEF is no longer needed because under version 2 the printer definitions don't have to be compiled.

ORATERM has replaced the TERMDEF allowing for a single terminal definition executable for all Oracle tools. For the new GUI or bit-mapped report capability no terminal definition is required.

```
SCRIPT          FUNCTION
SRW2DCEN.SQL    Drops the SQL*ReportWriter centralized tables.
SRW2DROP.SQL    Drops one or more modules (reports, external queries, external
                PL/SQL libraries).
SRW2GRNT.SQL    Grants privileges to the specified user(s).
SRW2ICEN.SQL    Installs central SQL*ReportWriter tables.
SRW2LMT.SQL     Limits the number of output pages for a user.
SRW2PUP.SQL     Creates the product profile and user profile tables and user views.
SRW2RVKE.SQL    Revokes privileges from specified user(s).
TOOLDCEN.SQL    Deletes the integrated Oracle Tools tables.
TOOLGRNT.SQL    Grants privileges to specified users on the integrated tools tables.
TOOLICEN.SQL    Installs the integrated Oracle Tools tables.
TOOLRVKE.SQL    Revokes privileges of the specified users so they can no longer
                use the integrated Oracle tools tables.

The scripts for UNIX will be lowercase (toolrvke.sql vice TOOLRVKE.SQL).
```

Figure 9.7 ORACLE7 ReportWriter administration scripts.

```
EXECUTABLE      PURPOSE
SQLREP          Define and generate reports.
RUNREP          Execute reports that have been generated.
CONVREP         Converts reports from one format (.REP, .REX) to another format.
MOVEPRT         Converts version 1.1 printer definitions to version 2 format.
MOVEREP         Converts version 1.1 reports to version 2.0 format.
```

Figure 9.8 ORACLE7 ReportWriter executables.

The reports SRW80, SRW132, and SRW175 are no longer valid under version 2. Instead of external reports, this functionality has been added to the file menu in version 2. Additionally, there are two new reports; SRWDOCPB.RDF (portrait output) and SRWDOCLB.RDF (landscape output), which can be run with RUNREP for documentation or reports.

9.5 Management of the Oracle CASE Tools

The Oracle CASE suite of tools consists of CASE*DICTIONARY, CASE*DESIGNER, and CASE*GENERATOR. The generator product was further split into CASE*GENERATOR for forms and menus and CASE*GENERATOR for SQL and reports. There are several DBA activities that will concern these tools including installation, security, user assignment, and environmental variable assignment.

It is suggested that a CASE administrator be assigned to handle user assignment and CASE maintenance. In small shops this may be the same as the DBA. In large shops the DBA will probably have his or her hands full and a second person should be assigned to this task.

9.5.1 Installation of the CASE Toolset

As far as the Oracle database is concerned, the CASE toolset consists of executables, a set of definition tables owned by a CASE administration account (usually SYSCASE), one or more sets of object tables, and a set of indexes. The definition tables hold the core definitions and menus for the CASE system and are usually shared between applications. The object tables hold the definitions for each object created in CASE by a developer or group of developers. These tables may or may not be shared.

CASE Tablespaces. The major decision for the DBA during the installation is whether or not to install the CASE toolset in its own set of tablespaces. It is highly recommended that this be done. The toolset should be installed in two tablespaces, one for definition tables and one for indexes.

CASE Object Tables. Another decision the DBA may have input on is whether or not each developer or development team has their own set of object tables or if all developers share a common set of central object tables. The answer to this decision is entirely environment dependent. If your applications won't be sharing entities, attributes, domains, and so on, then separate sets of object tables are acceptable. If on the other hand your applications will be closely related, sharing entities, and such, then use a centralized set of object tables. If a central set of object tables is used, they should be placed in the same tablespace as the definition tables. If noncentralized object tables are used, they should be placed in the working tablespaces for the developer(s) who will be using them.

Application Tablespaces. The final installation question is whether or not to create a separate tablespace for each application under development or to place all application test tables in a centrally managed tablespace. During development the application test tables will generally contain a small subset of the actual table's data. It makes sense to store these application test tables in a central tablespace rather than creating several small tablespaces, one for each application. A central tablespace called APPLICATIONS and a second called APPL_INDEXES can be used to store these development test tables and their associated indexes. Each application should have a single owner. One thing to remember when making this decision is that a single user can only have access to one set of object tables at a time. If your users will be accessing several applications it would be best to use a central set of object tables.

9.5.2 User Assignment in CASE

User assignment in the CASE toolset is essentially a seven-step process:

1. Create the user's account in Oracle. If they will be creating new systems they will need resource on the applicable tablespace. It is suggested that for a centralized set of object tables, the application's development tables be placed in a central tablespace called APPLICATIONS. The developers who will be creating tables can then be granted RESOURCE on this one tablespace rather than requiring numerous resource grants on several small tablespaces.

2. Grant user access to SQL*Menu. If they will be creating menus they will require ADMINISTRATE level access since they will also be creating roles as they create menus.

If they will be a read-only type of user, they should only be granted EXECUTE level access.

3. Grant the user the proper CASE role in SQL*Menu. The two role choices are CDICT for general users and CMAN for CASE Managers. Unless users will be adding new applications to CASE or assigning users, they should be given the CDICT role.

4. Login to CASE*Dictionary as a Manager (a user with CMAN menu role). From the Management Menu select item 2 (in version 5.0.22), CASE*Dictionary Access Menu. From the access menu you will have several choices; full access, read access, revoke access, read access for view users and the CASE dictionary user's screen. Choose the appropriate item. For a general CASE developer, this would be full access.

5. Login to CASE*Dictionary as the owner of the application the user will be working with and using the "Application Access Control Menu" from the "Management Menu" grant the user the appropriate privileges on the "Application System Access Rights Screen." For each application the user is to have access to, repeat this step.

6. Have the user login to the CASE system. If you know their password, log in the first time for them. The first time a new CASE user logs in to the CASE system they will be asked for the name of the CASE system table owner they received access permission from. Once the name of the CASE owner is entered, the system creates numerous aliases and synonyms that give the user access to the CASE tables for the application(s) to which they have access.

7. Assist the new user in altering their login procedure (LOGIN.COM on VMS, .login or .profile on UNIX) to reflect their printer requirements. There are several logicals/ environmental variables that each user should customize to point to the printers of their choice. For an installation where a central printer or/and plotter will be used, the DBA can place these definitions in a central procedure that can be called from the CASEDICTIONARYUSER procedure.

9.5.3 CASE Print-Related Logicals

CASE output in the form of reports and diagrams can be directed to general ASCII printers, laser printers, or plotters. These report destinations are controlled by the assignment of printer logicals or environmental variables. Figure 9.9 shows these logicals as they would be assigned for VMS. The specific assignments for use in UNIX are implementation specific.

9.5.4 Setup of the User Work Environment

Another user-related activity the DBA might want to perform would be the creation of a calling menu for the CASE products in SQL*Menu. This will provide a single point of entry for user name and password information. This menu can also have the other development tools such as SQL*Forms, SQL*Plus, SQL*ReportWriter, and SQL*Menu added to it. This allows the users ease of access to the system tools and will speed development efforts.

LOGICAL	EXAMPLE DEFINITION (VMS)	PURPOSE
CASE_HP_CMD	print /queue=plt_hbc5_draftpro	Define HPGL output for DESIGNER output.
CASE_PS_CMD	print/que=mh51021	Define PostScript output for DESIGNER.
CASE_RESOURCE	CASE_DEC:VT220	Define the default terminal definition.
CASE_SDPRINT	SYS$PRINT	Define default report printout location for DESIGNER.
SDD$PRINT	print /queue=prt_hbc5_a	Define portrait printout command for reports.
SDD$WPRINT	print /queue=prt_hbc5_l	Define landscape printout command for reports.

Figure 9.9 Listing of CASE printout logicals for VMS.

9.5.5 Node Identification for Workstations

If your environment consists of several PC or MAC workstations using X-Window emulation you may want to create a DCL or shell script that prompts for node identification (Decnet or TCPIP address or alias) and then passes this information to the menu mentioned above for CASE*Designer to use. If you have a fair amount of DCL or shell script ability, a procedure that places the user in the proper development environment, as discussed in Chapter 1, can be developed. It has been found that the less the developers/operators have to interact at the system command level, the better for both them and you as database administrator.

9.5.6 Application Ownership

The application owner in CASE is the user who defines the application on the "Application Definition Screen" in the "Application Access Control Menu" from the "Management Menu." The owner is the only user able to grant access to the application and the only user who can generate the application.

Forms of Ownership. Under CASE there are three ways to handle application ownership:

1. Central ownership of all applications
2. Ownership by individual users of the application they are working on
3. Creation of special-application owners.

Option 1. In the first option, all applications are defined and owned by the CASE object table owner. The advantage to this option is that there is a single point of contact with the CASE system for all application generation and user maintenance. The disadvantage is that either one person must do all generation and user addition, or several people must know the CASE object owner's password.

Option 2. In the second option there is essentially no control over applications development. In a small shop this may not be bad, in a large shop it can lead to chaos. The second option is not suggested.

Option 3. In the third option, the CASE object owner assigns ownership of individual applications to specially assigned user accounts whose sole purpose in life is to administer those applications. For example, for an application called SALES the owner would be SALES_DBA or some other standard name. Each application has its own owner. The owner does all generations, user additions and other application related tasks. This option has the advantage of having nonindividual user-based ownership of applications and single point of control for each application. The password for the application's owner can be given freely to the designers for that application, and if they screw up, it will only effect their application. Option three is the suggested method for ownership of applications.

9.5.7 User Preferences in CASE

The next topic for CASE administration is the assignment of system, user, and Application preferences within CASE*Generator for forms and reports. These user preferences tell the generator how you as the designer or administrator want to handle headers, help forms, and a plethora of other design issues. Since these preferences are added to or subtracted from with each release it would be difficult if not impossible to cover all of them. The DBA should completely review the applicable sections in the CASE*Dictionary and CASE*Generator manuals for a complete picture of these user preferences. Figure 9.10 shows the preferences as they exist with version 5.0.22 of CASE.

	SQL*FORMS GENERATOR PREFERENCES	
PREFERENCE	DEFAULT	PURPOSE
SQL*Forms Version	2.0	Specify whether 2.0, 2.3, 30 forms will be generated.
Screen Depth	22	The number of usable lines.
Validation Unit	Field	The point at which validation checks are performed. Block, Field, Form or Record.
Date Format	Date	Format of Dates Date: DD-MON-YY Edate: DD/MM/YY Jdate: MM/DD/YY
Company Name	None	Allow specification of company name for application screens.
Application Display Title	None	Allow specification of application title.
Create Default Help Block?	Y-Yes	Includes help for screen blocks. Help is populated from text on the Column Definition Screen.
Automatic Field Help/Hint	Y-Yes	Include field help on screen comment line.
Include Comments	Y-Yes	Includes comments in the generated form at form, block, field and trigger level.

Figure 9.10 User preferences listing. (continued)

PREFERENCE	DEFAULT	PURPOSE
Allow Split Prompts?	Y-Yes	Shows whether prompts can be split across more than one line.
Synchronize Blocks?	Y-Yes	Tells the generator to create synchronization triggers between blocks where a foreign key link exists.
Query Detail Blocks?	A	Forces a query on dependent blocks. Values are: A Always query detail blocks E Query on entry of block N Never Query Automatically.
Query Detail Blocks on Next Page?	Y	Should dependent (detail) blocks on a seperate page?
Order Option	P	Sequencing spec for a block with multiple rows. Values: P -- Order by Primary Key D -- Order by descriptor N -- No ordering
User Ref. Values Validation	Y	Indicates entered values should be validated against application reference values.
Create Referential Integrity Triggers	Y	Forces generation of foreign key update, delete and insert triggers that maintain referential integrity.
Create Descriptors for Foreign Keys?	Y	Indicate if descriptor columns will be included on forms.

SQL*REPORTWRITER AND SQL*PLUS PREFERENCES

PREFERENCE	DEFAULT	PURPOSE
Coding Styles:		
DOCFMT	NN.MD	Documentation format string.
IGNFWD	N	Ignore first word when generating pneumonic.
MAXMLN	0	Module short name maximum length (0-30).
Default Usage:		
ANDSUM	N	Generate default summaries.
IMPJNS	Y	Imply usages for join columns.
USEDIJ	N	Use descriptors on implied joins.
Display:		
BTITLE	NONE	Default bottom title (132 CHR).
CONAME	NONE	Company name (60 CHR).
DTEMSK	NONE	Parameter and display date mask (80 CHAR).
DTOTPG	Y	Display total of pages.
HLPTXP	N	Create pages of help about report.

Figure 9.10 (continued)

PREFERENCE	DEFAULT	PURPOSE
MNYMSK	9,999,990.00	Money display format (240 CHR MAX).
NATLNG	AMERICAN	End User National Language for text.
PREFERENCE	**DEFAULT**	**PURPOSE**
PARHNT	NONE	Use TEXT for hint line of parameter form hint line (80 CHR).
SELUSR	SELECT USER FROM SYS.DUAL	SQL statement to get user name (200 CHR).
TITLEP	Y	Create title page.
TRAILP	Y	Create trailer page.
UDLGHD	Y	Underline group headers.

Generator Runtime:

ANDESC	NONE	Include descriptors.
ANJOIN	NONE	Accept joins.
ANOVRW	NONE	Overwrite any existing module(s).
CMPRPT	Y	Compile report after generation.
DFTCRT	System Dependent	Default terminal mapping to use.
HIDPAR	Y	Hide parameters with default values.
RUNRPT	NONE	Run report after generation.
SAVPRF	Y	Preference values saved by module.

Layout:

BLKTOP	2	Blank lines between top title and data (0 -- 10).
HEIGHT	60	Report height (10 -- 999).
MARBOT	0	Bottom margin (0 -- 80).
MARLFT	NONE	Left margin.
MARRGT	0	Right margin (0 -- 80).
MARTOP	0	Top margin (0 -- 80).
MLTPAN	Y	Generate multi-panals if required.
SPLTPR	Y	Allow split prompts.
TOPBRK	N	Page break at top level.
VSPCBM	0	Master/Detail report control break groups record spacing (0 -- 5).
WIDTH	80	Report width (10 - 999).

SQL Generation Preferences:

ANDIST	N	If required, use 'SELECT DISTINCT'.
ANNOTR	NONE	For subqueries use 'NOT'.
DOJOIN	Y	Wherever possible, use joins.
SQLPRS	NONE	Always pre-parse SQL.
TABOWN	NONE	For SQL, use this table owner (30 CHR).

Figure 9.10 (continued)

9.5.8 Other DBA Tasks in the CASE Toolset

In addition to the above listed tasks, the DBA, if there isn't a CASE administrator, may be expected to control application versions, provide CASE extensions, export or import applications, and provide for customized terminal definitions for applications. Let's quickly look at these additional responsibilities.

Application Version Control. An application can be in one of three possible states; active, frozen, or dropped. If an application is active, valid users can make changes to it. If an application is frozen, no changes are allowed, and if an application is dropped, no further work can be done on it, and it cannot be generated or accessed. Multiple versions of an application are allowed, when a new version is created the other older versions are automatically frozen. The DBA can unfreeze these older versions if desired.

Applications are frozen via the "Application Version Control Menu" which is called from the "Management Menu." This "Application Version Control Menu" is also used to create a new version of the application. If a new version is created, the old version is locked during the process. One thing to note is to be sure to have sufficient rollback segment space when creating a new version of an application. The amount required will depend on the size of the application. Only the application owner can change the status of an application.

If a new version of an application is created, all shadow applications (shared entities may cause shadow applications) will also be duplicated. All shadow applications are automatically frozen and you may not change their status.

Extensions to CASE. CASE, beginning with version 5.0, allows user extensions to the CASE systems. User extensions consist of new element/association types and their properties. There are a maximum of 99 element/associate types allowed in the CASE Dictionary. The DBA may use any element/association that is marked as "not used" in their NAME column.

The following are additional readings the DBA can use to get more information on managing the Oracle toolset.

SQL*Forms 3.0 Designer's Reference Version 3.0, Part# 3304-v3.0-0191, 1991, Oracle Corp.

SQL*ReportWriter Reference Manual Version 1.1, Part# 641-v1.1-0991, 1991, Oracle Corp.

SQL*Menu User's Guide and Reference Version 5.0, Part# 3303-V5.0-0490, April 1990, Oracle Corp.

Oracle for DEC VAX/VMS Installation and User's Guide Version 6.0, Part# 1001-V6.0, March 1991, Oracle Corp.

Oracle for HP 9000 Series 700/800 Installation and User's Guide Version 7.0.9, Part# 1035-70-0492, May 1992.

Oracle*Terminal User's Guide Version 1.0, Part# 5206-V1.0-1290, 1990, Oracle Corp.

SQL*Forms User's Guide Version 4.0, Part# 7044-40-0293 Developer's Release, Feb. 1993, Oracle Corp.

SQL*Forms Reference Manual Volume 2 Version 4.0, Part# 7051-50-0293, Developer's Release, Feb. 1993, Oracle Corp.

SQL*ReportWriter Reference Manual Volume 2 of 2 Version 2.0, Part# 741-20-0193, Developer's Release, Jan. 1993, Oracle Corp.

DBA SQL Commands

This appendix lists the SQL commands used throughout the book. It is not intended to be a complete list of all SQL commands. The DBA is referred to the *SQL Language Reference Manual* for their particular version of the Oracle database system for a complete listing of available SQL commands, functions, and formats. This is especially improtant if you are in the throes of switching from version 6 to ORACLE7 since many of the command formats have changed and new commands and options have been added.

It is also suggested that the DBA refer to the SQL*Plus and PL/SQL manuals for their version of the database. The database administration manuals also will provide numerous examples of the use of the SQL and SQL*Plus commands for administration purposes.

Rather than just an alphabetical list of SQL commands, the commands in this section have been grouped by the type of object they effect. For example, the CREATE, ALTER, and DROP commands for tables are all listed together.

There are some standard commands and options that can be covered first. The major option is the STORAGE option. This option's format is shown below.

```
STORAGE (INITIAL integer   NEXT integer
   MINEXTENTS integer   MAXEXTENTS integer
   PCTINCREASE integer (0-100))
```

Where:

   INITIAL—This is the size in bytes of the initial extent of the object. The default is 10,240 bytes. The minimum is 4096. The maximum is 4095 megabytes. All values are rounded to the nearest Oracle block size.

   NEXT—This is the size for the next extent after the INITIAL is used. The default is 10,240 bytes, the minimum is 2048, the maximum is 4095 megabytes. This is the value that will be used for each new extent if PCTINCREASE is set to 0.

   MINEXTENTS—This is the number of initial extents for the object. Generally, except for rollback segments, it is set to 1. If a large amount of space is required, and there is not enough contiguous space for the table, setting a smaller extent size and specifying several extents may solve the problem.

MAXEXTENTS—This is the largest number of extents allowed the object. This defaults to 99. The limit for VMS is block size dependent, for UNIX, a maximum of 121 extents are allowed.

PCTINCREASE—This parameter tells Oracle how much to grow each extent after the INITIAL and NEXT extents are used. A specification of 50 will grow each extent after NEXT by 50 percent, *for each subsequent extent*. This means that for a table created with one initial and a next extent, any further extents will increase in size by 50 percent over their predecessor. If the table grows by 20 more extents, the final one will be 1.50 raised to the 20 - 2 power larger (1478 times) than the extent specified by the NEXT parameter. This is set to 50 percent as a default. Be sure you reset it. Under ORACLE7 this parameter is only applied against the size of the previous extent.

The general commands we will cover are SELECT, INSERT, UPDATE, and DELETE. This is not intended to be a detailed listing of each command covering all possible options. These are more a general look to familiarize the DBA with the command. There are numerous examples of the use of the commands throughout the rest of the book. For a more detailed treatment of these commands the DBA is referred to the *SQL Language Reference Manual*, either for version 6 or ORACLE7.

The first command we will cover will be the SELECT command. The format for the SELECT command follows.

```
SELECT [ALL --or-- DISTINCT] ( * --or-- table.* --or-- column --or--
           table.column --or-- expr) [c_alias],...
    FROM [user --or-- schema.]table [t_alias], ...
    [WHERE condition]
    [CONNECT BY condition [START WITH condition]]
    [GROUP BY expr[, expr]... [HAVING condition]]
    [ (UNION --or-- INTERSECT --or-- MINUS) SELECT ...],...
    [ ORDER BY ( expr --or-- position) [ASC --or-- DESC],...]
    [ FOR UPDATE OF column,... [NOWAIT]];
```

Where:

ALL—This is the default (doesn't have to be specified). It indicates all rows, including duplicates be returned.

DISTINCT—Indicates only unique rows be returned.

*—Indicates all rows from all tables in the FROM clause be returned.

table.*—Indicates all rows from specified table be returned.

expr—A valid expression.

c_alias—A different name for the column or expression. Makes handling of complex expressions or long column names easier. For example:

```
100*(SUM(USED_BLOCKS)/SUM(MAX_BLOCKS)) PCT_USED
```

Would be referenced by PCT_USED instead of the entire expression.

[user —or— schema.]table—Specifies the tables to be used. If owner or schema isn't specified, defaults to current user.

t_alias—Table alias. This allows shortening of names for use in long WHERE clauses. Replaces table name.

condition—One of the allowed conditions such as =, <,>,!= statements.

position—The numeric position evaluated left to right of the column to order on. The first column or expression is 1, the next 2, and so on.

ASC —or— DESC—The way to order the column. Asc (ascending) is the default.

column—This is a column name from one of the tables in the FROM clause.

NOWAIT—This specifies that the select should return control to user instead of waiting if it encounters lock contention for a row.

The SELECT, FROM, and WHERE clauses must be in order. CONNECT BY, START WITH, GROUP BY, and HAVING can be in any order. The order of the ORDER BY and FOR UPDATE OF may be interchanged.

CONNECT BY—This is used for hierarchical relationships. This cannot be used in subqueries or joins.

START WITH—This identifies the root row(s) for the hierarchical relationship.

GROUP BY, HAVING—This clause is used for summary information. Used with functions such as MAX, MIN, SUM, AVG in the select.

UNION —or— INTERSECT —or— MINUS—These are set operators. UNION returns all distinct rows. INTERSECT returns all rows that are common for the selects; MINUS returns all rows that don't meet the selection specified by the second select but do meet those of the first select.

ORDER BY—This is used to specify an ordering hierarchy. It orders by columns or positions in either ascending or descending order.

FOR UPDATE OF—This is used to update the specified column(s).

The next general command is the INSERT command. The INSERT command is used to insert rows in a table or tables underlying a view. The format of the INSERT command follows.

```
INSERT INTO [user --or-- schema.]table [column list]
   (VALUES (value list (one to one match with column list))    or - query)
```

Where:

[user —or— schema.]—This specifies the table owner (user) or, owning schema for ORACLE7, of the specified table.

column list—This is a list of columns that will be inserted with this statement. Must include all NOT NULL columns in the table.

value list—This includes a list of all values to insert. The list must maintain a one-to-one relationship with the column list. Character fields are surrounded by single quotes. If there is no column list provided, all columns in the table must have a value or place holder (double commas) in the value list.

query—This is a query that returns a value or set of values for each column in the column list.

If values in a table need to be altered, the UPDATE command is used. The format of the UPDATE command follows.

```
UPDATE [user --or-- schema.]table [alias]
   SET (column = value --or-- expr, ...)
   [WHERE condition]
```

Where:

[user —or— schema.]—Specifies the owner (user) or the owning schema in ORACLE7.

column—Specifies a valid column in the table.

value —or— expr—This is either a valid value or an expression that will resolve to a valid value for the column.

condition—This is a valid conditional statement.

To remove data from a table the user will issue a DELETE or TRUNCATE command. The format for the DELETE command follows.

```
DELETE [FROM] [user --or-- schema.]table [alias]
   [WHERE condition]
```

Where:

> [user —or— schema]—Specifies the table owner (user) or owning schema for ORACLE7.
> alias—Specifies a short version of the table name for use in the condition statement.
> WHERE—This is a valid conditional statement. If a WHERE clause is not included, all data in the table
> is dropped.

A DELETE generates redo and rollback information and consumes lots of resources for large tables. Under ORACLE7 a new command, TRUNCATE, is available that doesn't generate redo or rollback information, making it much faster. However, you can recover from a delete if you don't commit. You can't recover from a TRUNCATE. The format of the TRUNCATE command follows.

```
TRUNCATE TABLE --or-- CLUSTER [schema.]table --or-- cluster
    [DROP --or-- REUSE STORAGE]
```

Where:

> schema—This is the schema that owns the cluster or table.
> DROP—This is the default, it drops the space used by the table except that specified for the initial
> extents.
> REUSE—This leaves all allocated space as it is.

This concludes the generic section. The next sections deal with database or object specific commands. The next set of commands are those dealing with the database itself.

Databases are created from SQLDBA using the CREATE DATABASE command. This command is covered below.

```
CREATE DATABASE database name
    CONTROLFILE REUSE
    LOGFILE file specifications
    MAXLOGFILES integer
    DATAFILE datafile specifications
    MAXDATAFILES integer
    MAXINSTANCES integer
    ARCHIVELOG or NOARCHIVELOG;
    Additional ORACLE7 parameters:
    MAXLOGMEMBERS n
    MAXLOGHISTORY  n (Only used for Oracle in shared multi-thread operation)
    CHARACTER SET charset
```

Where:

- Database name is the name of the database, max of eight characters long.
- File specifications for data files are of the format: 'filename' SIZE integer K or M REUSE. K is for kilobytes; M is for megabytes; REUSE specifies that if the file already exists, reuse it.
- File specifications for log files depend on the operating system.
- The MAXLOGFILES, MAXDATAFILES and MAXINSTANCES set hard limits for the database; these should be set to the maximum you ever expect.
- For ORACLE7, MAXLOGMEMBERS and MAXLOGHISTORY are hard limits.
- For ORACLE7, CHARACTER SET determines the character set that data will stored in; this value is operating and system dependent.
- If you need archive logging, set ARCHIVELOG; if you will never need it, set NOARCHIVELOG.

Databases are created in EXCLUSIVE mode. There is an EXCLUSIVE clause that is entirely optional (not shown).

The database may require periodic modification. The ALTER DATABASE command is used for this purpose.

```
ALTER DATABASE database name
   ADD LOGFILE filespec, filespec ....
   DROP LOGFILE 'filename', 'filename' ...
   RENAME FILE 'filename', 'filename' ....
   TO 'filename', 'filename' ...
   ARCHIVELOG   or NOARCHIVELOG
   MOUNT EXCLUSIVE or SHARED (EXCLUSIVE is the default)
   MOUNT or DISMOUNT
   OPEN
   CLOSE NORMAL or IMMEDIATE (NORMAL is the default)
```

Where:

database name—is the max of 8 character database name. If it is not specified, the value in the INIT.ORA file will be used.

filespec—is a file specification in the format of:

'filename' SIZE integer K or M REUSE with:
filename a OS specific full-path name
K or M specifies integer as kilobytes or megabytes.
REUSE specifies to reuse existing file if it exists.
If SIZE isn't specified 500K will be used.
REUSE is optional.

filename—is a full-path file name.

MOUNT—Database is available for some DBA functions, but not normal functions.

DISMOUNT—Database is dismounted.

OPEN—Database is mounted and opened for general use.

CLOSE—Database is not available for use, and may still be mounted. Immediate does it now; normal does it politely; abort does it rudely.

The following are examples of the ALTER DATABASE command for adding redo logs, threads, and groups:

```
ALTER DATABASE database name
   ADD LOGFILE file specification, file specification;
```

or for ORACLE7:

```
ALTER DATABASE database name
   ADD LOGFILE  THREAD y GROUP n (file specification, file specification) SIZE x;
```

or:

```
ALTER DATABASE database name
   ADD LOGFILE  MEMBER 'file specification'  REUSE TO GROUP n;
```

or:

```
ALTER DATABASE database name
   ADD LOGFILE  MEMBER 'file specification'  REUSE TO
   ('file specification', 'file specification');
```

Where:

> For ORACLE7—*n* is the group number. If the GROUP *n* clause is left out, a new group will be added that consists of the specified log files.
>
> For ORACLE7—*x* is the size for all members of the group.
>
> For ORACLE7—*y* is the tread number to which the group is assigned. File specification is a system specific full-path file name: UNIX:

```
'/etc/usr/ora_redo1.rdo'  SIZE 1M REUSE
```

(For ORACLE7 the size parameter is not with the file specification) VMS:

```
'DUA1:[M_ORACLE_1.DB_EXAMPLE]ORA_REDO1.RDO' SIZE 1M REUSE
```

The SIZE clause specifies the size of the new log (it should be the same size as all of the other redo logs). M means megabytes, K kilobytes, and no specification—just a number—means bytes. REUSE tells Oracle if the file exists, reuse it.

The following are examples of the ALTER DATABASE command for removing redo logs, threads, or groups:

```
ALTER DATABASE database name
    DROP LOGFILE  'filename';
```

For ORACLE7:

```
ALTER DATABASE database name
    DROP LOGFILE   GROUP n --OR--('filename', 'filename');
```

or:

```
ALTER DATABASE database name
    DROP LOGFILE  MEMBER 'filename';
```

Where 'filename' is just the file name, no SIZE or REUSE clause.

To change a datafile name:

```
ALTER DATABASE database name
    RENAME DATAFILE 'OLD FILE NAME' TO 'NEW FILE NAME';
```

Once in a great while, entire databases may need to be dropped. The command to accomplish this feat is the DROP DATABASE COMMAND. The format of this command is simple:

```
DROP DATABASE database name;
```

The following are examples of other database-related commands. The database is started using the STARTUP command under SQLDBA. Under version 6 you cannot be connected to a database when performing a startup. Under ORACLE7 you must be connected to perform a startup.

```
STARTUP  [DBA] [FORCE] [PFILE=filename]
    [EXCLUSIVE or SHARED]
    [MOUNT or OPEN] dbname
    [NOMOUNT]
```

The Database is shut down using the SHUTDOWN command under SQLDBA. For version 6 you must not be connected to use shutdown. Under ORACLE7 you must be connected.

```
SHUTDOWN [NORMAL --or-- IMMEDIATE --or-- ABORT]
```

1. No option means SHUTDOWN NORMAL—the database waits for all users to disconnect, prohibits new connects, then closes and dismounts the database, then shuts down the instance.
2. SHUTDOWN IMMEDIATE—cancels current calls like a system interrupt, and closes and dismounts the database, then shuts down the instance. PMON gracefully shuts down the user processes. No instance recovery is required on startup.
3. SHUTDOWN ABORT — This doesn't wait for anything. It shuts the database down now. Instance recovery will probably be required on startup. You should escalate to this by trying the other shutdowns first.

With databases you will also need to manage ROLLBACK SEGMENTS; the commands to do this follow.

Rollback segments are created with the CREATE ROLLBACK SEGMENT command:

```
CREATE [PUBLIC] ROLLBACK SEGMENT rollback name
   TABLESPACE tablespace name
   STORAGE storage clause;
```

Where:

Rollback name is the name for the rollback segment; this name must be unique.

Tablespace name is the name of the tablespace where the segment is to be created.

Storage clause is a storage clause that specifies the required storage parameters for the rollback segment. It is strongly suggested the following guidelines be used:

```
INITIAL = NEXT
MINEXTENTS = 2 (See note below for ORACLE7.)
MAXEXTENTS = a calculated maximum based on size of the rollback segment
   tablespace, size of rollback segment's extents and number of rollback
   segments.
PCTINCREASE - 0 (See note below for ORACLE7.)
```

For ORACLE7 a new parameter, OPTIMAL is allowed. This parameter reflects the size that the system will restore the rollback segment to after it has been extended by a large transaction.

For ORACLE7 the MINEXTENTS will default to 2 and the PCTINCREASE will always be 0. In fact, if PCTINCREASE is specified in the create command, an error will result unless compatibility is set to version 6.

Rollback segments are modified by use of the ALTER ROLLBACK SEGMENTS command. Its format is:

```
ALTER [PUBLIC] ROLLBACK SEGMENT rollback name
   STORAGE storage clause
```

Where the storage clause cannot contain new values for INITIAL or MINEXTENTS. For ORACLE7 a new OPTIMAL value can be set as well.

Rollback segments are dropped using the DROP ROLLBACK SEGMENT command.

```
DROP [PUBLIC] ROLLBACK SEGMENT rollback name;
```

A rollback segment must not be in use or it cannot be dropped. Once dropped it must be removed from the INIT.ORA - ROLLBACK SEGMENT clause or the database cannot be restarted.

The next set of commands deals with tablespaces. The commands to manage tablespaces follow. The first command is the CREATE TABLESPACE command.

```
CREATE TABLESPACE tablespace name
   DATAFILE filespec, filespec ....
   DEFAULT STORAGE storage
   ON-LINE or OFFLINE
```

Where:

> tablespace name—This is the name you choose for the tablespace, it can be up to 30 characters long.
> filespec—This is the file specification for the data file(s) that the tablespace needs. The format for this is: 'filename' SIZE integer K or M REUSE

> Where:

>> filename—This is an OS specific file name.
>> integer—This is the size in either kilobytes (K) or Megabytes (M) of the file.
>> REUSE—This is an optional parameter that instructs Oracle to reuse the file if it exists and is the proper size.

> storage—This is the storage clause that will be used for any table in the tablespace that isn't created with its own STORAGE clause.
> ONLINE/OFFLINE—This tells Oracle to either create the tablespace for immediate access, ONLINE (default), or leave it idle, OFFLINE.

Periodically a tablespace may need to be altered. This is accomplished with the ALTER TABLESPACE command.

```
ALTER TABLESPACE tablespace name
   RENAME DATAFILE 'filespec_old' TO 'filespace_new'
   DEFAULT STORAGE storage
   ONLINE
   OFFLINE NORMAL or IMMEDIATE
   BEGIN or END BACKUP
```

At least one of the lines following the ALTER command must be supplied (or else why issue the command?). The definitions for the arguments are the same as for the CREATE command. One thing to note is the RENAME DATAFILE option. This option is used when you need to (A). Alter the name of a datafile, or (B). Relocate a datafile.

Command sequence to rename a datafile:

```
ALTER TABLESPACE tablespace OFFLINE;
ALTER TABLESPACE tablespace
   RENAME DATAFILE 'old name' TO 'new name';
ALTER TABLESPACE tablespace ONLINE;
```

Periodically a tablespace may need to be dropped. This is accomplished with the DROP TABLESPACE command.

```
DROP TABLESPACE tablespace name INCLUDING CONTENTS;
```

The INCLUDING CONTENTS clause is optional, but if it isn't included, the tablespace must be empty of tables or other objects. If it is included, the tablespace will be dropped regardless of its contents. The SYSTEM tablespace cannot be dropped.

The next set of commands deals with TABLES. The first command to be covered is the CREATE TABLE command.

```
CREATE TABLE table name
( table column   column format   column constraint,
   table column   column format   column constraint...)
    [PCTFREE integer(0-100)   PCTUSED integer(0-100)
    INITRANS integer   MAXTRANS integer]
    [TABLESPACE tablespace name]
    [CLUSTER cluster name (column, column ....)]
    [AS query]
```

Where:

Table name—This is formatted either user.name or just the name, defaulting to the current user. This must be a unique name by user. This unique name applies to tables, views, synonyms, clusters, and indexes. For uniqueness, the user portion counts.

Column name—This is a unique name by table. The column name can be up to 30 characters long and cannot contain a quotation mark, slash, or character other than A–Z, 0–9, _, $, and #. A column name must not duplicate an Oracle reserved word (see the SQL Language Manual for a list of these words). To use mixed case, include the mixed case portion in quotation marks. For example:

```
EMPNAME
DOG
AULT.EXPENSE
"SELECT" (Even though select is a reserved word, if it is enclosed in
   quotes it is okay to use.)
"NIP AND TUCK" (Even spaces are allowed with quotes.)
```

Names should be meaningful, not a bunch of symbols like A, B, C. The Oracle CASE products always pluralize the names of tables. If you will be using CASE, you might want to follow this convention.

Column format—This is one of the allowed SQL data types. They are listed in the SQL language manual. A brief list is:

CHAR(size)—Character type data, max size 255. Under ORACLE7 this is replaced by VARCHAR2. Under ORACLE7 CHAR will be right-side padded to specified length.

VARCHAR2—Variable-length character up to 2000.

DATE—Date format, from 1/1/4712 BC to 12/31/4712 AD. Standard Oracle fomat is dd-mmm-yy (10-APR-93).

LONG—Character, up to 65,535 long. Only one LONG per table. 2 gig under ORACLE7.

RAW(size)—Raw binary data, max of 255 size in version 6, 2000 under ORACLE7.

LONG RAW—Raw binary data in hexadecimal format, 65,535 long. 2 gig under ORACLE7.

ROWID—Internal data type, not user definable, used to uniquely identify table rows.

NUMBER(p,s)—Numeric data with p being precision and s being scale. Defaults to 38 p, null s.

DECIMAL(p,s)—Same as numeric.

INTEGER—Defaults to NUMBER(38), no scale.

SMALLINT—Same as INTEGER.

FLOAT—Same as NUMBER(38).

FLOAT(b)—NUMBER with precision of 1 to 126.

REAL—NUMBER(63).

DOUBLE PRECISION—Same as NUMBER(38).

No scale specification means floating point.

NOTE: If you are currently using version 6 and are planning to convert to ORACLE7 in the near future, specify CHAR columns as VARCHAR2, or they will become fixed length when you switch to ORACLE7.

Column Constraint—This is used to specify constraints. Constraints are limits placed either on a table or column. Oracle version 6 supports the format of constraints and stores constraint definitions but does not enforce them. It is a statement of the format:

CONSTRAINT name constraint type

Constraints also may be of the form:

```
NULL CONSTRAINT constraint type
NOT NULL CONSTRAINT constraint type
PRIMARY KEY CONSTRAINT constraint type
UNIQUE CONSTRAINT constraint type
UNIQUE PRIMARY KEY CONSTRAINT constraint type
CHECK condition CONSTRAINT constraint type
REFERENCES table name (column name) CONSTRAINT constraint type
```

In the above formats the "CONSTRAINT constraint type" is optional.
Tables may also have the additional constraints:

```
FOREIGN KEY (column, column)
REFERENCES table name (column, column)
CONSTRAINT constraint type
```

The foreign key constraint IS enforced. However, no index is automatically generated. It is suggested that indexes be maintained on foreign keys or else excessive full-table scans may result.

In order for tables to use COST-based optimization, they must have statistics loaded in the database. This is only for ORACLE7. The ANALYZE command accomplishes this.

```
ANALYZE TABLE [schema.]table COMPUTE  or  ESTIMATE
(for estimate) SAMPLE n ROWS --or-- PERCENT
STATISTICS ;
```

ANALYZE can also be used to verify the integrity of a table, and its indexes structure as far as blocks, rows, and cross references are concerned. The format for the ANALYZE command in this case is:

```
ANALYZE TABLE [schema.]table
VALIDATE STRUCTURE [CASCADE]
```

The results are supplied to the DBA on screen. Use of the CASCADE option causes the command to validate all indexes against the base table.

Periodically a table may need to have a column changed or added, a constraint added or modified, or its space utilization or storage parameters adjusted. This is accomplished with the ALTER TABLE command.

```
ALTER TABLE tablename
   ADD (column name  table constraint, column name table constraint)
   MODIFY (column name)
   DROP CONSTRAINT constraint
   PCTFREE integer  PCTUSED integer
   INITRANS integer   MAXTRANS integer
   STORAGE storage
   And new for ORACLE7:
   DEFAULT (Part of the MODIFY clause above) expr
   DROP drop_clause
   ALLOCATE EXTENT [SIZE n [K --or-- M] [DATAFILE 'filespec'] [INSTANCE n]]
```

```
[ENABLE --or-- DISABLE]   enable or disable clause
```

Some notes on the ALTER TABLE command:

Things you can do:

1. Add columns that can have NULL values to any table.
2. Modify columns to a larger size.
3. Modify columns that have all null values to be shorter, or to a different data type.
4. Alter the PCTFREE, PCTUSED, INITRANS, or MAXTRANS for any table.
5. Alter the storage clause for any table.
6. Tell the data dictionary that the table has been backed up as of the date of the ALTER command by use of BACKUP clause.

Things you cannot do:

1. Modify a column that has values to be shorter or to a different data type.
2. Add a NOT NULL column to a table that has rows.
3. Alter a column to NOT NULL if it has rows with NULL values in that column.

It may become necessary to drop a table. This is accomplished with the DROP TABLE command. The format of the drop table COMMAND follows:

```
DROP TABLE table name;
```

Where:

table name—This is the table including the user or owning schema if the current user is not the owner.

Oracle will drop the table regardless of its contents. The only time a drop will fail is when a table's primary key is referenced by another table's foreign key via a restraint clause.

The next type of object commands we will look at refer to indexes. Indexes are created with the CREATE INDEX command. Its format follows.

```
CREATE [UNIQUE] INDEX Index name ON
    table name (column ASC|DESC, column ASC|DESC ...)
    CLUSTER cluster name
    INITRANS n  MAXTRANS n
    TABLESPACE tablespace name
    STORAGE storage clause
    PCTFREE
    NOSORT
```

Where:

Index name—is a user unique index name.

Table name—is the name of the table to be indexed; the table must exist.

Column—is the name of the column to include in the index, maximum of 16.

The Order of a concatenated key is important. Only queries that access columns in this order will use the index. For example, table EXAMPLE has 16 columns. The first three are used as the concatenated index.

Only queries that contain columns 1,2,3 —or— 1,2 —or— 1 will use the index.

Tablespace name—is the name of the tablespace in which to store the index.

Storage clause—is a standard storage clause.

NOSORT—tells oracle to not sort the index, since the table is already loaded into Oracle in ascending Order.

The UNIQUE clause causes Oracle to enforce uniqueness of the entire key. If UNIQUE is left out, the index is nonunique. In ORACLE7 the primary key and unique key constraints automatically generate the required indexes. This renders the UNIQUE clause obsolete in ORACLE7.

For ORACLE7 the ANALYZE command can be used to get the average index size from an example index. The format of this command follows.

```
ANALYZE INDEX [schema.]index COMPUTE--or--ESTIMATE
(for estimate) SAMPLE n ROWS --or-- PERCENT
STATISTICS ;
```

The results appear in the DBA_INDEXES view.

When it is required for the DBA to alter an index, the ALTER INDEX command is used. The ALTER INDEX command's format follows:

```
ALTER INDEX  index
   INITRANS integer  MAXTRANS integer
   STORAGE storage clause;
```

Where the parameters are as described in the CREATE TABLE command.

Indexes may also have to be dropped. This is accomplished via the DROP INDEX command. When a table is dropped, so are its related indexes.

```
DROP INDEX  index;
```

Under version 6 the structure of an index can be checked for consistency using the VALIDATE INDEX command. The format of this command follows.

```
VALIDATE INDEX [user.]index
```

Under ORACLE7 the ANALYZE command replaces the VALIDATE command. The format for the ANALYZE command for this function is shown below.

```
ANALYZE INDEX [schema.]index
VALIDATE STRUCTURE;
```

The results are supplied to the DBA on screen and are placed in a view called index_stats which is dropped upon session exit.

The next set of object related commands deals with synonyms. Synonyms are made with the CREATE SYNONYM command. The format of the CREATE SYNONYM command follows.

```
CREATE [PUBLIC] SYNONYM  synonym FOR owner.table [@database link]
```

Where:

    Synonym—is an allowed name (it cannot be the name of an existing object for this user. For purposes of uniqueness, the owner name is considered as a part of the name for an object.)

    Owner.table—is an existing table, view or sequence name.

    Database link—is an existing database link (covered later).

Synonyms provide both data independence and location transparency. With proper use and assignment, they allow an application to function regardless of table ownership, location, or even database.

Synonyms are dropped via the DROP command.

```
DROP [PUBLIC] SYNONYM synonym;
```

The next set of object commands deals with sequences. Sequences are created by use of the CREATE SEQUENCE command. The command's format follows.

```
CREATE SEQUENCE sequence name
   INCREMENT BY n
   START WITH n
   MAXVALUE n or NOMAXVALUE
   MINVALUE n or NOMINVALUE
   CYCLE or NOCYCLE (default)
   CACHE n or NOCACHE
   ORDER or NOORDER
```

Where:

Sequence name—is the name you want the sequence to have. This may include the user name if created from an account with DBA privilege.

n is an integer, positive or negative.

INCREMENT BY—tells the system how to increment the sequence. If it is positive the values are ascending, negative, descending.

START WITH — tells the system what integer to start with.

MINVALUE—tells the system how low the sequence can go. For ascending sequences it defaults to 1; for descending the default value is 10e27-1.

MAXVALUE—tells the system the highest value that will be allowed. for descending sequences the default is 1, for ascending sequences the default is 10e27-1.

CYCLE—This option causes the sequence to automatically recycle to minvalue when maxvalue is reached for ascending sequences. For descending sequences it will cause recycle from minvalue back to maxvalue.

CACHE—This option will cache the specified number of sequence values into the buffers in the SGA. This speeds access, but all cached numbers are lost when the database is shut down. Default value is 20; maximum value is maxvalue-minvalue.

ORDER—This option forces sequence numbers to be output in order of request. In cases where they are used for time stamping, this may be required. In most cases, the sequence numbers will be in order anyway and ORDER is not required.

Sequences may need to be changed. This is accomplished through the ALTER SEQUENCE command. The format of the ALTER SEQUENCE command follows.

```
ALTER SEQUENCE sequence name
   INCREMENT BY n
   MAXVALUE n or NOMAXVALUE
   MINVALUE n or NOMINVALUE
   CYCLE or NOCYCLE
   ORDER or NOORDER
```

Only future sequence numbers are affected by this statement.

Sequences are dropped using the DROP SEQUENCE command. The format of this command follows.

```
DROP SEQUENCE sequence name
```

The next set of object commands deals with database clusters. Clusters are created with the CREATE CLUSTER command. The format of this command follows.

```
CREATE CLUSTER cluster name
   (cluster key)
   PCTUSED n   PCTFREE n
   SIZE n
   INITRANS n   MAXTRANS n
   TABLESPACE tablespace
```

```
STORAGE storage
INDEX --or-- HASH IS column [HASHKEYS n]
```

Where:

> cluster name—is the name for the cluster. If the user has DBA privilege, a user name may be specified (user.cluster).
>
> cluster key—is a list of columns and their data types. The names for the columns do not have to match the table column names, but the data types, lengths, and precisions do have to match.
>
> n—is an integer (not all of the n's are the same value, n is just used for convenience).
>
> SIZE—This is the expected size of the average cluster. This is calculated by:

> 19 + (sum of column lengths) + (1 × num of columns)

> SIZE should rounded up to the nearest equal divisor of your block size. For example, if your block size is 2048 and the cluster length is 223, round up to 256.
>
> storage—This storage clause will be used as the default for the tables in the cluster.
>
> INDEX—This specifies to create an indexed cluster (default).
>
> HASH IS—This specifies to create a HASH cluster. The specified column must be a zero precision number. (ORACLE7)
>
> HASHKEYS—This creates a hash cluster and specifies the number (n) of keys. The value is rounded up to the nearest prime number. (ORACLE7)

The other parameters are the same as for the CREATE TABLE command.

Hand in hand with the cluster creation comes the cluster index creation (unless you have ORACLE7 and are creating a hash cluster). Before any tables can be created in the cluster, a cluster index must be built. This is accomplished through the CREATE INDEX ON CLUSTER command. This command's format is shown below.

```
CREATE  INDEX index name ON CLUSTER cluster name
```

Note that you don't specify the columns. This is taken from the CREATE CLUSTER command that was used to create the named cluster.

The cluster is not complete until a table is assigned to it. The table is assigned to a cluster by the CREATE TABLE command with the CLUSTER clause. This command is shown below.

```
CREATE TABLE cluster table
   ( column list)
   CLUSTER cluster name (cluster column(s))
```

Where:

> cluster table—is a table name for a table that will be a part of the cluster.
>
> Column list—is a list of columns for the table, specified identically to the CREATE TABLE command's normal format.

Remember: The cluster columns don't have to have the same name but must be the same data type, size, and precision, and must be specified in the same order as the columns in the CREATE CLUSTER command.

Just as with other database objects, clusters may need to be altered. The command for altering clusters is shown below.

```
ALTER CLUSTER cluster name
   PCTUSED n PCTFREE n
   SIZE n
   INITRANS n  MAXTRANS n
   STORAGE  storage
```

The definitions for the above parameters are the same as for the CREATE TABLE, CREATE CLUSTER, and storage clause definitions.

In ORACLE7 the structure of a cluster and its associated index and tables can be analyzed for consistency and for sizing data using the ANALYZE CLUSTER command. The format of this command follows.

```
ANALYZE CLUSTER [schema.]cluster COMPUTE--or--ESTIMATE
(for estimate) SAMPLE n ROWS --or-- PERCENT
STATISTICS ;
```

The results appear in the DBA_CLUSTERS view.

To verify a clusters integrity, the following version of the ANALYZE command is used under ORACLE7.

```
ANALYZE CLUSTER [schema.]cluster
VALIDATE STRUCTURE  [CASCADE]
```

The CASCADE option forces analysis of all indexes and tables in the cluster.

A cluster is dropped with the DROP CLUSTER command. There is an INCLUDING TABLES clause that will allow the DBA to drop both the cluster and tables at the same time. The format of the command follows.

```
DROP CLUSTER cluster name
   [INCLUDING TABLES]
   [CASCADE CONSTRAINTS] (New with ORACLE7)
```

If the INCLUDING TABLES clause is excluded, all cluster tables must be dropped before issuing this command. If the CASCADE CONSTRAINTS clause is included, all referential constraints from tables outside of the cluster are also dropped. If the CASCADE clause is left out and there are outside constraints, the cluster cannot be dropped.

The next set of object commands deals with database links. Database links are created via the CREATE DATABASE LINK command. This command's format follows.

```
CREATE [PUBLIC] DATABASE LINK link name
   [CONNECT TO user IDENTIFIED BY password]
   USING 'connect string'
```

Where:

database link—Under version 6 this was a user specified name. Under ORACLE7 this is the GLOBAL db name and the DB_DOMAIN.

PUBLIC—This is specified for database links that are to be used by all users. The user must have DBA privilege to specify a PUBLIC link.

CONNECT TO—This clause is used to force connection to a specific database user at the database being connected to. This allows the DBA to restrict access to confidential or sensitive information to one user instead of all users. If this clause isn't specified, the user's user name and password will be used in its place.

'connect string'—This is the protocol-specific connection command. For VMS the format is:

```
D:NODE"""USER PASSWORD"""::"""TASK=ORDNsid"""
```

Note: The TASK specifies a file that is located in the user's login directory. This can lead to management problems if multiple people need access. One way around this is specify a network object that all users log in through, or by specifying a special user that all users log in to, such as SQLNET.

The ORDNsid.COM file on a VMS machine contains:

```
$ DEFINE ORA_SID sid
$ DEFINE ORA_RDBMS oracle location
$ SRV=="$ORA_RDBMS:SRV.EXE"
$ SRV DECNET_NSP
```

The use of proxies and net objects needs to be coordinated with the system administrator. *The SQL*Net For DEC VAX/VMS Installation and User's Guide* should be consulted for a more detailed explanation.

For a TCPIP (UNIX) installation, the connect string would be of the format:

```
T:HOST:SYSTEM ID,BUFFER
```

Where:

T—Tells Oracle this is TCPIP

HOST—Name of a node that is in your system HOSTS file.

SYSTEM ID—This is one or more characters that correspond to the sid for the database on the remote system. It must exist in the database listing file.

BUFFER—This is the size in bytes of the context area used between TCPIP and ORACLE. The value can be set between 4 and 4096. The default is 4096.

Some or all of these parameters can be aliased on UNIX.

Connect strings are very system specific, and DBAs should read all documentation provided by Oracle on their system's SQL*Net version before attempting to use them.

Database links cannot be altered. To change a link it must be dropped and recreated. Database links are dropped via the DROP DATABASE LINK command. For public database links the word *public* must be inserted after DROP. Only DBAs can drop public database links. The format of the DROP command follows

```
DROP [PUBLIC] DATABASE LINK link
```

The next set of object commands deals with VIEWS. Creation of views is accomplished with the CREATE VIEW command. This commands format follows.

```
CREATE VIEW view name (alias, alias,...)
AS query
[WITH CHECK OPTION   [CONSTRAINT constraint]]
```

Where:

view name—is the name for the view.

alias—is a valid column name, it isn't required to be the same as the column it is based on. If aliases aren't used, the names of the columns are used. If a column is modified by an expression, it must be aliased. If four columns are in the query, there must be four aliases.

query—This is any valid SELECT statement that doesn't include an ORDER BY or FOR UPDATE clause.

WITH CHECK—This clause specifies that inserts and updates through the view must be selectable from the view. This can be used in a view based on a view. (ORACLE7)

CONSTRAINT—This specifies the name associated with the WITH CHECK constraint. (ORACLE7)

Under version 6 views cannot be altered. To change a view it must be dropped and recreated. However, under ORACLE7, if a view is invalidated due to a change in an underlying table, it can be recompiled using the new ALTER VIEW command. This command's format follows:

```
ALTER VIEW  view name COMPILE
```

Where:

> view name—is a valid view name with schema name if you are not the owner.

> Views are dropped with the DROP VIEW command. Its format follows.

```
DROP VIEW view name
```

Where:

> view name—is a valid view name with schema name if you are not the owner.

A new type of database object under ORACLE7 is the database trigger. The database trigger is created using the CREATE TRIGGER COMMAND. A trigger is ENABLED when it is created. This command's format follows.

```
CREATE [OR REPLACE] TRIGGER [schema.]trigger
BEFORE--or--AFTER  DELETE--or--INSERT--or--UPDATE
OF column --or-- ON  [schema.]table
(The above is mandatory section, what follows is optional)
[[REFERENCING OLD--or--NEW AS old--or--new] --or-- [FOR EACH ROW]
WHEN (condition)]
pl/sql block
```

Where:

> OR REPLACE—replaces trigger if it exists. This can be used to change the definition of a trigger without dropping it first.
> schema—This takes the place of the owner argument in version 6.
> trigger—This is the trigger's name.
> BEFORE—This specifies the trigger is fired before the specified action.
> AFTER—This indicates the trigger is fired after the specified action.
> DELETE / INSERT / UPDATE—These are the specified actions, only one per trigger.
> OF—This limits the action response to the listed columns.
> ON—This specifies the table name of the table the trigger is for.
> REFERENCING—This deals with correlation names. This allows specification of old and new values for a column.
> FOR EACH ROW—This forces the trigger to fire on each effected row, making it a row trigger. The trigger is fired for each row that is affected by the trigger and that meets the WHEN clause constraints.
> WHEN—This specifies any constraints on the trigger. This is a trigger restriction clause. This contains a standard SQL clause.
> pl/sql Block—This is the trigger body and is in the standard pl/sql format.

Triggers can be altered like most database objects. The command used is the ALTER TRIGGER. The only alter option allowed is to either enable or disable the trigger. To change a trigger, the CREATE OR REPLACE command should be used. The format of the ALTER command for triggers follows. For completeness the ALTER command for tables that can be used to enable triggers is also shown.

```
ALTER TRIGGER [schema.]trigger ENABLE--or--DISABLE;
```

or:

```
ALTER TABLE [schema.]table ENABLE [UNIQUE] (column, column...)
PRIMARY KEY --or-- CONSTRAINT constraint [EXCEPTIONS INTO [schema.]table]
USING INDEX (index clause)
ALL TRIGGERS;
```

Where the index clause consists of:

```
INITRANS n  MAXTRANS n  TABLESPACE ts_name
  STORAGE (storage clause)  PCTFREE n
```

Where n are integers.

There can be multiple enables on a single alter. The ALTER TABLE command can also use a DISABLE clause.

```
DISABLE UNIQUE
   --or-- CONSTRAINT constraint
   --or-- PRIMARY KEY
   --or-- ALL TRIGGERS
   (column, column)
   [CASCADE];
```

Where CASCADE disables any integrity constraints that depend on a specified constraint. If a unique or primary key is referenced in this clause the CASCADE option must be specified.

One limit on the usefulness of the ALTER TABLE in either disabling or enabling triggers is that is an all-or-nothing proposition. It is better to use the ALTER TRIGGER command unless you want all triggers enabled or disabled at one time.

Triggers are dropped using the DROP TRIGGER command.

```
DROP TRIGGER [schema.]trigger;
```

Another set of objects new with ORACLE7 are functions and procedures. Functions and procedures are created using the CREATE command. The format for each differs slightly.

For functions the format is:

```
CREATE [OR REPLACE] FUNCTION [schema.]function
[( argument IN datatype, argument IN datatype,...)]
RETURN datatype IS--or--AS pl/sql body
```

For procedures the format is:

```
CREATE [OR REPLACE] PROCEDURE [schema.]procedure
[( argument IN--or--OUT--or--IN OUT datatype,
argument IN--or--OUT--or--IN OUT datatype,...)]
IS--or--AS pl/sql body
```

For both procedures and functions the command arguments are listed below.

OR REPLACE—This optional statement specifies that if the procedure or function exists, replace it; if doesn't exist, create it.

schema—This is the schema to place the procedure or function into. If other than the user's default schema, the user must have CREATE ANY PROCEDURE system privilege.

procedure or function—This is the name of the procedure or function being created.

argument(s)—This is the argument to the procedure or function, may be more than one of these.

IN—This specifies that the argument must be specified when calling the procedure or function. For functions, an argument must always be provided.

OUT—This specifies the procedure passes a value for this argument back to the calling object. Not used with functions.

IN OUT—This specifies both the IN and OUT features are in effect for the procedure. This is not used with functions.

datatype—This is the data type of the argument. Precision, length, and scale cannot be specified—they are derived from the calling object.

pl/sql body—This is a SQL, PL/SQL body of statements.

The only option for the ALTER command for functions and procedures is the COMPILE option. This option recompiles the procedure or function after a modification to their references objects has occurred. The format of this command follows.

```
ALTER FUNCTION--or--PROCEDURE [schema.]function --or-- procedure
COMPILE;
```

Periodically it may be required for a DBA to remove a function or procedure from the database. This is accomplished with the DROP command. The format of this command follows.

```
DROP FUNCTION--or--PROCEDURE [schema.]function--or--procedure;
```

Another new feature with ORACLE 7 is the package. Packages are collections of procedures, functions, and constraints. The command for creating package definitions follows.

```
CREATE [OR REPLACE] PACKAGE [schema.]package
IS--or--AS pl/sql package specification;
```

Where:

OR REPLACE—This is used when the user wishes to create or replace a package. If the package definition exists, it is replaced; if it doesn't exist, it is created.

schema—This is the schema the package is to be created in. If this is not specified, the package is created in the user's default schema.

package—This is the name of the package to be created.

pl/sql package specification—This is the list of procedures, functions, or variables that make up the package. All components listed are considered to be public in nature.

The previous command creates the package definition. You also need a package body. The format for the CREATE PACKAGE BODY command follows.

```
CREATE [OR REPLACE] PACKAGE BODY [schema.]package
IS--or--AS pl/sql package body;
```

Where:

OR REPLACE—When this is used if the package body exists it is replaced if it doesn't exist, it is created.

schema—This specifies the schema to create the package in. If this is not specified, the package body is created in the user's default schema.

pl/sql package body—This is the collection of all of the SQL and pl/sql text required to create all of the objects in the package.

There is also an ALTER PACKAGE BODY command that is used only to recompile the package body. The format of the ALTER command follows.

```
ALTER PACKAGE [schema.]package COMPILE PACKAGE--or--BODY;
```

Package definitions or complete packages are dropped with the DROP PACKAGE command. The format of this command follows.

```
DROP PACKAGE [BODY] [schema.]package;
```

Exclusion of the keyword BODY results in the drop of both the definition and the body. Inclusion of BODY drops just the package body leaving the definition intact.

Another new feature with ORACLE7 are snapshots and snapshot logs. The CREATE SNAPSHOT LOG command is used to create a snapshot log. The format of the command follows.

```
CREATE SNAPSHOT LOG ON [schema.]table
[PCTFREE n]
[PCTUSED n]
[INITRANS n]
[MAXTRANS n]
[TABLESPACE tablespace]
[STORAGE ( storage clause)];
```

Where:

schema—This is the schema in which to store the log. If not specified, this will default to the user's own schema.

table—This is the table name to create the snapshot log for.

PCTFREE—These are the values for these creation parameters to use for

PCTUSED   the created log file.

INITRANS

MAXTRANS

TABLESPACE—This specifies the tablespace in which to create the snapshot log. This will default to the user's default tablespace if not specified.

STORAGE—This is a standard storage clause.

Snapshot logs can be altered. The format for the ALTER SNAPSHOT LOG command follows.

```
ALTER SNAPSHOT LOG ON [schema.]table
[PCTFREE n]
[PCTUSED n]
[INITRANS n]
[MAXTRANS n]
[STORAGE ( storage clause)];
```

Where:

schema—This is the schema in which to store the log. If not specified, this will default to the user's own schema.

table—This is the table name to create the snapshot log for.

PCTFREE—These are the values for these creation parameters to use for

PCTUSED—the created log file.

INITRANS

MAXTRANS

STORAGE —This is a standard storage clause.

To change a snapshot log's location either an export/import or a drop/create of the snapshot log is required. A snapshot log is dropped using the DROP SNAPSHOT LOG command. The format for the command follows.

```
DROP SNAPSHOT LOG ON [schema.]table;
```

Snapshots are built using the CREATE SNAPSHOT command.

```
CREATE SNAPSHOT [schema.]snapshot
[[PCTFREE n]
[PCTUSED n]
[INITRANS n]
[MAXTRANS n]
[TABLESPACE tablespace]
[STORAGE ( storage clause)]]--or-- [ CLUSTER (column, column,....)]
[REFRESH FAST--or--COMPLETE--or--FORCE
[START WITH date]
[NEXT date]]
AS subquery;
```

Where:

>schema—This is the schema in which to store the snapshot. If not specified, this will default to the user's own schema.
>
>table—This is the table name to create the snapshot for.
>
>PCTFREE—These are the values for these creation parameters to use for
>
>PCTUSED   the created snapshot file.
>
>INITRANS
>
>MAXTRANS
>
>TABLESPACE—This specifies the tablespace in which to create the snapshot. This will default to the user's default tablespace if not specified.
>
>STORAGE—This is a standard storage clause.
>
>CLUSTER—This is used to designate the snapshot as part of the specified cluster. The values before the —or— will default to the clusters values so they are not used. In addition, the STORAGE clause for the cluster is used, so it is not needed.
>
>REFRESH—This specifies the refresh mode, either FAST, COMPLETE or FORCE. FAST uses a SNAPSHOT LOG, COMPLETE re-performs the subquery and is the only valid mode for a complex snapshot, FORCE causes the system to first try a FAST and if this is not possible, then a COMPLETE. FAST is the default mode.
>
>START WITH—This specifies the date for the first refresh.
>
>NEXT—This specifies either a date or a time interval for the next refresh of the snapshot. START WITH and NEXT values are used to determine the refresh cycle for the snapshot. If just START WITH is specified only the initial refresh is done. If both are specified, the first is done on the START WITH date and the NEXT is evaluated against the START WITH to determine future refreshes. If just the NEXT value is specified it computes based on the date the snapshot is created. If neither is specified, the snapshot is not automatically refreshed.

A snapshot is altered using the ALTER SNAPSHOT command. The user may alter such items as storage and space usage parameters and type and frequency of refresh. The format for this command follows.

```
ALTER SNAPSHOT [schema.]snapshot
[[PCTFREE n]
[PCTUSED n]
[INITRANS n]
[MAXTRANS n]
[STORAGE ( storage clause)]]--or-- [ CLUSTER (column, column,....)]
[REFRESH FAST--or--COMPLETE--or--FORCE
[START WITH date]
[NEXT date]];
```

Where:

schema— This is the schema in which to store the log. If not specified, this will default to the user's own schema.

table— This is the table name to alter the snapshot for.

PCTFREE— These are the values for these creation parameters to use for

PCTUSED   the created snapshot file.

INITRANS

MAXTRANS

STORAGE- This is a standard storage clause.

REFRESH- This specifies the refresh mode, either FAST, COMPLETE, or FORCE. FAST uses a SNAP-SHOT LOG; COMPLETE re-performs the subquery and is the only valid mode for a complex snapshot; FORCE causes the system to first try a FAST and if this is not possible, then a COMPLETE. FAST is the default mode.

START WITH—This specifies the date for the first refresh.

NEXT—This specifies either a date or a time interval for the next refresh of the snapshot.

START WITH and NEXT values are used to determine the refresh cycle for the snapshot. If just START WITH is specified, only the initial refresh is done. If both are specified, the first is done on the START WITH date, and the NEXT is evaluated against the START WITH to determine future refreshes. If just the NEXT value is specified, it computes based on the date the snapshot is created. If neither is specified, the snapshot is not automatically refreshed.

A snapshot is dropped using the DROP SNAPSHOT command. The command's format follows.

```
DROP SNAPSHOT [schema.]snapshot;
```

Another new feature with ORACLE7 is the concept of a schema. For our purposes, user name and schema are interchangable as far as definition. A user can create a schema, but it must be named the same as the user. The actual purpose of schemas is to bring Oracle into compliance with ANSI standard SQL. Schemas are populated via the CREATE SCHEMA command.

The CREATE SCHEMA statement can include the creation commands for tables, views, and grants. The user issuing the command must have the appropriate privileges to create each of the objects mentioned in the CREATE SCHEMA command. The format of this command follows.

```
CREATE SCHEMA AUTHORIZATION schema
[CREATE TABLE command]
[CREATE VIEW command]
[GRANT command];
```

Where:

schema—This is the user's schema. It must be their user name.

command—This corresponds to the appropriate CREATE object command.

The individual create commands are not separated with a command terminator. The terminator is placed at the end of the entire create sequence of commands for the schema. You cannot specify storage parameters in the create commands; they will only support the extensions of standard rather than Oracle extended SQL.

Users also have some SQL commands associated with them. A user's database-level privileges are altered using the GRANT and REVOKE commands. For instance, to grant global resource to a user, use the following format for the GRANT command:

```
GRANT RESOURCE TO user name;
```

To remove a privilege, the revoke command is used. The format to remove RESOURCE from a user would be:

```
REVOKE RESOURCE FROM user name;
```

The user's default and temporary tablespaces, as well as their password, can be altered with the ALTER USER command. The format for the ALTER USER command follows:

```
ALTER USER user
DEFAULT TABLESPACE new default
TEMPORARY TABLESPACE new temporary
IDENTIFIED BY password;
```

In Oracle version 6, you can't drop a user. The only way to remove access from a user is to revoke connect from them. The command is:

```
REVOKE CONNECT FROM username;
```

Database users under ORACLE7 are created using the CREATE USER command. This command replaces the GRANT CONNECT TO user IDENTIFED BY password; command in version 6. The format of this command follows.

```
CREATE USER user IDENTIFIED BY password--or-- IDENTIFIED EXTERNALLY
[DEFAULT TABLESPACE tablespace]
[TEMPORARY TABLESPACE tablespace]
[QUOTA n K--or--M --or-- UNLIMITED ON tablespace]
[PROFILE profile]
```

Where:

user—This is the user name of the user to be created. Use of the prefix specified in the OS_AUTHENT_PREFIX parameter of the INIT.ORA file will create a user accessible only to the user whose operating system login matches the specified user name plus the prefix. The prefix defaults to OPS$ but can be changed if desired.

password—This is the password the user must enter to use Oracle.

IDENTIFIED EXTERNALLY—This says that if the user can log on the system, he can use the account.

Tablespace—This is the name for the specific tablespace the command option applies to. If DEFAULT or TEMPORARY tablespaces aren't assigned, they are defaulted to the SYSTEM tablespace.

QUOTA—This is used to assign quota on a tablespace. Multiple quota assignments can be made in the same command.

n—This is the amount of quota assigned in the specified tablespace. If not specified it defaults to 0.

PROFILE—This assigns a specific profile to a user. If this is not specified, the user is assigned to the default profile.

Under ORACLE7 the ALTER USER command's format is changed. The new format follows.

```
ALTER USER user
[INDENTIFIED BY password] --or-- [IDENTIFIED EXTERNALLY]
[DEFAULT TABLESPACE tablespace]
[TEMPORARY TABLESPACE tablespace]
[QUOTA n K--or--M--or--UNLIMITED ON tablespace] (this can be repeated)
[PROFILE profile]
[DEFAULT ROLE [role,role,...]--or--[ALL [EXCEPT role,role,...]--or--[NONE]];
```

Where:

> user—This is the user to be altered.
> password—Allows alteration of specified user's password. Must be single byte. This is not case sensitive and is not delimited by quotes.
> tablespace—This is a specific tablespace.
> n—Integer specification for quota in bytes, Kbytes or Mbytes.
> UNLIMITED—This means the user has unlimited quota on the specified tablespace.
> profile—This changes the user's profile.
> role—one of the predefined roles available to be assigned.
> ALL—This assigns all of the roles GRANTED to be DEFAULT roles.
> NONE—This assigns none of the roles GRANTED to be DEFAULT roles.
> EXCEPT—This grants all the roles except those listed.

Under ORACLE7 a user can be dropped. Before the user is dropped, his or her tables and other objects must be dropped. The command to drop a user follows.

```
DROP USER user [CASCADE];
```

Where:

> user—This is the user name to be dropped.
> CASCADE—This tells ORACLE7 to also drop all of the user's objects.

If the cascade option is used, ORACLE7 also drops all referential integrity constraints associated with the objects. The system will also invalidate views, synonyms, procedures, functions, and packages that are associated with the dropped objects.

If you wish to use tablespace quotas under version 6—that is, limit the amount of space a user can take up in a tablespace—add the quota variable followed by K for kilobytes or M for megabytes after the GRANT RESOURCE command. Thus, if you use M:

```
GRANT RESOURCE &quota||'M' on &&default_ts to &&user_name;
```

Privileges are bestowed using the GRANT statement. To use the GRANT statement, the user must either have DBA privilege or have been granted their privileges on the table or tables on which they are using the grant option. The format of this command is:

```
GRANT priv, priv, priv...ON object TO username;
```

To grant all privileges on an object, the format is:

```
GRANT ALL PRIVILEGES ON object TO username;
```

To grant the ability for the user to grant the privileges to other users:

```
GRANT priv, priv, priv...ON object TO username WITH GRANT OPTION;
```

As was stated before, for tablespaces there is only one grant, and that is resource. The format of this command is:

```
GRANT RESOURCE ON tablespace TO username;
```

To establish a resource quota, specify the limit with either K for kilobytes or M for megabytes after the RESOURCE specified, for example:

```
GRANT RESOURCE 1M ON tablespace TO username;
```

Note: Under versions prior to 6.0.37 you could not grant on a view that referenced a database link.

Under ORACLE7 it is suggested that security be implemented with roles. Roles are collections of privileges and even other roles. The commands dealing with roles are in this section.

Roles are created with the CREATE ROLE command. The format of the CREATE ROLE command follows.

```
CREATE ROLE role NOT IDENTIFIED --or-- IDENTIFIED
[BY password] --or-- [EXTERNALLY];
```

Where:

> role—This names the role to be created.
>
> NOT IDENTIFIED—This indicates the user using the role doesn't need to be verified (docsn't have to supply a password) to use the role. This is the default option.
>
> IDENTIFED—This indicates all users are verified with a specified password or by the operating system.
>
> BY password—This gives the password that the users must use to access the role.
>
> EXTERNAL—This indicates verification will be performed by the operating system.

The roles have unique names and have one or more system and object privileges assigned to them. Roles can also be assigned to other roles. You don't grant the privileges with the CREATE ROLE command. The role is granted privileges via the GRANT or ALTER commands. To assign the privileges or roles to a new role, use the following command:

```
GRANT priv1, priv2,...,role1, role2,... TO role name or user name;
```

The ALTER USER command can also be used to assign roles to a user, its format follows.

```
ALTER USER user DEFAULT ROLE role,role,...;
```

Only roles that have been granted to the user with the GRANT command can be assigned via the default role option of the ALTER command.

The object level grants deal with the insert, update, delete, select, and so on of data within database objects. The object level privileges can be granted at the object, or in somce cases, column level. The format for granting these privileges follows.

```
GRANT object_priv, object_priv,...--or-- ALL PRIVILEGES [(column, col-
            umn,...)]
ON [schema.]object TO user--or--role--or--PUBLIC
[WITH GRANT OPTION];
```

Where:

> object_priv—This corresponds to:

```
ALTER for tables, sequences
DELETE for tables, views, columns in tables
EXECUTE for procedures, packages, functions
INDEX for tables
INSERT for tables, views, columns in tables
REFERENCES for tables (not to a role)
SELECT for tables, views, sequences, columns in tables, and snapshots
UPDATE for tables, views, columns in tables
```

> ALL PRIVILEGES—Grants all privileges applicable to the item to the user or role.
>
> column—This is a column in the table referenced in the command.

ON—This identifies the object on which the privileges are granted. If schema is not specified, the user's default schema is used. In addition to tables, views, sequences, functions, procedures, packages, and snapshots, synonyms that refer to these objects can be used here.

TO—This identifies the user or role to which the privilege is granted. If PUBLIC is used, all users receive the grant.

WITH GRANT OPTION—This allows the user to grant the privilege. This cannot be given to a role.

The method of authorization or the authorization password may be changed for a role using the following command:

```
ALTER ROLE roll name IDENTIFIED authorization password;
```

or

```
ALTER ROLE roll name IDENTIFIED EXTERNALLY;
```

To use this command you must have the ALTER ANY ROLE privilege or have been granted the role with the ADMIN OPTION.

To remove a role from a database, use the DROP ROLE command.

```
DROP ROLE role;
```

Where:

role—This is the role name to be dropped.

To drop a role you must have been given the role with the ADMIN OPTION or have the DROP ANY ROLE privilege at the system level.

Profiles are the way you can restrict resource consumption in ORACLE7. Profiles are created using the CREATE PROFILE command. The format of the CREATE PROFILE format follows.

```
CREATE PROFILE profile LIMIT
SESSIONS_PER_USER n --or--
CPU_PER_SESSION n (in hundreths of seconds)--or--
CPU_PER_CALL n (in hundreths of seconds)--or--
CONNECT_TIME n (in minutes)--or--
IDLE_TIME n (in minutes)--or--
LOGICAL_READS_PER_SESSION n (in blocks)--or--
LOGICAL_READS_PER_CALL n (in blocks)--or--
COMPOSIT_LIMIT n (in service units)--or--
PRIVATE_SGA [n K--or--M]--or--UNLIMITED--or--DEFAULT
```

Each of the n's above can be replaced with the keyword UNLIMITED or DEFAULT. Unlimited means there is no limit on this resource; default causes the resource to use the value from the default profile.

A profile can be altered using the ALTER PROFILE command. It has the same format as the CREATE PROFILE command.

A profile is dropped using the DROP PROFILE command. The commands format follows.

```
DROP PROFILE profile [CASCADE];
```

Users assigned to the profile are automatically reassigned to the DEFAULT profile.

SQL Scripts From Book

Appendix B contains all of the SQL scripts shown in this book. These scripts either use the tables and views created in the CTDBAEN.SQL script or the DBA_ or V$ views that are provided with the database system itself. The scripts can also be found on the companion disk that is available with this book.

Every attempt has been made to keep the scripts simple so that beginning DBAs can use them as a model for their own scripts. In some cases this hasn't been possible, but there is still a lot to learn from the techniques shown.

The DBA needs to be very familiar with SQL, SQLPlus, and PL/SQL. The SQLDBA program is an excellent place to start, but as you mature as a DBA you will want to create custom reports and monitoring scripts so that you can do it "your way." It is hoped that these scripts will help.

The following script is used to produce a SQL script that can be used to re-create the existing tablespaces in a database. One thing to notice in this script is how the concatenation symbol "||" is used to pull the different database columns into a CREATE command. This script also makes use of dynamic SQL—that is, SQL that generates SQL.

```
rem
rem   NAME: TS_RCT.sql
rem
rem   HISTORY:
rem   Date       Who                  What
rem   -------    ------------------   --------------------------------
rem   12/22/92   Michael Brouillette  Creation
rem
rem   FUNCTION: Build a script to re-create tablespaces in a database.
rem
rem   NOTES:  Must be run by a DBA.
rem
rem   ********************************************************************
SET LINESIZE 79
COLUMN X WORD_WRAPPED
SPOOL TS_RCT.LIS
```

```
SELECT 'CREATE TABLESPACE '||UPPER('&&1')||' DATAFILE '||
       ''''||FILE_NAME||''''||' SIZE '||BYTES/1024||'K REUSE'||
       ' DEFAULT STORAGE(INITIAL '||INITIAL_EXTENT||' NEXT '||NEXT_EXTENT||
       ' MINEXTENTS '||MIN_EXTENTS||' MAXEXTENTS '||MAX_EXTENTS||
       ' PCTINCREASE '||PCT_INCREASE||');' X
  FROM DBA_TABLESPACES, DBA_DATA_FILES
 WHERE
                  DBA_TABLESPACES.TABLESPACE_NAME=
                  DBA_DATA_FILES.TABLESPACE_NAME
   AND DBA_TABLESPACES.TABLESPACE_NAME = UPPER('&&1')
   AND DBA_DATA_FILES.FILE_ID =
          (SELECT MIN(FILE_ID)
             FROM DBA_DATA_FILES
            WHERE DBA_DATA_FILES.TABLESPACE_NAME=UPPER('&&1'));
SELECT 'ALTER TABLESPACE '||UPPER('&&1')||' ADD DATAFILE '||
       ''''||FILE_NAME||''''||' SIZE '||BYTES/1024||'K REUSE;' X
  FROM DBA_TABLESPACES, DBA_DATA_FILES
 WHERE DBA_TABLESPACES.TABLESPACE_NAME =
                  DBA_DATA_FILES.TABLESPACE_NAME
   AND DBA_TABLESPACES.TABLESPACE_NAME = UPPER('&&1')
   AND DBA_DATA_FILES.FILE_ID !=
          (SELECT MIN(FILE_ID)
             FROM DBA_DATA_FILES
            WHERE DBA_DATA_FILES.TABLESPACE_NAME=UPPER('&&1'));
SPOOL OFF
EXIT
```

The following script is probably the most complex one you will see in this book. The script is actually a compilation of several utility scripts that create numerous useful tables for the database administrator to use. The first script defines a database administration account, creates a tablespace for the account to use, and then assigns synonyms to point to SYS and SYSTEM-owned objects. The second half of the script creates views and tables needed by the various scripts throughout this book.

```
rem   ********************************************************************
rem   NAME: CT_DBAEN
rem   HISTORY:
rem   Date       Who                  What
rem   --------    ------------------    ----------------------------------------
rem   12/09/92   Michael Brouillette   Creation
rem   04/09/93   Michael Ault          Appended script to build DBA tables.
rem   FUNCTION: This script builds the initial environment for the DBA to work
rem             in. Specifically it:
rem                       Creates a separate tablespace for the DBA's objects.
rem                       Creates the DBA user id and sets its default
rem                       tablespace to the one just created and sets the
rem                       temporary tablespace to the one specified by &1.
rem                       Builds & runs script to grant access to SYS objects
rem                       and create synonyms for those objects.
rem                       Builds & runs script to grant access to SYSTEM objects
rem                       and create synonyms for those objects.
```

```
rem   INPUTS:
rem                      tsn     = Name of temporary tablespace for the DBA user
rem                      dbau    = User ID for the new DBA user
rem                      dbap    = Password for the new DBA user
rem                      sysp    = Password for the 'SYS' account
rem                      systemp = Password for the 'SYSTEM' account
rem
rem   NOTES: Runtime changes will probably have to be made to the command to
rem          create the tablespace. Format is for VMS, for UNIX must be
rem          changed to proper format.
rem   ***********************************************************************
rem
accept tsn     prompt 'Name of temporary tablespace for the DBA user? '
accept dbau    prompt 'User ID of the DBA user? '
accept dbap    prompt 'Password for the DBA user? '
accept sysp    prompt 'Password for the SYS account? '
accept systemp prompt 'Password for the SYSTEM account? '
rem
set echo off termout off heading off pagesize 999 newpage 1
set verify off feedback off
rem
rem   Create the DBA_TS tablespace
rem
create tablespace &tsn   - you will modify this line to be database specific
      datafile 'dia1:[oracle.db_oralims]dba_ts.dbs' size 3M
      default storage (initial 10k  next 10k
              pctincrease   0
              minextents 1  maxextents  999)
            on-line;
rem
rem Create the DBA id
rem
grant connect, resource, DBA to &dbau identified by &dbap;
alter user DBA
      default tablespace dba_ts,
      temporary tablespace &tsn;
rem
rem   create grants and synonyms for all necessary SYS owned objects.
rem
spool sys_gr$.sql
rem
select 'grant select on '||object_name||' to &dbau.;' from user_objects
 where object_type in ('TABLE', 'VIEW', 'SEQUENCE', 'CLUSTER');
select 'connect &dbau./&dbap'   from dual;
select 'create synonym '||object_name||' for sys.'||object_name||';' from user_objects
 where object_type in ('TABLE', 'VIEW', 'SEQUENCE', 'CLUSTER')
   and object_name not in (select synonym_name from user_synonyms);
rem
spool off
start sys_gr$
ho delete sys_gr$.sql;*
rem
rem   create grants and synonyms for all necessary SYSTEM owned objects.
```

```
rem
connect system/&systemp
spool syst_gr$.sql
rem
select 'grant select on '||object_name||' to &dbau.;' from user_objects
 where object_type in ('TABLE', 'VIEW', 'SEQUENCE', 'CLUSTER');
select 'connect &dbau./&dbap'   from dual;
select 'create synonym '||object_name||' for system.'||object_name||';'
   from user_objects
 where object_type in ('TABLE', 'VIEW', 'SEQUENCE', 'CLUSTER')
   and object_name not in (select synonym_name from user_synonyms)
   and object_name not like 'SRW%';
rem
spool off
start syst_gr$
ho delete syst_gr$.sql;*
undef sysp
undef systemp
rem
rem *****************************************************************************
rem NAME: CT_DBAOB.sql
rem HISTORY:
rem Date            Who                   What
rem --------        ------------------    --------------------------------------
rem 12/09/92        Michael Brouillette   Creation
rem 04/09/93        Michael Ault          Appended to CT_DBAEN, altered creates
rem                                       to default to dba_ts tablespace.
rem FUNCTION. Creates objects needed for various DBA and APS Utility users.
rem INPUTS:   None, assumes DBA tablespace is dba_ts.
rem *****************************************************************************
rem
connect &dbau/&dbap
set termout off
drop view ALL_LOCKS_VIEW;
rem
create view ALL_LOCKS_VIEW as
  select type, lmode, pid, to_char(id1) id1, to_char(id2) id2, request
     from v$lock       /* processes waiting on or holding enqueues */
 union
  select 'LATCH', 6, pid, rawtohex(laddr), ' ', 0   /* procs holding latches */
     from v$latchholder     /* 6 = exclusive, 0 = not held */
 union
  select 'LATCH', 0, pid, latchwait,' ',6      /* procs waiting on latch */
     from v$process
    where latchwait is not null;
rem
drop view APS_SESSTAT;
create view APS_SESSTAT as select * from v$sesstat;
grant select on APS_SESSTAT to public;
drop public synonym APS_SESSTAT;
create public synonym APS_SESSTAT for aps_sesstat;
rem
drop view APS_PROCESS;
```

```
create view APS_PROCESS as select * from v$process;
grant select on APS_PROCESS to public;
drop public synonym APS_PROCESS;
create public synonym APS_PROCESS for aps_process;
rem
drop view APS_SESSION;
create view APS_SESSION as select * from v$session;
grant select on APS_SESSION to public;
drop public synonym APS_SESSION;
create public synonym APS_SESSION for aps_session;
rem
drop view APS_PARAMETER;
create view APS_PARAMETER as select * from v$parameter;
grant select on APS_PARAMETER to public;
drop public synonym APS_PARAMETER;
create public synonym APS_PARAMETER for aps_parameter;
rem
drop view APS_DATA_FILES;
create view APS_DATA_FILES as
  select tablespace_name, sum(bytes) bytes from dba_data_files
   group by tablespace_name;
grant select on APS_DATA_FILES to public;
drop public synonym APS_DATA_FILES;
create public synonym APS_DATA_FILES for aps_data_files;
rem
drop view APS_ROLLNAME;
create view APS_ROLLNAME as
  select rownum id, name from v$rollname;
grant select on APS_ROLLNAME to public;
drop public synonym APS_ROLLNAME;
create public synonym APS_ROLLNAME for aps_rollname;
rem
drop view APS_ROLLSTAT;
create view APS_ROLLSTAT as
  select rownum id, extents, rssize from v$rollstat;
grant select on APS_ROLLSTAT to public;
drop public synonym APS_ROLLSTAT;
create public synonym APS_ROLLSTAT for aps_rollstat;
rem
drop view APS_ROLLBACK_SEGS;
create view APS_ROLLBACK_SEGS as
  select n.name name, s.extents extents, s.rssize rssize
    from aps_rollname n, aps_rollstat s
   where n.id = s.id;
grant select on APS_ROLLBACK_SEGS to public;
drop public synonym APS_ROLLBACK_SEGS;
create public synonym APS_ROLLBACK_SEGS for aps_rollback_segs;
rem
drop view APS_STATNAME;
create view APS_STATNAME as select * from v$statname;
grant select on APS_STATNAME to public;
drop public synonym APS_STATNAME;
```

```
create public synonym APS_STATNAME for aps_statname;
rem
drop view APS_SYSSTAT;
create view APS_SYSSTAT as select * from v$sysstat;
grant select on APS_SYSSTAT to public;
drop public synonym APS_SYSSTAT;
create public synonym APS_SYSSTAT for aps_sysstat;
rem
drop view APS_TS$;
create view APS_TS$ as select * from ts$;
grant select on APS_TS$ to public;
drop public synonym APS_TS$;
create public synonym APS_TS$ for aps_ts$;
rem
drop view APS_FET$;;
create view APS_FET$ as select * from fet$;
grant select on APS_FET$ to public;
drop public synonym APS_FET$;
create public synonym APS_FET$ for aps_fet$;
rem
drop table APS_CFET$;
create table APS_CFET$ (
   file#   number,   block#   number,  length   number)
storage (initial 5k next 5k pctincrease 0)
tablespace &tsn;
rem
drop view BAD_STORAGE;
create view BAD_STORAGE as
select 'table  ' type, owner, table_name name, initial_extent "INIT EXT",
       decode(mod(initial_extent, next_extent),
            0, substr(to_char(next_extent),1,13),
            substr(to_char(next_extent)||' BaD',1,13)) "NXT EXT",
       decode(to_char(pct_increase),'0','0',
            substr(pct_increase||' BaD',1,7)) "PCT_INC"
  from dba_tables
 where mod(initial_extent, next_extent) <> 0 or pct_increase <> 0
union
select 'index  ', owner, INDEX_name, initial_extent,
       decode(mod(initial_extent, next_extent),
            0, substr(to_char(next_extent),1,13),
            substr(to_char(next_extent)||' BaD',1,13)),
       decode(to_char(pct_increase),'0','0',
            substr(pct_increase||' BaD',1,7))
  from dba_indexes
 where mod(initial_extent, next_extent) <> 0 or pct_increase <> 0
union
select 'CLUSTER ', owner, cluster_name, initial_extent "INIT EXT",
       decode(mod(initial_extent, next_extent),
            0, substr(to_char(next_extent),1,13),
            substr(to_char(next_extent)||' BaD',1,13)),
       decode(to_char(pct_increase),'0','0',
            substr(pct_increase||' BaD',1,7))
  from dba_clusters
```

```
    where mod(initial_extent, next_extent) <> 0 or pct_increase <> 0;
rem
drop view BLOCKING_LOCKS;
create view BLOCKING_LOCKS as
select h.type   lock_type,
                decode( h.lmode,
                0, 'NONE',            /* Mon Lock equivalent */
                1, 'Null Mode',       /* N */
                2, 'Row-S (SS)',      /* L */
                3, 'Row-X (SX)',      /* R */
                4, 'Share (S)',       /* S */
                5, 'S/Row-X (SSX)',   /* C */
                6, 'Exclusive (X)',   /* X */
                h.lmode) lock_mode,
                h.pid             orcl_pid,   /* oracle process id */
                s.username        orcl_user,  /* oracle user name */
                p.spid            os_pid,      /* OS specific process id */
                p.username        os_user,    /* OS specific name */
                program,                       /* program that user is running */
                terminal,                      /* terminal that user is using */
              h.id1 rsrc_id1, /* the value of these depends on the type of lock */
                h.id2 rsrc_id2
    from v$session s, v$process p, all_locks_view h, all_locks_view r
    where   r.request  > 1     /* someone is waiting for (requesting) the lock  */
    and   h.lmode      > 1            /* h is holding the lock */
    and   h.type       = r.type
    and   h.id1        = r.id1
    and   h.id2        = r.id2
    and   h.pid        = p.pid
    and   p.lockwait is null
    and   p.latchwait is null
    and   p.addr       = s.paddr;
rem
drop view DBA_FREE_SUM;
create view DBA_FREE_SUM as
    select tablespace_name, sum(bytes) Total, trunc(avg(bytes)) average,
    max(bytes) Max, min(bytes) Min, count(*) Count
      from sys.dba_free_space
     group by tablespace_name;
drop table DBA_OBJ_TEMP;
create table DBA_OBJ_TEMP (
                otype     char(30),
                object    char(30),
                owner     char(30),
                osize     number)
storage( initial 10k next 10k pctincrease 0)
tablespace dba_ts;
rem
drop table HIT_RATIOS;
create table HIT_RATIOS (
                check_date  date, check_hour  number, db_block_gets number,
                consistent  number, phy_reads  number, hitratio  number,
                period_hit_ratio number, period_usage number, users  number)
```

```
storage (initial 10k next 10k pctincrease 0)
tablespace &tsn;
rem
drop table LOCK_HOLDERS;
create table LOCK_HOLDERS (
  pid number(18),  type char(4),  id1 char(10),  id2 char(10),  req number,
  hpid number,  hmod number)
storage (initial 10k next 10k pctincrease 0)
tablespace &tsn;
rem
drop table PLAN_TABLE;
create table PLAN_TABLE (
               statement_id char(30), timestamp date, remarks  char(80),
               operation char(30), options  char(30), object_node char(30),
               object_owner char(30), object_name char(30),
               object_instance numeric, object_type  char(30),
               search_columns  numeric, id numeric, parent_id numeric,
               position numeric, other long)
storage (initial 5k next 5k pctincrease 0)
tablespace &tsn;
rem
drop table TEMP_SIZE_TABLE;
create table TEMP_SIZE_TABLE (
               table_name char(30), blocks number)
storage (initial 10k next 10k pctincrease 0)
tablespace &tsn;
rem
drop table TRUE_SPACE_T;
create table TRUE_SPACE_T
  (tablespace_name  char(30), segfile#  number, segblock# number, file_id number,
   block_id  number, blocks number, bytes number, next number, lvl  number,
   t_file_id  number, t_block_id number)
storage (initial 200k next 50k pctincrease 0)
tablespace &tsn;
rem
drop index TRUE_SPACE_T_I1;
create index TRUE_SPACE_T_I1
on  true_space_t (file_id, block_id, next)
tablespace &tsn
  storage (initial 100k next 50k pctincrease 0);
rem
drop view TRUE_SPACE_V;
create view TRUE_SPACE_V as
     select a.tablespace_name,
            a.t_file_id file_id, a.t_block_id block_id, sum(a.blocks) blocks,
            sum(a.bytes) bytes,
            nil(obj$.name,'*** TEMPORARY ***') object_name,
            nil(sys_objects.object_type,'* T=S *') object_type,
            nil(user$.name, 'SYSTEM') object_owner,
            count(*) extents
        from true_space_t a, obj$, sys_objects, user$, seg$
       where a.segfile# = seg$.file#(+)
```

```
              and a.segblock# = seg$.block#(+)
              and a.segfile# = sys_objects.header_file(+)
              and a.segblock# = sys_objects.header_block(+)
              and seg$.user# = user$.user#(+)
              and sys_objects.object_id = obj$.obj#(+)
              and a.segfile# > 0 and a.segblock# > 0
          group by a.tablespace_name, a.t_file_id, a.t_block_id,
                  obj$.name, sys_objects.object_type, user$.name
union
       select tablespace_name,
              t_file_id, t_block_id, sum(blocks), sum(bytes),
              'FREE EXTENT', 'EXTENT', 'ORACLE',
              count(*)
        from true_space_t
       where segfile#  = 0 and segblock# = 0
       group by tablespace_name, t_file_id, t_block_id;
drop view TS_CONFLICT;
create view TS_CONFLICT as
select 'table  ' type, table_name name, owner
  from dba_tablespaces dts, dba_tables dt
 where dts.tablespace_name = dt.tablespace_name
   and (  dts.initial_extent <> dt.initial_extent
       or dts.next_extent    <> dt.initial_extent
       or dts.min_extents     <> dt.min_extents
       or dts.max_extents     <> dt.max_extents
       or dts.pct_increase    <> dt.pct_increase)
union
select 'index  ', INDEX_name, owner
  from dba_tablespaces dts, dba_indexes di
 where dts.tablespace_name = di.tablespace_name
   and (  dts.initial_extent <> di.initial_extent
       or dts.next_extent    <> di.initial_extent
       or dts.min_extents     <> di.min_extents
       or dts.max_extents     <> di.max_extents
       or dts.pct_increase    <> di.pct_increase)
union
select 'CLUSTER', cluster_name, owner
  from dba_tablespaces dts, dba_clusters dc
 where dts.tablespace_name = dc.tablespace_name
   and (  dts.initial_extent <> dc.initial_extent
       or dts.next_extent    <> dc.initial_extent
       or dts.min_extents     <> dc.min_extents
       or dts.max_extents     <> dc.max_extents
       or dts.pct_increase    <> dc.pct_increase);
rem
exit
```

The following SQL script is used to consolidate contiguous areas of free space within a database's tablespaces. Under ORACLE7 this script will no longer be needed. Consolidation will be done automatically by the SMON process.

```
rem    ***********************************************************************
rem    NAME:    CONS_FS.sql
rem    HISTORY:
rem    Date        Who                    What
rem    --------    ------------------     ------------------------------------------
rem    12/04/92    Michael Brouillette    Creation
rem    12/15/92    Michael Brouillette    Changed to use FET$ and TS$ instead of
rem                                        DBA_FREE_SPACE
rem    12/18/92    Michael Brouillette    Incorporated option to keep temp file CONS$
rem    01/05/93    Michael Brouillette    Split CONS$ file into CREATE$ and DROP$.
rem                                        When the code was combined consolidation
rem                                        would not always occur due to timing. This
rem                                        may still happen but can be worked around
rem                                        by executing the CREATE$ and DROP$ scripts
rem                                        directly.
rem    01/06/93    Michael Brouillette    Modified creation of CREATE$ to include
rem                                        ALTER SYSTEM command to avoid timing
rem                                        problem. Not guaranteed but seems to work.
rem    04/09/93    Michael Ault           Added in script BLOKSIZ.SQL
rem    FUNCTION:   This routine shows the true contiguous extents and will allow
rem                the user the option of consolidating one or more tablespaces.
rem
rem                If the user DOES consolidate it is IMPORTANT that the tablespace
rem                names be provided in the exact format shown.  That format is:
rem
rem                        'tsname1','tsname2',... ('keep')
rem
rem                The specification of the fake tablespace KODP causes the temp
rem                files CREATE$ and DROP$ to be kept.
rem
rem    NOTES: There is an assumption that the following table, index, and view
rem           exist.  The DBA routine CT_DBAEN.SQL will create the objects.
rem           The table and view are required.  The index is needed only for
rem           performance reasons.
rem
rem      TABLE:   TRUE_SPACE_T
rem      INDEX:   TRUE_SPACE_T_I1
rem      VIEW:    TRUE_SPACE_V
rem
rem    ***********************************************************************
rem
set echo off  feedback off  verify off  heading off  sqlcase upper
set pagesize 9999   termout off
column bls             new_value BLOCK_SIZE
rem
select blocksize bls from sys.ts$ where name='SYSTEM',
column t_old1          new_value t_new1
column t_old3          new_value t_new3
column a$a             heading "TABLE SPACE"
column b$b             heading "CONSOLIDATED|FREE EXTENTS"
column c$c             heading "UN-CONSOLIDATED|FREE EXTENTS"
column dum2            noprint
```

```
column dum3          noprint
column dum4          noprint
rem
rem   clean out true_space_t table
delete true_space_t;
rem
commit;
rem
rem load true_space_t with FREE extent information
rem
prompt
prompt WORKING . . . .
prompt
insert into true_space_t
    select B.name, 0, 0,
           A.file#, A.block#, A.length, A.length*&block_size,
           A.block# + A.length, 0, A.file#, A.block#
      from SYS.fet$ A, SYS.ts$ B
     where A.ts# = B.ts#;
commit;
rem
rem   set t_file_id, t_block_id and lvl for all extents
rem
declare
  xx number(5)  := 0;
  ll number(3)  := 2;
begin
update true_space_t a
   set lvl = -1
 where block_id in
                 (select next
                    from true_space_t
                  where next = a.block_id
                    and file_id = a.file_id
                    and segfile# = a.segfile#
                    and segblock# = a.segblock#);
update true_space_t
   set lvl = 1,
       t_file_id = file_id,
       t_block_id = block_id
 where lvl = 0;
loop
select count(*)
  into xx
  from true_space_t
 where lvl = -1;
if xx = 0
   then exit;
end if;
update true_space_t a
  set lvl = ll,
      t_file_id =
                (select t_file_id
```

```
                       from true_space_t
                      where a.block_id = next
                        and file_id  = a.file_id
                        and segfile# = a.segfile#
                        and segblock# = a.segblock#
                        and lvl = ll - 1),
           t_block_id =
                   (select t_block_id
                       from true_space_t
                      where a.block_id = next
                        and file_id  = a.file_id
                        and segfile# = a.segfile#
                        and segblock# = a.segblock#
                        and lvl = ll - 1)
    where lvl = -1
      and (file_id, block_id, segfile#, segblock#) in
                          (select file_id, next, segfile#, segblock#
                             from true_space_t where lvl = ll - 1);
ll := ll + 1;
end loop;
end;
rem
set heading on  termout on  newpage 1
prompt
prompt Tablespaces that can be consolidated :
rem
select c.name a$a,
       count(a.block_id) b$b,
       count(b.block#) c$c
from true_space_v a, SYS.fet$ b, SYS.ts$ c
where a.file_id(+) = b.file#
  and a.block_id(+) = b.block#
  and b.ts# = c.ts#
group by c.name
having count(a.block_id) <> count(b.block#)
   and count(b.block#) > 1;
set heading off
rem
prompt
prompt Enter tablespace names or <CR> for none
prompt Specify a tablespace of "KEEP" to keep the scripts CREATE$ and DROP$
prompt Format is: 'TS_NAME_1', 'TS_NAME_2.....'
accept ans prompt 'Enter tablespace names (NONE):  '
prompt
set termout off
rem
rem  set value to NONE if <CR> is given
rem  this technique depends on the select "blowing up" if the user enters
rem  anything
rem
define t_new1 = "&ans"
rem
select nil('&ans', '''NONE''') t_old1
```

```
    from dual;
rem
select decode(count(*),0, 'x', 'KEEP') t_old2 from dual
 where 'KEEP' in (&&t_new1);
rem
rem  Build the temporary file that will perform the CREATE and DROP necessary
rem  to consolidate the tablespace.
rem
spool create$.sql
select '$'||file_id||'$'||block_id dum2, bytes dum3, tablespace_name dum4,
       'create table t$'||file_id||'$'||block_id||' (c datc) '
  from true_space_v
 where blocks > 1
   and object_name = 'FREE EXTENT'
   and tablespace_name in (&&t_new1)
union
select '$'||file_id||'$'||block_id, bytes, tablespace_name,
       'storage (initial '||bytes||') tablespace '||tablespace_name||';'
  from true_space_v where blocks > 1
   and object_name = 'FREE EXTENT' and tablespace_name in (&&t_new1)
order by 3, 2 desc, 1, 4;
select distinct 'select * from sys.fet$;' from dual
 where 'NONE' not in (&&t_new1);
select 'alter system switch logfile;' from dual
 where 'NONE' not in (&&t_new1);
rem
spool off
spool drop$.sql
rem
select 'drop table t$'||file_id||'$'||block_id||';'
  from true_space_v
 where blocks > 1
   and object_name = 'FREE EXTENT'
   and tablespace_name in (&&t_new1);
rem
spool off
rem
rem  execute temp files CREATE$ and DROP$ if any tablespaces specified
rem  and cleanup all temp files unless KEEP specified then keep CREATE$ and
rem  DROP$
rem
spool clean$up.sql
rem
select 'start create$.sql'  from dual where 'NONE' not in (&&t_new1);
rem
select 'ho delete create$.sql;*'  from dual where 'KEEP' not in (&&t_new1);
rem
select 'start drop$.sql' from dual where 'NONE' not in (&&t_new1);
rem
select 'ho delete drop$.sql;*' from dual where 'KEEP' not in (&&t_new1);
rem
select 'ho delete clean$up.sql;*' from dual;
rem
```

```
spool off
start clean$up
undef 1
undef 2
undef 3
undef 4
undef ans
undef t_new1
column a$a clear
column b$b clear
column c$c clear
column dum2 clear
column dum3 clear
column dum4 clear
set termout on  feedback 10  verify on heading on  sqlcase mixed
commit;
exit
```

The following SQL script is used to determine the "bound" objects in a database. Bound objects are objects that have extents bounded by free space. This is a result of "Swiss-cheese" fragmentation. To correct this, the DBA must export the object, drop it, and then re-create it. This will also require the indexes, constraints, and grants to be re-done under version 6. Under ORACLE7 the object is exported, truncated, and then re-imported since a dropped objects space is automatically returned to the free pool.

```
rem   NAME:    BOUND_OB.sql
rem   HISTORY:
rem   Date       Who                 What
rem   -------    ------------------  ------------------------------------------
rem   12/04/92   Michael Brouillette   Creation
rem   01/07/93   Michael Brouillette   Switched to title80
rem   04/09/93   Michael Ault    Included code for Bloksiz.sql
rem   FUNCTION: Shows the object name, type and owner for all objects with one
rem             or more extents bounded by free space.
rem
start title80 'Objects With Extents Bounded by Free Space'
rem
spool b_ob|&db|..lis
column e      format a23           heading "TABLE SPACE"
column a      format a6            heading "OBJECT|TYPE"
column b      format a20           heading "OBJECT NAME"
column c      format a15           heading "OWNER ID"
column d      format 99,999,999    heading "SIZE|IN BYTES"
column bls    new_value BLOCK_SIZE
rem
break on e skip 1 on c
rem
set feedback off verify off  termout off
rem
select blocksize bls from sys.ts$
where name='SYSTEM';
```

```
rem
select h.name e, g.name c, f.object_type a, e.name b, b.length*&&blocksize d
  from uet$ b, fet$ c, fet$ d, obj$ e, sys_objects f, user$ g, ts$ h
 where b.block# = c.block# + c.length
   and b.block# + b.length = d.block# and f.header_file = b.segfile#
   and f.header_block = b.segblock# and f.object_id = e.obj#
   and g.user# = e.owner# and b.ts# = h.ts#
order by 1,2,3,4;                        /* group by g.name, f.object_type, e.name */
rem
column a clear
column b clear
column c clear
column d clear
set feedback 10
spool off
exit
```

The following script is used to compute the average row size of an existing example table. This data is then used to calculate the size of the production database table.

```
rem    *******************************************************************
rem    NAME: TB_RW_SZ.sql
rem    HISTORY:
rem    Date        Who                  What
rem    --------    -----------------    ------------------------------------------
rem    01/20/93    Michael Brouillette  Creation
rem    FUNCTION:  Compute the average row size for a table.
rem    NOTES:  Currently requires DBA.
rem    INPUTS:
rem            tname   = Name of table.
rem            towner  = Name of owner of table.
rem                         cfile  = Name of output SQL Script file
rem    *******************************************************************
rem
column dum1      noprint
column rsize     format 99,999.99
column rcount    format 999,999,999 newline
rem
accept tname  prompt 'Enter table name: '
accept towner prompt 'Enter owner name: '
accept cfile  prompt 'Enter name for output SQL script file: '
rem
set pagesize 999  heading off  verify off  termout off
set feedback off  sqlcase upper  newpage 3
spool &cfile..sql
rem
select 0 dum1,
      'select ''Table '||'&towner..&tname'||
      ' has '',count(*) rcount,'' rows of '', ('    from dual
union
```

```
select column_id,
      'sum(nvl(vsize('||column_name||'),0)) + 1 +'  from dba_tab_columns
 where table_name = '&tname' and owner = '&towner'
   and column_id <> (select max(column_id)
                     from dba_tab_columns
                                   where table_name = '&tname'
                                   and owner = '&towner')
union
select column_id,
      'sum(nvl(vsize('||column_name||'),0)) + 1)'
  from dba_tab_columns
 where table_name = '&tname' and owner = '&towner'
   and column_id = (select max(column_id)
                     from dba_tab_columns
                                   where table_name = '&tname'
                                   and owner = '&towner')
union
select 997,  '/ count(*) + 5 rsize, '' bytes each.'''  from dual
union
select 999, 'from &towner..&tname.;'  from dual;
rem
spool off
set termout on  feedback 15   pagesize 20   sqlcase mixed    newpage 1
start &cfile
exit
```

The following SQL script generates a SQL script to re-create the tables for a given user. This can be used to document existing systems and to re-create the tables of a user after system maintenence or disasters. Notice how the UNION operator is used in conjuction with the concatenation operator "||" to build the CREATE commands from several different tables. Note this script must be run from the table owner's account since it uses the USER_ series of views. By using the DBA_ views and using a variable to capture the user name, this script could be run from a DBA account for any user.

```
rem    ********************************************************************
rem    NAME:  TB_RCT.sql
rem    HISTORY:
rem    Date        Who                 What
rem    _____    _____    _____
rem    02/25/91    R. Gaydos           Created
rem    03/18/92    Gary Dodge          Improved format, changed SPOOL file name
rem    FUNCTION:  Build a script to re-create tables
rem    ********************************************************************
rem
COLUMN CPR NOPRINT
COLUMN NPR NOPRINT
rem
SET PAGESIZE 0
SPOOL creatab2
rem
```

```
Select table_name cpr, 10 npr, 1 npr,
       'Create table '||table_name||' ( '  from user_tables
UNION
select table_name cpr, 20 npr, column_id npr,
           '             '||
       decode( column_id, 1, ' ',',')||
       rpad(column_name,31)||decode(data_type,
                     'CHAR', 'CHAR ('||data_length||')',
                     'RAW', 'RAW ('||data_length||')',
                     'NUMBER','NUMBER '||
                          decode( nvl(data_precision 0 , ' ',
                                 '('||data_precision||','||data_scale||')' ),
                     'DATE', 'DATE','LONG', 'LONG',
                     'Error in script '||data_type||' not handled '
                     ||' length '||to_char(data_length)
                     ||' precision '||to_char(data_precision)
                     ||' scale '||to_char(data_scale) )
             ||decode( nullable, 'Y', '        ', ' NOT NULL' ) from user_tab_columns
 where table_name in ( select table_name from user_tables ) UNION
select table_name cpr, 30 npr, 1 npr,  ' )   ' from user_tables UNION
select table_name cpr, 40 npr, 1 npr, '        pctfree '||pct_free  from user_tables
UNION
select table_name cpr, 45 npr, 1 npr, '        pctused '||pct_used  from user_tables
UNION
select table_name cpr, 50 npr, 1 npr, '        initrans '||ini_trans  from user_tables
UNION
select table_name cpr, 55 npr, 1 npr, '        maxtrans '||max_trans  from user_tables
UNION
select table_name cpr, 60 npr, 1 npr, '        tablespace '||tablespace_name
   from user_tables  UNION
select table_name cpr, 70 npr, 1 npr,  ' Storage ('  from user_tables
UNION
select table_name cpr, 80 npr, 1 npr, ' initial    '||initial_extent  from user_tables
UNION
select table_name cpr, 90 npr, 1 npr,  'next        '||next_extent  from user_tables
UNION
select table_name cpr, 100 npr, 1 npr, '        minextents '||min_extents
   from user_tables UNION
select table_name cpr, 110 npr, 1 npr, '        maxextents '||max_extents
   from user_tables UNION
select table_name cpr, 120 npr, 1 npr, '        pctincrease '|| pct_increase
   from user_tables UNION
select table_name cpr, 130 npr, 1 npr,  '        ) ' from user_tables UNION
select table_name cpr, 140 npr, 1 npr, ' ; ' from user_tables UNION
select table_name cpr, 150 npr, 1 npr, '   ' from user_tables
 order by 1,2,3;
SPOOL OFF
exit
```

The following SQL script is used to calculate the size of production index based on the size of the columns entered as the candidate index.

```
rem    ***********************************************************************
rem    NAME: IN_ES_SZ.sql
rom    HISTORY:
rem    Date        Who                 What
rem    --------    ------------------  ------------------------------------------
rem    01/20/93    Michael Brouillette    Creation
rem    FUNCTION:  Compute the space used by an entry for an existing index.
rem    NOTES:  Currently requires DBA.
rem    INPUTS:
rem          tname  = Name of table.
rem          towner = Name of owner of table.
rem          clist  = List of column names enclosed in quotes.
rem                   i.e 'ename', 'empno'
rem                     cfile  = Name of output SQL Script file
rem    ***********************************************************************
column dum1     noprint
column isize    format 99,999.99
column rcount   format 999,999,999 newline
accept tname  prompt 'Enter table name: '
accept towner prompt 'Enter table owner name: '
accept clist  prompt 'Enter column list: '
accept cfile  prompt 'Enter name for output SQL script file: '
set pagesize 999 heading off verify off termout off feedback off sqlcase upper
   set newpage 3
spool &cfile..sql
select -1 dum1,
      'select ''Proposed Index on table ''||' from dual
union
select 0,
   '''&towner..&tname'||' has '',count(*) rcount,'' entries of '', ('  from dual union
select column_id,
      'sum(nil(vsize('||column_name||'),0)) + 1 +'
   from dba_tab_columns
  where table_name = '&tname'  and owner = '&towner'
   and column_name in (&clist)
   and column_id <> (select max(column_id)
                     from dba_tab_columns
                         where table_name = '&tname' and owner = '&towner'
                     and column_name in (&clist)) union
select column_id,
      'sum(nil(vsize('||column_name||'),0)) + 1)'
   from dba_tab_columns
 where table_name = '&tname'
   and owner = '&towner' and column name in (&clist)
   and column_id = (select max(column_id)
                     from dba_tab_columns
                         where table_name = '&tname'  and owner = '&towner'
                     and column_name in (&clist)) union
select 997, '/ count(*) + 11 isize, '' bytes each.''' from dual union
select 999,
      'from &towner..&tname.;'  from dual;
spool off
```

```
set termout on feedback 15 pagesize 20 sqlcase mixed newpage 1
start &cfile
exit
```

The following SQL script is used to calculate the estimated space used for an entry in an index based on a specified column for a table without that column indexed. No example index has to exist to use this script.

```
rem  ******************************************************************
rem
rem  NAME:  IN_CM_SZ.sql
rem
rem  HISTORY:
rem  Date       Who                 What
rem  --------   ------------------  -------------------------------------------
rem  01/20/93   Michael Brouillette  Creation
rem
rem  FUNCTION:  Compute the space used by an entry for an existing index.
rem
rem  NOTES:  Currently requires DBA.
rem
rem  INPUTS:
rem          tname  = Name of table.
rem           towner = Name of owner of table.
rem           iname  = Name of index.
rem           iowner = Name of owner of index.
rem                    cfile  = Name of output file SQL Script.
rem  ******************************************************************
column dum1      noprint
column isize     format 99,999.99
column rcount    format 999,999,999 newline
accept tname  prompt 'Enter table name: '
accept towner prompt 'Enter table owner name: '
accept iname  prompt 'Enter index name: '
accept iowner prompt 'Enter index owner name: '
accept cfile  prompt 'Enter name for output SQL script file: '
set pagesize 999 heading off verify off termout off feedback off
set sqlcase upper newpage 3
spool &cfile..sql
select -1 dum1,
       'select ''Index '||'&iowner..&iname'||' on table '
  from dual
union
select 0,
       '&towner..&tname'||' has '',count(*) rcount,'' entries of '', ('
  from dual
union
select column_id,
      'sum(nil(vsize('||column_name||'),0)) + 1 +'
  from dba_tab_columns
 where table_name = '&tname'
```

```
    and owner = '&towner' and column_name in
                    (select column_name from dba_ind_columns
                      where table_name = '&tname'
    and table_owner = '&towner'
    and index_name = '&iname'
    and index_owner = '&iowner')
    and column_id <> (select max(column_id)
                      from dba_tab_columns
    where table_name = '&tname'
      and owner = '&towner'
                        and column_name in
                            (select column_name from dba_ind_columns
                              where table_name = '&tname'
                                and table_owner = '&towner'
                                and index_name = '&iname'
                                and index_owner = '&iowner'))
union
select column_id,
      'sum(nv(vsize('||column_name||'),0)) + 1)'
  from dba_tab_columns
 where table_name = '&tname' and owner = '&towner'
   and column_name in
                    (select column_name from dba_ind_columns
                      where table_name = '&tname'
                        and table_owner = '&towner'
                        and index_name = '&iname'
                        and index_owner = '&iowner')
   and column_id = (select max(column_id)
                    from dba_tab_columns
   where table_name = '&tname' and owner = '&towner'
                    and column_name in
                            (select column_name from dba_ind_columns
                              where table_name = '&tname'
                                and table_owner = '&towner'  and index_name = '&iname'
                                and index_owner = '&iowner'))
union
select 997,
      '/ count(*) + 11 isize, '' bytes each.'''  from dual
union
select 999,  'from &towner..&tname.;'  from dual;
spool off
set termout on feedback 15 pagesize 20 sqlcase mixed newpage 1
start &cfile
clear columns
undef tname
undef towner
undef iname
undef iowner
undef cfile
exit
```

The following SQL script generates a SQL script file that will regenerate indexes for an existing application. This script can be used to document existing indexes.

```
rem     **********************************************************************
rem     NAME:   IN_RCT.sql
rem     HISTORY:
rem     Date        Who                 What
rem     01/27/93    Michael Brouillette    Created
rem     FUNCTION:  Build a script to re-create indexes.
rem     **********************************************************************
rem
column dum1 noprint
column dum2 noprint
column dum3 noprint
rem
set termout off feedback off verify off echo off heading off pagesize 0
spool in_rct.lis
rem
select index_name dum1, 10 dum2, 0 dum3,
       'create '||decode(uniqueness,'UNIQUE', 'UNIQUE','')||
       ' index '||index_name||' on ' from user_indexes
union
select index_name, 20, 0, table_owner||'.'||table_name||' ('  from user_indexes
union
select index_name, 30, column_position,
       decode(column_position,1,' ',',')||column_name from user_ind_columns
UNION
select index_name, 40, 99,' )    '  from user_indexes
UNION
select index_name, 50, 99,'        pctfree  '||pct_free  from user_indexes
UNION
select index_name, 70, 99,'        initrans '||ini_trans  from user_indexes
UNION
select index_name, 80, 99,'        maxtrans '||max_trans  from user_indexes
UNION
select index_name, 90, 99,'        tablespace '||tablespace_name  from user_indexes
UNION
select index_name, 100, 99, ' Storage ('  from user_indexes
UNION
select index_name, 110, 99,'        initial      '||initial_extent from user_indexes
UNION
select index_name, 120, 99,'        next         '||next_extent from user_indexes
UNION
select index_name, 130, 99,'        minextents   '||min_extents from user_indexes
 UNION
select index_name, 140, 99,'        maxextents   '||max_extents from user_indexes
 UNION
select index_name, 150, 99,'        pctincrease '|| pct_increase from user_indexes
 UNION
select index_name, 160, 99, '        ) from user_indexes
UNION
```

```
select index_name, 170, 99, '; ' from user_indexes
UNION
select index_name, 180, 99, '   '  from user_indexes
 order by 1,2,3,
rem
SPOOL OFF
exit
```

The following scripts create a view of the DBA_FREE_SPACE and V$SESSTAT views for use in various reports.

```
create view free_space
    (tablespace, file_id, pieces, free_bytes, free_blocks, largest_bytes,
    largest_blks) as
select tablespace_name, file_id, count(*),
    sum(bytes), sum(blocks),
    max(bytes), max(blocks) from sys.dba_free_space
group by tablespace_name, file_id;

REM Title   : DD_VIEW.SQL
REM Purpose        : View of the Data Dictionary caches
REM                   showing only parameters that have usage
REM                   and the percent of GETMISSES/GETS
REM USE           : Use as a selectable table only
REM Limitations   : User must have access to V$ views.
REM Revisions:
REM   Date      Modified By   Reason For change
REM   4/28/93   Mike Ault     Initial Creation
REM
CREATE VIEW dd_cache
AS SELECT PARAMETER,GETS,GETMISSES,GETMISSES/GETS*100 PERCENT   ,COUNT,USAGE
FROM V$ROWCACHE
WHERE GETS > 100 AND GETMISSES > 0;
```

The following SQL script can be used against an ORACLE7 database to document functions, procedures, or packages.

```
rem  ***********************************************************************
rem  NAME: FPRC_RCT.sql
rem  HISTORY:
rem  Date        Who             What
rem  _____    _____    _____
rem  05/22/93    Michael Ault    Created
rem  FUNCTION:   Build a script to re-create functions, procedures,
rem              packages or package bodies.
rem  ***********************************************************************
set verify off  feedback off lines 80 pages 0 heading off
```

```
spool cre_fprc.sql
rem
select 'create '||s1.type||' '||s1.owner||'.'||s1.name,
                substr(s2.text,1,80)||';'
from
                DBA_SOURCE s1,
                DBA_SOURCE s2
WHERE
                s1.type = UPPER('&object_type') AND
                s1.owner = UPPER('&object_owner') AND
                s1.type = s2.type AND
                s1.owner = s2.owner AND
                s1.name = s2.name
GROUP BY
                s1.owner,
                s1.name
ORDER BY
                s2.line;
rem
spool off
exit
```

The next script automates the creation of a user's account for Oracle version 6.

```
REM NAME          : add_user.sql
REM PURPOSE       : adds a user to the database
REM USE           : called from SQL*Plus, SQL*Menu or OS script
REM Limitations   : None
REM Revisions   :
REM               Date       Modified By   Reason For change
REM               5 DEC 90   Mike Riggs    Initial Checkin
REM               3 AUG 91   MIKE AULT     DONT USE SYSTEM AS
set verify off
grant connect to &user_name identified by &password;
alter user &&user_name default tablespace &default_ts;
alter user &&user_name temporary tablespace &temporary_ts;
grant resource on &&default_ts to &&user_name;
exit
```

The next script is used to create a script to drop all of a user's objects.

```
rem    ***************************************************************************
rem    NAME: RM_US.sql
rem    HISTORY:
rem    Date       Who                    What
rem    -------    ------------------     ---------------------------------------
rem    10/25/92   Cary Millsap           Creation
rem    FUNCTION: To build a script to remove all the object owned by a specified
rem              user.
rem    INPUTS:
```

```
rem           1 = User name
rem           2 = File name of the resulting script.
rem  ************************************************************************
set verify off  feedback off  heading off    pagesize 0
def uname          = &&1
def fname          = &&2
spool &fname
rem
select 'set echo on' from system.dual;
rem
select
  'DROP '||object_type||' '||owner||'.'||object_name||';'
from  dba_objects
where
  (object_type not in ('INDEX'))
    and
  (owner = upper('&uname'));
select 'set echo off' from system.dual;
rem
spool off
set newpage 1
select 'To drop &uname''s objects:' from dual;
select '  1. Examine the file &fname' from dual;
select '  2. SQL> start &fname' from dual;
select '  3. Remove the file &fname' from dual;
start login
```

The next script will generate a report on tablespace quotas for Oracle version 6.

```
rem  ************************************************************************
rem  NAME: TS_QO_US.sql
rem  HISTORY:
rem  Date       Who                 What
rem  -------    ------------------  ------------------------------------------
rem  06/17/91   G. Godart-Brown     Creation
rem  07/14/91   G. Godart-Brown     Clears & clean up
rem  12/14/92   Michael Brouillette Add ability to specify only one user
rem  05/11/93   Mike Ault           Remove use of ALL and use wild card
rem  FUNCTION: Print the tablespace quotas of users.
rem  ************************************************************************
prompt Percent signs are wild cards
accept username prompt 'Enter user name or wild card '
prompt Print the details of the Users Tablespace Quotas
start title80 "Database Users Space Quotas by Tablespace"
col un               format a25 heading 'User Name'
col ta               format a25 heading 'Tablespace'
col usd              format 9,999,999 heading 'K Used'
col maxb             format 9,999,999 heading 'Max K '
```

```
set verify off feedback off newpage 0 heading on
spool tsquotas&db..lst
set break on ta skip 2
select
 TABLESPACE_NAME          ta,
 USERNAME                 un,
 BYTES/1024               usd,
 MAX_BYTES/1024           maxb
from dba_ts_quotas
   where username = upper('&&username)
order by tablespace_name,username;
prompt End of Report
spool off
set verify on
undef username
clear breaks
clear columns
clear computes
exit
```

The next report generates a user report for version 6.

```
REM
REM NAME         : USER_REPORT.SQL
REM PURPOSE      : GENERATE USER_REPORT
REM USE          : CALLED BY USER_REPORT.COM
REM Limitations  : None
REM Revisions:
REM  Date         Modified By   Reason For change
REM 21-AUG-1991   MIKE AULT     INITIAL CREATE
REM
set flush off  term off  set pagesize 58  set linesize 131
rem
column username              heading User
column default_tablespace    heading Default
column temporary_tablespace  heading Temporary
column dba_priv              heading DBA
column resource_priv         heading RESOURCE
column connect_priv          heading CONNECT
rem
start title132 'ORACLE USER REPORT'
define output = 'ORA_STATUS_REPORTS:user_report&db..lis'
spool &output
rem
select username, default_tablespace, temporary_tablespace,
dba_priv, resource_priv, connect_priv from sys.dba_users
where connect_priv != 0
order by username;
rem
spool off
exit
```

The following is an example of the above reports output.

```
Date: 04/05/93              "Your Companies Name"                   Page:    1
Time: 06:55 AM                 ORACLE USER REPORT                   "User's Name"
                            "Database Name" Database

User              Default        Temporary       DBA     RESOURCE    CONNECT
------------      ------------   ------------    -----    ---------   --------
ADHOC_DBA         DEF_USER       TEMP_USER         0         0          1
CASE              CASE_WORK      TEMP_USER         0         0          1
CASE$TEST         DEF_USER       TEMP_USER         0         0          1
   .                 .              .              .         .          .
   .                 .              .              .         .          .
   .                 .              .              .         .          .
OPS$NM90950       DEF_USER       TEMP_USER         0         0          1
OPS$NM90964       DEF_USER       TEMP_USER         0         0          1
OPS$NM90995       DEF_USER       TEMP_USER         0         0          1
OPS$NM91469       DEF_USER       TEMP_USER         0         0          1
OPS$NM91498       DEF_USER       TEMP_USER         0         0          1
PC_DBA            DEF_USER       TEMP_USER         0         0          1

52 rows selected
```

Under ORACLE7 the protection structure is changed. For the user report to work, it must be altered to reflect these changes. The following script is the version 6 code modified to work on ORACLE7.

```
REM
REM NAME       : USER_REPORT.SQL
REM PURPOSE: GENERATE USER_REPORT
REM USE        : CALLED BY USER_REPORT.COM
REM Limitations : None
REM Revisions:
REM Date         Modified By    Reason For change
REM 08-Apr-1993  MIKE AULT      INITIAL CREATE
REM
set flush off  term off  pagesize 58  linesize 131
column username                heading User
column default_tablespace      heading Default
column temporary_tablespace    heading Temporary
column granted_role            heading Roles
column default_role            heading Default?
column admin_option            heading Admin?
column profile                 heading 'Users Profile'
start title132 'ORACLE USER REPORT'
spool user7_report
select             username,
                   default_tablespace,
                   temporary_tablespace,
                   profile,
```

```
                    granted_role,
                    admin_option,
                    default_role
from
                    sys.dba_users a,
                    sys.dba_dba_role_privs b
where
                    a.username = b.grantee and
                    b.granted_role='CONNECT'
group by
                    username,
                    default_tablespace,
                    temporary_tablespace,
                    profile;
spool off
exit
```

The following is an example of the output from the above ORACLE7 user report script.

```
Date: 06/12/93                          "Your Company"                      Page:   1
Time: 07:56 AM                       ORACLE USER REPORT                     DEV7_DBA
                                      "Your Database"

User       Default Tablespace   Temporary Tablespace   Users Profile   Roles               Admin?   Default?
--------   ------------------   --------------------   -------------   -----------------   ------   --------
DEV7_DBA   DBA_TS               ORA_TEMP               DEFAULT         DBA                 NO       YES
SYS        SYSTEM               ORA_TEMP               DEFAULT         CONNECT             YES      YES
                                                       DBA             YES                 YES
                                                                       EXP_FULL_DATABASE   YES      YES
                                                                       IMP_FULL_DATABASE   YES      YES
                                                                       RESOURCE            YES      YES
SYSTEM     ORA_TOOLS            ORA_TEMP               DEFAULT         DBA                 YES      YES

7 rows selected.
```

Under ORACLE7 there are new user related items to monitor. These are roles and profiles. The following scripts allow the DBA to monitor and document these items.

```
REM
REM NAME         : ROLE_REPORT.SQL
REM PURPOSE      : GENERATE ROLES REPORT
REM USE          : CALLED BY ROLE_REPORT.COM
REM Limitations  : None
REM Revisions:
REM Date         Modified By     Reason For change
REM 08-Apr-1993  MIKE AULT       INITIAL CREATE
REM
set flush off term off pagesize 58  linesize 78
rem
column grantee heading 'User or Role'
column admin_option heading Admin?
```

```
rem
start title80 'ORACLE ROLES REPORT'
define output = 'role_report&db.lis'
spool &output
rem
select grantee, privilege, admin_option
from sys.dba_sys_privs
group by grantee;
rem
spool off
exit
```

The following is an example of the report generated by the above script.

```
Date: 06/09/93                "Your Company Name"              Page:    1
Time: 03:12 PM                ORACLE ROLES REPORT              SYSTEM
                               "Your Database"


User or Role       PRIVILEGE                      Adm
------------------ ----------------------------   ----
CONNECT            ALTER SESSION                  NO
                   CREATE CLUSTER                 NO
                   CREATE DATABASE LINK           NO
                   CREATE SEQUENCE                NO
                   CREATE SESSION                 NO
                   CREATE SYNONYM                 NO
                   CREATE TABLE                   NO
                   CREATE VIEW                    NO

DBA                ALTER ANY CLUSTER              YES
                   ALTER ANY INDEX                YES
                   ALTER ANY PROCEDURE            YES
                   ALTER ANY ROLE                 YES
                   CREATE SEQUENCE                YES
                   CREATE SESSION                 YES
                   CREATE SNAPSHOT                YES
                          .
                          .
                          .

DEV7_DBA           UNLIMITED TABLESPACE           NO
```

```
REM NAME      : PROFILE_REPORT.SQL
REM PURPOSE   : GENERATE USER PROFILES REPORT
REM USE       : CALLED BY PROFILE_REPORT.COM
REM Revisions:
REM Date           Modified By    Reason For change
```

```
REM 08-Apr-1993    MIKE AULT      INITIAL CREATE
rem
set flush off term off pagesize 58 linesize 78
column profile              heading Profile
column resource_name        heading 'Resource:'
column limit                heading Limit
rem
start title80 'ORACLE PROFILES REPORT'
define output = ORA_STATUS_REPORTS:profile_report&db.lis'
spool &output
rem
select profile, resource_name, limit  from sys.dba_profiles
group by profile;
rem
spool off
exit
```

The following is an example of the report generated by the above script. This is the actual output for the DEFAULT profile. As you can see, you will want to adjust the default if you intend to use profiles to restrict use of resources.

```
Date: 06/09/93              "Your Company's Name"         Page:   1
Time: 03:10 PM              ORACLE PROFILES REPORT        SYSTEM
                              "Your" Database

Profile        Resource:                      Limit
------------   -----------------------------  -------------------------------
DEFAULT        COMPOSITE_LIMIT                UNLIMITED
               CONNECT_TIME                   UNLIMITED
               CPU_PER_CALL                   UNLIMITED
               CPU_PER_SESSION                UNLIMITED
               IDLE_TIME                      UNLIMITED
               LOGICAL_READS_PER_CALL         UNLIMITED
               LOGICAL_READS_PER_SESSION      UNLIMITED
               PRIVATE_SGA                    UNLIMITED
               SESSIONS_PER_USER              UNLIMITED

9 rows selected.
```

The next script generates a report on the free-space view shown in one of the previous scripts.

```
REM   TITLE      : FREE_SPACE.SQL
REM   PURPOSE    : Generate a report showing Tablespace free space and
REM                fragmentation
REM   USE        : Called from SQLPLUS, a user menu or other front end
REM   LIMITS     : None
REM   REVISIONS:
REM                DATE      NAME        CHANGE
```

```
REM               12/15/91   Mike Ault    Initial Creation
clear columns
set pages 56 linesize 80 feedback off verify off
rem
column tablespace        heading Name format a10
column file_id           heading File# format 99999
column pieces            heading Frag format 9999
column free_bytes        heading 'Free Byte'
column free_blocks       heading 'Free Blk'
column largest_bytes     heading 'Biggest Bytes'
column largest_blks      heading 'Biggest Blks'
rem
start TITLE80 "FREE SPACE REPORT"
spool free_space&DB.report
rem
select tablespace,file_id,pieces,free_bytes,
              free_blocks,largest_bytes,largest_blks
              from free_space;
rem
spool off
exit
```

This is an example report generated by the free space script.

```
Date; 04/26/93            "Your Company Name"              Page:   1
Time: 11:07 AM         ORACLE FREE SPACE REPORT          RCRUN_DBA
                          "Your" Database
```

Name	File#	Frag	Free Byte	Free Blk	Biggest Bytes	Biggest Blks
DBA_TS	6	1	2527232	1234	2527232	1234
ORA_TEMP	3	1	10483712	5119	10483712	5119
ORA_USERS	2	1	10483712	5119	10483712	5119
RCRUN	4	1	15235072	7439	15235072	7439
RCRUN_ROLL BACKS	5	1	6387712	3119	6387712	3119
SYSTEM	1	1	38270976	18687	38270976	18687

```
6 rows selected.
```

The next script is used to generate a table report.

```
REM
REM NAME        : TABLE_RP.SQL
REM PURPOSE     : GENERATE TABLE REPORT
REM USE         : FROM BOW_WEEKLY_STATUS.COM
```

```
REM Limitations    : None
REM Revisions:
REM Date           Modified By   Reason For change
REM 21-AUG-1991    MIKE AULT     INITIAL CREATE
REM 28-OCT-1992    MIKE AULT     ADD CALL TO TITLE132
rem
clear columns
column table_name             heading Table
column tablespace_name        heading Tablespace
column cluster_name           heading Cluster
rem
START TITLE132 "ORACLE TABLE REPORT"
DEFINE OUTPUT = 'table_report&DB..lis'
spool &OUTPUT
rem
select
             owner,
             table_name,
             tablespace_name,
             cluster_name
from
             sys.dba_tables
where
             OWNER NOT IN ('SYSTEM', 'SYS')
order by
             tablespace_name,
             owner;
rem
spool off
clear columns
EXIT
```

This is an example report output from the above script.

```
Date: 05/10/93              "Your Company Name"            Page:    5
Time: 08:00 AM              ORACLE TABLE REPORT            OPS$NM91263
                             "Your" Database

OWNER          Table                    Tablespace            Cluster
------------   ------------------------  --------------------  ---------------
CASE           CDI_DELTAB                CASE_WORKING_AREA
CASE           CDI_DICTIONARY_VERSION    CASE_WORKING_AREA
CASE           SDD_CC_ATTRIBUTES         CASE_WORKING_AREA
CASE           SDD_CC_COLUMNS            CASE_WORKING_AREA
CASE           CDI_NON_DFLT_USER_PREFS   CASE_WORKING_AREA
CASE           CDI_TEXT                  CASE_WORKING_AREA
CASE           SDD_ELEMENTS              CASE_WORKING_AREA
CASE           SDD_ERRORS                CASE_WORKING_AREA
KCGC_DBA       TEMP_SIZE_TABLE           DBA_TS                TEMP_CLUST
```

```
KCGC_DBA         LOCK_HOLDERS          DBA_TS
KCGC_DBA         DBA_TEMP              DBA_TS                    TEMP_CLUST
  .                .                     .                         .
  .                .                     .                         .
  .                .                     .                         .
RND_DBA          SDD_CC_ATTRIBUTES     DEFAULT_USER
RND_DBA          CG_FORM_HELP          DEFAULT_USER
405 rows selected.
```

The next script generates a report on extents used by tables and indexes.

```
REM
REM NAME            : EXTENTS.SQL
REM PURPOSE         : Generate extents report
REM USE             : From SQLPlus or other front end
REM Limitations     : None
REM Revisions:
REM Date        Modified By    Reason For change
REM 15-jan-91   Mike Ault      Initial Creation
REM
CLEAR COLUMNS
rem
column segment_name heading 'Segment' format a30
column tablespace_name heading 'Tablespace' format a20
rem
set pagesize 58 NEWPAGE 0 LINESIZE 79
set feedback off  echo off   termout off   newpage 0
rem
BREAK ON TABLESPACE_NAME SKIP PAGE
rem
START TITLE80 "EXTENTS REPORT"
DEFINE OUTPUT = 'EXTENT&DB..LIS'
spool &OUTPUT
rem
select
            TABLESPACE_NAME,
            segment_name,
            EXTENTS "Extents"
FROM
            SYS.DBA_SEGMENTS
order by
            tablespace name,
            segment_name;
SPOOL OFF
EXIT
```

This is an example of the above script's output.

```
Date: 05/10/93                "Your Company"             Page:   1
Time: 08:19 AM               EXTENTS REPORT             RECDEV_DBA
                             "Your" Database

Tablespace          Segment                          Extents
----------------    -----------------------------    ----------

DBA_TS              APS_CFET$                         1
                    DBA_OBJ_TEMP                      1
                    DBA_TEMP                          1
                    HIT_RATIOS                        3
                    HR_INDEX                          2
                    LOCK_HOLDERS                      1
                    PLAN_TABLE                        1
                    TEMP_SIZE_TABLE                   1
                    TRUE_SPACE_T                      1
                        .                                .
                        .                                .
                        .                                .
                    TRUE_SPACE_T_I1                   1
```

This is a script that reports on the allocated and actual sizes for database objects. The script is run from the object's owner's account.

```
rem   NAME: ACT_SIZE.sql
rem   HISTORY:
rem   Date        Who                  What
rem   --------    ------------------   ---------------------------------------
rem   09/??/90    Maurice C. Manton    Creation for IOUG
rem   12/23/92    Michael Brouillette  Changed to assume TEMP_SIZE_TABLE
rem                                    exists
rem                                    Changed to use DBA info and prompt for  the
rem                                    user name
rem                                    Changed spool file name to = owner
rem   FUNCTION:  Will show actual block used vs allocated for all tables for a user.
rem   INPUTS:
rem             owner = Table owner name.
rem
accept owner prompt 'Enter table owner name:
start title80 "Table Space Utilization Effectiveness | for | &&owner'
set term off  pagesize 0  verify off  heading off  recsep off  feedback off ttitle off
rem
delete temp_size_table;
rem
SPOOL fill_size_table.sql
rem
SELECT 'INSERT INTO temp_size_table',
              ' SELECT ','&'||'temp_var.' || segment_name ||'&'||'temp_var',
              ',COUNT( DISTINCT( SUBSTR( ROWID,1,8))) blocks',
              ' FROM &&owner..'||segment_name, ';'
FROM dba_segments
```

```
WHERE segment_type = 'TABLE' AND owner = upper('&&owner');
SPOOL OFF
DEFINE temp_var = ''''
rem
START fill_size_table;
HOST    DEL fill_size_table.sql;*
SET TERM ON TTITLE ON
SET VERIFY ON  HEADING ON  LINESIZE 79  PAGESIZE 58  NEWPAGE 0
rem
COLUMN t_date           NOPRINT new_value t_date
COLUMN user_id          NOPRINT new_value user_id
COLUMN segment_name     FORMAT A20 HEADING "SEGMENT|NAME"
COLUMN segment_type     FORMAT A7 HEADING "SEGMENT|TYPE"
COLUMN extents          FORMAT 999 HEADING "EXTENTS"
COLUMN bytes            FORMAT A6 HEADING "BYTES"
COLUMN blocks           FORMAT 9,999,999 HEADING "ORACLE|BLOCKS"
COLUMN act_blocks       FORMAT 9,999,999 HEADING "ACTUAL|USED|BLOCKS"
COLUMN pct_block        FORMAT 999.99 HEADING "PCT|BLOCKS|USED"
SPOOL &&owner
rem
SELECT segment_name, segment_type, extents, to_char( bytes/1024)||'K' bytes,
 a.blocks, b.blocks act_blocks, b.blocks/a.blocks*100 pct_block
  FROM sys.user_segments a, temp_size_table b
 WHERE segment_name = UPPER( b.table_name );
SPOOL OFF;
   delete temp_size_table;
exit
```

The following is an example of the report generated from the above script.

```
Date: 03/16/93                "Your Company Name"                 Page:    1
Time: 04:41 PM         SYS ACTUAL VS ALLOCATED STORAGE REPORT      SYS
                            "Your" Database


                                                      ACTUAL     PCT
SEGMENT     SEGMENT                                   ORACLE     BLOCKS
NAME        TYPE      EXTENTS    BYTES     BLOCKS      BLOCKS     USED
--------    -------   -------    -----     ------      ------     ------
AUD$        TABLE     1          10K       5           4          80.00
COLAUTH$    TABLE     1          10K       5           .00
COM$        TABLE     5          96K       48          44         91.67
CON$        TABLE     4          60K       30          23         76.67
DUAL        TABLE     1          10K       5           1          20.00
FILE$       TABLE     1          10K       5           1          20.00
INCEXP      TABLE     8          356K      178         138        77.53
INCFIL      TABLE     2          20K       10          5          50.00
INCVID      TABLE     1          10K       5           1          20.00

9 rows selected.
```

Under ORACLE7 there are a number of new statistics that the DBA needs to monitor. The following script will generate a report of these new statistics.

```
rem
rem  NAME: tab_stat.sql
rem  HISTORY:
rem  Date        Who                 What
rem  --------    ------------------  ---------------------------------------
rem  5/27/93     Mike Ault           Initial creation
rem
rem  FUNCTION:  Will show table statistics for a user's tables or all tables.
rem
 set pages 56 lines 132 newpage 0 verify off echo off feedback off
rem
column owner format a12 heading "Table Owner"
column table_name format a20 heading "Table"
column tablespace_name format a20 heading "Tablespace"
column num_rows format 999999999 heading "Rows"
column blocks format 999999 heading "Blocks"
column empty_blocks format 999999 heading "Empties"
column space_full format 9999999999999 "Percent Full"
column chain_cnt format 999999 "Chains"
column avg_row_len format 999999999999999999 "Avg Length (Bytes)"
rem
start title132 "Table Statistics Report"
spool tab_stat&db
rem
select owner, table_name, tablespace_name, num_rows, blocks,
                empty_blocks,
                1-((blocks * avg_space)/(blocks * 2048)) space_full,
                chain_cnt, avg_row_len
from dba_tables
where owner = upper('&owner') and tablespace_name = upper('&tablespace')
order by owner, tablespace_name;
spool off
exit
```

The following shows an example of the report generated from the above script. In order for the statistics to be available for use in this report, the ANALYZE command must have been run on the tables of interest.

```
Date: 06/10/93                        "Your Company Name"                   Page:   1
Time: 01:14 PM                       Table Statistics Report                SYSTEM
                                        "Your Database"


Table Owner  Table            Tablespace  Rows Blocks Empties Percent Full  Chains  Avg Length (Bytes)
-----------  ---------------- ----------  ---- ------ ------- -----------   ------  ----------------
SYSTEM       MENU_B_APPL      ORA_TOOL       6            1      22.56                              77
             MENU_B_CIRCLE                                1        .00
             MENU_B_GROUP                      1          1        .98                              20
             MENU_B_GRP_PRIV                 164          3      61.39                              23
             MENU_B_OBJ_TEXT                 142          5      72.11                              52
```

```
        MENU_B_OPTION                    141            8         80.90                  94
        MENU_B_PARAM                                    1          .00
        MENU_B_PARM_XREF                                1          .00
        MENU_B_PRIV                      141            3         75.73                  33
        MENU_B_PROCEDURE                                1          .00
        MENU_B_REF                                      1          .00
        MENU_B_USER                        2            1          1.95                  20
        PRODUCT_ACCESS                                  1          .00
        PRODUCT_PROFILE                    1            1          2.00                  41
        SRW_CMD_NAMES                     77            1         67.68                  18

17 rows selected.
```

The next SQL script generates a listing of primary keys based on these keys being documented with constraints.

```
rem    **********************************************************************
rem    NAME: PKEYLIST.sql
rem
rem    HISTORY:
rem    Date       Who                What
rem    --------    ------------------    --------------------------------------------
rem    06/18/91   Gary Dodge         Creation
rem    12/14/92   Michael Brouillette   Modified to accept an owner name.
rem
rem    FUNCTION:  This routine prints a report of all primary keys defined
rem               in the data dictionary (for owners other than SYS and SYSTEM).
rem               As written, it must be run by a DBA.  By changing the query to
rem               run against ALL_CONSTRAINTS, etc. it could be used by any user
rem               to see the primary keys which are "available" to them.
rem
rem    NOTES:
rem
rem    INPUTS: Owner for tables
rem
rem    **********************************************************************
ACCEPT OWNER PROMPT 'ENTER OWNER NAME OR "ALL" '
rem
COLUMN OWNER  FORMAT A15  NOPRINT NEW_VALUE OWNER_VAR
COLUMN TABLE_NAME        FORMAT A25 HEADING 'Table Name'
COLUMN CONSTRAINT_NAME  FORMAT A20  HEADING 'Constraint Name'
COLUMN COLUMN_NAME    FORMAT A25 HEADING' Column Name'
rem
BREAK ON OWNER SKIP PAGE ON TABLE_NAME SKIP 1 ON
              CONSTRAINT_NAME
rem
start title80 "Primary Keys For Database Tables"
SPOOL pkeylist
rem
SELECT C.OWNER, C.TABLE_NAME, C.CONSTRAINT_NAME,
              CC.COLUMN_NAME
  FROM DBA_CONSTRAINTS C, DBA_CONS_COLUMNS CC
```

```
WHERE C.CONSTRAINT_NAME = CC.CONSTRAINT_NAME
  AND C.OWNER = CC.OWNER
  AND C.CONSTRAINT_TYPE = 'P'
  AND C.OWNER <> 'SYS'
  AND C.OWNER <> 'SYSTEM'
  AND C.OWNER = UPPER('&&OWNER') OR UPPER('&&OWNER') = 'ALL'
 ORDER BY C.OWNER, C.TABLE_NAME, CC.POSITION;
rem
SPOOL OFF
UNDEF OWNER
exit
```

The following is an example report generated by the above script.

```
Date: 05/11/93            "Your Company Name"            Page: 1
Time: 02:03 PM       PRIMARY KEY REPORT FOR ADHOC_DBA       SYSTEM
                          "Your" Database

Table Name              Constraint Name           Column Name
--------------------    --------------------      ------------------------
ACCOUNT_CATEGORIES      CAT_PK                    ACT_CAT

ACCOUNT_CODES           ACT_PK                    ACT_COD

ACTIVITIES              ACY_PK                    ATY_COD

COST_CENTERS            CCTR_PK                   COST_CTR

CURRENCY_RATES          CURR_PK                   PST_DT
                        SCENARIO
                        SIT_COD

FUNCTIONS               FUNC_PK                   FCT_COD

HEAD_COUNTS             HDCNT_PK                  COST_CTR
                        SCENARIO
                        PST_DT

MTD_EXPENSES            MTDEXP_PK                 SEQ

PRODUCTS                PROD_PK                   PRD_ID_COD

REGIONS                 REGION_PK                 REGION

REPORTING_ENTITIES      REPORTING_PK              RPT_ENT

SCENARIOS               SCEN_PK                   SCENARIO

SITES                   SITE_PK                   SIT_COD
```

STRATEGIC_OBJECTIVES	SR_PK	SR_COD
SUB_ACTIVITIES	SAC_PK	SAC_COD
SYSTEM_TYPES	SYS_PK	SYS
UNIT_OF_CURRENCIES	UOC_PK	CURR_DSC
WORK_EFFORTS	WKEFF_PK	SEQ

The next script documents foreign keys for the entire database. You might try rewriting it to restrict it to a single user's tables.

```
rem     ************************************************************************
rem     NAME: FKEYLIST.sql
rem
rem     HISTORY:
rem     Date        Who                 What
rem     --------    ------------------  -----------------------------------------
rem     06/18/91    Gary Dodge          Creation
rem     06/28/91    Gary Dodge          Alter sort order
rem     05/10/93    Mike Ault           Alter select order to speed query,
rem                                     alter line and page size
rem     FUNCTION: This routine prints a report of all foreign keys defined in the
rem               data dictionary (for owners other than SYS and SYSTEM).  As
rem               written, it must be run by a DBA.  By changing the query to run
rem               against ALL_CONSTRAINTS, etc. it could be used by any user to
rem               see the foreign keys which are "available" to them.
rem     ************************************************************************
SET LINES 130 PAGES 56
rem
COLUMN OWNER                    FORMAT A10   NOPRINT NEW_VALUE OWNER_VAR
COLUMN TABLE_NAME               FORMAT A24   HEADING'TABLE NAME'
COLUMN REF_TABLE                FORMAT A24   HEADING'REF TABLE'
COLUMN R_OWNER                  FORMAT A10   NOPRINT
COLUMN CONSTRAINT_NAME          FORMAT A30   HEADING 'CONST NAME'
COLUMN R_CONSTRAINT_NAME        FORMAT A30   NOPRINT
COLUMN COLUMN_NAME              FORMAT A20   HEADING'COLUMN'
COLUMN REF_COLUMN               FORMAT A20   HEADING'REF COLUMN'
rem
start ORACLE$SQL:title132 "FOREIGN KEY REPORT"
rem
BREAK ON OWNER SKIP PAGE ON TABLE_NAME SKIP 1 -
          ON CONSTRAINT_NAME ON REF_TABLE
SPOOL fkeylist&DB
rem
SELECT C.OWNER, C.TABLE_NAME, C.CONSTRAINT_NAME,
          CC.COLUMN_NAME,
          R.TABLE_NAME REF_TABLE, RC.COLUMN_NAME REF_COLUMN
```

```
    FROM DBA_CONSTRAINTS C,
             DBA_CONSTRAINTS R,
             DBA_CONS_COLUMNS CC,
             DBA_CONS_COLUMNS RC
    WHERE C.CONSTRAINT_TYPE = 'R' AND C.OWNER NOT IN ('SYS','SYSTEM')
      AND C.R_OWNER = R.OWNER and
      C.R_CONSTRAINT_NAME = R.CONSTRAINT_NAME
      AND C.CONSTRAINT_NAME = CC.CONSTRAINT_NAME
      AND C.OWNER = CC.OWNER AND
      R.CONSTRAINT_NAME = RC.CONSTRAINT_NAME
      AND R.OWNER = RC.OWNER AND CC.POSITION = RC.POSITION
    ORDER BY C.OWNER, C.TABLE_NAME, C.CONSTRAINT_NAME, CC.POSITION;
    SPOOL OFF
    EXIT
```

The following is an example foreign key report.

```
Date: 05/11/93            "Your Company Name"          Page:   1
Time: 03:10 PM             FOREIGN KEY REPORT          SYSTEM
                            "Your" Database

TABLE NAME        CONST NAME             COLUMN        REF TABLE         REF COLUMN
--------------    ---------------------  ------------  --------------    ------------
ACCOUNT_CODES     ACT_CATEGORIED_BY      ACT_CAT       ACCOUNT_CATS      ACT_CAT

ACTIVITIES        ACY_CHARGED_AGNST      SR_COD        STRATEGIC_OBJ     SR_COD

COST_CENTERS      CCTR_A_SUBSET_OF       SIT_COD       SITES             SIT_COD
                  CCTR_RESPNSBLE_TO      FCT_COD       FUNCTIONS         FCT_COD

CURRENCY_RATS     CURR_CLASSIFIED_BY     SCENARIO      SCENARIOS         SCENARIO
                  CURR_TIED_TO           SIT_COD       SITES             SIT_COD

HEAD_COUNTS       HDCNT_CLSSIFD_BY       SCENARIO      SCENARIOS         SCENARIO
                  HDCNT_RPRTED_BY        COST_CTR      COST_CENTERS      COST_CTR

MTD_EXPENSES      MTDEXP_ALLCTD_TO       COST_CTR      COST_CENTERS      COST_CTR
                  MTDEXP_CTGRZD_BY       SCENARIO      SCENARIOS         SCENARIO
                  MTDEXP_CHRGED_TO       ACT_COD       ACCNT_CODES       ACT_COD
                  MTDEXP_CHRGED_TO2      ATY_COD       ACTIVITIES        ATY_COD
                  MTDEXP_CHRGED_TO3      SR_COD        STRAT_OBJ         SR_COD
                  MTDEXP_CHRGED_TO4      SAC_COD       SUB_ACTIVITIES    SAC_COD
```

The next SQL script generates an onscreen display of chained rows in a table. Under ORACLE7 this report won't be needed since the ANALYZE command with the ORACLE7 table statistics report listed earlier will replace this function.

```
rem   NAME: CHAINING.sql
rem   HISTORY:
rem   Date        Who                 What
rem   01/11/93    Michael Brouillette    Creation
rem   FUNCTION:  Produce a report showing the number of chained rows in a table.
rem               REQUIREMENTS:
rem 1.The user running this routine must have DBA privileges.
rem 2.The table must have at least one column that is both the leading portion of an
rem    index and defined as not null.
rem                      WARNINGS:
rem 1. This routine will use the V$SESSTAT table where the USERNAME
rem     is the current user.  This will cause a problem if there is
rem     more than one session active with that USERID.
rem 2. This routine uses the V$SESSTAT statistics.  These statistics
rem     may change between releases and platforms.  If the routine
rem     fails, check to make sure that the name of the statistic has
rem     not changed.  The current name is: 'table fetch continued row'
rem   INPUTS:  obj_own = Name of table owner,  obj_nam = Name of the table
rem   *********************************************************************
rem
accept obj_own prompt 'Enter the table owners name: '
accept obj_nam prompt 'Enter the table name: '
set echo off  feedback off  verify off  heading off  termout off
rem
rem find out what statistic we want
rem
column statistic# new_value stat_no
rem
select
              statistic#
from
              v$statname n
  where
              n.name = 'table fetch continued row';
rem
rem  find out who we are it terms of sid
rem
col sid new_value user_sid
rem
select
              sid
from
              sys.v_$session
  where
              audsid = userenv('SESSIONID');
rem
col  column_name new_value last_col
rem
select
              column_name
from
              sys.dba_tab_columns
```

```
 where
                table_name = upper('&&obj_nam')
 order by
                column_id;
rem
col name new_value indexed_column
rem
select
                c.name
from
                sys.col$ c,
                sys.obj$ idx,
                sys.obj$ base,
                sys.icol$ ic
 where
                base.obj# = c.obj#
                and ic.bo# = base.obj#
                and ic.col# = c.col#
                and base.owner# =
                (select user# from sys.user$  where name = upper('&&obj_own'))
                and ic.obj# = idx.obj#
                and base.name = upper('&&obj_nam')
                and ic.pos# = 1 and c.null$ > 0;
rem
col value new_value before_count
rem
select
                value
from
                v$sesstat
 where
                v$sesstat.sid = &user_sid
                and v$sesstat.statistic# = &stat_no;
rem
select
                &last_col from &obj_own..&obj_nam
 where
                &indexed_column <=(select max(&indexed_column))
from
                &obj_own..&obj_nam;
rem
col value new_value after_count
rem
select
                value
from
                v$sesstat
 where
                v$sesstat.sid = &user_sid
                and v$sesstat.statistic# = &stat_no;
rem
set termout on
rem
```

```
select
                upper('&obj_own')||'.'||upper('&obj_nam')||' contains '||
                (to_number(&after_count) - to_number(&before_count))||' chained rows.'
    from
                sys.dual;
rem
select
                'No indexed not null columns in table '||
                upper('&obj_own')||'.'||upper('&obj_nam') from sys.dual
where
                rtrim('&indexed_column') is null;
set heading on feedback on
exit
```

The following SQL script generates a report on object level grants for version 6.

```
rem   NAME: GRANTS.sql
rem   HISTORY:
rem   Date        Who                     What
rem   05/24/91    Gary Dodge              Creation
rem   12/12/92    Michael Brouillette     Allow specification of a owner.
rem   FUNCTION: Produce report of table grants showing GRANTOR, GRANTEE and
rem             specific GRANTS.
rem   INPUTS: Owner name
rem   ***********************************************************************
ACCEPT OWNER PROMPT 'ENTER OWNER NAME OR "ALL" '
rem
COLUMN GRANTEE              FORMAT A15
COLUMN OWNER               FORMAT A15
COLUMN TABLE_NAME          FORMAT A25
COLUMN GRANTOR             FORMAT A15
COLUMN SELECT_PRIV         FORMAT A1       HEADING'S|E|L'
COLUMN INSERT_PRIV         FORMAT A1       HEADING'I|N|S'
COLUMN DELETE_PRIV         FORMAT A1       HEADING'D|E|L'
COLUMN UPDATE_PRIV         FORMAT A1       HEADING'U|P|D'
COLUMN REFERENCES_PRIV     FORMAT A1       HEADING'R|E|F'
COLUMN ALTER_PRIV          FORMAT A1       HEADING'A|L|T'
COLUMN INDEX_PRIV          FORMAT A1       HEADING'I|N|D'
COLUMN CREATED             FORMAT A11      HEADING'GRANTED ON:'
rem
BREAK ON OWNER SKIP 4 ON TABLE_NAME SKIP 1 ON REPORT
SET LINESIZE 130
start title132 "TABLE GRANTS BY OWNER AND TABLE'"
rem
BTITLE SKIP 2 CENTER -
   'Y = Granted, N = Not Granted, G = Granted WITH GRANT OPTION, ' -
   'S = Granted on Specific Columns, A = Granted on All Columns' -
   left 'produced by ' &aps_prog
SPOOL grants
rem
```

```
SELECT
                OWNER,
                TABLE_NAME,
                GRANTEE,
                GRANTOR,
                CREATED,
                SELECT_PRIV,
                INSERT_PRIV,
                DELETE_PRIV,
                UPDATE_PRIV,
                REFERENCES_PRIV,
                ALTER_PRIV,
                INDEX_PRIV
  FROM
                DBA_TAB_GRANTS
  WHERE
                OWNER NOT IN ('SYS','SYSTEM')
                AND OWNER = UPPER('&&OWNER') OR
                UPPER('&&OWNER') = 'ALL'
  ORDER BY
                OWNER,
                TABLE_NAME,
                GRANTOR,
                GRANTEE;
rem
SPOOL OFF
exit
```

The following is an example of the report generated by the grants script.

```
Date: 05/10/93                "Your Company Name"                    Page:   1
Time: 09:43 AM Table authorizations by Grantor, Grantee, Owner Object name RECRUN_DBA
                             "Your" Database


                                                 S I U D A I R
                                                 E N P E L N E
GRANTOR    GRANTEE    Object Owner   Object Name  L S D L T D F   Created
--------   --------   ------------   -----------  - - - - - - -   --------

SYSTEM     REC_DBA    SYSTEM         MENU_B_A     G G G G N N N   26-APR-93
                                     MENU_B_CIRC  G G G G N N N   26-APR-93
                                     MENU_B_GRP   G G G G N N N   26-APR-93
                                     MENU_B_INFO  G G G G N N N   26-APR-93
                                     MENU_B_OPT   G G G G N N N   26-APR-93
                                     MENU_B_PRM   G G G G N N N   26-APR-93
                                     MENU_B_PRIV  G G G G N N N   26-APR-93
                                     MENU_B_PRC   G G G G N N N   26-APR-93
                                     MENU_B_REF   G G G G N N N   26-APR-93
                                     MENU_B_USR   G G G G N N N   26-APR-93
                                     MENU_V_APL   G G G G N N N   26-APR-93
                                     MENU_V_CiRC  G G G G N N N   26-APR-93
```

```
MENU_V_GRP          G G G G N N N    26-APR-93
MENU_V_INFO         G G G G N N N    26-APR-93
MENU_V_OPT          G G G G N N N    26-APR-93
MENU V PRM          G G G G N N N    26-APR-93
MENU_V_PRIV         G G G G N N N    26-APR-93

17 rows selected.
```

The next SQL script has been altered for ORACLE7, the grants are fully declared in the DBA_ view so no decodes are required.

```
rem    ***********************************************************************
rem    NAME: GRANTS.sql
rem
rem    HISTORY:
rem    Date       Who                  What
rem    --------   ------------------   -------------------------------------------
rem    05/24/91   Gary Dodge           Creation
rem    12/12/92   Michael Brouillette  Allow specification of a owner.
rem    05/27/93   Mike Ault            Updated to ORACLE7
rem
rem    FUNCTION: Produce report of table grants showing GRANTOR, GRANTEE and
rem              specific GRANTS.
rem
rem    INPUTS: Owner name
rem    ***********************************************************************
ACCEPT OWNER PROMPT 'ENTER OWNER NAME OR "ALL" '
rem
COLUMN GRANTEE         FORMAT A15
COLUMN OWNER           FORMAT A15
COLUMN TABLE_NAME      FORMAT A25
COLUMN GRANTOR         FORMAT A15
COLUMN PRIVILEGE       FORMAT A10  "Privilege"
COLUMN GRANTABLE       FORMAT A19   HEADING "With Grant Option?"
rem
BREAK ON OWNER SKIP 4 ON TABLE_NAME SKIP 1 ON REPORT
REM
SET LINESIZE 130 PAGES 56 VERIFY OFF FEEDBACK OFF
start title132 "TABLE GRANTS BY OWNER AND TABLE"
SPOOL grants&db
REM
SELECT
                OWNER,
                TABLE_NAME,
                GRANTEE,
                GRANTOR,
                PRIVILEGE,
                GRANTABLE
   FROM
                DBA_TAB_PRIVS
```

```
    WHERE
                        OWNER NOT IN ('SYS','SYSTEM')
                        AND OWNER = UPPER('&&OWNER') OR
                        UPPER('&&OWNER') = 'ALL'
        ORDER BY
                        OWNER,
                        TABLE_NAME,
                        GRANTOR,
                        GRANTEE;
    REM
    SPOOL OFF
    exit
```

The following shows an example of the output from the above ORACLE7 grants script.

```
Date: 06/09/93                  "Your Company Name"                Page:   1
Time: 03:09 PM         TABLE GRANTS BY OWNER AND TABLE             SYSTEM
                            "Your Database"


OWNER        TABLE_NAME        GRANTEE      GRANTOR      Privilege    With Grant Option?
---------    ----------------  ---------    ----------   ----------   ------------------

DEV7_DBA     APS_ROLLBACK_SEGS PUBLIC       DEV7_DBA     SELECT       NO
             INSTANCE          PUBLIC       DEV7_DBA     SELECT       NO
```

The following SQL script generates a report on sequences.

```
rem   NAME: Sequence.sql
rem
rem   HISTORY:
rem   Date        Who                  What
rem   --------    ------------------   ------------------
rem   5/10/93     Mike Ault            Creation
rem   FUNCTION:
rem               Generate report on Sequences
rem   INPUTS:
rem
rem               1 - Sequence Owner or Wild Card
rem               2 - Sequence Name or Wild Card
rem
rem   *********************************************************************
SET HEADING OFF VERIFY OFF PAUSE OFF
PROMPT ** Sequence Report **
PROMPT
PROMPT Percent signs are wild
rem
ACCEPT sequence_owner char  'Enter Oracle account to report on (or wild):';
ACCEPT sequence_name char   'Enter object name to report on (or wild): ';
rem
```

```
PROMPT
PROMPT Report file name is SEQUENCE_DBNAME.LIS
rem
SET HEADING ON
SET LINESIZE 130 PAGESIZE 56 NEWPAGE 0 TAB OFF SPACE 1
SET TERMOUT OFF
BREAK ON SEQUENCE_OWNER SKIP 2
rem
COLUMN SEQUENCE_OWNER    FORMAT A30       HEADING 'Sequence Owner'
COLUMN SEQUENCE_NAME     FORMAT A30       HEADING 'Sequence Name'
COLUMN MIN_VALUE                          HEADING 'Minimum'
COLUMN MAX_VALUE                          HEADING 'Maximum'
COLUMN INCREMENT_BY      FORMAT 9999      HEADING 'Incr.'
COLUMN CYCLE_FLAG                         HEADING 'Cycle'
COLUMN ORDER_FLAG                         HEADING 'Order'
COLUMN CACHE_SIZE        FORMAT 99999     HEADING 'Cache'
COLUMN LAST_NUMBER                        HEADING 'Last Value'
START TITLE132 "SEQUENCE REPORT"
SPOOL SEQUENCES&DB.LIS
rem
SELECT
                 SEQUENCE_OWNER,
                 SEQUENCE_NAME,
                 MIN_VALUE,
                 MAX_VALUE,
                 INCREMENT_BY,
                 DECODE(CYCLE_FLAG,'Y','YES','N','NO') CYCLE_FLAG,
                 DECODE(ORDER_FLAG,'Y','YES','N','NO') ORDER_FLAG,
                 CACHE_SIZE,
                 LAST_NUMBER
FROM
                 DBA_SEQUENCES
WHERE
                 SEQUENCE_OWNER LIKE UPPER('&SEQUENCE_OWNER') AND
                 SEQUENCE_NAME LIKE UPPER('&SEQUENCE_NAME')
ORDER BY  1,2;
SPOOL OFF
EXIT
```

The following is an example of the output from the sequence report.

```
Date: 05/11/93              "Your Company Name"              Page:   1
Time: 11:03 AM              SEQUENCE REPORT                  SYSTEM
                           "Your" Database

Sequence Own  Sequence Name  Minimum  Maximum     Incr.  Cyc  Ord  Cache  Last Value
------------  -------------  -------  --------     -----  ---  ---  -----  ----------
ADHOC_DBA     MTD_EXPENSE    1        1.0000E+27   1      NO   NO   20     1
              WORK_EFFRT     1        1.0000E+27   1      NO   NO   20     1

CT_DBA        AUDITOR        1        1.0000E+27   1      NO   NO   20     21
```

GRTS_DBA	COUNTRY	1	999	1	NO	NO	20	10
	DEGREE	1	99999	1	NO	NO	20	28
	DEGREE_T	1	99999	1	NO	NO	20	3
	DEPT	1	999	1	YES	NO	20	4
	MMD_PER	1	99999999	1	NO	NO	20	5
	POSITION	1	99999999	1	NO	NO	20	44
	REGION	1	999	1	NO	NO	20	6

10 Rows Selected

The following SQL script generates a report on indexes for version 6.

```
rem     *************************************************************************
rem     NAME: Index_rp.sql (Originally ODD005.sql)
rem     HISTORY:
rem     Date        Who                  What
rem     --------    ------------------   ------------------------------------------
rem     7/25/91     Tim Olesen           Creation
rem     01/07/93    Mike Ault            Switched to title132 altered line size
rem     05/10/93    Mike Ault            Added Header
rem     FUNCTION: Generate report on Indexes.
rem      INPUTS:
rem            1 = Oracle Account
rem            2 = Table name
rem     *************************************************************************
SET HEADING OFF VERIFY OFF PAUSE OFF
PROMPT **  Index Column Report  **
PROMPT
PROMPT Percent signs are wild
rem
ACCEPT OWNER CHAR PROMPT 'Enter Oracle account to report on (or wild): ';
ACCEPT TABLE_NAME CHAR PROMPT 'Enter table name to report on (or wild): ';
rem
PROMPT
PROMPT Report file name is  INDEXES.LIS
SET HEADING ON
SET LINESIZE 130 PAGESIZE 56 NEWPAGE 0 SPACE 1 TAB OFF
SET TERMOUT OFF
BREAK ON TABLE_OWNER SKIP PAGE ON TABLE_TYPE ON TABLE_NAME
ON UNIQUENESS ON INDEX_NAME SKIP 1
rem
COLUMN TABLE_OWNER        FORMAT A30    HEADING 'Object Owner'
COLUMN TABLE_TYPE         FORMAT A6     HEADING 'Type'
COLUMN TABLE_NAME         FORMAT A30    HEADING 'Object Name'
COLUMN INDEX_NAME         FORMAT A30    HEADING 'Index Name'
COLUMN UNIQUENESS         FORMAT A1     HEADING 'U|N|I|Q|U|E'
COLUMN COLUMN_NAME        FORMAT A30    HEADING 'Column Name'
START ORACLE$SQL:TITLE132 "Index Columns by Owner and Table Name"
SPOOL  indexes&db.LIS
rem
```

```
SELECT
                I.TABLE_OWNER,
                DECODE(TABLE_TYPE,'CLUSTER','CLUSTR','TABLE') TABLE_TYPE,
                I.TABLE_NAME, I.INDEX_NAME,
                SUBSTR(UNIQUENESS,1,1) UNIQUENESS,
                IC.COLUMN_NAME
    FROM
                DBA_INDEXES I,
                DBA_IND_COLUMNS IC
    WHERE
                I.INDEX_NAME = IC.INDEX_NAME
                AND OWNER = INDEX_OWNER
                AND I.OWNER LIKE upper('&OWNER')
                AND I.TABLE_NAME LIKE upper('&TABLE_NAME')
ORDER BY
                1,2,3,5 DESC,4,COLUMN_POSITION;
SPOOL OFF
EXIT
```

The following is an example of the output from the index report.

```
Date: 05/11/93                 "Your Company Name"                    Page:   1
Time: 11:06 AM          Index Columns by Owner and Table Name         KCGC_DBA
                              "Your" Database
                                                            U
                                                            N
                                                            I
                                                            Q
                                                            U
Object Owner Type      Object Name          Index Name      E    Column
------------ ------    --------------------  ---------------  --   ------------
ADHOC_DBA    TABLE     ACCOUNT_CATEGORIES   CAT_PK_PRIM     U    ACT_CAT
                       ACCOUNT_CODES        ACT_PK_PRIM     U    ACT_COD
                                            ACT_CAT_BY_FR   N    ACT_CAT
                       ACTIVITIES           ACY_PK_PRIM     U    ATY_COD
                                            ACY_AGST_FRN    N    SR_COD
                       ADHOC_RPT_FRM_HLP    X_AH_RP_FM_HP   N    HLP_IDX
                                                                 HLP_TYPE
                                                                 HLP_APPLN
                                                                 HLP_SEQ
                       AD_FUNTREE           AD_FUNTREE1     N    EL_ID
                       AD_FUNTREE?          PARENT
                       AD_MODNOTES          ADM_PRIME       N    MOD_ID

12 rows selected.
```

The next SQL script generates a report on index statistics for version 6 databases.

```
rem   NAME: IN_STAT.sql
rem   HISTORY:
rem   Date        Who                      What
rem   10/25/92     Cary Millsap             Creation
rem   01/07/93     Michael Brouillette      Switched to title80
rem   05/11/93     Mike Ault    Reformatted
rem   FUNCTION: Report on index statistics
rem   INPUTS:    1 = Index owner    2 = Index name
def iowner= &&1
def iname        = &&2
set heading off
col name                 newline
col headsep              newline
col height               newline
col blocks               newline
col lf_rows              newline
col lf_blks              newline
col lf_rows_len          newline
col lf_blk_len           newline
col br_rows              newline
col br_blks              newline
col br_rows_len          newline
col br_blk_len           newline
col del_lf_rows          newline
col del_lf_rows_len      newline
col distinct_keys        newline
col most_repeated_key    newline
col btree_space          newline
col used_space           newline
col pct_used             newline
col rows_per_key         newline
col blks_gets_per_access newline
validate index &iowner..&iname;
start title80 "Index Statistics for &iowner..&iname"
spool in_stat
select name, '-------------------------------------------------------'  headsep,
   'height               '||to_char(height,      '999,999,990') height,
   'blocks               '||to_char(blocks,      '999,999,990') blocks,
   'del_lf_rows          '||to_char(del_lf_rows,'999,999,990') del_lf_rows,
   'del_lf_rows_len      '||to_char(del_lf_rows_len,'999,999,990') del_lf_rows_len,
   'distinct_keys        '||to_char(distinct_keys,'999,999,990') distinct_keys,
   'most_repeated_key    '||to_char(most_repeated_key,'999,999,990')
    most_repeated_key,
   'btree_space          '||to_char(btree_space,'999,999,990') btree_space,
   'used_space           '||to_char(used_space,'999,999,990') used_space,
   'pct_used                '||to_char(pct_used,'990') pct_used,
   'rows_per_key         '||to_char(rows_per_key,'999,999,990') rows_per_key,
   'blks_gets_per_access '||to_char(blks_gets_per_access,'999,999,990')
    blks_gets_per_access,
   'lf_rows              '||to_char(lf_rows,      '999,999,990')||'         '||+
   'br_rows              '||to_char(br_rows,      '999,999,990') br_rows,
   'lf_blks              '||to_char(lf_blks,      '999,999,990')||'         '||+
```

```
    'br_blks                  '||to_char(br_blks,     '999,999,990') br_blks,
    'lf_rows_len              '||to_char(lf_rows_len,'999,999,990')||'        '||+
    'br_rows_len              '||to_char(br_rows_len,'999,999,990') br_rows_len,
    'lf_blk_len               '||to_char(lf_blk_len, '999,999,990')||'        '||+
    'br_blk_len               '||to_char(br_blk_len, '999,999,990') br_blk_len from
            index_stats;
spool off
exit
```

The following is an example of the report generated by the index report script.

```
Date: 05/12/93              "Your Company Name"              Page:   1
Time: 02:06 PM        Index Statistics for case.elem_10      SYSTEM
                              "Your"                          Database


ELEM_10
-----------------------------------------------
height                                 2
blocks                                86
del_lf_rows                            2
del_lf_rows_len                       32
distinct_keys                          6
most_repeated_key                  4,843
btree_space                      149,262
used_space                        78,820
pct_used                              53
rows_per_key                         808
blks_gets_per_access                 407
lf_rows              4,848  br_rows                 77
lf_blks                 78  br_blks                  1
lf_rows_len         77,588  br_rows_len          1,232
lf_blk_len           1,889  br_blk_len           1,920
```

Under ORACLE7 the index statistics are stored in the DBA_INDEXES view. A revised index statistics report for ORACLE7 follows.

```
rem   NAME: IN_STAT.sql
rem   HISTORY:
rem   Date        Who          What
rem   05/27/93    Mike Ault     Initial creation
rem
rem   FUNCTION: Report on index statistics
rem   INPUTS:   1 = Index owner    2 = Index name
rem
def iowner= &&1
def iname  = &&2
set pages 56 lines 130 verify off feedback off
```

```
rem
column owner format a20 heading "Owner"
column index_name format a20 heading "Index"
column status format a11 heading heading "Status"
column blevel format 9,999,999,999 heading "Tree Level"
column leaf_blocks format 999,999,999 heading "Leaf Blk"
column distinct_keys format 999,999 heading "# Keys"
column avg_leaf_blocks_per_key format 999,999,999 heading "Avg. LB/Key"
column avg_data_blocks_per_key format 999,999,999 heading "Avg. DB/Key"
column clustering_factor format 999,999,999 heading "Clstr Factor"
rem
start title132 "Index Statistics Report"
spool ind_stat&db
rem
select
                owner,
                index_name,
                status,
                blevel,
                leaf_blocks,
                distinct_keys,
                avg_leaf_blocks_per_key,
                avg_data_blocks_per_key,
                clustering_factor
from
                dba_indexes
where
                owner like upper('&&iowner') and
                index_name like upper('&&iname')
order by 1,2;
rem
spool off
exit
```

The following is a listing generated by the ORACLE7 index statistics report.

```
Date: 06/12/93                    "Your Company Name"                  Page:   1
Time: 11:21 AM                  Index Statistics Report                DEV7_DBA
                                    "Your Database"

Owner     Index            STATUS  Tree Level  Leaf Blk  # Keys  Avg. LB/Key  Avg. DB/Key  Clstr Factor
--------  ---------------  -----   ----------  --------  ------  -----------  -----------  ------------
DEV7_DBA  DBA_OB_DESC      VALID        1          33      254         1           3            835
          INDEX_LIST_1_PK  VALID
          SYS_C00440       VALID        2          88    1,013         1           1            353
          SYS_C00441       VALID
          TABLE_LIST_1_PK  VALID
          TRUE_SPACE_T_1   VALID
```

The following SQL script generates a report on synonyms in the database for a user.

```
REM
REM NAME          : SYNONYM.SQL
REM PURPOSE       : GENERATE REPORT OF A USERS SYNONYMS
REM USE           : FROM SQLPLUS
REM Limitations   : None
REM Revisions:
REM Date          Modified By    Reason For change
REM 12/MAY/93     Mike Ault      Initial Creation
REM
prompt Percent signs are Wild Cards
prompt
rem
accept own prompt 'Enter the user who owns synonym: '
set pages 56 lines 130 verify off feedback off term off
start oracle$sql:title132 "Synonym Report"
spool synonym&db
rem
column host        format a24 heading "Connect String"
column owner       format a15
column table       format a35
column db_link     format a6 heading Link
column username    format a15
rem
select
               a.owner,
               synonym_name ,
               table_owner ||'.'|| table_name "Table" ,
               b.db_link,
               username,
               host
from
               dba_synonyms a,
               dba_db_links b
where
               a.db_link = b.db_link(+) and
               a.owner like upper('&own');
spool off
exit
```

The following listing shows an example of the report generated by the synonym report.

```
Date: 05/12/93              "Your Company Name"                Page:    1
Time· 05:35 PM                Synonym Report                   OPS$NM91263
                             "Your" Database

OWNER          SYNONYM_NAME    Table                 Link    USER          Conn String
-----------    ------------    ----------------      ------  -----------   -----------
OPS$NM91263    DEV_INSTANCE    DEV_DBA.INSTANCE      DEV     OPS$NM91263   d:devcon
```

```
OPS$NM91263    DEV_HIT_RATIOS    DEV_DBA.HIT_RATIO    DEV     OPS$NM91263  d:devcon
OPS$NM91263    KCGC_INSTANCE     KCGC_DBA.INSTANCE    KCGC    OPS$NM91263  d:casecon
OPS$NM91263    KCGC_HIT_RATIO    KCGC_DBA.HIT_RATIO   KCGC    OPS$NM91263  d:casecon
    .              .                  .                .        .            .
    .              .                  .                .        .            .
    .              .                  .                .        .            .
OPS$NM91263    CDI_MCUI          CASE.CDI_MCUI
OPS$NM91263    ENTITIES          CASE.ENTITIES
OPS$NM91263    CDI_MTUI          CASE.CDI_MTUI
OPS$NM91263    CDI_NET_CHDRN     CASE.CDI_NET_CHILDREN
OPS$NM91263    CDI_NET_PRNTS     CASE.CDI_NET_PARENTS
OPS$NM91263    CDI_SEQUENCES     CASE.CDI_SEQUENCES
OPS$NM91263    SDD_DATASTRS      CASE.SDD_DATASTORES
OPS$NM91263    SDD_DATAFLWS      CASE.SDD_DATAFLOWS
OPS$NM91263    SDD_COLUMNS       CASE.SDD_COLUMNS
```

The following SQL script shows an example report for Database Links.

```
REM NAME          : DB_LINKS.SQL
REM PURPOSE       : GENERATE REPORT OF DATABASE LINKS
REM USE           : FROM SQLPLUS
REM Limitations   : None
REM Revisions:
REM Date          Modified By    Reason For change
REM 12/MAY/93     Mike Ault      Initial Creation
set pages 56 lines 130 verify off feedback off term off
start oracle$sql:title132 "Database Links Report"
spool db_links&db
rem
column host format a60 heading "Connect String"
column owner format a15 heading "Creator"
column db_link format a10 heading "Link Name"
column username format a15 heading "User"
column password format a15 heading "Password"
column create heading "Date Created"
rem
select
                host,
                owner,
                db_link,
                username,
                password,
                created
   from dba_db_links;
exit
```

This listing shows an example of the output from the database links report.

```
Date: 05/12/93                 "Your Company Name"              Page:    1
Time: 05:35 PM               Database Links Report            OPS$NM91263
                               "Your" Database

Connect String                        DB Link    Creator  Passwd   Date Created
-------------------------------       ---------  ------   --------  ------------
D:MMRD01"SQLNET SNET"::"TASK=ORDNKCGC" CASECON    KC_DBA   CASE_DB  15-MAY-1993
D:MMRD15"SQLNET SNET"::"TASK=ORDNDEV"  DEVCON     KC_DBA   CASE_DB  10-APR-1993
D:MMR203"SQLNET SNET"::"TASK=ORDNDREC" DLBDCON    KC_DBA   CASE_DB  10-MAY-1993
D:MMR203"SQLNET SNET"::"TASK=ORDNRREC" DLBRCON    KC_DBA   CASE_DB  10-MAY-1993
D:MMR102"SQLNET SNET"::"TASK=ORDNLIMSA" LIMSACON  KC_DBA   CASE_DB  12-MAY-1993
D:MMR102"SQLNET SNET"::"TASK=ORDNLIMSB" LIMSBCON  KC_DBA   CASE_DB  12-MAY-1993
T:ELWOOD                               ELCON      KC_DBA   CASE_DB  10-APR-1993
D:WINLIMS"WINNET WNET"::TASK=ORDNWINS" WINCON     KC_DBA   CASE_DB  05-FEB-1993
```

The next SQL script generates a rollback segment report.

```
rem  ************************************************************************
rem  NAME: DB_RBS.sql
rem  HISTORY:
rem  Date       Who                  What
rem  --------   ------------------   -------------------------------------
rem  10/25/92   Cary Millsap         Creation
rem  01/07/93   Michael Brouillette  Switched to title80
rem  06/16/93   Mike Ault            Added spool to file
rem                                  added sets
rem  FUNCTION: To report on database rollback segments.
rem  NOTES:
rem          The outer join (+) is needed on RBSNAMESTAT because there are only
rem          rows in RBSNAMESTAT for segments in DBA_ROLLBACK_SEGS with
rem          status='IN USE'. We want this report to list all rollback
rem          segments, regardless of status.
rem  ************************************************************************
set pages 56  lines 130  verify off  feedback off
start title132 "Database Rollback Segments"
col segment      format   a20        heading 'Segment Name'  justify c trunc
col status       format   a14        heading 'Status'        justify c
col tablespace   format   a20        heading 'Tablespace'    justify c trunc
col extents      format   9,990      heading 'Extents'       justify c
col rssize       format   9,999,999,990 heading 'Size|in Bytes' justify c
col owner        format   a6         heading 'Type'
spool rbs_rpt&db
select
  r.segment_name      segment,
  r.status            status,
  r.tablespace_name   tablespace,
  n.extents           extents,
  n.rssize            rssize,
  r.owner             owner
from
```

```
  sys.dba_rollback_segs   r,
  aps_rollback_segs   n
where
  (r.segment_name = n.name(+))
order by   r.status, r.segment_name;
spool off
exit
```

This is an example listing from the rollback segment report.

```
Date: 05/20/93              "Your Company Name"              Page:   1
Time: 11:10 AM           Database Rollback Segments          KCGC_DBA
                             "Your" Database


                                                     Size
Segment Name   Status     Tablespace       Extents   in Bytes    Type
-------------  ---------  ------------------ --------  ----------- ------
RBS2           AVAILABLE  SYSTEM                                   SYS
ROLLBACK_1     IN USE     CASE_ROLLBACK_SEGMEN  3      1,508,486   SYS
ROLLBACK_2     IN USE     CASE_ROLLBACK_SEGMEN  3      1,508,486   SYS
ROLLBACK_3     IN USE     CASE_ROLLBACK_SEGMEN  3      1,508,486   SYS
ROLLBACK_4     IN USE     CASE_ROLLBACK_SEGMEN  11     5,536,486   SYS
ROLLBACK_5     IN USE     CASE_ROLLBACK_SEGMEN  11     5,536,486   SYS
SYSTEM         IN USE     SYSTEM                3      175,218     SYS
```

The DBA also needs to check on active rollback status prior to taking them offline for maintenance. The following script will provide this information.

```
rem    Name      : TX_RBS.SQL
rem    Purpose   : Generate a report of active rollbacks
rem    Use       : From SQL*Plus
rem    History:
rem    Date       Who             What
rem    Sept 91    Lan Nguyen      Presented in paper at IOUG
rem               Walter Lindsey
rem    5/15/93    Mike Ault       Added Title80, sets and output
rem********************************************************************
column   name    format a20            heading "Rollback Segment Name"
column   pid     format 9999999999     heading "Oracle PID"
column   spid    format 9999999999     heading "Sys PID"
set pages 56  lines 130 verify off feedback off
start title132 "Rollback Segments in Use"
spool tx_rbs&db
select
                  r.name,
                  l.pid,
                  p.spid,
```

```
                         NVL(p.username, 'no transaction) "Transaction",
                         p.terminal "Terminal"
from
                         v$lock l,
                         v$process p,
                         v$rollname r
where
                         l.pid = p.pid (+)
                         and TRUNC(l.id1(+) / 65536) = r.usn
                         and l.type(+) = 'TX' and l.lmode(+) = 6
order by
                         r.name;
spool off
exit
```

This is an example report listing from the active rollback segment report script.

```
Date: 05/20/93               "Your Company Name"                Page:   1
Time: 10:44 AM              Rollback Segments in Use            KCGC_DBA
                               "Your" Database

Rollback Segment Name  Oracle PID   Sys PID   Transaction    Terminal
---------------------  -----------  --------- -------------  -----------
ROLLBACK_1                                    no transaction
ROLLBACK_2                  23      2C401AE9  NM91498-T      FTA125-T
ROLLBACK_3                                    no transaction
ROLLBACK_4                                    no transaction
ROLLBACK_5                                    no transaction
SYSTEM                                        no transaction

6 rows selected.
```

The DBA also may need to monitor the amount of redo space required in a rollback segment for a specific transaction. This data would then be used to size a rollback segment for the transactions use. This is especially useful when the DBA is planning the use of rollbacks for batch or large transactions.

```
rem*************************************************************
rem  Name          : UNDO.SQL
rem  Purpose       : Document rollback usage for a single transaction
rem  Use           : Note: You must alter the UNDO script and add a
rem                    call to the transaction at the indicated line
rem  Restrictions: : The database should be placed in DBA mode and
rem                    these be the only transaction running.
rem  History:
rem    Date      Who            What
rem    Sept 91   Lan Nguyen     Presented in paper at IOUG
rem              Walter Lindsey
```

```
rem    5/15/93   Mike Ault          Changed to use one table
rem
set feedback off  termout off
column name format a40
define undo_overhead=54
drop table undo_data;
create table undo_data (tran_no number, start_writes number, end_writes number);
insert into undo_data
select 1, SUM(writes) from v$rollstat;
set feedback on  termout on
rem
rem   INSERT TRANSACTION HERE
rem
set feedback off  termout off
update undo_data end_writes = SUM(writes) from v$rollstat;
 where tran_no=1;
set feedback on  termout on
select  ((end-writes - start_writes) - &undo_overhead)
"Number of Rollback Bytes Generated"
from undo_data;
set termout off feedback off
drop table undo_data;
exit
```

The DBA inserts either a call to the script that holds the transaction of interest or the transaction itself into the center of the above script and then executes the script. No other users should be active during the test.

The next script is used to monitor redo usage. The script can be used during tuning of the redo process.

```
REM
REM NAME         : rdo_stat.sql
REM PURPOSE      : Show REDO latch statisitics
REM USE          : from SQLPlus
REM Limitations  : Must have access to v_$ views
REM Revisions:
REM Date         Modified By   Reason For change
REM 20 May 93    Mike Ault     Initial creation
REM (From "Using SQL to ID DB Performance Bottlenecks"
REM   by Deepak Gupta and Sameer Patkar of Oracle Corp)
REM************************************************************************
set pages 56 lines 78 verify off feedback off termout off
start oracle$sql:title80 "Redo Latch Statistics"
spool rdo_stat&db
column name format a30
column percent format 999.999
select
                 name,
                 waits Total,
                 immediates Successes,
                 timeouts,
                 100.*(timeouts/waits) Percent
```

```
from
                sys.v_$latch l1,
                sys.v_$latchname l2
where
                l1.latch#=l2.latch# and
                l1.latch# in (11,12);
rem
start title80 "Redo Log Statistics"
select
                n.name name,
                sum(st.value) value
from
                sys.v_$sesstat st,
                sys.v_$statname n,
                sys.v_$session s,
                sys.v_$process p
where
                st.statistic# = n.statistic# and
                s.paddr = p.addr and
                p.pid = '5' and
                n.statistic# between 64 and 78
group by
                n.name;
spool off
exit
```

This is a listing showing what the output from the redo statistics report looks like.

```
Date: 05/20/93              "Your Company Name"                 Page: 1
Time: 12:51 PM              Redo Latch Statistics               KCGC_DBA
                             "Your" Database

NAME                 TOTAL           SUCCESSES        TIMEOUTS       PERCENT
-------------------- ----------      -------------    ------------   ----------
redo allocation      481621          481058           778             .162
redo copy            3               0                3            100.000

Date: 05/20/93              "Your Company Name"                 Page: 1
Time: 12:51 PM              Redo Log Statistics                 KCGC_DBA
                             "Your" Database

NAME                             VALUE
------------------------         --------
redo blocks written              174537
redo buffer allocation retries        5
redo chunk allocations              855
redo entries                       1044
redo entries linearized               0
redo log space requests               3
redo log space wait time              0
```

```
redo log switch interrupts               0
redo log switch wait failure             0
redo size                           211082
redo small copies                     1027
redo wastage                       1050943
redo write time                          0
redo writer latching time                0
redo writes                           7338
```

The next SQL script is used to generate a cluster report.

```
rem
rem File:       CLU_REP.SQL
rem Purpose:    Document Cluster Data
rem Use:        From user with access to DBA_ views
rem When        Who        What
rem ------      ----       ------
rem 5/27/93     Mike Ault   Initial Creation
rem
column owner format a10
column cluster_name format a15 heading "Cluster"
column tablespace_name format a20 heading "Tablespace"
column table_name format a20 heading "Table"
column tab_column_name format a20 heading "Table Column"
column clu_column_name format a20 heading "Cluster Column"
rem
set pages 56 lines 130 feedback off
start title132 "Cluster Report"
break on owner skip 1on cluster on tablespace
spool cluster&db                        .
select
                a.owner,
                a.cluster_name,
                tablespace_name,
                table_name,
                tab_column_name,
                clu_column_name
from
                dba_clusters a,
                dba_clu_columns b
where
                a.owner = b.owner and
                a.cluster_name=b.cluster_name
order by 1,2,3,4;
spool off
exit
```

The following is an example listing from the report.

```
Date: 05/26/93                "Your Company Name"              Page:   1
Time: 09:17 PM                   Cluster Report                KCGC_DBA
                                "Your" Database
```

OWNER	Cluster	Tablespace	Table	Table Column	Cluster Column
SYS	C_COBJ#	SYSTEM	CCOL$	OBJ#	OBJ#
			CDEF$	OBJ#	OBJ#
	C_FILE#_BLOCK#		SEG$	BLOCK#	SEGBLOCK#
			SEG$	FILE#	SEGFILE#
			UET$	SEGFILE#	SEGFILE#
			UET$	SEGBLOCK#	SEGBLOCK#
	C_OBJ#		CLU$	OBJ#	OBJ#
			COL$	OBJ#	OBJ#
			ICOL$	BO#	OBJ#
			IND$	BO#	OBJ#
			TAB$	OBJ#	OBJ#
	C_TS#		FET$	TS#	TS#
			TS$	TS#	TS#
	C_USER#		TSQ$	USER#	USER#
			USER$	USER#	USER#

The DBA is also interested in the cluster creation statistics. The following SQL report will provide this data.

```
rem
rem File:      CLU_SIZ.SQL
rem Purpose:   Document Cluster Space
rem Use:       From user with access to DBA_ views
rem
rem When       Who          What
rem ------     ----         ------
rem 5/27/93    Mike Ault    \Initial Creation
rem
column owner format a10
column cluster_name format a15 heading "Cluster"
column tablespace_name format a10 heading "Tablespace"
column pct_free format 999999 heading "% Free"
column pct_used format 999999 heading "% Used"
column key_size format 999999 heading "Key Size"
column ini_trans format 999 heading "IT"
column max_trans format 999999 heading "MT"
column initial_extent format 999999999 heading "Initial Ext"
column next_extent format 999999999 heading "Next Ext"
column max_extents format 9999 heading "Max Ext"
column pct_increase format 9999 heading "% Inc"
set pages 56 lines 130 feedback off
start title132 "Cluster Sizing Report"
break on owner skip 1 on tablespace_name
```

```
spool cluster_size&db
select
                        owner,
                        cluster_name,
                        tablespace_name,
                        pct_free,
                        pct_used,
                        key_size,
                        ini_trans,
                        max_trans,
                        initial_extent,
                        ncxt_extent,
                        min_extents,
                        max_extents,
                        pct_increase
from
                        dba_clusters
order by 1,3
/
spool off
exit
```

This is an example listing from the above SQL report script.

```
Date: 05/26/93                      "Your Company Name"                    Page:   1
Time: 09:57 PM                      Cluster Sizing Report                  KCGC_DBA
                                       "Your" Database
```

OWNER Ext	Cluster % Inc	Tablespace %	Free %	Used	Key Size	IT	MT	Initial Ext	Next Ext	Min Ex	Max
SYS 50	C_COBJ#	SYSTEM	50		300	2	255	51200	10240	1	99
50	C_FILE#_BLOCK#		10	40	225	2	255	20480	10240	1	99
50	C_OBJ#		5	40	800	2	255	122880	10240	1	99
50	C_TS#		10	40		2	255	10240	10240	1	99
50	C_USER#		10	40	315	2	255	10240	10240	1	99

Under ORACLE7 there are several new fields in the DBA_CLUSTER view. The next script generates a report on these new columns.

```
rem Name:        clu_typ.sql
rem Purpose:     Report on new DBA_CLUSTER columns
rem Use:         From an account that accesses DBA_ views
rem
```

```
rem    When       Who          What
rem    --------    --------     ------------------
rem    5/26/93    Mike Ault     Initial Creation
rem
column owner format a10 heading "Owner"
column cluster_name format a15 heading "Cluster"
column tablespace_name format a10 heading "Tablespace"
column avg_blocks_per_key format 999999 heading "Blocks per Key"
column cluster_type format a8 Heading "Type"
column function format 999999 heading "Function"
column hashkeys format 99999 heading "# of Keys"
set pages 56 lines 79 feedback off
start title80 "Cluster Type Report"
spool cluster_type&db
select
                    owner,
                    cluster_name,
                    tablespace_name,
                    avg_blocks_per_key,
                    cluster_type, function,
                    hashkeys
from dba_clusters
order by 2
/
spool off
exit
```

The following is an example of the output of the ORACLE7 cluster report.

```
Date: 06/12/93                "Your Company Name"              Page:   1
Time: 12:15 PM              Cluster Statistics Report          DEV7_DBA
                              "Your" Database

Owner   Cluster Name       Tablespace    Blk/Key   Type    Function   # of Keys
------  ----------------   ------------  --------  -------  ---------  -----------
-
SYS     C_COBJ#            SYSTEM                  INDEX
        C_FILE#_BLOCK#
        C_MLOG#
        C_OBJ#
        C_TS#
        C_USER#
        HIST$
```

Under ORACLE7 there is a new database object called a SNAPSHOT. The following script generates a report on these SNAPSHOTS.

```
rem
rem Name:         snap_rep.sql
rem Purpose:      Report on database Snapshots
rem Use:          From an account that accesses DBA_ views
rem
rem    When        Who             What
rem    --------     --------        ------------------
rem    5/27/93     Mike Ault        Initial Creation
rem
set pages 56 lines 130 feedback off
rem
column owner format a10 heading "Owner"
column snapshot format a30 heading "Snapshot"
column source format a30 heading "Source Table"
column link format a20 heading "Link"
column log heading "Use Log?"
column refreshed heading "Refreshed?"
column error format a20 heading "Error?"
column type format a10 heading "Refresh Type"
column refreshed heading "Last Refresh"
column start format a13 heading "Start Refresh"
column error heading "Error"
column type heading "Type Refresh"
column next format a13 heading "Next Refresh"
rem
start oracle$sql:title132 "Snapshot Report"
spool snap_rep&db
rem
select
                    owner,
                    name||'.'||table_name Snapshot,
                    master_view,
                    master_owner||'.'||master Source,
                    master_link Link,
                    can_use_log Log,
                    last_refresh Refreshed,
                    start_with start,
                    error,
                    type ,
                    next,
                    start_with Started,
                    query
from
                    dba_snapshots
order by 1,3,5;
rem
spool off
exit
```

This is an example listing from the snapshot report.

```
Date: 06/10/93                        "Your  Company Name "                          Page:   1
Time: 04:28 PM                         Snapshot Report                              DEV7_DBA
                                       "Your Database"


Owner    Snapshot        VIEW     Source Table  Link Log  Last Ref   Start Ref  R Type  Next Ref   STARTED   QUERY
DEV7_DBA TEST.SNAP$_TEST MVIEW$_  DEV7_DBA.      YES       10-JUN-93  10-JUN-93  FAST    SYSDATE+7  10-JUN-93 SELECT CHECK_DATE
                         TEST     HIT_RATIOS                                                                 FROM   HIT_RATIOS
```

In addition to snapshots, there are snapshot logs that allow for fast refresh of the snapshots. The following SQL script generates a report of snapshot logs.

```
rem Name:       snap_log_rep.sql
rem Purpose:    Report on database Snapshot Logs
rem Use:        From an account that accesses DBA_ views
rem
rem    When        Who          What
rem    --------    --------     ------------------
rem    5/27/93     Mike Ault    Initial Creation
rem
set pages 56 lines 130 feedback off
start title132 "Snapshot Log Report"
spool snap_log_rep&db
rem
column log_owner format a10 heading "Owner"
column master format a20 heading "Master"
column log_table format a20 heading "Snapshot"
column trigger format a20 heading "Trigger Text"
column current heading "Last Refresh"
rem
select
                log_owner,
                master,
                log_table table,
                log_trigger trigger,
                current_snapshots current
from
                dba_snapshot_logs
order by 1;
rem
spool off
exit
```

Under ORACLE7 the DBA nees to periodically run the ANALYZE command on the objects in the
database in order for cost-based optimization to work. The following script generates a script that runs ANA-
LYZE on the objects for a user. You may want to alter this to do an estimate rather than a full compute if you
have large tables.

```
rem
rem name           : ANLYZIT.SQL
rem purpose        : Build analyze script and run it for a user's tables
rem use            : Gather statistics for cost based optimization
rem limitations    : None
rem revisions:
rem Date:     Who:        What:
rem 6/10/93   Mike Ault    Initial Creation
rem
set lines 80 pages 0 heading off feedback off echo off
prompt Creating analyze script for tables
set termout off
spool analyze.sql
rem
select
                'analyze table '||table_name||' compute statistics;'
from
                user_tables;
rem
spool off
set termout on
prompt Analyzing all tables for user
start analyze
exit
```

The following report generates a report for optimizing the data dictionary caches for a version 6 database. The report restricts output to active caches and caches where getmisses have occurred.

```
REM
REM NAME           : DD_CACHE.SQL
REM PURPOSE        : GENERATE REPORT TO SHOW DATA DICTIONARY CACHE CONDITION
REM USE            : FROM EOW_WEEKLY_STATUS.COM
REM Limitations    : None
REM Revisions:
REM Date           Modified By     Reason For change
REM 21-AUG-1991    MIKE AULT       INITIAL CREATE
REM 27-NOV-1991    MIKE AULT       ADD % CALCULATION TO REPORT
REM 28-OCT-1992    MIKE AULT       ADD CALL TO TITLE PROCEDURE
SET FLUSH OFF
SET TERM OFF
SET PAGESIZE 59
SET LINESIZE 79
rem
COLUMN PARAMETER FORMAT A20;
COLUMN T_DATE NOPRINT NEW_VALUE T_DATE;
COLUMN PERCENT FORMAT 999.99 HEADING "%";
rem
```

```
SELECT
                SYSDATE T_DATE
FROM
                DUAL;
rem
START TITLE80 "DATA DICTIONARY CACHE STATISTICS REPORT"
DEFINE OUTPUT = 'CACHE_STAT&DB..LIS'
SPOOL &OUTPUT
rem
SELECT
                PARAMETER,
                GETS,
                GETMISSES,
                ( GETMISSES / GETS * 100) PERCENT,
                COUNT,
                USAGE
FROM V$ROWCACHE
WHERE
                GETS > 100 AND
                GETMISSES > 0
ORDER BY PARAMETER;
SPOOL OFF
EXIT
```

The next listing shows the output from the DD Cache report.

```
Date: 06/04/93              "Your Company Name"              Page:  1
Time: 04:17 PM         DATA DICTIONARY CACHE STATISTICS      DEV_DBA
                            "Your" Database

PARAMETER              GETS        GETMISSES    %       COUNT        USAGE
--------------------   ----------  ----------   ------  ----------   ----------
dc_columns             141779      15072        10.63   1000         1000
dc_indexes             27280       188          .69     150          149
dc_object_ids          4293        7            .16     75           6
dc_objects             27178       757          2.79    500          500
dc_rollback_segments   8456        6            .07     25           7
dc_sequences           375         4            1.07    30           4
dc_synonyms            3721        209          5.62    350          209
dc_table_grants        4704        257          5.46    150          110
dc_tables              26963       296          1.10    250          249
dc_tablespaces         171         12           7.02    30           12
dc_usernames           5636        40           .71     100          40
dc_users               5735        30           .52     100          30

12 rows selected.
```

One indicator of database health is hit ratio. Unfortunately, this is a dynamic parameter, and in order to monitor it the DBA must capture the data into a DBA defined table. The next few scripts allow the DBA to capture and monitor not only the ratio but the number of users and usage as a function of IO. Other parameters of interest could be added to the selects in the PL/SQL script if the DBA wishes to monitor them over time.

This first script is designed to be run hourly via an automated operating system procedure.

```
REM
REM NAME            :RUN_B_HRATIO.SQL
REM PURPOSE         :RUN PL/SQL PROCEDURE TO LOAD HIT RATIO AND USAGE DATA
REM USE             :FROM RUN_B_HRATIO.COM
REM Limitations     : None
REM Revisions:
REM   Date          Modified By     Reason For change
REM   10-JUL-1992   M. AULT         INITIAL CREATE
REM
get batch_hratio.sql
run
exit
```

The above script calls this next PL/SQL routine to calculate and load pertinent values into the hit ratio table.

```
DECLARE
    C_DATE DATE;
    C_HOUR NUMBER := 0;
    H_RATIO NUMBER := 0;
    CON_GETS NUMBER := 0;
    DB_GETS NUMBER := 0;
    P_READS NUMBER := 0;
    STAT_NAME CHAR(64);
    temp_NAME CHAR(64);
    STAT_VAL NUMBER := 0;
    USERS  NUMBER := 0;
BEGIN
  select to_char(sysdate,'DD-MON-YY') into c_date from dual;
  select to_char(sysdate,'HH24') into c_hour from dual;
  STAT_NAME := 'db block gets';
      select a.name, b.value  into temp_name, db_gets from v$statname a, v$sysstat b
                where a.statistic# = b.statistic# AND A.NAME = STAT_NAME;
  STAT_NAME := 'consistent gets';
      select a.name,b.value into temp_name, con_gets from v$statname a, v$sysstat b
                where a.statistic# = b.statistic# AND A.NAME = STAT_NAME;
  STAT_NAME := 'physical reads';
      select a.name,b.value into temp_name, p_reads from v$statname a, v$sysstat b
                where a.statistic# = b.statistic# AND A.NAME = STAT_NAME;
  select count(*)-4 into users from v$session;
  H_RATIO := (((DB_GETS+CON_GETS-p_reads)/(DB_GETS+CON_GETS))*100);
  INSERT INTO  hit_ratios
```

```
      VALUES (c_date,c_hour,db_gets,con_gets,p_reads,h_ratio,0,0,users);
commit;
update hit_ratios set period_hit_ratio =
        (select  round((((h2.consistent-h1.consistent)+(h2.db_block_gets
               h1.db_block_gets)-
    (h2.phy_reads-h1.phy_reads))/((h2.consistent-h1.consistent)+
         (h2.db_block_gets-h1.db_block_gets)))*100,2) from hit_ratios h1, hit_ratios
              h2
       where h2.check_date =  hit_ratios.check_date  and  h2.check_hour  =
              hit_ratios.check_hour
     and ((h1.check_date = h2.check_date and h1.check_hour+1 = h2.check_hour) or
    (h1.check_date+1 = h2.check_date and h1.check_hour = '23' and h2.check_hour='0')))
where period_hit_ratio = 0;
  COMMIT;
update hit_ratios set period_USAGE =
    (select ((h2.consistent-h1.consistent)+(h2.db_block_gets-h1.db_block_gets))
    from hit_ratios h1, hit_ratios h2 where h2.check_date = hit_ratios.check_date
    and h2.check_hour = hit_ratios.check_hour  and ((h1.check_date = h2.check_date
    and h1.check_hour+1 = h2.check_hour) or (h1.check_date+1 = h2.check_date and
    h1.check_hour = '23' and h2.check_hour='0'))) where period_USAGE = 0;
  COMMIT;
EXCEPTION
    WHEN ZERO_DIVIDE THEN
    INSERT INTO  hit_ratios  VALUES
               (c_date,c_hour,db_gets,con_gets,p_reads,0,0,0,users);
    COMMIT;
END;
```

Once the data is collected, the DBA needs a method of retrieving and listing the information. The data can be displayed as a report or as a graph. The following SQL script report generates a tabular format report of hit ratios, usage, and users.

```
REM
REM NAME          :HITRATIO_SUMMARY.SQL
REM PURPOSE       :GENERATE SUMMARY REPORT OF PERIOD HIT RATIOS AND USAGE
REM PURPOSE       :BETWEEN TWO DATES
REM USE           :FROM STATUS_REPORTS.COM
REM Limitations   : None
REM Revisions:
REM   Date          Modified By     Reason For change
REM   10-JUL-1992   M.AULT          INITIAL CREATE
REM
set verify off pages 58 newpage 0
start title80 "HIT RATIO AND USAGE FOR &&CHECK_DATE1 TO &&CHECK_DATE2"
define output = 'hitratio_summary&db..lis'
spool &output
select
               CHECK_DATE,
               CHECK_HOUR,
               PERIOD_HIT_RATIO,
```

```
                PERIOD_USAGE,
                USERS
from
                hit_ratios
where
                CHECK_DATE BETWEEN '&&CHECK_DATE1' AND '&&CHECK_DATE2'
order by
                CHECK_DATE,CHECK_HOUR;
SPOOL OFF
PAUSE PRESS RETURN TO CONTINUE
EXIT
```

The following listing shows an example of the output of the above script.

```
Date: 06/05/93                "Your Company Name"                Page:  1
Time: 03:39 PM    HIT RATIO AND USAGE FOR 18-may-93 TO 18-may-93    DEV_DBA
                         "Your" Database

CHECK_DAT    CHECK_HOUR    PERIOD_HIT_RATIO    PERIOD_USAGE    USERS
---------    ----------    ----------------    ------------    ----------
18-MAY-93    0             18.78               2172            1
18-MAY-93    1             19.01               2178            1
18-MAY-93    2             19.01               2178            1
18-MAY-93    3             18.78               2172            1
18-MAY-93    4             18.78               2172            1
18-MAY-93    5             18.78               2172            1
18-MAY-93    6             18.78               2172            1
18-MAY-93    7             18.78               2172            1
18-MAY-93    8             21.7                2253            4
18-MAY-93    9             24.41               2360            5
18-MAY-93    10            55.27               3946            6
18-MAY-93    11            92.95               28578           6
18-MAY-93    12            50.21               3547            5
18-MAY-93    13            18.78               2172            5
18-MAY-93    14            20.89               2259            5
18-MAY-93    15            19.08               2180            5
18-MAY-93    16            20.07               2207            5
18-MAY-93    17            19.08               2180            5
18-MAY-93    18            19.08               2180            1
18-MAY-93    19            19.21               2186            1
18-MAY-93    20            19.08               2180            1
18-MAY-93    21            19.08               2180            1
18-MAY-93    22            19.08               2180            1
18-MAY-93    23            19.08               2180            1
24 rows selected
```

The following graphs show hit ratio over time. A script similar to the ones that generated these graphs follows.

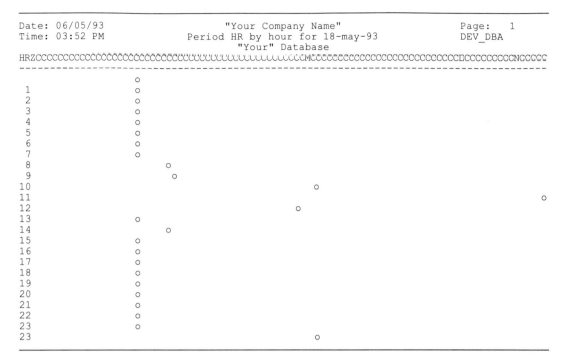

```
Date: 06/05/93                          "Your Company Name"                        Page:    1
Time: 03:52 PM                     Period HR by hour for 18-may-93                  DEV_DBA
                                          "Your" Database
HRZCCCCCCCCCCCCCCCCCCCCCCCCCCCCCCCCCCCCCCCCCCCCCCCCCCMCCCCCCCCCCCCCCCCCCCCCCCCCCCCCCCCCDCCCCCCCCCCNGGGGC
---------------------------------------------------------------------------------------------------
 1                  o
 2                  o
 3                  o
 4                  o
 5                  o
 6                  o
 7                  o
 8                      o
 9                        o
10                                           o
11                                                                                              o
12                                      o
13                  o
14                      o
15                 o
16                 o
17                 o
18                 o
19                 o
20                 o
21                 o
22                 o
23                 o
23                                      o
```

Periodic hit ratio for 18 May 1993

```
Date: 06/05/93                          "Your Company Name"                        Page:    1
Time: 03:52 PM                   HR on the hour by hour on 18-may-93                DEV_DBA
                                          "Your" Database
HRZCCCCCCCCCCCCCCCCCCCCCCCCCCCCCCCCCCCCCCCCCCCCCCCCCMCCCCCCCCCCCCCCCCCCCCCCCCCCCCCCCCCCCCCCCCNCCCCCCCCC
---------------------------------------------------------------------------------------------------
                                             o
 1                                           o
 2                                        o
 3                                        o
 4                                      o
 5                                      o
 6                                    o
 7                                    o
 8                                    o
 9                      o
10                      o
11                                  o
12                                  o
13                                 o
14                                  o
15                                o
16                                o
17                                o
18                              o
19                              o
20                              o
21                            o
22                            o
```

Graph of cumulative hit ratio for 18 May 1993

This is the example report script for the hit ratio graphs. This should work for any 132-column format printer.

```
REM
REM NAME          :HRATIO_REPORT.SQL
REM PURPOSE       :CREATE PLOT OF PERIOD HIT RATIO FOR 1 DAY
REM USE           :FROM STATUS_REPORTS.COM
REM Limitations   : None
REM Revisions:
REM   Date          Modified By      Reason For change
REM   10-JUL-1992   M. AULT          INITIAL CREATE
REM
host SET TERM/WID=132 REM: For VMS only, won't work under UNIX
set lines 131 newpage 0 VERIFY OFF pages 180 space 0 feedback off
column hr format 99
start title132 "Period HR for &&check_date1 TO &&check_date2"
define output = 'hratio_graph_BT_DATES&db.lis'
spool &output
select
    check_hour hr,
    decode(round(period_hit_ratio),0,'o',null) zchk0,
    decode(round(period_hit_ratio),1,'o',null) chk1,
    decode(round(period_hit_ratio),2,'o',null) chk2,
    decode(round(period_hit_ratio),3,'o',null) chk3,
    decode(round(period_hit_ratio),4,'o',null) chk4,
    decode(round(period_hit_ratio),5,'o',null) chk5,
                     .
                     .
                     .
    decode(round(period_hit_ratio),94,'o',null) chk94,
    decode(round(period_hit_ratio),95,'o',null) chk95,
    decode(round(period_hit_ratio),96,'o',null) chk96,
    decode(round(period_hit_ratio),97,'o',null) chk97,
    decode(round(period_hit_ratio),98,'o',null) chk98,
    decode(round(period_hit_ratio),99,'o',null) chk99,
    decode(round(period_hit_ratio),100,'o',null) chk100
from hit_ratios
WHERE CHECK_DATE BETWEEN '&&CHECK_DATE1' AND '&&CHECK_DATE2'
order by CHECK_DATE,check_hour;
spool off
PAUSE 'PRESS RETURN TO CONTINUE'
host SET TERM/WID=80  rem: Only for VMS, will not work on UNIX
exit
```

The decodes have to be done from 0 to 100. The decodes between 5 and 94 have been removed from the listing to shorten it. To function properly, they will have to be entered back into the script. If the script is reentered by hand. The copy on the accompanying disk is complete. The host commands are only valid for VMS. They change the display to 132-column format. Check your operating system for the proper command to achieve this if you are on UNIX.

The database buffers are tuned via the v$kcbrbh and x$kcbcbh tables. The v$kcbrbh table shows the results from increasing the number of buffers. The x$kcbcbh table shows the results from decreasing the number of buffers. Some example queries and reports to take advantage of these tables follow.

This is a select that sums the possible loss of hits for the specified dropped increment of buffers.

```
SELECT SUM(count) "interval total"
   FROM v$kcbrbh
   WHERE indx BETWEEN ( interval start, interval end);
```

This is a select that groups the results in ranges. This can be adjusted to any desired step level.

```
SELECT
   50 * TRUNC(indx/50)+1||' to '||50 * (TRUNC(indx/50)+1) "interval",
   SUM(count) "Buffer Cache Hits"
FROM  sys.x$kcbrbh
GROUP BY TRUNC(indx/50);
```

The following is an example of the output from the above query.

```
Interval        Buffer Cache Hits
1 to 50         17350
51 to 100       9345
101 to 150      404
151 to 200      19568
```

This is a listing of a more detailed report generated from the v$kcbrbh table.

```
rem   ***********************************************************************
rem
rem   NAME: SGA_INC.sql
rem
rem   HISTORY:
rem   Date        Who                  What
rem   --------    ------------------   -----------------------------------------
rem   10/25/92    Cary Millsap         Creation
rem   01/07/93    Michael Brouillette  Switched to title80
rem   06/05/93    Mike Ault            Added capability to input buffer interval
rem
rem   FUNCTION: Examine the statistice in the X$KCBRBH table with the intent to
rem             increase the size of the SGA.
rem
```

```
rem    *******************************************************************
col bufval new_value nbuf noprint
col thits new_value tot_hits noprint
select   value  bufval
from  v$parameter
where
  lower(name) = 'db_block_lru_extended_statistics';
select sum(count)  thits from v$kcbrbh;
start title80 "Prospective Hits if &nbuf Cache Buffers were Added"
col interval   format        a20 justify c heading 'Buffers'
col cache_hits format 999,999,990 justify c heading -
  'Cache Hits that would have been|gained by adding Buffers'
col cum format 99.99 heading 'Percent of Gain'
set termout off feedback off verify off echo off
spool sga_inc&db
select
  lpad(to_char((&nbuf/&incr)*trunc(indx/(&nbuf/&&incr))+1,'999,990'),8)||' to '||
  lpad(to_char((&nbuf/&&incr)*(trunc(indx/(&nbuf/&&incr))+1),'999,990'),8)||
            interval,
  sum(count) cache_hits, sum(count)/&tot_hits * 100 cum
from
  v$kcbrbh
group by
  trunc(indx/(&nbuf/&&incr));
spool off
set termout on feedback 15 verify on
undef nbuf
exit
```

The next query shows the results of decreasing the number of buffers for the specified buffer interval.

```
SELECT SUM(count) "Hit Misses"
   FROM x$kcbcbh
   WHERE indx >= 100;
```

To generate a listing for a series of decrements, the following query should be used.

```
SELECT 10*TRUNC(indx/10)+1||' to '||10*(TRUNC(indx/10)+1) "Interval",
SUM(count) 'Buffer Hits'
FROM x$kcbcbh
WHERE indx > 0
GROUP BY TRUNC(indx/10);
```

This is an example of the output from the above query.

```
Interval    Buffer Hits
1 to 10     2500
11 to 20    1345
21 to 30    1097
31 to 40    896
41 to 50    110
```

This is a listing of a SQL report script to show details of decrementing the number of buffers.

```
rem  ***********************************************************************
rem  NAME: SGA_DEC.sql
rem
rem  HISTORY:
rem  Date       Who                 What
rem  --------   ------------------  -------------------------------------------
rem  10/25/92   Cary Millsap        Creation
rem  01/07/93   Michael Brouillette Switched to title80
rem  06/05/93   Mike Ault           Added selectable ranges
rem  FUNCTION: Examine statistice in the X$KCBCBH table with intent to shrink
rem            the SGA.
rem  ***********************************************************************
col bufval new_value nbuf noprint
col thits new_value tot_hits noprint

select value  bufval
from v$parameter
where
  lower(name) = 'db_block_buffers';
select sum(count) thits
from x$kcbhcbh;
start title80 "Lost Hits if &nbuf Cache Buffers were Removed"
col interval   format        a20 justify c heading 'Buffers'
col cache_hits format 999,999,990 justify c heading -
  'Hits that would have been lost|had Cache Buffers been removed'
col cum fromat 99.99 'Percent of loss'
set termout off feedback off verify off echo off
spool sga_dec&db

select
            lpad(to_char(&&incr*trunc(indx/&&incr)+1,'999,990'),8)||' to '||
            lpad(to_char(&&incr*(trunc(indx/&&incr)+1),'999,990'),8) interval,
            sum(count)  cache_hits,
            sum(count)/&tot_hits * 100 cum
from
            x$kcbcbh
where
            indx > 0
group by
            trunc(indx/&&incr) ;
spool off
```

```
set termout on feedback 15 verify on
exit
```

The DBA also needs to monitor the efficiency of file IO operations. This will show the status of buffers, indexes, and table placement. The following script calculates file IO efficiency.

```
REM
REM NAME        :FILE_EFF.SQL
REM PURPOSE     :GENERATE FILE IO EFFICIENCIES REPORT
REM USE         :FROM STATUS_REPORTS.COM
REM Limitations :MUST BE RUN FROM ORACLE DBA ACCOUNT
REM Revisions:
REM Date           Modified By     Reason For change
REM 10-JUL-1992    M. AULT         INITIAL CREATE
REM 07-JUN-1993    M.AULT          Added reads to writes, reformatted
REM
$SET TERM/WIDT=132
$set term/noecho
connect  sys/&sys_password
$set term/echo
SET PAGES 58 NEWPAGE 0
SET LINES 131
COLUMN EFFICIENCY FORMAT 999.99 HEADING '% Eff'
COLUMN RW FORMAT 9,999,999,999 HEADING 'Phys Block read/writes'
COLUMN TS FORMAT A22 HEADING 'TABLESPACE NAME'
start title132 "FILE IO EFFICIENCY"
BREAK ON TS
DEFINE OUTPUT = 'file_io_eff&DB..rep'
spool &OUTPUT
SELECT
                SUBSTR(TS.NAME,1,30) TS,
                SUBSTR(i.kcffinam,1,40) name,
                x.kcfiopbr+x.kcfiopbw RW,
                decode(x.kcfiopbr,0,null,round(100*x.kcfiopyr/x.kcfiopbr,2))
            efficiency
from
            x$kcfio x,
            ts$ ts,
            x$kcffi i,
            file$ f
where
            i.kcffiidn=f.file#
            and ts.ts#=f.ts#
            and x.kcfiofno=f.file# AND i.kcffinam IS NOT NULL
ORDER BY
            I.KCFFINAM;
spool off
PAUSE 'PRESS RETURN TO CONTINUE'
$ SET TERM/WID=80
exit
```

The following listing shows the output from the efficiency report.

```
Date: 06/07/93                    "Your Company Name"                Page.   1
Time: 10:46 AM                    FILE IO EFFICIENCY                 SYS
                                   "Your" Database

TABLESPACE NAME   NAME                                      Phys Block read/writes    % Eff
---------------   ----------------------------------------  ----------------------    --------
CASE_RLBK_SEG     M_DISK6:[M_ORACLE6.DB_CASE]ORA_CASE_ROLL  14,411                    100
APPL_INDEXES      M_DISK8:[M_ORACLE6.DB_CASE]ORA_APPL_IDX_  791                       95.92
CASE_INDEX        M_DISK8:[M_ORACLE6.DB_CASE]ORA_CASE_INDE  3,279                     100
APPLICATIONS      M_DISK9:[M_ORACLE6.DB_CASE]ORA_APPL_1.DB  45,765                    23.07
CASE_TRAINING     M_DISK9:[M_ORACLE6.DB_CASE]ORA_CASE_TRAI  2,942                     21.47
                  M_DISK9:[M_ORACLE6.DB_CASE]ORA_CASE_TRAI  878                       18.36
CASE_W_AREA       M_DISK9:[M_ORACLE6.DB_CASE]ORA_CASE_WORK  259,531                   9.28
                  M_DISK9:[M_ORACLE6.DB_CASE]ORA_CASE_WORK  24,513                    13.75
DBA_TS            M_DISK9:[M_ORACLE6.DB_CASE]ORA_DBA_TS.DB  254                       61.72
DEFAULT_USER      M_DISK9:[M_ORACLE6.DB_CASE]ORA_DEFAULT_U  1,880                     36.09
SYSTEM            M_DISK9:[M_ORACLE6.DB_CASE]ORA_SYSTEM.DB  205,815                   22.85
                  M_DISK9:[M_ORACLE6.DB_CASE]ORA_SYSTEM_2.  198,757                   9.64
                  M_DISK9:[M_ORACLE6.DB_CASE]ORA_SYSTEM_3.  28,509                    21.12
                  M_DISK9:[M_ORACLE6.DB_CASE]ORA_SYSTEM_4.  20,507                    40.82
                  M_DISK9:[M_ORACLE6.DB_CASE]ORA_SYSTEM_5.  181,513                   10.11
                  M_DISK9:[M_ORACLE6.DB_CASE]ORA_SYSTEM_6.  193,892                   19.62
TEMP_USER1        M_DISK9:[M_ORACLE6.DB_CASE]ORA_TEMP_USER  3,703

17 rows selected.
```

The DBA also needs to monitor for all types of contention. The following script reports on some PL/SQL calculated statistics that will help the DBA to determine status of contention and other tuning variables.

```
REM
REM NAME          :CAL_STAT_REPORT.SQL
REM PURPOSE       :GENERATE CALCULATED STATISITICS REPORT USING CAL_STAT.SQL
REM USE           :FROM STATUS_REPORTS.COM
REM Limitations   :
REM Revisions:
REM Date          Modified By     Reason For change
REM 05-MAY-1992   Mike Ault       Initial Creation
REM
SET PAGES 58  NEWPAGE 0
COLUMN TODAY NEW_VALUE _DATE
GET ORACLE$SQL:CAL_STAT.SQL
R
START TITLE80 "CALCULATED STATISTICS REPORT"
DEFINE OUTPUT = 'CAL_STAT_REPORT&DD..LIS'
SPOOL &OUTPUT
SELECT * FROM DBA_TEMP;
SPOOL OFF

Listing of CAL_STAT.SQL - The called PL/SQL routine
```

```
DECLARE
    STAT_VAL NUMBER := 0;
    P_COUNT NUMBER := 0;
    PC_U NUMBER := 0;
    R_CALLS NUMBER := 0;
    H_RATIO NUMBER := 0;
    W_CONT  NUMBER := 0;
    DB_GETS NUMBER := 0;
    CON_GETS NUMBER := 0;
    P_READS NUMBER := 0;
    BB_WAITS NUMBER := 0;
    U_CALLS NUMBER := 0;
    CALLS_U NUMBER := 0;
    RLOG_WAIT NUMBER := 0;
    STAT_NAME CHAR(64);    /*Change to VARCHAR2 in ORACLE7*/
    TEMP_NAME CHAR(64);    /*Change to VARCHAR2 in ORACLE7*/
BEGIN
  DELETE DBA_TEMP;
  STAT_NAME := 'parse count';
      select a.name,b.value into TEMP_NAME, p_count
              from v$statname a, v$sysstat b  /* Selects can be made entirely */
              where a.statistic# = b.statistic#
              AND A.NAME = STAT_NAME;          /* from v$sysstat under ORACLE7*/
  STAT_NAME := 'recursive calls';
      select a.name,b.value into TEMP_name, r_calls
              from v$statname a, v$sysstat b
              where a.statistic# = b.statistic#  AND A.NAME = STAT_NAME;
  STAT_NAME := 'user calls';
      select a.name,b.value into TEMP_NAME, u_calls
              from v$statname a, v$sysstat b
              where a.statistic# = b.statistic# AND A.NAME = STAT_NAME;
  STAT_NAME := 'db block gets';
      select a.name,b.value into TEMP_NAME, db_gets
              from v$statname a, v$sysstat b
              where a.statistic# = b.statistic# AND A.NAME = STAT_NAME;
  STAT_NAME := 'consistent gets';
      select a.name,b.value into TEMP_NAME, con_gets
              from v$statname a, v$sysstat b
              where a.statistic# = b.statistic#  AND A.NAME = STAT_NAME;
  STAT_NAME := 'physical reads';
      select a.name,b.value into TEMP_NAME, p_reads
              from v$statname a, v$sysstat b
              where a.statistic# = b.statistic#  AND A.NAME = STAT_NAME;
  STAT_NAME := 'buffer busy waits';
      select a.name,b.value into TEMP_NAME, bb_waits
              from v$statname a, v$sysstat b
              where a.statistic# = b.statistic#  AND A.NAME = STAT_NAME;
    PC_U    := (P_COUNT/U_CALLS);
    CALLS_U := (R_CALLS/U_CALLS);
    H_RATIO := (100*(DB_GETS+CON_GETS)/(DB_GETS+CON_GETS+P_READS));
    W_CONT  := (BB_WAITS/(DB_GETS+CON_GETS));
  STAT_NAME := 'RECURSIVE CALLS PER USER';
    INSERT INTO DBA_TEMP VALUES (STAT_NAME, CALLS_U);
```

```
   STAT_NAME := 'CUMMULATIVE HIT RATIO';
      INSERT INTO DBA_TEMP VALUES (STAT_NAME, H_RATIO);
   STAT_NAME := 'BUFFER ACCESS WAIT CONTENTION';
      INSERT INTO DBA_TEMP VALUES (STAT_NAME, W_CONT);
   STAT_NAME := 'CALLS PER PARSE';
      INSERT INTO DBA_TEMP VALUES (STAT_NAME, PC_U);
   STAT_NAME := 'dbwr free needed';    /* Obsolete in ORACLE7*/
         select a.name,b.value into TEMP_NAME, stat_val
                  from v$statname a, v$sysstat b
                  where a.statistic# = b.statistic# AND A.NAME = STAT_NAME;
      INSERT INTO DBA_TEMP VALUES (STAT_NAME, STAT_VAL);
   STAT_NAME := 'dbwr free low';    /*Obsolete in ORACLE7*/
         select a.name,b.value into TEMP_NAME, stat_val
                  from v$statname a, v$sysstat b
                  where a.statistic# = b.statistic# AND A.NAME = STAT_NAME;
      INSERT INTO DBA_TEMP VALUES (STAT_NAME, STAT_VAL);
    STAT_NAME := 'enqueue timeouts';
         select a.name,b.value into TEMP_NAME, stat_val
                  from v$statname a, v$sysstat b
                  where a.statistic# = b.statistic# AND A.NAME = STAT_NAME;
      INSERT INTO DBA_TEMP VALUES (STAT_NAME, STAT_VAL);
  STAT_NAME := 'table scans (short tables)';
         select a.name,b.value into TEMP_NAME, stat_val
                  from v$statname a, v$sysstat b
                  where a.statistic# = b.statistic#  AND A.NAME = STAT_NAME;
      INSERT INTO DBA_TEMP VALUES (STAT_NAME, STAT_VAL);
   STAT_NAME := 'table scans (long tables)';
         select a.name,b.value into TEMP_NAME, stat_val
                  from v$statname a, v$sysstat b
                  where a.statistic# = b.statistic#  AND A.NAME = STAT_NAME;
      INSERT INTO DBA_TEMP VALUES (STAT_NAME, STAT_VAL);
   STAT_NAME := 'table fetch continued row';
         select a.name,b.value into TEMP_NAME, stat_val
                  from v$statname a, v$sysstat b
                  where a.statistic# = b.statistic#  AND A.NAME = STAT_NAME;
      INSERT INTO DBA_TEMP VALUES (STAT_NAME, STAT_VAL);
   STAT_NAME := 'sorts (memory)';
         select a.name,b.value into TEMP_NAME, stat_val
                  from v$statname a, v$sysstat b
                  where a.statistic# = b.statistic#  AND A.NAME = STAT_NAME;
      INSERT INTO DBA_TEMP VALUES (STAT_NAME, STAT_VAL);
   STAT_NAME := 'sorts (disk)';
         select a.name,b.value into TEMP_NAME, stat_val
                  from v$statname a, v$sysstat b
                  where a.statistic# = b.statistic#  AND A.NAME = STAT_NAME;
      INSERT INTO DBA_TEMP VALUES (STAT_NAME, STAT_VAL);
   STAT_NAME := 'redo log space wait time';
         select a.name,b.value into TEMP_NAME, stat_val
                  from v$statname a, v$sysstat b
                  where a.statistic# = b.statistic#  AND A.NAME = STAT_NAME;
      INSERT INTO DBA_TEMP VALUES (STAT_NAME, STAT_VAL);
   COMMIT;
EXCEPTION
```

```
    WHEN ZERO_DIVIDE THEN
    INSERT INTO DBA_TEMP VALUES (STAT_NAME,0);
    COMMIT;
END;
```

Note the statisitics that are invalid for ORACLE7 that must be removed before running this routine against an ORACLE7 database, or it will fail.

This next PL/SQL select should be substituted into the above PL/SQL routine for it to function under ORACLE7. The call to the V$STATNAME table is no longer needed since the STAT_NAME is stored in the V$SYSSTAT table under ORACLE7.

```
select name, value into TEMP_NAME, stat_val
from  v$sysstat where NAME = STAT_NAME;
```

The following is an example listing from the above report for a version 6 database.

```
Date: 06/04/93                   "Your Company Name"              Page:   1
Time: 04:09 PM             CALCULATED STATISTICS REPORT           KCGC_DBA
                                 "Your" Database

STAT_NAME                              STAT_VALUE
---------------------------------- ----------
RECURSIVE CALLS PER USER               1.28859702
CUMULATIVE HIT RATIO                   88.2306292
BUFFER ACCESS WAIT CONTENTION          .000085936
CALLS PER PARSE                        .08003804
dbwr free needed                       0            Obsolete in ORACLE7
dbwr free low                          295          Obsolete in ORACLE7
enqueue timeouts                       17
table scans (short tables)             4255
table scans (long tables)              7497
table fetch continued row              61
sorts (memory)                         12745
sorts (disk)                           6
redo log space wait time               0

13 rows selected.
```

This next script provides the details on any contention indicated by the "buffer busy waits" statistic.

```
REM
REM   NAME      : CONTEND.SQL
REM   PURPOSE   : SHOWS WHERE POSSIBLE CONTENTION FOR RESOURCES IN
REM               BUFFER BUSY WAITS
```

```
REM   USE        : TO PINPOINT ADDITIONAL TUNING AREAS.
REM REV 0. DOCUMENTED ON PAGE 5-6 OF TUNING MANUAL. M. AULT 14-AUG-1992
REM
SET VERIFY OFF FEEDBACK OFF
SET PAGES 58
SET LINES 79
START TITLE80 "AREA OF CONTENTION REPORT"
DEFINE OUTPUT = 'CONTEND_AREA&DB..LIS'
SPOOL &OUTPUT
SELECT
            CLASS,
            SUM(COUNT) TOTAL_WAITS,
            sum(time) TOTAL_TIME
FROM
            V$WAITSTAT
group by
            class;
SPOOL OFF
PAUSE PRESS RETURN TO CONTINUE
EXIT
```

The following is an example output from the above report.

```
Date: 06/03/93            "Your Company Name"              Page:   1
Time: 08:25 AM         AREA OF CONTENTION REPORT         ELWOOD_DBA
                          "Your" Database

CLASS                   TOTAL_WAITS      TOTAL_TIME
------------------      ------------     -----------
data block              68               0
free list               0                0
save undo block         0                0
save undo header        0                0
segment header          1                0
sort block              0                0
system undo block       0                0
system undo header      0                0
undo block              0                0
undo header             1                0

10 rows selected
```

Another form of contention is latch contention. The next SQL script allows the DBA to monitor latches without the need to wade through several SQLDBA screens in monitor for the few latches of interest.

```
REM
REM NAME         : LATCH_CO.SQL
REM PURPOSE      : Genereate latch contention report
```

```
REM USE          : From SQLPlus or other front end
REM Limitations  : None
REM Revisions:
REM Date       Modified By      Reason For change
REM 5 DEC 92   Mike Ault        Initial Creation
REM
COLUMN NAME FORMAT A30
COLUMN RATIO FORMAT 999.999
SET PAGES 58 NEWPAGE 0
start title80 "LATCH CONTENTION REPORT"
define output = 'CONTENTION&db..LIS'
SPOOL &output
rem
SELECT
           A.NAME,
           100.*B.TIMEOUTS/B.WAITS RATIO
FROM
           V$LATCHNAME A,
           V$LATCH B
WHERE
           A.LATCH# = B.LATCH# AND
           B.TIMEOUTS > 0;
SPOOL OFF
PAUSE PRESS RETURN TO CONTINUE
EXIT
```

Notice that only latches showing timeouts are reported.
Under ORACLE7 the following query will give latch status.

```
SELECT
A.NAME,
100.*B.MISSES/B.GETS RATIO1
100.*B.IMMEDIATE_MISSES/(B.IMMEDIATE_GETS+b.IMMEDIATE_MISSES) RATIO2
FROM
V$LATCHNAME A, V$LATCH B WHERE
A.LATCH# = B.LATCH# AND B.MISSES > 0;
```

The following listing is an example report from the latch contention script.

```
Date: 06/04/93              "Your Company Name"            Page:   1
Time: 04:04 PM             LATCH CONTENTION REPORT         KCGC_DBA
                             "Your" Database
NAME                            RATIO
------------------------------  --------
process allocation              .101
session allocation              .003
messages                        .002
enqueues                        .014
```

```
cache buffers chains              .000
cache buffers lru chain           .030
cache buffer handles              .001
multiblock read objects           .005
redo allocation                   .032
redo copy                      200.000
dml/ddl allocation                .005
row cache objects                 .008

12 rows selected.
```

```
rem
rem Name           : Lib_cache.sql
rem Purpose        : Provide report on library cache in the SGA
rem Use            : From SQLPLUS
rem Limitations    : Must have access to v$ tables.
rem History
rem When           Who                What
rem ----------     ----------------   -----------------------------------
rem 7/5/93         M. Ault            Initial creation
rem
column namespace                    heading "Library Object"
column gets                         heading "Gets"
column gethitratio    format 999.99 heading "Get Hit%"
column pins                         heading "Pins"
column pinhitratio    format 999.99 heading "Pin Hit%"
column reloads                      heading "Reloads"
column invalidations                heading  "Invalidations"
column db format a10
rem
set pages 58 lines 132
start title132 "Library Caches Report"
define output = lib_cache&db
rem
spool &output
rem
select
          namespace,
          gets,
          gethitratio*100 gethitratio,
          pins,
          pinhitratio*100 pinhitratio,
          RELOADS,
          INVALIDATIONS
from
          v$librarycache
/
spool off
exit
```

The next script is an example of a database creation script used to document and allow recreation of a database.

```
rem     File:  M_ORA_Disk0:[M_Oracle.Oracle6.DB_prod]create_all_ts.SQL
rem  Created:  11jun93  M.Ault
rem
rem !!! Short !!! abstract about application
rem
rem ----------------- Disk Capacity Plan (MB) -------------------------
rem
rem
rem    M_ORA_DISK#->     1      2      3      4      5      6      7
rem                     ----   ----   ----   ----   ----   ----   ----
rem Data  -LOTS                 5
rem Index -LOTS                        5
rem Roll Back                                 20
rem Redo              4
rem Archive                                         1-10 vary w/ activity
rem DBA space                  .3
rem Ora_temp                   10
rem Ora_user                   10
rem system           10
rem tools            20
rem Control Files    .19    .19    .19
rem                  ----   ----   ----   ----   ----   ----   ----
rem  Disk Totals (MB) 34.2   28.2   5.2    20    10 (max)
rem
rem
rem GRAND TOTAL DISK CONSUMPTION ==> 97.6 MB <==
rem -----------------------------------------------------------------

remark - Created by ORA_RDBMS_CDB.COM on 25-MAY-1993 13:16:29.62
remark - added monitor script call, database tablespace creates 27-may-1993 M. Ault

spool ora_instance:create_PROD.log
set echo on

remark - This will take some time, please wait.

startup nomount
connect internal
create database PROD controlfile reuse
      datafile 'm_ORA_DISK1:[M_ORACLE6.DB_PROD]ORA_SYSTEM_1.DBS' size 30M reuse
      logfile  'M_ORA_DISK1:[M_ORACLE6.DB_PROD]ORA_LOG1.RDO' size 1M reuse,
               'M_ORA_DISK1:[M_ORACLE6.DB_PROD]ORA_LOG2.RDO' size 1M reuse,
               'M_ORA_DISK1:[M_ORACLE6.DB_PROD]ORA_LOG3.RDO' size 1M reuse,
               'M_ORA_DISK1:[M_ORACLE6.DB_PROD]ORA_LOG4.RDO' size 1M reuse
   maxdatafiles 190
   maxlogfiles  32
   maxinstances 16
            archivelog;
```

```
set termout off
@ora_system:catalog.sql    rem: This remains CATALOG.SQL in ORACLE7
@ora_system:expvew.sql     rem: This is called CATEXP.SQL in ORACLE7
@ora_system:monitor.sql    rem: This is called UTLMONTR.SQL in ORACLE7

create tablespace tools
datafile 'm_ora_disk1:[m_oracle6.db_prod]ora_tools_1.dbs' size 20m reuse
default storage (minextents 1 maxextents 110 initial 50k next 50k
pctincrease 50);

create tablespace ora_users
datafile 'm_ora_disk2:[m_oracle6.db_prod]ora_users_1.dbs' size 10m reuse
default storage (minextents 1 maxextents 110 initial 50k next 50k
pctincrease 0);

create tablespace ora_temp
datafile 'm_ora_disk2:[m_oracle6.db_prod]ora_temp_1.dbs' size 10m reuse
default storage (minextents 1 maxextents 110 initial 50k next 50k
pctincrease 0);

create tablespace ora_lots_data
datafile 'm_ora_disk2:[m_oracle6.db_prod]ora_lots_data_1.dbs' size 5m reuse
default storage (minextents 1 maxextents 110 initial 4k next 10k
pctincrease 0);

create tablespace ora_lots_index
datafile 'm_ora_disk3:[m_oracle6.db_prod]ora_lots_index_1.dbs' size 5m reuse
default storage (minextents 1 maxextents 110 initial 4k next 10k
pctincrease 0);

create tablespace ora_rollbacks
datafile 'm_ora_disk4:[m_oracle6.db_prod]ora_rollbacks_1.dbs' size 20m reuse
default storage (minextents 2 maxextents 40 initial 100k next 100k
pctincrease 0);
rem: No need to specify PCTINCREASE for ORACLE7, for rollback segments
rem: it defaults to 0 and cannot be specified.
exit

rem
rem   Name        : CREATE_TS_ALL_PROD.SQL
rem   Purpose     : Create all tablespaces for the PROD database
rem   Use         : From SQLDBA or SQLPLUS and a DBA account
rem   Limitations : VMS or UNIX user must have create permission on disks used
rem   History
rem   When        Who            What
rem   --------    ------------   ----------------------
rem 27-May-93   M. Ault         Initial Creation
rem
create tablespace tools
datafile 'm_ora_disk1:[m_oracle6.db_prod]ora_users_1.dbs' size 10m reuse
default storage (minextents 1 maxextents 110 initial 50k next 50k
pctincrease 0);
```

```
create tablespace ora_users
datafile 'm_ora_disk2:[m_oracle6.db_prod]ora_users_1.dbs' size 10m reuse
default storage (minextents 1 maxextents 110 initial 50k next 50k
pctincrease 0);

create tablespace ora_temp
datafile 'm_ora_disk2:[m_oracle6.db_prod]ora_temp_1.dbs' size 10m reuse
default storage (minextents 1 maxextents 110 initial 50k next 50k
pctincrease 0);

create tablespace ora_lots_data
datafile 'm_ora_disk2:[m_oracle6.db_prod]ora_lots_data_1.dbs' size 5m reuse
default storage (minextents 1 maxextents 110 initial 4k next 10k
pctincrease 0);

create tablespace ora_lots_index
datafile 'm_ora_disk3:[m_oracle6.db_prod]ora_lots_index_1.dbs' size 5m reuse
default storage (minextents 1 maxextents 110 initial 4k next 10k
pctincrease 0);

create tablespace ora_rollbacks
datafile 'm_ora_disk4:[m_oracle6.db_prod]ora_rollbacks_1.dbs' size 20m reuse
default storage (minextents 2 maxextents 40 initial 100k next 100k
pctincrease 0);   rem : PCTINCREASE  not used for ORACLE7 rollbacks.
exit
```

The following is a script to build a re-create user's SQL script under version 6.

```
set heading off verify off termout off feedback off echo off
set pages 0 lines 132
spool recreate_users.sql
select
                'grant connect to '||username||' identified by new_user;'
from
                dba_users
where
                username not in ('SYSTEM','SYS','_NEXT_USER','PUBLIC')
/
                select
                'alter user '||username||
                ' default tablespace '||default_tablespace||
                ' temporary tablespace '||temporary_tablespace||';'
from
                dba_users;
where
                username not in ('SYSTEM','SYS','_NEXT_USER','PUBLIC')
/
spool off
exit
```

The following is a script to build a re-create user's script for ORACLE7.

```
set heading off verify off termout off feedback off echo off
set pages 0 lines 132
spool recreate_users.sql
select 'create user '||username||
'default tablespace '||default_tablespace||
'temporary tablespace '||temporary_tablespace||
'profile '||profile||';'
/

spool off
exit
```

The following is an example of a script to build or rebuild rollback segments.

```
rem
rem Name          : Create_prod_rollbacks.sql
rem Purpose       : Create production instance rollback segments
rem Use           : From SQLPLUS or SQLDBA using a DBA level account
rem Limitations   : None
rem History
rem When          Who             What
rem -----------   -------------   ------------------------
rem 5/28/93       M. Ault         Initial Creation
rem
create rollback segment rollback1
tablespace ora_rollbacks
storage (
                initial 100k next 100k
                minextents 2 maxextents 40
                pctincrease 0);

create rollback segment rollback2
tablespace ora_rollbacks
storage (
                initial 100k next 100k
                minextents 2 maxextents 40
                pctincrease 0);

create rollback segment rollback3
tablespace ora_rollbacks
storage (
                initial 100k next 100k
                minextents 2 maxextents 40
                pctincrease 0);

create rollback segment rollback4
tablespace ora_rollbacks
```

```
storage (
                initial 100k next 100k
                minextents 2 maxextents 40
                pctincrease 0);
exit
```

The following script documents file placement and file sizes for an Oracle database.

```
REM Name       : SPACE.SQL
REM Purpose    : Document  file sizes and locations
REM Use        : From SQLPLUS
REM History:
REM When          Who          What
REM ----------    ----------   ------------------------------------------
REM 7/5/93        M. Ault      Initial creation
REM
CLEAR COLUMNS
COLUMN FILE_NAME FORMAT A55
COLUMN TABLESPACE_NAME FORMAT A20
START ORACLE$SQL:TITLE80 'DATABASE DATAFILES'
SPOOL FILE_LIST&DB..LIS
SELECT
                TABLESPACE_NAME,
                FILE_NAME BYTES/1048576 MEG
FROM
                DBA_DATA_FILES
ORDER BY
                TABLESPACE_NAME
/
SPOOL OFF
EXIT
```

Sample DCL and Shell Scripts

The database administrator will be expected to clean his or her own house in most shops. This means that they will write their own support scripts and help users and even developers with system-related questions—sometimes questions having nothing to do with the Oracle database at all.

To this end this appendix provides some examples of how to do some basic scripts using DCL and KORNE script languages. The scripts show basic menuing techniques, variable substitution, and calling the various Oracle tools from both types of scripts.

This appendix doesn't provide a complete menu system. The disk that is a companion to this book contains a complete set of scripts, menus, and SQL scripts that will provide a template for the DBA to use to create their own menu-driven management system. For those with a good handle on VMS or one of the shell scripts provided by the various flavors of Oracle, deriving a home-brewed menu system to support DBA operations should be a snap.

Also provided on the disk are several SQL*Menu unload SQL scripts that will build several SQL*Menu 5.0 menu applications, DBTOOLS, DBSTATUS, DBUTILS, DDVIEW, and even a CASE_MENU application. These are called by the scripts mentioned in the previous paragraph. Many of the DBA tasks that are shown in the accompanying scripts in this appendix can also be automated via SQL*Menu 5.0 scripts or SQL*Forms 4.0 menu scripts if the DBA desires.

As is shown in the accompanying scripts it is suggested that full-path specifications be avoided and logicals in VMS and environmental variables in UNIX be used in their place. This facilitates moving the scripts from platform to platform. It has been demonstrated that using this technique the entire menu system can be installed and operating in less than two hours (on a VMS system). The logical or variable assignment script can be a focus point for system logicals, symbols, and other definitions that involve the entire Oracle installation. This gives a single file that the DBA has to maintain instead of several.

The methods shown in these scripts may not be the best or the fanciest, but they do work and are easy to maintain. Too often all of us have seen scripts that may execute beautifully but contain such convoluted, arcane code that they are impossible to decipher (on VMS look at the VMSINSTAL procedure sometime). This is fine if you are looking for job security, but it can be tough five years from now when you want to upgrade a script and can't figure it out.

It is hoped that as this book goes through future revisions the scripts will become better as well. Your comments, suggestions, and scripts that you have developed are always welcome. Who knows? They may show up in future editions! With permission, of course.

The first set of scripts we will show are digital command language (DCL) scripts. It is practical to provide a central file to provide logical and symbol definitions. Therefore the first script will be a file that does just this. The file is called ORACLE_LOG.COM.

```
$! This command procedure DEFINES logicals used by the Oracle Management
$! menu.
$! MRA, REV 0, 10/23/92
$!
$! First, get logicals defined:
$!
$ DEFINE/NOLOG ORACLE$COM           M_ORA_DISK0:[m_oracle.dba_tools.dbstatus.COM]
$ DEFINE/NOLOG ORACLE$SQL           M_ORA_DISK0:[m_oracle.dba_tools.dbstatus.SQL]
$ DEFINE/NOLOG ORACLE$MENU          M_ORA_DISK0:[m_oracle.dba_tools.dbstatus.MENUS]
$ DEFINE/NOLOG ORACLE$DOC           DUA2:[NM91263.ORACLE6.DOC]
$ DEFINE/NOLOG ORACLE$ODDS          M_ORA_DISK0:[m_oracle.dba_tools.ddview.sql]
$ DEFINE/NOLOG oracle$log           DUA2:[nm91263.oracle6.log]
$ DEFINE/NOLOG ORACLE$EXP           m_ora_disk2:[m_ORACLE6.db_case.exportS]
$ DEFINE/NOLOG ORA$DBA_REP          M_ORA_DISK0:[m_oracle.dba_tools.dbstatus.reports]
$ DEFINE/NOLOG ORA$EXP_COM          DUA2:[NM91263.ORACLE6.COM.EXPORTS]
$ DEFINE/NOLOG ORA$ODDSFRM          M_ORA_DISK0:[m_oracle.dba_tools.ddview.sql]
$ define/nolog/TRANS=CONC           ORA$ARCHIVE M_ORA_DISK0:
$ DEFINE/NOLOG ORA_ANSI             MH5102P
$ DEFINE/NOLOG ORA_LAND             PRT_HBC5_R1_L
$ define/nolog ORA$IOUG             M_ORA_DISK0:[m_oracle.dba_tools.dbutil.sql]
$ define/nolog ora$com_rep          M_ORA_DISK0:[m_oracle.dba_tools.dbstatus.reports]
$ define/nolog ora_status_reports   M_ORA_DISK0:[m_oracle.dba_tools.dbstatus.reports]
$ define/nolog CASE_HP_CMD          "print /queue=plt_hbc5_draftpro"
$ define/nolog CASE_PS_CMD          "print /queue=prt_hbc5_r1_p"
$ define/nolog CASE_SDPRINT         "SYS$PRINT"
$ define/nolog  SDD$PRINT           "print /queue=prt_hbc5_r1_a"
$ define/nolog  SDD$WPRINT          "print /queue=prt_hbc5_r1_l"
$ define/nolog  SDD_QUEUE           "PRT_HBC5_r1_A"
$ define/nolog adhoccon             NODE1"""sqlnet slnet"""::"""task=ordnadhoc"""
$ define/nolog casecon              NODE1"""sqlnet slnet"""::"""task=ordnkcgc"""
$ define/nolog DEVcon               NODE1"""sqlnet slnet"""::"""task=ordnDEV"""
$ define/notran elcon               "UNIX1:oracle"
$ define tcpcase                    "157.206.11.15:"""CASE""":4096,5,YES"
$!
$! Symbol definitions:
$!
$! Report related symbols:
$!
$ PREP              :== "@ORACLE$COM:PRINT_REPORTS.COM"
$ GREP              :== "@ORACLE$COM:GEN_REPORTS.COM"
$!
$! Menu related symbols:
$!
$ ddview            :== "''runmenu' ddview -m f"
```

```
$ dbstatus          :== "''runmenu' dbstatus -m f"
$ DBUTILS           :== "''RUNMENU' DBUTILS -M F"
$ DB_TOOLS          :== "''RUNMENU' DBTOOLS -M F"
$ DBTOOLS           :== "''RUNMENU' DBTOOLS  M F"
$ CASE_MENU         :== "''RUNMENU' CASE_MENU -M F"
$!
$! Specific Instance Startup and Shutdown symbols:
$! The instance specific ORAUSER must be run for symbol to work.
$!
$ start_kcgc        :== "@ORA_INSTANCE:startup_EXCLUSIVE_CASE.com"
$ stop_kcgc         :== "@ORA_INSTANCE:shutdown_CASE.com"
$ start_APPL        :== "@ORA_INSTANCE:startup_EXCLUSIVE_PROD.com"
$ stop_APPL         :== "@ORA_INSTANCE:shutdown_PROD.com"
$ start_ADHOC       :== "@ORA_INSTANCE:startup_EXCLUSIVE_ADHOC.com"
$ stop_ADDHOC       :== "@ORA_INSTANCE:shutdown_ADHOC.com"
$ START_RECDEV      :== "@ORA_INSTANCE:STARTUP_EXCLUSIVE_RECDEV.COM"
$ STOP_RECDEV       :== "@ORA_INSTANCE:SHUTDOWN_RECDEV"
$ START_RECRUN      :== "@ORA_INSTANCE:STARTUP_EXCLUSIVE_RECRUN.COM"
$ STOP_RECRUN       :== "@ORA_INSTANCE:SHUTDOWN_RECRUN"
$!
$! Management Menu related symbols:
$!
$ MAN               :=="@ORACLE$COM:MANAGE_ORACLE.COM"
$ DEV_DIR           :=="ORACLE.DEV"
$ LIMS_DIR          :=="ORACLE.LIMS"
$ KCGC_DIR          :=="M_ORACLE6.DB_CASE"
$ APPL_DIR          :=="M_ORACLE6.DB_APPL"
$ ADHOC_DIR         :=="M_ORACLE6.DB_PROD"
$ GORECDEV          :== -
"@M_ORA_DISK0:[M_ORACLE.ORACLE6.DB_RECDEV]ORAUSER_RECDEV.COM
$ GORECRUN          :== -
 "@M_ORA_DISK0:[M_ORACLE.ORACLE6.DB_RECRUN]ORAUSER_RECRUN.COM
$!
$EXIT
```

This script is run by all users who will be using the menu system.

Once the logicals and symbols are set, the users should be sent to a central menu that accesses all other menus. This ensures that the menus are properly invoked and things are done in a standard form. The central management menu for DBA activities in these examples is called MANAGE_ORACLE.COM appropriately enough. Its listing follows.

```
$!
$! NAME         : MANAGE_ORACLE.COM
$! PURPOSE      : ALLOW EASE OF ORACLE SYSTEM MANAGEMENT
$! USE          : @ORACLE$COM:MANAGE_ORACLE
$! Limitations  : None
$! Revisions:
$!    Date          Modified By    Reason For change
$!    03-AUG-1991    MIKE AULT      INITIAL CREATE
$!    23-AUG-1991    MIKE AULT      ADDED DBA*ASSIST
```

```
$!   04-SEP-1992    MIKE AULT      ADDED CASE ACCESS
$!   23-OCT-1992    MIKE AULT      REP FP WITH LOGS
$!
$ ON CONTROL_Y THEN GOTO START
$!
$! Define local use logicals
$!
$ DEFINE/NOLOG REPORT$LOCATION oracle$sql
$ define/nolog report$dest ora_status_reports
$!
$! define local symbols
$!
$ DELETE :== ""
$ SEE :== "DEFINE/USE SYS$INPUT SYS$COMMAND"
$ say :== "WRITE SYS$OUTPUT"
$ CON_STR:==""
$ node = f$getsyi("NODENAME")
$ USER == F$GETJPI("","USERNAME")
$ USER == F$EDIT("''USER'","TRIM")
$ define node 'node'
$!
$ START:
$!
$ CLS   ! If not defined by SYS. Manager, set to SET/TERM/WID=80
$!
$! The next line displays a static menu file, can be generated via FMS or by editor.
$!
$ TYPE ORACLE$MENU:MANAGE_oracle.MEN
$!
$ DB == F$TRNLNM("ORA_SID")
$!
$ READ/PROMPT=-
"     USER: ''USER' NODE: ''NODE' DB: ''DB' ENTER CHOICE:" SYS$COMMAND ANS
$!
$! The next several if constructs check for special commands
$!
$ IF (ANS .EQS. "LO" .OR. ANS .EQS. "lo")
$   then
$   lo
$ ENDIF
$!
$ IF (ANS .EQS. "EX" .OR. ANS .EQS. "ex")
$   then
$   cls
$   goto END_IT
$ ENDIF
$!
$ IF (ANS .EQS. "SLEEP" .OR. ANS .EQS. "sleep")
$   then
$   @ORACLE$COM:idle.com
$   GOTO START
$ ENDIF
$!
```

```
$!
$ IF (ANS .EQS. "spawn" .OR. ANS .EQS. "SPAWN")
$    then
$    SEE
$    SPAWN
$    GOTO START
$ ENDIF
$!
$ IF (ANS .EQS. "ed" .OR. ANS .EQS. "ED")
$    then
$    SAY " "
$    @ORACLE$COM:EDIT_IT
$    WAIT 00:00:03
$    GOTO START
$ ENDIF
$!
$ IF (ANS .EQS. "MAIL" .OR. ANS .EQS. "mail")
$    then
$    SAY " "
$    SAY "INVOKING VMS MAIL ...."
$    SEE
$    MAIL
$    GOTO START
$ ENDIF
$!
$ IF (ANS .EQS. "PHN" .OR. ANS .EQS. "phn")
$    then
$    SAY " "
$    SAY "INVOKING VMS PHONE ...."
$    SEE
$    PHONE
$    GOTO START
$ ENDIF
$!
$ IF (ANS .EQS. "PRT" .OR. ANS .EQS. "prt")
$    then
$    SAY " "
$    @oracle$com:prt_it
$    GOTO START
$ ENDIF
$!
$! the next set of if constructs allow changing the database instances accessed
$!
$ IF (ANS .EQS. "PROD" .OR. ANS .EQS. "prod")
$    then
$    SAY " "
$    see
$    @M_ORA_DISK0:[M_ORACLE.ORACLE6.DB_PROD]ORAUSER_PROD
$    GOTO START
$ ENDIF
$!
$ IF (ANS .EQS. "adhoc" .OR. ANS .EQS. "ADHOC")
$    then
```

```
$   SAY " "
$   see
$   @M_ORA_DISK0:[M_ORACLE.ORACLE6.DB_ADHOC]ORAUSER_ADHOC
$   GOTO START
$ ENDIF
$!
$ IF (ANS .EQS. "case" .OR. ANS .EQS. "CASE")
$   then
$   SAY " "
$   see
$   @M_ORA_DISK0:[M_ORACLE.ORACLE6.DB_CASE]ORAUSER_CASE
$   GOTO START
$ ENDIF
$!
$! Actual Menu section
$!
$ ON ERROR THEN GOTO START
$ ANS = F$INTEGER(ANS)
$!
$ IF (ANS.LT.1) .OR. (ANS.GT.14)     ! This line changes as menu items added/deleted
$ THEN
$   GOTO START
$ ENDIF
$!
$! Process Menu options, wish DCL had a CASE statement like UNIX!
$! Notice all options call other procedures, this allows ease of maintenance
$!
$ IF (ANS.EQ.1)
$ THEN
$   @ORACLE$COM:MANAGE_USER.COM
$!
$ GOTO START
$ ENDIF
$!
$ IF (ANS.EQ.2)
$ THEN
$   @ORACLE$COM:MANAGE_TABLESPACE.COM
$!
$ GOTO START
$ ENDIF
$!
$ IF (ANS.EQ.3)
$ THEN
$   @ORACLE$COM:QUEUE_MENU.COM
$!
$ GOTO START
$ ENDIF
$!
$ IF (ANS.EQ.4)
$ THEN
$   @ORACLE$COM:EXPORT_MENU.COM
$!
$ GOTO START
```

```
$ ENDIF
$!
$! This option calls the Oracle supplied report writer administration menu.
$!
$ IF (ANS.EQ.5)
$ THEN
$    SRW_ADMIN
$!
$ GOTO START
$ ENDIF
$!
$! This option calls the Oracle supplied installation menu.
$!
$ IF (ANS.EQ.6)
$ THEN
$    ORACLEINS
$!
$ GOTO START
$ ENDIF
$!
$! This option uses the startup symbols createdin ORACLE_LOG.COM
$!
$ IF (ANS.EQ.7)
$ THEN
$ ORA_SID == F$TRNLNM("ORA_SID")
$    READ/PROMPT = "STARTUP INSTANCE ''ORA_SID'? (Y OR N): ->" -
          SYS$COMMAND INS
$    INS = F$EDIT("''INS'","UPCASE")
$    IF ("''INS'" .EQS. "Y")
$ THEN
$    START_'ORA_SID'
$ ENDIF
$!
$ GOTO START
$ ENDIF
$!
$! The next option uses the shutdown symbols defined in ORALCE_LOG.COM
$!
$ IF (ANS.EQ.8)
$ THEN
$ ORA_SID == F$TRNLNM("ORA_SID")
$    READ/PROMPT = "SHUTDOWN INSTANCE ''ORA_SID'? (Y OR N): ->" SYS$COMMAND INS
$    INS = F$EDIT("''INS'","UPCASE")
$    IF ("''INS'" .EQS. "Y")
$ THEN
$    STOP_'ORA_SID'
$ ENDIF
$!
$ GOTO START
$ ENDIF
$!
$ IF (ANS.EQ.9)
```

```
$ THEN
$    @ORACLE$COM:ARCHIVE_MENU.COM
$!
$ GOTO START
$ ENDIF
$!
$ IF (ANS.EQ.10)
$ THEN
$    @ORA_install:ora_insutl
$!
$ GOTO START
$ ENDIF
$!
$ IF (ANS.EQ.11)
$ THEN
$    ora_sid == f$trnlnm("ORA_SID")
$    ora_sid:== "'''ora_sid'"
$    @ORACLE$COM:ORACLE_LOG_MENU.COM
$!
$ GOTO START
$ ENDIF
$!
$! The next few options call SQL*Menu menus, the symbols are defined in ORACLE_LOG.COM
$!
$ IF (ANS.EQ.12)
$ THEN
$    define/nolog report$location ORACLE$COM
$    define/nolog report$DEST ORA_STATUS_REPORTS
$    ORA_SID == F$TRNLNM("ORA_SID")
$    ORA_SID:=='ORA_SID'
$       GOSUB GET_USER_DATA
$       SEE
$       DBSTATUS 'un'/'pw'
$!
$ goto start
$ ENDIF
$!
$ IF (ANS.EQ.13)
$ THEN
$    define/nolog report$location ora$ioug
$    define/nolog report$dest ora_STATUS_REPORTS
$    ORA_SID == F$TRNLNM("ORA_SID")
$    ORA_SID:=='ORA_SID'
$       see
$       dbutils
$!
$ GOTO START
$ ENDIF
$!
$ IF (ANS.EQ.14)
$ THEN
$    DEFINE/NOLOG REPORT$LOCATION ora$oddsfrm
```

```
$    DEFINE/NOLOG REPORT$DEST ora_STATUS_REPORTS
$    ORA_SID == F$TRNLNM("ORA_SID")
$    ORA_SID:=='ORA_SID'
$      SEE
$      DDVIEW
$!
$ GOTO START
$ ENDIF
$!
$ IF (ANS.EQ.15)
$ THEN
$    GOSUB GET_USER_DATA
$    SEE
$    DBTOOLS 'UN'/'PW'
$!
$ GOTO START
$ ENDIF
$!
$ IF (ANS.EQ.16)
$ THEN
$    GOSUB GET_USER_DATA
$    SEE
$    RUNMENU CASE_MENU 'UN'/'PW' -M F
$!
$ endif
$ GOTO START
$!
$ GET_USER_DATA:
$!
$ READ/PROMPT = "INPUT USER NAME: ---->" SYS$COMMAND UN
$ SET TERM/NOECHO
$ READ/PROMPT = "INPUT USER PASSWORD: ---->" SYS$COMMAND PW
$ SET TERM/ECHO
$ RETURN
$!
$ end_it:
$!
$ EXIT
```

As you can see, this main menu does very few direct actions. It allows the user access to system features such as the editor, printing, spawn to the OS, mail, and phone, but still keeps them within the menu structure. If desired, the spawn option can be removed, and a "captive" user will result.

The menu also allows the user to switch between available instances—in this case "CASE," "ADHOC," and "PROD." Options can also be added to "go" to different nodes using "SET HOST."

One of the drawbacks of the DCL system is lack of a "case" command such as in UNIX shell languages. This requires the developer to result to the IF-THEN-ELSE-type structure shown. In spite of this lack, some very easy to use scripts can be built.

The MANAGE_ORACLE.MEN file is shown below.

```
                    DATABASE MANAGEMENT MENU

ED-EDIT  PHN-PHONE  PRT-PRINT MAIL-VMS MAIL EX-EXIT MENU

1. MANAGE ORACLE USERS MENU    9.  ARCHIVE MENU
2. MANAGE TABLESPACES MENU     10. INSTALL TOOLS SHARED
3. QUEUE MENU                  11. MANAGE ORACLE LOGS
4. EXPORT MENU                 12. DB STATUS MENU
5. REPORT WRITER ADMIN MENU    13. DB UTILITIES MENU
6. ORACLEINS MENU              14. DATA DIC. VIEWS
7. STARTUP DATABASE            15. DB TOOLS MENU
8. SHUTDOWN DATABASE           14. CASE ACCESS MENU
```

Menu items 12, 13, and 14 can be combined into a DBA Tools SQL*Menu menu. Item 15's SQL*Menu menu calls SQL*Forms, SQL*Plus, SQL*ReportWriter, and SQLDBA. Item 16's SQL*Menu menu calls CASE*Dictionary, CASE*Designer, and CASE*Generator.

Menu Item 12 calls a SQL*Menu menu that allows the generation, display, and print of most of the DBA-related reports shown in Chapter 4. Menu Item 13 calls a SQL*Menu menu that allows the generation, display and print of several useful reports gleaned from the Oracle IOUG (International Oracle User's Group) distribution disks. Menu Item 14 calls a SQL*Menu menu that runs Tim Olesen's Oracle Data Dictionary (ODDS) system of forms and reports.

The scripts used in menu items 13 and 14 can be obtained from the IOUG. The menus developed to run the scripts are provided on the disk that is the companion to this book.

Let's look at a few of the secondary menus and see how processing is handled in them. The first submenu does user-related tasks. It would probably be better to do this through a combination of SQL*Menu and SQL*Forms, but this method is simpler and it works. The DCL script is called MANAGE_USERS.COM. The listing of this script follows.

```
$!
$! NAME          : MANAGE_USER.COM
$! PURPOSE       : ASSIST DBA IN MANAGING ORACLE USERS
$! USE           : FROM MANAGE_ORACLE.COM
$! Limitations   : None
$! Revisions:
$!    Date          Modified By    Reason For change
$!    21-AUG-1991   MIKE AULT      INITIAL CREATE
$!    23-OCT-1992   MIKE AULT      REPLACE FULLPATH WITH LOGICALS
$!
$ DELETE :== ""
$!
$ START:
$!
$ CLS
$!
$! Display menu
$!
$ TYPE ORACLE$MENU:USER_MENU.MEN
$!
```

```
$ READ/PROMPT="              ENTER CHOICE:" SYS$COMMAND ANS
$!
$ ANS = F$INTEGER(ANS)
$!
$ IF (ANS.EQ.99) THEN GOTO END
$ IF (ANS.LT.1) .OR. (ANS.GT.6) THEN GOTO START
$!
$ IF (ANS.EQ.1)
$ THEN
$ @ORACLE$COM:ADD_USER.COM
$!
$ GOTO START
$ ENDIF
$!
$ IF (ANS.EQ.2)
$ THEN
$ @ORACLE$COM:SWITCH_USER.COM
$!
$ GOTO START
$ ENDIF
$!
$ IF (ANS.EQ.3)
$ THEN
$ @ORACLE$COM:GRANT.COM
$!
$ GOTO START
$ ENDIF
$!
$ IF (ANS.EQ.4)
$ THEN
$ @ORACLE$COM:REVOKE.COM
$!
$ GOTO START
$!
$ ENDIF
$!
$ IF (ANS.EQ.5)
$ THEN
$ @ORACLE$COM:REVOKE_CONNECT.COM
$!
$ GOTO START
$ ENDIF
$!
$ IF (ANS.EQ.6)
$ THEN
$ @ORACLE$COM:USER_REPORT.COM
$!
$ GOTO START
$ ENDIF
$!
$ END:
$!
```

```
$ EXIT
```

Again, as with the main menu, this menu does no actual processing. This menu calls subroutines that actually do the work. This allows wholesale replacement of subroutines without affecting the calling menu. The menu actually displayed is shown below.

```
    DATABASE USER MANAGEMENT MENU

1. ADD ORACLE USER
2. CHANGE ORACLE USERS DEFAULT TABLESPACE
3. GRANT RESOURCE TO ORACLE USER
4. REVOKE RESOURCE FROM ORACLE USER
5. REMOVE ORACLE USER
6. GENERATE USER REPORT

99. RETURN TO MAIN MENU
```

Let's look at one of this menu's subroutines. The first menu item allows a user to create a new Oracle account. The script is called ADD_USER.COM and is listed below.

```
$!
$! NAME          : add_user.com
$! PURPOSE       : add an oracle user to the database
$! USE           : use from command line
$! Limitations   : NONE
$! parameters    : NONE
$! Revisions:
$!   Date        Modified By   Reason For change
$!   5 DEC 90    Mike Riggs    Initial Checkin
$!   23 OCT 92   MIKE AULT     REPLACE FULLPATHS WITH LOGICALS
$!
$ INQUIRE S_USER    "Enter DBA userid-->"
$!
$! To protect the DBA password from prying eyes, set so terminal doesn't echo
$!
$ SET TERM/NOECHO
$ INQUIRE S_PW      "Enter DBA password->"
$ SET TERM/ECHO
$!
$ cls
$!
$ INQUIRE U_ID      "Enter new account name---------->"
$ INQUIRE PW        "Enter new account password------>"
$ INQUIRE TS        "Enter user default tablespace-->"
$ INQUIRE TST       "Enter user Temporary tablespace->"
$!
$ sqlplus -s 'S_USER'/'S_PW' -
```

```
@ORACLE$SQL:add_user 'u_id' 'PW' 'TS' 'TST'
$!
$ INQUIRE ANS "Is this user a developer?"
$!
$ IF ANS .NES. "Y" THEN GOTO ADD_USER_DONE
$!
$! add sqlreportwriter developer's access
$!
$ WRITE SYS$OUTPUT "For SQL*Reportwriter access, enter user name here."
$ SEE
$ sqlplus 'S_USER'/'S_PW' @ORA_ROOT:[SQLREPORTWRITER.BIN]SRW_GRNT
$!
$! add sqlmenu 50 developer's access
$!
$ 'GENMENU'  's_user'/'s_pw' -gd 'u_id' -s
$!
$ADD_USER_DONE:
$   EXIT
```

Finally, we see some processing done. Note the call to the SQL script to actually insert the user. This allows upgrades to the SQL script without modifications to the calling DCL script. For example, switching from the GRANT CONNECT followed by ALTER USER type of user assignment to the ORACLE7 CREATE USER type of assignment. The version 6 SQL code called is shown below.

```
REM
REM NAME         : add_user.sql
REM PURPOSE      : adds a developer user to the database
REM                 includes access for all products
REM
REM USE          : called by add_user.com
REM Limitations  : None
REM Revisions    :
REM   Date         Modified By    Reason For change
REM   5 DEC 90     Mike Riggs     Initial Checkin
REM   3 AUG 91     MIKE AULT      DONT USE SYSTEM AS TEMP!
grant connect to &1 identified by &2;
alter user &1 default tablespace &3;
alter user &1 temporary tablespace &4;
exit
```

Several utility scripts written in DCL need mentioning. If we wanted to do several different printout styles—say, portrait, landscape, or to a terminal—we would either have to come up with the command each time we wanted to do a different style or create a DCL routine we could pass a minimum of parameters and have them do the work. PRINT_REPORT.COM that is referenced by the PREP symbol in ORALCE_LOG.COM is one such DCL routine. This routine is used by several of the support menus to specify how a report should be printed. Of course, the report has to be generated first. This is accomplished with GEN_REPORTS.COM and GEN_BATCH_REPORTS.COM. These two report generation scripts work together to allow the user to generate a report whether it be from REPORT, SQL*ReportWriter, or SQL*Plus. The listing for these utility scripts follow.

```
$! GEN_REPORTS.COM
$!
$! PROCEDURE TO ALLOW FOR THE GENERATION OF REPORTS FROM THE
$! DATABASES
$!
$! REV. 0 12-MAY-1992 M. AULT
$!
$! REV:   DATE:       REASON:                 PERSON:
$! ----   --------    --------------------    ------
$! 0      12-MAY-1992 INITIAL CREATE          M. AULT
$! 1      23-OCT-1992 REP FP WITH LOGS        M. AULT
$!-------------------------------------------------------------
$! PARAMETERS:
$!
$! P1 : REPORT TO RUN
$! P2 : USERNAME (ORACLE)
$! P3 : PASSWORD (ORACLE)
$! P4 : TYPE OF REPORT 1-RPT, 2-REPORTWRITER, 3-SQL
$! P5 : B FOR BATCH, N FOR NORMAL
$! P6 : Y TO USE PARAMETER FORM, N TO NOT USE FORM
$! P7 : TO PASS VARIABLE TO SQLPLUS REPORT
$!_____
$!
$! ASSUMPTIONS:
$!
$! 1. EACH NON-RPT REPORT MUST SPECIFY ITS OWN DESTINATION
$! 2. REPORT$LOCATION IS A LOGICAL POINTING TO THE DIRECTORY FOR THE
$!    REPORT SPECIFICATION FILE
$! 3. IF REPORT$LOCATION IS NOT SPECIFIED, IT WILL DEFAULT TO SYS$LOGIN
$! 4. REPORT$DEST IS A LOGICAL POINTING TO THE LOCATION OF THE REPORT
$!    OUTPUT
$!    IF IT IS NOT SPECIFIED IT DEFAULTS TO THE REPORT$LOCATION VALUE
$!-------------------------------------------------------------
$!
$ INQUIRE ANS "CONTINUE?"
$ SET NOON
$!
$ NODE = F$GETSYI("NODENAME")
$!
$! CHECK VALUE OF REPORT$LOCATION
$!
$ IF F$TRNLNM("REPORT$LOCATION") .EQS. ""
$ THEN
$   DEFINE/NOLOG REPORT$LOCATION SYS$LOGIN
$ ENDIF
$!
$! CHECK VALUE OF REPORT$DEST
$!
```

```
$ IF F$TRNLNM("REPORT$DEST") .EQS. ""
$ THEN
$    DEFINE/NOLOG REPORT$DEST REPORT$LOCATION
$ ENDIF
$!
$! VERIFY SPECIFICATION FILE EXISTS
$!
$ FILE = F$SEARCH("REPORT$LOCATION:''P1'")
$ IF (FILE .EQS. "")
$ THEN
$   WRITE SYS$OUTPUT "BAD FILE SPECIFICATION"
$   GOTO GET_OUT
$ ENDIF
$!
$ WRITE SYS$OUTPUT "GENERATING REPORT FOR ''FILE'"
$!
$! CHECK IF BATCH REQUESTED:
$!
$ IF "''P5'" .EQS. "B"
$ THEN
$   if "''p2'".eqs."N" then p2 = " "
$   if "''p3'".eqs."N" then p3 = " "
$   SUBMIT/NOTIFY/NOPRINT/QUEUE='NODE'$BATCH -
 ORACLE$COM:GEN_BATCH_REPORTS.COM/-
 PARAMETERS=('FILE','P2','P3','P4','P1','P7')/LOG=SYS$LOGIN:ORA_BATCH_REPORT.LOG
$   GOTO GET_OUT
$ ENDIF
$!
$! RPT FILES:
$!
$ IF F$INTEGER(P4) .EQ. 1
$ THEN
$    if "''p2'".eqs."N" then p2 = " "
$    if "''p3'".eqs."N" then p3 = " "
$ DEFINE/USE/NOLOG SYS$INPUT SYS$COMMAND
$ RPT REPORT$LOCATION:'P1' REPORT$DEST:'P1' 'P2'/'P3'
$ RPF REPORT$DEST:'P1' REPORT$DEST:'P1' -F
$ GOTO GET_OUT
$ ENDIF
$!
$! SQL*REPORTWRITER FILES:
$!
$ IF F$INTEGER(P4) .EQ. 2
$ THEN
$   if "''p2'".eqs."N" then p2 = " "
$   if "''p3'".eqs."N" then p3 = " "
$ IF "''P6'" .EQS. "" THEN P6 = "NO"
$ IF "''P6'" .EQS. "Y" THEN P6 = "YES"
$ IF "''P6'" .EQS. "N" THEN P6 = "NO"
$ DEFINE/USE/NOLOG SYS$INPUT SYS$COMMAND
$ RUNREP 'FILE' PARAMFORM='P6' USERID='P2'/'P3'
$ GOTO GET_OUT
$ ENDIF
```

```
$!
$! SQLPLUS REPORTS:
$!
$ IF F$INTEGER(P4) .EQ. 3
$ THEN
$   if "''p2'".eqs."N" then p2 = " "
$   if "''p3'".eqs."N" then p3 = " "
$ SQLPLUS -S 'P2'/'P3' @'FILE' 'P7'
$ GOTO GET_OUT
$ ENDIF
$!
$ WRITE SYS$OUTPUT "IMPROPER REPORT TYPE SPECIFIED"
$ GOTO GET_OUT
$!
$ GET_OUT:
$!
$ EXIT
```

Since this script calls GEN_BATCH_REPORTS.COM, we will look at it next.

```
$! GEN_BATCH_REPORTS.COM
$!
$! PROCEDURE TO ALLOW FOR THE GENERATION OF REPORTS FROM THE
$! DATABASES IN BATCH MODE
$!
$! REV. 0 12-MAY-1992 M. AULT
$!
$! REV:   DATE:        REASON:                PERSON:
$! ----   --------     --------------------   ------
$!  0     13-MAY-1992  INITIAL CREATE         M. AULT
$!
$!-------------------------------------------------------------------
$! PARAMETERS:
$!
$! P1 : REPORT TO RUN
$! P2 : USERNAME (ORACLE)
$! P3 : PASSWORD (ORACLE)
$! P4 : TYPE OF REPORT 1-RPT, 2-REPORTWRITER, 3-SQL
$! P5 : FILE NAME FOR RPT REPORTS
$!_____
$!
$! ASSUMPTIONS:
$!
$! 1. EACH NON-RPT REPORT MUST SPECIFY ITS OWN DESTINATION
$! 2. REPORT$LOCATION IS A LOGICAL POINTING TO THE DIRECTORY FOR THE
$!    REPORT SPECIFICATION FILE
$! 3. IF REPORT$LOCATION IS NOT SPECIFIED, IT WILL DEFAULT TO SYS$LOGIN
$! 4. IF REPORT$DEST IS NOT SET, IT WILL DEFAULT TO REPORT$LOCATION
$!-----------------------------------------------------------------------
$!
```

```
$ SET NOON
$!
$! RPT FILES:
$!
$ IF F$INTEGER(P4) .EQ. 1
$ THEN
$ DEFINE/USE/NOLOG SYS$INPUT SYS$COMMAND
$ RPT REPORT$LOCATION:'P1' REPORT$DEST:'P1' 'P2'/'P3'
$ RPF REPORT$DEST:'P1' REPORT$DEST:'P1' -F
$ GOTO GET_OUT
$ ENDIF
$!
$! SQL*REPORTWRITER FILES:
$!
$ IF F$INTEGER(P4) .EQ. 2
$ THEN
$ P6 = "NO"
$ DEFINE/USE/NOLOG SYS$INPUT SYS$COMMAND
$ RUNREP 'FILE' PARAMFORM='P6' USERID='P2'/'P3'
$ GOTO GET_OUT
$ ENDIF
$!
$! SQLPLUS REPORTS:
$!
$ IF F$INTEGER(P4) .EQ. 3
$ THEN
$ SQLPLUS -S 'P2'/'P3' @'FILE'
$ GOTO GET_OUT
$ ENDIF
$!
$ WRITE SYS$OUTPUT "IMPROPER REPORT TYPE SPECIFIED"
$ GOTO GET_OUT
$!
$ GET_OUT:
$!
$ EXIT
```

Once the report is ready, we will want to get a look at it, either in hard copy or on screen. PRINT_REPORTS.COM does this for us. This script is referenced by the PREP symbol in the ORACLE_LOG.COM procedure. Its listing follows.

```
$! PRINT_REPORTS.COM
$!
$! PROCEDURE TO ALLOW FOR THE PRINTING OF REPORTS FROM THE
$! DATABASES
$!
$! REV. 0 12-MAY-1992 M. AULT
$!
$!  REV:   DATE:      REASON:              PERSON:
$!  ----   --------   --------------------  ------
```

```
$!   0     12-MAY-1992  INITIAL CREATE          M. AULT
$!
$!------------------------------------------------------------------
$! PARAMETERS:
$!
$! P1 : REPORT TO PRINT (FULL PATH UNLESS GENERATED IN DEFAULT DIRECTORY)
$! P2 : WHERE TO PRINT REPORT (QUEUE NAME FROM MMD_QUEUES OR SPECIFY)
$!      "TERM" WILL DISPLAY TO TERMINAL
$! P3 : SIZE OF REPORTS LINES 1-80, 2-132 (DEFAULTS TO 80), 3->132
$!_____
$!
$! ASSUMPTIONS:
$!
$! EACH REPORT IS ANSI FORMAT
$!
$!------------------------------------------------------------------
$!
$ SET NOON
$ DEFINE/USE/NOLOG SYS$INPUT SYS$COMMAND
$!
$ IF F$TRNLNM("REPORT$LOCATION") .EQS. ""
$ THEN
$   DEFINE/NOLOG REPORT$LOCATION SYS$LOGIN
$ ENDIF
$!
$ IF F$TRNLNM("REPORT$DEST") .EQS. ""
$ THEN
$   DEFINE/NOLOG REPORT$DEST REPORT$LOCATION
$ ENDIF
$!
$ FILE = F$SEARCH("REPORT$DEST:''P1'")
$ IF (FILE .EQS. "")
$ THEN
$   WRITE SYS$OUTPUT "BAD FILE SPECIFICATION"
$   WAIT 00:00:03
$ GOTO GET_OUT
$ ENDIF
$!
$ IF "''P2'" .EQS. "TERM"
$ THEN
$ GOTO DISPLAY_REPORT
$ ENDIF
$!
$ QUE_TEST = F$GETQUI("DISPLAY_QUEUE","QUEUE_NAME","''P2'")
$ IF "''QUE_TEST'" .EQS. ""
$ THEN
$   WRITE SYS$OUTPUT "BAD QUEUE SPECIFICATION"
$   WAIT 00:00:02
$   GOTO GET_OUT
$ ENDIF
$!
$ WRITE SYS$OUTPUT "PRINTING REPORT ''FILE'"
$!
```

```
$ IF P3 .EQS. ""
$ THEN
$   P3 = "1"
$   WRITE SYS$OUTPUT "DEFAULTING TO 80 COLUMNS"
$   WAIT 00:00:02
$ ENDIF
$!
$ IF F$INTEGER(P3) .EQ. 1
$ THEN
$   PRINT/QUEUE='P2'/param=(numb=1) 'FILE'
$   GOTO GET_OUT
$ ENDIF
$!
$ IF F$INTEGER(P3) .EQ. 2 .OR. F$INTEGER(P3) .EQ. 3
$ THEN
$   PRINT/QUEUE='P2'/PARAMETERS=(numb=1,PAGE_O=LANDSCAPE) 'FILE'
$   GOTO GET_OUT
$ ENDIF
$!
$ WRITE SYS$OUTPUT "IMPROPER LINE SIZE SPECIFIED"
$ WAIT 00:00:03
$ GOTO GET_OUT
$!
$ DISPLAY_REPORT:
$ IF F$INTEGER(P3) .EQ. 2 .OR. F$INTEGER(P3) .EQ. 3
$ THEN
$   SET TERM/WIDTH=132
$ ENDIF
$ TYPE/PAGE 'FILE'
$ READ/PROMPT="PRESS ENTER WHEN FINISHED" SYS$COMMAND NULL_IN
$ set term/wid=80
$ GOTO GET_OUT
$!
$ GET_OUT:
$!
$ EXIT
```

Another form of this script is called PRINT_IT.COM and is used by some of the menus. The listing for PRINT_IT.COM follows.

```
$!
$! NAME        : PRINT_IT.COM
$! PURPOSE     : AUTOMATE THE PRINTING OF STATUS REPORTS FOR THE DBA
$! USE         : FROM DBSTATUS MENU
$! Limitations : None
$! Revisions:
$!   Date          Modified By    Reason For change
$!   07-AUG-1992   MIKE AULT      INITIAL CREATE
$!   23-OCT-1992   MIKE AULT      REPLACE FULLPATHS WITH LOGICALS
$ START:
```

```
$ HOST = F$GETSGI("NODENAME")
$!
$ PRINT_IT:
$ purge/nolog ora_status_reports
$ READ/PROMPT = "DO YOU WANT A PRINTOUT?: " SYS$COMMAND YN
$ YN = F$EDIT(YN,"UPCASE")
$ IF "''YN'" .EQS. "Y"
$ THEN
$  READ/PROMPT = "ENTER QUEUE NAME: " SYS$COMMAND PRT
$  PRT = F$EDIT(PRT,"UPCASE")
$   PRINT/QUE='PRT'/PARAM=(num=1) ORA_status_reports:'P1'
$ ENDIF
$!
$ END:
$!
$ EXIT
```

As you can see, PRINT_IT.COM isn't nearly as sophisticated as PRINT_REPORTS.COM, but for noncritical applications, it works just fine.

The final example script is one to do hot backups. This is just a bare-bones script, and lots of error checking and self-protection can be added, but as a starting point, it is sufficient.

```
$!*************************************************************************
$! Name        : Hot_backup.com
$! Purpose     : Perform a hot backup of an Oracle Database
$! Use         : @Hot_backup.com
$! Limitations : Creates a read consistent image, but doesn't backup in process
$!               transactions
$!
$! Revision History:
$! Date         Who          What
$! --------     ----------   -------------------------------
$! June 1993    K. Loney     Featured in Oracle Mag. Article
$! 29-Jun-93    M. Ault      Modified, commented
$!*************************************************************************
$!
$! Define symbol for backup command so don't have to fully specify it each time
$ dup_it = "backup/ignore=(noback,interlock,label) /log"
$ !
$ sqldba
    connect internal
    alter tablespace system begin backup;
    exit
$ dup_it m_ora_disk2:[m_oracle.oracle6.db_example]ora_system_1.dbs
  mua0:ora_system.bck/save                          ! could use * wildcard to
$                                                   ! get all system files
$                                                   ! ORA_System_*.dbs
$!
 sqldba
   connect internal
```

```
   alter tablespace system end backup;
   alter tablespace tools begin backup;
   exit
$ dup_it m_ora_disk3:[m_oracle.oracle6.db_example]ora_tools_1.dbs
  mua0:ts_tools.bck/save
$!
sqldba
   connect internal
   alter tablespace tools end backup;
   alter tablespace user_tables begin backup;
   exit
$ dup_it m_ora_disk3:[m_oracle.oracle6.db_example]ora_user_tables_1.dbs
  mua0:ts_tools.bck/save
$!
   sqldba
   alter tablespace user_tables end backup;
   exit
$! force write of all archive logs
$!
$ sqldba
   connect internal
   alter system switch logfile;
   archive log all;
   exit
$!
$ rename m_ora_disk5:[m_oracle.oracle6.db_example.archives]*.arc *.oldarc
$! Now backup a control file
$!
$ sqldba
   connect internal
   alter database example
   backup controlfile to
   'm_ora_disk1:[m_oracle.oracle6.db_example]ora_control.bac
   reuse;
   exit
$ dup_it m_ora_disk1:[m_oracle.oracle6.db_example]ora_control1.con -
mua0:ora_control.bac/save
$! now backup all archive logs
$!
$! you don't want to delete logs if an error causes them not to be backed up
$ on error goto end_it
$!
$ dup_it m_ora_disk5:[m_oracle.oracle6.db_example.archives]*.oldarc  -
mua0:ora_archives.bck/save
$! Now delete logs
$!
$ delete/log m_ora_disk5:[m_oracle.oracle6.db_examples.archives]*.oldarc;*
$ end_it:
$ exit
```

Using the example scripts shown, a DBA, perhaps with the assistance of the system manager or someone familiar with DCL, can create their own menu system using DCL, SQL*menus, and other utilities. A complete menu system based on the MANAGE_ORACLE.COM procedure is available on the disk that is the companion to this book and comes with complete installation instructions.

Of course, we couldn't call this a book about UNIX and Oracle if we didn't show a few UNIX Shell script examples to go along with the VMS examples in DCL. As with VMS and DCL it is suggested a central environmental symbol script be created. An example follows.

```
# Oracle path, executable and symbol definition file
#
# M. Ault 22-Feb-1993
# Rev 0.
#
ORACLE_MENUS="$HOME/dba_tools/menus"
ORACLE_SCRIPT="$HOME/dba_tools"
ORACLE_HOME="/oracle"
ORACLE_SID="oracle"
sqlplus="$ORACLE_HOME/bin/sqlplus"
sqlforms="$ORACLE_HOME/bin/sqlforms30"
sqlmenu="$ORACLE_HOME/bin/sqlmenu50"
export ORACLE_HOME
export ORACLE_SID
export sqlplus
export sqlforms
export sqlmenu
runmenu="$ORACLE_HOME/bin/runmenu"
runform="$ORACLE_HOME/bin/runform"
export runmenu
export runform
```

As you can see, this looks simpler than the DCL script. Of course, not as many variables are being defined. Note the export commands. If the variable isn't exported, it is not kept active.

Next, let's look at the UNIX version of the MANAGE_ORACLE.COM script.

```
#
# Menu Shell script for Oracle Management
#
# Rev 0. Mike Ault 22-Feb-1993
#
#
# Be sure "logicals" are set
#
 sh oracle_log
#
# Display Menu
#
validchoice=""
until [ -n "$validchoice" ]
do
clear
```

```
  echo '
           _____

                         Oracle Database Management Menu
                                   Rev 0.
           _____

              1. MANAGE ORACLE USERS MENU     7. STARTUP DATABASE
              2. MANAGE TABLESPACES MENU       8. SHUTDOWN DATABASE
              3. CRON MENU                     9. DBA TOOLS MENU
              4. EXPORT MENU                   10. ARCHIVE MENU
              5. REPORT WRITER ADMIN MENU      11. MANAGE ORACLE LOGS
              6. ORACLEINS MENU                12. DEV TOOLS MENU

                            99. Exit Menu
           _____

              Enter Choice (1-12,99): \c'
#
# Read and Process choice
#
  read choice
  echo
#
# Process menu choice
#
    case "$choice"
    in
       1) sh manage_users
          validchoice=TRUE;;
       2) sh manage_ts
          validchoice=TRUE;;
       3) sh que_menu
          validchoice=TRUE;;
       4) sh export_menu
          validchoice=TRUE;;
       5) /oracle/sqlreport/admin/srw.admin;;
       6) /oracle/install/oracle.install
          validchoice=TRUE;;
       7) /oracle/bin/dbstart
          validchoice=TRUE;;
       8) /oracle/bin/dbshut
          validchoice=TRUE;;
       9) runmenu dbatools -m f
          validchoice=TRUE;;
      10) sh archive_menu
          validchoice=TRUE;;
      11) sh log_menu
          validchoice=TRUE;;
      12) runmenu devtools -m f
          validchoice=TRUE;;
      19) exit;;
       *) echo "Not a valid Choice";;
    esac
done
```

This script is simpler than the previously shown DCL script; of course, it also does less. It doesn't do the specialized processing of commands from the input line, nor does it do the switching between in stances. Other than these few items, which can be added in, it is functionally equivalent to the DCL MANGE_ORACLE.COM.

Notice only two SQL*Menu menus are called, DEVTOOLS and DBATOOLS. These menus call all of the other menus that are on the MANAGE_ORACLE.COM menu. DEVTOOLS calls SQL*Forms, SQL*Plus, SQL*Menu, SQL*ReportWriter, and SQLDBA. DBATOOLS calls DBSTATUS, DBUTILS, and DDVIEW.

Let's look at the equivalent of the MANAGE_USER.COM procedure in HPUX KORNE shell script.

```
#
# Menu Shell Script for Managing Oracle User Accounts
#
# Rev 0, 24-Feb-1993 M. Ault
# called from manage_oracle
#
#
# Display Menu
#
validchoice=""
until [ -n "$validchoice" ]
do
clear
  echo '


                      Oracle Users Management Menu
                              Rev 0.


                      1. Add Oracle User
                      2. Switch users default tablespace
                      3. Grant Resource to user
                      4. Revoke Resource from a user
                      5. Revoke connect from a user
                      6. Generate User report
                     99. Exit


                  Enter Choice (1-6,99): \c'
#
# Read and process choice
#
  read choice
  echo
    case "$choice"
    in
          1) sh add_user
             validchoice=TRUE;;
          2) sh switch_user
             validchoice=TRUE;;
          3) sh grant_user
             validchoice=TRUE;;
          4) sh revoke_user
```

```
                   validchoice=TRUE;;
              5)   sh revoke_all_user
                   validchoice=TRUE;;
              6)   sh user_report
                   validchoice=TRUE;;
             99)   sh manage_oracle
                   exit;;
              *)   echo "Not a valid choice";;
        esac
done
```

Finally, let's look at an example processing script that is called from this last menu script. As with the DCL procedures, let's examine the ADD_USER shell script that compares with the ADD_USER.COM procedure shown before.

```
#
# add_user shell script
# Rev 0  9-March-1993 MRA
#
# Called from manage_users shell script
#
clear
echo '
Enter Oracle User Name to create: \c'
read uname
#
echo '
Enter Oracle User password for new account: \c'
read password
#
echo '
Enter default tablespace: \c'
read def_ts
#
echo '
Enter temporary tablespace: \c'
read temp_ts
#
echo '
Enter System user password: \c'
read sys_pwd
#
$sqlplus -s system/$sys_pwd @$ORACLE_SCRIPT/ct_us.sql $uname $password $def_ts $temp_ts
#
exit
```

As you can see, this script gathers the data and sends it to the ct_us.sql script for processing. Again, this is to allow the underlying SQL scripts to be changed as dictated by the changing Oracle product releases without requiring changes to the controlling scripts.

The ct_us.sql script is shown below.

```
REM
REM NAME          :ct_us.sql
REM PURPOSE       : adds a  user to the database
REM                 includes access for all products
REM
REM USE           : called by add_user shell script
REM Limitations : None
REM Revisions   :
REM   Date        Modified By    Reason For change
REM   5 DEC 90    Mike Riggs     Initial Checkin
REM   3 AUG 91    MIKE AULT      DONT USE SYSTEM AS TEMP!
REM   OCT 92      MIKE AULT      Modified for UNIX
grant connect to &1 identified by &2;
alter user &1 default tablespace &3;
alter user &1 temporary tablespace &4;
exit
```

If this script looks familiar, it should. It is identical to the one used for the DCL menus. This shows the true power of Oracle, the platform independence of code.

The next script can be used as a basis for a hot backup shell script for performing a hot backup on an Oracle Database.

```
#************************************************************************
# Name       : Hot_backup.com
# Purpose    : Perform a hot backup of an Oracle Database
# Use        : @Hot_backup.com
# Limitations  : Creates a read consistent image, but doesn't backup in process
#               transactions
#
# Revision History:
# Date         Who             What
# ----------   ---------------  --------------------------------
# June 1993    K. Loney        Featured in Oracle Mag. Article
# 29-Jun-93    M. Ault         Modified, commented
# 02-Aug-93    M.Ault          Converted to UNIX script
#************************************************************************
#
# Define symbol for backup command so don't have to fully specify it each time
 dup_it = "tar Ncf /dev/rfd.0"
 #
 sqldba << ending1
     connect internal
     alter tablespace system begin backup;
     exit
ending1
#
 dup_it rd2/usr/m_oracle/oracle6/db_example/ora_system_1.dbf
#
  dup_it = "tar N Rf /dev/rfd.0"
 sqldba << ending2
```

```
   connect internal
   alter tablespace system end backup;
   alter tablespace tools begin backup;
   exit
ending2
#
 dup_it rd3/usr/m_oracle/oracle6/db_example/ora_tools_1.dbf
#
sqldba << ending3
   connect internal
   alter tablespace tools end backup;
   alter tablespace user_tables begin backup;
   exit
ending3
#
 dup_it rd3/usr/m_oracle/oracle6/db_example/ora_user_tables_1.dbf
#
   sqldba << ending4
   connect internal
   alter tablespace user_tables end backup;
   exit
ending4
# force write of all archive logs
#
 sqldba << ending5
   connect internal
   alter system switch logfile;
   archive log all;
   exit
ending5
#
 cp rd5/usr/m_oracle/oracle6/db_example.archives/*.arc *.oldarc
# Now backup a control file
#
 sqldba << ending6
   connect internal
   alter database example
   backup controlfile to
   'rd1/usr/m_oracle/oracle6/db_example/ora_control.bac
   reuse;
   exit
ending6
#
 dup_it rd1/usr/m_oracle/oracle6/db_example/ora_control.bac
# now backup all archive logs
#
# you don't want to delete logs if an error causes them not to be backed up
 trap 'exit' 0 2 3 4 5 10 12
#
 dup_it rd5/usr/m_oracle/oracle6/db_example.archives/*.oldarc
# Now delete logs
```

```
#
rm rd5/usr/m_oracle/oracle6/db_examples.archives/*.oldarc;*
#end_it:
exit
```

If the DBA has knowledge of Shell scripting, or has access to someone with the required skills, a complete menu-driven system to manage the Oracle database can be developed using the above techniques. A menu system based in the HP-UX KORNE Shell is available on the companion disk to this book.

Version 6 and ORACLE7 INIT.ORA Parameters

The following is a list of the version 6 and ORACLE7 INIT.ORA parameters, their default values, and dependencies.

PARAMETER	DEFAULT VALUE	PURPOSE	ORACLE7?	DEPENDANCIES
LIST	N/A	List param. during startup.	Y	None
AUDIT_TRAIL	false/NONE	Enables or disables the writing of rows to the audit table.	Y	None
BACKGOUND_DUMP_DEST	O/S Dependent	Path name for destination of DUMP files.	Y	None
CALLS	Derived	Number of allowed recursive calls.	N	PROCESSES and AUDIT_TRAIL
CLEANUP_ROLLBACK_ENTRIES	20	Number of rollback entries to cleanup in single pass.	Y	None
CONTEXT_AREA	4096 bytes	Initial size of a user's context area.	N	O/S dependent.
CONTEXT_INCR	4096 BYTES	Number of bytes context area will grow by.	N	O/S dependent.
CONTROL_FILES	O/S Dep.	The names for the instance control files.	Y	Full path O/S names or logicals.
CPU_COUNT LOG_SIMULTANEOUS_COPIES	Sys. Dep.	The number of CPUs installed in the system.	Y	
DB_BLOCK_BUFFERS	32	The number of buffers in the SGA.	Y	Way to small. Set higher. DB_BLOCK_SIZE
DB_BLOCK_LRU_EXTENDED_STATISTICS	0	Enables statistics on buffer usage if > zero.	Y	Value corresponds to number of additional buffers.
DB_BLOCK_LRU_STATISTICS	false	Enables statistics compilation to the X$KCBCBH table.	Y	See previous entry.
DB_BLOCK_MAX_SCAN_CNT	30	Number of buffers scanned for free buffers.	N	
DB_BLOCK_SIZE	O/S Dep.	Size in bytes of one database block.	Y	2048 for VMS and HP-UX
DB_BLOCK_WRITE_BATCH	8	Number of blocks written by DBWR.	Y	
DB_WRITER_MAX_SCAN_CNT	Derived	Used for multi-block I/O	N	10% of DB_BLOCK_BUFFERS

PARAMETER	DEFAULT VALUE	PURPOSE	ORACLE7?	DEPENDANCIES
DB_FILE_MULTIBLOCK_READ_CNT	O/S Dep.	Number of blocks read in one read.	Y	Max of 65 K on VMS 40 K on UNIX.
DB_FILE_SIMULTANEOUS_WRITES	4	Number of writes at one time for a file.	Y	MAX_BLOCK_WRITE_BATCH
DB_FILES	32	Maximum number of data files (can be changed).	Y	<= MAXDATAFILES in CREATE DATABASE.
DB_NAME	NULL	The name of the database.	Y	
DC_COLUMN_GRANTS	50	Number of column grants cached in buffers.	N	
DC_COLUMNS	300	Number of column names cached.	N	
DC_CONSTRAINT_DEFS	200	Number of constraints cached.	N	
DC_FILES	25	Number of file names cached.	N	
DC_FREE_EXTENTS	50	Number of entries in the free extent cache.	N	
DC_INDEXES	50	Number of index names cached.	N	
DC_OBJECT_IDS	50	Number of object ids cached.	N	
DC_OBJECTS	100	Number of Object Names cached.	N	
DC_ROLLBACK_SEGMENTS	25	Number of entries in the rollback segment name cache.	N	
DC_SEGMENTS	50	Number of entries in the segment ID cache.	N	
DC_SEQUENCE_GRANTS	20	The number of sequence grants that can be cached.	N	

PARAMETER	DEFAULT VALUE	PURPOSE	ORACLE7?	DEPENDANCIES
DC_SEQUENCES	20	Number of entries in the sequence description cache.	N	
DC_SYNONYMS	50	The number of entries in the sequence cache.	N	
DC_TABLE_GRANTS	50	Number of table grants cached.	N	
DC_TABLES	100	Number of table names cached.	N	
DC_TABLESPACE_QUOTAS	25	Number of tablespace quotas cached.	N	
DC_TABLESPACES	25	Number of tablespace names cached.	N	
DC_USED_EXTENTS	50	The number of entries in the used extents cache.	N	
DC_USERNAMES	50	Number of usernames cached.	N	
DC_USERS	50	Number of user ids to cache.	N	
DDL_LOCKS	5*Sessions	Number of parse locks.	N	SESSIONS
DML_LOCKS	4*Transactions	Number of DML locks.	Y	TRANSACTIONS
ENQUEUE_RESOURCES	Process Dep.	Number of resources that can be locked by lock manager.	Y	((PROCESSES-3)*5+20 If PROCESSES >3<10 ((PROCESSES-10)*2)+55 If processes>10
FREE_LIST_PROC	1	Number of free lists per instance.	N	
GC_DB_LOCKS	0	Number of innstance locks.	Y	
GC_FILES_TO_LOCKS	0	Hashing control string.	Y	
GC_ROLLBACK_LOCKS	20	Number of modified rollback blocks (simultaneous).	Y	

PARAMETER	DEFAULT VALUE	PURPOSE	ORACLE7??	DEPENDANCIES
GC_ROLLBACK_SEGMENTS	20	Number of rollback segments in all shared instances.	Y	
GC_SAVE_ROLLBACK_LOCKS	20	Number of all deferred roll-backs in all instances.	Y	
GC_SEGMENTS	10	Simultaneous segments undergoing modification.	Y	
GC_TABLESPACES	5	Total number of transient tablespaces (online/offline).	Y	
IFILE	NULL	Full path name of additional parameter file.	Y	
INIT_SQL_FILES	NULL	Contains SQL file names to execute on startup.	Y	
INSTANCES	16	Maximum number of instances in a shared environment.	N	
LANGUAGE	AMERICAN	NLS Language for instance	N	
LOG_ALLOCATION	200	Number of redo blocks allocated to each instance in a shared environment.	N	
LOG_ARCHIVE_DEST	O/S Dep.	The location to send archive logs to.	Y	ARCHIVELOG
LOG_ARCHIVE_START	false	Begin archive logging.	Y	ARCHIVELOG
LOG_BUFFER	O/S Dep.	Size of redo log buffers in SGA.	Y	
LOG_CHECKPOINT_INTERVAL	O/S Dep.	Number of filled redo blocks that will trigger a checkpoint.	Y	
LOG_ENTRY_PREBUILD_THRESHOLD	0	Maximum size of a redo entry before it is pre-built	N	
LOG_FILES	16	Number of log files.	Y	<MAXLOGFILES

PARAMETER	DEFAULT VALUE	PURPOSE	ORACLE7?	DEPENDANCIES
LOG_SIMULTANEOUS_COPIES	CPU_COUNT	Number of REDO_COPY latches.	Y	2 * CPU_COUNT
LOG_SMALL_ENTRY_MAX_SIZE LOG_SIMULTANEOUS_COPIES	OS Dep.	The largest copy size for redo allocation latch.	Y	
MAX_DUMP_FILE_SIZE	500 Blocks	Max trace file size.	Y	
MI_BG_PROCS	0	Number of LCK processes.	N	
NLS_SORT	false	Sort order based on NLS Language if true.	Y	LANGUAGE
OPEN_CURSORS	50	Max number of open cursors for a process.	Y	
OPEN_LINKS	4	Max number of open database links per user.	Y	
PROCESSES	25	Max number of simultaneous connects to Oracle.	Y	
ROLLBACK_SEGMENTS	NULL	All private rollback segments that you want online need to be listed here.	Y	
ROW_CACHE_CURSORS	10	Cached recursive cursors.	Y	
ROW_CACHE_ENQUEUES	100	Number of all objects in all row caches accessed concurrently.	Y	
ROW_LOCKING	ALWAYS	Should row locking be used?	Y	
SAVEPOINTS	5	Number of simultaneous savepoints per user.	N	
SEQUENCE_CACHE_ENTRIES	10	Number of SEQUENCES that can be cached at one time.	Y	
SEQUENCE_CACHE_HASH_BUCKETS	7	Number of hash buckets used for locating sequences.	Y	<SEQUENCE_CACHE_ENTRIES
SERIALIZABLE	false	If true you get read locks.	Y	

PARAMETER	DEFAULT VALUE	PURPOSE	ORACLE7?	DEPENDANCIES
SESSIONS	DERIVED	Total number of user and system processes.	Y	1.1*PROCESSES
SINGLE_PROCESS	false	If true databse is brought up single user.	Y	
SORT_AREA_SIZE	O/S Dep.	Size of sort area. Doesn't effect SGA.	Y	
SORT_SPACEMAP_SIZE	O/S Dep.	Context area sort spacemap size. Change for large sorts.	Y	
SQL_TRACE	False	Enables trace facility if true	Y	
TIMED_STATISTICS	false	Enables time based statistics	Y	
TRANSACTIONS	DERIVED	Max number of concurrent transactions.	Y	1.1*PROCESSES
TRANSACTIONS_PER_ROLLBACK_SEGMENT	20	Number of concurrent transactions for a rollback segment.	Y	30 for ORACLE7
USER_DUMP_DEST	O/S Dep.	Where to write user trace files to.	Y	

NEW INIT.ORA PARAMETERS FOR ORACLE7:

PARAMETER	DEFAULT VALUE	PURPOSE	ORACLE7?	DEPENDANCIES
CHECKPOINT_PROCESS	false	Start up a seperate checkpoint process.		
COMMIT_POINT_STRENGTH	NULL	For use with two phase commit.		
COMPATIBLE	Ver. Dep	Earliest version this one is compatible with.		
COMPATIBLE_NO_RECOVERY	Ver. Dep.	Earliest version this one is compatible with without being recoverable.		
CURSOR_SPACE_FOR_TIME	false	Uses more space to save time.		
DB_BLOCK_CHECKPOINT_BATCH	DERIVED	Max blocks in one checkpoint DB_BLOCK_WRITE_BATCH/4 write.		
DB_DOMAIN	WORLD	Sets domain for db links		
DISCRETE_TRANSACTIONS_ENABLED	false	Enables faster rollback for special transactions.		

Parameter	Default	Description
DISTRIBUTED_LOCK_TIMEOUT	60 SEC.	The amount of time a distributed transaction will wait for locked resources.
DISTRIBUTED_TRANSACTIONS	0	If set > zero can have that many distributed transactions active.
GC_LCK_PROCS	0	Replaces MI_BG_PROCS from version 6.
GLOBAL_NAMES	false	Enables db link name checking.
INSTANCE_NUMBER	0	If set, sets the instance number for use with threads.
LICENSE_MAX_SESSIONS	0	Set to your session license value.
LICENSE_MAX_USERS	0	Set to your user license value.
LICENSE_SESSION_WARNING	0	Set to < LICENSE_MAX_SESSIONS
LOG_ARCHIVE_BUFFER_SIZE	O/S Dep.	Size of archive buffer in O/S blocks.
LOG_ARCHIVE_BUFFERS	O/S Dep.	Number of buffers to allocate to redo logs.
LOG_ARCHIVE_FORMAT	O/S Dep.	Sets format for archive log files.
LOG_CHECKPOINT_TIMEOUT	0 SEC	Max. amount of time between checkpoints.
MAX_ENABLED_ROLES	20	Max number of roles for a user.
MAX_ROLLBACK_SEGS	20	Max. number of rollback names cached.
MTS_DISPATCHERS	NULL	Set type and number of dispatchers.
MTS_LISTENER_ADDRESS	NULL	Configure listener process.
MTS_MAX_DISPATCHERS	5	Maximum number of concurrent dispatchers.
MTS_MAX_SERVERS	20	Maximum number of server processes.
MTS_SERVERS	0	Number of servers to startup with.
MTS_SERVICE	NULL	Name of service, defaults to DB_NAME.
NLS_CURRENCY	DERIVED	Defaults to currency for NLS_LANGUAGE.
NLS_DATE_FORMAT	DERIVED	Defaults to date format for NLS_LANGUAGE.
NLS_DATE_LANGUAGE	DERIVED	Defaults to NLS_LANGUAGE
NLS_ISO_CURRENCY	DERIVED	Defaults to currency symbol of NLS_LANGUAGE.
NLS_LANGUAGE	American	The language the instance should use.
NLS_NUMERIC_CHARACTERS	DERIVED	Defaults to the normal for NLS_LANGUAGE.
NLS_TERRITORY	O/S dep.	Name of territory whose conventions to use.

OPTIMIZER_MODE	COST	Specifies what optimizer mode to use.
OS_AUTHENT_PREFIX	OPS$	Specifies what prefix for autologin accounts.
OS_ROLES	FALSE	OS system manages roles if set to true.
REMOTE_OS_AUTHENT	false	Allows remote users to automatically login.
REMOTE_OS_ROLES	False	Allows OS roles for remote users.
RESOURCE_LIMIT	False	Enable or disable use of resource limits.
SHARED_POOL_SIZE	3.5 MEG	Size of SQL shared pool area.
SMALL_TABLE_THRESHOLD	4 blocks	Size of small table (used in small table reads)
SORT_AREA_RETAINED_SIZE	DERIVED	Size to shrink sort area to after sort = SORT_AREA_SIZE
TEMPORARY_TABLE_LOCKS	DERIVED	Number of temporary tables that can be created in the temporary area = SESSIONS
THREAD	0	Number of redo thread for this instance.

Index

A

Access violation error, 38
ACT_SIZE.sql listing, 157–158, 391–392
active sessions, 142
  resources or events waiting, 144
add_user shell script listing, 470
add_user.com listing, 457–458
add_user.sql (ORACLE7) listing, 458
add_user.sql listing, 117, 381
ADMIN OPTION privilege, 131
administrative users, 28
administrator security, 133
AFTER ROW triggers, 101
AGGREGATE action, 205
ALL_ view, 215
ALL_ROWS hint, 222
ALTER [PUBLIC] ROLLBACK SEGMENT
  command, 61
ALTER ANY CLUSTER privilege, 125
ALTER ANY INDEX privilege, 125
ALTER ANY PROCEDURE privilege, 126
ALTER ANY ROLE privilege, 127
ALTER ANY SEQUENCE privilege, 127
ALTER ANY TABLE privilege, 128
ALTER ANY TRIGGER privilege, 130
ALTER CLUSTER command, 95, 346–347
ALTER command, 52, 61-62, 104
  RENAME DATAFILE option, 63

STORAGE clause, 52–53
ALTER DATABASE command, 54–55, 59–61,
  337
  CLOSE parameter, 337
  database name parameter, 337
  DISMOUNT parameter, 337
  examples, 337–338
  filename parameter, 337
  filespec parameter, 337
  MOUNT parameter, 337
  OPEN parameter, 337
  SIZE clause, 60
ALTER DATABASE privilege, 125
ALTER FUNCTION command
  COMPILE option, 104, 351
ALTER INDEX command, 86, 88, 344
ALTER PACKAGE BODY command, 107, 351
ALTER PROCEDURE command, 351
  COMPILE option, 104
ALTER PROFILE command, 133, 358
ALTER PROFILE privilege, 126
ALTER RESOURCE COST command, 132
ALTER RESOURCE COST privilege, 126
ALTER ROLE command, 131
ALTER ROLLBACK SEGMENT command, 61,
  268-269, 339
ALTER ROLLBACK SEGMENT privilege, 127
ALTER SEQUENCE command, 92, 169, 345
ALTER SESSION command, 200

E

W

X